THE CHURCHILLS

BOOKS BY A. L. ROWSE

Literature

SHAKESPEARE'S SOUTHAMPTON: PATRON OF VIRGINIA

CHRISTOPHER MARLOWE: HIS LIFE AND WORK

WILLIAM SHAKESPEARE: A BIOGRAPHY

SHAKESPEARE'S SONNETS
(edited, with Introduction and Notes)

THE ENGLISH SPIRIT: ESSAYS IN LITERATURE AND HISTORY

THE ENGLISH PAST: EVOCATIONS OF PERSONS AND PLACES

POEMS OF A DECADE, 1931–1941

POEMS CHIEFLY CORNISH

POEMS OF DELIVERANCE

POEMS PARTLY AMERICAN

A CORNISH CHILDHOOD

A CORNISHMAN AT OXFORD

WEST COUNTRY STORIES

History

THE ELIZABETHANS AND AMERICA

SIR WALTER RALEGH

THE ENGLAND OF ELIZABETH

THE EXPANSION OF ELIZABETHAN ENGLAND

TUDOR CORNWALL

SIR RICHARD GRENVILLE OF THE *Revenge*

THE EARLY CHURCHILLS

THE CHURCHILLS

THE USE OF HISTORY

APPEASEMENT: A STUDY IN POLITICAL DECLINE

A HISTORY OF FRANCE, by Lucien Romier
(translated and completed)

A. L. ROWSE

THE CHURCHILLS

THE STORY OF A FAMILY

HARPER & ROW, PUBLISHERS

New York and Evanston

This is an abridgement of *The Early Churchills* and *The Churchills*

FIRST U.S. EDITION

LIBRARY OF CONGRESS CATALOG CARD NUMBER: 67-15970

Contents

Book I

Book II

ILLUSTRATIONS

The following are grouped in a separate section after page 206:

Preface

The Churchill family, take them all in all, are probably the most striking and variegated of all the families in which English history has been so rich. I was first drawn to the subject by their West Country origin, but this was confirmed by the inspiration afforded in our own time by the career of the family's greatest son. Probably no figure in history has himself been more inspired, as he went along, by awareness of the history of his own family and country. I have been fascinated, looking back over it again, to see how significantly and revealingly, how richly and diversely, they are intertwined.

The family is naturally the chief unit in history, often the necessary condition for individual achievement. Yet, for the hundreds of excellent historical biographies that exist, there are extremely few family-histories that are comparable works of literature. They are more usually genealogical mausoleums.

This family-history originally appeared in two volumes, *The Early Churchills* and *The Later Churchills*. For this edition I have combined them in one, cutting out a great deal of detailed research-material; for this and for full notes and references, if anyone wants to consult them, the original volumes are available. But I hope not to have sacrificed anything material to the story, or diminished its richness or lessened its diversity. All the characters remain, though the leading ones—John and Sarah, first Duke and Duchess of Marlborough, Lord Randolph Churchill and Sir Winston, the original Sir Winston, the Cavalier Colonel, and indeed Blenheim itself—can now stand out more simply and clearly in the perspective of the whole.

The many obligations I incurred in the course of my researches are acknowledged in the original Prefaces. Here I can only say how much the book owed to the personal interest and encouragement of Sir Winston, who himself went through the early chapters making suggestions, and to the Duke of Marlborough, who gave me generous permission to work in the archives at Blenheim, without which the book could not have been written.

A. L. ROWSE

THE CHURCHILL FAMILY

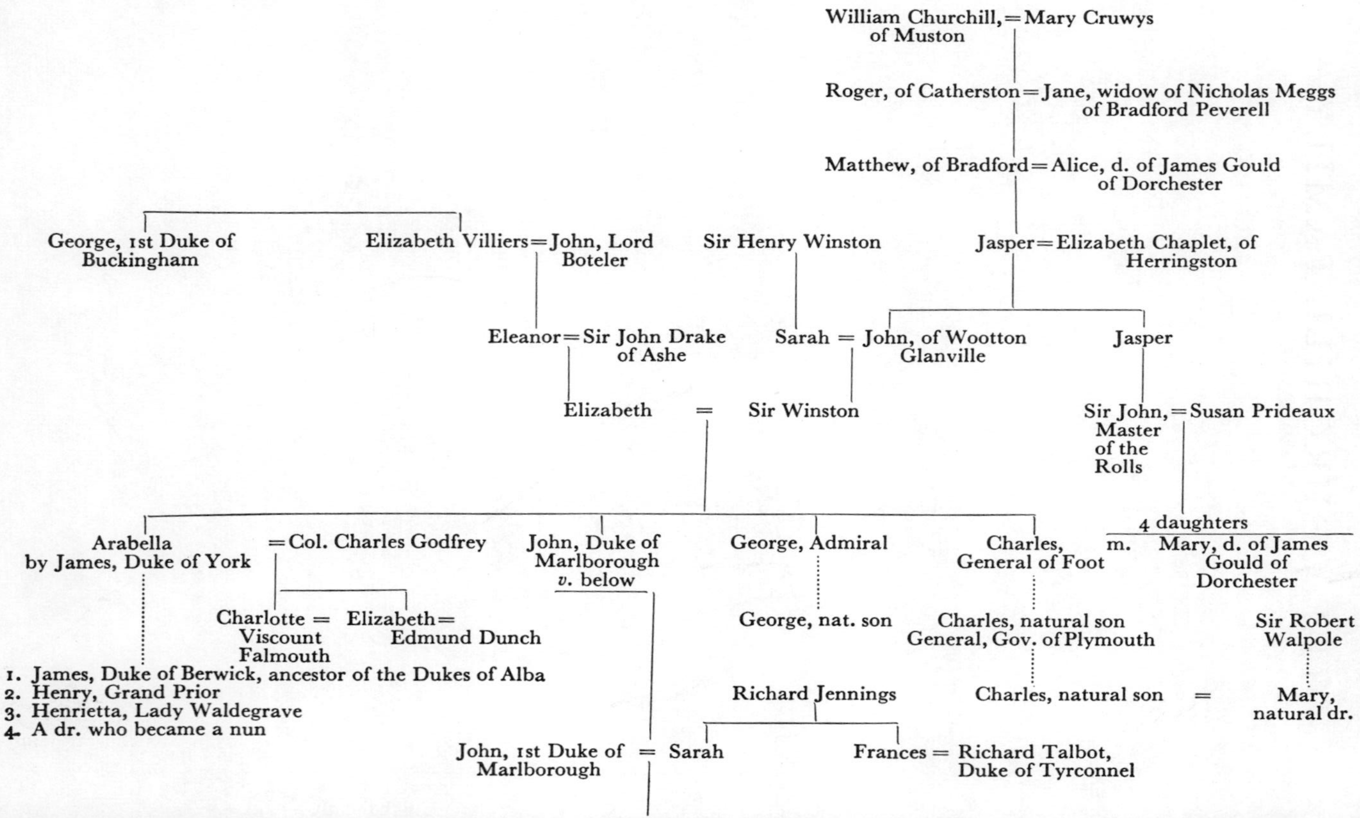

William Churchill, = Mary Cruwys
of Muston
Roger, of Catherston = Jane, widow of Nicholas Meggs
of Bradford Peverell
Matthew, of Bradford = Alice, d. of James Gould
of Dorchester
George, 1st Duke of
Buckingham
Elizabeth Villiers = John, Lord
Boteler
Sir Henry Winston
Jasper = Elizabeth Chaplet, of
Herringston
Eleanor = Sir John Drake
of Ashe
Sarah = John, of Wootton
Glanville
Jasper
Elizabeth = Sir Winston
Sir John, = Susan Prideaux
Master
of the
Rolls
4 daughters
Arabella
by James, Duke of York
= Col. Charles Godfrey
John, Duke of
Marlborough
v. below
George, Admiral
Charles,
General of Foot
m. Mary, d. of James
Gould of
Dorchester
Charlotte = Viscount
Falmouth
Elizabeth =
Edmund Dunch
George, nat. son
Charles, natural son
General, Gov. of Plymouth
Sir Robert
Walpole
1. James, Duke of Berwick, ancestor of the Dukes of Alba
2. Henry, Grand Prior
3. Henrietta, Lady Waldegrave
4. A dr. who became a nun
Richard Jennings
Charles, natural son =
Mary,
natural dr.
John, 1st Duke of
Marlborough
= Sarah
Frances = Richard Talbot,
Duke of Tyrconnel

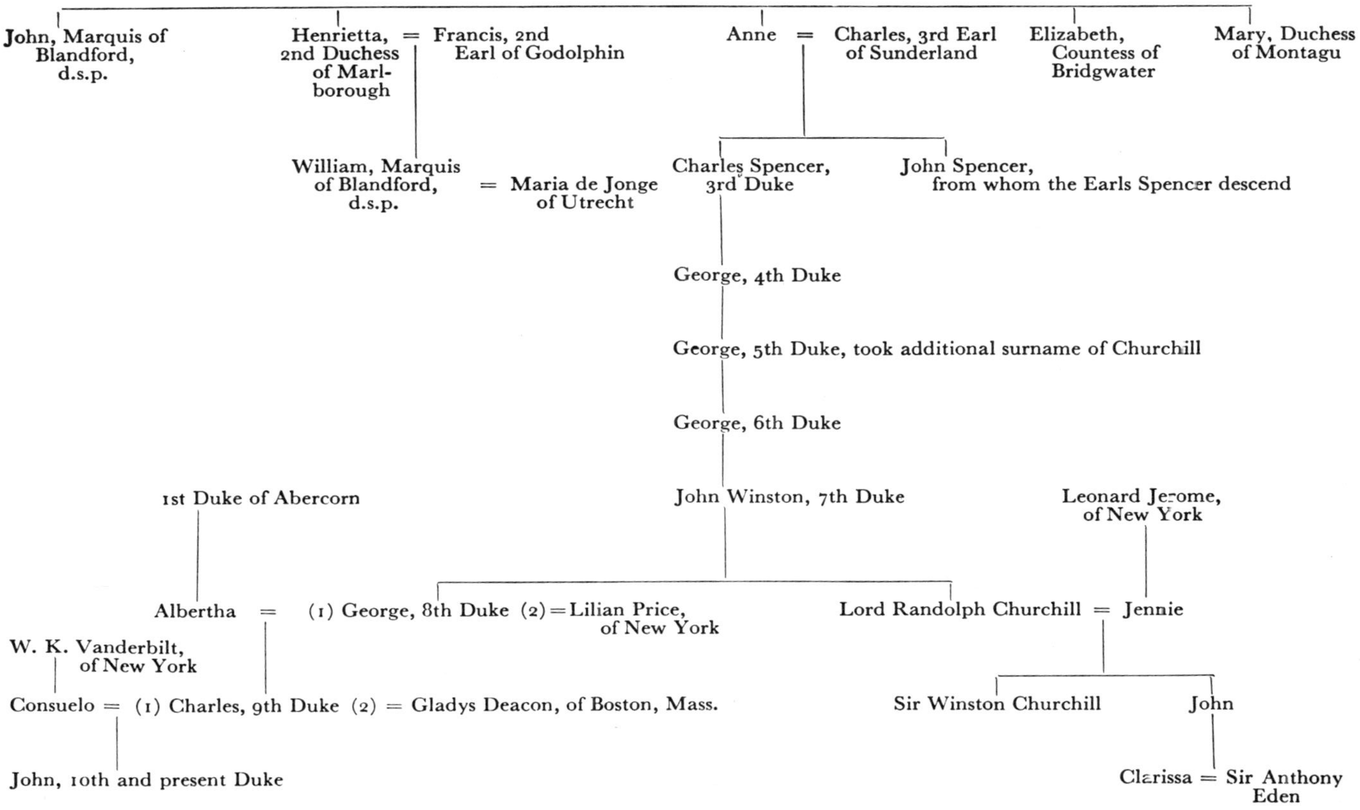

John, Marquis of Blandford, d.s.p.
Henrietta, 2nd Duchess of Marlborough = Francis, 2nd Earl of Godolphin
Anne = Charles, 3rd Earl of Sunderland
Elizabeth, Countess of Bridgwater
Mary, Duchess of Montagu
William, Marquis of Blandford, d.s.p. = Maria de Jonge of Utrecht
Charles Spencer, 3rd Duke
John Spencer, from whom the Earls Spencer descend
George, 4th Duke
George, 5th Duke, took additional surname of Churchill
George, 6th Duke
John Winston, 7th Duke
1st Duke of Abercorn
Leonard Jerome, of New York
Albertha = (1) George, 8th Duke (2) = Lilian Price, of New York
Lord Randolph Churchill = Jennie
W. K. Vanderbilt, of New York
Consuelo = (1) Charles, 9th Duke (2) = Gladys Deacon, of Boston, Mass.
Sir Winston Churchill
John
John, 10th and present Duke
Clarissa = Sir Anthony Eden

BOOK I

CHAPTER ONE

Dorset Beginnings

THE Churchills are good West Country stock, of considerable antiquity. When they first appeared on the public scene in the good days of the Restoration, with the original Sir Winston Churchill and his famous progeny, the old Cavalier insisted that they had come over with the Conqueror. This did not impress the positive, Whiggish spirit of Duchess Sarah later on, who was no historian but commented on a fulsome life of the great Duke, her husband: 'this history takes a great deal of pains to make the Duke of Marlborough's extraction very ancient. That may be true for aught I know; but it is no matter whether it be true or not, in my opinion. For I value nobody for another's merit.'

In fact, the Churchills were pretty thick upon the ground, and very close to the soil, in Dorset, Somerset and East Devon. We find them scattered over that Dorset countryside with the delightful, evocative names—Melbury Osmond, Melbury Sampford, Melbury Bubb; Bishop's Caundle, Purse Caundle and Caundle Marsh; Piddlehinton and Piddletrenthide; Winterborne Herringston and Winterborne Came. The name of the family, it seems, derives from the farm of Churchill in the parish of Broad Clyst in Devon, where Jocelyn de Churchill is recorded as early as the middle of the twelfth century.

But we are interested in the country on either side of the main road from Dorchester to Sherborne, at first upheaved and hilly as the way goes through the narrow valley to Cerne Abbas and Minterne Magna, then broadening out towards Sherborne into what was once the Forest of Blackmore, with its heaths and copses and its medieval legend. This is the soil upon which the family we are pursuing emerged. An enemy of theirs in the eighteenth century asserted that 'John Churchill's great-grandfather was a blacksmith, who worked in the family of the Meggs'. Certainly the Duke's great-great-great-grandfather, Roger Churchill, married the widow of Nicholas Meggs of Bradford Peverell. This Roger had a son Matthew, who had a son called Jasper, who married a girl from Herringston. They had two sons, John the elder, Jasper the younger. John took to the law and made a marked step up in the world; he became a gentleman. He was followed by his nephew, Jasper's son, another John, who became an eminent figure at the Bar and ended up as Attorney-General to the Duke of York and Master of the Rolls: Sir John Churchill.

His uncle John did not attain such eminence, nor did he have such luck as the younger generation: his generation came to an end with the Civil War. Before this catastrophe he had had time to do well enough out of the law. A member of Middle Temple, he rose to be a Deputy-Registrar of Chancery. He was enabled to buy the pleasant little estate of Newton Montacute in the parish of Wootton Glanville, not half a dozen miles from Sherborne. In addition, John Churchill leased Minterne from Winchester College: a pretty little estate deep in the valley towards Dorchester, the house conveniently near the road next the church, woods all round and a sounding trout-stream below. He had, besides, house-property in and near Dorchester, and one or two farms in the neighbourhood. In short, the typical estate of a small West Country gentleman, the status to which he had risen.

Just like such a man going up in the world, he married into the class above him: Sarah, daughter of a Gloucestershire knight, Sir Henry Winston of Standish. She bequeathed the Gloucestershire name of Winston to the Churchills. It was to have a resounding reverberation. She presented her husband with two sons: John, the elder, who died shortly after birth, and Winston who survived. He was born about the year 1620. At some time before the Civil War, the mother died, for John Churchill made a second marriage in 1644.

When the Civil War opened and party-alignments sharpened, the western counties were dominantly with Church and King. Particularly with the conservative society of a county like Dorset. There, the sympathies of almost all the gentry were Royalist. Of the leading families only the Trenchards, the Sydenhams, the Erles and Denzil Holles were Parliamentarians. The coastal and clothing towns were apt to be Parliamentarian: both Poole and Lyme undeviatingly so—the resistance of the latter, in a prolonged siege, gave heart to the Parliamentarians and seriously impeded Royalist progress in the West. Dorchester, too, was with Parliament in its sympathy—the Churchills of that place took the protective colouring of the environment. The celebrated minister of Holy Trinity, John White, an eminent Puritan and a leading figure in the founding of Massachusetts, 'one of the subtlest and wisest of that sort of men', was much to the fore in managing the affairs of the town and keeping the burgesses to the path of virtue. There were two Royalist strongholds which were important—Sherborne Castle in the north of the county, Corfe Castle in the south—for each was very strong and they held the keys of communications with the West.

It was natural that John Churchill and his son Winston should share the sympathies of the rest of the Dorset gentry: the father in a quiet enough way, as befitted an elderly man in retirement, the son furiously in action, fighting in the field, a gallant captain of horse. At Wootton Glanville they were within the aura of, and naturally looked to, Sherborne Castle. In these years of Royalist ascendancy in the West, John Churchill acted as one of the King's commissioners, while his son was away fighting in the King's army.

When the fighting was over and the King had lost, the Churchills had to pay heavily for their delinquency. The victorious Parliament, much more competent at administration than the King had ever been, rapidly brought into play its instruments for reorganising a disrupted society and making its opponents pay: the Committee for Compounding, which sat at Goldsmiths' Hall, with its commissioners in every county. It is impressive how effectively it got to work. How it must have piled up rancour and resentment in the defeated—who got their long-delayed revenge with the return of Charles II in 1660.

At some time during the Civil War—probably about the year 1644—John Churchill had married again. From a case that came into Chancery after the father's death, we can see that there was no love lost between Winston and his stepmother and can descry something of the state of affairs at Wootton. One sees something of the picture: Winston Churchill, kept out of his own home by the exigencies of these hard times. How Winston Churchill was affected by it all we shall shortly see.

CHAPTER TWO

Cavalier Colonel

WINSTON CHURCHILL is the first member of the family whom we can depict at something near full-length, in whom we can descry the lineaments of his personality, grasp the gist of his character, give a framework to his life and career. We have seen that he was born about the year 1620, for in 1636 he matriculated at Oxford as a member of St. John's College, on 8 April, at the age of sixteen. The college was at the full tide of Laudian favour and Laudian principles. Its former President was now Archbishop of Canterbury and only a short time before had endowed his college with the most beautiful of Caroline buildings—the Canterbury building, where Winston Churchill shared a room with an Oxfordshire lad, John Meeze of Over Worton, for his first year. He left in the term ending Michaelmas 1638. The two and a half years he spent at Oxford, as a member of St. John's College, may now be seen to have their proper importance. For it was there that he imbibed the Laudian principles—in politics devotion to the Crown, in religion High Church, himself remaining undeviatingly Protestant—to which he adhered all his life.

Meanwhile, he had been entered as a student at Lincoln's Inn, and admitted on 30 January 1637[1]. The Inns of Court were an alternative university, where it was the regular thing for the sons of country gentlemen to study, to complete their training with the more practical and worldly accomplishments of the law. Such a course was doubly indicated in his case, the son of one who had made his way by the law: here he was entered, the 'son and heir of John Churchill of Glanville Wootton, gentleman'. Three years later his cousin John followed him there, to make a distinguished career as a professional lawyer.[2]

Life at the Inns of Court was very much the same for the students as at the university, with the same framework and following the same routine, except that there was rather more liberty and there were the opportunities and excitements of the capital. Within the Inn, the students were summoned to dinner and supper in hall

[1] Admission Register of Lincoln's Inn, I. 229. [2] *Ibid.* 238.

by the blowing of a horn. Their proper wear in hall was cap and gown, as at the university; but fashion challenged this sobriety and the young men ruffled it booted and spurred, in cloak and lace collar, and wearing their hair long. Hall and chapel were the scene of an intensive, crowded life. In the former took place the readings, moots and bolts—the public exercises that tested the knowledge acquired by the students from their seniors, sharpening their wits against each other. The same bell that rang them to the chapel, then newly built, still clangs upon the scene. The young men shared chambers in those crowded buildings, some of which still stand—having survived fire and bombs—looking out on Chancery Lane.

Within, their life proceeded: readings every week, services and sermons in chapel (Donne's sermons had not long ceased to echo within those walls), meals in common in the hall, feasts at All Saints, Candlemas and Ascension-tide; at Christmas, revels and the young men dancing before the assembled Benchers.

Of Winston Churchill's progress in the law we have no knowledge; it must have been that of any other young lawyer. But here in these years at the end of the 1630's, he laid the foundations of the stock of knowledge, acquired the rudiments of legal training, which stood him in sufficient stead for a career after the long interruption of the Civil War.

Churchill was in his twenty-second year when the Civil War broke out and desultory fighting first crackled in the West. The situation changed with the march of the Cornish army into Somerset: the war became professional, and we know that he fought in the Royalist horse at the battles of Lansdown and Roundway Down. In the midst of these excitements, the young captain of horse married, it seems in May 1643, just before he went off on campaign. War has never been averse to love; but no doubt other calculations entered into this marriage that was to be so important to the Churchills. John Churchill, like a sensible man, had married above him in marrying a Winston. He must have had a hand in making a further step upwards in his son's marriage to Elizabeth Drake, a daughter of Sir John Drake of Ashe. For the Drakes of Ashe were one of the leading families of Devon, a medieval family that had been going for generations, intermarried with the oldest Norman gentry of Devon, Grenvilles, Fortescues and such. Sir John Drake had married Eleanor, daughter of Lord Boteler, who had married the sister of George Villiers, first Duke of Buckingham. Since that handsome young man had been promoted to the favours of the susceptible James I, three generations of Villiers exerted an irresistible fascination, in various members—men and women alike—upon three generations of Stuarts. It is an extraordinary story. Something in that errant, vivacious blood, with its wonderful looks, passed an electric current into the stocks with which it mingled. Nothing in the Churchills so far, earthy and commonplace, could have foretold their astonishing future—nothing until that marriage.

Sir John Drake died young, in 1636; but his wife was not a Villiers for nothing: she was a personality, and she took charge. We learn from complicated proceedings they were subsequently involved in, through the troubles brought down on them all by the times, that Elizabeth had been left by her father 1000 marks towards her marriage portion. She was then only a girl. Now she was twenty-one. Lady Drake agreed with John Churchill to give her a dowry of £1500, in return for which he was to settle upon her lands worth £160 a year. The marriage went forward.

However, with the Royalist ascendancy in the West, Lady Drake was the first to taste adversity. Her fine house of Ashe—a large Elizabethan E-shaped mansion—lay right on the main road, on the right-hand side going south, from Axminster to the sea. There a fragment of it, one wing with its detached chapel, still remains, looking out over the fat pastures of that shallow valley on one side, across to Colyton and up to the dark woods of Shute lining the horizon to the west. To the east, there is the little village of Musbury, with its Devon church-tower and, within, the monuments of generations of Drakes. It is a pleasant place, though only a fragment, within its formal gardens, the remains of the old fish-ponds, the *emplacements* of the earlier great house: surrounded now by its orchards, a white foam of apple-blossom in spring, the red and russet and gold of autumn. Ashe lay exposed to the road, and to whoever was passing up and down. It stood on the direct route between Axminster in Cavalier hands, and Lyme that was obstinately, irreducibly, Parliamentarian. It was hardly possible that the mansion of a flagrantly Parliamentarian lady should escape attention.

At Christmas 1643, a friendly neighbour heard talk at the Royalist headquarters at Axminster, where Lord Paulett was commander-in-chief, that there would have to be a garrison placed at Ashe or else it would have to be burned. This neighbour, a Devon yeoman, at once sent word by his sister to Lady Drake, warning her to ask Lord Paulett to place some musketeers in the house to save it from destruction. But she had already got the Parliamentarian garrison of Lyme to put in a few soldiers. So that it was hardly surprising that, a week later, Lord Paulett let loose his Irish soldiery on the place, who burned it down. When the war ended with the victory of the Parliament, Lady Drake was awarded £1500 compensation out of Lord Paulett's estate; while he had to settle £200 a year on faithful Lyme—a permanent knock to the finances of that noble house. It took the active and clamorous lady some years, however, before she got her money.

To return to the summer of 1644: Lyme, with Lady Drake within it, was regularly besieged by Prince Maurice's army, from April to the end of June. We do not know where Winston Churchill was in this year 1644; but it is reasonable to suppose that he was fighting in the field, either with the forces in his own native county under Prince Maurice, or with the King's forces that pursued Essex into Cornwall, cooped him up in the peninsula and forced him to surrender. The war, however, was not decided in the West; but by the superior resources of the eastern counties and London, Parliament's control of the navy and sea-power, and, ultimately by the fruition of Pym's long-term strategy in bringing Scotland in to make the balance against the King certain and secure. The result was to be seen in the great defeat of Marston Moor in 1644, by which the King lost the North, and in the disaster of Naseby, 1645, by which he lost the Midlands and his cause received a fatal blow.

In the West, he still had a considerable army, which, in May, moved upon the sorely tried and already once-besieged Parliamentarian town of Taunton. The heroic defender of Lyme, Blake, threw himself with indomitable spirit into its defence. Already relief was at hand; Parliament could not allow Taunton to fall: Fairfax and Cromwell were sent into the West at the head of a strong, tried army. At the news of their approach, just as Blake had exhausted his ammunition, the Royalists for the second time broke up the siege and moved away. The way was open to the assault on Bristol. The city was in a terrible plight, under the visitation of the plague, with a hundred people a week dying. The Parliament's ships blockaded it by sea; the suburb of Bedminister was burnt to the ground; from 21 August it was invested on all sides. Prince Rupert made constant sallies from the city; but early on the morning of 10 September, the assault was delivered. Prior's Hill fort resisted stoutly: almost everyone inside was put to the sword On the Somerset side, the Parliamentarians were beaten to a retreat. The city was now on fire in several places, and Rupert asked for a parley. Now some 3000 Gloucestershire countrymen came in to Parliament: nothing succeeds like success. Rupert surrendered on good terms, the garrison marching out, while the country people cried, 'Give him no quarter! No quarter'. The city was in a ghastly state of privation, its trade throttled, people starving, the streets noisome with pestilence and destruction. In all this last phase of the fighting Winston Churchill was present; for we know that he was wounded in the arm by the forces under his fellow Dorsetman, Colonel Starr, that he was at the siege of Taunton and engaged in the defence of Bristol, and that he was still in arms against Parliament as late as December 1645.

The Civil War was over. It remained to gather up the threads of life, resume the broken diurnal routine, accustom oneself to the new and unprecedented situation in which England found itself; for the country to find, if possible, a basis of settlement; for the individual, to make the best of things. In the year 1647, in the summer of which Lady Drake left London, the Cavalier captain was at length free to come together with his wife; for on 23 February next year their first child, Arabella, was born at Ashe, and baptised in the chapel there on 16 March. Thereafter, Mrs. Churchill presented her husband with fruitful increase, with monotonous annual regularity, till the complement of a dozen was reached. As usual in those days, most of them died in infancy. Winston, the first-born son, born in 1649 did not live. Their next son, the famous John, was born at Ashe in 1650 and baptised there on 26 May. Of their remaining children, those who survived were George, born at Ashe in 1653, who became an Admiral; Charles, born in 1656, who was a General under his brother, the Duke; Theobald, born in Dublin in 1663, who took orders but died in his twenties.

We see that the family life centred upon Ashe. His father was still alive at Wootton Glanville, with a second wife. There was Minterne: why did not Winston occupy that? We have evidence that he was not on good terms with his stepmother and, perhaps, his father. Then, too, they were all impoverished.

The experience of civil war and revolution explains the intense bitterness of party spirit in the years to come. It also explains much in the outlook and characteristics of the Churchills. Defeat and frustration gave an edge to long-smothered ambition, sharpened the determination to make the most of opportunity when it came.

Wants denied and financial stringency all through their youth must have determined them that they would *not* be poor when they grew up: they would make money and hold on to it—as every one of them did. Those dark years must have had a subtler impact: it made each of those children reserved, capable of keeping his or her own counsel, bent on inner independence.

In these years Winston Churchill made one appearance that we know of in London, 23 June 1652, when he was called to the Bar; but this seems to have been a purely formal, much belated measure: he made no use of it and did not keep term. Down in the country, in remote east Devon, sunk in glum resentment, he had, at any rate, the consolation that intelligent people have who are defeated and out of favour: reading and writing. He was reading hard, for he was going to write a book. Now that the sword had been struck from his hand, he would take up the quill in defence of his cause. His spirit was not defeated: it burns with unquenched ardour in what he wrote. He had plenty of time for reading and writing in those long winter nights when the south-westerlies blew up the valley from the sea and the candles guttered in the draughty damaged house; or when snow lay upon the pastures and up the slopes to Musbury church, where a Puritan intruder held forth in place of the pulpit's rightful occupant. The Colonel was not likely to patronise his ministrations or to entrust the education of his children to him. It is said that he used the services of a neighbouring sequestrated clergyman, whose sympathies he shared.

The book helped to fill the black years when Oliver ruled at Whitehall and the faithful waited, almost without hope, for the King to come back to his own. It was not published till long after the Restoration, in 1675, when it was dedicated to 'His most Sacred Majesty, Charles II', and the old Cavalier offered it 'as the only instance of duty I could give at that which was indeed the worst of times; being begun when everybody thought that monarchy had ended and would have been buried in the same grave with your martyred father.... When none of us that served that blessed Prince had any other weapons left us but our pens to show the justice of our zeal by that of his title; when, for want of ink black enough to record the impieties that followed, we designed to write them in blood: writing and fighting being alike dangerous, and necessary.'

The book is a history of England, only a monarchical history: that the government of this isle has always been monarchical is its theme. Its title: *Divi Britannici*: *being a Remark upon the Lives of all the Kings of this Isle.* It is pleasant to observe that the wheel has come full circle with Sir Winston's namesake, who also has written his history of England, though, with the wider scope of our age, his has broadened out into the history of the English-speaking peoples.

We soon discern that the dominant influence upon Churchill in writing his book was that of his fellow West Countryman, Ralegh's *History of the World,* even before we come to a marked tribute, which may record something of family tradition in Devon as to Ralegh's fate. 'Herein those that were his particular friends and relations were not more surprised than all the world beside. For as they expected to have been indebted to his sword for bringing home more gold than would have paid the price of his forfeited head, so everybody else hoped to have been no less indebted to his pen for finishing that most excellent piece of his, the History of the Old World, which ended as untimely as himself, by attempting a discovery of the new one.'

CHAPTER THREE

The Restoration: in England and Ireland

THE early months of 1660 witnessed a landslide in favour of the King in exile. Neither Parliament nor the Army, Republican politicians nor generals, Presbyterians nor Independents, had been able to give the country a permanent settlement or provide a firm constitutional structure. Only the prestige, the power of Cromwell had been able to hold things together; even after his death, that mighty shadow had prevailed for more than a year. Now, cracks appeared on every side; innumerable schemes were put forward by clever doctrinaires—all to no avail; a gulf opened beneath men's feet. The whole country was demanding a free Parliament; everyone knew that that meant the restoration of the exiled King.

Slowly General Monk marched south from Scotland with his army, watching the currents of opinion, keeping his thoughts to himself. At last arrived in London, he formed the conclusion that nothing but the restoration of King, Lords and Commons—the country's ancient constitution—would do. In glad May-time, Admiral Montagu was sent over with the fleet to fetch home the King, with his brothers, the Dukes of York and Gloucester. Pepys was with the Admiral on board the *Naseby,* so that we know all about the homecoming. When the King came aboard, the royal standard was hoisted; cheers resounded through the fleet, and the sailors threw their caps and even their doublets into the sea. The ships were renamed: the *Naseby*—name of ill-omen—became the *Royal Charles.* On board, the King surprised Mr. Pepys by his activity and affability. 'All the afternoon the King walked here and there, up and down (quite contrary to what I thought him to have been) very active and stirring.' The King's mind was full of the last days he had spent in England, and Mr. Pepys was touched to tears by his Majesty's stories of his escape and the hardships he had undergone on his flight, after Worcester, to the coast.

At Dover, crowds lined the shore. There was General Monk kneeling, whom the King embraced and raised up, hailing him as

'Father'. The mayor approached with a large Bible, which Charles accepted with the memorable words that 'it was the thing that he loved above all things in the world'. The English have always been more susceptible than most peoples to humbug, and some humbug is no doubt necessary to government. This was designed to appeal to the Protestantism of the nation; it will be seen later how far the remark was true.

The King's first proclamation, against drinking, swearing and whoring, was read to the ships' companies in the fleet, where it seems to have given particular satisfaction. In London, the enthusiasm was immense; similar scenes were enacted. At St. Paul's door, the ministers presented Charles with another Bible for his collection, to whom he replied that 'he would make that book the rule of his life and government'. But he left it behind him. John Evelyn watched the King's entry into London on his birthday, 'with a triumph of above 20,000 horse and foot, brandishing their swords and shouting with inexpressible joy; the ways strewed with flowers, the bells ringing, the streets hung with tapisserie, fountains running with wine, the Mayor, Aldermen and all the companies in their liveries, chains of gold and banners; lords and nobles clad in cloth of silver, gold and velvet; the windows and balconies well set with ladies; trumpets, music and myriads of people flocking even so far as from Rochester, so as they were seven hours in passing the city, even from two in the afternoon till nine at night. I stood in the Strand and beheld it and blessed God!'

The thaw had come; it was happy springtime; the King was home to enjoy his own again. With his pleasant cynical turn of humour, he 'said, smiling to some about him that he doubted it had been his own fault that he had been absent so long, for he saw no one that did not protest he had ever wished for his return'.

On his father's death, Winston Churchill—or the Colonel, as we henceforth find him popularly called—went to live at Minterne. He made that his seat in the country. At the Restoration, he was a man of forty; if ever he was to make a mark in the world, now was the moment. Even so, it was rather late. The Convention Parliament of 1660 having called home the King and passed an Act of Indemnity and Oblivion—which the Cavaliers described as 'Indemnity for the King's enemies and Oblivion for his friends'—dissolved itself. The full tide of Royalist reaction became evident in the Parliament that was elected next year, the Cavalier Parliament. It contained a large number of the younger generation that had grown up since the Civil War. On someone commenting on these beardless young men, Charles said that he would keep them until they had beards. And so he did; this Parliament was kept in existence for eighteen years, from 1661 to 1679. So overwhelming a majority for one side, so strong a reaction, was neither representative of the nation nor good for it. It represented the victory of the Anglican country gentry, the alliance between squire and parson henceforth in every parish, not to be broken until the social revolution of our own time: it expressed their accumulated resentments at their sufferings, the insults and humiliations they had received at the hands of their inferiors. Never again! was their watchword.

In March 1661, Winston Churchill was returned as a member for Weymouth, and so he remained till the end of the Cavalier Parliament in 1679. At once we find him one of the most energetic and active members of the House, serving on most of its important committees. His legal background was useful; his long service in the field gave him an advantage over the younger men. There were three kingdoms to get in order, a new deal to be worked out and as securely grounded as the shifting circumstances of the Restoration permitted. The Colonel was one of the foremost committee-men in the House and a faithful follower of the King. His service was at length taken notice of by the Court.

Churchill owed his introduction at Court to the patronage of Sir Henry Bennet, later Earl of Arlington. Arlington came from a similar family, of Berkshire small gentry who had risen through the law. He, too, was an Oxford man—one sees his grand portrait over the door of Christ Church hall, very dignified in his deportment and his sweeping robes, with the black patch he always wore on the bridge of his nose to remind people of his service to the Crown. For, like Churchill, he too had received a wound: a sabre-cut in a skirmish at Andover. It did not amount to much, but he made the most of it. Anthony Hamilton said that 'the plaster-patch so well suited his mysterious looks, that it seemed an addition to his-gravity and self-sufficiency'. He was a favourite with the King, for he was an amusing man, with 'the best turns of wit in particular conversation that I have known', said Sir William Temple; he had the art, wrote Bishop Burnet, 'of observing the King's temper and managing it beyond all the men of that time'. Even Clarendon admitted, generously—for Arlington in the end supplanted him—'he may well be reckoned in the number of the finest gentlemen of the time. . . . The King received him with great kindness, as a man whose company he always liked.' One thing Arlington understood better than the Chancellor was foreign affairs; and another was the art of intrigue. He was engaged now in bringing together a group of the new generation in the Commons, whom the Chancellor neglected: country gentlemen on whose votes the King could rely and who, when the time came, could be turned against the antiquated, honest, monopolising Chancellor.

Such was the Colonel's political patron, and, in time to come, he was to suffer—or, at any rate, be traduced—for his associations.

It may be thought that the royal recognition was exiguous enough. Charles had little to give, except to his personal favourites and intimates who took advantage of his good nature to pester him—anything rather than be bored! It was typical of the circumstances of the Restoration that the Parliamentarian John Drake received a knighthood within a fortnight of the King's return. The faithful Colonel had to work and wait four years for his. All that he got now was an augmentation of honour to his coat of arms. A cheap enough way of recognising service; but we may take it as an earnest of better to come. As for the Colonel, he blazoned above his new coat of arms an uprooted oak with the motto *Fiel pero desdichado* ('Faithful but unfortunate')—again with the personal touch of the sense of his own misfortunes. Such is the motto his descendants continue to bear. 'Faithful' certainly, but never was the cant of heraldry more belied than in the second epithet, 'unfortunate'.

Even the Colonel's fortunes were turning. Churchill's assiduity in the House at length brought him to the notice of the King, by Arlington's means. We have Clarendon's sub-acid account of it in his autobiography; self-satisfied, as always, he did not see the necessity of bringing in the younger men. 'These men had parts, indeed, and good affections, and often had resorted to the Chancellor, received advice from him and thought themselves beholden to him. . . . But now these gentlemen had got a better patron; the new courtier had raised their value and talked in another dialect to them, of recompenses and rewards, than they had heard formerly. He carried them to the King and told his Majesty in their own hearing "what men of parts they were, what services they had done for him and how much greater they could do"; and his Majesty received and conferred with them very graciously and dismissed them with promises which made them rich already.'

Charles naturally asked Clarendon's opinion of these men, 'and particularly named Mr. Clifford and Mr. Churchill and some other men of better quality and much more interest, who he said, "took it ill that they were not particularly informed what the King desired and which way they might best serve him"; and bade him that "at the next meeting of the rest, these men might likewise have notice to be present".' This was the nightly meeting that took place at Court during the session to discuss government business. Clarendon could not but give a good character of Clifford and Churchill, 'who were honest gentlemen, and received the advice they were to follow from Sir Hugh Pollard, who had in truth a very particular influence upon all the Cornish and Devonshire men'.

Upon this, the King said that 'he would have Sir Harry Bennet, Mr Clifford and Mr. Churchill called to the next meeting; and because they were to be introduced into company they had not used to converse with, that it should be at the Chancellor's chamber, who should let the rest know the good opinion his Majesty had of those who were added to the number'.

We observe the Chancellor's art, in the days of his power, of making enemies, of alienating those who should have been his supporters. Sir Hugh Pollard was a good friend of his; now two of Pollard's most forward recruits were added to the number of Arlington's friends.

It was to him that Churchill owed his introduction at Court, and shortly the connexion brought him the reward of an employment under the Crown, a job at last.

The Restoration was presented with a far more intractable, and a more complex situation, in Ireland. The rebellion of Celtic and Catholic Ireland in 1641 had been a prelude to the civil war in England; it was accompanied by massacres and barbarities which made a fearful impression on the English and forfeited all claims of the Irish to sympathy now. After years of warfare, civil war, calling in papal nuncios to do what they could not do for themselves, *i.e.* govern, the Cromwellian conquest made a clean sweep—swept the native Irish landowners west of the Shannon and settled the rest with Puritan soldiers and adventurers. Whereas the majority of Irish landowners up to 1641 had been Catholic, they were now Protestant. In 1660, the Cromwellian colonists had accepted the Restoration; the King's declaration gave them guarantees. Through all the subsequent tangle of negotiations, bargaining, resettlement, this remained the fundamental factor: the Cromwellian conquest of Ireland remained essentially unchanged.

The situation within Ireland was sufficiently intractable: the bulk of the claims were incompatible and abstract justice could not be achieved. To this was added the rapacity of English courtiers. The Civil War, like all such wars, had resulted in a decline of public virtue and private morals: gone was the old idealism that had led men to die for their principles: there had been too much of that, and too much suffering in consequence of it. The new generation, led by Charles himself—who had grown up in the penurious squalor, the seedy circumstances of hanging round foreign courts and capitals, often not knowing where their next meal was coming from—were all on the make.

In 1662, the government made the best choice it could of seven Commissioners to carry out the Act of Settlement. There was Henry Coventry, who had served on committees of the Commons with Churchill; but the King found he could not dispense with him at home and his place was taken by Sir Allen Brodrick. There was Sir Edward Dering of Kent; three judges, Rainsford, Beverley, Smith; Colonel Cooke; and Winston Churchill, whose legal training gave him a qualification. Clarendon describes them as 'gentlemen of very good extractions, excellent understandings and above all suspicion for their integrity and generally reputed to be superior to any base temptation'.

In the late summer, after the Parliamentary session was over, the Commissioners went across to Dublin and by October they were well into their work. The job was not a lucrative one, but it offered opportunities to advance the interests of his patron, from whom Churchill might expect some reward. The work, which was expected to take some weeks, in fact took years. The Colonel transported his family to Dublin, where they spent most of the year 1663, and in subsequent years they were in Dublin part of the time. The youngest son, Theobald, was born there and was baptised in St. Bride's Church, 11 January 1663. The eldest son, John, for some time attended the Dublin Free Grammar School. The Commissioners met at the King's Inns—where the Four Courts now stand, on the bank of the Liffey on the way to Phoenix Park, which was just now being imparked: one thing that Dublin owes to the Restoration.

The first thing the Commissioners discovered was that there was an immense amount of land being withheld from the King, which should be at his disposal. Arlington had been made Secretary of State in October 1662, and all Irish affairs now passed through his hands. Like everybody else—or perhaps more than most, for he was very extravagant—he was avid to make up for the years that the locusts had eaten. Not far from Dublin, in the pleasant country of the upper Barrow, in King's and Queen's Counties, lay the large estate of Lord Clanmalier, head of the O'Dempseys. Lord Clanmalier had been a rebel, though not one of the worst. He was held to have forfeited his estate and the King now granted it to Arlington, for services which he had for long been unable to recompense. Ormonde was against the grant. There was no love lost between him—so great a magnate that he had no need to be any other than honest—and Arlington. As the greatest of Irish landowners, Ormonde's sympathies were with his class: he would have restored Clanmalier and many others. Moreover, the lands were occupied by a large number of Cromwellian soldiers and adventurers. The King had granted it to Arlington, but the problem was how to secure it for him. It became a vexed issue, tied up with Irish politics and perplexing legal difficulties.

It was not improper for the Colonel to advise his patron on the matter and to look after his interests. There is a long series of letters from him to Arlington about it—all of his correspondence, unfortunately, that remains. From this one-sided correspondence, we derive glimpses of the Commissioners and their work. Colonel Richard Talbot became a friend of Churchill: he afterwards married Duchess Sarah's beautiful sister and, as Duke of Tyrconnel, became James II's Catholic Lord Lieutenant: a light-headed adventurer. Talbot advised Arlington that there was so much opposition to the grant that he would do better to beg an equal estate in compensation. It was worth £3000 a year, even unimproved. Churchill advised that the best course would be to proceed by private Bill in the Irish House, and he spoke to the Speaker, a friend, to promote it. He also informed Arlington of an adventure of Henry Cromwell that had come to light, an estate worth £600 a year: 'I suppose 'tis a good fat spot by Henry Cromwell's choice of it, who at that time had all under his grip.' However, nothing came of this.

The Colonel went on pressing Arlington's claims, with the aid of Talbot and Lord Aungier; but so far in vain. Arlington wished to recall Coventry and Churchill to aid in the January session of Parliament. The Colonel was not so well disposed to a winter journey to London as Coventry was: 'we single men are the franker travellers'. Mrs. Churchill was expecting her youngest child next month. Coventry returned; Churchill remained. It must have been a gloomy winter in murky Dublin. The King's Inns were crowded with a perpetual train of clamorous suitors: threadbare Cromwellian captains (Ironsides underneath), seedy Royalist squires who had first been ousted by Catholic Irish and then squatted upon by Cromwell's soldiery, tattered Irish peers of noble birth and extravagant pretensions, a mob of native Celts who had started the trouble in 1641 and now were, as usual, to come worst out of it.

The Commissioners were much impeded in their work by being divided three to three, so that at present almost every case was dismissed, 'and the parties, though never so innocent, without any visible remedy'. The common saying in Dublin was that the Commissioners were loyal and honest, at least Rainsford, Beverley, Brodrick and Churchill were; but that they were divided, three for the King—Rainsford, Beverley and Churchill; three for the English interest—Smith, Dering and Cooke; and one for himself—Brodrick.

The most important business was the new Bill of Settlement, sent over for the King's and Arlington's opinion. The Lord Lieutenant had refused the Commissioners leave to go over, in order, it was said, to gratify the English interest, who wanted to put things in their own light to the King. The Colonel writes, 'that part of myself at my own dispose I have sent over before. . . . If my sister or daughter can serve you they are at your service, though I design them not for courtiers. My wife I leave to her own inclinations'. This is the first, and last, we hear of a sister of the Colonel's; what sort of courtier his daughter became we shall see. In October, he had to send over his wife to look to his private affairs. He much wanted leave, after more than a year in Dublin, to come over himself. He sent his observations on the new Bill: it needed a few changes, but these must be carried 'with somewhat more than ordinary resolution on the King's part, who will never decide the disputes of this nation but by being absolute in his own judgment and director'.

The King was considering summoning Churchill over to hear his views on the Bill. For his part, the Colonel found that it was not enough to send his wife over to look after his private affairs: he needed to go himself. The King left the matter to the Lord Lieutenant, and Churchill got his leave. His last words to Arlington before coming were the advice 'not to pen the Act so as to suffer any parties to be judged'. This, at any rate, was virtuous counsel. He went on to add, 'for, as I have ever told you in the business of Ireland, you will find yourself strangely deceived if the King be not absolutely despotical. I shall say no more till we meet.' The Colonel's mind was of a disconcerting simplicity. He never concealed what he thought, and such thoughts gained him much opprobrium later. On his return, he received a somewhat belated recognition of his services: on 22 January 1664, he was knighted by the King at Whitehall. No one can say that he had not had to work hard for it.

CHAPTER FOUR

Sir Winston Churchill: Whitehall and Dublin

SIR WINSTON was able to spend the years 1664 and 1665 happily in England. The new Act of Settlement for Ireland had as yet taken no satisfactory form; it was for long under discussion, bandied about between the English Council and Ormonde's government in Ireland. Through Arlington, Churchill could represent his views. His presence was much needed in the House of Commons, for one of the chief weaknesses of the Restoration government was that it was quite inadequately represented there. Arlington saw the point, though he had been no good in the House himself: he had never once opened his mouth there—popular assemblies were not the place for his secret and insinuating arts. He had done what he could in bringing together a group of King's friends, who could be relied on in all weathers, in the fluctuating conditions of Charles II's reign. Of these the most reliable and unquestioning was the Colonel—he did not cease to be known as such for having been knighted. And it was an index to the estimation in which he was held: though no fool, an educated and even a bookish man, he was too much of a piece, cut after too obvious a pattern, to weigh much with that assembly, where the strings were pulled by more sophisticated, more disingenuous men. As a regular dependable Court-member, soon to become an official of the royal household, he remained a prominent House of Commons man throughout the Cavalier Parliament, serving on committees and frequently speaking for royal policy. As that policy became increasingly unpopular and distrusted, the Colonel became a target for attack. With the Whig triumph in 1679 he was made a victim; fortunately for him he was a secondary figure, he was not important enough for anything more than extrusion.

All that was in the future: for the present he could enjoy himself, and no year was more propitious to him than the year 1664.

The brief session of Parliament which began 16 March 1664 was yet an important one. Attendance at the House was not very regular in those days, and even for important divisions not much more than a couple of hundred members registered their votes. The Colonel was back and busy on committees: on a Bill for taking away Damage Clear, on various private members' Bills, measures for the relief of the Merchant Adventurers' creditors, for distributing £60,000 among loyal and indigent commissioned officers, and for considering the petitions of merchants, tradesmen, victuallers, et cetera.

This cannot have taken up all his time: his own private affairs needed attending to. Let us hope that he was able to spend the summer at agreeable Minterne. All the more so since at the end of the summer he forfeited his freedom to become a permanent official of the royal household. On 13 September 1664, he was appointed Junior Clerk Comptroller to the Board of Green Cloth: the first-fruits of the King's favour, which he had besought through Arlington, and the limit of the King's generosity. It was no very grand post, but through it came that intimate contact with the Court from which flowed, in the next generation, all the fortune of the Churchills.

The Board's business was to take the accounts of the daily expenditure of the royal household, make the necessary provisions for it, undertake the contracts and the payments, control the discipline and pay the wages of the household servants below stairs. The head of the Board was the Lord Steward of the Household, who, throughout the reign, was Ormonde; so perhaps Sir Winston owed his promotion to the Duke, who thought well of him, as much as to Arlington, who was a man of professions rather than performance: a cold heart, where the Duke was warm. Under the Duke, who can hardly have attended the Board much, for he was absent for long periods in Ireland, there were eight officers. Sir Winston entered at the bottom as Junior Clerk Comptroller; and in twenty-two years he moved up only two places to become the Junior Clerk of the Green Cloth. The four Clerks received their full board and wages of £88 13*s.* 4*d.* a year; when the Court was absent they got board wages at the rate of £365 a year. On James II's accession, they were moved up to £500 a year. This post gave them a lodging at Court, wherever it was, at Whitehall, Windsor or Hampton Court. As with all Court posts, there were fees and tips, perquisites and considerations, more rewarding than the salary. Sir Winston's private affairs, so long under a cloud, the outlook discouraging, begin to take a more cheerful hue. By 1667 he was able to lend the

King £2000 in his necessity.

The Board must have been an agreeable little body; but it was no sinecure providing for Whitehall with its scores of servants, liveried and otherwise. Altogether there must have been hundreds of them, though the Board had to provide for only its own section, of which the core was the kitchen—always a fruitful source of profit. Whitehall was a small town in itself, the residence not only of the royal family and the Court, but the seat of government. It covered the whole area from the present Great Scotland Yard on the north to Richmond Terrace on the south, from St. James's Park on the west to the river-bank. There was a wide thoroughfare down the middle, more or less following the present one, terminating in a fine Tudor gateway, with a lesser gate at the southern exit. Inigo Jones's much admired Banqueting Hall was the latest addition to the congeries of buildings. The royal apartments were on the side of the river. There were the stairs leading up to the apartments *en suite*: the Great Chamber, with the Yeomen of the Guard in attendance; the Presence Chamber, where public audiences took place; the Privy Chamber, where only nobles and privy councillors had the right of entry; the Privy Gallery, which was near the Council Chamber and led down the stairs on the other side into the Park. Behind these was the King's Bedchamber, which, for all that few had the entry to it, was often occupied by a crowd of Charles's cronies laughing with the King over his broad and frequently repeated stories. Unlike his father, he was very friendly, familiar and all too accessible. Sir William Temple, after some experience of his ways, wrote: 'the first thing that a king should learn is to say No, so resolutely as never to be asked twice, nor once importunately'. This Charles could hardly ever bring himself to do, and never to women. He had an agreeable nature.

In addition, there were chapels and closets, the Queen's apartments and the Duke of York's and, no less important, Lady Castlemaine's at the Cockpit—for that was her abode: on the site of the garden of 10 Downing Street. Altogether it was a rabbit-warren of perhaps a couple of thousand rooms: a jumble with its little privy gardens, its naughty alleys and its open spaces: not magnificent like the Louvre, but far more convenient and comfortable in the English manner, for it housed everybody of importance attached to the Court. There was virtually free access to it, as we may read in Pepys's and Evelyn's Diaries, with hundreds of people bustling about, hurrying in and out on business, or lounging about the galleries, waiting for the great to appear, tattling, gossiping, quarrelling, eyeing each other or ogling the ladies, who 'in good King Charles's golden days' were not at all averse, and few were those who were all that they should be.

At the Restoration the Court was reorganised on former lines, though only Clarendon remained to continue the gravity and decorum of the old ways and to become the butt of the ridicule of the brilliant but graceless Buckingham, Tom Killigrew, Charles's favourite wag, Lady Castlemaine and their set. Nevertheless, the ancient routine, the elaborate ritual, the external splendour and formality remained. When the King dined in public, he was served by peers on bended knee. When he went to chapel—and there was daily chapel—the 'ladies of the Bedchamber to our Dearest Consort the Queen' sat in the first seat 'on the left hand of Our Closet.' That was where Lady Castlemaine sat, one of the ladies of the Queen's Bedchamber—until she chose to announce her conversion to Catholicism. Amid the ritual and the frolics moved the familiar figure of the King, with natural dignity, but free and easy; tall and slender, with his swarthy Bourbon complexion, his long stride followed by his spaniels in the Park, sauntering with the ladies or paying his nocturnal visits to the Cockpit, recognised by the sentries on his return.

Such was the scene upon which Sir Winston Churchill was a well-known figure for the rest of his life; taking a regular official part, which, though a secondary one, was not negligible.

One of the characteristic creations of the Restoration was the Royal Society. After the ravages of fanaticism, all too certain about the universe, the spirit of inquiry got its chance—from which the astonishing developments of modern science proceeded. Along with the scientific experiments and investigations of serious people like Wilkins, Wren, Hooke, Boyle, Sir William Petty, there were not wanting curiosities, like the promise of the Duke of Buckingham to bring to the Society a piece of a unicorn's horn—like most of his promises, unfulfilled. Sir Kenelm Digby reported that the calcinated powder of toads reverberated, being applied in bags upon the stomach of a pestiferate body, cured it by several applications. The sky was said to have rained seeds and ivy berries in Warwickshire, Shropshire and other counties. The spirit of wonder was abroad in the world. Captain Silas Taylor related that Virginians, when they would kill rattlesnakes, tied some of the plant called dittany of Virginia in a cleft stick and held it to the snake to smell, 'who presently coils herself up, turning her head away from the plant as long as she can; then she opens herself on a sudden and, being stretched out in length, is found quite dead'. Dr. Charlton was to provide two male vipers against the next meeting. Dr. Hooke had observed with a microscope how leaping cheese-maggots put their tail into their mouth and, when they leap, spring it out with great force to leap a great way like fleas.

Meetings of the Royal Society must have been amusing in those days. One cannot doubt where Swift got his inspiration from for his picture of the professors in the Island of Laputa, his satire on projectors elsewhere. Along with the diversions, there went the serious intellectual aim of the Society: to analyse things as they are, not to picture them as they are supposed to be. Science became fashionable. The King himself was amused by scientific experiments and was willing to become the Society's Patron and Founder. It attracted an aristocratic membership. Viscount Brouncker became its President; the Duke of Buckingham, the Earl of Devonshire, Lord Shaftesbury, Lord Cavendish and other peers sparkled among the scientists and physicians, the general gentlemanly membership.

At the end of this year, 21 December 1664 Sir Winston Churchill's name was proposed by Sir William Petty: evidently they had become friends in Dublin. At the next meeting, 28 December, Sir Winston was elected, along with Sir William Portman, another Dorset squire. On 4 January they were admitted Fellows. They heard three accounts of the new comet, which had caused such perturbation in December. Mr. Pepys was with child to see it; the King and Queen sat up all night to glimpse it, and did, it seems. Of course, it portended dreadful horrors: the horrors were not slow in coming. Mr. Hooke showed a way of applying a thermometer to a weather clock. Francis Willoughby, home from his travels, was desired to communicate his philosophical observations made abroad. Mr. Boyle reported on his experiments on the congelation of animals and vegetable substances. What a future this line of investigation was to have, to be sure!

Whether it was that this menu was too much for Sir Winston Churchill or no, true it is that he never appeared *there* again. Some years later, when that excellent administrator, Samuel Pepys, was President, a list of members who were in arrears, contrary to the statute, was drawn up and it was ordered that their names should be left out of the next list. Among them was the Duke of Buckingham, which was not surprising, considering that he was well on the way to bankruptcy. With him—some fifty all told—were Sir William Portman and Sir Winston Churchill. His lack of interest in science offers a contrast with his descendant, who kept remarkably *au fait* with the portentous developments of which his ancestor saw the beginnings without curiosity.

An equally striking contrast across the centuries is provided by their respective contributions, in the Commons, to the Poor Law: the original Sir Winston playing his part in constructing the code that kept the poor and the unemployed in their place all through the classic period of the rule of the squirearchy, his descendant contributing constructively to the social revolution of our time with his Labour Exchanges, Trade Boards and introduction of Unemployment Insurance. In January 1665, Sir Winston was placed on a committee to supply defects in the Act for the Relief of the Poor, as it was euphemistically called. He was regularly placed on committees dealing with this subject, concerned in each development of it. In February he was a member of a large committee on a Bill for regulating the assize and measure of wood and coal to meet at two in the afternoon—and a cold winter's day—in the Speaker's chamber.

That summer, in the middle of the fiercely fought sea-war with Holland, befell one of the horrors portended by the comet: the Great Plague that ravaged London. It began in April; by June the death-rate was 600 a month, in August it reached the appalling total of 26,000. All well-to-do people left the City; business was suspended. The Court fled from Whitehall; many thought the Plague a judgment for its licentiousness. They were certain when, in 1666, a second visitation hit the City. Yet, oddly enough, the Great Fire spared Whitehall.

The autumn session of Parliament met in October at Oxford, away from the Plague. This gave Sir Winston an opportunity to renew acquaintance with his old college of St. John's; for when Parliament met at Oxford, it was usual for members to stay in the colleges where they had been students. The House of Commons sat in the Convocation house; the Commons' committees conveniently near by in the Schools—it is pleasant to think of that long-dead heart of the University humming with Parliament men coming to and fro. It is agreeable, too, to find Sir Winston, at the beginning of the month, on arrival at Oxford, being admitted as a reader to the Bodleian Library. No doubt, with his bookish interests, he found it enjoyable, as well as useful, to vary attendance at the committees of the House meeting in the Schools below, to mount the stairs to Duke Humphrey's library in all the panoply of bookcases and painted ceiling furnished by Sir Thomas Bodley.

The Anglican reaction reached its high-water mark in this Laudian centre; the Oxford Parliament passed the Five Mile Act, by which nonconformist ministers and schoolmasters were forbidden to reside in cities and corporate towns. It remained entirely inoperative; the best comment on the Act was that in Oxford itself a supposedly excluded Dissenter presently became mayor. Sir Winston sat on the committee in the Divinity School, from which this pious Bill emerged. He was on another to amend the Bill for regulating the press. This committee, with all the Members of Parliament that were of the long robe (*i.e.* lawyers) and the university members, met in the Law School: they were empowered to consider defects in the Acts against conventicles and to report what temporary Acts were to be continued.

Actually, in the English environment, it was impossible to operate these Acts. They were understandable enough, after the long and intolerant rule of the sectaries. But the Anglican reaction had passed its peak and was already receding. Clarendon and his friends were exceedingly, and undeservedly, unpopular; Buckingham, Arlington, Shaftesbury were rising to power. The membership of the House of Commons was changing; new men were entering all the time, altering its inflection; new currents of opinion were flowing, with which these men were in touch.

Far more important in its effects than any Five Mile Act was the exclusion of Irish cattle. An Act of 1663 had excluded Ireland from the colonial trade and forbidden the importation of Irish cattle every year from 1 July to the end of the year. The jealous interests of English landowners, particularly of the West Country and the North, were in the ascendant. Cromwell's policy had been more enlightened: union with Ireland, Irish members sitting at Westminster, free trade between the two countries, Ireland sharing in the benefits of the Navigation Act. Clarendon and Ormonde were anxious for the repeal of the restrictions on Irish cattle, in the interests of Ireland, and if the English settlers there were ever to make a success of the country. They were true statesmen.

Pepys tells us that the Prohibition Bill was the work of the Western members, 'wholly against the sense of most of the rest of the House, who think, if you do this, you give the Irish again cause to rebel'. The eastern counties, whose interest was feeding, not breeding, cattle were in favour of allowing Irish cattle in. But the eastern counties, responsible for Cromwell's victory and rule, were now under a cloud: the Restoration was the heyday of the West Country.

The King entirely shared Ormonde's views on the matter, who represented to him 'the cruelty of such a treatment of a colony, which all wise states, especially the Roman, thought it their interest to encourage'. Now, in 1665, there was an agricultural depression. The brilliant, unscrupulous Shaftesbury was intelligent enough to know that the depression had nothing to do with the importation of Irish cattle; but to gain popularity with the Western members against Clarendon, he inflamed their passions and led them on with that compelling voice of his with its irresistible cadences. So far from the majority being in favour of repeal, they pushed for total prohibition. In committee the debates were continued and the strongest opposition to the majority was put up by Sir Winston Churchill and Sir Allen Brodrick, much to their credit. In the Lords the Duke of York and the Chancellor were outspoken against it and the King several times declared that he could not give the royal assent to it with a safe conscience. Nevertheless, the second reading was carried by 103 votes to 52, and so the matter stood when Parliament was prorogued—to meet at Oxford in the autumn.

There, towards the end of October, the struggle was resumed. On 20 October a committee of the whole House met in the Divinity School 'to summon and hear such persons of the Irish Privy Council as are in town'. Sir Winston continued to fight as stoutly as ever for justice for Ireland, and the cause even made some progress. But the situation was rendered hopeless by a complete change in the attitude of the King. With the cost of the Dutch war, the losses by the Plague and the Fire, he was desperate for money to carry on the government. If he had remained firm, he could have carried the peers with him. Charles II, however, usually took the line of least resistance: he was now as anxious to carry the Bill, and placate the majority, as he had previously been to oppose it. Sir Winston and Sir John Talbot fought on in vain: at the end they were Tellers for the Noes, who mustered 68, as against 81 Yeas. It had been a gallant fight; but 'so it was resolved in the affirmative'.

During these two years when Sir Winston Churchill was in England, a great deal of time and attention was given to the Act of Explanation, which was to define and make clear the Act of Settlement. Ormonde had had to come over from Ireland; the Solicitor-General drew up the Bill with the aid of a committee consisting of the Duke, all the Irish Privy Councillors then in London and the Commissioners of Claims, so that Sir Winston had his part in drawing up the measure he went back to Ireland to execute. In Ireland the English interest had consented to surrender one-sixth of what the Act of Settlement gave them. In London the Irish agents thought that too little, and in the end the English interest agreed to raise the one-sixth to one-third. On that basis the Act was drawn up. Having made this considerable concession, the Protestants—Royalists, Cromwellians, Adventurers, soldiers—expected theirs to be the first claim upon the Act; and they were now confirmed in possession of two-thirds of their former holdings. The rest, along with the mass of forfeitures to the Crown, of rebels and regicides, constituted a reservoir from which to allot reprisals and make grants to those qualified under the Act.

The Act was considerably more generous to the Irish and represented a larger measure of justice, considering the historic tangle of rebellion, reconquest and new settlement. All would depend on how it was implemented. Full powers were given to five of the former Commissioners to execute it: Chief Justice Smith, Dering, Colonel Cooke, Brodrick and Churchill. Lord Orrery wrote that the English interest was very much startled at Sir Allen Brodrick's and Sir Winston Churchill's being Commissioners, 'but for the last of them I have, I hope, given satisfaction'. These two were both sympathetic to Irish claims. Once more Sir Winston transferred himself and his family to Dublin, to the tedious treadmill of the Court of Claims. We have indications that his lady, who inherited something of her mother's temperament, did not relish this Irish sojourn and longed for England. Moreover, the children were growing up, of an age to be placed and provided for; in Ireland they were out of sight and out of mind.

In January 1666, Sir Winston wrote to thank Arlington for recommending his younger son to Lord Sandwich, 'for though (as times go now) it is no great preferment to be a page, I am not ignorant of the benefit of disposing of him (in such a juncture of time as this) into that country where all the boys seem men and all the men seem wise'. Residence in Ireland for any length of time is apt to put such reflections into people's heads. He was glad that the boy would have Lord Sandwich's example before him. (Lord Sandwich was the Cromwellian Admiral Montagu who had brought over the King in 1660.) The boy being so provided for must be the second son, George, who went to sea and had a prominent naval career, ending up as an Admiral and administrative head of the Admiralty, in the day of his brother the Duke's power.

The Commissioners sat all through that winter and spring, by which time they had dealt with the bulk of the claims that were fairly clear. In the spring, Sir Winston was anxious to get back to England, or his presence was desired at Whitehall, where he had other duties to perform. At the end of May, the Court adjourned till October: 'today [25 May] Sir Winston Churchill and Colonel Cooke have gone to sea'. He was in England that exciting, distracted, contentious summer of 1667. During the peace-negotiations, when the government decided to send no fleet to sea in order to economise, the Dutch took the opportunity in June to break the boom at Chatham, burn four ships of the line and coolly tow the *Royal Charles* off home undamaged. It was a national humiliation, and let loose a fury of contempt and anger against Charles's government. While he was largely occupied with Lady Castlemaine, the only man to show any capacity for war or resolution was the old Cromwellian Monk.

To divert popular clamour and share responsibility, Charles called a session of Parliament in July. Sir Winston was thus able to be in his place. The King gained nothing by his move. Parliament passed a unanimous resolution demanding the disbandment of the 12,000 men he had raised under the guise of resisting the Dutch. The Commons were beginning to suspect him, and rightly, for he was already negotiating secretly with France for support: a course contrary to the interests of the nation, which culminated later in the disgraceful, the treacherous, Secret Treaty of Dover. The King hastily prorogued Parliament till October, when the Commons were able to employ their time in impeaching Clarendon, and the King his in sacrificing him. That summer before his fall, the old man was able to prove himself much abler in diplomacy than in conducting a war he had never sought and tried to avert. He managed to make peace with Holland on a favourable basis, one which brought an acquisition of the utmost importance for the future. The Dutch ceded New Netherland, so closing the gap in the English possessions along the American coastline, and giving the colonists the command of the trade-route from the Great Lakes to what was to become the greatest city in the world. New Amsterdam became New York.

By now Sir Winston was back in Dublin. He and Sir Edward Dering arrived together, two days within their appointed time, so that apprehensions that the Commission would lapse were allayed. They had had a stormy October passage. Work, and such diversions as Ireland could afford, went on till June. In that month a most important issue, which could have had very awkward consequences for Sir Winston—considering the stand he took up—came to a head. This was the question of the Duke of York's claim. He had been granted practically all the lands of the regicides, Cromwell's, Ireton's, Ludlow's and others; something between 100,000 and 150,000 acres. And this without any protection for the old proprietors. The Duke left his claims to be prosecuted by a rapacious set of agents, of whom the most shameless was a Captain Thornhill. These delayed the settlement of the Duke's claim as long as they could, in order that they might enjoy the gifts upon lettings from year to year. This held up a large number of other claimants and suitors whose affairs could not be settled until the Duke's were.

Sir Winston, who, as we have seen, was never wanting in courage, took the lead against the Duke's agents, and gave Captain Thornhill a dressing down in open court. In a passion Sir Winston attacked the Duke's agents, calling them all a pack of knaves and cheats engaged in betraying their master. Thornhill then tried to provoke the Colonel into saying something that might be reportable as treasonable. Captain Thornhill visited him in his chamber that afternoon and asked whom he meant by 'the Duke's agents'. Sir Winston replied hotly, 'What, are you come to challenge and hector me? I meant you.' Thornhill returned that the words were 'the Duke's agents' and it could not be that Churchill meant only him. 'No,' said Sir Winston, 'I meant you and Dr. Gorges and the whole pack of you.' The Captain, drawing Sir Winston into committing himself—never a difficult operation—pointed out that the influential Sir Jerome Alexander was the Duke's chief agent: he presumed that Sir Winston durst not call him a knave. ' "Yes," in passion replied the Knight. "He's the chief knave and so I can prove you all"—and with that directed the Captain to the stairs, who seeing the necessity of either running down the stairs or being thrown down, as the least of two evils elected the former.' Churchill's colleague, Colonel Cooke, reported that this passage at arms did nothing but good. And, in fact, the courageous stand of Sir Winston's fortified his brother Commissioners in docking the Duke of York's lists of 30,000 acres, which were to be distributed in reprisals, while a similar acreage was to follow.

What makes Sir Winston's courage in standing up against the Duke's claims all the more admirable is that his daughter had been given a place at Court as maid-of-honour to the Duchess of York, and was now the Duke's mistress. In later years, enemies would say that the old Cavalier had promoted his daughter to the Duke's favours. We see how unjust an aspersion that was; he had not even wanted his daughter to go to Court. It is far more probable that Lady Churchill managed to get her daughter a Court post. We have seen that she detested being in Ireland, and we have had some indication that she inherited her mother, Lady Drake's temper: Sir Winston may not have had too comfortable a life with her.

That summer a great change threatened the direction of Irish affairs. After the fall of Clarendon, there remained only the magnificent figure of Ormonde between the young men and the attainment of full power. The weakness of the Clarendonian régime had always been finance. That gifted jackanapes and spoiled crony of the King, the second Buckingham, made himself—of all people—the spokesman of financial reform. A hopeless squanderer, he was already on his way to bankruptcy. This did not impair his popularity with the Commons. He deserved everything that Dryden said of him:

A man so various that he seemed to be
Not one; but all mankind's epitome.
Stiff in opinions, always in the wrong;
Was everything by starts, and nothing long:
But in the course of one revolving moon
Was chemist, fiddler, statesman and buffoon . . .
In squandering wealth was his peculiar art:
Nothing went unrewarded but desert.
Beggared by fools, whom still he found too late:
He had his jest and they had his estate.

This man, in the cause of financial virtue and out of resentment that Ormonde had not been more lavish with him over the marriage of his niece, made himself the Duke's leading opponent.

Ormonde thought that he had reached an understanding with the subtle Arlington, who had married his son's sister-in-law. Arlington feared above all things that Ormonde would lead a party to bring Clarendon back. He assured the Duke that he would prevent an attack on him from Buckingham. Ormonde, secure in these assurances, went down to Moor Park 'to enjoy the company of friends and the coolness of the place'. No sooner was his back turned than commissioners were appointed to examine into the malversation of the government and revenue of Ireland. This was but a foreshadowing of what was to come.

In October, the Commissioners of Claims returned to Dublin to wind up their work. It took them another three months to complete it. On 21 January 1669, Churchill, Dering, Brodrick and Cooke arrived at Holyhead in the King's pleasure-boat, *Mary*. Irish matters followed Churchill over to Whitehall; for we find him sending an Order in Council 'grounded upon a petition of Thornhill, and some of that gang'. Ormonde had advised Churchill to solicit the King about the Commissioners' diet-money—so it was still in arrear: Churchill's regular attendance gave him the opportunity. But he was about to 'begin my journey . . . towards my new home' and would not be back till April. This must mean that Sir Winston was now building at Minterne.

When we consider its long endurance, we may regard the Restoration settlement of Ireland, as human affairs go, as a not unsatisfactory achievement. As for the great man who had presided over it, in spite of Buckingham's calumnious campaign, the King repeatedly affirmed his confidence in Ormonde. Then suddenly, in February 1669, he was dismissed. Pepys regarded it as 'a great stroke to show the power of Buckingham and the poor spirit of the King, and little hold that any man can have of him'. Little Mr. Pepys was not wrong: the best days of the Restoration were over.

CHAPTER FIVE

House of Commons : Court-Member

WHEN Sir Winston Churchill came back from his Irish exile he found that the world had moved on without him, leaving him rather behind. The disappearance of Charles's tiresome mentor, the great man, Clarendon, left the King free to conduct a policy of his own—and a very disingenuous affair it turned out to be. Politics were, in any case, in a state of confusion, for the bounds of the royal power and that of Parliament, the boundaries of jurisdiction between Lords and Commons, were by no means clearly defined; they were in course of definition in the political struggles of the time. This is what makes these years so interesting constitutionally. Finance was a fundamental trouble of the period. The Commons here had undoubted power, but could they trust the King, with adequate supplies, to conduct a policy of which they and the nation approved?

Here was the issue that dominated politics up to its resolution in 1688; for, of course, the Stuarts could not be trusted. Charles II was a clever, indolent man, willing to make concessions, to compromise in order to keep his throne and not have to go on his travels again. But, underneath, he was not much more willing to conduct the nation's business in accordance with its will than his father had been. So far as he could, he followed his own personal policy of a French alliance, subsidies from Louis XIV in order to rule independently of Parliament, favour for Catholics and—since this was a necessary coating for the pill—for Dissenters. (Not that he liked Dissenters: he thought theirs was 'no religion for a gentleman'.) This line was in accordance with neither the interests nor the wishes of the nation. When his brother succeeded, who had no conception of compromise ('Nobody will kill me, Jamie, to make you King'), it took James a mere three years to lose the throne.

This condition of affairs made the situation of loyal supporters of the monarchy, who were at the same time Protestants, increasingly uncomfortable. It created acute difficulties under James II, difficulties that dominated, as their solution decided, the careers of the

Churchills. They were all monarchists, but they were all Protestants. They would not succumb to the inducements of the King to become Papists.

The truth is that the backbone of the nation was the House of Commons. In spite of everything. In spite of bribery and corruption, the extremes of partisanship, the asininities of which all collective assemblies are capable, the disloyalties, the mutual antagonisms, the contradictions, the panic that seized them over the Popish Plot. The Commons represented the nation, assembled and embattled. Everybody who was anybody in his county was there: the gentry who not only ruled, but ran, English society. This institution, and its power, distinguished this country from all others. It was not, as supercilious monarchs like Louis XIV thought, a mark of inferiority; it was a mark of the greater political maturity of the English people and their governing class. This peculiar institution, which grew to express the political instinct of the nation, was to have an astonishing career wherever English-speaking people settled in the world, and to have its influence wherever other peoples were capable of self-government.

In spite of crises and distractions, Parliament followed, in the event, a moderate course, that attained its objective in 1688. Beneath the excitements and alarms of the time, and in spite of the opposition of the monarchy fighting a rear-guard action to preserve power for itself, the work of building a constitutional state went forward. Parliament wanted a monarchy, but a Protestant one. It wanted a foreign policy in the interests of the nation, *i.e.* an alliance with other European powers, particularly Holland, to check the growing ascendancy of France. It wanted responsible Parliamentary government, not the irresponsible absolutism of a Louis XIV. It was now ready for a measure of toleration for Protestant Dissenters, but not for Catholics with their exclusive claims and their record of persecution.

In circumstances of great complexity and confusion, Parliament's achievement in these years was remarkable. An American scholar has summed it up: 'it settled the relations of church and state, of Anglican and Nonconformist, which have endured in part almost to our own day, in part still remain. It made good in principle and practice the control of finance by the Commons. It determined the status of Catholics for a century and a half. It enunciated those protests against illegal taxation and against government by a standing army—with its consequent abuses, the quartering of soldiers and martial law—which have found place in every Anglo-Saxon constitution since. It reformed the judicial system,' and secured the liberty of the individual, by the enactment of Habeas Corpus, which remains today a fundamental difference between democratic freedom and the absence of any personal security where there are no representative institutions. . . . 'The House of Commons indeed supplies the real connexion between the Civil War and the Revolution of 1688; and it is the Commons, rather than the leaders, which give us the correct measure of public opinion.'[1]

In all this activity of the Commons, Sir Winston Churchill took a regular, a fairly prominent, but not a central, part. He was now, first and foremost, an official of the royal household; that not only circumscribed his freedom, but turned him into a Court-member—someone whose line on any important matter of policy in dispute could be foretold. He was there to defend the King's policy, and his wishes. As Charles's government became more unpopular and lost command of any majority in the Commons, so Sir Winston was considered simply a place-man of the Crown. One watches the decline of his personal position, the sacrifice he made; for, with the victory of the Whigs, he became a target of abuse, was eventually driven from his post at the Board of Green Cloth and lost his seat in Parliament.

He sacrificed his independence; but then, as we have seen, any independence of the Crown was contrary to his high monarchical principles: he may be described as a Passive Obedience Tory. He was a man set in his ways, simple and rigid, in that snake-pit of a Court with its twisting, turning, reptilian creatures, glittering, deceitful and insincere. He had become fixed somewhat early and had now reached the limit of his development. There was something obstinate, even *borné,* about him: something of a West Country bull.

In the House, besides being a Court-member, he had a secondary classification as a lawyer: one of the 'gentlemen of the long robe', more frequently put on committees than others, apt to be called on for an opinion on legal points. Even so, he was a lawyer of the second rank. His interventions in debate were not weighty; he usually delivered himself of one simple point, and that an emotional one. All the same, he usually spoke *to* the point: and his speeches had the importance that they always expressed the official point of view. As a leading spokesman of the Court

[1] Wilbur C. Abbott, *The Long Parliament of Charles II,* E.H.R., 1906, 283.

in the House—throughout the whole period—he incurred unpopularity when opinion turned more and more against the Court. And in the public prints he was traduced for the undignified situation he was placed in by his daughter's relation to the heir to the throne. It was a strange turn of fortune for a respectable West Country squire. But there was nothing to be done: his fate was fixed by his position at Court. It may have been a source of unhappiness and disquiet to him; one will never know. There is a look of anxiety and sadness in his eyes, all the more striking in the big, heavy, masculine features, tricked out in all the Court-finery of slashed sleeves and satin. At the same time, what made him a target for abuse and subsequent depreciation in history opened up the astonishing possibilities that made his children's fortune.

In the session that began on 19 October 1669, Sir Winston was back in his place to play a full part. We find him serving, as usual, on committees to consider the poor laws and seditious conventicles. In this session and the next, he was busy with the question of the import duties on brandy, wines and other liquors. In March, Churchill was called upon to defend both the government and the King's prerogative in ecclesiastical matters. Into the Bill amending the Conventicle Act the Lords inserted a proviso reserving the King's ancient prerogative in ecclesiastical matters or any power at any time enjoyed by any of his ancestors. Andrew Marvell reported to his Whiggish constituents, the Mayor and corporation of Hull, 'there never was so compendious a piece of absolute universal tyranny': he thought it would leave it in the King's power to dispense with the execution of the whole Bill. Sir Winston, of course, defended the Lords' proviso. He thought it 'necessary to recognise the King's Supremacy now. It is not whether his ecclesiastical right be infringed, but whether the King thinks so or no. The Lords, the two estates, have thought this requisite; the Lords think the Supremacy in question, and they advise it. He cannot give his negative till he hears the Lords' reasons.' One detects the note of cant on both sides—but perhaps some cant is necessary in politics. As Lord Halifax observed, 'the comfortable opinion men have of themselves keepeth up human society, which would be more than half destroyed without it'. In spite of Sir Winston, the House negatived the proviso by 122 to 88.

At the end of March there was a committee of the whole House on the Bill for Lord Roos's divorce, a case which made a tremendous scandal; but the political importance of it was greater, for the

Whigs intended it as a precedent for a divorce for the King and the provision of a Protestant succession. So far as the King was concerned, all were fooled. As a secret Catholic he had no intention of marrying again—and no intention of giving up his pleasures. Halifax, who was 'near him', observes: 'men that were earnest Protestants were under the sharpness of his displeasure, expressed by raillery, as well as by other ways. Men near him have made discoveries from sudden breakings out in discourse etcetera, which showed there was a root. It was not the least skilful part of his concealing himself, to make the world think he leaned towards an indifference in religion.'

This was a very busy session, for Churchill as for others. Marvell wrote his excuses to Hull, that 'the crowd of business now toward our rising obliging us to sit both forenoon and afternoon, usually till nine o'clock, which indeed is the occasion that I have the less vigour left at night, and cannot write so frequently to you'. He added, 'that which is extraordinary is that his Majesty hath for this whole week come every day in person to the House of Lords and sat there during their debates and resolutions. And yesterday the Lords went in a body to give him thanks for the honour he did them therein.' What Marvell may not have known was his Majesty's reason for going: he thought it 'better than a play'.

This was the last session that gave Charles any satisfaction; for he was now engaged in the underground negotiations with Louis XIV that led to the Secret Treaty of Dover. After that, when news of its purport leaked out and suspicions were confirmed, there was never any more confidence in Charles on the part of the majority in the House. That treaty was his greatest mistake. Not so much the secret clauses by which he promised to declare himself a Catholic and to bring the country over to Catholicism—as if that were possible! The rumour of this design did immeasurable damage; but he was left free to declare himself when he liked, and he had the political sense never to do so. What was unforgivable was that the collusion of the King of England with Louis XIV, in a treacherous attack on Holland and in the general course of French policy, immensely aided Louis to achieve that domination of Europe which, in consequence, it took twenty years of European war later to reduce. The Treaty of Dover was personally a clever instrument: Charles got the cash and was free to keep his promises or no as he liked. One-half of the Cabal government was duped as to what the other half had agreed; everybody was fooled, not only one-half of the government and the English Parliament, but to some extent Louis and the Catholics too. It is better, in the end, to be direct and sincere, where the fates of nations are concerned.

The collective capacities of the Cabal were very considerable; the trouble was that they could not be collected. Two of them were crypto-Catholics, the other three crypto-Protestants. Only one of them had any genuine belief, and he the least intelligent: Churchill's old West Country associate, Clifford. Clifford's ability was purely financial and administrative. One notices in this session how frequently and to the point he speaks on all such matters. He had quite outdistanced Churchill, was now Treasurer of the Household and on his way to become, at the momentary full deployment of Charles's Catholic policy, Lord High Treasurer. The response of the Commons to all this was the Test Act, driving all Catholics from public life. Clifford died shortly after—it was said, by his own hand.

Sir Winston Churchill, however, was not aware of the King's real plans; nor was anyone else. The strangest thing about this affable, talkative monarch was his silence and secrecy. No one knew what his real convictions were: he could never utter them. No one knew his plans, not even his mistresses; he had the advantage that his relations with them were not those of any love. Among them all, he moved a solitary, lonely man, very *désabusé*; underneath the gaiety and easy nature, really rather a sad man, as one perceives between the lines of Halifax's discerning *Character*.

From April 1671 to February 1673 Charles kept Parliament in recess: nearly two years in which to unfold his own policy and try out, as his father had done, his personal rule. He had got large supplies out of Parliament by a trick, further subsidies from Louis by his promises. With these, Louis had sent over Louise de Quérouaille, a former waiting woman of Charles's favourite sister, Henriette, to keep him quiet and, if possible, attached. The Breton beauty became a figure in English politics; to Charles a cosier one than the exacting, the clamorous, the tempestuous Castlemaine; all the same, she needed to be subsidised largely too. Supported on both fronts, Charles felt in a position to launch his religious policy at home and to attack the Dutch, alongside of Louis abroad. In March 1672, he issued his Declaration of Indulgence, suspending by his own absolute authority all the country's repressive laws against Roman Catholics and Protestant Dissenters. On this, the King said he would never withdraw. Two days later, he declared war against Holland.

The importance of the war in the long run was that it produced a complete revulsion of opinion with regard to Holland, and revealed in a flash the overriding danger from France. The tough little Republic had to sustain the onslaught of the immense forces the greatest power in Europe could bring to bear on her land-frontier and, at sea, the weight of attack of the one sea-power that rivalled her own, *plus* Louis's growing navy. It was a moment fraught with danger for Europe. In Holland, the dykes were broken, the sea let in: the irresistible might of the French army was held up at the water's edge; a revolution threw out the appeasers of France and brought the young William of Orange to power, to save the state and launch himself on his lifelong task of reducing Louis. From the grave, through the brain and arm of Winston Churchill's son, he accomplished it in the end.

At sea the Dutch saved themselves by the drawn battle of Sole Bay. It was a tremendously hard-fought contest between English and Dutch, in which the French, obviously under instructions, held off and left the contestants at it hammer-and-tongs. When this happened again at the battle of the Texel next year, it became too obvious that the French game at sea was to watch the English and Dutch immolate each other for France's benefit. Public opinion in England, which had devoted to these sea-battles the intense feeling usually reserved for sport, veered sharply from the treacherous ally to the gallant opponent. What was the purpose of the war? What could possibly be gained by it? It could only result in ensuring the domination of Louis XIV over Europe. Holland had saved herself by her exertions and was now to save Europe by her example.

William set to work to bring together the Grand Alliance which alone could keep France within bounds—an alliance of which this country should have been the keystone, if its king had not virtually been a traitor to the interests of the naion. That is, briefly, the reason for the Revolution of 1688, and why William became king in England.

During those two years, Charles had, as the historian of the reign observes, 'committeed acts which had a profound reaction on the fate of his dynasty and the history of his country'.[1] When he was forced, in February 1673, to summon Parliament for supplies for a war which now had no purpose, he was faced with a House of Commons inflamed with rage and frustration. The real purport of the Secret Treaty of Dover had leaked out. There were going to be no supplies until the Catholic advisers of the King were removed and a Protestant succession assured. The nation was determined

[1] David Ogg, *England in the Reign of Charles II,* I. 351.

not to allow Catholics in power—at a time of European crisis, when Louis was driving his Protestant subjects into exile, and the House was constantly engaged upon Bills for naturalising them. His policy pointed straight to the Revocation of the Edict of Nantes, the expulsion of scores of thousands of his best and most industrious subjects, the forced conversion of others, the *dragonnades* of fire and slaughter in the Protestant Cévennes. The atmosphere of the time was very much of the Nazi 1930's, the issues for English policy not dissimilar.

The Commons were not going to have it, and in a continuous campaign drove the King from position to position, marked out the course the nation would have him follow. Otherwise: no supplies. Within a month Charles 'took a step which no other male Stuart would have taken': he withdrew the Declaration of Indulgence.[1] Such toleration as there was going to be was not by royal grace and favour, but by Parliamentary authority, and for Protestants only. This was followed up by the Test Act, which forced the heir to the throne to resign his public offices and withdraw, and drove the Lord Treasurer into retirement. The Cabal was split in pieces. Shaftesbury, furious at having been outsmarted over the Treaty of Dover, when he thought nobody smarter than himself, went over to the Opposition. Buckingham and Arlington were made to give an account of themselves to Parliament.

The temper of the Cavalier Parliament was changing with its composition: by now one-third of its members were new men who knew not David or the blithe promise of May 1660. Churchill remained a prominent member, not to be ignored.

The character of the House was changing too. Gone were the more idealistic days of Clarendon: with the organisation of parties, the struggle for influence and votes, the House was becoming much more open to bribery. After the disaster to the Cabal, Charles turned to a House of Commons man, Danby, who bribed members right and left to secure a party for the King. In January the House took note that a member had been reported to say that he hoped to make this session worth £5000 to him. The House was very delicate about this matter: no lady is so conscious of virtue as a lady of easy virtue. Sir Winston was on the committee to look into the matter; and on another to consider the more interesting question of the water-pumps invented by Sir Samuel Morland, a fascinating figure in an age full of them.

On the decisive matter of the independence of the judiciary, Sir

[1] *Ibid,* I. 368.

Winston took, as usual, the Crown's line. The issue was the historic one that had come up under Charles I, whether the Judges' patents were to be made out according to the form *Durante bene placito* (during pleasure) or *Quamdiu se bene gesserint* (during good behaviour): according to the first, they held office at the pleasure of the Crown; by the second, Parliament could be the only court to determine their record of behaviour. The future independence of the judiciary, throughout the English-speaking world, depended on this decision.

The old poet, Edmund Waller, had become a kind of Father of the House and its most admired speaker. His speeches stand out by their style and by their allusions, even in the crabbed reporting of those days. On this issue Waller, who had become the memory of the House, said: 'Fifty years ago this came in question; the House of Commons ever favoured *Quam diu se bene gesserint*. . . . Lord St. John said, it was no great matter their fining Justices; the only arbitrary power was fining one hundred pounds, it may be, for a wry look, and no remedy.' The poet, who was very famous in his old age, put his finger on the crucial issue here—as it remains today with those countries that have no justice independent of political power.

When Parliament met again on 13 April 1675, after fourteen months' prorogation, the Commons at once pressed forward with anti-Popery measures. Bills were introduced applying tests of such specific Catholic doctrines that every loophole against Papists in power might be stopped. Every loophole, that is to say, except the largest: the throne itself; for the heir to the throne was a Catholic, and nothing would induce James to compromise his faith. In November the Commons introduced a measure that 'the children of the royal family should be educated in the Protestant religion and no Popish priest to come near them'. Popish priests were crawling in the corridors of Whitehall and Somerset House. Marvell reports drily to his Protestant constituents at this moment: 'the Pope hath given a Cardinal's hat to Father Howard, the Queen's almoner'. Why could not the Stuarts take warning from the temper and will of the nation? Charles did, and at the opening of this session he asseverated 'that for his part he should always maintain the religion and the Church of England as now established, and be all his life constant in that profession'. Nor did he ever dare to withdraw publicly from that position.

From the constitutional point of view, the historian of the reign tells us that 'the central theme is the attempt to establish a clearly defined relationship within the trinity which consisted of Crown and both Houses'.[1] The formative years of his life Charles had passed in exile; his ideal of government, as of conduct, was that of his cousin, Louis XIV, the grandest monarch in Europe. He associated 'absolute kingship with order, and political experiment with anarchy. Of English patriotism, or respect for English tradition, there was no trace in his career.' Subsequent history has underlined the relative values, the respective worth, of French and English models of government. Neither Charles nor James was English, however: they were five-eighths French, the rest a mixture of Scot, Dane, German. Of course, Charles, like Louis, was a fine gentleman—though Halifax thought that 'his fine gentlemanship did him no good'. The House appreciated that he was a gentleman, but was increasingly of the opinion that he could not be trusted. In the circumstances of gathering tension between them, the unfailing courtesy that was preserved was a triumph, 'a distinctively English achievement'.[2]

The Commons became more and more sensitive as to its rights and privileges, and this led to conflicts not only with the King, but with the Lords. Sir Winston Churchill took a prominent part in the dispute over Shirley *v.* Fagg, which had the importance of settling the appellate jurisdiction of the House of Lords. Over this, Sir Winston was, for once, and not the last time, on the winning side. It also fell to him to defend his cousin, Sir John Churchill, Jasper's son, whom we last saw following him as a student at Lincoln's Inn. He was a more distinguished lawyer than Sir Winston, and no less of a royalist; Attorney-General to the Duke of York, on James's accession he was made Master of the Rolls.

[1] Ogg, *op. cit.* II. 450.
[2] *Ibid.* 458.

CHAPTER SIX

Parliament and Popish Plot

PARLIAMENT met again in October 1675. Sir Winston was as prominent as ever on the Commons' committees. A new Bill to prevent the growth of Popery was brought in. With the tension in Europe and the advances being made by Louis XIV, the Commons were determined to maintain the Protestant foundation of the state. Even James might have survived as king, if he had had sense to respect this determination.

Not content with the largest army in Europe, Louis XIV was now engaged in building a navy to rival England's. It was like the determination of pre-1914 Germany, and had the same result: it brought on a clash between the two countries. Why should they expect to be dominant on both land and sea? No English government could survive such a threat to the nation. Even Charles's government took defensive measures and proposed a programme of naval building—which would cost money. Some members were in favour of going slow and saving the burden of taxes. Not so Sir Winston. 'Saving money is no argument, when saving the nation is the case. We are now upon the shallows, upon the fewest ships; but we consider not the great man on t'other side of the water, the King of France.' He was called upon to name him 'the French king'—the King of England never having retracted his title to France. Sir Winston wanted the larger number of ships put to the question first. If you put five before nine, if we vote not five, how shall we vote nine? If nine be put first, then five may come naturally.

How strange a foreshadowing it seems of his descendant's introduction of the Naval Building programme of 1912 and the popular cry—

We want eight,
And we won't wait!

There followed a typical wrangle over procedure—nothing more boring—whether the greater or lesser sum necessary should be put to the question. The debate is enlivened for us by a nostalgic phrase of Colonel Birch. 'The more diffusive the work, the better it is for the nation. He has had occasion to ride through the Forest of Dean; for half a mile together he saw not one tree in fifty decayed, and of great height—the bravest echo of woods he ever heard.' It is a phrase in which the beauty of Restoration England stands revealed.

The House resolved that one first-rate, five second-rates and fourteen third-rates be built and that the money, £300,000, should be raised by Land Tax. This was voted by 176 to 150, which gives us the rough division of parties, the Whigs being mainly in favour of raising money from the land, rather than from trade and excise. This division of interest between parties becomes the usual one for the next half century.

The next step was to see that this sum was appropriated to the proper object. In such efforts we see the forms of our constitution gradually taking shape—against the wishes of a Tory like Sir Winston. A Committee of the whole House resolved that the moneys for the ships be kept separate and distinct in the Exchequer: they did not trust Charles's government. Churchill was named as being against appropriation. He explained, with moderation, that he was against it only until there was proof given that such a branch of the revenue was misapplied, as had been said. 'Till that be, we ought not to appropriate.' Distrust of Charles was responsible for this; though actually it seems that money voted for the Navy was not misappropriated and that Churchill was in the right. It must have been a thankless task defending the government in these mistrustful years—the fruits of Charles's personal policy; and the temper of public opinion was rising the whole time. A motion for the adjournment was lost by 147 to 117, Churchill being a teller for the Yeas. Candles were called for, *i.e.* that the debate might continue; Mr. Boscawen commenting from long experience, 'one candle may always be on the table, when it grows dark, without a question; and at a division, that you may see who goes out and who in'.

We may still see these vanished gentlemen, as by the mellow light thrown by candles, upon their canvases in the corridors of English country houses: in their wigs, full-faced or half turned away, with their long, coarse country faces, their hawk noses and their curled wigs, their lace cravats, their wine-coloured velvets and silver buttons. One still sees these names that occur so frequently in the Commons' proceedings—Sir Courtenay Pole, Sir Copleston Bamfylde, Sir Jonathan Trelawny, Sir Joseph Tredenham, Mr. Boscawen—upon the walls of West Country houses, their former occupants gone to join the shadows that fell from those candles.

For the present, the King had had enough of them. Besides, his simultaneous negotiations for a subsidy from Louis enabled him to dispense with their services. Since 1671 Charles had got £600,000 out of his cousin. Louis now paid him £100,000 to prorogue Parliament for a year—which would enable him to go forward unhampered on the Continent—and offered the same amount to keep Parliament in recess during 1677, with an addition if this disagreeable institution might be prevented from meeting till 1678. Charles could not see his way so far; but he kept Parliament prorogued for fifteen months, while Louis went ahead.

During the interval, public anxiety grew with the French advances on the Continent. Cambrai and Valenciennes fell to Louis XIV and the Netherlands were again in danger. Louis offered Charles two million livres to delay the meeting of Parliament. Charles attempted to stave off Parliament's anger by forwarding the Protestant marriage of James's daughter, Mary—heiress-presumptive to the throne—to William of Orange: a marriage that had revolutionary consequences. Charles even entered into an alliance with the Dutch; but he renegued, and maintained his secret understanding with Louis. Besides, the Duchess of Mazarin had now come over, to vary her more masculine attractions with the feminine appeal of the Duchess of Portsmouth.

Party-feeling in the Commons was becoming more and more inflamed. The Whig party, under the impulse of the organising and demagogic talents of Shaftesbury, was gaining strength. The Court was losing ground rapidly in the Commons.

Up to this time Churchill had been a respected figure in the House; he was a House of Commons man in spite of his holding a place at Court. But it is clear what a struggle he increasingly had to put the government point of view to the House. In the hectic atmosphere of the last sessions of the Cavalier Parliament, he was sometimes cried down or laughed out of court. (It was a reversal of fortune of which his descendant was not without experience too.)

The moment Parliament met after the long interval, it questioned the validity of the prorogation, and we detect, in Churchill's speeches, an increasingly defensive note. He speaks without conviction that he will convince anybody. Nobody was going to be convinced anyway. Many people thought the days of the Long Parliament had come again.

The situation was rendered more critical by the posture of foreign affairs, the constantly growing power of France. Charles was using this to demand large supplies from the Commons; but they had no guarantees as to his foreign policy. It was much like the situation in the 1930's, when the Opposition could hardly be expected to vote supplies for a policy they rightly distrusted. At both junctures, the right policy was that of a Grand Alliance against the aggressor. The Opposition in 1667 had no more confidence in Charles II than that in our own day had in Neville Chamberlain. One was engaged in appeasing Louis XIV, as the other in appeasing Hitler. In either case it increased the danger the country would have ultimately to meet. Waller summed up the situation in a sentence: 'No man can love England that seeks not after the balance of our neighbours'.

The Churchill of that day, unlike the Churchill of ours, took no part in the tense debates on foreign policy. The House was ready to vote Charles large supplies for war, requesting him to submit to no treaty leaving Louis in a better situation for aggression than he had enjoyed by the Treaty of the Pyrenees, at the outset of his rule. The government's reply was that foreign policy was the King's prerogative: if the Commons wanted alliances, they should vote supplies. 'You have asked for a treaty,' said the Secretary of State; 'a treaty you have. Now vote supply.' 'What kind of a treaty?' inquired the leaders of the House: 'Show us the treaty, and if it meets our wishes we will vote supply.' The Commons voted a large sum, a million pounds, but with the proviso 'to enter into actual war against the French king'. They proceeded to address Charles II, advising and desiring him to enter into a Grand Alliance against Louis XIV, for the safety of England. Louis was offering Charles six million livres to dissolve Parliament—which Charles dared not accept for fear of revolution. He contented himself with proroguing Parliament for a year, and dressing down the Commons for trenching upon his prerogative in foreign policy, for prescribing the manner and circumstances of alliances in such a way that no foreign power would believe sovereignty rested in the Crown.

Parliament was recalled in January 1678, in circumstances of mounting tension. The European war was still going on; the Commons were determined to force the King into the Grand Alliance against Louis. Charles was playing an even subtler game than usual. He was preparing to yield to their demand, in order to increase the pressure on Louis for subsidies. A general alliance was, in fact, signed at Westminster in March, but never ratified by Charles. He meant to have an easier life, and was engaged in bidding up both sides. Louis's reply to that was to direct a barrage of bribery against the Commons, and use them against Charles. The French now had two powerful emissaries in London: Barillon, to look after the Court, its master and its ladies; Ruvigny, now dispatched with large sums to operate with the Commons. To assert some control of the nation's affairs against France, Danby organised a counter-campaign of bribery against Ruvigny. The effect was, at this juncture, that England was completely neutralised in European affairs. And so she remained until this intolerable situation was resolved by the Revolution of 1688. To such a state had the Stuarts reduced their—but one can hardly say 'their'—country!

One result was that Charles had now, on the expectation of his entering the war, got his standing army. Another was that the very threat of our joining the allies and making an effective Grand Alliance had some effect in inducing Louis to make peace on moderate terms—the Peace of Nijmeguen. It showed what could be done, if England would only play her part and not leave it too late. (As in the 1930's—the whole burden of speech after speech in the Commons by Sir Winston's descendant, while the locusts ate up the years.)

The agitated state of opinion was reflected in a crowded opening of Parliament. On the return of the Commons to their own House, Sir Winston complained, in his impulsive manner, that 'we cannot follow the Speaker to the Lords' House without hazard of our lives, the disorder is so great, by reason of crowding. You, Mr. Speaker, tell us many great things, declared from my Lord Chancellor in his Speech. I desire he would give you a copy of what he spoke to us.' This was a move in the hope, no doubt, of mitigating the ill effect of the Speech, and worse reports of it, by a copy of the text.

For the first time Sir Winston was omitted from the committee of Elections and Privileges. No doubt the dominant majority left him out as merely the spokesman of the Court—as he was. He was placed on one or two other committees of not much importance: on a Bill to erect a register of pawnbrokers; on another to prevent the export of wool, in the interest of English manufacture. A more important committee was that to inquire whether Quakers or any dissenting Protestants had been convicted as Popish Recusants, and whether the penalties on the latter had not been levied. The committee was to frame a distinction between Popish Recusants and other Dissenters. The day after their meeting, the House would consider the danger the Church of England was in by the growth of Popery.

The truth is that the Catholics in England were an inconsiderable minority and, as such, no danger. What injected fever into feeling on the matter was the influence of Catholics at Court, the constant proselytising that went on in the proximity of the royal family—though it is true, as the Archbishop said on Lady Castlemaine's conversion, that if the Church of Rome gained no more than the Church of England lost by her, it was no great matter. There was, above all, the certainty of a Catholic on the throne—and James was known to be resentful, vindictive, implacable.

The House set itself to take what steps it could to safeguard the future—the extreme section of the Whigs, led by Shaftesbury, wanted to exclude James altogether from the succession. The Commons passed a Bill disabling all Papists from sitting in either House of Parliament, with a proviso exempting the Duke of York from taking the oaths. The Lords accepted the principle of the Bill, but sent it back with amendments, which the Commons would not agree to. This disagreement was referred to a committee, upon which Churchill had to be placed.

In the debate, he spoke up for the proviso and the Duke: it took some courage, in the awkward relationship in which he stood to the Duke. 'Upon this disadvantage, when I hear so loud a cry, "To the Question", I should not speak, but to discharge my conscience. Though I think not to prevail, when I heard so loud a cry against what I am moving. The Lords are so near the government, that they see more than we. . . . I think that the monarchy of England is concerned in this. Consider the consequence, if you reject this Proviso. How far will you force so great a prince to declare? . . . Suppose the Duke takes not the oaths, etcetera. All that do not take them, will you make them Papists? There were some at your bar that were Quakers, who would not take them; will you drive all that herd of swine into the sea of Rome at once? If those that sit in Parliament must take them, those out of Parliament must too.' The report records, 'And so he sat down abruptly'.

Emotions ran very high in the debate, particularly among the loyalist West Countrymen. Sir Jonathan Trelawny, who was a pensioner of the Crown, burst out—What would happen on the King's death? 'For God's sake, accept the Proviso.' It is noted that 'those against the Proviso sat silent'. Sir William Killigrew, who was a place-man, cried, 'I dread taking the Duke from the King', and broke down in a flood of tears. We see, in all this, how impossible a position was that in which the Stuarts were placing their most loyal Protestant subjects. These last had to bear the accusation of advancing the Papist projects of their masters—unfairly in the case of Sir Winston. Actually the Proviso passed by only two votes, 158 to 156. It is an indication how near the Cavalier Parliament was to Exclusion, and how determined they were on a Protestant succession.

Already the political situation was boiling over, the first manifestations of the monstrous experience of the Popish Plot. Titus Oates, who had seen something of Catholic society and been at the Jesuit College of St.-Omer, had already made his depositions before the King and Council, as to a plot to bring England under Catholic sway. The Council took his depositions seriously; the people were hardly likely to reject what those hardened sinners, the Privy Councillors, had swallowed—whatever their motives. This was the spark that ignited a raging prairie fire: there was the combustible material of all the distrust that had been mounting up for years, the frustration of the efforts to deal with Catholicism in the highest quarters, the indignation and humiliation at our rôle, when Europe was burning. The nation was convulsed by panic and hysteria. A concatenation of circumstances made people crazy with fear and suspicion—we must remember the crudity and brutality, the credulity and volatile emotionalism of the age. It was a time of informers, spies, perjurers; of confessions extorted, made, recanted and again sworn to; of clubs with their oaths and secret rites; of meetings in dark alleys, hired assassins, duels and beatings-up. Mysterious documents were found in unexpected places, in garden or thatch—though no one appears to have thought of a pumpkin in a field.

Indeed, we in our time can well visualise the horror of the experience the nation went through: it was not very dissimilar to that which the United States experienced under MacCarthy. The point about each indefensible episode is that there *was* a certain amount of justification for it; then fear, fanned and made use of by designing politicians, made the thing pass all bounds. Again, the seventeenth-century experience in England has this in common with the American version in the twentieth century, that in each case it was absorbed and overcome by the normal functioning of the political system, without resorting to any extra-constitutional measures: tribute to the fundamental health and soundness of the respective politics, the English and American conception of constitutional, representative government.

What wrought public feeling to such a pitch was that, beneath the wicked lies of Titus Oates—who had the psychological intuition of the pathological, the half-insane, for he was an informer of genius—there really *was* a Popish Plot. It was not a very important matter, but it came from an exalted quarter. There had been a secret Jesuit consult that spring, not—as Oates thought—at the 'White Horse' tavern, but at St. James's Palace itself. The papers of Father Coleman, who was the Duke of York's secretary and then the Duchess's, were impounded and revealed, to a maddened public, negotiations for substituting James for Charles in the French king's favour and for advancing Catholicism in England. Coleman was a megalomaniac exhibitionist; of all the people who went to the gallows or the scaffold in that time of horror, he was the only one who, in some sense, partly deserved it. The murder—or was it suicide?— of Sir Edmund Berry Godfrey finally clinched the terror; for he was mysteriously associated with Coleman, had shown alarm and apprehension at having, as a magistrate, to take Oates's depositions and, shortly after, had been found transfixed with a sword through the back on some waste ground on Primrose Hill.

On 28 November Titus Oates was called to the bar of an already convinced House to give his evidence. He claimed that at Whitehall he had been placed under restraint and denied the use of pen, ink and paper. Sir Winston dared to contradict the liar, and said that he had seen him busy writing something as if for print, only a week ago at Whitehall. The House knew better; the report says that 'he was laughed at'. The cataract was in full career; nothing could now stop it. Five Catholic peers—harmless, retired backwoodsmen—were impeached and sent to the Tower. All through next year, 'Charles was forced to acquiesce in the judicial murders which were removing men whom he knew to be innocent'. Such were the fruits of the distrust he had sown. Men thought it was 1641 come again; and the parallel appeared very close when the King's chief minister, Danby, was sent to the Tower.

In December, the House purged itself. The names were called of all members who had defaulted in their attendance, and not taken the oaths of allegiance and supremacy or subscribed to the declaration against Transubstantiation according to the Test Act. The case of Sir Richard Graham was put to the question. It was lost, and it was then ordered that the list of members be sent for in custody of the Serjeant-at-Arms. Sir Winston Churchill bravely acted as a teller for the minority, and this is the last time that he saw the inside of Parliament in the reign of Charles II.

For the next two years the King was not in control of events: the reaction against his rule swept him off his feet and almost swept the traditional constitutional boundaries away. He was driven at last to dissolve Parliament and to call a new one. This represented the high-water mark of the reaction against the Stuarts and the height of the power attained by the Whig extremists, who drove events forward furiously.

There was no place for a Winston Churchill in this overwhelmingly Whig Parliament or in any of the three elected in these years, 1679, 1680, 1681. A dead set was made against all who were attached to the Court, and apparently Sir Winston dared not stand for the seat at Weymouth he had held so long. He was certainly not returned. It seems that he even lost his place at the Board of Green Cloth for a time. At least, unkind Anthony Wood reports this as appearing in a news-letter at the end of the year 1678. And he does not fail to record the attack on Churchill in an anonymous pamphlet of 1677, *A Seasonable Argument to persuade all the Grand Juries to petition for a new Parliament*. This accused him of being a pensioner in Parliament, of being a principal labourer in the great design of bringing in Popery and arbitrary government, of getting £10,000 in boons and of preferring his own daughter to the Duke of York. The same charges were repeated in the vituperative *Flagellum Parliamentarium*. Not one of these charges was true; but such were the amenities of Restoration politics.

In the way that often happens in fatuous public affairs, the grand opportunity having come to the Whigs, they behaved disgracefully—far more cruelly than ever Charles had behaved, for they sent innocent people to their deaths. Under the leadership of that vindictive spirit, Shaftesbury, the former Cromwellian, the Whigs tried not merely to exclude James from the throne, but to make Charles's eldest bastard, Monmouth, king. Instead of attempting to unite the nation on a moderate course, in which they could easily have reached agreement with Charles for limitations on his successor, whose stupidity and folly none knew better than he, they drove furiously on, affronting the moderate sentiments of the nation, which did not want a Venetian oligarchy, but an ordered, constitutional monarchy. In 1679 Charles had a stroke and James, who had been sent into exile at Brussels, returned to be with him in case of his death. When Charles recovered there was no keeping James by him. He was packed off to Holyrood, with his favourite, Winston Churchill's son, John, with him.

In time the Whigs wore out their welcome; the popular

enthusiasm for extreme courses diminished rapidly, in the English fashion. The King recovered his popularity and, skilful politician that he was, took advantage of the reaction against the Whigs to defeat and disperse them. He called no more Parliaments. A verbal treaty with Louis in 1681 obviated the disagreeable necessity: Charles was to receive two million *écus* for the first year and half a million in each succeeding year. Louis felt secure in the knowledge that Charles, 'étant dans une alliance secrète avec moi, ne fera rien contre mon intérêt'. Nor did he: he gracefully—or, rather, disgracefully—accepted a supplement of a million livres to raise no opposition to Louis's acquiring Luxemburg. Retrenchment in the Navy indicated appeasement. With that, and these subsidies, Charles was able to jog along without Parliament. With Nell Gwyn as the staunchest supporter of Protestantism in the most intimate sector of the royal circle, in comfortable domesticity with her and the Duchess of Portsmouth, Charles had peace for the last four years of his life.

James succeeded quietly to the inheritance which Charles had so skilfully—and, on the whole, successfully—manoeuvred to hand on to him unimpaired. During the Tory reaction in those last four years, the borough corporations, which had been the strongholds of the Whigs, were remodelled in the Tory interest. So that it is not surprising that a Tory majority was returned to James's one and only Parliament. Never had the Court so exerted itself to secure the return of well-affected members.

The reconstructed corporation of Lyme Regis returned its old opponent Sir Winston Churchill—perhaps the shade of Lady Drake lent piquancy to the transaction. In any case, he had for a number of years been on the commission of the Peace, one of the deputy Lieutenants for Dorset, a name in the county, though he himself was usually away at Court.

At once Sir Winston resumed his activity as spokesman for the Court. If he had temporarily lost his post at the Board of Green Cloth in the Whig blizzard, he soon recovered it. On James's accession, the remuneration of the four clerks was fixed at £500 a year. Next year, on Sir William Boreman's death, Sir Winston moved up to the second place.

In the House, he was more active than ever—though in very different circumstances; he could now speak with authority: he had the majority behind him. We find him serving on a large number of committees, lesser and greater. In June, there was a committee to inspect the accounts of the Commissioners for disbanding the forces which had been raised to deal with Monmouth's rebellion. Another committee was to inspect the Journals of the House and report what was fit to be expunged—which strikes an ominous note. There were Bills to create a new parish in Westminster, to be called after the King's patron saint, St. James: of which the church, which we know as St. James's, Piccadilly, was to be built by the Tory architect, Wren. Later in that month of June, we find Sir Winston serving agreeably with Sir Christopher on the committee for the Bill for St. Paul's Cathedral.

James was treated far more generously by this Tory Parliament, than ever Charles had been by his. Even so, the Commons did not hesitate to address him to enforce the laws against *all* dissenters from the Church of England. James proceeded to use his dispensing power and instruct the Exchequer not to collect the statutory fines on recusants. Parliament held firm to both Habeas Corpus and the Test Acts, which James was initiating a campaign to undermine and overthrow. And both Houses were uncompromising about James's employment of Catholic officers. In spite of Parliament's generosity to him, James regarded their attitude as merely vexatious and went on appointing Papists to posts in his standing army. It was all very ominous—and he could take no warning.

When Parliament met again in November he read them a lesson about his Catholic officers and his intention to be obeyed—a speech from the throne at once provoking and undignified. Charles had never made such mistakes of tact. Poor gouty old Lord Belasyse, who—though a backwoods Catholic peer—was not without sense, said to the faithful Ailesbury, taking him by the hand, 'My dear Lord, who would be the framer of this speech? I date my ruin and that of all my persuasion from this day'.

But James had got a standing army; and, though this was not yet clear, he intended to use it to enforce his Catholic policy—after all the experience of Charles's reign! The Opposition was set against a standing army, and wished to rely on a militia under Parliamentary control. It fell to Sir Winston, as the spokesman of the Court, to move supply for the army: 'some other than the militia is necessary to be found'. Sir Richard Temple countered by asking leave for a Bill to strengthen the militia. Sir Winston: 'The Beef-eaters at this rate may be called an army'. To this Sir Thomas Hussey retored, 'The Colonel may say what he will of the Beef-eaters, as he nicknames them; but they are established by act of Parliament'. (We need not assume that Sir Winston Churchill was responsible for this famous nickname, but it is interesting that he should have been first to use it in Parliament.)

Supply was voted. Next came the question how it was to be apportioned. The government wanted £1,200,000. There was a motion to grant £200,000 for the present; more to come later. The Colonel: '£200,000 is much too little: soldiers move not without pay. *No Penny, No Paternoster.*' No, indeed. It was an unfortunate proverb to quote just then; for it spoke the unspoken thought in everybody's mind—if they lost control over the revenue, the King could enforce his religious policy and arbitrary rule. A motion for £700,000 was introduced; but rather than endure any criticism of his measures James prorogued Parliament. He did not call them together again. They had been dangerously generous to him, in the beginning, in voting him Customs and Excise for life. It was enough for him to get on without them—and gave him rope enough to hang himself.

Sir Winston Churchill was getting an elderly man now; and it is not surprising to find him concerning himself more with Minterne in these last years. His father had been buried there, not at Wootton Glanville. When one enters the dark, narrow-chested little church by the roadside up from Cerne Abbas, a stone's throw away from the big house looking out upon that exquisite valley and up the wooded slope beyond, one stumbles upon John Churchill beneath his stone in the central aisle: 'Here lies the body of John Churchill esq., who died the 6th of April, 1652. This stone was erected and laid here at the cost of Mrs. Mary Churchill, widow, out of her affection, and in commemoration of her beloved husband, John Churchill, esq.' Do we not detect a slight note of reproach that it was left to the widow to place the grave-stone at her own cost?

It is evident that Sir Winston was not prosperous. He got little enough for his long service to the Stuarts. He died in debt, and the large amount he had lent the impecunious Charles II in 1667—£2,000—was still unpaid at his death. He did not possess the cool, clear, calculating head of his famous son. Sir Winston had the hot impulsive head of the Cavalier Colonel, only a little disciplined by his legal training.

Sir Winston had already, in 1684, made his will. He wished to be buried in his father's grave at Minterne—after all, his father had been his only effectual ancestor, maker of the place he had attained in the world. He left to his wife the farm and demesne of Minterne, as her jointure, on condition of paying the dues to Winchester College. She was to have all the plate, hangings and household stuff, for life, from London, Windsor and Minterne; with 'the profits of my fair at Hermitage, Dorset, and of King's Drift in Blackmore, and 90 acres in the new enclosure at Wootton'. The manor of Newland was to be sold for the payment of his debts; and any moneys due from the King devoted similarly. He had appointed certain lands to be offered to John Churchill, his eldest son, 'if he would give as much for them as anyone else'. This is a pretty cold reference to his famous son, already a well-known figure in the world, and a peer. (There is no reference at all to Arabella.) It seems that Sir Winston was not buried with his father after all. Anthony Wood tells us that he died 26 March 1688 and was buried three days after in St. Martin's-in-the-Fields.

CHAPTER SEVEN

Arabella

IT was Sir Winston's children, Arabella and John, who made the fortunes of the Churchills, though their father's post at Court put them in the way of it.

Never in English history, before or since, has there been a Court so given up to pleasure, particularly the pleasures of sex, as that of Charles II. Anthony Hamilton, who lived at the heart of it—or rather, at the centre, for it had no heart—describes it as 'entirely devoted to love and gallantry. . . . The Court was an entire scene of gallantry and amusements, with all the politeness and magnificence which the inclinations of a prince naturally addicted to tenderness and pleasure could suggest. The beauties were desirous of charming and the men endeavoured to please. All studied to set themselves off to the best advantage: some distinguished themselves by dancing; others by show and magnificence; some by their wit, many by their amours, but few by their constancy.'

After the morose respectability of the Puritans, the seriousness and sobriety, the Restoration was a time of extravagance and opulent ostentation, of voluptuousness in decoration and clothes—as one sees from the half-naked women, who always appear to be in *négligé,* in spite of all the flowing silks and velvets, looking down from the canvases of Lely—of French luxuries and *objets d'art.* 'Perfumed gloves, pocket looking-glasses, elegant boxes, apricot paste, essences and other small wares of love arrived every week from Paris. But, with regard to solid presents, such as ear-rings, diamonds, brilliants, bright guineas, all this was to be met with of the best sort in London, and the ladies were as well pleased with them as if they had been brought from abroad.' French taste, French standards, prevailed; the plays of Corneille and Racine, the verse of Boileau were the models; the airs of Lully were the favourites—the King listening peaceably after dinner, politics suspended for an hour, himself beating time with his hand. The Court was essentially, devotedy, French; though following the fashions of Louis XIV, it was, in its gaiety, its lightness and lack of restraint, in spirit more like that of Louis XV. (That, too, led to a Revolution.)

The dance was led by Charles—'that known enemy to virginity and chastity, the monarch of Great Britain', as a crony agreeably called him. The second place was occupied by the Duke of York. There was little that the brothers resembled each other in. Where Charles was affable and familiar, James was cold and arrogant; Charles was apt to be generous and was certainly extravagant, James mean and parsimonious. Above all, Charles was good-tempered and humorous; James had no sense of humour whatever: not a joke is recorded from him. Only one thing the brothers shared: that 'terrible Bourbon temperament' which Madame de Maintenon complained of in her royal husband in his seventies.

Here, too, the brothers differed. Where Charles was selective and discriminating, and rather considerate, James was omnivorous. He was described as 'very amorous, and more out of a natural temper than for the genteel part of making love, which he was much a stranger to'. Charles himself, who is usually thought of as the chief offender, said to a French ambassador, 'I do not believe there are two men who love women more than you and I do; but my brother, devout as he is, loves them still more'.

James's affairs are less well known, partly because they were not politically important, unlike the King's. But they were, if anything, more numerous. There was Miss Price, then there was Lady Southesk, then Lady Denham. He was so clumsily obvious, that he was apt to be caught in undignified postures. Hamilton says of one of his affairs, 'as he was the most unguarded ogler of his time, the whole Court was informed of the intrigue before it was well begun'. Then he took to ogling the beautiful Lady Robartes, in the zenith of her glory and youth, married to a strait-laced Presbyterian, 'an old, snarling, troublesome, peevish fellow, in love with her to distraction and, to complete her misery, a perpetual attendant on her person'. Defeated, the Duke turned his attentions to Lady Chesterfield. James, who played the guitar tolerably, desired to try out a fashionable new piece upon Lady Chesterfield's instrument, which was the finest in England. When he arrived at her apartments, he found her husband was present; and a very awkward trio they made of it. The Duke paid the Lady a complimentary visit at her house, while her husband was engaged at Court: who, on his return, was surprised and annoyed to find the Duke's coach blocking his way. Lord Chesterfield thought best to whisk his wife off to the country, where she endured what everyone thought the hardship of spending her Christmas at a country-house, a hundred and fifty miles from London.

James was laughed at by all the clever ones; but, in truth, he was no laughing matter.

He was married to an excellent woman, Anne Hyde, Clarendon's daughter. He had compromised her—or rather, since he was a royal person, himself with her—in the seedy, impoverished days of exile. She was good enough for him then—indeed, a great deal too good; and, secretly, he contracted himself to marry her. The marriage, as Hamilton says, 'was deficient in none of those circumstances which render contracts of this nature valid in the eye of heaven: the mutual inclination, the formal ceremony, witnesses, and every essential point of matrimony had been observed'. But when the Restoration Court began to burgeon in all its glory, to bloom with beauties and 'he considered he was the only prince who, from such superior elevation, had descended so low, he began to reflect upon it'.

These reflections were aided by some superior wits, though very inferior characters. The Court, which made such a point of fine gentlemanship, abounded in cads. Nothing could be more caddish than the proposal put to James by a group of fine young men, who detested Clarendon—a proposal to which James was cad enough to lend himself. James opened his heart to Lord Falmouth, the King's favourite, who engaged himself to fix it for the Duke: the marriage was invalid without the King's consent, it was 'a mere jest even to think of the daughter of an insignificant lawyer, whom the favour of his sovereign had lately made a peer of the realm, without any noble blood, and chancellor, without any capacity'.

In the secrecy of the royal cabinet there was a prolonged wrangle; Charles was a gentleman, if James was not. 'The Duke of York appeared to be in such agitation when he came out, that they no longer doubted that the result had been unfavourable for poor Miss Hyde.' They all met an hour later in her chamber: 'a few tears trickled down her cheeks, which she endeavoured to restrain. The Chancellor, leaning against the wall, appeared to be puffed up with something, which they did not doubt was rage and despair.' The Duke of York announced: 'As you are the two men of the court whom I most esteem [*i.e.* Falmouth and Ossory], I am desirous you should first have the honour of paying your compliments to the Duchess of York: there she is.' Surprised and astonished, the two young peers yet knew their duty: 'they immediately fell on their knees to kiss her hand, which she gave to them with as much majesty as if she had been used to it all her life'.

Hamilton, who had a very sharp pair of eyes and no illusions about people, pays the new Duchess a marked tribute. He says that the moment her marriage was made public, 'the whole Court was eager to pay her that respect, from a sense of duty, which in the end became very sincere'. After her elevation, she 'conducted herself with such prudence and circumspection as could not be sufficiently admired: such were her manners and such the general estimation in which she was held that she appeared to have found out the secret of pleasing everyone—a secret yet more rare than the grandeur to which she had been raised'. She was a kind woman, though, like her father, apt to stand rather more on her dignity than was altogether necessary; and she was an intelligent one. She became the patron of Lely, and brought him into fashion and favour: in that, leaving some legacy of herself to us and posterity, besides her children, Mary and Anne, each of whom became Queen. It was a pity she did not live to become Queen herself: such influence as she could exert upon James would have been in the direction of sense and moderation.

As for him, 'the Duke of York, having quieted his conscience by the declaration of his marriage, thought that he was entitled by this generous effort, to give way a little to his inconstancy. He therefore immediately seized upon whatever he could first lay his hands upon: this was Lady Carnegie, who had been in several other hands.' And so on.

Such was the Court to which Sir Winston Churchill had not been anxious to promote his daughter. But a Court in which her cousin, Lady Castlemaine, reigned could not be without prospects for the daughter of an impecunious knight; and he could hardly have resisted the offer of a place for her as maid-of-honour to the Duchess of York.

All the maids-of-honour were fair game to James, who paid his addresses to them one after another. Arabella was a mere slip of a girl, sixteen or seventeen: tall and thin, with a very pale complexion, as yet undeveloped. James became infatuated with her: no one could understand why. 'The Court was not able to comprehend how, after having been in love with Lady Chesterfield, Miss Hamilton and Miss Jennings, he could have any inclination for such a creature.' On this occasion, the Duchess's jealousy was really aroused: 'the Duchess beheld with indignation a choice which seemed to debase her own merit in a much greater degree than any of the former'. There may have been another motive: the Duchess may well have been indignant at the Duke engaging in a serious pursuit of a girl so young. It is clear that for some time his attentions were resisted, and his ardour began to cool.

In the summer of the Plague-year, 1665, the Duke and Duchess made a progress to York. There were various motives: to separate the royal family, so that the brothers might not both be struck down by the Plague; to make the most of the popularity James had temporarily gained by his conduct at the battle of Lowestoft; to give the North a sight of restored royalty. Hamilton tells us that 'the votaries of love' made the most of the expedition and of the opportunities it afforded. 'There were continual balls and entertainments upon the road; hunting, and all other diversions, wherever the Court halted in its progress. The tender lovers flattered themselves with the thought of being able to crown their happiness as they proceeded in their journey; and the beauties who governed their destiny did not forbid them to hope.'

James had two passions, hunting and women—which he was apt to combine; in course of time he added a third—religion, which was more disastrous. On their way north, he amused himself by teaching Arabella to ride. She was gawky, gauche and timid; now a girl of seventeen, he a man of thirty-one. It was his idea of fun to scold her for sitting so ill on horseback. (We know what his conversation was like from his attempts to entertain Miss Hamilton: 'telling her miracles of the cunning of foxes and the mettle of horses; giving her accounts of broken legs and arms, dislocated shoulders, and other curious and entertaining adventures; after which, his eyes told her the rest, till such time as sleep interrupted their conversation'.)

The maids-of-honour were usually the worst mounted of the whole Court, but in order to distinguish Arabella, 'on account of the favour she enjoyed, they had given her a very pretty, though rather a high-spirited horse: a distinction she would very willingly have excused them'. One day, the horse ran away with her, and she had a bad fall. 'A fall in so quick a pace must have been violent; and yet it proved favourable to her in every respect; for, without receiving any hurt, she gave the lie to all the unfavourable suppositions that had been formed of her person, in judging from her face. The Duke alighted, in order to help her. She was so greatly stunned, that her thoughts were otherwise employed than about decency on the present occasion; and those who first crowded around her found her rather in a negligent posture. They could hardly believe that limbs of such beauty could belong to Miss

Churchill's face.' In short, beneath her clothes, Arabella had the Villiers figure, famous for its perfection in women and men alike.

'After this accident, it was remarked that the Duke's tenderness and affection for her increased every day; and, towards the end of the winter, it appeared that she had not tyrannised over his passion, nor made him languish with impatience.'

James's liaison with Arabella was not one of his numerous casual affairs; it was on a completely different footing. It was the chief affair of his life, lasting for ten or twelve years; it gave him some domesticity—for Arabella was an entirely domestic sort of woman—and left him with a family to provide for. There were four children who survived. The first was Henrietta, who married a Waldegrave and was the mother and grandmother of the Waldegraves who made their mark in the eighteenth century. Another daughter, who became a nun, had an immensely long life and lived (in France) to see the accession of George III to her father's throne. Of the two sons, the younger, Henry, was given the Jacobite title of Duke of Albemarle in France after 1688, but was better known as the Grand Prior; the elder, James, Duke of Berwick, became perhaps the finest soldier in Europe after his uncle, the Duke of Marlborough.

There must have been something remarkable in the stock: we need not suppose that it was the Stuart blood that made it so. There was nothing remarkable about James's progeny by anybody else, Anne Hyde, Catherine Sedley or Mary of Modena. Our Sir Winston comments on his ancestor that he 'has been accounted one of the most notable and potent of sires. Had he lived . . . he would have witnessed within the space of twelve months his son gaining the battle of Ramillies and his daughter's son that of Almanza; and would have found himself acknowledged as the progenitor of the two greatest captains of the age at the head of the opposing armies of Britain and of France and Spain. Moreover, his third surviving son, Charles, became a soldier of well-tried distinction, and his naval son virtually managed the Admiralty during the years of war. The military strain flowed strong and clear from the captain of the Civil Wars, student of heraldry and history, and champion of the Divine Right. It was his blood, not his pen, that carried his message.' Berwick's life and career have always been treated in their Stuart setting, but it is clear that his military genius came from the Churchills.

Little is known of Arabella's life and personality; she was not one of the blatant, exhibitionist beauties always in the public eye, at

Court or at the play-house, making trouble or causing scenes and scandals, like Castlemaine, Portsmouth, La Belle Stuart, Nell Gwyn and the rest of them. She led a quiet, hidden life; after all, she was very young and her time was much taken up with child-bearing: it was no sinecure being mistress to the Duke. Pepys mentions her only once. In the cold weather of January 1669—bright moonshine at night and hard frost by day, in which the King and Duke walked abroad, attended sometimes by the little man—one day he ran into his crony, Mr. Pierce, the Duke's doctor. 'I asked him whither he was going; [he] told me as a great secret that he was going to his master's mistress, Mrs. Churchill, with some physic; meaning for the pox, I suppose, or else that she is got with child.'

The latter supposition was the correct one; though—the Restoration being what it was—everyone talked of the former. Marvell writes:

> His meagre Highness, now he's got astride,
> Does on Britannia, as on Churchill ride.

And on James's marriage to young Mary of Modena:

> Then draw the Princess with her golden locks,
> Hastening to be envenomed with the pox,
> And in her youthful veins receive a wound,
> Which sent Nan Hyde before her underground;
> The wound of which the tainted Churchill fades,
> Preserved in store for the next set of maids.

This was quite unforgivable; but it may be held that the Stuarts had asked for it. Unforgivable, and also untrue; Anne Hyde died of cancer of the breast; Arabella lived to a hale and hearty old age, dying at eighty-two. It is generally held that James had taken some such infection and that this accounts for some of his mental characteristics: the abnormal fixity, the wooden rigidity, the complete crack-up and loss of nerve at the defection of the nation in 1688, the fainting fits and nose-bleedings. But I do not think we need go so far to account for a humourless fool

When children began to arrive, James moved Arabella out of Whitehall, and set her up in a house in St. James's Square. This was the new salubrious neighbourhood being opened up by Henry Jermyn, who got the grant of the land from the Crown: what with the unearned (or doubtfully earned) increment and the profits of the gaming table (he did not lose), he became very well off. His name is suitably recalled to us by the lower associations of Jermyn

Street. Here, in the new square, Arabella set up house: the Marquis de Blanquefort, afterwards Earl of Feversham, to whom James as king confided the command of his army, the Countess of Warwick, and the Earl of Oxford, in the south-east corner; Clarendon's two sons, the second Earl and his brother Laurence Hyde, later Earl of Rochester, on the north side; on the west, Lord Halifax, Lord Purbeck, Sir Allen Apsley, Madame Churchill and, as her next-door neigbour, Madame Davis. Madame Davis, appropriately called Moll, was the dancer who danced her way from 'a bed on the cold ground to a bed royal'. Pepys thought her dancing infinitely beyond Nell Gwyn's; but her hold on Charles's affections was much shorter. Moll Davis's was the first, and Aabella's the second, house on the left-hand side as you enter the Square from the south-west.[1]

Here Arabella lived, discreetly and noiselessly, leaving no traces, except her children, and an occasional entry in the Treasury Books. James was not generous by nature; but a pension of £1000 a year (multiply by, perhaps, ten)—though a very different matter from the hundreds of thousands squandered on Castlemaine and Portsmouth—enabled Arabella to live comfortably for the rest of her life. She travelled to France, for we learn from the Memoirs of her son, Berwick, that he was born at Moulins in the Bourbonnais, 'whither Mrs. Churchill had retired to conceal her pregnancy'.

Three years later, 28 December 1674, there is a warrant from the Lord Treasurer to the Customs to deliver at Madame Churchill's house—no doubt, duty-free, whatever the Commons might say about imported luxuries from France—a box with brass andirons, a box with two Mantua gowns, some muffs, two or three garnitures of buttons and loops, stuffs for a petticoat directed to Mr. Founds for the Duke of York, and a trunk and portmanteau for Sir Henry FitzJames with his wearing clothes in it, which are imported in the *Anne* yacht. It is rather a touching trace of that hidden life to come across in those pedestrian Treasury Books. Two years later, there is a warrant to deliver, on payment of customs, some looking-glasses, tables, stands and hanging candlesticks sent from France for Madame Churchill. These things were all the rage just then: one sees them still in Restoration houses.

The death of Anne Hyde freed James for what he could regard as a respectable, *i.e.* a royal, marriage. All Europe was scoured for

[1] Arabella paid £3 6*s*. poor rate to the parish. In the Victorian Age the house was occupied by the blameless Bishops of Winchester. A. I. Dasent, *History of St. James's Square*, 18, 21, 244.

suitable candidates. James made it clear that he would marry no one who was not a Catholic. The country was very much aroused. The King insisted on the news that poor Anne had died a Catholic being kept secret. He told the French ambassador, Croissy, that he recognised two weaknesses in his brother—religion and marriage; that the first had already produced effects enough and that he had reason to fear worse consequences in the future. The phrase 'la sottise de mon frère' was frequently on his lips in these conversations. In the end, James took his wife at the hands of their grand patron, Louis XIV, and, for all his haughtiness, wrote him an obsequious letter assuring him of his lasting devotion.

The great man's choice had fallen on Maria Beatrice, sister of the young Duke of Modena: she was only fifteen, lively and healthy, capable of bearing Catholic children for the throne of England. The Commons were certain to protest; the marriage by proxy was hurried on before they could get to work. The news of its having taken place was brought to the Duke in the Drawing-room at Whitehall by the French ambassador: James turned round and said, 'Then I am a married man'. He went down to meet his wife at Dover, where Nathaniel Crewe, the sycophantic Bishop of Oxford, pronounced what both the recipients must have regarded as a bogus benediction. The donor must, however, have considered it worth the fat see of Durham which he got for it. He was among the first to go over to William in 1688. He lived to enjoy Durham a long time and salved what he regarded as his conscience by his benefactions to Oxford.

Such a marriage was no interruption to James's liaison with Arabella; within a month he was said to have resumed domestic relations with her. In any case, it was some time before the girl-Duchess took to her husband, and she was slow in producing children. The girl was good-natured and not unintelligent, in spite of her ridiculous *dévote* upbringing. Her worst influence on James was to increase his religious bigotry, and cut him off still further from common sense and the English people. Danby, who did his best to save the Stuarts, complained that whereas the Archbishop of Rheims, when in England, came to our churches and knelt during the services, James would not so much as come to the door. A King of England who drew the line at the Church of England was an intolerable contradiction.

What did interfere with his liaison with Arabella, and bring it to an end, was not his marriage, but a new liaison with another maid-of-honour. This was Catherine Sedley, in every way a contrast with

Arabella. She was the only child of Sir Charles Sedley, the dramatist and wit, rake and poet. Catherine inherited her father's wit, and was to inherit his fortune. It was this that made Sir Winston and Lady Churchill so anxious to have her as a catch for their son John. That cool young man was much attracted by her fortune; he could not have been by her looks, for she had none. Next year, in 1678, when she was twenty, she became a maid-of-honour to the new Duchess, and that was fatal.

Catherine was not at all attracted by James and had no illusions about her looks. She herself could not understand his infatuation and, with engaging candour, said so: 'It cannot be my beauty, because I haven't any; and it cannot be my wit, because he hasn't enough to know that I have any'. The fact was that Catherine fascinated James as no one else—as only a clever woman can a really stupid man, whatever her looks. Catherine caused the Duchess much more grief than Arabella had done, for James was unable to emancipate himself from the spell of her personality. When he became King he created her Countess of Dorchester, to the Queen's annoyance and distress. When he ceased to be King, Sir Charles Sedley was one of the Commons who voted his daughter Mary to the throne: 'her father made my daughter a Countess; I have been helping to make his daughter a Queen'. And Catherine said of Queen Mary: 'if I broke one of the Commandments *with* her father, she broke another *against* him'.

Arabella got no countess-ship; but her children were recognised and brought to Court—to Mary of Modena's disapprobation and jealousy: she still had none of her own when, in September 1685, young James and Henry, future Dukes of Berwick and Albemarle, were introduced. Their sister, Henrietta, was married to Sir Henry Waldegrave; in January 1686, he was made a peer. With the beginning of James's liaison with Catherine Sedley, about 1678-9, his relations with Arabella Churchill ceased: she was free to live her own life. On 7 April 1679 she got a pass to go abroad with two of her children, a younger brother Mountjoy Churchill as her escort, Elizabeth Peacock, Elizabeth Becher, Francis Sarsfield and a maidservant. About this time, or later, she sold her fine house in St. James's Square for a large sum, £8000. With this, with a pension of £1000 a year secured on Irish lands, still only thirty, she was a desirable *parti*.

As the children grew older, James took them away from their mother to provide for their upbringing and education. They were sent to France to be brought up—irresistible magnet for the

Stuarts, the model for royal manners and the proper conduct of subjects. Some letters of James to his daughter Henrietta throw light into this dark corner. From Windsor in 1682 he writes, with a characteristic combination of lofty condescension and stiff kindness, that he is glad to hear from his cousin, Princess Louise, that 'you behave yourself so well and that she gives you so good a character. I hope you will do nothing to give her reason to alter her opinion of you, and that you will do nothing to make me less kind to you than I am, and you shall upon all occasions find me as kind as you can desire.' Next year, he sends over Sir Henry Tichborne, a reliable Catholic, to fetch her back to England, and at Tichborne she is to stay, 'where I shall have the opportunity of seeing you when we go to Winchester this summer, and letting you see that I shall always be very kind to you'.

By next year, he had found her a suitable marriage: the heir to the old Catholic family of Waldegrave. We see, in everything he did, what a consistent *dévot* James was. In June 1684, the head of the family having died, 'now that Sir Henry is come to the estate I must recommend you both to be good managers, and to be sure to live within what you have and be sure to have a care not to run out at first'. We also see what a careful man he was about money.

Next we hear news of the two boys. 'I was very sorry to hear this morning of the accident which happened to your brother Harry, and send this footman on purpose to you, to have an account from you how he does. They tell me his face will not be marked with it.... Remember me to your brother James, and tell him I am sorry his journey should be stopped for some days, especially by such an accident; and tell Harry I hope he will be carefuller for the time to come, and now that he do what the chirurgeons will have him....'

The two boys had been sent early to school in France, under the care of an Oratorian, Father Gough, at the Oratory school at Juilly, and afterwards at Plessis. In 1684, they were brought to England to be presented to their uncle, Charles II, and were then sent back, on the advice of the egregious Father Petre, to the Jesuit College of La Flèche. At seventeen, the elder boy had his first experience of war, fighting in the plains of Hungary against the Turks. At the great victory of Mohács, it was rumoured that Berwick had been killed. James, now king, wrote, 1 September 1687: 'Two days ago I was very much alarmed by the letters which came from France about your brother Berwick; but now, God be thanked, I am at ease concerning him, for ... I find he was very well recovered though still a little weak; and I believe the Earl of Kinnoull, who died at Mohács, was the occasion of that report.'

It seems that James was fond of his daughter by Arabella. In this same year, 1687, he made her husband Comptroller of the Household; next year, a month before his flight from the realm, James sent Waldegrave to France with a large sum of money for future use. It was needed. A year later, Waldegrave died at the exiled court at St.-Germain. Henrietta was free to follow her inclinations. These led her to fall in love with Lord Galmoye, a Catholic member of the Butler clan. In 1695, Dangeau says, she found herself in a state in which no widowed lady should be: she was sent into a convent. On her emergence—convents had their uses—it was rumoured, though not certain, that she married Galmoye: they had loved each other for a long time and had, says Dangeau, given each other proofs of it. But James and his wife would not receive them. Shortly after, his daughter, sick of exile and silliness, made terms with William III and returned alone to England, where she lived the rest of her days. She may be said to have opted for the Churchills against the Stuarts, for her mother's side against her father's. For she lived in amity with her mother, and was remembered in her will. She died in the same year as Arabella, and was buried at Navestock in Essex, where a monument in the chancel recalls her memory.

It has usually been assumed that after James threw Arabella over, life had nothing more for her; that impoverished and faded, she passed from the scene. The truth, however, provides no such morosely moral a conclusion.

Charles Godfrey was a fellow-officer of her brother, Jack Churchill. Lady Drake had a sister, Mrs. Godfrey; she may have been Charles Godfrey's mother or grandmother, in which case he and Arabella would be cousins. He was with Churchill and a dozen young Life Guards serving under Vauban at the siege of Maastricht in 1673. These Englishmen, led by Monmouth, were responsible for a gallant exploit: the storming of the half-moon in front of the Brussels gate. Captain Godfrey was given the honour of conveying the news of the fall of Maastricht to Charles II; but he did not get the expected knighthood. At some point, he succeeded in storming Arabella's unoccupied heart, and they made a happy marriage of it.

We do not know when they were married; but in July 1681 we find Arabella appearing in the family circle as godmother to John's eldest daughter, Henrietta, afterwards Duchess of Marlborough in her own right. Arabella and her husband followed her brother's career, and supported his interests, faithfully. They received their reward, which was not inconsiderable.

In the heyday of the Churchills, with the accession of Queen Anne, Godfrey became one of the Clerks of the Green Cloth—it is pleasant to think of him following in Sir Winston's steps—and Master of the Jewel Office. He was a very good sort of fellow, approved of by Swift, though a Whig. Swift tells Stella, 20 September 1711: 'Today I was invited to the Green Cloth by Colonel Godfrey, who married the Duke of Marlborough's sister, mother to the Duke of Berwick by King James: I must tell you those things that happened before you were born.'

Honest Colonel Godfrey died in the same year as the Queen: 1714. We have seen from Lady Churchill's will that there were four children of the marriage, of whom two survived. Charlotte married Hugh Boscawen, son of the influential Mr. Boscawen of Charles II's Parliaments, that very characteristic country-member who was a touchstone of English political life, moderate, grave, responsible. His son, Hugh, was even more capable: a leading Whig, he was made Lord Warden of the Stannaries by Godolphin in 1708; on George I's accession, he became Comptroller of the Household and was created Viscount Falmouth. Vice-Treasurer of Ireland for many years, he was the maker of the Boscawens' fortunes.

Colonel Godfrey left all his lands, furniture, jewels, plate, etcetera 'unto my dear and loving wife, Arabella Godfrey', whom he appointed his executrix. There is evidence of entire affection, complete confidence. The second daughter, Elizabeth, had married another Whig politician: Edmund Dunch, Master of the Household in the Whig years, 1708 and 1714. To each of his daughters and sons-in-law Godfrey left £100; token payments of affection, for they were all well provided for. He left an annuity of £100 a year to his sister, wife of John Waldegrave: a brother-in-law of Arabella's daughter by James, Henrietta. What a small circle theirs was—for all its European connexions through the Stuarts and Marlborough himself!

Nor did the Duke forget his sister. In his immense will, made in 1722, the year of his death, with its elaborate dispositions of the vast wealth he had accumulated, there was included 'an annuity of £400 in trust for his sister Godfrey for life'.

When Arabella came to die, she was full of money. She left £4000 in trust for her daughter, Lady Falmouth, and £1000 to her grandson, James, Lord Waldegrave. This young man had had the sense to return from France, where he had been brought up; he dropped the family Catholicism and became a leading Whig diplomat, ambassador at Vienna and then at Paris, a follower of Sir Robert Walpole. This changed the direction, and the tradition, of the Waldegraves to their advantage. To Lady Falmouth, Arabella left 'one pair of my diamond ear-rings, of four great diamonds each', which she usually wore (had they been a gift from James?). She left £500 to Lady Waldegrave, and 'my best pearl necklace'. All the rest of her property, which must have been considerable—stocks in the Bank and South Sea Company, ready money, plate, jewels, etcetera, she left to 'my dear daughter', Elizabeth Dunch, evidently her favourite, whom she appointed her executrix.

She left £5 to each of her children to buy a mourning-ring. No mention of the most famous of them, the Duke of Berwick, long since a naturalised Frenchman and now a Marshal of France. During the long wars that filled his early life, in which he and his uncle commanded armies on opposite sides, there is only one inquiry recorded from him of his mother. When only a boy, on campaign in Hungary, he writes home an account of his first battle to his brother Henry: 'I have taken two lusty tall fellows and one sabre', and asks him to write his sister that Mr. Thorp was killed. At the battle of Landen in 1694, Berwick was captured by his uncle, Charles Churchill, and exchanged for the Duke of Ormonde. With his uncle Marlborough, in the war of the Spanish Succession, he maintained more important relations.

What kind of a woman was she, whose fate was so curiously interwoven in our history?

An ordinary enough woman, whose inclinations were wholly domestic—if they had not been early wrested out of their course by her royal lover. Hamilton tells us that she was an indolent creature; and that may well have been true: though she inherited the Villiers figure, she inherited none of their vivacity. She was a kindly, prudent, reserved woman, whose horizons were entirely bounded by the family. Nothing unpleasant or unkind is recorded of her; like all those children born in the ambivalent circumstances of Ashe, she knew well how to hold her tongue. Only a rumour of resentment at her treatment by James reached posterity, and that through Dangeau some years later. He evidently got wind of the view held at St.-Germain that Arabella regarded James with detestation after his departure—and this was thought unreasonable of her since he had recognised her children in spite of the Queen's strong opposition. But such a reaction is not unknown in such circumstances: no one ever said that she loved James: he merely took advantage of her.

When Hamilton describes her, she was only a girl, thin and pale. Time remedied that and filled out her lines, though she retained her pale complexion, her milk-white skin. From Lely's portraits of her she seems to have had her father's long nose, a more sensual face; there are the voluptuous lips, the amorous eyes, the hand invitingly defending the too explicit breasts. Lely gave all his beauties this look—it was the mood, the fashion, the foible of the time: the smouldering eyes, the languor of the expression, the seductive disarray of dress, the suggestiveness of pose.

For the rest, when Arabella died in 1730, a very old woman of eighty-two, she could look back over it all, in the flickering intervals of her memory, with some satisfaction. Though no countess, and open—like everybody else—to the tart remarks of her sister-in-law, Sarah, it had been a strange, richly fulfilled fate after all, taking an unexpected course from those unpromising, unprosperous beginnings. She died 4 May, and was buried 10 May, in Westminster Abbey, in the grave of her brother George, the Admiral, near the choir door.

Horace Walpole, who had the true historian's unappeasable nostalgia for the life of the past and treasured its evidences in scraps and oddities, carried the memory of Arabella—it is extraordinary to think—up to the end of the eighteenth, the threshold of the nineteenth, century. One day in the hot summer of 1759, we find him visiting Navestock, with its alleys of limes and green canal; within were the French mirrors, the commodes, screens and portraits, 'a deal of noblesse *â la St.-Germain*'. There were James II, Charles II, the Duke of Berwick and the rest, 'above all, *la Godfrey*, and not at all ugly, though she does not show her thighs'. Two years later : 'I have picked up at Mrs. Dunch's auction the sweetest Petitot in the world—the very picture of James II, that he gave Mrs. Godfrey—and I paid but six guineas and a half for it—I will not tell you how vast a commission I had given'.

One day in 1764, the Berwicks—the third generation of them—came to visit Horace. 'They have the grace to call themselves Lirias here, yet they do not go to Court, and say that they are only come to see their relations. . . . He had never heard that his great-grandmother married Mr. Godfrey; he told me today that she called herself Churchill, but that her family name was Marlborough.' Horace forgot nothing of the past: he was fond of recalling that he had known six generations of the Waldegraves. When very old, in

1785, he recalled his memory of Arabella: 'I was a schoolfellow of the two last Earls of Waldegrave, and used to play with them in the holidays when I was about twelve years old. They lived with their grandmother, natural daughter of James II. One evening while I was there, came in her mother, Mrs. Godfrey, that King's mistress —ancient, in truth ,and so superannuated that she scarce seemed to know where she was. I saw her another time in her chair in St. James's Park, and have a perfect idea of her face, which was pale, round and sleek.'

This was a whole century after the events and days we have been recording. We must return.

CHAPTER EIGHT

John and Sarah

MEANWHILE, Arabella's brother John was growing up into handsome young manhood.

He had been at school in Dublin and, for a time, it seems, at St. Paul's. But he was never much of a scholar, unlike his father. His genius was for action: action—and diplomacy. He took more after the Villiers side of the family; he certainly had their ravishing looks. To these he added the courtesy and manners that had so distinguished the first Duke of Buckingham. Courts are much more responsive to beauty, whether in women or men; and the youth's striking looks did not go unnoticed. James made him his page and used to take him with him to Hyde Park when drilling the Guards—a favourite amusement with that dull head. He noticed his young attendant's keenness and, one day, asking him what career he wished for, John fell on his knees dutifully and asked for 'a pair of colours' in one of the Guards regiments. On 14 September 1667 his commission was made out as ensign to the King's own company in Colonel Russell's regiment of Foot Guards. John was just turned seventeen; so began the long connexion of the greatest of English soldiers with the Grenadiers.

Next year, he was sent to Tangier and spent the greater part of the three years in that African outpost, which had been added to our dominions by Charles's self-sacrificing marriage to Catherine of Braganza. This was the most tangible asset that came to us from the Portuguese marriage, and we should have done well to hold on to it. The King and his advisers realised the strategic value of the place—key to the Western Mediterranean; but it was expensive to garrison and it became a bugbear to the House of Commons, to whose ignorance it was sacrificed in the end. Not till we won Gibraltar in 1704 did we have an equivalent.

These three years were of great importance in the formation of that masterly military mind. Field-Marshal Wolseley says, 'we know little of Churchill's doings at Tangier, beyond the fact that he was constantly engaged with the enemy, who closely invested the place. He took part in frequent sallies made by the garrison, and showed remarkable daring in numerous skirmishes with the Moors, whose enterprise often took the form of cutting off, by means of cleverly laid ambushes, those who ventured to straggle beyond the British lines. Churchill was thus able whilst a boy to test his nerve, and to accustom himself to danger and to the curious sensation of being shot at.' Coolness of nerve was, indeed, one of Churchill's many gifts; he often exposed himself on the field of battle in later years as Commander-in-Chief, but he was never known to be rattled.

More important, it was these apprentice-years that implanted the appreciation of the strategic value of the Mediterranean that Marlborough never lost sight of in all the vast complexities and burdens, military, political and diplomatic, that rested upon him as Generalissimo of the Grand Alliance. To this we must add an equal appreciation of the importance of sea-power in the conduct of overall military operations.

We now know that the young subaltern, eager for experience, in his third year at Tangier exchanged land service for sea, and took part in the expedition against Algiers. We have an order from the King to the Vice-Treasurer of Ireland, 21 March 1670, commanding him to pay Sir Winston his arrears of £140 for diet and lodging during service in Ireland, since it had been represented that Sir Winston had bestowed that sum on John 'for and towards his equipage and other expenses in the employment he is now forthwith by our command to undertake aboard our fleet in the Mediterranean seas. We, being graciously willing to give all due encouragement to the forwardness and early affections of the said John Churchill to our service, and also in just satisfaction to the father', ordered this sum to be paid from any moneys coming to hand, dispensing with any order to the contrary, 'in particular bounty to the said John Churchill'.

In the winter of 1670-1, Churchill returned from the Mediterranean, bronzed and fit, eager not only for military experience, to his place at Court, where other arms awaited him. His cousin Barbara, now made Duchess of Cleveland, was still the reigning beauty, though she and the King—like the restless, promiscuous spirits they were—had tired of each other.

In any case, no one could have supported Barbara long, in either sense of the word 'support'; for she was both wildly extravagant and of an intolerable temper. Only Charles would have put up with her: he was easy-going and, being king, had the nation's purse to dip into. Gone were the rapturous early days of the

Restoration, when Dryden could address the favourite with a perhaps pardonable exaggeration—Dryden was always a gentleman, and always a sycophant:

> You sit above, and see vain Men below
> Contend, for what you only can bestow;
> But those great actions others do by chance,
> Are, like your beauty, your Inheritance:
> So great a soul, such sweetness joined in one,
> Could only spring from noble Grandison:
> You, like the stars, not by reflection bright,
> Are born to your own Heaven and your own light;
> Like them are good, but from a nobler cause,
> From your own knowledge, not from Nature's laws.
> Your Power you never use but from Defence,
> To guard your own, or others' Innocence. . . .

Really! . . . We know what she was capable of in her cabal against Clarendon. She was certainly not without resource. When Charles's feelings for Moll Davis grew to a height, Barbara had entertained the dancer to supper on her way to the King and administered her a jalap in the sweet, which had the effect of very much disappointing the King in his intentions with her.

Since Dryden wrote his lines, Barbara had presented the King with a whole family of children—though there was doubt about the paternity of one or two. After some protest and mutual recriminations, Charles accepted (and provided for) them all. But she never put herself out to make the King easy; indeed, after she found out that ease was what he valued most, she made him purchase it at a constantly heightened price: scenes, propitiation, gifts, demands; scenes, forgiveness, grants and titles followed in the regular order of the dance she led him. When, on the grounds of her intimacy with Harry Jermyn's nephew, Charles refused to own the child she was expecting, she threatened she would bring it to Whitehall and dash its brains out against the walls. The King had to go down on his knees and beg forgiveness. What was more to the point, she got 5600 ounces of plate from the Jewel-House.

She was a relentless gold-digger. To console her for the libels circulated about her and the insults she received, Charles was made to present her with Berkshire House at St. James's. Two years later, she sold the whole site with its gardens for building plots, making large sums on the transaction: her memory is preserved in this quarter, Cleveland Court and Square, Cleveland Row, St. James's. Next year, she got what became an annual grant of £4700 from the

Post Office, and later she got grants for a term of years from excise and customs, in addition to the income she obtained from the sale of offices, the rents she exacted from place-holders. From Charles she extorted large sums—on one occasion £30,000—and grants of plate from the Jewel-House. But her extravagance was such that she was still always out of funds. And no wonder—when she could appear at the theatre one afternoon wearing jewels worth £40,000 (multiply!) or at night lose half as much at cards. She reached her apogee in 1670 when Charles created her Duchess of Cleveland—with remainder to her first and third sons, omitting the second for obvious reasons—and gave her outright Elizabeth I's favourite palace and park of Nonsuch. This the miscreant proceeded to dismantle and to sell all the contents.

By this time her amorous activities were as variegated as her financial depredations: she made the King share her favours with Jacob Hall, the rope-dancer, whom she had picked up at Bartholomew Fair and whom she paid for his services. He must have been more satisfying than the King. Hamilton tells us that 'his strength and agility charmed the public, even to a wish to know what he was in private; for he appeared, in his tumbling dress, to be quite of a different make from the fortunate Jermyn. The tumbler did not deceive Lady Castlemaine's expectations, if report may be believed, and as was intimated in many a song, much more to the honour of the rope-dancer than of the countess. But she despised all these rumours, and only appeared still more handsome.'

At this point, her cousin John, 'grown a man, bronzed by African sunshine, close-knit by active service and tempered by discipline and danger,' says our Sir Winston, 'arrived home from the Mediterranean. He seems to have been welcomed . . . and by none more than Barbara, now become Duchess of Cleveland. She was twenty-nine and he twenty. . . . Affections, affinities and attractions were combined. Desire walked with opportunity and neither was denied. John almost immediately became her lover, and for more than three years this wanton and joyous couple shared pleasures and hazards.' Certainly, 'the cynical, promiscuous, sagacious-indulgent sovereign was outwitted or outfaced'.

The situation was not without its comedy, or its escapades. Two stories are well known. One is that John was in Barbara's bedroom when they heard the King approaching, and John, to save the Duchess's 'honour'—that flexible, expendable commodity—leaped from the high window into the court below. For this, he was said to have been rewarded with a large sum. The other story is that

Charles once surprised the couple *in flagrante delicto*; but the easy-going monarch, well appreciating such situations, let his young officer off with—'You are a rascal, but I forgive you, for you do it to get your bread'.

There was a sting to this insult. For after a year or two of this, John was able to invest, in 1674, the considerable sum of £4500 in purchasing an annuity of £500. It was the foundation of his financial security—no doubt always in view, from the impoverished days at Ashe—and of his immense fortune. It was only from Barbara that he could have got such a sum—and she was as generous with (other people's) money as she was with her own charms. What shocked contemporaries was not that the money had been thus earned, but that the young officer, instead of spending it in the expected fashion, should have proceeded prudently to invest it.

Barbara's last child, a daughter, Barbara, born 16 July 1672, was another fruit of this affair. It was generally held that this was John's child, and the Duchess had to provide for her herself. When she left the English Court in high dudgeon in 1677, she gave the nuns of the Immacuate Conception of the Rue Charenton in Paris £1000, to bring the child up. The little girl grew up and made her profession as a nun, by the name of Sister Benedicta. But convent walls did not prevent the Earl of Arran from coming to her, by whom she became the mother of Charles Hamilton; nor did this prevent her ending happily as prioress of the convent of St. Nicholas at Pontoise.

Altogether, we may consider that, for a young Guards officer, to have known the Duchess must have been a very liberal education.

For the rest, during these years Churchill was living the life of a young soldier of the time who happened to be favoured by his family's intimate position at Court. It was a small society in which points of 'honour'—or dishonour—were quickly taken up and duels ensued, in which men were idiots enough to kill and get killed for a mere nothing. John, at twenty-one, was not above such nonsense. On 6 January 1671 we hear: 'Yesterday was a duel between Mr. Fenwick and Mr. Churchill, who had for their seconds Mr. Harpe and Mr. Newport, son to my Lord Newport; it ended with some wounds for Mr. Churchill, but no danger of life'. The quarrel had begun, apparently, at a masquerade. These two were to meet on the more dangerous ground of politics years later, when it proved fatal to Fenwick. In August there was a 'recounter' between Captain Herbert and 'young Churchill. I know not the quarrel; but Herbert ran Churchill twice through the arm, and Churchill him into the thigh, and after, Herbert disarmed him. But what is the worse, I hear that Churchill has so spoke of it that the King and Duke are angry with Herbert.' We see that Churchill is something of a favourite already; in time to come this same correspondent describes him as 'the only favourite of his master'.

Meanwhile, the remedy for this sort of thing was action.

Next year, with the joint war of France and England against the Dutch, it came. At the murderous battle of Sole Bay, the 1st Company of the Guards served immediately under James, upon the deck of the flagship, the *Prince*—main target of the attack. There was a ghastly slaughter of officers, and, after the battle, Churchill received a double promotion: from Guards ensign to Marine captaincy. Next year, the Admiralty regiment in which he now held a company was serving on land under the French king. The exploit of the English company under Monmouth, under whom Churchill and Godfrey served, when the half-moon work in front of the gate at Maastricht was carried, took place under Louis's eye. Afterwards, Churchill, who had been wounded at Monmouth's side, was publicly congratulated on parade by the great man himself. Another young subaltern had joined in the gallant assault, against orders: Villars. Monmouth wrote home to his father commending Churchill: 'here is the brave man who saved my life'. What ironic vistas war opens up: Marlborough defeating Monmouth at Sedgemoor, Villars at Malplaquet!

When England withdrew from this indefensible war—product of the Secret Treaty of Dover—a number of troops were left on the Continent in French pay. They were rapidly reduced in number, and units were combined. Churchill received the reward of his gallantry at Maastricht by being promoted Colonel of a regiment in the service of France. One sees how ambivalent his career was made by the circumstances of the time, from his earliest days: it was not without its effect on his personality. Before taking command of his regiment he had to be presented at Versailles and Louis greeted once more the 'young Adonis in scarlet and gold' who as an elderly man proved the old King's greatest opponent. In the English army Churchill retained the rank of Captain till next year, when he was promoted Lieutenant-Colonel.

Before his return he took part under the famous Turenne in the grim battle of Enzheim. On this October day, 1674, Turenne made a surprise attack on the Imperialists' army with only half their numbers. The brunt of the fighting fell upon the English and Irish regiments, especially upon Churchill's, which had half its officers killed or wounded in the bitter struggle for a wood that lay between the two armies. Feversham reported: 'One and all accomplished marvels. . . . No one in the world could possibly have done better than Mr. Churchill has done and M. de Turenne is very well pleased with all our nation.' Churchill had been allotted the post of honour by Turenne, who clearly had confidence in him. What is more arresting is the cool assessment of the battle made by the young Colonel, with its laconic, implied criticism of the great Turenne. Churchill wrote to Monmouth: 'Half of our foot was so posted that they did not fight at all'. There is a quiet but damaging criticism of the master's dispositions; there speaks, at twenty-four, an instinct for economy in war which was a leading characteristic in Turenne's most brilliant pupil.

More than a quarter of a century elapsed before Churchill had the opportunity fully to display his military genius. 'From 1671 to 1675 he exhibited all those qualities which were regarded as the forerunners in a regimental officer of the highest distinction. He won his way up from grade to grade by undoubted merit and daring. . . . At twenty-four he was a colonel. He was fifty-two before he commanded a large army. . . . By the time he arrived at the highest command he was passing the prime of life, and older than many of the leading generals of the day.'

It offers a parallel with his famous descendant, who did not arrive at supreme power until he was sixty-five, at that moment of supreme danger in 1940: *annus mirabilis.*

The young Colonel came home in 1675, to engage in operations which proved the most difficult he ever had to conduct against a formidable opponent. This was Sarah Jennings, then at the mature age of fifteen. He was ten years older, and—in spite of his experience with his cousin—by no means a match for her.

Sarah was the younger sister of Frances, 'la belle Jennings', whose dazzling looks made such an impression at the Court of Charles II. But it was no use: both of them as masterful as they were beautiful, they were impregnable. They took part in all the public activities of the Court—the masquerades and balls, the dancing and routs—but they were proof against more dangerous allurements. Marriage was the only way to their favours, as Churchill had to learn. 'La Belle Jennings' married first Anthony Hamilton's brother, and, later, tall Dick Talbot, whom we have come across with Sir Winston in Ireland. James II made him Lord

Lieutenant of Ireland; so that Frances Jennings ended up as Jacobite Duchess of Tyrconnel, though she managed, in an ambivalent world, to maintain good relations with the Marlboroughs.

Sarah was not quite so startlingly lovely as her sister; but she was quite beautiful enough, with cherry lips, inclined to be petulant, her flashing blue eyes and regular nose, with its indication of wilfulness and determination, the gold hair that was washed in honey, people said, and showed never a grey hair even when she was a grandmother. Though younger, she was a more powerful personality than her sister. She early showed her mettle by pushing her mother out of Court: though under age she was well capable of looking after herself.

The Jennings family were a more established family than the Churchills and better off; they, too, had been West Country by origin. They had owned the manor of Churchill in Somerset, and sold it to Sir John Churchill. They were Royalists, and now the father was dead; so the sisters were heiresses—though not in a large way, enough to add to their spirit of independence. They owned the estate of Holywell, near St. Albans, which remained always a favourite residence with Sarah, who later bought her sister's share of the inheritance.

The sisters had their place in the household of the new Duchess of York; but Sarah's hold was due to the place she had in the affections of Anne Hyde's younger daughter, the Princess Anne, a favourite with her father, James. Years afterwards, Sarah wrote: 'the beginning of the Princess's kindness for me had a much earlier date than my entrance into her service. . . . We had used to play together when she was a child, and she even then expressed a particular fondness for me. This inclination increased with our years. I was often at Court, and the Princess always distinguished me by the pleasure she took to honour me, preferably to others, with her conversation and confidence. In all her parties for amusement, I was sure, by her choice, to be one.' There is no reason to doubt the essential veracity of this. Poor Anne, to be sure, would not be much good at amusing herself.

A bundle of letters remains to testify to the difficulties John encountered in these years of his courtship.[1] When they open, he is already in love—and, it would seem, for the first time. 'My Soul, I love you so truly well that I hope you will be so kind as to let me see you somewhere today, since you will not be at Whitehall. I will not

[1] These are given in full in Churchill, *Marlborough,* I. 119-40, from which I quote.

name any time, for all hours are alike to me when you will bless me with your sight.' That sounds like the genuine eloquence of love, and he already swears, 'You are, and ever shall be, the dear object of my life, for by heavens I will never love anybody but yourself'.

To that Sarah could reply, and no doubt did: 'What about Barbara? Did you not love her?' The answer was, apparently not.

John sends note after note, urging a meeting. 'I fancy by this time that you are awake, which makes me now send to know how you do, and if your foot will permit you to give me the joy of seeing you in the Drawing Room this night.' It seems he was not vouchsafed that joy: 'My Soul, it is a cruel thing to be forced in a place when I have no hopes of seeing you, for on my word last night seemed very tedious to me; wherefore I beg you will be so kind to me as to come as often as you can this week, since I am forced to wait' (*i.e.* on the Duke).

Not at all: the girl's heart is not touched: she does not come, sends word she is not well. She keeps him waiting: she well knows the art, young as she is. And, indeed, the experienced young officer, who knows the ways of women, always did have more heart than Sarah and was at a corresponding disadvantage in dealing with her. Now he is sick, and we hear several times of the headaches that tortured him in the field in later life—perhaps psychological manifestations of the strain he was under and the price he paid for the marvellous self-control he showed, in everything except his love for Sarah. He was now completely under her spell: 'I was last night at the ball, in hopes to have seen what I love above my own soul, but I was not so happy, for I could see you nowhere, so that I did not stay above an hour'.

Another time: 'I stayed last night in the Drawing Room expecting your coming back, for I could have wished that we had not parted until you had given me hopes of seeing you, for, my soul, there is no pain so great to me, as that when I fear you do not love me'. There is the authentic note, not merely of passion, but of love itself. But there are shadows in the path: 'do not be so ill-natured as to believe any lies that may be told you of me, for on my faith I do not only now love you, but do desire to do it as long as I live'.

What were these shadows, the lies told about him? They can only refer to continuing relations with Barbara, or to gossip—in that small circle, where everybody knew everybody else's most intimate affairs—about him and other women. Now he is going away, perhaps being sent by James on a confidential mission to France. 'My soul, I go with the heaviest heart that ever man did, for by all that is good I love you with my heart and soul, and I am sure that as long as I live you shall have no just reason to believe the contrary. If you are unkind, I love so well that I cannot live, for you are my life, my soul, my all that I hold dear in this world.'

For an untutored soldier, he was not expressing himself badly—'Love bade me write'. And to think that this little minx kept the handsomest young man at Court dangling at her beck! 'By all that is good' is the favourite phrase by which he swears when thinking of her: evidently he did not think of his relations with Barbara as coming into that category. That was the clue: her youth and innocence, her virtue and chastity. What was it that he wanted? If it were just that and no more, he could wait for ever. There had been no word of marriage from his eloquent pen. If she yielded what so many other ladies at Court made no such fuss about, that would be the end of any thought of marriage, his passion satisfied. Fortunately, she was not tempted: she had not been aroused physically: she could wait. Instinctively, with a true strategic sense, she played her woman's game, she conducted her operations.

She made a quarrel with him: she turned her back on him in the Duchess's Drawing Room. At once he is at her feet. 'To show how unreasonable you are in accusing me, I dare swear you yourself will own that your going from me in the Duchess's Drawing Room did show as much contempt as possible. I may grieve at it, but I will no more complain when you do it, for I suppose it is what pleases your humour. I cannot imagine what you meant by your saying I laughed at you at the Duke's side, for I was so far from that, that had it not been for shame I could have cried. And, for being in haste to go to the Park, after you went, I stood near a quarter of an hour, I believe, without knowing what I did.'

John was plainly in love; the tricks of this girl, now sixteen, were what anyone of his age and experience should have seen through. Perhaps he did see through them, but could not help himself; he could not say the word 'Marriage', he had not the means to make her an offer, certainly not to support a family. It was for her to bring him to the point—and, with superior tactical sense, she goes straight to it. She takes up the pen: 'If it were true that you have that passion for me which you say you have, you would find out some way to make yourself happy—it is in your power. Therefore press me no more to see you, since it is what I cannot in honour approve of, and if I have done too much, be so just as to consider who was the cause of it.'

John can only fall back on his defences, like many another man in a similar predicament. He begins to despair: 'as for the power you say you have over yourself, I do no ways at all doubt of it, for I swear to you I do not think you love me. . . . You must give me leave to beg that you will not condemn me for a vain fool that I did believe you did love me, since both you and your actions did oblige me to that belief, in which heaven knows I took so much joy that from henceforward my life must be a torment to me for it. You say I pretend a passion to you when I have other things in my head. I cannot imagine what you mean by it, for I vow to God you do so entirely possess my thoughts that I think of nothing else in this world but your dear self.' There speaks the usual man's hope of establishing the innocence of his intentions by asseverating ignorance.

This did not take Sarah in: 'As for seeing you I am resolved I never will in private nor in public if I could help it. As for the last I fear it will be some time before I can order so as to be out of your way of seeing me. But surely you must confess that you have been the falsest creature upon earth to me. I must own that I shall suffer a great deal of trouble, but I will bear it, and give God thanks, though too late I see my error.'

From this exchange of letters we perceive several things. The girl at last is touched, even agitated; we can see as much in the hurry of the letter, almost without punctuation, even apart from what she says. From what both she and John say, a real obstacle raises its head. This can be nothing else but the pressure of John's parents to marry him to Catherine Sedley. This was a good idea, an obvious one. John had no money and little of an inheritance to look forward to; she would one day be rich, inheriting a fortune from her father; she was intelligent and a good sort. It was one of those projects that had everything in common sense to recommend it, and John's parents pressed it hard. Duty and inclination pulled him in different directions; for he had a strong sense of duty, and no man was more ambitious. Considering all this, it is a strong tribute to his heart that it prevailed—almost the only time it ever did—against his head. For Sir Winston was certainly in negotiation with Sir Charles Sedley—and this was what was alarming Sarah, perhaps unconsciously acting as a precipitant upon her as yet unfixed affections.

John held firm. By the spring of 1677, the Sedley marriage was off. A more exalted fate for Catherine was in view: the Duke had become infatuated with her. Instead of marrying John, she was on her way to ousting John's sister from the place of *maîtresse en titre* to the Duke.

In 1677 another obstacle from the path of true love was removed by Barbara packing all her traps and departing in disgust with everybody and everything to France, taking her child with her. This must have been as much of a relief to John as it was to the King, who sank back into the more consoling, if hardly less scrounging, arms of the Duchess of Portsmouth and Nell Gwyn.

The correspondence between John and Sarah could be resumed, the deadlock broken. He returned to the assault on her emotions, now that they had been touched. 'It is not reasonable that you should have a doubt but that I love you above all expression, which by heaven I do. . . . But Oh, my soul, if we might be both happy, what inexpressible joy would that be! . . . I will not dare to expect more favour than you shall think fit to give, but could you ever love me, I think the happiness would be so great that it would make me immortal.'

We see that John is the romantic, the rhapsodist, the one with the ranging imagination; Sarah the rationalist, the woman of practical common sense. This contrast in their characters appears later in other relations, other aspects of their lives. She replies: 'I am as little satisfied with this letter as I have been with many others, for I find all you will say is only to amuse me and make me think you have a passion for me, when in reality there is no such thing. . . . Therefore pray consider if, with honour to me and satisfaction to yourself, I can see you; for if it be only to repeat those things which you said so oft, I shall think you the worst of men, and the most ungrateful; and 'tis to no purpose to imagine that I will be made ridiculous in the world, when it is in your power to make me otherwise.'

It is evident from this that tokens of affection had passed between them, and that Sarah, now seventeen, is willing to be married. But he need not imagine that she is going to be made a fool of by him, however fond she may be of him. The fear of being 'made ridiculous in the world' always remained with her, a constant motive: it led her to actions later in life which had precisely that effect and made her a raging eccentric; but by then she was too rich, too independent, too careless of what anybody thought, and perhaps too odd, to mind.

John writes, 'I have been so extreme ill with the headache all this morning that I have not had courage to write to know how you do; but your being well is what I prefer much above my own health. . . . If the Duchess sees company, I hope you will be there; but if she does not, I beg you will then let me see you in your chamber, if it be but for one hour. If you are not in the Drawing-Room, you must then send me word at what hour I shall come.' Dangerous? Apparently their understanding is now so clear that there is no danger. The girl replies: 'At four o'clock I would see you, but that would hinder you from seeing the play, which I fear would be a great affliction to you, and increase the pain in your head, which would be out of anybody's power to ease until the next new play. Therefore, pray consider, and without any compliment to me, send me word if you can come to me without any prejudice to your health.'

At that, John blew up. With hurt feelings, he wrote a letter of resentful protest to Sarah's waiting-woman. He got what he deserved from her mistress: 'I have done nothing to deserve such a kind of letter as you have writ to me, and therefore I don't know what answer to give; but I find you have a very ill opinion of me, and therefore I can't help being angry with myself for having too good a one of you; for if I had as little love as yourself, I have been told enough of you to make me hate you, and then I believe I should have been more happy than I am like to be now.' The cat shows her claws in that: the unhappy reminder of Barbara and Catherine, the stories, the rumours, true and false, that circulated about him and them, making him 'ridiculous in the world'. There was no point in arguing with Sarah: John was not clever enough to keep his own end up; nothing to do but capitulate: 'I am resolved to take nothing ill but to be your slave as long as I live, and so to think all things well that you do'.

And that, in the event, was what came about.

These in truth were lovers' quarrels: the crisis in their relations was safely past; it was taken for granted that they were for each other: it was a question of finding ways and means. John still had reason to complain: 'it was unkind of you to go away last night since you knew that I came for no other purpose but to have the joy of seeing you; but I will not believe it was for want of love, for you are all goodness, the thought of which makes me love you above my own soul'.

Perhaps Sarah's tantrums were going too far—as they certainly were to do in the future. She reproaches John with loving her less than he did. It is necessary to bring him finally, irrevocably, to the point. She announces her intention of going to France with her sister. It was a superbly executed manoeuvre. John was forced to bring his talks with the Duchess, who is their one hope and looks on it all with a friendly eye, an open purse, to a conclusion.

The catch was on the hook, the landing about to be made; now Sarah turns to offer a piece of practical woman's advice as to how best to manage the Duchess in the matter: 'I have made many reflections upon what you said to me last night, and I am of the opinion that could the Duchess obtain what you ask her, you might be more unhappy than if it cannot be had. Therefore, as I have always shown more kindness for you than perhaps I ought, I am resolved to give you one mark more—and that is to desire you to say nothing of it to the Duchess on my account; and your own interest, when I am not concerned in it, will probably compass what will make you much happier than this can ever do.' It did. It was a shrewd piece of advice that Sarah offered, and it clinched the matter. The marriage was made possible for them. Not all the advice that the Duke of Marlborough received from his Duchess, in the distant future, was as sound or as happy.

What the Duchess of York did for the couple we do not know—evidently some arrangements were made with regard to John's post, for he was now gentleman of the bed-chamber to the Duke. The sad thing was that Sir Winston could do nothing for his son: he was in debt, and John, upon whom the estate was entailed, had to sacrifice some part of his inheritance to raise cash for his father and himself at this juncture. With whatever he could manage to raise, the salary of his post and the annuity he had so gallantly earned, and with Sarah's perhaps equivalent income—she had expectations of more when her mother died—the couple came together. It was not much to live on in such a very grand society, still less to provide for a family; they would have to be very careful: fortunately, by disposition they both were.

When, years after, Sarah came to sum it all up, looking back upon it from an immense distance of age and fame, she said: 'I don't know whether it is proper or necessary to add what I am going to write, though I think it a merit, that Sir Winston Churchill had about £1000 a year from his father,[1] who liked his grandson better than his own son, settled it upon him, that his father could only enjoy it for his life. But the Duke of Marlborough, when he was but eight and twenty [*i.e.* at the time of his marriage] joined

[1] I think that this must be an over-estimate on Sarah's part, or that her memory betrayed her after so many years. Perhaps she had never known exactly what Sir Winston's estate was worth. A likely explanation is that the income from his estate and his salary from the Board of Green Cloth together equalled £1000 p.a.

with his father, who was in debt, and let him sell his estate. From the very beginning of his life, he never spent a shilling beyond what his income was. He began with the first commission of an ensign in the army, and went on regularly through every step in that profession; and in King Charles II's time served in France under Marshal Turenne, from whom he learnt a great deal.' Then Sarah's political prejudices took charge of her pen: 'And I think it more honour to rise from the lowest step to the greatest than, as the fashion is now, to be Admirals without ever having seen water but in a basin, or to make Generals that never saw any action of war and only felt from the generosity of their temper that they were not to pursue a flying enemy.' One can hear the very accents of her voice, positive, cutting, contemptuous, always in the right.

No-one knows when or where precisely the marriage took place —probably in the privacy of the Duchess's apartments, and for several months it was kept secret.

It was, unlike most of the marriages in that age and society, a love-match; and the most courageous and imprudent action that that prudent couple ever committed. From this time to their dying day, they were in love with each other. Neither of them ever looked at anyone else. Sarah's strength of character, extraordinary for a mere girl, conditioned John in the course of that protracted and argumentative courtship. He had promised to become her slave, and all his life he remained so: in fact, he spoiled her, letting her have her way in all things.

Their passion for each other lasted always. The famous Duke, departing for the wars, many years later, wrote: 'It is impossible to express with what a heavy heart I parted with you when I was at the waterside. I could have given my life to have come back, though I knew my own weakness so much I durst not, for I should have exposed myself to the company. I did for a great while have a perspective glass looking upon the cliffs in hopes I might have had one sight of you.' We know by verbal tradition that on his home-comings the Duke 'pleasured' his wife before ever taking off his boots.

On her part: 'Wherever you are, whilst I have life, my soul shall follow you, my ever dear Lord Marlborough, and wherever I am I should only kill the time wishing for night that I may sleep and hope the next day to hear from you'.

When he was dead, she became his slave, devoting herself to his memory. Hence one of the greatest sayings of any woman in history, when her hand was sought by the proud Duke of Somerset:

'if I were young and handsome as I was, instead of old and faded as I am, and you could lay the empire of the world at my feet, you should never share the heart and hand that once belonged to John, Duke of Marlborough'.

In the long empty years without him, she often turned over the letters she had kept: 'Some copies of my letters to Mr. Churchill before I was married and not more than fifteen years old', she wrote, folded them up and put them carefully away. She meant to burn them before she died; but in the last year of her life, in the shaky hand of extreme old age: 'Read over in 1743 desiring to burn them, but I could not do it'.

CHAPTER NINE

Court Life and Home Life

WITH his private life and happiness now on a settled foundation, Churchill could go forward, with a more contented mind, on his career. At first the only home he and Sarah had in the country was with his parents at Minterne. We find him toiling up and down the dusty roads to his native Dorset in summer, going to and from Whitehall at the Duke's summons. Sarah was more at Minterne, with what consequences we can imagine. John's diplomacy was needed between the two women: he thanks Sarah for writing to his mother: 'if she takes anything ill that is in that letter, you must attribute it to the peevishness of old age, for really there is nothing in it that she ought to take ill. I take it very kindly that you have writ to her again, for she is my Mother, and I hope at last that she will be sensible that she is to blame in being peevish.'

Diplomacy was called for in every relation of—what his descendant has well called—John's 'anxious, toilsome and troubled life', perhaps from the earliest days at Ashe. It came as more than 'second nature' with him: it became his nature itself; so that by temperament he was exceedingly well fitted for the other half of his life's work.

These next years were filled with such labours: the chief confidant of James, going to and fro between the King and the Duke—he was the chief channel of communication between the two brothers when they were away from each other—between Whitehall and Versailles, James and Louis XIV. We may regard it all as his apprenticeship for the years when he was not only the military arm, but the diplomatic brain-centre, of the Grand Alliance.

In March 1678, he was summoned up from Minterne by the Duke: 'I got to town by a little after three, very weary. However, I dressed and went to the Duke for to know what he had to command me.' What was in question at this time was Britain's joining with Holland in the alliance to contain Louis's aggressions in Europe. Such was Danby's policy, and it would have united the nation behind the monarchy. Even James favoured it; Charles kept his own counsel. Churchill was sent over to Holland to make the military arrangements for intervention; Sidney Godolphin was sent to manage the political negotiations.

Godolphin, who was five years Churchill's senior, was a coming man in politics: one of the 'Chits', the three young men supposed to possess the King's confidence at this moment. Of a Cornish Royalist family—Sidney had been called after his uncle, the Cavalier poet killed in the Civil War—Godolphin and Churchill had long been known to each other and they had much in common. They had both begun as pages in royal service; then their courses diverged: Churchill going into the army and serving abroad, Godolphin remaining always at Court. They had a similar West Country background, small gentry, not rich—though the Godolphins were of more consequence in their county. They came from the house that still largely remains, with its grey granite colonnade at the northern foot of Godolphin Hill, near Helston, out of which came their wealth. But Sidney's mother was a Somerset woman—one sees a portrait bust of another uncle of his, a splendid Caroline bronze, on the wall of the chancel in Bruton church.

Godolphin, too, had had a long and difficult courtship, of Margaret Blague—well known to Sarah, since they were both maids-of-honour. In Margaret's case, the difficulties were chiefly made by John Evelyn, who was her spiritual mentor—and perhaps something of a satyr, since he wished to keep her away from married happiness for religion, and himself. Evelyn's *Life of Margaret Godolphin* was a work of religious piety very popular with Victorians: we understand better the psychological nature of his relation to her and his motives. Margaret appears as no such paragon in the pages of Hamilton, though she was a lady of virtue: she had that commodity in common with Sarah. With great difficulty and in secrecy Godolphin married her and they were happy. In the autumn of this very year she died, leaving Godolphin and Evelyn alike disconsolate. The latter erected his memorial to her; Godolphin never married again. Later, he developed a platonic affection for James's young Duchess; and when they came to the throne, Godolphin was made Chamberlain to her household.

Godolphin and Churchill were both West Country Royalists by origin, Tories by conviction and affiliation. They had more in common. That shrewd judge of men, Charles II, said of Godolphin that he was 'never in the way and never out of the way'. He and Churchill were essentially servants of the state. There was a certain impersonality in their attitude to affairs; they were both reserved, prudent, dependable and loyal, and they were honest men. Churchill was more ambitious and he had a not unworthy passion for money. Godolphin did not care greatly for power, and for money not at all; his passion was for horse-racing. He was essentially an administrator rather than a party-politician; and though he spent a lifetime at the Treasury, he died not a rich man.

We do not hear of Godolphin and Churchill together until this mission to Holland in 1678: it must have had the importance of cementing their friendship and alliance. Henceforth their careers and lives became more and more closely interwoven; until, under Queen Anne, they achieved the famous partnership that brought Louis XIV low: Marlborough in command abroad, Godolphin as Lord Treasurer at home. Before this they had achieved a closer tie: Godolphin's only son married Marlborough's eldest daughter, and their son, if he had lived, would have inherited Marlborough's dukedom. Except for Marlborough, Godolphin was the only person who had much sway with Sarah and who had her unreserved regard and affection. She recognised his goodness and disinterestedness, his unselfishness and care for her and hers. When he died, she wrote in her Bible that he 'was the best man that ever lived'.

The mission to Holland had the further importance that for the first time Godolphin and Churchill were doing business with William of Orange. That young man, who was without the social graces of his ancestor William the Silent, nevertheless became by his achievement, like him, one of the grand figures of European history. All his life, from the time of the terrible threat to his country in 1672, he pursued unswervingly the aim of checkmating Louis XIV; all his life the Dutch Stadtholder fought the Grand Monarch; he was the architect of the alliance that accomplished his life's object. Nephew of the King of England, married to James's elder daughter Mary, who was the next heir to the throne, William was a factor of the first importance in English politics.

William was the same age as Churchill; though he had not Churchill's genius as a soldier, he possessed an even greater spirit, a lofty and indefeasible moral courage. Equally silent and far-sighted, he must have welcomed the opportunity to make the acquaintance of these two young Englishmen, his future subjects, whose minds were ultimately ruled by the idea of the well-being of their country.

In the negotiations the proposal was that James should be Commander-in-Chief. Perhaps it was as well that they came to nothing. Charles had no intention of intervening in the war:

sufficient for him if the threat of it induced Louis to incline to peace. Churchill wrote to allay Sarah's anxiety: 'You may rest satisfied that there will be certain peace in a very few days ... therefore be not concerned when I tell you that I am ordered over and that tomorrow I go. ... I believe it will be about the beginning of October before I shall get back, which time will appear an age to me, since in all that time I shall not be made happy with the sight of you. ... So, dearest soul of my life, farewell. My duty to my Father and Mother.' Later, when all these things were over, Sarah wrote on the treasured letter: 'Lord Marlborough to ease me when I might be frighted at his going into danger'.

On his return, England was thrown into the panic of the Popish Plot, with all its incalculable political consequences. Charles was forced to send his brother into exile, and no doubt was glad to get him off his hands. James fixed himself at Brussels, with his intimate attendants, and there a small Court took shape. Churchill and Legge, whom old snobs like Reresby regarded as 'scarce gentlemen', accompanied him. Then there were one or two ladies, of whom Lady Belasyse must have been a consolation—for she got twice Arabella's pension on the Irish establishment. The Princess Anne joined her father; Sarah was summoned over from Minterne and shortly afterwards her beautiful sister arrived. So the ladies were happy; for James there was plenty of stag-hunting and it looked as if the fox-hunting would be very good too.

At this time an attempt was made to make James see reason on the religious issue: his obstinacy was rocking the throne, threatened to wreck his chances of the succession and was uniting the nation against him. It is not too much to say that at this time he was detested. It was no joke to be, with all one's belongings, in the boat with such a man, utterly dependent on him. All James's best friends tried to move him; it was left to Hyde to put the point directly, since he was his brother-in-law. The answer came back: 'I assure you I will never try that way mentioned in yours to Churchill, and which also has been hinted to me by several of my best friends [they were, indeed], though I were sure it would restore me into the good opinion and esteem of the nation, which I once had; and therefore, I desire that neither you nor none of my friends will ever mention it to me, or flatter themselves that I can ever be brought to it: what I did was never done hastily, and I have expected many years and been prepared for what has happened to me, and for the worst that can yet befall me.'

He thus banged the door on his future in England: he got what he deserved in 1688.

At that moment Charles was struck down by his first stroke. Churchill was in England; it was agreed to send him over to bring James back hurriedly, in case the King died and the Whigs tried to set Monmouth on the throne. James came over in obvious disguise, in a black perruque and a plain suit without his Star and Garter, attended only by Lord Peterborough, Churchill and a couple of footmen not in livery; Churchill, 'like a French officer in his scarf represented the best man in the company'. And so to Windsor in the early morning, where James found his brother recovering; but the King did not dare to keep him in the country that was seething with anger and hysteria.

James had to go back to Brussels. Churchill was sent to Versailles, ostensibly to congratulate the Queen of Spain on her marriage. The real purpose of the mission was to get Louis's support for James, on condition the latter identified his interests completely with Louis. Louis did not think it worth offering an adequate sum. Nothing for James but continued exile, though he would not remain abroad. It was decided to send him to Holyrood, whence he could try his hand at governing Scotland.

That autumn James took the road to Edinburgh, with Churchill at his side. Sarah, expecting her first baby, had to be left behind in Jermyn Street, where her sister joined her to look after her. The child was born at the end of October, Sarah being then nineteen. John, on the road north: 'You may guess by yourself how uneasy I have been since I left you, for nothing breathing ever loved another so well as I do you, and I do swear to you as long as I do live I will never love another. . . . Mr. Legge leaves us this night, so that then I will write to you again; till when, my soul's soul, farewell.' The baby had arrived; John was weary with riding: from Stilton, 'Pray kiss the child once for me'.

At York, James was very coldly received, 'which he never forgot afterwards'. John's thoughts were further south, on the house in Jermyn Street: 'you cannot be truly sensible how much I desire to be with you. I swear to you the first night in which I was blessed in having you in my arms was not more earnestly wished for by me than now I do to be again with you, for if ever man loved woman truly well, I now do you, for I swear to you were we not married I would beg you on my knees to be my wife.' At the moment, he has been suffering from his violent migraine again: 'which makes me melancholy, for I love you so well that I cannot think with patience of dying, for then we must part for ever, which is a dreadful thing to me that loves you above all expression'. This does not say much for John and Sarah's hopes of a future state; but they were both too rational to entertain such illusions.

It is likely enough that John's recurring migraines were due to the increasing strain that he was under in serving James, the superhuman control that such a life demanded. He was anxious to obtain a post, a command, anything that would give him some independence, and his family some security. As it was, he had none: he was utterly dependent, all his fortunes embarked in that crazy vessel. As early as 1672 there was talk of his having the Vice-Chamberlainship of the Household: his friend, Harry Savile, was anxious to sell it and make the best of it, but John had no money and the Duke did not wish anyone else to have it. Now there was talk of Churchill being made ambassador to Versailles or at the Hague.

Churchill got none of these appointments: the truth was that he was too indispensable to James. James confessed as much: 'So long as I am from him [*i.e.* the King], I would not willingly have Churchill from me'. He could not get on without him. Churchill took no profit from this indispensability: he was in part its victim. Among the numerous politicians of both parties who appeared in Barillon's pay-books, our Sir Winston is quite right to point out: one name is conspicuous by its absence from these lists of shame—Churchill's'. In that age of unprincipled men, who made all the more fuss of their principles, it was Trimmers like Halifax and Godolphin and Churchill who were remarkable for not taking bribes. Of the 'ubiquitous go-between', the ambivalent agent, who made no such song and dance about high principle, Sarah wrote the truth: 'the Duke of Marlborough never took a bribe'.

James was free to turn his accumulated resentment against the temper of the Scots—a foretaste of what he would do in England, given the power and the chance. It is true that the Covenanters were tiresome and lugubrious fanatics; but so was he, on the other side. Torture was no way to cure them of their illness: it merely aggravated the disease. Reason, tolerance, scepticism are the only cure for such states of mind. Of this James was totally incapable. The result was a parallel to Louis's *dragonnades* of the Huguenots in France, which had James's enthusiastic approval. He brought in wild, but Catholic, Highlanders to hold down the more civilised Lowlands; torture of the boot, hangings followed, chasing the Calvinist *dévots* out of their homesteads with fire and slaughter. The historical upshot was the creation of a saga of the martyrs, a tradition, a legend; the practical consequence, an unquenchable spirit of resistance: when the crisis came in 1688 all Lowland Scotland turned against the King and went over to Dutch William.

What the Churchills had to put up with while witnessing James's fatuous conduct, Sarah has told us long after. Argyle, the ablest brain in Scotland, was brought up before the Duke. 'Marlborough told me he never heard a man speak more reason than he did to the Duke; and after he had said what he first resolved, the Duke would never make answer to anything but "You shall excuse me, my lord; you shall excuse me, my lord". And so continued for a long time, whatever he said, without answering otherwise.' The fact was that the royal dunderhead was incapable of answering. What Sarah felt about James's rule, she has herself described: 'for I saw it myself, and was much grieved at the trials of several people that were hanged for no reason in the world, but because they would not disown what they had said, that King Charles II had broke his covenant. I have cried at some of these trials, to see the cruelty that was done to these men, only for their choosing to die rather than tell a lie.' All this had its influence in the end in making Sarah, with her rationalist frame of mind, into—what Marlborough never became—a partisan Whig.

For Argyle's insistence that he took the oath of allegiance with the reservation 'so far as it was consistent with the Protestant religion', James had him sentenced to death for high treason. Churchill deplored the sentence, and hoped, when Argyle escaped from prison, that no notice would be taken of it. Charles took no notice; when James became king, Argyle returned to raise rebellion.

Were James's private qualities much better than his public ones?

He showed up very badly in the episode of the sinking of the *Gloucester* in May 1682. He was returning to Scotland for the last time, attended by Churchill; a small squadron and several yachts accompanied the vessel. Suddenly she struck a dangerous sandbank off Cromer and in an hour had foundered. There was plenty of time to get everybody off; but James's fatal obstinacy and hopeless judgment supervened. He was afraid to be thought a coward, so he would not give the order to abandon the ship until it was too late to save the people on board. He himself managed to get into the long boat—'so near was this poor kingdom to its deliverance', one might say, as Clarendon did of Cromwell's threat to leave England for America. James took with him his priests and his dogs, and a few of his friends, including Churchill.

We may take it as an omen, with implications in several directions, of what happened in 1688.

These years of Popish Plot, Whig ascendancy, the King's first stroke and James's exile, were a time of constant negotiations and much anxiety for Churchill. James was incessantly pestering the King with his advice: nothing but strong measures were any use against rebels; badgering him to allow him to come back to his side: how could Charles get on without him at his side? Indeed the King could get on a great deal better without this nuisance on his hands. Churchill was sent south in 1681 to urge James's representations: not to allow Parliament to meet, an absolute monarchy and a French alliance, himself to be recalled from exile. But he cautioned Churchill not to communicate these matters to Halifax—the soundest brain of them all, who had saved James in the Exclusion debates in the Lords—'as not likely to enter into such measures'. Certainly not; nor is it likely that they had Churchill's own agreement: his political line closely followed that of the wise and philosophic Trimmer, and may well have been influenced by it. Their best friends sent him back with the advice to keep James out of harm's way at all costs. James merely registered resentment at the advice. Charles was engaged in a skilful rearguard action to save the prerogatives of the monarchy, and the succession, for his brother; taking full advantage of the excesses of the Whigs and their divisions, encouraging and exploiting the country's reaction against them, wearing them down with patience, waiting for the turn of the tide to come into haven at last.

Having won his last battle for the monarchy and its rights, supported by the Tory reaction, Charles could sink back into the peace and quiet he had achieved. In 1682, James was allowed to return from exile to his brother's side; in these last years he took full share in government as the second person in the kingdom, the accepted successor. Churchill received the reward of his labours with a Scottish peerage and, what was worth more, the command of the second troop of the Life Guards. He was spoken of for Secretary of State along with Sunderland. The Court said that this was grounded upon his having been learning to write lately. When the rumour came to Charles, he said pleasantly that he was not resolved to have two idle Secretaries. It was true that Churchill was not well-educated, certainly not so far as book-learning goes—though what an education he had received in more important matters!

It would seem that he was under-estimated, like his father, by these gay, clever people. It was all taken in good part. The atmosphere had cleared: there was a *détente*: people could enjoy themselves. Churchill and Godolphin, both excellent players, were favourite tennis-partners with the King, who tried to make up by excessive exercise for the ravages his other excesses made on his constitution. Then, one night at the end of January 1685, he had his second stroke; after enduring tortures at the hands of his physicians, with his customary courtesy and philosophic resignation, he died.

James was king at last.

Meanwhile, a step had been taken in Sarah's fortunes which was more fruitful for the Churchills than anything in the relationship of John to the Duke, which was without an emotional element on either side. This was far from the case with the Princess Anne and Sarah: their relation was rooted in emotion, grew to a possessive intensity on one side and ended in a tragic breach—all of which exerted powerful effects upon history. The story has all the elements of a personal tragedy; what makes it the more exciting, and important, is that is was closely interwoven with public affairs and historic events.

We have noted the marked favour with which the Princess regarded Sarah from her early days at Court. It is not too much to say that Anne had a school-girl fascination for the companion who was five years her senior. Their characters and temperaments were complementary. There was a masculine element in the mind of the dazzling Sarah: forthright and fearless, she had a keen, incisive intelligence that was, as we have seen, more than a match for John, though he was ten years older. Though not well-educated, she was a clever woman and by nature an intellectual: that gave her the advantage of inexhaustible resource, of constant interest and vivacity of mind that never failed her, when ordinary mortals faltered and paltered and were dull, a prey to boredom. Sarah never: she had the indefeasible quality of the true intellectual: in herself she was never bored. I think this must have been a strong element in the unbroken fascination she had for John and in the intellectual ascendancy she came to exert over the most famous Englishman of the time.

No one was a more feminine character than Anne; and, in spite of her plainness, her prosaic dullness, she is rather a touching figure. Left motherless by Anne Hyde's death, she was neglected and unloved all through her childhood: a pathetic little soul in that false and glittering Court. No one bothered to educate her; no one bothered to love her: these early impressions left their lifelong mark on her saddened heart. Like such children, she longed intensely for love: she rated it higher than anything else in the world. And she was very capable of returning it, with all the ardour of a sincere and simple nature. For she had a generous heart: nothing she would not give to those she loved. Then, too, she was truly religious—far more so than people who made a parade of their convictions: for her it took the place of a mental life, it was the consolation for loneliness. The most English of the Stuarts, she had a fund of common sense so conspicuously lacking in the line. In time she developed a responsiveness to the moods and needs of her people that was wanting in cleverer and more intellectual persons: she was nearer them; it made her right when those were wrong. It was easy to underrate Anne, as Sarah—who had done so all her life—found in the end.

But now they were young, and they were necessary to each other: Sarah, in all the pride and flourish of her spring; Anne still a girl, unsure of herself, but ready to give her heart unstintingly. All the more so to someone so self-confident and positive, where Anne was as yet so negative. Our Sir Winston says that there was 'a romantic, indeed perfervid, element in Anne's love for Sarah', and thinks the affection 'strangely intense'. This is rather a masculine judgment: these things happen. And what more natural? Where Anne was silent and withdrawn, Sarah was lively and extrovert; Anne was reserved and restrained, Sarah was most unreserved and quite unrestrainable. She had the appeal that someone of high spirits and exceptional vitality has for the low-spirited and easily discouraged—especially perhaps when the latter is a person set apart by her birth for a position and a fate for which she lacks confidence.

In 1683, the Princess Anne was eighteen and marriageable. Her marriage was a matter of state, and even of European importance, since she was next in succession to the English throne after her sister Mary, married to William of Orange, and they had no children. Their cousin, Prince George of Hanover—son of that redoubtable woman, the Electress Sophia—had been invited over to England for inspection as a possible husband. Whether he did not like the prospect, or Louis XIV—who took such a paternal interest in our affairs—did not approve, the young man departed without making a proposal. Anne was much mortified and, with true Stuart temper, never forgave him. As Queen, later, she could not bear the thought of him as her successor and refused to allow him to come over and acquaint himself with the country he was to rule. It was a pity. George, though not a nice man, was an able one; the Hanoverian line more sagacious than the Stuart. It would have short-circuited a great deal of trouble, and provided a joint reign—after William and Mary—of Anne and George, 1702-27.

There remained the possibility of Prince George of Denmark, far better-looking and much less intelligent. The Grand Monarch had no objection to him: a Lutheran who might at any time be converted to the true faith, perhaps carrying the Princess with him. (Pressure had already been brought upon her to become a Catholic, so far without effect. Her father's obstinacy, in her, stood her in good stead.) Prince George had already paid one visit to the country in the company of Charles Churchill, who had been appointed a page of honour to the brother, King Christian of Denmark, ten years earlier. In June 1683, John was sent over with the royal yachts to Glückstadt to meet the King and Prince and escort the bridegroom to England.

When the good-looking, heavy-feeding, stolid young Dane arrived, he found himself out of his depth in that sophisticated Court, where it was so easy to make a false step. Charles declared that he had tried him drunk and tried him sober and there was nothing in him. 'Est-il possible?' was all that he could safely venture to say—or perhaps all he could think of—in that world of *sauve qui peut*. So they all called him 'Est-il possible?' However, he settled down very contentedly with Anne, who became devoted to him; he gave her a child with uxorious regularity every year, but Anne had many miscarriages and only the little Duke of Gloucester survived into boyhood.

Anne's feelings for Sarah were far too deep, and of too long standing, to be affected by marriage. Indeed, she needed her more than ever, with family and political difficulties thickening. 'Kings and princes,' Sarah wrote in her uncompromising way, 'for the most part imagine they have a dignity peculiar to their birth and station, which ought to raise them above all connexion of friendship with an inferior.... The Princess had a different taste. A friend was what she most coveted: and for the sake of friendship (a relation which she did not disdain to have with me), she was fond even of that *equality* which she thought belonged to it. She grew uneasy to be treated by me with the form and ceremony due to her rank; nor could she bear from me the sound of words which implied in them distance and superiority. It was this turn of mind which made her one day propose to me that whenever I should happen to be absent from her, we might in all our letters write ourselves by feigned names, such as would import nothing of distinction of rank between us.' No doubt they read the French and English romances of the time together, and this was in keeping with the tone of their world. 'Morley and Freeman were the names her fancy hit upon; and she left me to choose by which of them I would be called. My frank, open temper naturally led me to pitch upon Freeman, and so the Princess took the other; and from this time Mrs. Morley and Mrs. Freeman began to converse as equals, made so by affection and friendship.' Though the Princess was well aware of her station and never did anything to impair its dignity, this testified to the human need to have someone with whom she could relax and be as equals. Prince George became Mr. Morley, Lord Churchill Mr. Freeman; only one name was added to this very select circle: Lord Godolphin became Mr. Montgomery.

Sarah herself summed up their relations from the vantage point of later life, looking back upon their youth with a certain impersonality. She speaks of herself in the third person: 'she now began to employ all her wit and all her vivacity, and almost all her time, to divert and entertain and serve the Princess; and to fix that favour which now one might easily observe to be increasing towards her every day. This favour quickly became a passion; and a passion which possessed the heart of the Princess too much to be hid. They were shut up together for many hours daily. Every moment of absence was counted a sort of tedious, lifeless state. To see the Duchess was a constant joy; and to part with her for never so short a time a constant uneasiness—as the Princess's own frequent expressions were. This worked even to the jealousy of a lover. She used to say she desired to possess her wholly; and could hardly bear that she should ever escape from this confinement into other company.'

Marriage may be said to have added depth to the relationship; they now had each other's expectancies, each other's experiences, their joys and disappointments and sorrows to share. Anne continued to be emotionally dependent, the one who demanded emotion. Sarah and John had at length achieved a secure and established family life. They even had a home. Had they not had to wait and work for it long enough? With the pay and perquisites of his posts, with the Colonelcy of the King's Own Regiment of Dragoons and that of a troop of the Life Guards, he was at last well off. How magnificent they must have looked in their scarlet dress with gold lace; the chief officers' horses had their bridles gilded—what a vivid, coloured world it was, with its ceremoniousness only just covering the passions beneath! Often the passion broke through the crust of courtesy; but never, since his early days as a young officer, with John Churchill. Everyone noticed that it was impossible to penetrate his armour of good manners, of unfailing and distinguished courtesy.

In these years they extricated themselves from dependence on Minterne. Sarah succeeded to her share of her mother's property near St. Albans. John was able to buy out her sister and there they settled, at Holywell, and rebuilt the house. They made a pleasant place of it, laying out the gardens and walks, planting fruit-trees, which the Duke saw in his mind's eye on battlefields abroad since they often appear in his letters, as with any other man much away from home. This was his home: 'the pomp and magnificence of Blenheim were for his posterity.'

Here the babies were arriving and growing into childhood. The first child had been born while John was in Scotland: 'I hope all the red spots of the child will be gone against I see her, and her nose straight, that I may fancy it be like the mother, for as she has your coloured hair, so I would have her be like you in all things else.' For all his solicitude, the child died. She was succeeded by another Henrietta, to whose christening Arabella came as godmother: whether the godmother imparted an influence or no, Henrietta, who lived to be Duchess of Marlborough in her own right, ended up with a phase reminiscent of Arabella: though she did not entertain a king, she maintained a king among the wits, the dramatist Congreve. In 1684, another daughter arrived, named for the Princess, Anne, who lived to be the toast of the Whigs, 'the Little Whig'.

A charming side of John comes out in his tenderness to his children. He was always their favourite: *Malbrouck s'en va-t-en guerre* could never be severe or even strict with them: he certainly spoiled them. He writes from Tunbridge Wells: 'you cannot imagine how pleased I am with the children; for they have nobody but their maid, they are so fond of me, that when I am at home, they will be always with me, kissing and hugging me. Their heats are quite gone; so that against you come home they will be in beauty. Miss is pulling me by the arm, that she may write to her dear mamma.' To gratify the child, he writes a postscript in her name: 'I kiss your hands, my dear mamma. Harriet.'

Time was to wreak a bitter irony upon that sentiment.

CHAPTER TEN

The Revolution

THE members of this little circle of close friends needed all their resources of private happiness and of confidence in each other to face the storms that were bound to come with James's rule. At first all was deceptively fair. The new King met the Privy Council with the promise to maintain the established order in state and church and to uphold the laws. James, like Mary Tudor, got an unexpectedly warm welcome from his subjects. Some instinct of the English people told them that he had been hardly treated; and there were unexhausted reserves of sentiment—not to say, sentimentality—that welled up to welcome a new king.

Parliament responded generously and James received a grant of revenues which amounted to something like twice the grant to Charles II on his accession. It was like the glad days of the Restoration again, with a Cavalier Parliament in a much more generous mood. Sir Winston came back to his former scene of action, after exclusion from the Parliaments of 1679 to 1681, now respected and listened to. His son was sent over to Versailles to negotiate the continuance of Louis's subsidies; before he arrived Barillon had laid half a million livres at James's feet. This was John Churchill's last call upon the Grand Monarch. All this made James financially freer than his brother—and he was a more careful manager. All would have been well if he could have responded fairly to the country's good-will, and governed it in accordance with its wishes.

Already indications of his unchanged intentions had been given. After his promises loyal Anglicans were shocked when, the second Sunday after his accession, the King went in state to Mass in the Queen's chapel at Whitehall, the doors thrown open invitingly for all to follow. At his coronation James promised once more to uphold the Church of England; but he refused to accept communion at its hands, and the Communion Service had to be omitted. After the coronation John Churchill received an English peerage for his services: Baron Churchill of Sandridge. His mentor, Halifax, was kicked upstairs and shortly removed from the government altogether.

This was a significant pointer, even something of a danger-signal. Halifax had saved the throne for James. He had fought for the life of the Catholic Lord Stafford against the fanatic Whigs, for the lives of the Whig Lord Russell and Algernon Sidney against the extreme Tories. The most brilliant brain in English politics was also the most humane: the great Trimmer was not only the brain, but the heart, of England. Of course he was ambitious; but such are the men who ought to rule. He would not agree to the repeal of the Test and Habeas Corpus Acts, the two chief constitutional milestones of Charles's Long Parliament. So he was dropped: the dropping of the pilot indeed. It was ominous.

In early June the Duke of Monmouth slipped away from Holland to raise rebellion in the West Country. Monmouth was the eldest and the handsomest of Charles's bastards, a favourite with his father. A soldier of dash, he was the candidate of the extreme Whigs for the throne. There could not have been a worse moment for his venture, with James's popularity at its height. How did he manage to slip off the leash under William's nose? That deep politician must have guessed: if Monmouth were (*per impossibile*) successful, William would have a Protestant England for ally in his lifelong struggle against Louis; if Monmouth were defeated, a rival candidate for the throne would have been removed from his path. William would be all right in either case; and so it happened, for it is the prudent, not the meek, who shall inherit the earth.

On 11 June Monmouth landed at Lyme—that town of Civil War memories and Puritan allegiance, now represented in Parliament by Sir Winston. At once the townspeople, who had not forgotten Blake and Lady Drake and their own heroic resistance for Parliament, joined the Duke's standard. He had some artillery and munitions with him, and he set out across country so familiar to the Churchills—especially Sir Winston who had fought all over it—across Dorset and Somerset, towards Bristol, second city in the kingdom, fortress and seaport, full of Protestant sympathisers. On his march hardly any of the gentry came in to him; but the simple folk, Protestant to the core, flocked to his standard. The militia, hurriedly mobilised, were disaffected and began to go over to the popular cause.

At once Churchill was given command and ordered to march west with what regular troops he had got, troops of the Blues and of his own Dragoons, with some horse. He marched with much rapidity and on 17 June was at Bridport. Monmouth had moved north and now had considerably superior numbers. Churchill reported to the King: 'I am sorry to send your Majesty this ill news; which is, unless speedy course be taken, we are like to lose this country [*i.e.* the West Country] to the rebels; for we have those two regiments run away a second time. . . . I do humbly submit this to your Majesty's commands in what I shall do in it, for there is not any relying on these regiments that are left, unless we have some of your Majesty's standing forces to lead them on and encourage them; for at this unfortunate news I never saw people so much daunted in my life.' That shows where the sympathies of the people lay.

Those were the men of the militia, and half of them went to join Monmouth. With his inferior forces Churchill hung on to Monmouth's skirts while reinforcements marched west to hem him in. On 18 June Sunderland, now in chief power with James, announced that the King had appointed Churchill to the command of the forces against Monmouth. The very next day the Frenchman Duras, Earl of Feversham, was appointed Lieutenant-General over Churchill's head. He had had no such experience of command in the field and, in addition to being twelve years older and fat and lazy, was a foreigner.

Churchill moved up to Bath, where—not far from his father's battlefields in 1643—he joined forces with Feversham. Thither, too, came his brother Charles with a train of artillery from Portsmouth. Headed off from Bristol Monmouth fell back upon Bridgwater. Together Feversham and Churchill countered the move by a more southerly route and arrived at Somerton. Sedgemoor, criss-crossed by its ditches and waterways, lay between the two armies.

From Somerton, 4 July, Churchill wrote Clarendon—the King's brother-in-law, uncle to Princess Anne—a very revealing letter. Perhaps we may cite it, for once, in his own spelling, just as he wrote. 'I doe ashure you, that you waire very Just to me in the opinion you had of me, for nobody living can have bene more obsarvant then I have bene to my Lord feaversham, ever since I have bene with him, in soe much that he did tell me that he would writt to the King to lett him know how diligent I was, and I should be glade if you could know whether he has done me that Justice.' In these phonetic spellings we hear the accents of that long dead voice—how he pronounced the word 'observant', for example. But we overhear a good deal more: the atmosphere of distrust, the King's distrust of Churchill, Churchill's uncertainty of the King's opinion, the correctness of his attitude under the slight put upon him, the anxiety that his correctitude be reported, the resentment beneath the submission and the courtesy.

That evening, after a day's march, the royal army encamped on Sedgemoor, behind the shelter of the Bussex rhine, too deep to be crossed on foot. The General had a good feed and went to bed. Not so Churchill. He knew Monmouth and had divined his intentions: a surprise attack was his only hope. Though tired with a long day, Churchill visited all his outposts in person and posted strong pickets. In the darkness of the night the rebel army was feeling its way across Sedgemoor to fall upon the royal camp asleep and unawares. The surprise might have been successful had not the rebels been halted by the rhine and Churchill awake and ready for them. He at once assumed command and took immediate action to prevent the royal forces being outflanked on the right, where the rebels had got round the ditch. Feversham, when awakened, approved the dispositions Churchill had made. This was the turning-point of the action in the dark, for on the greater part of the front the armies could not come to grips across the waterway: there was a duel of the guns, and indiscriminate firing exhausted the rebels' ammunition. In the grey light of dawn Monmouth saw that the battle was lost, and fled the field; the Puritan peasantry, staunch as their fathers, stood to the last by the ditch, fighting with the butt-ends of their muskets and their scythes, charged by the regulars, battered by the guns.

Next day Churchill was in rebellious Bridgwater, whither Feversham followed more slowly.

He moved quickly away from his own West Country and the sickening scenes that followed there. In truth, he was lucky not to bear the responsibility for the last battle against Englishmen on our soil; while, at the same time, the army appreciated professionally that, had it not been for him, the battle might have been lost.

Judge Jeffreys, who got promotion by lending himself to James's purposes, was sent hot-foot down to the West on the Bloody Assizes. No amount of apologetics can get round the fact that nearly four hundred West Countrymen were strung up, and over a thousand sold into slavery in the plantations. The vindictive King showed himself in his true colours in that last unforgiveable, unforgiving scene with his nephew. To a young West Country woman waiting to petition the King for her brothers' lives, Churchill is reported to have said, 'Madam, I dare not flatter you with any such hopes, for that marble is as capable of feeling compassion as the King's heart'. Improbable as it sounds, this represents the truth.

At last he had an opportunity of expressing openly what he thought. The extreme Whig, Lord Delamere, was sent for trial by his peers for complicity in Monmouth's rebellion, with Jeffreys as Lord High Steward. In the King's presence, it fell to Churchill as junior peer to give his vote first, 'Not guilty, upon my honour!' and all the other peers followed suit. That should have been a warning to James: the open defection of his favourite servant, his ablest soldier.

James was not one to take warning; he belonged to the class of men who will scarcely take 'Yes' for an answer. Like Mary Tudor, his faith was fortified by his triumph: 'God' was with him: *hubris* took control and led him step by step, with the certainty of a somnambulist, to his downfall.

Even the most loyal, the most Cavalier of Parliaments was not going to let him undermine the Protestant establishment. He saw that Parliament would interpose its veto upon the large Dispensing measure he contemplated to suspend all laws against Catholics. So suddenly in November he dissolved Parliament: he never met another.

Led on by the insidious and insinuating Sunderland and by the brazen Father Petre, his Jesuit confessor, James turned away all his best councillors. After Halifax, his Hyde brothers-in-law, Clarendon and Rochester, were thrown out. The control of Ireland was taken from Clarendon to be handed over to the Catholic adventurer, Tyrconnel, who was ready to execute James's scheme of providing Catholic Irish for an army to hold down England. An Ecclesiastical Commission was set up to dragoon the Church, though such a body was of doubtful legality. It gave dispensations to curates who turned Catholic to hold on to their benefices. The Tory University of Oxford, which carried loyalty to the point of frantic absurdity, was affronted and wounded at its tenderest spot by James's proceedings; appointing a Catholic Dean of Christ Church, driving out the Fellows of Magdalen from their freehold to turn it into a Popish seminary, with Fellows appointed by Father Petre! The Archbishopric of York was kept vacant, it was said, in hopes of Petre's eventual succession. His claims to a cardinalate were pushed at Rome—in vain, for the intelligent Pope thoroughly disapproved of these rash and crazy proceedings. Petre had been allotted James's own lodgings as Duke of York in the palace; now he and Sunderland ran the government. Petre was given the dubious charge of Sunderland's spiritual welfare, and Sunderland duly bent the knee. He said afterwards that he thought anybody who attempted to oppose a king's wishes a fool. The Jesuit priest was made Clerk of the Closet in place of its proper Anglican occupant. The Bishop of London, the redoubtable Compton, was dismissed from being Dean of the Chapel Royal, brought before the Ecclesiastical Commission and suspended from exercising his diocesan functions. Evelyn tells us that this 'very extraordinary way of proceeding was universally resented'. The Jesuit priest was finally made a member of the Privy Council.

Catherine Sedley was the last hope of the Protestants with James. Under her influence he occasionally deviated into sense; under the influence of his wife and the priests his feet were firmly back on the path of nonsense. On his accession he piously resolved to see her no more: she was packed off to Arabella's old house in St. James's Square, but with four times her allowance, *i.e.* £4000 a year. In 1686 she was made Countess of Dorchester, an honour quite unsought by her; there were hopes of her return and the Catholic king saw her again, in secrecy. A sharp struggle for his virtue was put up by the Queen and the priests, and James was reduced to the scourge to subdue his inclinations. (This devout implement, a 'curious love-token,' was subsequently bequeathed by the Queen to the nuns of Chaillot.) Virtue—or the Queen—triumphed; the Catholics at Court rejoiced; the new Countess was ordered to withdraw to Flanders. She replied that the number of convents there rendered the air too oppressive for her. She went off to Ireland, where she found the devout Irish 'melancholy'.

James proceeded on his crazy course, sawing off the bough on which he sat as monarch: the passive obedience of the Anglican Church, the unquestioning loyalty of the Tory party. Anglican passive obedience began to turn into passive resistance; Tories began to question. The King took to making tours about the country, partly for devotional reasons—the pilgrimage to St. Winifred's was supposed to be good for making women pregnant (the Queen had no children); partly to curry favour for his intending measures, to organise popularity. His public appearances, however, were apt to lack dignity: something always happened to put him in a false light and make him look ridiculous. He touched for the King's Evil with great assiduity—in Anglican cathedrals, with his Catholic priests officiating. On one of these occasions, walking in the garden of the deanery, after the ceremony at Winchester, James asked Churchill what the people thought, and got a very unsatisfactory answer. What Churchill seems to have said was that the people in general disapproved, for they regarded it as intended to pave the way for popery. After this he was not spoken to during dinner; the King held forth to the Dean on passive obedience. He was determined to make people obey. He did not know his people: it is impossible to *make* the English obey.

What were the Churchills to do in this situation?

Evidently not to make a false step, but to keep in close understanding with Princess Anne; to save money for a rainy day. For the rest not to mislead the King, to serve him dutifully—with a saving clause of conscience not to forward his unconstitutional and religious measures. It was not the part of a servant to obtrude his disagreement, but, when asked, to answer with truth and candour. And that is exactly what Churchill did: it was a difficult line to pursue—everyone was thrown into difficulties by the King's folly—but it was a perfectly clear line, both honest and patriotic, in the best interest both of the country and himself. It is difficult to see why it should have been so misunderstood—except that people always seem to find anything but simple partisanship, on one side or the other, hard to understand: they never understand the virtues, or the advantages, of ambivalence. Certainly Churchill has not only been misunderstood, but cruelly misrepresented.[1]

Bishop Burnet, who was no friend to Churchill and saw everything from the point of view of William of Orange, yet observes: 'as he never betrayed any of the King's secrets to the Prince, so he never set the King on violent measures, but on the contrary, as oft as he spoke to him of his affairs (which was indeed but seldom) he gave him moderate counsels'.

His financial affairs were at last prospering; though not opulent, he could save for the future of his family. For someone who had a peerage to provide for, with no foundation in land or money, this was doubly necessary. Fortunately it fitted in with his saving disposition. In addition to his lucrative Army appointments, he was a Lord of the Bedchamber—along with the Duke of Beaufort, the Earls of Ossory, Lichfield, Feversham and others—at £600 a year. His own private resources were exiguous—the famous annuity and anything that might come from his father's estate. Sarah had much more: her ultimate share of the Jennings estate may have been £2000 a year. (Perhaps that consideration contributed to John's bondage to the girl so much his junior.) At any rate he was able, for

[1] Above all, of course, by Macaulay, who riveted his crude and cruel caricature of Marlborough upon generations of readers of his *History*.

the first time, in January 1685 to lend £2000 to the Exchequer at 6 per cent. Further loans he made to the government, bearing interest at 6 per cent, were: in February 1687, £2000 and £3000; in June 1687, £2000, and in February 1688, £3000. In the absence of a Bank of England as yet, the government was perhaps the best channel for investment. But it also meant that Churchill had a vested interest in seeing that government was not overthrown. He was no revolutionary and far from an extremist; he was an ordinary Englishman—save for his military genius, which had not yet had a chance to reveal itself—adhering to the middle way.

Not enough attention has been drawn to the significant fact that Churchill, in spite of his lifelong service and favour with James, was promoted to no office by him during his reign. That speaks for itself. Legge, who was very much his junior in James's service, already Master of the Ordnance, a very lucrative post, was ultimately given the command of the fleet. It is clear that James recognised that Churchill was opposed to his policy. Though he remained the King's servant, the foundation of his political position shifted, and his potential importance increased, as the confidant and adviser of the Princess Anne.

Anne kept discreetly in the background in this time of tribulation. But the eyes of the nation were upon the little Court at the Cockpit. James had not given up hope of his daughter's conversion. His daughter, however, had more sense than he; the influence of the Churchills went along with that of her favourite cleric, the Bishop of London, to fortify her Protestantism and ensure her prospects. It was from this time that the nation began to look to her and her popularity started. The country was prepared to put up with a good deal from James, provided it was temporary. His Queen had no children; his heirs, Mary and Anne, were firm Protestants: all would be well in time.

It is not to be supposed that the Churchills were very religious persons, as Anne was: England was Protestant and they were English. John Churchill's religion was that of a sensible Englishman; Sarah had less. On his last visit to Versailles he had spoken his mind to the Huguenot Ruvigny, who left Louis to fight for William: 'he said then to him that if the King was ever prevailed upon to alter our religion, he would serve him no longer, but would withdraw from him.' Religion was, as so often in history, the convenient 'platform,' as we should call it: not in itself without significance, but of subordinate importance to adult minds. More important matters than religion were involved: the freedom of the

English people; constitutional government and our liberties. Were we going to become an absolute monarchy, like France? That was what James intended. Would that have been a good thing, either then or looking forward into the future—to the French Revolution, or, for that matter, to the political record of France subsequently?

While these contacts and understandings were being made, the more serious side to James's intentions was becoming apparent. He was building up a powerful army. It is not sufficiently realised that before the thing broke, he had an army of 40,000 men—the largest army that had ever been in England: larger than that with which Cromwell won the Civil War. He had placed a foreigner in command, Feversham; it contained large contingents of Catholic Irish, who would have had no compunction fighting the English; it was officered, so far as possible, by Catholic officers. Arabella's son, the Duke of Berwick, was now put in command at Portsmouth; Catholics commanded at Hull and at Dover; in the summer of 1688 a Catholic was in command of the fleet in the Channel. The people of England would never have been able to resist, if William had not come over with an army and virtually the whole Dutch fleet to support it. James thought he was all right: like Mary Tudor, he grew confident: had he not 'God' with him?

What were people in the situation of Churchill to do—true Englishmen, in the best interests of their country? The question became agonising, as things grew to a crisis.

The Princess Anne thought of leaving the country. Permission to pay a visit to her sister in Holland was refused. She wrote secretly to warn William and Mary not to come over: 'for though I dare swear the King could have no thought against either of you, yet since people can say one thing and do another, one cannot help being afraid'. Churchill tried to obtain the command of the English troops in Dutch service. That was too obvious a move: no hope of it. The net was closing round the small circle at the Cockpit. They were forced to declare themselves. Churchill was asked whether he would support the repeal of the laws against Catholics; like Halifax, he refused.

To gain support for altering the religious establishment of the country by his own authority, James was making up to the Dissenters. Not that he had anything but detestation for them. Some of the Dissenters took the bait; the Quaker, William Penn—who, like most idealists, never had his feet quite on the ground—lent himself to James's purposes. The bulk of the Dissenters stood firm by Protestantism: their common sense told them what to expect if

James won. Barillon reported, 'the King desires intensely that Catholics and Catholics alone should have freedom to practise their religion'. Of course—as always.

In France, the *dragonnades* were going forward hot-foot. In Europe, the Grand Alliance to resist Louis's domination was taking shape; the Pope, who had himself been subject to Louis's bullying, was sympathetic. Only England was being counted out. James, however, was too conceited to put himself entirely under Louis's protection. Besides, with him religion was more important than the facts of power. In April James issued his grand Declaration of Indulgence, by his own authority suspending the laws and undermining the Establishment. His brother had recognised the impossibility of carrying this through in 1672 and accepted defeat. The attempt itself had been responsible for worsening the situation by the Test Act. Now James would carry it through by force, with the army behind him. The governing figures in the country at large, the Lords Lieutenant, were dismissed, the Catholic backwoodsmen who had had no experience of power for a hundred and thirty years were brought out, rather dazed, into the light of day. They were a tiny, ineffectual minority and, even with the Dissenters together, made no counter-weight to the natural governing class of the nation backed by the people.

James not merely published his Declaration, but ordered it to be read in all the churches throughout the country. Those bishops who happened to be in London, led by the Primate, refused: they were the famous Seven. Furious that even these worms had turned, James—like his father with the Five Members of Parliament—determined to put them on trial. Sunderland and Jeffreys were alarmed by opposition from such a quarter; but James, fortified by his confessor, persisted. The reverend fathers were sent to the Tower: for the first and last time bishops became the heroes of the nation.

While they were awaiting their trial, a son was born to James: at last, a Catholic heir. Like Mary Tudor, when she fancied the child leaped in her womb and Cardinal Pole assured her with a 'Hail Mary'—*Benedictus fructus ventris tui*—James was confident that God was on his side: a conviction that is apt to ruin men. The nation was consternated. Was this kind of thing to go on for good? The governing class awaited a clear indication where the sympathies of the people lay.

This came with the acquittal of the Bishops: general rejoicings in London, bonfires, bell-ringing, people kneeling in the streets to receive the prelates' blessings—a very unwonted thing. The jubilation spread to the camp at Hounslow: the troops joined in; and so on throughout the country. The avalanche was set moving.

That night, 30 June, the invitation was sent to William to come over and defend the country's liberties and his wife's inheritance. It was signed by such leading, and representative, figures as the great Danby, the Earl of Shrewsbury, the Earl of Devonshire; for the Church, the Bishop of London; for the Navy, Admiral Russell. Churchill was not a signatory; but the little Court at the Cockpit must have been in touch with what was going forward. The legend that the Child at Whitehall had been smuggled in in a warming-pan was assiduously spread. Princess Anne wrote to her sister, 'I shall never now be satisfied whether the child be true or false. Maybe 'tis our brother. . . . Where one believes it, a thousand do not. For my part, unless they do give a very plain demonstration . . . I shall ever be of the number of unbelievers.' The legend was a lie; but it was a suitable response to people who believed the nonsense they did.

In August the national leaders sent over the handsome Sidney, who had already commended himself to William's attention; after the Revolution he was loaded with lands and favours. The clever men who were leading the nation were making no mistakes. Churchill was wholly with them. Sidney carried a letter from him to William: 'Mr. Sidney will let you know how I intend to behave myself: I think it is what I owe to God and my country. My honour I take leave to put into your royal Highness's hands, in which I think it safe. If you think there is anything else that I ought to do, you have but to command me and I shall pay an entire obedience to it, being resolved to die in that religion that it has pleased God to give you both the will and the power to protect.'

Sunderland was now thoroughly frightened and urged James to retreat. William's preparations went forward. The European war was about to break out, and Louis made one of the many mistakes he made out of self-conceit. He delivered an ultimatum to Holland: he took it upon him to declare William's military preparations a menace to England and to offer England his protection. Result: the Dutch, once more insulted, lined up behind William; James, humiliated publicly, refused France's protection. At that Louis made a further mistake: instead of going on to overawe Holland, he moved his forces south to attack Austria on the Rhine. William was free to move: the hour of the crowned ass in England had come.

Panic seized upon Whitehall. Sunderland persuaded the King to concede everything: abolish the Ecclesiastical Commission, restore the Fellows of Magdalen, put the Acts against the Catholics and Dissenters into force again. The Lords Lieutenant who had been dismissed were ignominiously asked back; the charters restored to the municipal corporations. These measures only revealed the weakness of James's position and his isolation. He now dismissed the reptilian Sunderland, who went over to William with all his secrets and all his information. With these he climbed on to the band-waggon.

In mid-October William set out on his combined operations: a small army in a large number of vessels, escorted by the Dutch fleet. They were scattered and blown back by a great gale. This was no surprise to James: 'it is not to be wondered at,' he said, 'for the Host has been exposed these several days.' Still his councillors pressed upon him the necessity of calling a Parliament. He refused. The comment of the profane Jeffreys, who was not without common sense, was much to the point: 'the Virgin Mary is to do all'.

The wind changed again, into a Protestant wind—as in 1588, Armada year, exactly a hundred years before. It was an encouraging memory. William was able to sail down the Channel and landed at Torbay on 5 November. When he was reminded that it was Gunpowder Plot day, William turned to Burnet and said, 'What do you think of Predestination now?' It was a joke between them; for William was by family tradition, and by personal conviction, a Calvinist.

The landing in the West Country was a great disappointment to Danby, who had gone to raise the northern counties and hoped to control events from there. Moreover, now that things had come to the arbitrament of force, James preferred to have William in the West: the King had double the number of William's forces, and with this superiority hoped to coop him up in the south-western peninsula. The royal army was ordered to concentrate at Salisbury; on 7 November Churchill was made Lieutenant-General in command of a division. It was the best James could do for himself: to keep Churchill close to him under his own eye, while not giving him the command of the army.

Before setting out from Windsor, disconcerting news was reported to James: a significant pointer. His brother-in-law Clarendon's son and heir, Lord Cornbury, had gone over to William. Indeed, he had nearly carried over three regiments of horse: if it had not been for the immediate reaction and speed of young Berwick, who at once realised what was happening, dashed after him and prevented it—a remarkable *début* for the military career of this lad of eighteen. He clearly took after the Churchill side, not the dilatory Stuarts.

When the King arrived at Salisbury the situation was one of touch-and-go. He contemplated arresting Churchill; but that would have advertised his insecurity to the world and been a shock to the morale of the troops. On the evening of 23 November there was a council of war. Churchill and the Duke of Grafton—Barbara's son—advocated an advance towards William; Feversham insisted on a retreat. Doubt, distrust, anxiety gnawed away James's nerve: he had a fainting fit and nose-bleedings which took a long time to stop. He refused to go forward: he was convinced that it was a plot on Churchill's part to hand him over to William. That night, having failed to gain control of the situation—indeed, having been defeated by James's refusal to move—Churchill and Grafton stole away from the camp, with some four hundred troopers, and rode through the night to join William.

Churchill left behind him a letter to the King, which exposes the dilemma in which he had placed his best servants: 'though my dutiful behaviour to your Majesty in the worst of times (for which I acknowledge my poor service is much overpaid) may not be sufficient to incline you to a charitable interpretation of my actions, yet I hope the great advantage I enjoy under your Majesty, which I own I can never expect in any other change of government, may reasonably convince your Majesty and the world that I am actuated by a higher principle, when I offer that violence to my inclination and interest as to desert your Majesty at a time when your affairs seem to challenge the strictest obedience from all your subjects, much more from one who lies under the greatest personal obligations to your Majesty.' This principle—or rather, interest—to which he appealed was that of Protestantism, with all that it implied in constitutional liberties, the liberty of the individual, the struggle for the liberties of Europe against the domination of Louis XIV. After all, to an English mind kings were not ends in themselves, their service an absolute law to the individual's conscience: they were the guardians of their country's interest and well-being, the service they could command conditional upon their fulfilling their trust.

Churchill's conduct at this crisis for the nation needs no defending, and we need waste no time upon it. He was bound to suffer the charge of ingratitude, then and for ever afterwards; but the responsibility was James's. In leaving him Churchill was doing what was best for the nation.

What is far more fascinating, and what no one has penetrated, is the secret of his intentions at this decisive moment in history. What did he mean to do as between James and William? Neither then nor afterwards did this reserved, inscrutable man, with the perfect command of himself, let fall one word as to what he had in mind. In consequence, historians have thought his conduct at the crisis very mysterious. It seems to me that if we put ourselves back into the circumstances of the time he had lived through, from the Restoration to the Revolution, the explanation is simple. It is surprising that no one seems to have thought of it as a clue to his conduct.

We have seen the rôle played at the Restoration by that other West Countryman, Monk: it must have been very present to the mind of John Churchill, as to others. After all, the powerful Danby had hoped to control affairs by William landing in the North, which Danby was raising. Why should not John Churchill hope to control affairs from his position high up in the command of the army, with Princess Anne as a further pawn in his hand? What Monk had done was in the nation's interest, and what the nation wanted. He had well deserved the reward he had earned: a dukedom, the wealth to support it, command of the Army for life. John Churchill was deeply ambitious; he had a serene confidence in his military star—Monk was no genius, just an ordinary competent general. If Churchill could have got the King in his control, he would have been the arbiter between James and William: he could have imposed the terms he thought best in the interests of the nation. We know what a humane and patriotic Englishman he was: he could have negotiated—a superb negotiator with a long and varied experience—a settlement that would have prevented any bloodshed. Actually, such a settlement would have worked out far better for James. James would have remained as king, nominally at least, with William perhaps as Regent. What William wanted more than anything in the world was that England should come into place in the Grand Alliance that was all he lived for. What Churchill cared for more than anything, we need not doubt, was the command of the English army playing its proper place in that Alliance. Other things would follow, as they had for Monk: a dukedom, the wealth to support it, a name and fame to posterity.

All that had been *in posse* for a moment at Salisbury. But things did not work out like that: they rarely do so sensibly. James, by losing his nerve and taking fright, had really defeated Churchill. If James had had any real will-power instead of a fanatic's fatalism, he might still have kept control of the situation or made William fight for it—the last thing the latter wanted to do. For Churchill, failing to gain control of the King, the only thing he could do was to go over to William. It must have been bitterly disappointing, even humiliating. William received him well; but that penetrating brain would realise acutely all that it meant for Churchill, as well as for himself. Henceforth, the Dutchman was in complete control of the national movement, with its prospects opening before him; he was in far more effective control on his side than the King on his; no Englishman could command him or hold up his designs. What adds corroboration to this view of it all is that it also provides the clue to Churchill's actions under William as king, accounts for his discontent and the nationalist form it took against the Dutchman.

These events set the avalanche in motion: the whole nation was turning against James. Danby had raised Yorkshire; the Earl of Devonshire the county of Derby; Delamere, Cheshire. Opinion in the fleet was moving over to William; the faithful Dartmouth was distracted and in the end surrendered it to William. In that movement George Churchill had his part, carrying his ship the *Newcastle* over, and taking a hand in the submission of Plymouth, of which the most loyal of Cavaliers, Bevil Grenville's son, the Earl of Bath, was governor. The King was on his way back to London. At Andover Prince George and the Duke of Ormonde left him for William. Of two squadrons of horse, Brigadier Trelawny and Colonel Charles Churchill deserted with twenty or thirty of their soldiers.

Clarendon's Diary reports for us the state of affairs in London. Sunday, 25 November: 'In the evening I went to Court: great crowds in the galleries and consternation in all men's looks. 26 November. As I was walking in Westminster Hall, on a sudden was a rumour all about that the Princess was gone away, nobody knew whither; that somebody had violenty carried her away. I went presently to the Cockpit. I found my Lady Frecheville and all the women in great consternation. All the light I could get was that last night after her royal Highness was in bed, the chamber doors locked, and Mrs. Danvers in bed in the outer room where she used to lie when in waiting, she rose again, went down the backstairs and, accompanied only by Lady Churchill, Mrs. Berkeley and a maid of Lady Churchill's, went into a coach and six horses, which stood ready at the street-gate.'

Clearly some move had been intended; but the news that the King was on his way back to Whitehall caught them by surprise. There is no reason to disbelieve Sarah when she says that 'this put the Princess into a great fright. She sent for me . . . and declared "That rather than see her father she would jump out of the window". This was her very expression.' Sarah went to the Bishop of London, who was lying in concealment, to make arrangments for their flight. 'The Princess went to bed at the usual time to prevent suspicion. I came to her soon after; and by the backstairs which went down from her closet, her royal Highness, my Lady Fitzharding and I, with one servant, walked to the coach, where we found the Bishop and the Earl of Dorset. They conducted us that night to the Bishop's house in the City, and the next day to my Lord Dorset's at Copt Hall. From thence we went to the Earl of Northampton's and from thence to Nottingham, where the country gathered about the Princess; nor did she think herself safe, till she saw that she was surrounded by the Prince of Orange's friends.'

At Nottingham, where her grandfather had raised his standard in unpropitious circumstances, the Princess was royally received. The Earl of Devonshire had raised several hundred horse; the townsfolk trooped out to meet her. Fifty years later old Colley Cibber, the dramatist, looked back on that day and the public banquet given her that night in Nottingham. What his romantic heart chiefly remembered was the dazzling figure beside the Princess, and the only words he heard Sarah utter as he waited at table, 'Some wine and water'.

A fortnight later Anne made a splendid entry into Oxford, a regiment meeting her some miles outside. 'The Earl of Northampton with five hundred horse led the van. Her Royal Highness was preceded by the Bishop of London, at the head of a noble troop of gentlemen, his lordship riding in a purple cloak, martial habit, pistols before him, and his sword drawn; and his cornet had the inscription in golden letters on his standard, *Nolumus Leges Angliae Mutari*. . . . The mayor and aldermen in their formalities met her at the North gate; and the Vice Chancellor with the heads of the university attended in their scarlet gowns, made to her a speech in English; and the Prince [*i.e.* George] received her royal Highness at Christ Church quadrangle with all possible demonstrations of love and affection, and they will be tomorrow at Windsor.'

Meanwhile, in London the issue was being settled. The day after his return James had a meeting with such of the lords as could be assembled. He told them that he looked upon his bleeding at the nose to be a great providence; for had it not returned upon him the day he intended to view some of his troops at Warminster, he had great reason that Lord Churchill then designed to give him up to the Prince of Orange. That was a great providence: no conception that what the Prince least wanted was to have his father-in-law on his hands. What he wanted was to have him out of the country.

There is no point in recounting the remainder of the story in detail, since Churchill had little hand in James's fate. Even in the hurry and scurry of his last days in England, James thought it worth while to discharge Churchill from his place as lord of the Bedchamber, score through his name in the Lord Chamberlain's book of the Household, and name someone else to the post. After packing off his wife and child to France, James fled once and was fetched back from Faversham. Evelyn saw him dine in public, 'a Jesuit saying grace'. From Windsor, William was giving his orders to the nation's forces; Churchill sent his commands to the Guards in London to assemble, and said he would unite with them in a few days.

It is unlikely that Churchill had contemplated William's accession to the throne. Few people can have expected such an upshot—except William, and he kept his designs to himself. He was in no hurry to reach London and had no intention of parleying with his father-in-law. He wanted the coast clear and was ready to rely on James's fatuity, of which he had taken the fullest measure. James made the way easy by flight. With infantile vindictiveness, on his first going, he had sent orders to his faithful Feversham and Dartmouth to disband the army and the fleet; he had himself thrown the Great Seal into the Thames in the hope of bringing government to a stop and producing anarchy. Such a man was unworthy of the throne. Feversham's disbanding the army was a shocking piece of irresponsibility, throwing thousands of soldiers unpaid, but not disarmed, upon the population. Broken-hearted, at his chief's desertion, Dartmouth surrendered the fleet to William. Fortunately William was there to step into the breach. James's mind was obstinately bent on flight: he feared for his life, and William did nothing to reassure him.

At last, 19 December, 'the King went off from Court, and this day about 3 o'clock the Prince arrived at St. James's with great acclamations of joy and huzzas'. Next day he went to Whitehall and from thence to Somerset House to call on his aunt, the Queen

Dowager; on his return, hearing that the Princess Anne and her husband had arrived in town, he called to see them at the Cockpit. On 23 December James embarked for France; at once William gave the French ambassador twenty-four hours to leave the country. England fell into its proper place in the coalition against France: William's essential purpose in coming over was fulfilled.

But what next? The throne was vacant. Acute divisions of opinion, conflicts of conscience within men's minds, appeared. Had James ceased to be King? By what right? All the dreary doctrines of political theory were trotted out by the doctrinaires. The pressure of events and the willpower of the one man who held the key to the situation decided. Would William consent to act as Regent for James, government being carried on in his Majesty's name? This was the Tory solution; but it would not have worked, and Churchill did not support it. Would William act as Regent for his wife? He was willing to accept the throne for himself alone, leaving his wife on one side. This shocked his best friends, and the nation would not have accepted that. English common sense, expressing itself through the Commons, proposed the joint rule of William and Mary. Where common sense was to be found, there was John Churchill also: he supported the sensible compromise solution of the Commons.

It was not what the nation had expected or really wanted: it was the best that could be obtained in the circumstances. Churchill, at the very centre of the nation and sharing its moods and apprehensions, must inwardly have been disappointed. The leading English soldier had failed to dominate the situation; the country had fallen under the control of a foreigner; nobody, and nothing, had been able to stop William. The instinct of an Englishman at such a juncture is to try and make things work. Churchill did his best by using his influence—still more, his wife's—with Princess Anne to surrender her right to succeed to the throne on Mary's death, so that William might enjoy the crown for life. Here, too, compromise was reached: any children there might be of William and Mary came first in the succession, then Anne's, then any William might have by a subsequent marriage.

It was not at all logical, let alone legitimist; it was very much of a compromise, in the English manner, and it worked.

CHAPTER ELEVEN

William III and Marlborough

THE long struggle Britain was engaged in against Louis XIV's domination of Europe covered two periods of war, separated by a truce. The Revolution of 1688 and William's accession to the throne committed us to the coalition which waged war with Louis for eight years, 1689 to 1697, until the peace of Ryswick; then followed the war of the Grand Alliance against him, from 1702 till 1713, when the Treaty of Utrecht re-established the balance of Europe for a period. Our long struggle with Louis XIV may be compared with that we waged against the aggressions of the French Revolution and Napoleon: two periods of war, 1793 to 1802 and from 1803 to 1815, separated by a truce. Or with the ordeal we have gone through in the twentieth century to save ourselves and the liberties of Europe from the intolerable aggressions of Germany: the two wars of 1914 to 1918 and of 1939 to 1945, divided by a longer period of peace.

From the first William distrusted the English. Perhaps that was understandable in the circumstances of the Revolution. But he did little enough to commend himself to them. Evelyn's first impression of him at St. James's was: 'he is very stately, serious and reserved'. A month later Evelyn says that to the general dissatisfaction must be added 'the morose temper of the Prince of Orange, who showed little countenance to the noblemen and others, who expected a more gracious and cheerful reception when they made their court'. The truth was that the great little man with the heroic spirit had the manners of a Dutch corporal. It was very different from the Stuarts: Charles II might betray his country and the cause of Europe, but he did it with an easy grace, an irresistible affability that made him personally popular to the end of his life. Even James's formal manners were good: though rigid and haughty, he had a royal condescension and courtesy. William cared for nothing but politics and power, the convolutions and combinations of states, the army and action.

At the very beginning Churchill was indispensable to William, and rendered him great service in reconstituting the Army after the disorganisation: Churchill knew all the personnel and all the ropes. Schomberg said that it was all 'at my Lord Churchill's disposition. . . . My Lord Churchill proposes all, I am sent for as to say the General consents, and Monsieur Bentinck is the Secretary for to write all.' Ailesbury tells us that the harvest Churchill made out of this was very large; he has a story of a footman holding a purse of a thousand guineas for his master, entering Churchill's lodgings at the Cockpit to obtain a regiment. He rendered an even more important service to William by obtaining Princess Anne's consent to the postponement of her right to the succession. Then there was Churchill's going over to William at the crucial moment at Salisbury.

For his services, he was rewarded with an earldom at the Coronation. He took the title of Marlborough after his cousin (on his mother's side), the Royalist sailor Earl, who had been killed at Sole Bay—a very respectable association. William increased the salaries of the Gentlemen of the Bedchamber to £1000 a year. Then Marlborough had his pay as Lieutenant-General, his colonelcies, his perquisites and so on; Sarah, her salary as lady of the Bedchamber to Princess Anne. At last the Marlboroughs were making money; and we find them lending to the government, investing £10,000 in the Bank of England when it was started, in the East India Company and in the Hudson's Bay Company. Of the last, Churchill had been made Governor in succession to James when James became king. The Company thrived under its Governor's careful and painstaking management. Churchill was no sleeping partner: he threw himself into all the concerns of the Company. By 1690 it was able to pay a dividend of 75 per cent. and to treble the value of its shares by splitting the original stock. It is very right and proper that a settlement on Hudson's Bay, Fort Churchill, should be named after him.

Prosperity was in view at last—and how welcome it must have been after all the years of living on a shoe-string! Even so, the Marlboroughs were the least well off among their class of peers; and they still had no land to speak of—indispensable to self-respect in such a society. Sarah told Ailesbury one day, walking alone with her in the garden at Holywell, 'Lord [a common word with her], they keep such a noise at our wealth. I do assure you that it doth not exceed £70,000, and what will that come to when laid out in land; and, besides, we have a son and five daughters to provide for.' This was some years later: it makes Marlborough's opposition to William all the more courageous: he sacrificed a great deal for it. He came into harbour with Anne's accession. By 1728 Sarah was able to offer the Crown a loan of £700,000 at 3 per cent.; and she and her daughter, Duchess of Marlborough, had near double that sum in land and money. It was certainly 'Good Queen Anne' for the Marlboroughs.

In 1689 Marlborough was given the command of the English contingent of 8000 men under the aged Prince of Waldeck in Flanders. They were in poor condition, and in three months Marlborough transformed them, paying particular attention, as he always did, to the comfort and well-being of the troops. The result was that when action came at Walcourt, the English won the honours in defeating the French assault on the town. The elderly Prince was generous in acknowledgments: 'the English did marvels . . . Marlborough, in spite of his youth, displayed in this one battle greater military capacity than do most generals after a long series of wars.' He was thirty-nine, and had had an extensive experience of war by land and sea since youth. But it was an axiom with people on the Continent that the English were no good at fighting on land: they ought to have remembered Cromwell and the Civil War.

At the end of the year James landed in Ireland, which was under the command of the Catholic Tyrconnel and had not gone over to William. James had done his best to undermine the Acts of Settlement, and the Catholics now had the ascendancy. He had some hundred thousand indifferent Irish troops and some French officers with him. William was forced to withdraw his attention from the European war and to lead an army in person to Ireland. He won the battle of the Boyne, and James fled, never to return to his refractory kingdoms. But Ireland was still full of troops and resistance continued; William was held up by the stubborn defence of Limerick. If Louis decided to send a French army, Ireland might still be lost. Marlborough realised that the southern landing-ports were the key to the situation, and himself proposed an expedition.

William's Dutch generals, convinced that no English general could make a success of it, were against. The King saw the point and allowed Marlborough to undertake it. That September with the minimum of fuss and the maximum of efficiency Marlborough captured both Cork and Kinsale. Gone were the chances of a French invasion now. Field-Marshal Wolseley says, 'in twenty-three days Marlborough had achieved more than all William's Dutch commanders had done both in Ireland and abroad during the whole of the previous year'. The Churchills were much to the fore. Charles, whom Marlborough made a Brigadier, took a leading part in the capture of Cork. At the conclusion of the operations he was made Governor of Kinsale. Henceforth we find him lending to the government, building up his patrimony at Minterne. Berwick, now nineteen, was left in command of James's forces in Ireland: this courageous and able young soldier was worthy of a better cause. He could do nothing to hold up Marlborough's operations: 'he was the spectator, by no means for the last time, of his uncle's success'. Even William was gracious: 'no officer living who has seen so little service as my Lord Marlborough is so fit for great commands'. That precisely expressed the inappreciative Dutch attitude.

The commands were not forthcoming. Next year William took the field himself in Flanders and carried Marlborough with him, inevitably subordinate. Nothing happened. There was a great deal of marching and counter-marching, in which William was checkmated; when he retired, he handed over the command to Waldeck, who had qualified for it by getting himself badly beaten at Fleurus the year before. And this in spite of what William's cousin, the Prince of Vaudemont, had said to him about the English generals: 'Kirke has fire, Lanier thought, Mackay skill and Colchester bravery; but there is something inexpressible in the Earl of Marlborough: all their virtues seem to be united in his single person'. This means the indefinable quality of genius. Marlborough was aware of it in himself; he was also aware that William, for all his invincible courage and resolution, was without it. William was a rarer spirit than Marlborough politically; but for all his much longer experience in the field he was no match for him as a soldier. Here William was merely competent, plodding, safe and without imagination: the solid Dutchman, who had all the authority as king, beside the brilliant Englishman, with 'something inexpressible' about him, who had had to make his way step by step for himself.

Without any doubt, there was an element of jealousy in William's attitude to Marlborough. Military glory was the one thing that that heroic spirit—caged in so miserable a carcase, asthmatic, hunched, tubercular—pined for; and it always eluded him. Beside him was the handsome Englishman, who knew all his secrets, understood every movement of his mind, who never gave himself away and had only to hold out his hand, it seemed, and all the fruits of life were his. No wonder a contemporary, watching the King's attitude to Marlborough, concluded that 'at heart he never esteemed him'. William—watching these English aristocrats, with their smooth courtiers' manners, who had all betrayed their master—must have thought them all false; indeed, he never fully trusted any one of them—except Sidney, of whom he was fond.

Marlborough's legitimate ambitions were thus frustrated, his services insufficiently rewarded. It was rumoured in London that he would be made a Duke—after all, Monk had been; that he would be given the Garter, appointed Master of the Ordnance, given the command in Ireland. Nothing came of any of these. He very much wanted to be Master of the Ordnance—a lucrative office; though at the Revolution he and Godolphin had generously joined in asking that Dartmouth might be continued in it. Now it was given to Sidney, a civilian with no qualifications whatever. Ginkel had been given the command in Ireland; the elderly and incompetent Waldeck continued to command the King's confidence in Flanders. A command was what Marlborough, with serene confidence in himself, wanted more than anything: an opportunity that would deploy his capacities, now at their prime, to the fullest. Was he to wait for ever? Under James he had had to take second place for a third-rate Frenchman, Feversham; under William he was to play second fiddle, in his own country, to a lot of Dutchmen.

To these discontents were added the poison, the irreparable hurts, of a women's quarrel: of Queen Mary and her sister over money, politics and, above all, Sarah.

We must remember that the only account we have of this famous affair comes from Sarah and is necessarily biased: there must have been something to be said on both sides.

Things were bound to be difficult between the two sisters in their position, with the constant pull of politics and rival Courts tugging them apart. Sarah believed that William was at the bottom of it; and no doubt there was the usual feeling between the occupants of the throne and the heiress presumptive waiting to step into their shoes. Moreover, Mary had no children; Anne was the mother of the little Duke of Gloucester and was still breeding. Though Mary was popular, William was decidedly not; he was jealous both of Anne's popularity and of her independence—for she had a party, as heir to the throne, at her service in the Commons, while the Tories and all the High Church people looked to her.

In addition there was a complete incompatibility of temper between the royal sisters. 'It was impossible they should be very agreeable companions to each other,' Sarah said, 'because Queen

Mary grew weary of anybody who would not talk a great deal; and the Princess was so silent that she rarely spoke more than was necessary to answer a question.' Sarah gives an unflattering account of Mary; but in truth she was gay and lively, full of extrovert interests, modest about her own capacities and touchingly devoted to the great, but inscrutable man, her husband, of whom she stood in awe and who gave her no children. We have seen what Anne was like—much more like her father: sullen and sad, capable of tremendous devotion, generous to those she took to, obstinate as a mule—but a common-sense mule.

The first clash took place with regard to the revenues to be settled on the Princess. William wanted these to be left to his discretion, to come out of his civil list, and expressed his wonder how the Princess could spend £30,000 a year 'though it appeared afterwards that some of his own favourites had more'. The Princess not unnaturally preferred a settlement on her by Parliament, which made her secure, rather than depend on William's grace and favour. Her friends were prepared to propose a grant of £70,000 a year. One night at Court the Queen asked the Princess what was the meaning of these proceedings in Parliament? To which the Princess answered, 'She heard her friends had a mind to make her some settlement.' The Queen replied with a very imperious air, 'Pray, what friends have you but the King and me?' It was one of those sallies that are delicious to deliver, and are never forgiven by the recipient. Anne had no answer, but she resented it all the more: she determined to accept no offer from William. Her friends answered for her: she got a Parliamentary grant of £50,000 a year.

A year after this, Sarah was surprised by a letter from the Princess: 'I have had something to say to you a great while, and I do not know how to go about it. I have designed, ever since my revenue was settled, to desire you would accept of a thousand pounds a year. I beg you would only look upon it as an earnest of my good will, but never mention anything of it to me; for I shall be ashamed to have any notice taken of such a thing from one that deserves more than I shall be ever able to return.' Sarah consulted her confessor, Godolphin, whether she might accept the pension; he saw no reason in the world for her to refuse it, and neither did she.

Ill-feeling between the royal sisters expressed itself in all sorts of ways: as to the Princess's lodging at Whitehall, for she wanted to exchange hers at the Cockpit; as to the Queen's house at Richmond, which Anne wanted for the air for her children, and Mary would not let her have, though she did not use it herself. William treated Prince George worse. The Prince was anxious to serve in Ireland; William would not allow him to go in the coach with him: he had to tag along with the troopers behind, and during the whole campaign the King took no more notice of him 'than if he had been a page of the backstairs'. Next year the Prince asked permission to serve at sea rather than on land and, taking the King's silent embrace for consent, prepared his equipage and sent everything on board. At the last moment he received the order that he was not to go to sea and that he was to make this appear as his own choice. It made Anne's husband, whom she adored, look still more of a fool. There was also policy in it: when William was so unpopular, it would not have done to give the Prince a chance of winning any laurels.

On top of this came Marlborough's disgrace. On 24 January 1692, Evelyn notes: 'Lord Marlborough, Lieutenant-General of the King's army in England, Gentleman of the Bedchamber etc. dismissed from all his charges military and other, for his excessive taking of bribes, covetousness and extortion on all occasions from his inferior officers'. This was the complexion it was given; but there was much more to the affair than this. Marlborough's superhuman patience had at last given way. Resentful of the deliberate frustration imposed upon his military abilities, contemptuous of the futile conduct of the last campaign in Flanders, he became an outspoken critic of the King. He made himself the spokesman of the English resentment at being led by the nose by the Dutch: at his headquarters he made no bones about what he thought of them. His indiscretions were calculated: he meant his remarks about the 'wooden' Bentinck and others of William's intimates to reach him. He told the King to his face what he thought about his disposal, on an enormous scale, of the property of the English Crown to his Dutch favourites. The King turned his back on him. When William proposed to take him abroad again on campaign with him—to witness similar futilities or worse—Marlborough refused: he never served William in the field again. For the whole of the rest of the war, for the five years 1692 to 1697, the genius of the most brilliant of English soldiers was given no chance to deploy itself, went unused. Meanwhile, William's third-rate commanders bumbled about and stumbled on disaster; he himself, though showing heroic tenacity in adverse circumstances, could never contrive a victory.

William was not the man to put up with insubordination, and Marlborough went further: he made himself the organiser of the opposition to the King. He set on foot moves both in the Lords and Commons for addresses to the Crown against the employment of foreigners. These might well have been carried in the unrest and discontent of 1692—and William would have been robbed of his Dutch guards, the guarantee of his authority. He had no intention of being a *roi fairéant,* dependent on the goodwill of the men who had thrown out James II. As part of his purpose of obtaining as wide support as possible, Marlborough was in touch with the Jacobites. Sir Winston with his political instinct has perceived, what historians have not, that it was not on this side that the danger to William lay. A nation-wide movement in favour of the Princess Anne was far more dangerous than any that concerned James—and this was precisely the combination that Marlborough, with his strategic sense and his hold on the Princess through Sarah, was forming. William could see 'Parliament, the Army and the Princess Anne—a fatal trident—in the hand of Marlborough, pointed at his heart.'

We may fairly observe that William was the more to blame for his treatment of Marlborough. On the other hand, since he was king, it was not for him to place himself at the mercy of his most menacing subject. Not that Marlborough would necessarily have removed William, but if he had been able to place the Princess Anne at the head of a combination of the Army, the Church and the Tories, backed by the sentiment of the nation against Dutch rule, Marlborough would have been in the controlling position that he had missed so bitterly at Salisbury in 1688.

The heroic little man had not come to England for this consummation. Without a word of warning, Marlborough was dismissed from all his offices, civil and military, and forbidden the Court. Worse was to follow. Then, for the next three years the King neither saw nor spoke to Marlborough.

Some weeks later, Sarah, who had refrained from appearing at Court, went to Kensington in attendance upon her mistress. The Princess was *enceinte*, and so the Queen spared her a scene; but she wrote her a letter next day: 'seeing that you brought Lady Marlborough hither last night, makes us resolve to put it off no longer, but tell you, she must not stay. . . . I must tell you, it was very unkind in a sister, would have been very uncivil in an equal, and I need not say I have more to claim. Which, though my kindness would make me never exact, yet when I see the use you would make of it, I must tell you I know what is due to me and expect to have it from you. 'Tis upon that account, I tell you plainly, Lady Marlborough must not continue with you in the circumstances her lord is.'

The Queen got a reply from Anne: 'your care of my present condition is extremely obliging. And if you would be pleased to add to it so far as upon my account to recall your severe command . . . I should ever acknowledge it as a very agreeable mark of your kindness.' To this the Queen did not reply, but sent a message by the Lord Chamberlain forbidding Lady Marlborough from continuing any longer at the Cockpit. The Princess was not going to give way to this. She determined to retire from Court and persuaded the Duke of Somerset to lend her Syon House for her approaching confinement.

The summer of 1692 was very critical for England. An invasion was at last being prepared by Louis in the Channel ports—and here were the central figures in the Revolution of 1688 divided and quarrelling. At the height of the invasion-scare papers were laid incriminating Marlborough and others in a dangerous conspiracy: their signatures were very cleverly forged. Coming at such a moment it looks like a frame-up. On 4 May Marlborough was sent to the Tower on the dangerous charge of high treason. While he was there, a private grief assailed John and Sarah: their younger son died, leaving only one boy to carry on the name and the line.

Anne's letters are full of solicitude: 'I hear Lord Marlborough is sent to the Tower; and though I am certain they have nothing against him . . . yet I was struck when I was told it; for methinks it is a dismal thing to have one's friends sent to that place. I have a thousand melancholy thoughts, and cannot help fearing they should hinder you from coming to me; though how they can do that without making you a prisoner, I cannot imagine.' The Princess was expecting that a guard would be set on her the moment the French invasion fleet set sail. 'But let them do what they please, nothing shall ever vex me, so I can have the satisfaction of seeing dear Mrs. Freeman, and I swear I would live on bread and water, between four walls, with her, without repining; for as long as you continue kind, nothing can ever be a real mortification to your faithful Mrs. Morley, who wishes she may never enjoy a moment's happiness, in this world or the next, if ever she proves false to you.'

Twelve years ahead and the breach between these two women was irreparable. Anne's passion for Sarah was too possessive, too overwhelming: Sarah could not requite it fully. She was really rather bored by it—husband and family were enough for her—and this must have been an element in the reaction that ultimately overwhelmed Anne's too passionate attachment and turned it, tragically, into detestation.

Whenever Sarah brought forward the idea of parting, to ease the situation between the royal sisters, the Princess 'fell into the greatest passion of tenderness and weeping that is possible to imagine'. Sarah said that if she could have known how long this was to last, she would have chosen to go to the Indies rather than endure it. That she was not exaggerating Anne's passion we can see from her language whenever Sarah broached the thought of their parting: 'I beg it again for Christ Jesus's sake, that you would never name it any more to me. For be assured, if you should ever do so cruel a thing as to leave me, from that moment I shall never enjoy one quiet hour. And should you do it without asking my consent (which if I ever give you, may I never see the face of heaven) I will shut myself up and never see the world more, but live where I may be forgotten by human kind.' The accents of passion are unmistakable; Anne was a very single-minded woman, who could love only one object at a time, but with all the intensity of her nature. We also catch the very English Princess, though no reading woman, echoing her Shakespeare.

Dutch William was detested by these two women. After all, he had little to commend him to women; and, for his part, he took little notice of them. Anne and Sarah called him Caliban, or the Dutch Abortion. Used as they were to the polished manners of the Restoration Court, they were horrified by his ill-breeding. There is the story of the dish of new peas brought to his table when Anne was dining with him and her sister one day. The Queen dared not touch them; and Anne, to her horror—for she was pregnant and had a longing for them—had to watch William eat up every one himself without offering her any. This was all the more mortifying in that Anne, besides her pregnancy, was also a glutton.

In June, Marlborough applied to the Council for his Habeas Corpus and asked for bail. The great Trimmer, Lord Halifax, went bail for him. Anne wrote to Sarah, 'it is a comfort they cannot keep Lord Marlborough in the Tower longer than the end of the term; and I hope, when the Parliament sits, care will be taken that people may not be clapt up for nothing, or else there will be no living in quiet for anybody but insolent Dutch and sneaking mercenary Englishmen.' That was the tone of the Cockpit circle: the assertion of a conscious English feeling against the foreigner ruling the country; and, of course, it appealed to national sentiment.

Marlborough was freed, indignant at his treatment and the King's ingratitude. He probably did not calculate that his tribulation rendered him a service in the long run. Hitherto, he had been regarded simply as a royal favourite, for whom things had been easy; the Churchills were disrespected and decidedly unpopular. This was the turning-point. Marlborough had shown that he could speak out, that he was not afraid to take the sole responsibility for opposing a powerful sovereign—a very different kind of man from James. He had made himself the spokesman of national feeling.

While Marlborough was in the Tower, the decisive victory of La Hogue took place at sea—the Trafalgar of the age. English supremacy in the Channel was established, to last throughout those wars: all danger of an invasion was at an end. Tension was relaxed; Marlborough was free. But he was not employed. The feud continued. Anne was immovable and William considered bringing financial pressure to bear by curtailing her Parliamentary grant. This would not make her budge one inch: she and the Prince took up their position. 'Can you think either of us so wretched that for the sake of twenty thousand pound, and to be tormented from morning to night with flattering knaves and fools, we should forsake those we have such obligations to, and that we are so certain we are the occasion of all their misfortunes? . . . No, my dear Mrs. Freeman, never believe your faithful Mrs. Morley will ever submit. She can wait with patience for a sunshine day, and if she does not live to see it, yet she hopes England will flourish again.'

It is evident that when that sunshine day came and Anne was Queen of England, hers was a character that would have to be taken into account, if only for its monumental obstinacy.

The stalemate was broken by the sudden illness of the Queen, who was stricken with smallpox—that scourge of all classes from highest to lowest: never were its ravages more striking than in the century from the Restoration onwards. Anne at once wrote asking if she might come to her sister's bedside. Sarah received the reply saying that it was necessary to keep the Queen as quiet as possible; Lady Derby added a postscript, 'Pray, madam, present my humble duty to the Princess.' From this Sarah, inured to the language of the courts, concluded, 'more than if the college of physicians had told it me, that the disease was mortal'.

Mary's death transformed the situation for the Princess Anne, and for all her friends and dependants. Hitherto, Mary's life had seemed a much better one than Anne's: she had much greater spirits and vitality. There was little enough prospect that Anne would survive her and come to the throne. And that must be said for the loyalty of the Marlboroughs in sticking by her: Sarah does not fail to say it and to hint that Mary would have welcomed the transfer of her allegiance earlier. I dare say: actually, Sarah's Whig outlook would have been more in keeping with the royal circle than with Anne's.

Now the Princess was fairly certain to succeed to the throne: only the rickety life of William stood between her and it. Anne wrote a dutiful and sympathetic letter to the King; the King received her with extraordinary civility at Kensington. Everyone knew his (or her) duty in the changed situation. Crowds of people flocked to pay their respects to the heiress to the throne—with that heartless display of unmeaning civility, with an eye to the main chance, characteristic of an aristocratic society. The Princess's Court was more crowded now than that of William, growing more solitary and caring only for his boon companions. Berkeley House was too small for her. Old Lord Sunderland, whose manners were even more insinuating than his politics—Sarah tells us that 'he had upon all occasions relating to her [Anne], showed himself a man of sense and breeding'—interposed himself to make things easy with William and persuaded him to give the Princess St. James's. Here, in suitable state, the heiress to the throne could await with patience the 'sunshine day' of which she had written to Sarah in the darkest of their troubles.

No one's prospects were more obviously transformed than Marlborough's: he could look forward to the future now with some confidence. William still did not employ him, and he continued to forgo the pay and profits of his offices: a very considerable sacrifice that has been overlooked. Much as Marlborough loved money he loved the proper exercise of his unique talents more; and this was denied him. The news of the near-disaster at Steinkirk in the summer of his troubles, 1692, must have been bitter to him. Solms, the wooden Dutch General to whom William confided the command of Marlborough's troops, led them into a frightful carnage and stubbornly refused to send for help. Half their number, some three thousand of them, were killed or wounded. Even William was moved to tears, 'O, mes pauvres Anglais', as he witnessed their being cut to pieces, unable to control the battle. Marlborough would have done better, if he had been there; he was never defeated in his life.

At home it was no longer Marlborough's business to make

trouble for the King. Excluded though he was, his friends were in the inner circle of government: his best friend, Godolphin, always there, dependable, loyal, indispensable. Marlborough, entrenched at St. James's, exerted himself increasingly to give the King much-needed support, and to keep relations with Anne on a good footing. It was not always easy, for William was determined to keep all power in his hands and, like most monarchs, was jealous at the thought of a successor.

Marlborough continued his polite exchanges with the exiled Court at St.-Germain. These had hardly ceased; any more than those of Godolphin, Shrewsbury and others among the government. William knew about them, and found them not inconvenient. It was a way of obtaining information. One thing we can be sure of about Marlborough: he received more information than he gave. He never told St.-Germain anything that they had not heard of already; and that seems to be the explanation of the famous case of the Brest expedition. Later on Berwick came secretly to England to weave together the threads of a Jacobite conspiracy: there is no likelihood that he saw his uncle. When the Fenwick conspiracy burst upon the country, and Marlborough's old antagonist charged him with complicity, William took no notice. There could be no better sign of the understanding at length established.

At length, in 1697, peace was made at Ryswick—it turned out only a truce, for the issue of French supremacy, of Louis XIV's domination, was not settled. Everybody was glad of a breathing-space. Tallard, whom Marlborough was to meet on a more famous occasion, came to England as the French envoy. Louis was ready to restore practically all his conquests; William to waive his demand for the extrusion of the exiled Court from France—indeed, he was so agreeable as to allow Mary of Modena £50,000 a year for her jointure, a polite way of making life easier for James in his last years.

In 1698 Marlborough was at last restored to his rank in the Army, and to the Privy Council. A more significant mark of confidence and a recognition of the rôle he would necessarily play in the future came with the constitution of a household for the little Duke of Gloucester—promising in every way, except his health. Marlborough was made his Governor. Even William was gracious on this occasion: 'my Lord, teach him but to know what you are, and my nephew cannot want for accomplishments'. The golden flow of favour was restored. In addition to his Army pay, as Lieutenant-General and his colonelcies of regiments, Marlborough now received £2000 a year as Governor and £1200 a year for his table. His own young son was made Master of the Horse to the little Duke, at £500 a year, quite a nice little sum for a playmate. Sarah obtained posts for her poor relations, the Hills: a younger daughter was made laundress at £200 a year, her brother Jack a groom of the Bedchamber at something similar. The little Duke was rather a favourite with his forbidding uncle, the King: the boy was mad about soldiers and that recommended him to that soldierly spirit. Then one day in 1700 the boy fell ill and swiftly died. William, then in Holland, was much affected: 'it is so great a loss to me, as well as to all England, that it pierces my heart with affliction', he wrote to Marlborough. We can imagine how much more of a blow it was to Anne, her last remaining hope: it is from this time that she begins to sign herself in her letters to Sarah, 'your poor unfortunate faithful Morley'.

Marlborough's daughters were growing up, and of an age to be married. In 1698, the eldest, Henrietta, was married to Godolphin's only son: it seems to have been a love-match between the young persons, but it was also another bond in the historic friendship between the parents. It was in every way a suitable match, except that the too virtuous Godolphin had not the wherewithal to endow his son. The Princess Anne, in her constant rôle of fairy godmother to the Marlboroughs, weighed in; nor could it have been done with more tact and good feeling. 'I have a request to make to my dear Mrs. Freeman. It is that, whenever dear Lady Harriet marries, you would give me leave to give her something to keep me in her thoughts. . . . I beg my poor mite may be accepted, being from a heart that is without any reserve with more passion and sincerity my dear Mrs. Freeman's than any other can be capable of.' The mite proposed was £10,000. Sarah says, with some complacency, that it always had been the custom of the Crown to give portions to the daughters of their favourites, but that since the Princess had but £50,000 a year, she would accept no more than £5000. It was on a par with Anne's constant generosity to the Marlboroughs, which Sarah took for granted and gave no very generous recognition of in return.

In 1698 Marlborough's favourite daughter, little Anne, vivacious and sparkling, was married to—of all people—Sunderland's son and heir. We have seen how Sunderland had retrieved himself from the shocking gamble for power into which he had plunged under James, and had wormed his way into William's confidence. He expressed a characteristic wish that his son would henceforth be governed in everything public and private by Marlborough. Of course, he was not: the son was an extreme, a doctrinaire, Whig and became a liability later for Marlborough with Queen Anne—all the more so because he fortified Sarah's outspoken Whig propensities. In the end his wife and son-in-law became too much for poor Marlborough. For the present all was well: the Princess came forward with another portion of £5000, and Marlborough, himself a Tory, gained the advantage of these important new Whig connexions.

The last years of William's heroic, laborious life were spent in a quicksand of diplomatic activities on a European scale. His strength was ebbing; but he would not relax his hold on power or give up till his last breath. All the subtle combinations of European politics, all the possibilities and alternatives, were in his brain as in no one else's. What he needed was a hand to execute for him in his failing strength. More and more he turned to Marlborough; he even began to make him confidences, of his troubles, his disappointments, his plans. William, with his European view-point, never could accommodate himself to the petty broils of English party politics: he was weary to death, of their self-sufficiency, their ignorance, their irresponsibility. This was his great, though very understandable, weakness; it was where Marlborough, with his extraordinary patience, had an advantage.

It is not our purpose to go into the diplomatic complexities that engaged William's last energies. The overwhelming problem that faced Western Europe was this: what was to happen to the vast inheritance of Spain, both in Europe and America, on the approaching extinction of the line of Spanish Habsburgs with the childless Charles II? The whole undivided inheritance could not be allowed to come to a grandson of Louis XIV: it would overthrow irrevocably the balance of Europe, which William had fought all his life to maintain, was the only security for the lesser states of Europe, was the essential and necessary objective of British policy.

In 1698 and again in 1700 William seemed to have reached agreement with Louis to partition the inheritance—in spite of the incomprehension of the House of Commons and their weakening the King's hand. But could Louis be trusted to keep his word? When at last Charles of Spain died, Louis accepted the whole vast inheritance for his grandson, contrary to his engagements. There was no reaction to the menace in England, no realisation of the danger in the Commons. 'Holland could not go it alone'. William was in despair; it looked as if his life's work were undone.

Then Louis came to his aid, as he had before, with a series of crashing mistakes, due to arrogant over-confidence: pride once more asserting itself and having to pay a heavy price. Without warning—a Hitler-like move—Louis seized all the Dutch barrier-fortresses along the frontier of the Spanish Netherlands, which were the line of Holland's security. The menace aroused the instinct of self-preservation among the Dutch, who now were ready to give William the complete support that had been wanting. At the same time, on James II's death at St.-Germain, Louis recognised his son as King of England. This at last aroused the complacent English to what was in store for them; they, too, came into line behind the King, who had been prescient all along.

It was now possible to knit together again the Grand Alliance of all the powers of Western Europe whose security—and the existence of some—was threatened by the domination, and the aggression, of Louis XIV. William called Marlborough to his aid. At last Marlborough was to be engaged upon a task that extended his fullest capacities, the work to which all his life had led up. In the summer of 1701 he went over to Holland with full powers. Nothing was omitted to declare to the world that he was the representative of the English state. He was appointed Ambassador Extraordinary and Plenipotentiary for negotiations with the Empire, the States General and other princes at the Hague and elsewhere, for securing the peace and liberty of Europe. At the same time he was made Commander-in-Chief of all the English forces serving in the Netherlands.

All his life Marlborough had been negotiating; but when he first appeared a prime figure on the European scene, the world did not know what a master was now taking a hand: subtler, more accommodating, less autocratic than William. Swiftly yet surely he drew together the strands, winning people's confidence, never offending them, forming the friendships that were to last through years of struggle and beyond. The treaties that Marlborough made were shaped and presented with more Parliamentary understanding than William would have shown, more patient forbearance for English foibles.

His strength failing, William gave helpful supervision from his country house, Het Loo: after all, Marlborough had learned much from him. When William got back to England he was visibly dying. He was worn out, his life-work done. At the same age—such are the injustices of life and fate—Marlborough was just beginning upon his.

CHAPTER TWELVE

The Duke

It is not my purpose to narrate Marlborough's military career in detail, write the history of his war, even if such a thing were possible within the bounds of this book: here the emphasis must be personal. Many are familiar with the outlines of Marlborough's military achievement, the unbroken record of success, the four great battles: the brilliant victories of Blenheim (1704), Ramillies (1706), Oudenarde (1708) and the bloody struggle of Malplaquet (1709). It may be well to ask at once, what were the qualities of Marlborough's generalship? To what did he owe his untarnished career of victory? It was a tremendous surprise to the Continent: the first time that an Englishman had given the French lessons in the art of fighting on land since Henry V. And it made an enormous impression in Europe: no wonder French school-children still sing *Malbrouck s'en va-t-en guerre*.

That other soldier-Duke in our history, Wellington, was also never defeated. There could hardly be more of a contrast between him and Marlborough. Where the Iron Duke was cold, competent to the *n*th degree, a hard man, stoical and taciturn, Marlborough was *sensible* in the French sense, a most sensitive register of all the impressions that came to him, an artist by temperament in his ups and downs—the depressions he got before the precipitant of action, the headaches that racked him at all the obstructions he had to put up with, and the self-control he exercised so habitually that it became second nature to him. It exacted its price. Where Wellington, for all the edge to that remarkable personality, was a rather impersonal man, forbidding, a man of whom others stood in awe, apt to be silent, Marlborough was affable, of an extreme courtesy, talkative, willing to communicate what he wished his hearers to know and think. For he was, in fact, as an experienced observer saw, 'brimful of policy'—and not only with regard to his immense European objectives, but in all the small change of personal life. Everything was calculated: personal attentions to a visiting Jacobite peer, the first lobster to his wife who is pregnant and longs for it; worn out after fourteen hours in the saddle after Ramillies and lying down on the ground to sleep in his cloak, then remembering to share it with some Dutch deputy who may be useful; offering empty *politesses* to the Court of St.-Germain, but not hesitating to suggest two million livres for himself if peace should be made.

What is exciting about John Churchill is that, beneath that handsome, polished, serene exterior, there was a most daring, far-ranging ambition. And that is characteristic of his generalship, as of the man as a whole. It is not for nothing that Blenheim Palace was his choice; his child, not Sarah's, whose common sense was affronted by anything so magnificent, so rhetorical—the nearest thing in England to Versailles. In John Churchill, there was a fascinating mixture of caution with extreme daring: we have seen it glimpsed and muffled in 1688, open and undisguised in his political action in 1692. We now see it displayed in warfare: in the Great Design of 1703, in the march to the Danube, the projects for a lunge into the heart of France, for another march across Europe to aid Eugene in Italy, to be co-ordinated with the use of the Mediterranean for an attack on Toulon. In the first years of his supreme command, his allies—especially the Dutch—were terrified of his audacity: they thought it rashness and clung on to his coat-tails, clogging his operations, holding up action.

Certainly Marlborough took risks that Wellington would never have taken. In action, in strategy, on the field of battle, he had the confidence of a virtuoso: everything was brought into play, with a sure, deft instinct. There was 'something inexpressible' about him—pure military genius. His old rival Ginkel, after doing everything to hinder Marlborough's first campaign, declared breathlessly at the end of it, 'the success of this campaign is solely due to this incomparable chief, since I confess that I, serving as second in command, opposed in all circumstances his opinions and proposals'. Marlborough brought a new spirit into warfare as William III and Louis XIV knew it, a rather static business of formal sieges, sedate marches and text-book battles ending in stalemate. In speed, flexibility, dash, Marlborough was the precursor of Napoleon; like Napoleon, too, Marlborough fought a battle to gain a decision. No wonder Napoleon made a special study of Marlborough: the only Englishman whom France, *mère des armes,* has ever thought worthy of that honour.

Marlborough, then, made war mobile.

There is something else to account for the consistent success of Marlborough's army in the field and the confidence it developed in itself, its faith in him—we must think of the army as his, for never more than one-third of it was British: the rest were Dutch infantry of stubborn, fighting quality, squadrons of Danish horse, the rest Germans, who always make excellent mercenaries. The key to the superiority of Marlborough's infantry was that they were armed with flintlocks, instead of matchlocks: the French were slow in catching up with this new weapon, which gave a much more effective volley. Marlborough exploited this advantage to the uttermost: he did not think of infantry as a static mass but as a moving flame, and all his training of his troops was directed to increasing precision and weight of fire. In consequence, Marlborough could afford to advance his infantry in four-line formations against the French six or eight, with extended wings to outflank the enemy; while his use of man-power was economical. The man who was so careful of cash was equally sparing of his men: he ended up the battle of Ramillies, completest of his victories, with a considerable number of fresh troops unused.

This enabled him to tackle superior numbers with confidence, and it helped to create the fluidity by which he gained a superiority of force at the decisive spot at the right moment. In the heat of the battle he calculated numbers as he counted his cash. At the crisis of Ramillies, his most perfect work of art, he suddenly came out with—'I have five horses to two'. Actually it was five to three; but it was sufficient to overwhelm the enemy. To obtain that preponderance was what he had been manoeuvring for, like a chess-player. As Sir Winston says of Blenheim, where Marlborough achieved the same result by taking advantage of the mistaken dispositions of the French: 'there is a grand simplicity in two or three to one at the decisive point. To procure it—there lies the secret.'

Marlborough used cavalry, as Cromwell had done, as a shock weapon rather than a missile; and in those days of extended battle-fronts, of four or five miles as against Waterloo's three, cavalry were still the decisive force, giving the *coup de grâce*. Marlborough kept the artillery under his own personal direction, and used it in mobile fashion: at Ramillies, for example, he had the guns brought up against the French right that was crumbling, and from thence he rolled up the whole French army. His methods were distinctly unorthodox: that was what alarmed the Dutch text-book generals and caught out the French. At Blenheim he was thought to have taken an excessive risk: his attack in the centre should have been overwhelmed by the enemy's wings. There were plenty of people who wanted to think that Höchstädt was a defeat from which Marlborough was only just saved by Eugene—as other fools think that Waterloo was a defeat from which Wellington was saved by Blücher. Marlborough's risks were always well calculated and deep-laid: others fell into the traps: what seemed so risky was not so risky after all. In fact, his three greatest victories were won at a very low cost in casualties.

He was not only economical of his men, but very considerate of them, a humane man: not made of iron like Wellington, with his well-known contempt for 'the scum of the earth'. Often enough the Commander-in-Chief went the rounds himself to see to the comfort of his men, just as he never minded exposing himself in the thick of battle—in this case, to a fault. The tremendous six-hundred-mile march to the Danube was conducted with such forethought that the men enjoyed it like a picnic. The day's march always began at dawn so that by the time it was really hot the troops had reached their next camp: 'the remaining part of the day's rest was as good as a halt'. Provisions had been laid 'before we arrived and the soldiers had nothing to do but to pitch their tents, boil their kettles and lie down to rest. Surely never was such a march carried on with more order and regularity and with less fatigue'. It was something that the Commander-in-Chief had an economical mind.

Marlborough's natural good temper and unfailing tact were immense assets to the common cause: no one else, without the dual authority of William III, could have kept English and Dutch together. The Jacobite exile, Ailesbury, observed him at close quarters in the Netherlands: his information is valuable to us. 'For his natural good temper he never had his equal. He could not chide a servant, and was the worst served possible; and in command he could not give a harsh word, no, not to the meanest serjeant, corporal or soldier.' This is very endearing in so great a man—though it certainly accounts for Sarah's getting so badly out of hand. There is a story of some Dutch officer getting in a rage and expressing himself very offensively in the Commander-in-Chief's presence: all that Marlborough did was to turn to someone and say peaceably, 'Now I would not be of that man's temper for anything in the world'.

He certainly would not have survived as Generalissimo if he had been. There were constant occasions for clashing between English and Dutch. Once when Athlone's (*i.e.* Ginkel's) men took the forage from Marlborough's in the field, many hard words passed, though fortunately no bloodshed. All that Marlborough said was, 'Advertise my Lord Athlone's men to beware of doing that twice'. To his own men he explained, 'the Dutch troops are in the wrong, but for reasons I will have you put up the affront'. Ailesbury concludes, 'if we had had a General of another disposition, the two nations might have come to hostilities'. When there were troubles and disputes over the commissariat, he would say to the Dutchman in charge, 'it is our business to look forward for the common cause, and'—putting his hand before his face—'let us wink at all this, and when we have a peace it will then be time to have a discussion'. To difficulties that were objected against some enterprise or other, Marlborough would always say: 'Done it must be, one way or the other: let us resolve on what way may be of less difficulty'. It is very English—the emphasis all on the practical, how to make things work with least trouble.

Along with this went a great deal of art and artifice. On his entry into Brussels he was careful to make a good impression by paying a formal visit to the first lady of the land, the Countess of Egmont. To the Archbishop, *à propos* of the feast of Corpus Christi, he said: 'If I can contribute anything towards your solemnizing the festival with more lustre than usual, my brother shall receive my orders'. (General Churchill had been made Governor.) To avoid disturbances the Army stood to arms in a square where the procession would not pass. In return, the Queen's birthday was celebrated with enthusiasm, and Marlborough's state-entry was performed with immense ceremony. 'Brimful of policy' and having made them every assurance as to religion and the laws, he had no trouble in getting them to pay large contributions to the war. In Belgium and Holland alike he made himself popular: that was no disadvantage to one who aspired, as he did, to be made Governor-General of the Netherlands—virtually an independent prince.

What ambition! It was like Wallenstein or Napoleon, quite unlike Wellington.

In fact, he was not in absolute command: he was never the master, but the servant, of the Grand Alliance. That added immensely to the complexity of the task, demanded all his powers of diplomacy, all his gifts of concealment, self-subordination, control. Sir Winston says truly, 'no one can read the whole mass of the letters which Marlborough either wrote, dictated or signed personally without being astounded at the mental and physical energy which it attests. The entire range of European affairs, all the intricate personal relations of the heads of states and governments, all the vital connexions with Holland, with the Empire, with Prussia, with the Archduke Charles and with a score of minor potentates, all the anxious and shifting combinations of English politics, all the ceremonious usage which surrounded the Queen, her husband and her Court, are disposed of day after day by a general manoeuvring equal or smaller forces in closest contact with a redoubtable enemy, who often might engage in a decisive battle at no more than one hour's notice. After twelve or fourteen hours in the saddle on the long reconnaissances often under cannon fire; after endless inspections of troops in camp and garrison; after ceaseless calculations about food and supplies, and all the anxieties of direct command in war, Marlborough would reach his tent and conduct the foreign policy of England, decide the main issues of its Cabinet, and of party politics at home. He thought for all, he acted for all.... But for the life-effort and tireless scheming of Marlborough the whole structure which resisted Louis XIV would have fallen to pieces.'

In addition, there was the management of Sarah: a full-time job in itself.

The accession of Anne inaugurated a brilliant age. Whether we consider its literary distinction—with Swift and Defoe, Addison and Steele, the young Pope writing; or science, with Newton, Halley and Hooke still active; or architecture, with Wren, Vanbrugh, Hawksmoor all at work; or the military achievements of Marlborough—the age has left its imprint on England still. There are its visible memorials: St. Paul's and Greenwich Hospital, Castle Howard and Blenheim Palace. What brings the intellectual energies of a society to a finer point, what releases its artistic impulses and gives them fuller expression at one moment rather than another, is a subtle and perhaps not wholly decipherable matter. But it is worth noting that the epochs associated with the rule of a woman—Elizabeth, Anne, Victoria—gave expression to some deep feeling of satisfaction among the English or perhaps allowed that feeling to well up more easily into expression.

Certainly Anne's first appearance before Parliament gave the nation reason to rejoice: here was a lady of regal dignity, a recognisably English figure who could address her subjects in their own language, express their sentiments and their own prejudices in that well-modulated voice—William did not speak his subjects' language, he spoke the language of the enemy. 'I know my own heart to be entirely English,' the Queen declared, with an implied comparison with the dead William, and that thrilled the nation. With the Queen at the head, to symbolise the nation, and Marlborough at her right hand, there could be no question of jealousy or conflict: the relation would be one of chivalry and service, of a knight towards his sovereign lady. And something of that was always present in Marlborough's attitude, until the last sad phase, when the irresistible pull of politics wrenched them apart.

Privately, the understanding between Mrs. Morley and Mr. Freeman, Mrs. Freeman and Mr. Montgomery, was complete: they four would stand against the world. In the autumn of 1703, when Marlborough was discouraged by the disappointments of the campaign, the Queen wrote him a remarkable letter. 'The thought that both my dear Mrs. Freeman and Mr. Freeman seem to have of retiring gives me no small uneasiness. . . . Give me leave to say you should a little consider your faithful friends and poor country, which must be ruined if ever you should put your melancholy thoughts in execution. As for your poor unfortunate faithful Morley, she could not bear it; for if ever you should forsake me, I would have nothing more to do with the world, but make another abdication; for what is a crown when the support of it is gone. I never will forsake your dear self, Mr. Freeman, nor Mr. Montgomery, but always be your constant faithful servant; and we four must never part, till death mows us down with his impartial hand.'

The Queen made Marlborough Captain-General of her armies at home and abroad. She at once conferred the Garter on him—which William had not seen fit to confer in the thirteen years of his reign. The office of Master of the Ordnance, with all its lucrative appointments and perquisites, so long withheld from Marlborough, was now given him. William's favourite, Sidney, was turned out; his Dutch comrades brushed aside, to go home and serve their own country. The English were going to rule England.

The Queen showed her confidence by the generosity she always displayed towards those she loved. Within a year or two, Marlborough's pay and appointments came to some £60,000 a year, besides the percentages he was allowed on the bread contracts of the Army abroad and the pay of foreign mercenaries for secret service, and besides the perquisites and gifts. By the time he died he was a millionaire. Sarah was at once made Groom of the Stole, Mistress of the Robes and Comptroller of the Privy Purse. As such she managed the Queen's personal finances economically and well. She saved the Queen money, and thought herself worth the £5600 a year (multiply by ten!) her appointments added up to. In addition, her two married daughters were made Ladies of the Bedchamber, with their independent salaries. With Prince George as Lord Admiral, George Churchill became his right-hand man and head of the Admiralty. The Queen was surrounded by Churchills. It was natural enough in a way; but other people did not take unalleviated pleasure in the monopoly of favour enjoyed by the fortunate family. And so great were the rewards of power and favour in those days: what remains of the English aristocracy is founded upon such things. Naturally, serving a democracy is a sufficient reward in itself—a joy, so long as it lasts, if not a thing of beauty.

So supported, with the government at home in the hands of his closest friend, Godolphin, Marlborough could go oversea with some confidence to conduct the war.

For some time it was not certain that the Dutch would give him the command of their army; they had generals of their own with far wider experience. To them Marlborough was a general by favour of the Queen of England: he had yet to prove himself. But he won the complete confidence—and, in the end, the true comradeship—of the Grand Pensionary, Heinsius; and this, from the leading figure in the Republic, was no small tribute. Marlborough was given command of the Dutch forces serving with the English. We may take this as marking the transition, in the long struggle against French ascendancy, from the leadership which lay with Holland so long as William lived to that of England henceforth. However, the Dutch attached two Deputies to him, 'civilians with powers of obstruction as unlimited as their inability to understand war'. Perhaps we should add a rider—war as Marlborough understood it; for he proceeded to give them several turns that made them quite dizzy.

The situation, as usual at the beginning of any war the English take part in, was unsatisfactory. Louis's seizure of the Spanish Netherlands gave the French a powerful advantage; they were on the frontiers of Holland, the Meuse fortresses were in their hands; they were in a position to outflank the Dutch with considerably superior forces. No static warfare would improve this situation. Marlborough was determined to seize the initiative and impose his will on the enemy. He proposed to invade Brabant: vetoed by the Dutch, who were afraid that it would expose them to invasion down the Meuse valley and the Rhine. Marlborough was confident that if he had had his way the French 'must then have had the disadvantages of governing themselves by our motions, whereas we are now obliged to mind them'.

Baulked of this Marlborough moved rapidly across the Meuse to place himself across the communications of the French army there and on the Rhine. This forced them to withdraw at a dangerous disadvantage. Marlborough had placed himself across their line of retreat when they were in disorder: the Dutch vetoed a battle. However, he gave himself the pleasure of taking their generals out with him 'to see the enemy pass the heath . . . hurrying over it in the greatest confusion and disorder imaginable. Upon this they all acknowledged that they had lost a fair opportunity of giving the enemy a fatal blow.'

Marlborough was exceedingly disappointed: he was out for decisision. He sent a trumpet to Boufflers and Berwick, his own nephew, in command on the other side, to assure them with his compliments that it was not his fault that he had not engaged them—a charming touch, so true to that polite, formal age. To Godolphin he expressed his feelings with a flash of patriotic spirit: 'England, that is famous for negligence, should any they employ be guilty of half what I see here, it would be impossible for them to avoid being justly torn to pieces by the Parliament'. All the same he had set things moving; and that autumn a series of successful sieges, Venloo, Stevensweert and Ruremonde, was crowned by the fall of Liège. The waterway of the Meuse was cleared from thence downward; the threat of Holland being outflanked was removed. With the capture of Kaiserswörth the French were driven from the lower Rhine and the Electorate of Cologne taken by the Allies.

These successes aroused much enthusiasm and won the confidence of the Dutch people for Marlborough. They would have constituted a triumph for any campaign of William; the only disappointed person was the Commander-in-Chief who knew what had been missed. On his way down the river he was nearly lost himself. A night-raid ambushed the Commander-in-Chief's boat. The Dutch Deputies had their passes on them, Marlborough none. While they were being held up, a clerk slipped into Marlborough's hand an out-of-date pass for General Charles Churchill, which he presented with his usual sang-froid. But a good deal else must have passed before the barge was allowed to go on its way. Marlborough gave that clerk a pension for life; the lieutenant who let the officers through deserted to Dutch service and was given a captaincy.

The rumour spread that the Commander-in-Chief had been captured and taken prisoner to France: it might have been the end of the war if he had been. His appearance in Holland occasioned a spontaneous outburst of feeling such as he had never received in his own country, and he was touched by it. 'Till they saw me, they thought me a prisoner in France, so that I was not ashore one minute, before I had great crowds of the common people, some endeavouring to take me by the hands, and all crying out welcome. But that which moved me most was, to see a great many of both sexes cry for joy.'

The Queen was equally enthusiastic and determined to make Marlborough a duke on his return. She wrote to Sarah, 'I hope you will give me leave. . . . I know my dear Mrs. Freeman does not care for anything of that kind nor am I satisfied with it, because it does not enough express the value I have for Mr. Freeman, nor nothing ever can how passionately I am yours, my dear Mrs. Freeman.' Sarah was not at all pleased; in fact, she was very much against it: 'there is no advantage in going in at a door; and when a rule is settled, I like as well to follow five hundred as one'. A dukedom?—ridiculous, without an appanage to support such useless grandeur. She wrote at once to John to refuse it. But this kind of thing was precisely where he differed from her: it is clear that he had every intention of being a duke. He brought in the Grand Pensionary to argue for him: Heinsius was all for it, urging that it would increase Marlborough's standing among the European princes and strengthen his hand in dealing with them.

The Queen came to his aid financially, as so often before, with a grant of £5000 a year from the Post Office. She wanted this to be in perpetuity; but there was strong objection in Parliament to this endowment of a title, and the grant was confined to her lifetime. In compensation, Anne wanted the Marlboroughs to accept £2000 a year from her Privy Purse; but this they refused. That winter there fell upon them a blow which seemed to make Sarah right about the vanity of dukedoms and to cheat John of his dynastic hopes: their remaining son and heir was struck down by smallpox and died at Cambridge, aged seventeen. When Ailesbury met him that spring in camp at Maastricht and condoled with him for the loss, 'the finest young man that could be seen,' the Duke said sadly, 'I have lost what is so dear to me, it is fit for me to retire and not toil and labour for I know not who: my daughters are all married'. He certainly did not know for whom he would be toiling.

The year 1703 was full of disappointment for Marlborough. He began the year by bringing forward his Great Design: an ambitious plan for converging movements on Antwerp, while moves were also being made against Ostend in the north-west and the Lines of Brabant defending Belgium from the east. To execute such a masterly plan demanded the closest co-ordination and supreme authority. That authority he could not exert. The Dutch general Cohorn, who was to attack Ostend, went off instead on a foraging expedition. Later when Opdam tried to fulfil his part of the attack on Antwerp, Cohorn left him with his flank dangerously exposed so that Marlborough had to come up from the Lines to the rescue. There was a rumour that Opdam was beaten: 'he is very capable of having it happen to him'.

In spite of his disappointment, with his usual resiliency Marlborough resolved on a second attempt to bring Villeroi to battle before Antwerp. The French prudently withdrew behind their fortifications and the Lines. Marlborough was all for an assault on these: he had probed and found a soft spot opposite Ramillies. Discussions raged, and this time everyone was with him except the Dutch generals: we see him gradually winning confidence. They maintained an obstinate refusal. Marlborough wrote Godolphin that he would return to England early: 'I shall not be very fond of staying with an army that is to do no more but eat forage'. To Heinsius he delivered an ultimatum before returning. 'Even if I were given millions I would not again serve in the field with such obstacles and forced to depend upon the unanimous consent of the generals. I would rather die than put up with anything like it again.' It seemed that he was bent on giving up the command, or perhaps handing it over to some royal prince—possibly Elector George of Hanover—who could command greater authority, while Marlborough acted as chief of staff.

In this mood he returned to England for the winter to meet the equal frustrations of party politics. The basic fact of the political situation was that the Tory party, which commanded the bulk of the country gentry and therefore normally the Commons, was opposed to intervention in the land war on the Continent. They would only fully support the war at sea. The Whigs, who continued William's policy, supported the war fully and with conviction. They had a majority in the Lords, they had the moneyed interest of the City and the Dissenters with them; their leaders were men of ability, who understood the realities of the European situation as the Tories did not. They knew what was necessary, and they were prepared to enforce it. But they were a minority. The Tories were far stronger, the majority party in the country and the Commons. They also had the sympathies of the Queen with them, and the Church: they were the Church party. How, in this intractable situation, to find a solid basis of support upon which to carry on the war? That was the problem. In the end these intractabilities broke

Godolphin and Marlborough, and the heart of Queen Anne.

When Marlborough went abroad in 1704 he had a solider foundation beneath him: Godolphin in undisputed control of the government; the subterranean, disingenuous, indispensable Harley to manage the Commons. The Duke was in a stronger position now to demand a freer hand from the Dutch, and he got it. Heinsius favoured a Moselle offensive. Though Marlborough's two previous campaigns had made Holland secure, the situation in Germany had grievously worsened. Bavaria had treacherously gone over to France; Hungary was in full revolt; Vienna was exposed and the Empire in mortal danger. A year before he had warned the Queen what the consequences of the Empire's supineness would be; now they were upon them: a Bavarian army in the field with a French army under Marsin to join it and strike down the Danube at Vienna. The Duke not only saw the strategy of the war as a whole, but was the only person on the Allied side who felt each move intensely and reacted like an artist.

The plan for the march to the Danube was germinating. It demanded elaborate planning and co-ordination: an army out of the Dutch and deceiving them as to its destination; providing for their safety during his absence; moving his army up the Rhine and across Germany; counteracting French moves and deceiving them as to his own; providing for supply on a six-hundred-mile march—the whole army was to be re-equipped with shoes, for example, at Frankfort; opening new communications with his advance along the Danube; arranging for a junction with Eugene; smashing Bavaria out of the war. All these, in the event, he accomplished: and it astonished Europe. He had one advantage: he would be moving on interior lines of communication; of this he would make the utmost advantage: 'if they should let me get ten days before them, they may come too late'.

The march in itself was a triumph, in strategic conception, in organisation and execution. The French were thoroughly deceived; first by a feint towards the Moselle; secondly, along the Rhine frontier, where he had boats constructed as if for an attack on Strasbourg. That he was a deceiving sort of man served his country well: 'the French had been deluded and could not now prevent the concentration of his army in the heart of Southern Germany'. There was his constant thought for his troops; on the Danube it was cold and rainy: 'the poor men, I am afraid, will suffer from these continual rains'. Later, 'I am extremely pleased to know that I have it now in my power that the poor soldiers shall not want bread'.

The news of Marlborough's march roused excitement and expectation in England: even William Penn came out with —'he will be Xenophon and Cyrus too if he beats the great Duke of Bavaria, so great a captain and a sovereign prince'.

Nothing interfered with his determination to inflict a decision. The key to the entry to Bavaria was a strong position, the Schellenberg, above the Danube. It was immensely strong by nature and the Margrave of Baden was aghast at Marlborough's determination to storm it. But time pressed: the Bavarians had neglected to fortify it and were only now throwing up defences; Tallard was on his way with an army to join the Bavarians. Marlborough was right to order an assault, though it was a bloody business and the losses fell heavy on the English. The Bavarians, however, lost twice as heavily, and this key-position was in Marlborough's hands while he proceeded to subjugate and devastate Bavaria.

This was a necessary operation of war; as he wrote to Sarah, 'you will, I hope, believe that my nature suffers when I see so many fine places burnt, and that must be burnt if the Elector will not hinder it'. His aim was to drive the Elector out of the war, to remove the threat to the Empire. But Tallard was now approaching with his army to join up with Marsin and the Elector. They would have an overwhelming preponderance, if Eugene, marching along a parallel route from the Rhine did not arrive in time. The anxiety revealed itself in one of Marlborough's violent headaches, lasting for days: 'I depend very much on the vigilance of Prince Eugene'. Armies were converging on a Napoleonic scale.

At last Eugene, whose movements had been concerted with Marlborough, arrived with 18,000 men. Those two allowed the Margrave to go off on a siege with as many men: they must have thought his absence was worth such a heavy price. The Franco-Bavarian army was approaching, with a slight superiority in numbers: 60,000 and more guns against 56,000. 'Deserters' were planted on Tallard and the Elector to give them the information that Marlborough was retreating. In consequence, when the armies were within range on 12 August, the French did not attack. That night the Duke spent some time in prayer and received the sacrament. (He was a more conventional person than Sarah and had a simple faith—she had as good as none.) Early next day the French found, instead of a retreating army, that they were going to be attacked. It was a complete moral surprise and contrary to the experience of a generation of war: by the rules, finding himself countered by a superior army, Marlborough should have retired.

More marching and counter-marching would have followed, as in the former days of the Grand Monarch and William.

That was not Marlborough's conception of war. There followed a tremendous battle which blew much of the Grand Monarch's scheme for Europe sky-high. It was also a most complicated battle, impossible to describe here: only a soldier of genius could keep all the operations in his head—as there is the best of evidence that Marlborough did. The simple outline is this. The French had a good position on ground rising from a marshy stream that ran into the Danube on their right. Forward on their right was the village of Blenheim. On their left, four miles away was the village of Oberglau, with Marsin and the Elector behind, forming the French left; Tallard in command of the centre and right. To their surprise they found that they were going to be attacked in the centre and that Marlborough's lines were crossing the marshy stream to re-form in novel formations on the other side: the first line of foot, the next two or three of horse, another of foot in the rear. With some complacency, Tallard allowed them to re-form, sure that a cavalry charge would throw them back into the stream. But he had weakened his own centre of infantry, of whom twenty-seven battalions were concentrated in Blenheim.

Marlborough's dominant idea was simple: to hold or mask the very strong French flanks, while *he,* not Tallard, delivered the assault in the centre, concentrating everything on that. On his left Cutts advanced with sixteen battalions to pen the twenty-seven French battalions within Blenheim; and was able to do it, though not to subdue them, since the space they were cooped up in prevented them from deploying their strength or playing anything like a proper part in the general action. On the right Eugene had difficulty in getting across the stream, but attacked Marsin and the Elector with extreme tenacity; and though he no more than Cutts could gain the upper hand, he held back superior forces. In the centre Marlborough was locked in struggle: 'from one end of the armies to the other, everyone was at grips and all fighting at once—a feature very rare in battles', wrote a French eye-witness. At the critical moment, when his second assault was wavering, Marlborough asked Eugene for the help of a brigade. Eugene was having a very tough struggle and could make no headway; but he sent the brigade at once, and this turned the scale in the centre. Up till this time, having taken the offensive everywhere, the Allied losses were perhaps double the French. No matter: a decision was being reached.

In mid-afternoon there was a lull, while the Duke brought into play the immense superiority he had collected at the centre—like the saving man he was. He now had nearly eighty squadrons of horse against Tallard's sixty and twenty-three battalions of foot against his nine. Tallard could get no help from the twenty-seven battalions penned within Blenheim, and was now himself rolled back and penned against Oberglau. Marlborough brought up his guns to mow down the French squares that would not give way, and ordered forward a general advance of the Allied cavalry under which the French centre now broke and gave way. They streamed off the field in two directions: some falling back on Marsin and the Elector, the others rushing to the right: these were pushed down the steep slopes of the bank into the Danube, where many hundreds perished. In the moment of victory Marlborough, with his usual command of himself, checked the pursuit of Marsin and the Elector's undefeated wing, to make sure of the twenty-seven battalions in Blenheim. Marshal Tallard was captured trying to make his way into Blenheim, which was now encircled.

At this moment of the evening the Duke paused to write his famous message to Sarah—first in his thoughts—pencilling it on the back of a bill of tavern expenses: 'I have not time to say more but to beg you will give my duty to the Queen, and let her know her army has had a glorious victory. Monsieur Tallard and two other Generals are in my coach and I am following the rest. The bearer, my aide-de-camp Colonel Parke, will give Her an account of what has passed.' From the coach, Tallard could observe the agony of his men in Blenheim: he offered to command them to stop firing if the poor fellows might retire. The Duke, astonished at this piece of French arrogance—Tallard had, of course, been received with every courtesy—gave a sharp reply: 'Inform Monsieur Tallard that in the position in which he now is, he has no command'.

While Marsin and the Elector withdrew in order, Blenheim surrendered. The grief and fury of these famous regiments knew no bounds: they burnt their flags, their officers would not sign the convention. By the time the Duke arrived, they were disarmed prisoners. Two-thirds of this large French army had been either destroyed or captured.

Orkney described Blenheim as 'the greatest and completest victory that has been gained these many ages'; and he attributed it, very properly, to the Duke, who had 'been everywhere from one attack to another and ventured his person too much'. No doubt about his generalship now. The effects of the victory were far-reaching. The remnants of the French army were quite demoralised and retreated from Germany to behind the Rhine. 'If they had not been the most frightened people in the world,' he wrote, 'they would never have quitted these parts.' The fabric of Louis' schemes for Germany fell to the ground: henceforth France would be fighting on the defensive. Louis gave orders that in future 'the best troops should be placed opposite the English'. Gone were the days of Charles and James when the French monarch could interfere at will in our internal affairs and, externally, offer to take England under his protection. Marlborough's war was the first round in the long struggle that ended at Waterloo. When the news of the glorious victory reached the Queen at Windsor, she was sitting, that summer's day towards the end of August, in the bay overlooking the terrace, playing a game of dominoes with Prince George—so tradition says. All is unchanged there in that bay; there are the dominoes still.

At once Mrs. Morley began planning a suitable reward for her faithful Mr. Freeman, who had raised the British name to such heights and shed such lustre thus early upon her reign. Already the Emperor was suggesting that he might make Marlborough a Prince of the Empire, with a principality and a vote in the College of Princes. This would need the Queen's permission. Sarah's attitude was one of disgust at more nonsense of this kind: Princess of the Holy Roman Empire was the last thing to commend itself to her rational spirit. She made no impression on John: he was bent on getting every recognition of his service and his genius. The Emperor, in the Austrian manner, was now going back on his generous impulse: perhaps the title without the principality would do? It would not: Marlborough was not going to accept an empty title. So the little principality of Mindelheim was constituted for him: an estate of a few square miles in Suabia, worth £2000 a year. At the peace, this Imperial generosity was subtracted, and there remained but a hollow name after all.

The strain of that summer told upon Marlborough's health and spirits; and there still remained much to be done. As after the storming of the Schellenberg, he gave the care of the wounded his own special attention. To Godolphin: 'I have been so employed about our own wounded men and the prisoners, that I have not one hour's quiet, which has so disordered me, that if I were in London I should be in my bed in a high fever'. Of all the leading figures on the field at Blenheim, we must remember that Marlborough was the oldest: he won his first great battle at fifty-four. At this age,

Wellington had won his last and Napoleon was dead. To Sarah Marlborough wrote: 'for thousands of reasons I wish myself with you. Besides, if I were with you quietly at the Lodge [in Windsor Park], I should have more health; for I am at this time so very lean . . . that your care must nurse me this winter, or I shall certainly be in a consumption.' He found the pressure on his brain relieved by bleeding, and decided to journey back to the Rhine more comfortably in his own coach.

There was still much to be done before he could return. He had to obtain the assurances of aid from the states of North Germany, if the war were to be finished next year. His personal prestige would clinch his diplomatic persuasions. The news of Blenheim had given universal joy at Berlin: now was the time to strike. So off he rumbled in his coach on his eight-hundred-mile tour of North Germany, jolted and shaken fourteen or fifteen hours a day on the bad roads. At Berlin he gained all he wanted: a sizeable contribution of troops, subsidised by England and Holland. On his return he visited the Court of Hanover, where he made a strong impression and conquered the very intelligent Electress Sophia, granddaughter of James I: the thought of whom Queen Anne could not bear, since that tough old lady was next in succession and might easily outlive her. It was a useful visit: the Duke made the acquaintance of his future sovereign and his family.

When Marlborough got back to England in December, he got, at last, the reception his labours had deserved. He brought back with him Marshal Tallard and sixteen French generals, a score more of high-ranking officers, a mass of standards and colours captured at Blenheim. These were paraded around London before being deposited—where he had been himself twelve years before—in the Tower. There were votes and addresses of the Lords and Commons; processions, bell-ringing, fireworks; receptions, banquets in the City. The question was what more permanent form could the nation's gratitude be given? Parliament now voted the grant of £5000 a year, which had been restricted to the Queen's life-time, in perpetuity.

The Queen came forward with her own well-considered plan, making over to the Duke and his heirs the historic royal manor of Woodstock with its offices and perquisites. There on its site, with all its memories of the English royal house—of Henry II and his fair Rosamond, of Queen Elizabeth as Princess, confined there under her sister Mary—was to rise a great building, the Castle of Blenheim, to be a reminder of that glorious victory to Englishmen for ever. It was an act not only of princely generosity but of historic imagination.

Godolphin had done his best, too: he had called in the talent of the promising Whig poet, Mr. Addison, to celebrate the campaign in verse. To encourage the young man's muse the Lord Treasurer had made him a Commissioner of Appeal in Excise in succession to the philosopher Locke. An aristocracy takes the arts seriously. Rarely has a government been so rewarded by a poem it has subsidised. Addison's *The Campaign* was published on the day the Duke landed; it expressed perfectly the mood of the moment, the mood of the nation, the spirit of national self-satisfaction, the objectives and the purpose of the war.

> Our British youth, with inborn freedom bold,
> Unnumbered scenes of servitude behold,
> Nations of slaves, with tyranny debased,
> (Their Maker's image more than half defaced)
> Hourly instructed, as they urge their toil,
> To prize their Queen and love their native soil.

We may not respond to this national self-esteem now; but that is partly because it has won its battles for the nation. Most admired was his description of the Duke, with the two lines that became among the most often quoted in the language:

> And, pleased th' Almighty's orders to perform,
> Rides in the whirlwind and directs the storm.

The poem won not only immediate success, but for more than a century was looked up to as the model of its kind. Strangely, too, it won admiration abroad. Voltaire, that professional Anglophile, described it as a 'monument plus durable que le palais de Blenheim'. In fact, it has been forgotten, while Marlborough still stands on the top of his column in the park at Blenheim, with the trees grouped in battle formation beneath him, still

> Rides in the whirlwind and directs the storm.

CHAPTER THIRTEEN

Summit and Fall

THE year 1705 was a disappointing one for Marlborough, according to the rhythm that was establishing itself: a series of successes as in 1702, or a great victory as in 1704, 1706, 1708 followed by counter-check, a year of disappointment and frustration. After Blenheim Louis withdrew his outlying forces from Germany and concentrated them behind the Rhine. Marlborough was full of confidence, at the height of his genius, and was preparing to attack across the river: it was always his idea to carry the war into France and teach Louis upon his own soil what his aggressions meant for other people. With their concentration of forces, the French were able to take the offensive down the Meuse valley. Perhaps, after all, Blenheim was a fluke, due to ill-luck, a mere exception in Louis' long career of glory? The Dutch reacted to the threat at once: appeals, Deputies, commands to the Duke to return and give up his plans. Finally, the threat to make a separate peace made him give way. All his life he had been having to give way: he never had the sovereign authority of a Napoleon to do what he thought best; always conflicting demands to reconcile, his own ideas how best to finish the war frustrated. No wonder it became second nature with him to give way: it had its effect on his character and must have sapped his will-power.

He opened his heart to his friend, Godolphin: 'I may assure you that no one thing—neither for the troops nor for the subsistence of the Army—that was promised me has been performed. . . . These considerations and the knowledge I have that it is in this place [*i.e.* on the Rhine] where we can do most hurt to France, vexes me so that I have made myself sick. . . . I have for these last ten days been so troubled by the many disappointments I have had that I think if it were possible to vex me so for a fortnight longer it would make an end of me. In short, I am weary of my life.' To Sarah: 'my dearest soul, pity me and love me'.

Back in the Netherlands, Marlborough was confronted by the immensely strong Lines of Brabant—a sort of Maginot Line—which extended all the way from Antwerp to Namur, from the

Scheldt to the Meuse. Faced with a problem like this, Marlborough's chess-player mind comes visibly into play. He had not only to cheat the enemy, but to deceive his masters, the Dutch. After some weeks of waiting, threatening now in the north, now in the south, there followed a series of dizzy marches and counter-marches, punctuated by feints—and, behold, Marlborough was through and across the celebrated lines and the enemy in full retreat from Louvain. Marlborough led the charge himself, riding like a trooper with the front rank, like the young man of thirty years before, fighting under Turenne.

Later that summer he led his men to the plain of Waterloo. By his masterly manoeuvres he had caught Villeroi's army at a decided inferiority—the only occasion, apart from the Schellenberg, when he had a large superiority of numbers. The Deputies would not allow him to engage. There followed an extraordinary scene: the Dutch Deputies arguing, while the Commander-in-Chief pleaded and sometimes burst out in anger, and the French dug themselves in. Slangenberg flatly refused to undertake the attack: it would sacrifice too many men, he said. 'Had Marlborough won the unfought battle of Waterloo in August 1705, all the French power in the Netherlands would have been thereby annihilated. The French stood with their faces towards France, just as the Dutch looked towards Holland. In such a situation there could have been no recovery in the Low Countries for the defeated side. Marlborough would have acquired that supreme authority which he always lacked to plan the campaign of 1706.... The year of victory, 1706, might also have been the year of peace.'

The frustration of his plans in 1705 enabled the French to take the offensive both on the Rhine and in Italy. Marlborough worked out complete plans and went far in his preparations for a march to the rescue of his comrade, Eugene, in Italy. Godolphin did not like the thought of his going so far away; still less the Dutch. The threat made them amenable. They would agree to a large reinforcement for Eugene, provided that the Duke would remain to command their armies in the Netherlands. He should be free from the hampering restrictions of the Deputies to conduct the campaign as he wished. Marlborough thought this a good offer, and it was. It enabled him to give the Dutch the completest and most artistic victory of his career.

The tactical situation on the battlefield of Ramillies closely resembled that at Blenheim. Villeroi had a good position above the slope down to the marshy Geet that covered his left, and to the little Mehaigne on which his right rested, protected by two villages, Tavières and Franquenay. Ramillies was just in front of the centre of his line. Marlborough began with two powerful thrusts upon the flanks. The Dutch Guards gained surprisingly quick possession of the two villages, and opened up an immediate threat to the whole French right. The French sent fourteen squadrons, dismounted, to retake Tavières and fend off the danger. At that moment a powerful charge of the Danish cavalry descended on them: the dismounted French dragoons never saw their horses again.

Meanwhile, on the right the British infantry had succeeded in crossing the marshes and were attacking the French left. There was a tough struggle here, but the British troops under Orkney made unexpected—and, apparently, unintended—progress. For Marlborough was contemplating a manoeuvre like that which had decided the issue at Blenheim. On the left centre he observed the Dutch cavalry and the rest of the Danish crash into the Maison du Roi. On the right centre his infantry was attacking Ramillies and its defences. But Villeroi was alarmed by the progress the English were making against his left flank, and just before the crisis of the battle began altering his dispositions, sending reinforcements from his centre to his left. That is to say, Villeroi was doing exactly what Marlborough wanted him to do: the Duke was imposing his will on the enemy, making them conform to his intentions. At this moment the Duke ordered all his remaining cavalry reserves to the left and himself rode into the whirlpool.

Here the decision was to be forced: Marlborough had brought about the superiority he intended. He led two charges of the Dutch himself at the crisis, a conspicuous figure with his staff in scarlet and gold amid the sober blue and grey of the Dutch. It was not right—any more than Nelson's pacing the deck of the *Victory*, a too recognisable figure, was right. A dead set was made at the Commander-in-Chief; he was thrown from his mount, and disappeared from view in the scrimmage. His faithful aides-de-camp closed in round him and at last got him mounted again. As he changed to a second charger the Colonel holding the horse's head had his own struck off by a cannonball.

Regaining control, the Duke sent order after order to the British to break off their attack on the right. Here he had difficulty in making his will prevail, and Orkney was furious, just when he had good prospects of capturing the French strongpoint in front of him. Marlborough saw that the battle was being won in the centre and on the left, and the entire French line being rolled back. As at

Blenheim there was a pause, while he and Auverquerque wheeled the whole of the Allied cavalry—some hundred squadrons—round to practically right angles from their original attack. It was a tremendous operation, and must have been a splendid spectacle. Not even the Maison du Roi could stand it, let alone withstand it. The French army was broken in two, before the final assault was delivered; they streamed from the field, while Marlborough still had reserves in hand, including the British infantry whom he had had to force to break off.

The victory was essentially a Dutch victory: won by their staunch, stubborn fighting qualities and by Marlborough's brain. He himself, with his retinue, remained with them in the centre the whole time. The Allied losses were some 4000, against 15,000 French; 5000 prisoners, all the French guns and baggage, fell to the victors. The French army, shattered by the battle, was dissolved by the pursuit that followed. Where after Blenheim there had been none and the French left got away, the pursuit after Ramillies was mercilessly effective: it 'may well rank among the great pursuits of history, with Napoleon's after Jena or Blücher's after Waterloo'.

The political consequences of the victory were even more spectacular. Town after town, for each one of which William III had fought a slow and stubborn campaign, fell to the more fortunate Marlborough. He soon saw, as he wrote to Godolphin, that 'the consequence of this battle is likely to be of greater advantage than that of Blenheim; for we now have the whole summer before us and, with the blessing of God, I will make the best use of it'. He certainly did: practically the whole of the Spanish Netherlands, *i.e.* Belgium, fell to the Allies. The authorities of the capital and the chief towns, disillusioned with French rule, declared for the Austrian candidate for the Spanish throne, Charles III, against Louis' grandson, Philip V.

From Godolphin came the sincere, unforced words of an honest man: 'the Queen is come to town to give God thanks next Thursday for your victory. I assure you I shall do it from every vein within me, having scarce anything else to support either my heart or my head. The animosity and inveteracy one has to struggle with is unimaginable, not to mention the difficulty of obtaining things to be done that are reasonable, or of satisfying people with reason when they are done.' Godolphin was now engaged in a more difficult campaign than Marlborough's, caught in a political situation that was intractable: between the Whigs who were the only people whose heart was in the war and who were willing to give it priority, and the Queen who loathed the Whigs and would not have them in the government. Godolphin was under constant pressure from the Whigs, being attacked by them while he knew that they must have a larger share in the government, if the war was to be won. In consequence, he had to put pressure on the Queen, who resisted every step of the way, with all her father's obstinacy and much more sense. The struggle was ruining the friendship, and indeed all good feeling, between Mrs. Morley and her faithful Mr. Montgomery. Nor did Sarah's ceaseless vexation of the Queen help: it was turning Mrs. Morley's love into detestation.

All these worries were transmitted regularly to Marlborough, who henceforth had to conduct his campaigns and fight his battles under this sense of strain and insecurity: the political support for the war threatening to cave in, the personal friendship of the intimate Cockpit circle breaking down, the atmosphere poisoned, their happiness in each other ruined.

In Brussels now Marlborough was suffering the usual effects of such exertions. To Sarah: 'I have been in so continued a hurry ever since the battle of Ramillies, by which my blood is so heated that when I go to bed I sleep so unquietly that I cannot get rid of my headache.... My dearest soul, I have now that great pleasure of thinking that I may have the happiness of ending my days in quiet with you.'

When Brussels had capitulated and the Estates of Brabant transferred their allegiance there was no source of authority to take over the government of these rich provinces. The Duke had had to take everything upon himself. It was then that Ailesbury saw him making his solemn entry into the capital, in immense state and, as usual, exploiting every circumstance—his handsome presence, his familiar courtesy, his fame and prestige—to win the favour of the people. It was obvious policy and, as usual, entirely successful. He guaranteed all the religious and civil rights of the country; he was particularly careful of Catholic susceptibilities; he laid down stringent orders to prevent any molestation of the inhabitants by the military. The result was even better than might be expected: food and forage poured in; the country came into the war alongside the Allies. It wanted no better Governor than the Duke.

At this point, the Emperor made him the formal offer of the Governor-Generalship in the name of Charles III. At once Marlborough informed Godolphin: 'I beg you to assure the Queen that I have in this matter, nor ever shall have in any other, any desire of my own, but with all the submission in the world, be pleased with what she shall think is for her interest'. The Queen and the English government were wholly in favour. The Duke was already most acceptable to the inhabitants. His rule there would, more effectively than anything else, knit together England and the distant Empire, make it more easy to co-ordinate the war and control the peace.

At once the Dutch were alerted, and jealous. This was their most sensitive spot. Since the breach in the unity of the Netherlands a century and a half before, some elements among the Dutch had perhaps never given up hope of restoring it. It could only come about now as the result of the ascendancy of North over South, of Dutch over Belgians. The Dutch saw no objection to that: they felt that the burden they had borne in the war, their tremendous efforts and sacrifices, Ramillies itself, entitled them to it. There has always been an element of obtuseness in the tough Dutch character. The truth was that the South would rather be governed by anybody than the North, the Belgians, as we may call them, by anybody but the Dutch—as Europe proved a century later again, after Waterloo, when it was tried.

Marlborough desired intensely to accept. He saw all its advantages to the common cause; even apart from his own personal interest, he knew it was best. For himself, it would be a tremendous elevation among the princes of Europe, where by nature and achievement he belonged. The appointments of the Governor-Generalship, the richest in Europe, were worth another £60,000 a year. Since he saw that the Dutch were against it, without any hesitation he declined the offer: the common cause was more important. He wrote to the Grand Pensionary: 'I infinitely prefer their friendship before any particular interest to myself; for I thank God and the Queen I have no need nor desire of being richer, but have a very great ambition of doing everything that can be for the public good. . . . And let me, on this occasion, assure the States that I serve them with the same affection and zeal that I do my own country.'

This was Marlborough's summit. If he had become Governor-General of the Netherlands, he would have had the authority, and the unity of direction, to finish the war. In the malign manner that is mixed into, but does not altogether govern, human affairs, things from this moment began to go wrong. Though Marlborough continued to win victories, his military genius to shine forth as brilliantly as ever, the seed of distrust between the Dutch and him, sown by the grand offer, grew evil fruits. The confidence between them, so hardly won, was broken; the understanding no longer complete; and this put peace further off than ever.

The year 1707 repeated the rhythm of 1705 in its disappointments; indeed the situation worsened. The Habsburgs, selfish as ever, made a separate peace on the Italian front, releasing a large number of French troops for service elsewhere. This enabled them to mount an offensive on the Rhine and break into Germany again. Meanwhile, the British were left to bear the brunt of supporting Charles's cause in Spain, and here their inadequate army suffered a complete defeat at the hands of Berwick at Almanza. (Berwick was granted a Spanish estate in gratitude; his son settled in Spain and the Berwick title came ultimately to the house of Alba, bringing a trickle of Churchill blood into that famous line.) On the Flanders front the French had been reinforced, and Vendôme, a much abler general than Villeroi, dispatched to hold Marlborough in check behind the fortesses of the French frontier. He had strict orders not to let himself be engaged in battle. As if this were not sufficient, the Dutch on their side vetoed a battle too.

There is a tide in the affairs of men,
Which, taken at the flood, leads on to fortune;
Omitted, all the voyage of their life
Is bound in shallows and in miseries.

That tide had been missed: all that Marlborough could do this campaigning season was to catch Vendôme's rear and some four thousand prisoners.

That winter the political issue in England was resolved, for the time. Godolphin caught Harley out in underhand intrigues against the government. By this time—with the aid of his cousin Mrs. Masham's favour with the Queen, in which she had supplanted Sarah—Harley was sure of the Queen's support. Godolphin and Marlborough both tendered their resignations. Anne was prepared to accept them. The Cabinet was not, and would not hear Harley when he proposed to take over the government. There was a deadlock. Still the Queen would not give way; it was Harley who gave in his hand and resigned. St. John and the rest of the Tories went with him into opposition; the Whigs were in control. The Queen was defeated and never forgave the affront. With something of her father's vindictive spirit, she went underground and bided the time of her revenge. The circle of old friends was irretrievably broken.

The victory of the Whigs meant that Marlborough and Godolphin—the men of the centre—were no longer in control either. Had Marlborough had an independent source of authority in the Netherlands, he might have forced a decision and put a term to the war. But the Whigs, who represented the commercial and imperial interests of England, were committed to wresting Spain and the Spanish Empire out of the hands of the Bourbons. The Spanish people had opted for the Bourbon Philip V. Was the war to go on for ever? From now on Marlborough lost control over the high political direction of the war: he became the military executant of Whig policy.

The Whigs gave themselves enthusiastically to its winning. Returned with a majority at the election, they voted large sums speedily for its financing. With this support behind him, Marlborough delivered his best: a great victory at Oudenarde, followed by a series of successes that more than retrieved the situation and left him poised for the invasion of France.

Oudenarde was quite different from Marlborough's previous battles in that it was an encounter-action, almost a running battle, touched off by chance, with the main armies coming piecemeal into action as and when they could. It was not at all a formal set-piece such as was dear to the heart of that classic world, like its cotillions and stately dances. Sir Winston describes it as a twentieth-century battle, with its looseness and flexibility, its improvisations and the wide encircling movement foreshadowing Tannenberg. In consequence, the element of chance and risk was much higher, while at the same time training, mutual confidence, skill, precision of movement paid even greater dividends.

Marlborough had spent that rainy spring in constant reviewing and training his veteran army, which had reached a high degree of perfection. Louis had concentrated a larger army than ever before against him, 90,000 men, under Vendôme and the heir in line, the Duke of Burgundy. With them was James II's young Prince of Wales, the pathetic Pretender. On the other side served the Elector of Hanover who was to occupy their throne. All the brilliant young men of Versailles were there: there was not much love lost between them and the rough, violent Vendôme. Of this Marlborough, whose intelligence-service was always of the first order, was well aware. It enabled him to take calculated risks that no one could take with him and Eugene, so perfect was their understanding.

When campaigning became possible very late that season, Eugene was on his way to reinforce Marlborough, against whom alone the French had a weighty superiority. Berwick made a parallel move to Eugene's, north from the Moselle; but Marlborough and Eugene were already in strategic touch, their moves achieving an instinctive co-ordination. The season began with the loss of Ghent and Bruges to the French: the citizens preferred the French to the Dutch so that they simply surrendered the towns. The Dutch, thoroughly alarmed, were now prepared to allow Marlborough's army alone to attack the French. Fortunately he and Eugene joined arms in time; for the French were making for the Scheldt crossing at Oudenarde. Marlborough's army now made one of its swift marches to head them off: fifty miles in some sixty hours. The French moves were hesitating: there were differences in the high command, between the royal prince and the elderly Marshal. Marlborough himself was getting elderly, two years from sixty: he had had fever that spring and was so weak from it that he could hardly sit his horse. He arrived, nevertheless, at the Scheldt crossing first: once he was in contact with the enemy, no sign of weakness, no hesitation: perfect clarity, the artist keyed up for action.

It was already afternoon and the troops had marched fifteen miles that day. Marlborough pushed Cadogan's redcoats across the pontoons, where they easily mopped up the small advance forces of the French, unaware of what they had blundered into. The Hanoverian cavalry with Cadogan scattered the French squadrons behind, and then found themselves engaged with the vast mass of the whole French left. Fortunately the ground was broken and marshy, and Burgundy held his punch. Marlborough fed the Prussian horse on to Cadogan's right to give him some protection: in danger as he was, Marlborough did not withdraw him: Cadogan's business was to engage the enemy in a holding action as long as he could stand, while the rest came up. He did this with dogged tenacity and to Vendôme's fury, who hurled brigade after brigade from his centre against the redcoats. The Marshal now ordered the entire French left wing under Burgundy to advance; and that could have overwhelmed Cadogan, while Marlborough's army was still not half across the Scheldt. For some reason, the French left did not advance: conflict of opinion about the state of the ground, still more conflict of pride between the prince with his courtiers and the rugged Marshal.

Cadogan was now being overlapped on his left by Vendôme's right advancing. But the pontoons and bridges were disgorging their men and Argyll moved up to join him with twenty more battalions. The centre of each army was now in close grip: 'always the French brought up superior numbers and reached round the Allied left. Always Marlborough's infantry poured across the bridges and advanced to make new head against them.' Now the entire Dutch army, 25,000 men, were crossing by the two bridges in Oudenarde: these could decide the battle. At this moment Marlborough sent Eugene off to command the right, including all the British troops, while he went left to concert the decisive junction of left with centre. There was a delay at the bridges: they could not deliver so many men so fast. At this juncture Eugene had to bear the full strain of the attack of Vendôme's centre. Marlborough sensed his comrade's stress and stripped himself of twenty Hanoverian battalions, which he withdrew from his own attack to send to Eugene. It was a generous gesture, and at the same time characteristically economical: for it gave those hard-pressed troops a rest from the firing line while they marched to the right to Eugene. Marlborough left himself with only eighteen battalions, as compared with Eugene's fifty-six.

The delay in Oudenarde held up the immense enveloping action the Duke was projecting by an hour; but the moment Auverquerque was in touch Marlborough sent his remaining regiments to join Eugene to resist the threatened onslaught of the French left. Here was a second gesture of confidence and selfless generosity at the height of action. The French right, fighting a confused action down in the valley, had not observed the immense turning operation of Auverquerque now in full swing. Vendôme had lost all control of the battle and even any conception of what was happening, in spite of the immense advantage of the position he had enjoyed all along, with the greater part of the Allied forces employed in crossing while the battle was joined. The whole French right and centre were now bent back into a vast horse-shoe, in which were 50,000 Frenchmen struggling in confusion. Up there on the ridge above was the French left wing, under the command of the royal princes, surrounded with a glittering retinue, taking no effective part in the battle at all.

Vendôme rode up to them to demand a last effort, or at least that they should remain in place to try to recover their fortunes next day. There was no point in it: two-thirds of the French army were surrounded. As after Blenheim, the left wing sought refuge in flight, the young dandies of Louis' Court trundling along with the rest. In the dark large numbers managed to slip through the Allied cordon in all directions. But many battalions and regiments surrendered whole. Eugene sent Huguenot officers out into the dark to call them in, 'A moi, Picardie', 'A moi, Roussillon': hundreds of prisoners were collected this way: it was a nice revenge for the idiocy of the Revocation of the Edict of Nantes. The prisoners taken were more than 9000; there were more than 6000 casualties, and more than 2000 deserters. 'If we had been so happy to have had two hours more of daylight,' the Duke wrote, 'I believe we should have made an end of this war.'

Queen Anne's first words, on hearing the news of yet another glorious victory, were: 'Oh, Lord, when will all this dreadful bloodshed cease?' In fact, the Allied casualties were remarkably small: only three thousand altogether; and, strangely enough, as John was able to assure Sarah, 'I thank God the English have suffered less than any of the other troops; none of our English horse having been engaged.' The Queen was a humane person: her sympathies were not confined to her own nation. Her young brother—who she sometimes hoped might succeed her—had been present on the other side. She had to tear herself away from the sick-bed of her dying husband to ride in state to St. Paul's to give thanks for the victory. On the way took place an open quarrel with the Duchess.

To the Duke, however, she wrote graciously and sincerely. She had not broken with him, as she had with Sarah and Godolphin. All that summer she bombarded him with letters, putting her own point of view, appealing to him against his wife and his friend. 'If you were here, I am sure you would not think me so much in the wrong in some things as I fear you do now.' What could he do, for her or for himself? He was responsible for the war; only the Whigs would fight it. He was as much the prisoner of the Whigs as the Queen was. But she had no intention of enduring it: a time would come ... meanwhile she took refuge in Stuart dissimulation. Marlborough could only reply to her—be advised by Godolphin, follow his advice. To Sarah: 'we are now acting for the liberties of all Europe, so that, though I love the Queen with all my heart, I can't think of the business of England till this great affair is decided, which I think must be by another battle'.

He was thinking out his most original and daring project: it was for the invasion of France by land and sea; combined operations: a strong task-force from the Isle of Wight and himself with his victorious army converging upon Abbeville and marching upon Paris. It might have ended the war: the project at least disproves those people who later argued that he had prolonged the war for his own advantage. His enemies in England were already saying—because he had had the magnanimity and the confidence to hand over the command on the right at Oudenarde to Eugene—that the Prince had won the battle for him. There will never be wanting such persons to detract from the achievements of great men or to fail to understand their greatness. Never a shadow ruffled the complete understanding between the two comrades or disturbed the admiration of the younger for the older and greater man.

The invasion project was vetoed by the Dutch: far too risky, far too imaginative. Marlborough was now raiding across the French frontier, deep into Artois and Picardy for forage, hostages, provisions. Louis, unable to protect them, authorised them to compound with Marlborough for a million and a half livres—quite a *renversement* from the days when such sums had enabled his cousin to keep England neutral on the side-lines.

A more terrible task than Oudenarde awaited Marlborough: the reduction of Lille, the great double fortress that was the hinge of the line of fortresses protecting the French frontier. It was the richest city in France after Paris, and certainly the strongest, with its inner pentagon within the enormous fortifications: Vauban's masterpiece. The city was indeed 'the most splendid fruit of Louis XIV's life-long aggressions'. Marlborough, like the man of genius he was, would have much preferred the flexibility of movement, the art and skill the invasion project would have demanded and where his genius would have told most.

Louis had given orders that a decisive battle should be fought rather than allow Lille to fall; and he had built up a superiority of forces to this end. Marlborough got ahead of the enemy, as usual, and encircled Lille. Vendôme and Berwick joined forces and together deployed 110,000 men against Marlborough's 75,000, on the position he took up south of the city. This is the only occasion on which we can study Marlborough on the defensive. He took up a position such as Tallard threw away at Blenheim and Villeroi at Ramillies. He posted his army on the top of a slope, flanks protected by streams and villages ahead to serve as strong-points. Where he differed was that, with his much inferior strength, he placed them on a narrow front, with his artillery posted along the whole front. He clearly meant to break the far more numerous French cavalry by artillery fire, then to charge down-hill upon them in confusion. The French command studied the position. The more they looked at it the less they liked it. Berwick, now Marshal of France for his splendid services—the capture of Nice, the victory of Almanza—knew his uncle's mind better than anyone: *cet animal est méchant, quand on l'attaque*. . . . He persuaded the French command not to attack. They drew off, leaving Lille to its fate.

The reduction of Lille proved a bloody business: the first big assault cost the Allies as many casualties as Oudenarde had done. There followed a long struggle of attrition. At one stage a large convoy was passed into the city. Then Eugene was wounded and Marlborough had to bear the entire burden of the siege, providing for the army, keeping open communications, parrying threats himself. A heavy convoy on its way through to the besiegers was threatened by superior forces, which were successfully fought off by the British at Wynendael. This was the turning-point: Lille was forced to surrender, but the price had been a terrible one in total casualties.

Anyone but a perfectionist would have been satisfied with the achievements of this campaign. Not so Marlborough: 'he was set on rounding off the campaign by recovering all that treachery had handed over to the French earlier in the year'. Frost made it easier for the Allies to surmount the water-defences of Ghent; at the turn of the year both Ghent and Bruges surrendered.

That winter there fell upon Louis XIV retribution for his long career of aggression. A prolonged frost held France in its grip: we remember the vivid impression from the pages of Saint-Simon, the courtiers at Versailles roasted on one side in front of the blazing fires, on the other freezing. Outside in the streets, in the exhausted countryside, bled white by so many years of war, poor people were frozen to death. The Great Frost was followed by famine: people died of hunger in the streets of Paris, bands of starving men roamed the country pillaging markets and *châteaux*, the women of Paris marched on Versailles demanding bread and peace. This was the end of sixty years' pursuit of glory. There is no doubt that the vainglorious Louis, *le Roi-Soleil,* was at last touched, smitten to the heart. He was prepared to consider almost anything in the way of peace terms.

Tentative discussions about peace had been going on for some time, the most important of them through the secret correspondence of Marlborough with his nephew, Berwick. They were now taken up again, with the renewal of the offer of two million livres to the Duke. He was not to be bribed. If peace came about, with himself as intermediary, he would accept, or even expect, recognition and reward for his services. He always did: he was building up a ducal patrimony, a monument to posterity. It may not, in modern times, be thought proper, and even in those days it was considered excessive, but one must observe that there is a difference.

Louis was prepared to give up the whole Spanish inheritance for which he had fought so long. This is where the fatal touch of pride betrayed the Whigs. They were fighting for the destruction of France; they were out for the trade of the Spanish Empire—what Britain did not achieve till a century later with the end of that empire. They were determined that it should not fall to France, and that was reasonable enough. Louis humbled himself to renounce Spain and her Empire for his grandson and to accept that it should all go to the Habsburg candidate. There was a snag: the Spanish people had rejected Charles III; they wanted the Bourbon, Philip V. The Whigs demanded that Louis himself should extrude his grandson from Spain. It is possible that the old and tarnished king might even have accepted that; but his son and heir would not: he rose in council and refused such a demand.

This was the climax of the war. Here was the one chance of the Allies to secure the complete defeat of France, thrown away by overplaying their hand. Louis threw himself, for the first time, upon his people—as the leaders of the Dutch had done in 1672. He appealed, no longer to glory, but to their patriotism, the sense of their country in danger: a more worthy sentiment. And not in vain: one more large army was got together and concentrated on the frontier against Marlborough; France's ablest soldier, Villars, was brought out against him. We see what the strength of the most powerful nation in Europe was, and how hard it was to get her down.

There is no reason to doubt the sincerity of Marlborough's wish for peace, 'which upon all accounts I long for, being extremely weary of the life I am obliged to live, for my spirit is so broke that I am become fit for nothing else but a lazy and quiet life'. He was weary and ill—as we can see from his symptoms—with high blood-pressure. The offer of the Governor-Generalship of the Spanish Netherlands was again being pressed on him by Charles III. It was impossible for him to accept now, though, speaking for himself, he saw no reason why he would not do as well as another. He still hoped that at the peace perhaps his claims might be considered. This naturally did not incline him to favour a Barrier Treaty which the Dutch were attempting to negotiate. Marlborough feared that if the Dutch were given the barrier fortresses in the Spanish

Netherlands, for which they had poured out their blood and treasure, they would have no motive for continuing in the Alliance.

These jars continued to disturb the Alliance to the end.

The French refusal of the Allied ultimatum came as a shock to Marlborough: 'is there, then, no counter-proposal?' There was not—merely the continuance of the war, when he had assumed that there would be peace. Marlborough concluded that only a victory inside France and the putting its government on a constitutional basis, with the States General functioning as a Parliament, would stop the aggressive tendencies of absolute government. In this he showed himself very prescient—as we can see from the career of Napoleon and other dictators. It also reveals his strong conviction in favour of English constitutionalism, in which he had been consistent all along, in spite of having been placed in a false light by his career as a royal favourite.

The responsibility for the breakdown of peace-negotiations rested fairly with the Whig government. Perhaps if Marlborough had realised that this would happen, he would have exerted himself more. But the Duke no longer had his former authority: he was the executant of Whig policy. In return the Whigs gave him all he could want for the next campaign. They poured out supplies and subsidies: he took the field with 25,000 men more than the previous year: for the first time he had a superiority over the French.

The character of the war was changing: the French were defending their homeland from invasion: the fighting became more desperate, more murderous. The ground that was being fought over was that so familiar, so blood-soaked, in 1914-18. It was not less difficult terrain: in Marlborough's time a lot of it was tangled woodland, cut up by canals and rivers, starred by fortresses. The reduction of Tournai cost 5000 casualties. No wonder the Queen by now hated the war: she thought in the terms in which Elizabeth I had prayed, for 'the least expenditure of English blood'.

The battle that followed, Malplaquet, was the bloodiest of the age. Villars had taken up a strong position behind two woods; the gap between he had fortified with entrenchments, redans, batteries. Marlborough and Eugene had some 100,000 men, to Villars' and Boufflers' 80,000. The Allied right had to fight its way through the wood, and suffered severe losses in doing so. In the gap in the centre there raged a bitter infantry struggle, and no quarter was given on either side. Here Marlborough was able to bring up a strategic reserve, as at Blenheim and Ramillies. There followed a vast cavalry battle in the open ground that had been won. Marlborough in person led up the British and Prussian squadrons. The Maison du Roi charged again and again, and were only pushed back by the arrival of the Imperialist cavalry under Eugene.

On the left flank the dare-devil young Prince of Orange had mounted three assaults and suffered shocking losses, until Marlborough countermanded any more. The French might have launched a counter-attack along the whole line if Villars had not been dangerously wounded at the crisis of the battle. Now the French position was being turned on their extreme left by Withers' division marching right round the wood and bearing down on the exposed flank. The French left was broken and began to retreat; a general retirement was ordered. The Allies were too exhausted to pursue: their losses that day had been far heavier than the French, over twenty thousand to the French ten or twelve thousand.

Europe was appalled by the carnage: not until Borodino was it equalled. Marlborough was deeply affected by it, and what with that and his exertions he was rendered ill: to that is attributable his failure to pursue the French over the frontier. Actually the British losses were relatively small, some 1800 killed and wounded out of 14,000 men—less than at Blenheim. Marlborough's enemies in England the opponents of the war fanned public feeling about the carnage at Malplaquet and blamed him as a 'butcher'. The nation was turning towards peace; the Whigs, in turn, were to pay the forfeit for their tempting of Providence.

In 1710, in the interests of peace, the Queen took the offensive. She was advised secretly by Harley, supported and consoled by Abigail. She had ceased to see—or hear—Sarah. She waited until the Duke had gone abroad to face another campaign, and then she embarked on hers. She began with small strokes and proceeded to heavier ones: one by one the blows descended that summer on Marlborough's patient back. After all, it was her duty as Queen to interpret the will of the country, and she was not sure of that: she was feeling her way until it crystallised. From the dark corners of her palaces, up the back stairs and into her closet, came Harley to hold one hand, Abigail the other.

The moves were well-concerted; every advantage was taken of the hesitation and division among the Whigs. Abigail's incompetent soldier-brother was promoted Brigadier; to put him there all the Colonels of 1705 had to be made Brigadiers. This was a direct affront to the Duke at a sensitive spot: his sense of professional propriety and efficiency. The Whigs foolishly did not support him: he had to give way. So, in June, his son-in-law Sunderland, whom the Queen had always detested, was turned out of office: a Tory took his place as Secretary of State. The Allies began to take alarm: did this change portend a separate peace? Four directors of the Bank of England waited on the Queen to express their fears of a financial panic. She replied that she did not contemplate any more changes at present. Harley began to organise opinion, making use of writers such as Swift and Defoe; surreptitiously he encouraged attacks on the two grand figures.

In the spring Godolphin had made a mistake: in an attempt to stop libellous traducers of himself and his government in the pulpit, he had embarked on the prosecution of the loud-mouthed Tory clergyman, Sacheverell. The cry, 'The Church is in danger,' had been most effectively propagated. Later when the Lord Treasurer sought a show-down with the Queen, he ended his harangue by asking whether it was her will that he should continue in office. She replied unhesitatingly: 'Yes.' Next morning he received his dismissal by letter brought by a servant. 'The uneasiness which you have showed for some time has given me very much trouble, though I have borne it,' wrote the Queen: 'and had your behaviour continued the same it was for a few years after my coming to the crown, I could have no dispute with myself what to do. But the many unkind returns I have received since, especially what you said to me personally before the lords, makes it impossible for me to continue you any longer in my service; but I will give you a pension of four thousand a year, and I desire that, instead of bringing the staff to me, you will break it, which, I believe, will be easier to us both.' Godolphin broke his white wand of office into pieces, threw them into the fire and refused the pension.

Such was the background at home against which Marlborough had to fight the campaign of 1710—fight his way through the barrier of frontier fortresses into France. Should he give up his command? That would be to betray the Allies, the loyalties, the comrades of many years' standing; it would probably mean the break-up of the Alliance—certainly the stultification of all his efforts, his planning, his life's work, denying it of its proper end. His ambition could ill support the thought of that. He began to doubt whether he would be allowed to complete his life's work: 'I am not so fully pleased with those sanguine thoughts as formerly, that God would protect and bless us.' He was now poised on those plains 'where two lucky hours might decide the fate of France'.

He was not to be given that chance: Villars had strict orders not to engage France's last army. The politicians in London were coming to Louis' rescue, as Marlborough felt acutely: 'the King of France is so encouraged by what passes in England that he had taken a positive resolution for the continuation of the war, and reckons upon my not being employed this next campaign'.

What remained for Marlborough was the costly business of reducing the frontier fortresses one by one: it was a race for time between him and Louis, with the new English government keeping time for Louis. Marlborough moved as quickly, and manoeuvred as skilfully, as ever: first upon Douai, no easy fortress to attack, protected by its river and by inundations. It held out for two months and cost the Allies 8000 casualties. Next Béthune, which took a month to reduce; St.-Venant a fortnight; Aire, which held out unexpectedly long, in miserable weather. Such were the achievements of a disappointing campaign: a serious breach of the fortress barrier that barred the road to Paris had been blasted. But there had been no hope of a battle that might have ended the matter. Instead, Villars was engaged in constructing an elaborate system of field fortifications, making use of every natural feature—rivers, canals, woods, inundations—stretching practically from the Channel to the Meuse: the *Ne Plus Ultra* Lines.

The new government at home, headed by Harley, won the election with a large majority and proved that the Queen was right in interpreting the nation's will as being for peace. The size of the Tory majority was a handicap to Harley, who was a man of the centre, and found himself in turn under the pressure of their extreme wing. In the way that often happens in human relations, the two enemies, Harley and Marlborough, now stood in need of each other. For Harley the Duke's command of the Allied armies became his chief asset in bargaining with France; moreover, Marlborough had the support of both Hanover and Prussia, which threatened to leave the Alliance if he laid down his command. Both interest and duty indicated an accommodation. Marlborough could remain the General of the Tory government until peace was assured; he could not have supposed at this stage that they would go so far as to make a separate peace and let down the Allies. That would force a decision. For the time he remained; relations with Harley were conducted on a basis of mutual civility.

The Duke started on his tenth campaign in a bad way: he complained to Sarah of much 'giddiness and swimmings in my head, which also gave me often sickness in my stomach'. This was his last campaign: another might well have brought on the stroke that partially incapacitated him five years later. A grave disappointment was added to oppress him. Before the campaign started he was counting on concentrating 140,000 men to Villars' 120,000, and on Eugene's comradeship. With the Emperor's death Eugene was ordered back to Germany with his army. Marlborough now had 90,000 with which to pierce the *Ne Plus Ultra* Lines and invade France, in face of a superior army, and with his health failing.

Actually, once he got going, never did his military genius shine more brilliantly than in this last campign. It was like Napoleon's last campaign in 1814—except that Marlborough was still on the offensive. There was the problem: to get across those lines in the face of a stronger army, commanded by the best of the French generals. Marlborough judged that the best place to pierce the line was at Arleux, near the fortress of Bouchain. To get his army across the river and the inundations there he would have to get Villars moving westward away from Arleux. He decided to practise a double-bluff, on the principle of telling your opponent the truth: he will not believe it. In the event he accomplished more: he got Villars to do his work for him.

As a preliminary Marlborough captured Arleux and strengthened its defences. He then marched in full force west, as if to mount his intended full-scale attack towards Arras. Villars followed him by a parallel march behind the lines, leaving a detachment to recapture Arleux and demolish its defences. Marlborough closed up to the lines as if to attack—while secretly sending his artillery in the opposite direction. It was a risk. At the end of his career, it is nice to think, he was as daring and as ready to take (calculated) risks as at the beginning. Other detachments he sent off to the rear. The men were dumbfounded: had the 'old Corporal' taken leave of his senses? Still they trusted him; only the Duke's chaplain knew what was in the wind. On the intended night, when the moon was at the full, the whole army was set in motion back to Arleux. 'We had the finest night in the world to march in', wrote the chaplain: everything, as usual, had been thought of. 'His attention and care was over us all', wrote a corporal.

It was a tremendous march, far longer than that before Oudenarde: nearly forty miles in sixteen hours. Villars discovered that Marlborough was missing three or four hours after the start; the French were on interior lines with a good road, ten miles fewer to go; Marlborough marching across open country. So that it was a most exhausting race; half the infantry fell out on the way. But by that afternoon Marlborough's army was across the river at Arleux and behind the enemy lines. The furious Villars riding anxiously ahead of his army with his staff was nearly captured. He had to accept the fact that the *Ne Plus Ultra* Lines had been turned—and with no casualties. Even the government at home were pleased. Eugene, away from the scene, was delighted: he understood, better than anyone, all that it involved. The excitement over, the work of art accomplished, the Duke was ill again: 'I must confess to you the last six weeks have given me frequent and sensible remembrances of my growing old.'

Still there was no battle: Villars dared not risk one with France's last army; his men were in poor condition, the country war-weary: 'Je ne trouvais plus le caractère national.' Nothing for it but for Marlborough to force open the road to Paris, fortress by fortress: it was another race for time, with the home government irrevocably committed to its secret peace negotiations. The Duke turned to the reduction of Bouchain, the strongest fortress in his direct road. It was protected by its river and practically surrounded by the inundations to which the French were reduced to defend their country—by historic justice—like the Dutch in 1672.

He had judged that Bouchain could be taken, and taken it was, in the presence of a French army of decidedly superior strength. Sir Winston describes it as 'an amazing operation'; and so it would appear, if Marlborough had not accustomed his own time and posterity to expect nothing but victory from him. This was his last operation: but for two minor fortresses, he now had the road clear down the Oise to Paris. Posterity, however, was to be cheated of that last and grandest spectacle. The Tory government at home was too far down its own road to peace to make any more sacrifices for further advances into France. In Marlborough's ten campaigns, 'he had broken the military power of France, and reduced the first of military nations to a condition in which they were no longer feared by any country.... During the whole of these ceaseless operations of war on the largest scale the world had seen, or was to see for several generations, confronted by the main armies of France and their best generals, he had never sustained a defeat or even a serious check.... The annals of war contain no similar record.'[1]

That winter of 1710-11 the campaign for the peace was decided

[1] Churchill, *Marlborough* IV. 457.

in London. When all is said, in the complexities of politics, the personal issues, the struggles, the feuds and hatreds, it is the simple overriding facts that matter. England wanted peace; so did France. The question was whether, in these circumstances, it was worth going on fighting any more. With the death of the Emperor a transformation had taken place that profoundly affected the political objectives of the war. The Austrian candidate for Spain was now Emperor himself: to combine Spain and her Empire with all the possessions of the house of Austria was as much of a danger for Europe as to have Louis' grandson enthroned in Madrid.

This consideration much strengthened the Tories in pushing forward with the peace negotiations. They needed every ounce of their strength: for they had arrayed against them the Allies—particularly Hanover; the reunited Whig party with their majority in the Lords; Marlborough and, behind him, the heir to the throne, the future George I. Against this formidable array there stood the Queen and the Tory party, with their majority in the Commons. Harley thought of trying to come to terms with Marlborough, but his party was too strong for him. In any case Marlborough embodied the Grand Alliance: he was the power engaged in rallying the Allies: he was the most dangerous enemy in the way.

In the debate on the Queen's Speech in the Lords, in the presence of the Queen—sitting there *incognita* in her box—Marlborough vindicated himself, replied to the aspersions that had been cast upon him and stated his view with a last challenge. 'I can declare with a safe conscience, in the presence of her Majesty, of the illustrious assembly, and of that Supreme Being, Who is infinitely above all the powers upon earth, and before Whom, according to the ordinary course of natutre, I must soon appear, to give an account of my actions, that I was ever desirous of a safe, honourable and lasting peace; and that I always have been very far from any design of prolonging the war for my own private advantage, as my enemies have most falsely insinuated.' At the same time he would not consider a separate peace without the Allies, 'for I am of the same opinion with the rest of the Allies, that the safety and liberties of Europe would be in imminent danger, if Spain and the West Indies were left to the house of Bourbon'.

The Queen herself was shaken and hesitated to take the last step. The atmosphere of crisis continued; the friends of the new ministry wondered how it would resolve itself. The ministry was in a minority in the Lords. At this juncture, Harley—now Earl of Oxford—did not hesitate; like a true leader he calculated his steps and coolly took them. Proceedings were on foot against Marlborough in the Commons for malversation of funds; the press-campaign against him was redoubled—Swift lent himself to these purposes and was much the most effective penman. With Harley to guide the Queen and with Abigail to warn her of the consequences of defeat, Anne took the last steps. She created twelve peers at once, one of them Abigail's husband, to secure a majority for the government, and the peace, in the Lords. She dismissed Marlborough: we do not know in what terms, for, moved beyond endurance and losing his habitual self-control, he threw her letter into the fire. But, resuming his serene manner, he replied to her with dignity: 'I am very sensible of the honour your Majesty does me in dismissing me from your service by a letter of your own hand, though I find by it that my enemies have been able to prevail with your Majesty to do it in the manner that is most injurious to me. . . . I wish your Majesty may never find the want of so faithful a servant as I have always endeavoured to approve myself to you.'

The comment of Louis XIV, on hearing the news, was much to the point: 'The affair of displacing the Duke of Marlborough will do all for us we desire.' There needs no further tribute to what Marlborough had accomplished.

CHAPTER FOURTEEN

Sarah and the Queen

WE must retrace our steps to tell the extraordinary story of the relations between Sarah and the Queen.

When William was dead and Anne was Queen, the Cockpit circle came into their own: nothing was too much, nothing was too good, for Sarah. She was at once made Groom of the Stole [*i.e.* the Stool, in actuality], Mistress of the Robes, Keeper of the Privy Purse. While the going was so good Sarah looked after her poor relations. Her mother's sister had married a Nonconformist merchant named Hill, in the City, and fallen upon bad times. Sarah afterwards said grandly that she 'never knew there were such people in the world'; but she was not without kindness of heart and she took the fortunes of her young cousins efficiently, as was her way, under her wing. The elder daughter, Abigail, she took to live with her at Holywell, 'and I treated her with as great kindness as if she had been my sister'. That may not have been Abigail's impression of the matter and, anyway, such relationships are apt to breed resentments. Before Anne's accession Abigail had been advanced to the post of a Bedchamber-woman (not-lady) to the Princess. The younger daughter was given the job of laundress to the little Duke of Gloucester; when he died she got a pension and, later, she too became a woman of the Bedchamber. The elder brother, at Sarah's request, was given a job in the Customs House by Godolphin; the younger, 'whom the bottle-men afterwards called *honest* Jack Hill, a tall boy, whom I clothed (for he was all in rags) and put to school at St. Albans', was taken into the army and given a regiment by Marlborough.

Sarah never learned what a mistake it can be to do people a good turn; but she had a warmer heart than her husband, and she sometimes burned her fingers by her good actions. For the moment all was well: it was 'good Queen Anne' for the Hills as well as for the Churchills. The endearments that passed give us the tone, and the temperature, of the circle: 'My dear adored Mrs. Morley,' and Mrs. Morley in reply, 'I am so entirely yours, that if I might have all the world given me, I could not be happy but in your love.' It was the language of the sentimental French romances, of Mademoiselle Scudéry and the rest, on which the ladies of the Restoration Court had been brought up. But that there was strong emotion we may see from an occasional sentence that throws a shaft of light upon present or past stresses.

Now it is Sarah's fondness for Abigail that arouses Anne's jealousy. Sarah has been away two or three days without writing, and the Queen must write if only to get a line or two. If Sarah is in town, no doubt she will be tempted to see the Opera: 'I hope Mrs. Freeman has no thoughts of going to the Opera with Mrs. Hill, and will have a care of engaging herself too much in her company; for, if you give way to that, it is a thing that will insensibly grow upon you. Therefore give me leave once more to beg for your own sake, as well as poor Mrs. Morley's, that you would have as little to do with that enchantress as 'tis possible, and pray pardon me for saying this.' From this we learn that Abigail had already been a subject of contention between Sarah and the Queen, and that Abigail had her own share of the Jennings charm.

So far the Cockpit circle remained firm. What neither of them realised was the profound change that came from the fact of Anne's accession to the throne. So long as William lived the Cockpit circle was united in opposition to, and detestation of, him. With him removed their own differences of temperament and opinion were bound to come into play: they were open to be forced apart by the irresistible pulls of politics.

Anne was devoted to the interests of the Church. The new Queen dismissed William's Parliament with the declaration: 'My own principles must always keep me entirely firm to the interests and religion of the Church of England, and will incline me to countenance those who have the truest zeal to support it.' This was a declaration of war upon William's coalition of Latitudinarians, Dissenters, Rationalists—the Whigs. All Anne's associations and predilections were Tory: her family principles were those of passive obedience and Divine Right (as channelled through the Church of England); her uncles were high Tories; the Church was the Tory party at prayer. Sarah tells us that the Queen really hated the Whigs: she associated them with the injuries she had received in William's reign, she regarded their principles as anti-monarchical. As a sovereign—and perhaps no less as a lady—she regarded her prerogative as a very personal matter, and any demeaning of it as a personal affront.

For Sarah's part, 'I had not the same prepossessions. The *word*

"Church" had never any charm for *me,* in the mouths of those who made the most noise with it; for I could not perceive that they gave any other distinguishing proof of their regard for the *thing*, than a frequent use of the *word,* like a spell to enchant weak minds.' In short the temper of Sarah's mind was that of a rationalising Whig. She had no patience with the humbugging cry of 'The Church in danger' with such a 'nursing mother' as the Queen—Sarah turned the Tories' cant phrase against them. Still less had she any patience with 'the high church nonsense of promoting religion by persecution'. And she scores a shrewd point with her remark: 'the gibberish of that party about non-resistance and passive obedience and hereditary right I could not think to forbode any good to my mistress, whose title rested upon a different foundation'.

The Queen, however, thought herself above party: a Whig government was a party-government; a Tory government was not. This fixed idea Sarah set herself, from the beginning of the reign, to eradicate from the Queen's mind. She apparently protested against that minatory phrase in the Queen's Speech, for Anne replied: 'I know the principles of the Church of England, and I know those of the Whigs; and it is that, and no other reason, which makes me think as I do of the last. And upon my word, my dear Mrs. Freeman, you are mightily mistaken in your notion of a true Whig: for the character you give of them does not in the least belong to them, but to the Church.'

One would have thought that this was warning enough of the Queen's temper. But Sarah was never one to take warning; moreover, she regarded it as her duty to make the Queen's mind more receptive to the rest of her subjects who deserved as well as the others. In former days the Princess had adjured her to speak her mind freely and with candour on all subjects: how was she to know the truth, if surrounded, like her father, with flattery and dissimulation? 'I did therefore speak very freely and very frequently to her Majesty upon the subject of Whig and Tory, according to my conception of their different views and principles.' We may be sure that she did. Here, again, comes in a difference: it was all very well for her to regard the diffident, taciturn Princess as in tutelage, but a change had overtaken the situation now that she was Queen.

This change is the sort of thing that clever people often understand less well then ordinary ones—and Sarah, though far more intelligent than Anne, was not gifted with tact or imagination. The same woman who had had little confidence in herself as Princess was now as Queen the source of sovereign power and authority: its very exercise was bound to strengthen the will. It would not be so easy to speak so very freely to the sovereign; and if one insisted, it would be certain to lay up stores of resistance and accumulated resentment that might one day overwhelm ancient friendship. One could hardly expect to batter at the Queen all day and every day with impunity; and that was what Sarah proceeded to do. To some extent the exigencies of politics, the overriding need to support Marlborough's war, forced Sarah to it. This was bound to ruin their friendship; the element of necessity, which was present in it, gives it the character of a true tragedy. After more than a year of such battering, even after Blenheim, the Queen could still write: 'I have the same opinion of Whig and Tory that ever I had. I know both their principles very well, and when I know myself to be in the right, nothing can make me alter mine.'

The Queen sought to keep her intimate relationship with Sarah on the old private footing, while Sarah as relentlessly pushed her views in the political sphere. In private matters the Queen was as kind as ever. Griefs and joys still drew them together. When Sarah's only remaining son died, the Queen was all sympathy and would have gone down to Holywell to console her. 'It would have been a great satisfaction to your poor unfortunate faithful Morley, if you would have given me leave to come to St. Albans, for the unfortunate ought to come to the unfortunate.' Sarah had nursed the boy struck down with smallpox: 'give me leave once more to beg you for Christ Jesus' sake to have a care of your dear precious self, and believe me with all the passion imaginable your poor unfortunate faithful Morley.' This way of referring to herself went back to her own loss of an only son, the extinction of her hopes of her blood inheriting the throne.

His son's death was a grievous blow to Marlborough's dynastic sense, his profoundly masculine instinct to found a family. For a time he hoped that Sarah might bear him another: 'whilst you are kind . . . I cannot but hope we shall yet have a son, which are my daily prayers'. Full of solicitude as ever for Sarah, he confided, not to her but to Godolphin, how much he missed his boy: 'Since it has pleased God to take him, I do wish from my soul I would think less of him'. Now he learned from Sarah that his hopes were vain and that she was ill: 'you and I have great reason to bless God for all we have', he consoled her, 'so that we must not repine at his taking our poor child from us, but bless and praise him for what his goodness leaves us'. There were the four daughters, all married now. At the marriage of the third who became Lady Bridgwater, and of the last who became Duchess of Montagu not long after—rather to her mother's annoyance—the Queen repeated her generosity: £5000 each, though the Marlboroughs were now rich.

In 1704 and 1705 circumstances came to the aid of Sarah's too insistent arguments, with the mistakes of the Tories. To make trouble and split the government, which rested on the moderate men of the middle, the extremer Tories were prepared to do a deal with the Whigs. The Queen grasped this firmly and sent two of the Tory *frondeurs* packing. She reported this with some satisfaction to Sarah and with curious Stuart deviousness: 'I am told by a very good hand that the Queen has sent a message to Lord Jersey and Sir Edward Seymour which they will not like. Sure this will convince Mrs. Freeman that I never had any partiality to any of these persons; for if that had been so, this would certainly never have been done. Something more of this nature, it is believed, will soon happen, that will not be disagreeable to Mrs. Freeman.' We observe the Queen anticipating the approbation of her adored friend; yet the situation is a little subtler than this: she remains, and is determined to remain, mistress of her actions: she is the Queen.

Next year the Tories made a further mistake: some of them raised the project of bringing over the Elector of Hanover, or his son, to take his seat in the House of Lords. Nothing could be more disagreeable to the Queen: she disliked the thought of the Hanover family as her successors, and could not bear the idea of one of them being in the country for a week. Godolphin's increasing co-operation with the Whigs delivered her from this horrid spectre. Anne was grateful: 'I believe dear Mrs. Freeman and I shall not disagree as we have formerly done, for I am sensible of the services those people have done me that you have a good opinion of, and will countenance them, and am thoroughly convinced of the malice and insolence of them that you have always been speaking against.'

Alas, for these hopes! The Whigs in turn now clamoured for their recompense, a greater share in power. This renewed the Queen's alarm. She wrote to Godolphin: 'I must own to you I dread the falling into the hands of either party, and the Whigs have had so many favours showed them of late, that I fear a very few more will put me insensibly into their power . . . I know my dear unkind friend has so good an opinion of all that party that, to be sure, she will use all her endeavour to get you to prevail with me to put one of them into this great post, and I cannot help being apprehensive that not only she but others may be desirous to have one of the heads of them in possession of the Seal.' It was no use the Queen's appealing to her Lord Treasurer: he was on Sarah's side, and anyway as a politician needed the Whigs' support for the war. They got the Privy Seal for one of their leaders.

Next year, 1706, the year of Ramillies, the Whigs demanded further representation in the government; they pressed for the key-post of Secretary of State for Lord Sunderland. The Secretary of State would be in constant contact with the Queen, and Anne detested Sunderland: he was the incarnation of all that she hated in pure Whiggery—an arrogant intellectual, tactless and inconsiderate, an oligarch whom Anne regarded, not without reason, as having no great respect for monarchy and meaning to subordinate the sovereign to the oligarchy. The Queen put her point of view forcefully to Godolphin: 'All I desire is my liberty in encouraging and employing all those that concur faithfully in my service, whether they are called Whigs or Tories, not to be tied to one or the other; for if I should be so unfortunate as to fall into the hands of either, I shall look upon myself, though I have the name of Queen, to be in reality but their slave; which as it will be my personal ruin, so it will be the destroying of all government, for instead of putting an end to faction, it will lay a lasting foundation for it.'

This passage is of striking interest to the historian, for it points to the transition in government to a party-basis. For Parliamentary government party-organisation is indispensable; when that evolution was complete real political power would inevitably shift from the sovereign to Parliament and party-government. We have observed an earlier phase of this development in the reign of Charles II; the reign of his niece constitutes a second chapter. The Queen was naturally a conservative; she had a profound sense of her duty as Queen, and was equally conscious of her prerogative and her rights. To her parties were factions: why could they not pull together for the country's good, leaving it to her to choose those who would govern best in the interests of the country as a whole? 'Why, for God's sake, must I, who have no interest, no end, no thought, but for the good of my country, be made so miserable as to be brought into the power of one set of men, and why may I not be trusted, since I mean nothing but what is equally for the good of all my subjects?'

We see that Anne—invalid as she was, crippled with gout—was a force not to be disregarded; and indeed she has been much underestimated. She proceeded to put up a strong resistance to Sunderland's appointment. She appealed to Marlborough, whose own sympathies, chivalrous as ever, were with the Queen: he did not want his son-in-law forced upon her. But he could not go against Godolphin, who was himself under pressure from the Whigs. The Queen held out for months. But they were all under the inevitable pressures of politics. The Whigs were obdurate and from their point of view they were right: they were the people whose heart was really in the war: they were the most competent and able to wage it: why should they not have their proper share in the government? Godolphin could not now maintain his government without their support; Marlborough could not conduct the war without Godolphin and the Whigs.

But Sarah? She might at least have sympathised with the Queen's agony of mind. Not a bit: she was herself much under the intellectual influence of her son-in-law; she really shared his point of view, rationalising, debunking the *mystique* of monarchy, libertarian and oligarchical. She took a passionate part in the controversy, bombarding the Queen with letters, arguments, interviews. To her the Queen's resistance was mere obstinacy and stupidity. The tone of her communications was peremptory: the incessant wrangling was killing all affection, and in these circumstances the appeal to old memories and endearments simply poisoned feeling. We can only say on Sarah's side that the situation was becoming disagreeable enough for her; for she was under pressure from the Whigs to exert her influence with the Queen, and the more she tried the more resistance she encountered. The situation had to be resolved one way or the other; on her own responsibility Sarah forwarded to the Queen a letter from Marlborough assuring Godolphin that he could not go on without him: the effect was to coerce the Queen. 'Upon recalling everything to my memory that may fill my heart with all that passion and tenderness I had once for Mrs. Morley I do solemnly protest I think I can no ways return what I owe her so well as by being plain and honest.' When love is dead this kind of language leaves a most unpleasant taste. Sarah then proceeded to say something unpardonable: 'as one mark of it, I desire you would reflect whether you have never heard that the greatest misfortunes that have ever happened to any of your family had not been occasioned by having ill-advice and an obstinacy in their tempers'.

This was a shocking thing to say, to remind the Queen, at such a moment, of her father's fate, to wound her at her conscience's most sensitive spot. Sarah had indeed forgotten herself—as she often enough did with other people: this was not only her friend from girlhood, the loved one of many years, to whom she and her husband owed everything: this was her Queen. The insult was beyond apology and it was never forgiven. The Queen had to give way, since government had to go on: Sarah's son-in-law became Secretary of State—in what conditions! The Whigs were on their way now to dominate and monopolise the government. The Queen bided her time and went underground. There was always the refuge of dignified dissimulation: courtesy on the surface, alienation at heart. We observe a new tone set in her letters to Sarah. At the same time the Queen found that she was not without resource. Mr. Harley discovered that he, too, was a cousin of Abigail's: he was ready to come up the backstairs with his information and advice. The Queen's relation to her Bedchamber-woman became a matter of the first political importance.

It took Sarah longer than it would have done most people to discover the footing upon which Abigail was with the Queen: she was so used to domineering over every one that she could not believe her place in Anne's affections might be taken by another, least of all by her own poor relation 'whom I took out of a garret'. And now we observe with fascination how helpless the strong overbearing character was, as often happens, in dealing with the disingenuousness and dissimulation of weaker natures: she had not the weapons to deal with Anne or Abigail. Her only chance would have been to try and retrace her steps, recover something of Anne's affection, even if the passion of love were over.

Offended pride made this impossible: she would not give way. Instead of going to the Queen, renewing her attentions, surrounding her with solicitude, she absented herself from Court for weeks at a time. Anne's was a lonely life, rendered doubly so by her position and her temperament. Sarah had often been bored, at the height of their intimacy, by the duties of attendance. Anne had no conversation, was low-spirited and preferred to be alone in a crowded Court. Sarah's vitality had cheered her up and supported her spirits when she had the spleen or was in actual pain. Now she chose to absent herself. It was unwise, as her daughter, Lady Sunderland, warned her. It played Abigail's game for her: the coast was clear.

It is certain that the Queen never intended Abigail to occupy the position of near-equality on which Sarah had been with her from girlhood; and for some time she laboured to keep relations with Sarah on a friendly footing. 'My dear Mrs. Freeman, I cannot go to bed without renewing a request that I have often made, that you would banish all unkind and unjust thoughts of your poor unfortunate faithful Morley, which I saw by the glimpse I had of you yesterday you were full of. Indeed I do not deserve them, and if you could see my heart you would find it as sincere, as tender and passionately fond of you as ever, and as truly sensible of your kindness in telling me your mind freely upon all occasions.'

In the summer of 1707 Sarah learned news of her cousin and protégé that astounded her: Abigail had been married secretly to Samuel Masham, groom of the Bedchamber to Prince George. Masham, of course, owed his promotion to Sarah; but the news had been kept from her. He was a gentleman of good birth, having a Plantagenet descent: a respectable marriage for the daughter of a Baptist merchant, no longer young. Sarah went to the Queen for confirmation of this; all that Anne would say was, 'I have a hundred times bid Masham tell it you, and she would not'. That is what one gets for being too domineering: Sarah suddenly saw the hold her cousin had upon the Queen and that there was some mystery in the affair into which she was not being admitted. She set inquiries on foot, 'and in less than a week's time I discovered that my cousin was become an absolute favourite; that the Queen herself was present at her marriage in Dr. Arbuthnot's lodgings, at which time her Majesty had called for a round sum out of the Privy Purse; that Mrs. Masham came often to the Queen when the Prince was asleep, and was generally two hours every day in private with her. And I likewise then discovered beyond all dispute Mr. Harley's correspondence and interest at Court by means of this woman.'

Sarah now called to mind several passages over a long period that indicated the intimate relations established between the Queen and Abigail. She recalled one night in particular when, having gone by a secret passage to the Queen's bedchamber, 'on a sudden this woman, not knowing I was there, came in with the boldest and gayest air possible, but, upon sight of me, stopped; and immediately changing her manner, and making a most solemn curtsy, "Did your Majesty ring?" And then went out again.'

Henceforth there was to be no quarter between Sarah and Abigail: the affair bore all the extremism of a women's quarrel. We know what Abigail felt towards her former patron from her correspondence with Harley. 'The 22nd day I waited [*i.e.* on the Queen], and in the evening about eight o'clock a great lady came and made a visit till almost ten. I was in the Drawing Room by good luck, and as she passed by me I had a very low curtsy, which I returned in the same manner; but not one word passed between us, and as for her looks, indeed they are not to be described by any mortal but her own self.'

The Duchess determined on a show-down with 'this woman'. She wrote reproaching her with keeping her marriage secret from her; to this she received an artful, obsequious, insincere reply. She demanded an interview, at which she reproached her cousin with doing her ill offices with the Queen. To this Mrs. Masham, 'very gravely answered that "she was sure the Queen, who had loved me extremely, would always be very kind to me". It was some minutes before I could recover from the surprise with which so extraordinary an answer struck me. To see a woman, whom I had raised out of the dust, put on such a superior air, and to hear her assure me, by way of consolation, that the Queen would be always very kind to me!' No doubt its effect had been calculated: Abigail was an intelligent woman. She must have hated Sarah: it was intended to madden.

Sarah could not let it rest there. She had once before protested to the Queen, and got a cool rebuttal of the 'suspicions you seemed to have concerning your cousin Hill, who is very far from being an occasion of feeding Mrs. Morley in her passion, as you are pleased to call it, she never meddling with anything. I believe others that have been in her station in former times have been tattling and very impertinent, but she is not at all of that temper; and as for the company she keeps, it is with her as with most other people. I fancy that their lot in the world makes them move with some out of civility rather than choice; and I really believe, for one that is so much in the way of company, she has less acquaintance than anyone upon earth.' This was true: Abigail was a great contrast to Sarah: a discreet, secret woman, who never raised her voice, a woman of confidences and *chuchotements*, who melted easily into the background.

Now the Queen replied to Sarah with a finality that showed it was useless to raise the subject any more. 'I beg you would not mention any more that person who you are pleased to call the object of my favour; for whatever character the malicious world may give her, I do assure you it will never have any weight with me, knowing she does not deserve it, nor can I ever change the good impressions you once gave me of her, unless she should give me a cause, which I am very sure she never will.'

All this was duly retailed by Sarah to Marlborough abroad, in the midst of all his other worries, the intricacies of European diplomacy, fighting his campaigns: she spared him nothing. He had judged the situation pretty correctly all along: he knew that the Queen would not give in. He knew, better than anyone, her father's obstinacy in her. As for his own wife, he was in part much to blame: he had always spoiled her; he should have ridden her with a much tighter rein: she would have been all the better for it, for the material was good.

These quarrels would not have had their importance, or been so bitter, if they had not been inextricably interwoven with the struggle of men for power. Sarah felt it incumbent on her to fight her husband's battles at home—actually he would have done better without her; but as long as the war went on it was necessary to support him. The Queen longed for peace: as early as the summer of Ramillies she wrote, 'I having no ambition . . . but to see an honourable peace, that whenever it pleases God I shall die, I may have the satisfaction of leaving my poor country and all my friends in peace and quiet.' The Tories were the peace-party, and it was this, in addition to Anne's determination to free herself from the Whigs, that gave Harley so much influence with her; Abigail was his intermediary and his instrument.

The quarrel between the Queen and the Duchess was becoming public property, and Sarah did not restrain herself from talking about it. The Queen saw its unwisdom and approached Marlborough in a letter which shows how much more sense she had. It also reveals a perfectly respectable conception of how their relations could continue: Sarah keeping to the exercise of her offices, showing courtesy and discretion, and ceasing to try and oust Abigail.

That summer of 1708 there was an open altercation between the two women on, of all days, the Thanksgiving for Marlborough's victory at Oudenarde, and, of all places, in the state-coach on the way to St. Paul's. In the exercise of her office Sarah had laid out the jewels the Queen was to wear in the accustomed way. The Queen chose to wear no jewels. Sarah was beside herself with rage: she was convinced that this was Mrs. Masham's doing, a fresh example of her insolence, and that it was intended as a humiliation on the very occasion of returning thanks for her dear lord's victory. Reproaches, recriminations poured forth all the way to St. Paul's. We know the difficulty the Queen had in speaking her mind immediately: it was not until they were in the Cathedral that she began to reply—and then Sarah commanded her to keep quiet, she afterwards explained, 'for fear of being overheard'.

Sarah felt that she had put herself in the wrong: she now wrote a dignified letter, in a tone which she would have done well to adhere to. 'Though I have always writ to you as a friend and lived with you as such for so many years, with all the truth, honesty and zeal for your service that was possible, yet I shall never forget that I am your subject, nor cease to be a faithful one.' This was one of the few occasions when Sarah condescended, quite simply, to touch the Queen's heart. The memory of their former love, if no longer love itself, softened their hearts, and from a renewed meeting both Anne and Sarah withdrew in tears.

Unfortunately the Duchess was one of those women on whose good resolutions one cannot rely from one moment to another. The next moment she was sending the Queen copies of the ballads and lampoons that were being circulated about her and Abigail. She could not resist the cutting remark that it was not to be expected that Mrs. Masham would acquaint her with them, 'though the town and country are full of them'. We may be sure that Sarah did not discourage their appearance. She dared to remind the Queen that her father had been 'sung out of his kingdom by silly ballads' and warned her not to risk everything similarly for a woman incapable of giving her any good advice, 'nobody but a chamber-maid, whom I took from a broom as the ballad says rightly'. Clearly, hatred of Abigail was making Sarah quite unbalanced. The wrangles, altercations, scenes continued.

That autumn the Queen, a sick woman herself, was nursing her dying husband. Prince George was always a good friend to the Churchills. Sarah now wrote, with repellent self-justification at such a moment: 'though the last time I had the honour to wait upon your Majesty your usage of me was such as was scarce possible for me to imagine, or for anybody to believe, yet I cannot hear of so great a misfortune and affliction to you as the condition in which the Prince is without coming to pay my duty, in inquiring after your health'. When Sarah presented herself she was very coolly received; but she came back next day and was present when the Prince died. On this occasion mindful of appearances, the Duchess knelt to the Queen and prevailed on her to withdraw from the death-chamber to her own closet. She took charge of the situation, as was her right, and persuaded Anne to leave Kensington, where the preparations for the funeral were going forward, for St. James's: Sarah would take her in her own coach.

At this moment of her grief all that Anne wanted was Abigail to console her. She gave Sarah her watch and, pointing to some little time later when she should come back, asked her meanwhile to send Abigail to her. Sarah felt humiliated and did not give the message; but when announcing that the carriage was ready, she added, your Majesty may send for her at St. James's when and how you please'. Anne acquiesced and passed out through the gallery, leaning on Sarah's arm for support. As Abigail's sister put on her hood, the Queen whispered a commission; shortly after Abigail appeared to see her off; and the Queen turned leaning fondly towards her, though neither spoke. At St. James's Anne wrote Sarah a touching little note, 'I scratched twice at dear Mrs. Freeman's door, as soon as Lord Treasurer went from me, in hopes to have spoke one more word to him before he was gone; but, nobody hearing me, I wrote this, not caring to send what I had to say by word of mouth; which was to desire him that when he sends his orders to Kensington, he would give directions there may be a great many Yeomen of the Guards to carry the Prince's dear body, that it may not be let fall, the great stairs being very steep and slippery'.

This was the last kindness that passed between them. If only Sarah could have left matters here, if only she had attended to Marlborough's words of wisdom: 'it has always been my observation in disputes, especially in those of kindness and friendship, that all reproaches, though ever so reasonable, do serve to no other end but the making the breach wider.' Instead of that the intolerable woman—perhaps the only extenuation of her conduct may be her change of life, and an element of hysteria—went on tormenting the Queen about Mrs. Masham. In 1709 the disreputable Mrs. Manley, who later became Swift's understrapper on the *Examiner*, published her *New Atalantis*, which drew attention to the situation at Court. It was intended to curry favour with Harley and Abigail; but it gave Sarah an opening to write to the Queen, for it commended Abigail's efforts as making for peace, 'and there is stuff not fit to be mentioned of passions between women'. The prim Sarah found it a disagreeable subject, but perhaps not so disagreeable to let the Queen know what she was opening herself to. It was a case of the characteristic Stuart infatuation for their favourites, like James I and Charles I's for Buckingham. Even when Sarah was still supreme at Court a mere man could write, 'but the Queen's fondness for t'other lady is not to be expressed'. Now Sarah's clever confidant, Maynwaring, wrote: 'since you have lost nothing but her passion, which it is plain you never cared for', and that may let us into the secret springs of Anne's resentment against the beautiful, and more masculine, Sarah. Anne at last, all kindness gone, replied in kind, charging the Duchess with inveteracy against her cousin and 'having nothing so much at heart as her ruin'. She told Sarah outright that it was impossible for her to recover her former kindness, though she would behave to her as the Duke of Marlborough's wife and her Groom of the Stole.

At this the Duchess drew up a long narrative of her services to Anne during the past twenty-six years, which she presented to her to read. The Queen replied that, when she had the time, she would. The Duchess added the directions given by the author of the *Whole Duty of Man* in regard to friendship; the instructions given in the Prayer Book in regard to reconciliation, together with Jeremy Taylor's rules on the matter. The Queen's reply to that was, when passing by to receive the Communion, to smile very graciously upon Sarah; 'but the smile and pleasant look I had reason afterwards to think were given to Bishop Taylor and the Common Prayer Book, and not to me'. To Marlborough, the Queen wrote: 'you seem to be dissatisfied with my behaviour to the Duchess of Marlborough. I do not love complaining, but it is impossible to help saying on this occasion I believe nobody was ever so used by a friend as I have been by her ever since my coming to the Crown. I desire nothing but that she would leave off teasing and tormenting me, and behave herself with the decency she ought both to her friend and Queen, and this I hope you will make her do.'

This was the year of Malplaquet, 1709. The Queen took no notice of Marlborough's victory. Impelled by a sense of insecurity, wanting to shore himself up to see the war through to a finish, he made a grave mistake: he asked to be made Captain-General for life. This corroborated his enemies in their accusation that he was aiming at a monopoly of power. The Queen had no difficulty in refusing his demand. Then the Whigs failed to make peace—which made the Queen right, at any rate more certain that she was right, in relying upon Harley's advice. Mrs. Masham's influence inevitably grew, even if the Queen did not rely on it in political matters as people supposed: Harley was the real figure in the background, on his way into the foreground now. Rumours flew round of Sarah's disrespectful talk about the Queen and Mrs. Masham: she wrote demanding to be heard in her own defence. The Queen desired that she would do it in writing. Sarah wrote again asking for an audience: no doubt she thought her presence would be more effective than mere writing. The Queen a few days later: 'whatever you can have to say to me may certainly be as well writ as said, I *desire* you once more to put your thoughts in writing'. Without permission, Sarah announced that she was coming to Kensington that afternoon and would wait every day till the Queen would grant her an audience. Arrived there the Duchess sat down in a window of the long gallery 'like a Scotch lady with a petition, instead of a trusted and life-long confidant'. She was kept waiting outside a long time—which must have given her bitter thoughts of the days when she was always within, when the Queen could not see enough of her.

At last she was called in. The Queen said that she was just going to write to her. When Sarah began to speak, Anne interrupted again and again, repeating, as her manner was, the phrase, 'whatever you have to say, you may put it in writing'. Sarah said that her Majesty never did so hard a thing to any as to refuse to hear them speak; and she assured her that she would not trouble her upon the subject she knew to be so ungrateful to her. At this Anne turned away: she must have been so sick of the subject, she had been through it all so many times before. In the next breath Sarah went on to say that there were those about her Majesty who had made her believe that she had said things about her which she was no more capable of saying than of killing her own children. (This was an unfortunate image, for Sarah was not on good terms with two of her children.) Anne said, with justice, to this: 'Without doubt there are many lies told.'

Sarah took advantage of this to ask the particulars of which she had been accused, that she might clear herself. The Queen, laying hold of a phrase in Sarah's letter, replied that she would give her no answer. Characteristically Sarah pressed again and again and would not desist; she said, with the so familiar implication, that she did not ask the names of the authors of these calumnies. To every attempt Sarah made, Anne replied, 'You desired no answer, and shall have none'. The Queen made a move towards leaving the room; Sarah followed. 'When she came to the door, I fell into great disorder; streams of tears fell down against my will and preventing my speaking for some time.' Sarah poured out passionate protestations, asking the Queen whether she had ever in the course of their long friendship played the hypocrite, or offended except by pressing too zealously what she thought necessary for her service. To everything Anne opposed, 'You desired no answer, and you shall have none.'

The repetition of a phrase like this was very characteristic of Anne: it was a defence against her own lack of confidence, her hesitation to speak and, perhaps in the present instance, to maintain her self-control against the solicitations of hysteria. Sarah appealed to Anne's own knowledge whether she was capable of disowning anything she knew to be true—always Sarah's first and last gambit: her candour, her sincerity. 'You desired no answer, and you shall have none.' 'This usage was so severe, and these words, so often repeated, were so shocking ... that I could not conquer myself, but said the most disrespectful thing I ever spoke to the Queen in my life ... and that was "I was confident her Majesty would suffer for such an instance of inhumanity." ' To this the Queen answered, 'That will be to myself.'

These, to my mind, are the most tragic words spoken in the course of that famous altercation—their last, for they never saw each other again. Those words reveal the Queen's full sense of the responsibility she was taking home to herself, the suffering that would be her lot, which she was ready to accept and endure. Nor was it long now in coming.

After Sarah emerged from the private apartments, she sat down again in the long gallery to wipe her eyes before confronting the world. A few days later the Queen wrote asking for the return of her letters; 'all my strange scrawls, it being impossible that they can now be agreeable to you'. Sarah neither complied nor replied.

There was a latent threat that she might publish them, with all their revelations of Anne's feelings towards her predecessor. When Marlborough came home that winter, he persuaded Sarah to make a complete submission to the Queen. His own position as Commander-in-Chief was in jeopardy, and Sarah, who would make no submission for herself, was willing to humble her pride for his sake. She wrote the Queen a letter of contrition and apology, promising never to raise the old topics of controversy, and abjectly begging that she might retain her offices. Marlborough himself bore this letter to the Queen; he had written before coming home: 'I would go upon all-fours to make it easy between you.'

It was too late. He could hardly get the Queen to open the letter, and then she said, 'I cannot change my resolution.' Her steps were resolved, her plans made. She demanded that Sarah's gold key of office be delivered up within three days. Marlborough begged for ten days' respite. Anne, now implacable like her father, cut it down to two; and she would discuss no business with him till she had the key.

The tradition is that when he delivered the message, Sarah flung the key on the floor and told him to take it back at once. Her offices were divided: the Duchess of Somerset became Groom of the Stole, but Abigail Keeper of the Privy Purse. Perhaps the saddest thing is that this long and famous friendship should end in the squalor of money. In the noonday of friendship and favour the Queen had offered Marlborough £2000 a year out of the Privy Purse to support his dukedom: Sarah had refused it. Now she claimed the arrears of it for the past nine years; the Queen—in contempt, we may be sure—made it good. Sarah was left to clear her things out of St. James's Palace: the Queen sent a message that she might take a lodging for 10s. a week to put her Lord's goods in. Sarah commented savagely, 'it sufficiently shows what a good education and understanding the wolf has, who was certainly the person who gave that advice'. The lodgings were wanted for someone else: Sarah had them stripped of every mortal thing that belonged to her, down to the locks on the doors, leaving a desert behind.

CHAPTER FIFTEEN

Exile and Return

MARLBOROUGH was dismissed from all his employments 30 December 1711. Next day twelve peers were created—Abigail's husband being one—to give the Tory government a majority in the Lords to carry the Peace. This did not resolve the crisis: indeed, we may regard the last years of the Queen's reign, until the safe realisation of the Protestant succession with George of Hanover, as one prolonged crisis. Nor did it mean that the European figure of the Duke ceased to be dangerous to the Tory Ministry. It was necessary to damage him in the eyes of the public, direct against him a 'smear-campaign'. In the art of manoeuvring opinion Harley was a past-master: Sarah described it, for once with some justification, as 'that wonderful talent Mr. Harley possessed, in the supreme degree, of confounding the common sense of mankind'.

All the wits were Whigs by origin: Addison and Steele, Prior and Swift, and that unattractive camouflaged figure, something apart on his own, Defoe. Harley had recruited Defoe to his intelligence service, bought him for the Tories. And he bought Jonathan Swift, no less, though not with cash: with a little influence and less power, which Swift valued even higher than money. Godolphin, who was too old-fashioned or too Philistine to care for such things, or too lofty to notice, lost both Prior and Swift. The Marlboroughs were made to smart for this.

Swift was born and bred a Whig; but, baulked of anything better, poor and without prospects, he took Orders. The Church was his regiment, and though it may be doubted—as Queen Anne doubted—whether he had much belief in God, he had unquestioning belief in himself and a determination, rendered savage by long frustration, to advance his own prospects. He had been sent over by the Church of Ireland to obtain the grant of first-fruits from the Crown. Godolphin, who had other things to think about, put him off and cold-shouldered him. Swift rewarded him with a satire, 'Sid Hamet the Magician's Rod', and did not hesitate to hint that Sarah was Godolphin's mistress. No one else sank so low—anyone who knew Sarah or Godolphin knew how improbable such a relationship was. It is to be feared that the misanthrope of genius himself makes a mean figure in all this. He went wholly and bitterly, as was his way, on to the other side.

Harley caressed and nursed the great satirist, who put his incandescent powers at the service of the new Ministry. Never was a political tractate more immediately effective than his *Conduct of the Allies*, which came out a month before Marlborough's dismissal. This brilliantly written pamphlet argued, persuasively enough, that the other allies had a greater stake in the Grand Alliance than Britain, and then suggested that she had borne a greater burden than they. 'Ten glorious campaigns are passed, and now at last, like the sick man, we are just expiring with all sorts of good symptoms.' Swift argued the Tory case for a sea-war, as against taking part on the Continent, and put the point of view of the country gentry, who paid the land-tax, as against the moneyed interest and the stock-jobbers, who were doing well out of the war. At the head of these stood out, above all, the Marlboroughs: 'so that whether this war were prudently begun or not, it is plain that the true spring or motive of it was the aggrandizing a particular family, and in short, a war of the General and the Ministry, and not of the Prince or people'.

This was a *suggestio falsi*. It was true that Marlborough had made an immense fortune out of the war; it was not true that that had been either the spring or motive of it. Ordinary people would be incapable of distinguishing between the two propositions, and no line of attack on the Duke was so damaging as this, however unwarranted. It would appeal to people's jealousy and envy, always on the alert against any singular degree of eminence, to people's cupidity and suspicion—as Swift, with his precise knowledge of the baser side of human nature, knew well. He went on to describe the exemplary partnership of Marlborough and Godolphin, really a national union of moderate non-party men, 'as a conspiracy founded upon the interest and ambition of each party'. We know what to think of that: we know that Godolphin had no ambition at all, and no wish to be where he was, except to serve his friend, and that that friend's overriding ambition had been to serve his Queen and country. Swift ended on the note of peculation, the suggestion of fraud, always grateful to common ears, which was bound to have the widest and most popular reverberation.

This was the note that was constantly struck in the campaign that was let loose week by week in the *Examiner* directed by Swift, in pamphlets, squibs, satires, epigrams—for this was a small and literate society, a literary age. It was as if Swift could not get away from Marlborough, as if he had a fixation on him: again and again he comes back to the theme of his avarice, his covetousness—almost the only thing that could be urged against the Duke—and the interesting thing is that Swift was fairly avaricious, pretty covetous himself. Then, too, Swift wanted power more than anything: all his life, though conscious of his own capacity, he had been frustrated. Marlborough had reached the summit of power, and was still not done for: he was a living danger to the Ministry, a threat to the Peace.

The pamphlet and press campaign did its work: it undermined the Duke's credit with the people and prepared the way for measures against him in Parliament. One week the *Examiner* would come out with the observation that some subjects' palaces were more splendid than those of the Queen herself; another week that Marlborough had more ready money at his disposal than all the monarchs of Christendom.

Then Sarah took a hand. Nothing of all this daunted her: she was guns for any of them, spoiling for a fight. She employed her own scribes to attack the Ministry: the obvious result was to redouble the attacks on the Marlboroughs. It is possible that she enjoyed the fight, for all her life she managed to be in the thick of one row after another. In some ways she was a more masculine spirit than her husband, far more aggressive and altogether less sensitive. John had the more feminine qualities of sensitivity and intuition; his gift as a soldier was something apart, it was pure genius, unfailing and inspired. In the ordinary commerce of life he was a man of infinite accommodation, not at all aggressive.

To this heroic soldier all this was unbearably painful, and he wrote touchingly to Harley, now Earl of Oxford, to deliver him from it. He received an exceedingly disingenuous reply: 'I hope my sentiments are so fully known of that villainous way of libelling, I need say little to your Grace upon that subject.' The campaign continued.

Swift was not the worst of the vilipenders, and sometimes he had his doubts. Even St. John felt sorry for the Duke, he looked so worn out at this time with his lifetime of labours, his fatigues and misfortunes. He had denied that he was covetous or ambitious to the Queen; in vain: she said, according to St. John, that if she could have conveniently turned about, she would have laughed, and could hardly forbear to, in his face. St. John told Swift that 'the Queen and Lord Treasurer mortally hate the Duke of Marlborough and to that he owes his fall, more than to his other faults'. Swift began to question 'whether ever any wise state laid aside a general who had been successful nine years together, whom the enemy so much dread; and his own soldiers cannot but believe must always conquer; and you know that in war opinion is nine parts in ten'. He wondered how far his dismissal might not encourage the French to play tricks with us. For Louis, it had been an almighty deliverance: Marlborough in Paris might have given the *ancien régime* the necessary propulsion towards liberty and constitutional government. We know that he had it in his mind: who knows what the consequences might have been for France, in an orderly evolution making the Revolution unnecessary? There was no limit to Marlborough's profound ambition to leave an immortal name in history. The fact that the artist in him was defrauded of the proper end of his life's work, the March on Paris—which he could certainly have accomplished in 1712—is enough to account for his personal hatred of Harley. There was no one else in his whole life against whom Marlborough felt so deeply or so bitterly.

St. John told Swift that the Duke was saying he desired nothing so much as to find some way to soften Dr. Swift. (If Marlborough had had a bishopric to dispose of, he could have done it easily enough.) This was very flattering to Swift's vanity, his inflamed inferiority-complex, always on the alert. The Doctor commented sagely, 'I do not love to see personal resentment mix with public affairs.' Really, the obtuseness of the satirist with regard to himself—as if the whole of his work did not spring out of personal resentment!

In March 1713 Swift went to sit with Lady Clarges and found Marlborough's eldest daughter, now Lady Godolphin, playing whist. 'I sat by her and talked of her cards, etc. but she would not give one look, nor say a word to me. She refused some time ago to be acquainted with me. You know, she is Lord Marlborough's eldest daughter. [This, for the benefit of Stella.] She is a fool for her pains and I'll pull her down.' What a scene it presents!—these ladies, with the insolent parson persisting at the elbow of the one whose father and mother he had vilified: intellectuals often do not know how to behave, but there can be few scenes more unpleasant than this, with its horrid sentiment at the end.

The government found that the most effective way of damaging their opponents was to keep charges of financial peculation on the boil. Ground was made for an attack on Marlborough. He had received about £6000 a year from Sir Solomon Medina, the contractor for bread for the army; and a deduction of $2\frac{1}{2}$ per cent on the pay of all the foreign troops, which yielded large sums. These perquisites had been regularly permitted to constitute a secret service fund; and all who knew recognised that Marlborough's intelligence service throughout the war had been superlative: one clue to his unbroken success. Harley offered to let the Duke off any severe censure, if he ceased to oppose the government's resolutions on the subject. For once Marlborough refused point-blank; he was deeply wounded and indignant. He had made a large fortune, but it was honourably made out of his employments; he had not needed to resort to fraud: all his accounts were in order, he refused to besmirch himself to help his enemies, even though they held hostages of his—above all, his unfinished Blenheim.

The government resolution that the taking of an annual sum from the bread-contractor was 'unwarrantable and illegal' was passed in the Commons by 276 to 165. It was a pure party-vote. The Tory ministers proceeded to authorise the Duke of Ormonde, whom they had appointed to succeed Marlborough as Commander-in-Chief, to draw the same deduction upon the bread-contract and the same $2\frac{1}{2}$ per cent on the pay of the foreign troops for precisely the same purposes as Marlborough had used it. So much for the humbug of politics. Meanwhile Harley—now Earl of Oxford—accepted £10,000 from the Queen for his services.

Far more important than any of this were the Restraining Orders which the Tory government gave their new Commander-in-Chief, not to hazard any battle or engage in any siege. In the Netherlands the war, without him, went not so much badly as disgracefully. Villars knew that Ormonde was not allowed to fight. Some 12,000 British troops were withdrawn. Villars was able to win a victory at Denain, which, Napoleon said, saved France. Marlborough's captures, Douai and Bouchain, were lost. Louis XIV was saved from himself and France able to make peace on far better terms than was justified by the course of the war.

The peace terms presented to Parliament were a disappointment to many of the government's supporters. Marlborough, Godolphin and the Whig Junto registered their solemn protest at what they regarded as inadequate terms and a shameful desertion of the Allies. But the terms were accepted by large majorities in both Houses. The fact was that the nation wanted peace: the Queen, that woman of ordinary composition and abilities, proved a more correct interpeter of her people than those lords of very superior parts and the one man of genius. The courage and determination with which she had fought and at length defeated them were anything but ordinary.

On Blenheim Day the Duke gave a feast to his old companions and the Whig leaders at Holywell. The magnificent tent, in which so many historic decisions had been made on his campaigns, was pitched on the bowling-green, and all that summer crowds visited it. The attacks on him were redoubled. The aftermath of the war would be a dangerous period, for Marlborough's veterans were returning in no good mood, either at his treatment or theirs. The Duke offered a vulnerable target, if quite unjustly. After the resolution in the Commons he might at any moment be sued for the repayment of all the money he had spent on his intelligence-service. Work at Blenheim was stopped; a suit to make him repay at least £30,000 was threatened. The government wanted him out of the way, and Marlborough was glad to go.

This summer of 1712 Godolphin was at Holywell, nursed by Sarah in his last illness. On his death-bed he recommended the young Walpole to her care as a future leader; it will be seen how she carried out his wishes. Godolphin's death removed Marlborough's last objection to going abroad. He transferred £50,000 to The Hague for all eventualities, and on 1 December embarked with a small retinue; Sarah was to follow. The Queen approved of his going into exile: 'the Duke of Marlborough has done wisely to go abroad'.

At once the alarm was set going in England. Swift: 'Here is the Duke of Marlborough going out of England (Lord knows why), which causes many speculations. Some say he is conscious of guilt and dare not stand it. Others think he has a mind to fling an odium on the government, as who should say that one who has done such great services to his country cannot live quietly in it by reason of the malice of his enemies.' What was he up to now? His enemies found that he was up to a great deal in the twenty months before the Queen's death and his return.

In the Netherlands, where he might have ruled, he was received with almost sovereign honours. He was anxious not to give the Queen cause for complaint, so he travelled quietly by by-ways, across the scenes so familiar to him, to Maastricht and Aix-la-Chapelle. He asked that his old comrade-in-arms, Cadogan, might be released from duty to travel with him. The Queen gave Cadogan permission, and shortly after dismissed him from all his appointments. In the New Year Sarah went to join the Duke.

It does not seem that Sarah had ever been abroad before, and in her letters home a new character appears, which helps one to understand something of the charm that must have existed underneath so much that was intolerable. The school-girl stands before us, very innocent and much surprised at what she saw; sometimes shocked, excited by the newness of it all, corroborated in her insular prejudices; a very English figure, patriotic among all those foreigners, in the end longing for home. Here she is at Maastricht, writing with all the authority of a few weeks abroad, to home-keeping Mr. Jennings, yet another relation. 'All the places one passes through in these parts have an air very different from London. The most considerable people I have seen have but just enough to live, and the ordinary people, I believe, are half starved. But they are all so good and so civil that I could not help wishing (if it were possible to separate the honest from the guilty) that they had the riches and the liberties that our wise citizens and countrymen have thrown away, or at best put in great danger, and that *they* were punished as they deserve to be by an arbitrary prince and war, as these poor people have been for fifty years. . . . The honours they have done me in all places upon the Duke of Marlborough's account is not to be imagined, which is not disagreeable now, because as it cannot proceed from power, it shows he made a right use of it when he was General.'

It was not long before Sarah's strong Protestant common sense was affronted by what she saw 'in visiting nunneries and churches, where I have heard of such marvels and seen such ridiculous things as would appear to you incredible if I should set about to describe them'. At Frankfort, Sarah watched Eugene's troops pass by from a window. 'They paid all the respects as they went by to the Duke of Marlborough, as if he had been in his old post. . . . To see so many brave men marching was a very fine sight, but it gave me melancholy reflections and made me weep. But at the same time I was so much animated that I wished I had been a man that I might have ventured my life a thousand times in the glorious cause of liberty.'

Soon Sarah's thoughts were turning homewards: she could not believe that she would be content to live the rest of her life in 'these dirty countries . . . I think 'tis much better to be dead than to live out of England'. Her mind rattles on and on: 'I will own to you that I am not so much to be pitied as some people, having never seen any condition yet that was near so happy as 'twas thought. When I was a great favourite, I was railed at and flattered from morning to night, neither of which was agreeable to me; and where there were but few women that would not have poisoned me for the happiness they thought I enjoyed, I kept the worst company of anybody upon earth. . . .' Still, she reflected, thinking of home, 'we are like a sort of banished people in a strange country'.

We may be sure that the Duke was a good deal more contented: he had spent so much of his life abroad, one way or another, that he was used to it. Besides, after a lifetime of exertions and fatigues he was enjoying a rest, not even putting pen to paper. He had plenty to turn over in his mind. 'I wish he would write himself sometimes because his hand would not trouble you so much to read; but he is intolerable lazy, and has not writ once to any of his daughters since he left England.' Early in 1714 came the news of the death of one of these daughters, Lady Bridgwater—a favourite with her father, for she was gentle and turned after him. Not a word passed those reserved lips, though, it is said, when the news came he leaned against the marble chimneypiece, losing consciousness for a moment.

All the time, at the back of her mind, Sarah was wondering what would happen when the Queen died: 'for let the sorcerers give out what they will of Mrs. Morley's good health, it is next to impossible that one with such a complication of diseases can last long'. Would the villains at home bring in the Pretender? Sarah's mind ran much upon this theme as the year 1714 advanced. She was inclined to think they would bring in the Prince of Wales—as she often referred to him. If so, she agreed with Mr. Steele, 'Farewell Liberty, all Europe will soon be French.' It is fairly clear that on these matters the Duke kept his own counsel.

At home things were going badly with the Tory government. They had held together well enough to put through the Peace of Utrecht; and we must admit that, though the manner of doing it was ill, they provided very well for the interests of the country. Once the Peace was out of the way the Government had to confront a still more dangerous issue—that of the succession to the throne. The Queen's health was visibly worsening: she was seriously ill in 1713 and again early in 1714. She detested the Hanover family, and they were unknown in England. She wanted her brother—no more nonsense about the warming-pan now—to succeed her. Both Harley and Bolingbroke, the Tory leaders, would have preferred James's son, if he were prepared to become a Protestant. He was not—and for this it is customary to commend him. I do not see why: it only shows him to have been as much of a fool as his father. His refusal left the Queen and the government with no policy but to drift with events.

The difficulties of the political situation were exacerbated by the overwhelming Tory majority in the Commons, with its powerful wing of extreme Tories, who were the foundation of Bolingbroke's strength and to whom he appealed. Harley—Earl of Oxford and Lord Treasurer—was a moderate; the Queen was no more inclined to be the cat's-paw of a Tory government than she had been of a Whig one. No one knows the trouble that Harley had with her; he in turn could now appreciate the difficulties Godolphin had had to contend with. Nor was the Queen unaware of the failings of her beloved Abigail, as we can descry from a little note to Harley: 'my Lady Masham told me she heard one of the chaises that are come out of France was intended to be given to her. Do not take any notice of it to her but find out if it be so and endeavour to prevent it; for I think it would not be right.' When the pamphleteers had not hesitated to charge Sarah with fraud in her accounts as Keeper of the Privy Purse, the Queen herself had given them the answer: 'Everybody knows, cheating is not the Duchess of Marlborough's crime.' We cannot say as much for Abigail. She was in league with Bolingbroke to get money out of the Asiento contract, for trade with Spanish South America, provided for by the Treaty of Utrecht. Bolingbroke had made a good £3000 out of the grants of passports to France upon the Peace, besides abstracting sums from secret service funds to pay off his mortgages. Tory finance was by no means incorruptible, as Godolphin's had been—but then they had been kept away from the trough a long time.

Harley's veto on Abigail's sharing in the Asiento contract earned him her hostility: she went over to Bolingbroke. The last months of the reign were riven by the factions within the government. All the while there was the prospect of ruin opening before them, if the Queen died and no steps had been taken to make themselves secure: the House of Hanover would come in and the Whigs would be in for good. The Lord Treasurer himself said to Swift, 'Whenever anything ails the Queen, these people are out of their wits; and yet they are so thoughtless that, as soon as she is well, they act as if she were immortal'. The Tory ministry was ruining itself by its intestine quarrels, which made any policy impossible; the party would go down into the night.

What was Marlborough up to abroad? What were the steps he was engaged on—of which Sarah was plainly kept in ignorance?

Like the strategist he was, he first made sure of his rear. The communications with St.-Germain that had never been completely dropped were taken up again through his nephew Berwick. Dividends might always accrue from courtesy, politeness, assurances. His wealth, estates, Blenheim itself, were at the mercy of the government at home: could not St.-Germain influence the French government to moderate the hostility of the ministry to him? Perhaps his nephew Berwick could obtain a pardon for him in the event of James III's restoration? Berwick was not deceived by these protestations; but neither was he so impolite as to allow it to appear that he was not deceived. He passed them on, without enthusiasm but with no reluctance.

These intelligences did not disturb the confidence of Hanover in the Duke: all his real preparations were made on that front. He gave his advice that on the Queen's death George of Hanover should at once go over to England; in the same contingency he and Cadogan were given authority in the name of the King to take command of all the troops. Marlborough and his commanders, colleagues of the war, drew together, made their preparations. In England all depended on a dying woman. Marlborough moved slowly towards England with the cool deliberation with which he had moved on objectives in the field. He sent a message in mid-June to Hanover: 'my best friends think my being in England may be of much more use to the service than my continuing abroad, *upon which I design to return as soon as the Parliament is up*'.

That last week of July took place the last struggle around the Queen. Harley had really given up hope and wanted to resign: he knew the chasm that was opening under their feet for the Tory party with the accession of the House of Hanover. It was far too late for them ever to put themselves right. Bolingbroke was trying all in all to oust the Treasurer and take his place. The time came when Abigail refused to carry any more messages for the latter to the Queen—she had carried so many in the years before—and when she said to her 'cousin': 'You never did the Queen any service, nor are you capable of doing her any'. The time came when the Queen dismissed him, as she had done Godolphin; but telling all the Lords with contumely her reasons: that he neglected all business, that he was seldom to be understood, that she could not depend on the truth of what he said, that he never came to her at the time she appointed, that he often came drunk, that he behaved himself towards her with ill manner, indecency and disrespect.

The Lord Treasurer was out, but could the Queen put the staff into the hands of a man whom, however brilliant, she knew to be a debauchee, a dissolute adventurer? Her sense of duty forbade. On

27 July 1714 the struggle raged for hours in the Cabinet Council in the presence of the Queen, determined to abide it to the last. Before the end she was mortally stricken and had to be carried from the room.

It was all too late, as Swift had seen all along it would be. 'At the time I am writing, the breath is said to be in the Queen's nostrils; but that is all. No hope left of her recovery. Lord Oxford is in Council; so are the Whigs.' The whole Council was in constant session. In her last moments the Queen's hand was guided into giving the staff into the hands of Shrewsbury, Marlborough's friend of many years, one of the grandees at the Revolution, one of those men of the centre who really rule England.

Marlborough was on his way home and would have been present at that last scene if contrary winds had not detained him. There were rumours before the Queen died that he was to take over the government. The day after her death he landed at Dover. His home-coming was a triumphal progress such as he had never had in the days of his victories. At Rochester 3 August, 'today, about 12 o'clock, the Duke and Duchess of Marlborough passed through this city; they were received with great expressions of joy from the people, especially those at Chatham, who strewed their way with flowers, as they adorned their houses with green boughs, and welcomed them with repeated shouts and acclamations'. Everywhere they passed they were given an official reception. On entering the City they were received and escorted by the civic authorities, a train of coaches and a troop of militia with drums and trumpets. This welcome was not much appreciated by the Tories; but the future was not with them. At this moment of uncertainty when people could not see their way, with a spontaneous movement they turned instinctively to the Duke for confidence as never before.

When the King landed later that summer, Marlborough was first to receive him: 'My lord Duke,' George I said graciously, 'I hope your troubles are now all over.' Marlborough was at once restored to his offices—Captain-General, Master-General of the Ordnance, Colonel of the 1st Guards—by the first warrant the King signed. As before in 1702 when Anne came to the throne, as in 1689 when William became king, Marlborough was there at the right hand of a new monarch, in this case a new dynasty.

CHAPTER SIXTEEN

Blenheim Palace

DURING all these years of struggle and victory, set-backs and disappointments, exile and return, the great house that was the nation's monument to an unexampled English victory in the heart of Europe was taking shape—and with a similar rhythm. It too had its prodigious beginnings, its gathering difficulties, criticism and spreading disparagement, a crisis when all the work was stopped; then continued slowly upon political contingencies; at last finished quietly under changed auspices, a new reign. In all this Blenheim Palace offers an eloquent parallel to, almost a physical expression of, Marlborough's career.

Never was a house carried on with such difficulties, under such cumulative vexation and trouble, carrying into stone the hazards, the ups and downs, of politics. But rarely has there been such an undertaking. It is the English parallel to Versailles—intended as such by Marlborough, that reserved, inexpressive man who thus expressed both his profound ambition and his sense of art. At last it stood forth, the grandest, the most splendid conception of a house in this island, to celebrate the grandest victory, the splendour of his feats of arms.

Blenheim has hardly ever been understood, or properly appreciated for what it was intended to be. It was not much liked in its own time: too vast, too grandiose, that 'wild unmerciful house' Sarah called it, who could not bear it. Shortly after, when Palladian standards ruled, it was disapproved of: too rhetorical and declamatory, too dramatic and unrestrained. The Victorian age detested such an immense, classic pile. Perhaps in this age we are beginning to descry its true meaning at last. In the first place, it is a national monument, a building of state, and always has been intended as such; only secondarily is it a house, intended for the posterity of John, Duke of Marlborough, victor of Blenheim. The private apartments in the east wing, the Duke's Grand Cabinet, his study, and so forth are on a reasonable, modest scale—like Philip II's at the Escorial.

Then there is all the drama of the site and the composition, the complex changing masses, the rhetoric of the roofscape, the astonishing grandeur of the lay-out. As one enters Sarah's triumphal arch—an expression of her love for the Duke—and one looks across the crescent of lake with its monumental bridge, to see the skyline dominated by the Palace with spreading wings reaching out towards the bridge, one reflects that not for nothing was Vanbrugh a dramatist: there is the scene set in stone. If St. Paul's Cathedral is the *Paradise Lost* of our architecture, Blenheim Palace is one of Dryden's heroic poems or heroic plays.

Imagine the private citizen, however, the subject of Queen Anne, who meant to rival Louis XIV! Only as one stands in the middle of the grand saloon and grasps that one is on the centre of an axis extending a couple of miles or more—from Bladon's classical church tower, where the later Churchills are buried, through the house and portico across the bridge, to Marlborough standing on his Victory Column and the avenue beyond—that one realises the heroic grandeur of the conception and that one is in touch with the spirit of John, Duke of Marlborough, who conceived it.

The response of the ordinary uncritical person has always been one of incomprehension and of a certain dumbfounded awe. And that is right in a way, since no one has understood the spirit of Marlborough: not even Sarah, though she accepted his incomprehensible genius, and what she did for this house—she recognised it as 'his passion' and thought it his greatest weakness—is the ultimate evidence of her submission.

Perhaps least of all has the rational critic understood it, as we see from Pope's clever epigram:

See, sir, here's the grand approach;
This way is for his Grace's coach:
There lies the bridge, and here's the clock,
Observe the lion and the cock,
The spacious court, the colonnade,
And mark how wide the hall is made!
The chimneys are so well designed,
They never smoke in any wind.
This gallery's contrived for walking,
The windows to retire and talk in;
The council chamber for debate,
And all the rest are rooms of state.
Thanks, sir, cried I, 'tis very fine,
But where d'ye sleep, or where d'ye dine?
I find, by all you have been telling,
That 'tis a house, but not a dwelling.

Of course Pope was being deliberately obtuse for the sake of the joke; but his poem does represent what people said at the time. Moreover, Pope's genius was non-dramatic: he was out of sympathy with the drama of the house, which for the rest was on too big a scale for him.

On successive visits to Louis XIV, on missions for Charles II and James II, Marlborough was able to see Versailles rising upon its ungrateful site. Blenheim Palace was his Versailles, rival to the great monarch he at length defeated. About this Marlborough never said a word. We have already seen what an impersonal sort of man he was, and he seems to have held to a distinction between himself as an individual person and his achievements which were public property, for the country and for posterity. It is the tradition of his family that has best preserved the sense of this, and that thus offers us the truest guide to the understanding of the man. Sir Winston Churchill says justly, 'about his achievements Marlborough preserved a complete silence, offering neither explanations nor excuses for any of his deeds. His answer was to be this great house.'

No one knows why Sir Christopher Wren was not chosen to build Blenheim, or why it should have been Vanbrugh. It must have been Marlborough's own choice. There is an historic propriety that it should have been an artist of Dutch extraction and French training who was chosen. Wren, one would have said, was obviously much closer to Marlborough's personality: the classic form, the calm courtesy, the romanticism underneath, the subtlety, the elegance and coolness. But that was not all that Marlborough wanted: he wanted the clash of battle, the drama and bravura of magnificence, military glory in stone. Vanbrugh too had been a soldier. There was an instinctive understanding between them—even apart from Vanbrugh's deep admiration, a real hero-worship, for the Duke. They would have been friends for life if it had not been for that *femme fatale*, the Duchess. Never a cross word passed between the two men, in all the campaigns, lasting longer than Marlborough's in the field, before the Palace was finished; while the quarrels that raged between Sarah and Vanbrugh created a complex on both sides. In the architect's correspondence with the Duke we note a tone of entire confidence, the assumption of mutual understanding; the Duke never criticises or crabs, or suggests cutting down the design—his only suggestions are for more. In Vanbrugh's letters to Sarah he is constantly on the defensive, having to explain himself, observe caution or he will be taken up; the boisterous dramatist becomes a

Winston Churchill, The Cavalier Colonel, by Sir Peter
y (*Permission of the Duke of Marlborough*)

John and Arabella Churchill as children, by Sir Peter Lely (*Permission of the Duke of Marlborough*)

Sarah, Duchess of Marlborough, with her Gold Key of Office (*Courtesy National Portrait Gallery, London*)

John, Duke of Marlborough (*Permission of Lord Spencer*)

King William III, by Godfrey Schalcken (*Permission of the Duke of Marlborough*)

Louis XIV, by Rigaud (*Courtesy the Louvre*)

King James II, by Sir Godfrey Kneller (*Courtesy National Portrait Gallery, London*)

Bust of King Charles II, by Honoré Pelle (*Courtesy The Victoria and Albert Museum, London*)

Sidney, Earl of Godolphin, after Kneller (*Courtesy National Portrait Gallery, London*)

Admiral George Churchill, by Sir Godfrey Kneller (*Courtesy National Maritime Museum, Greenwich*)

Francis, 2nd Earl of Godolphin and Lady Henrietta Churchill (*Courtesy of National Museum, Stockholm*)

James, Duke of York, with his first wife and the Princesses Mary and Anne, by Sir Peter Lely (*Gracious permission of H.M. the Queen*)

Charles, 3rd Duke of Marlborough, attributed to Charles Phillips (*Permission of Lord Spencer*)

Elizabeth, 3rd Duchess of Marlborough, by Van Loo (*Permission of Lord Spencer*)

George, 4th Duke of Marlborough and his family, by Sir Joshua Reynolds (*Copyright Country Life*)

John, 7th Duke of Marlborough (*Illustrated London News*)

Leonard W. Jerome (*Culver Service*)

Lord Randolph Churchill

Lady Randolph Churchill

Charles and Consuelo, 9th Duke and Duchess of Marlborough, with their sons, John, Marquess of Blandford, and Lord Ivor Spencer Churchill, by John Singer Sargent (*Copyright Country Life*)

Blenheim Palace, Seat of the Dukes of Marlborough

Lower Terrace at Blenheim (*Combine Photos*)

The room where Winston Churchill was born

Mr. Churchill with Lloyd George in 1910 (*Reuter Photos Ltd.*)

Winston Churchill with his mother in 1911 (*European*)

The Prime Minister arriving in the U.S. with Mrs. Churchill during the war (*European*)

Mr. Churchill in the bombed House of Commons, 1941 (*Kemsley Picture*)

Winston Churchill at work during a train journey (*Imperial War Museum*)

cat on hot bricks. Never can an artist have had such an experience as he had with Sarah.

When Queen Anne gave Marlborough after Blenheim the royal manor of Woodstock with the forest and its appurtenances, the place was in considerable disrepair. Much of the castle had been a ruin since the Civil War, only a few of its rooms were at all habitable. The forest was rough, scraggy ground, with magnificent oaks and a deer-park; the course of the little river Glyme was very marshy; the manor-house looked down on a picturesque swamp. All the same, it was a princely gift, with some two thousand acres, and what a scene to challenge the imagination, the will-power and art, of John, Duke of Marlborough and John Vanbrugh!

Vanbrugh produced his design in the spring of 1705, and it was an inspired site that he selected. Not that of the original manor-house, where the space was confined by the steep slopes of the hill, but across the ravine from there: a vast expanse of level ground looking to the south, while on the west there was the sharp fall-away to the valley giving magnificent prospects to all this side of the house. Vanbrugh already had the experience of designing Castle Howard to go on—a sight of the design may have decided Marlborough that this was the architect he wanted. And now Vanbrugh was in a position to improve upon even that superb and lovely house. Blenheim, as it emerged, has a higher degree of integration in its composition, with the raising of the central mass to dominate the whole and with the powerful corner pavilions to reinforce it. So imposing a centre-piece can easily ride the spreading wings, joined by the segmental colonnades that remember Bernini's colonnade at St. Peter's. Where Castle Howard has the dispersed grace of a feminine composition, Blenheim—it was originally thought of as the Castle of Blenheim—has a more masculine strength and concentration. There is something Michelangelesque about it.

Both Godolphin and Sarah wanted a more modest scheme. Not so the Duke: it was no objection to his frugal mind that the nation was paying for it; the house was planned to cover, with its courts, seven acres. The boy from the roofless house at Ashe had travelled a long way: it was no wonder his enemies said that he was as covetous as Hell and as ambitious as the Prince thereof! It is indeed a Lucifer of a house: pride and ambition are its keystones. Vanbrugh at once hurried on the foundations for the whole thing; and all through we see his determination as an artist to carry up the building as a whole, without finishing any part of it, for fear that the Duchess might intervene once the living part were finished and countermand the rest. This motive of Vanbrugh's has not been realised by any of the writers on Blenheim; and yet it might easily have happened, had the Duke been killed or died. Vanbrugh knew that the Duchess was well capable of it: she grew to hate the thing and thought it all madness.

A more serious threat to the completion of Blenheim, and what gave rise to difficulties of all kinds and to complicated legal proceedings, was a certain ambivalence in the initial financial arrangements. The house was the nation's gift to the Duke and to be built at its expense. Marlborough accepted no financial responsibility for it and was careful to interfere in no part of the financial arrangements. Godolphin, however, issued a warrant to Vanbrugh to make agreements with the contractors, who had no direct dealings with the Crown: their money was issued from the Treasury as to the Duke. This provision was probably intended by Godolphin to protect the Crown from spoliation and keep rates down; but it had the effect of making either the Duke or Vanbrugh liable, when work outran the Treasury payments and large liabilities were incurred. In the end the Duke had to meet a portion of this—contrary to the original intention, contrary to his wishes—and this was the result not so much of the size of the building, for the sums paid out were vast, but of the intolerable delays in its completion. To the Duchess, with whom patience was not a strong point, it was all maddening.

That very summer of 1705 Marlborough was bidding Sarah: 'Pray press on my house and gardens; for I think I shall never stir from my own home, being very sensible that it is impossible to serve with any satisfaction, where it is in so many people's power to do mischief.' Sarah sent on a draught of house and gardens, which fell into the hands of the French, who politely forwarded it unopened. Vanbrugh promised that the gardens should be formed and planted in a year from their beginning; to form the grand parterre alone some 17,000 yards of earth had to be removed, and good earth and dung dug in. Plants, fruit-trees and trees were bought and planted on an equally colossal scale: scores of junipers, laurels, cedars, apricots, quinces; hundreds of peaches, pears, vines, apples, wych-elms, sycamores, limes; flowering shrubs, espalier limes, hedge hollies, hornbeams and sweet briar in thousands. Flowers were brought in scores of thousands: irises, hyacinths, narcissi, Dutch yellow crocuses, tulips, jonquils. Henry Wise was the gardener who planned and planted it all, and he made a splendid job of it.

It is touching to find Marlborough writing, immediately after Ramillies, 'I am so persuaded that this campaign will bring us a good peace, that I beg of you to do all you can that the house at Woodstock may be carried up as much as possible, that I may have a prospect of living in it.' Thus propelled, Sarah went down for a few days, finding fault as she went. Difficulties were already accumulating, but Marlborough would not have Godolphin worried about them: 'though Woodstock is extremely at my heart . . . upon my word, I had rather never be in the house than put any difficulty upon him.'

Hawksmoor, an artist hardly less original than Vanbrugh, was now collaborating happily with the latter; and Hawksmoor made important contributions to the design of the interior, the conception of the rooms and details in them, cornices, chimney-pieces, door-cases. As the great house gathered wing, it is most impressive to watch the concentration of talent and craftsmanship upon it: a forum for the best craftsmen of the time. The St. Paul's men were here, headed by their redoubtable contractor, Strong. Much of the carved stonework was done by Grinling Gibbons; above his princely door-cases rose the frescoes of Laguerre, the painted ceilings of Thornhill. The clocks and sundials were by Langley Bradley and John Rowley, the plaster work by Weatherill and Isaac Mansfield. Nearly all of them had had their apprenticeship at St. Paul's. Wren himself was called in to advise about the approach, though his characteristic suggestion of compromise was rejected and Vanbrugh's uncompromising bridge across the ravine prevailed. When it came to completing the statuary of the house, Rysbrack was recruited. Indeed, it was a national monument. It would take all Marlborough's fortune to carry it on safely to posterity.

This year took place one of the major interruptions in the building of the house, owing to Vanbrugh's drastic alteration of scale and consequent replanning of the façades and towers at the corner-pavilions. For this he must have had the Duke's approbation; though there is nothing to show that the Queen was informed of what the alterations amounted to: she had taken much interest in the original model which was deposited in the Gallery at Kensington for her to study. Now, though Vanbrugh said nothing about it, it was departed from drastically: nothing less than raising the main block by perhaps a third in height and changing the whole order from Doric to Corinthian. It would have the effect of making the house less austere and forbidding, more of a triumph and a festival: turning it from a Castle into a Palace. It necessitated pulling down yards of existing building and altering the level of the windows already built in the south front. At the same time stone was more difficult to get and payments were coming in more slowly from the Treasury.

That autumn Vanbrugh found the Duke 'out of patience about it; for this morning, telling him I feared it would be three weeks yet before the scaffolds could be struck about the great tower, he was quite peevish upon it, being resolved to go down by that time'. A month elapsed before his visit: Vanbrugh ordered 'the clearing of every place about the building that can be, both within and without, to show it to the best advantage; for my Lord Duke comes down full of expectation'. In April, before setting out on campaign, the Duke went down again to gaze upon his darling house. From camp he wrote to Sarah, 'You say nothing of going to Blenheim, but the weather is so fine I could wish you there, by which the finishing within doors, I believe, would go on the faster. If it were possible, I would flatter myself that I might be so happy to see it the next summer.'

And what, meanwhile, was Vanbrugh doing? Pushing forward the building of the bridge: it was not possible to inhabit that (could he really intend to make a habitable house of it?); repairing and doing up the ruined manor as a very nice residence for himself. When Sarah came down, he rigged up a temporary ceiling to her bedroom and a temporary door, to give her the impression that things were farther advanced than they were; but she was not taken in. She was furious about the work going on at the manor: had she not told him again and again that making the main body of the house habitable for the Duke was what mattered? It was all very well for Vanbrugh to plead that he haunted the building like a ghost, from six o'clock when the workmen left off till it was dark—that was literature; his claim that he was studying 'to make this the cheapest as well as (if possible) the best house in Europe, *which I think my lord Duke's services highly deserve*' was a pretence and an insult to the meanest intelligence. (The Duchess never thought meanly of her intelligence.)

In 1709 a new distraction came to complicate the family building operations. For some time Sarah had been desirous of a town-house, and while Godolphin was still in power she obtained a Crown lease of the land next door to St. James's Palace, to build Marlborough House. She would show the Duke and Vanbrugh how to do it. The first condition was that Vanbrugh should have nothing whatever to do with *her* house. She went to Sir Christopher, who would have been her choice for Blenheim. She laid down two conditions: that the contracts should be reasonable and not as Crown work, that the house was to be 'strong, plain and convenient . . . and not have the least resemblance of anything in that called Blenheim, which I had never liked but could not prevail against Sir John'. The agreeable Sir Christopher obliged with a very sober design, the only nonsense being four statues in niches on the front and decorative figures along the roof. The Duchess was convinced that *her* building operations would proceed without trouble.

Notwithstanding her dislike for Blenheim, Sarah saw no objection to drawing on the craftsmen there for her own operations: the Strongs, the Bankses, the Hopsons, Henry Wise were all mobilised. The Duke was unhappy about it: 'I am so desirous of living at Woodstock that I should not much care to do anything but what is necessary anywhere else. . . . But I would have you follow your own inclination in it. You know I never liked to built it at all. And I am confident you will find 'twill cost you much more money than the thing is worth. You may build a better apartment than you have now, but you will never have as many conveniences as in your lodgings. And you may depend on it, 'twill cost you double the money they have estimated.'

Having said his say, the Duke gave way to her, as he usually did, and made arrangements to advance the money. He never grudged money for this kind of thing; and shortly he was asking for the measurements of the rooms to have tapestry woven for them. Sarah was able to assure him that *her* house met with general applause. The Duke was glad, since it gave her pleasure, and 'for the same reason be not uneasy that it costs more money than you thought it would, for upon my word, I shall think nothing too much for the making you easy.' Of course it did cost too much. Instead of the Blenheim way of going on, Sarah agreed upon a sum, £30,000, which—woman of her word, as she was—she paid over before the house was finished. But, in spite of her efforts and her tantrums, it cost nearer £50,000. Was Sir Christopher no better than Sir John? To admit as much offended her pride: the poor old man—Wren was seventy-eight—must have been imposed upon. Sir Christopher was sacked. Sarah took the finishing of the house upon herself, and was persuaded that it was done to everybody's satisfaction. At any rate it was ready for her occupation by 1711, when she herself was sacked and had to remove from St. James's: so perhaps, as usual, she could consider herself to have been right. Even if it had cost £50,000: 'almost incredible, but not really as extravagant as it appears, because it is the strongest and best house that ever was built'. She had built it herself. The horrid Sir John observed maliciously that Wren had paid higher prices than would have been paid at Blenheim: ' 'tis true she would have gone to law with them, but the Duke would not let her'. But then, she consoled herself with the thought, *all* architects were mad.

While the roof was not yet on at Blenheim, Vanbrugh was planning a further grand addition: a superb Orangery on the western side, 'having a very beautiful situation (the west end of it coming to the very brow of the hill and so looking directly down the valley and the river) may perhaps be thought proper for a distinct retired room of pleasure, furnished with only some of the best greens, mixed with pictures, busts, statues, books and other things of ornament and entertainment. These kind of detached buildings have ever been extremely valued, where there has happened anything particularly fine for their situation, and I believe there is not in Europe a finer than this.' Sarah killed it: 'the second greenhouse, or a detached gallery, I thank God I prevented being built; nothing, I think, can be more mad than the proposal, nor a falser description of the prospect'. No doubt it was too much; but we have lost thereby what might have been one of the noblest rooms in Europe.

Though his roof was still not on, the Duke had long been collecting furnishings, fabrics, treasures from all over Europe for his Palace. A very fine set of hangings at Antwerp had been bespoken for William III. They were offered to Marlborough for £1800, worth much more. Should he buy them? He was 'so fond of some pictures I shall bring with me, that I could wish you had a place for them till the Gallery at Woodstock be finished'. Vandyck's famous equestrian portrait of Charles I was among these: it had been given by the Elector of Bavaria to the Emperor. Marlborough took as much interest in the furnishing of the house as Sarah did. 'I have been to see the hangings for your apartment and mine; as much as are done of them I think are very fine . . . I should be glad, at your leisure, you would be providing everything that may be necessary for furnishing these two apartments, and that you would direct Vanbrugh to finish the breaks between the windows, in the great cabinet, with looking glass; for I am resolved to furnish the room with the finest pictures I can get.' Splendid tapestries, depicting scenes from his battles, were being woven at Brussels; marble from Alicante, silks from Genoa, pictures, busts, statuary, gems. The Duke spared no expense for the temple of his glory, did not even complain. Two suites of hangings made at Brussels cost £800. William III just before his death had been negotiating for four fine statues from a palace at Florence; Marlborough ordered their purchase for the niches designed for the Grand Saloon. Unfortunately he was disappointed and the scheme never took effect. He was in treaty for brass figures to be cast at Florence, which cost £1000, and the Spanish ambassador in Rome presented him with a full-scale model of a Bernini fountain in the Piazza Navona. At the siege of Tournai chance offered him an immense marble bust of Louis XIV over the gateway: the very thing, to set his great opponent's head on the roof of his house. There it stands, with its reference to Versailles, high above the garden-front, looking out across what was once the hunting grounds of medieval English kings, now subjugated to Augustan order, where everything remembers Marlborough.

By the end of 1709, when the position of the Marlboroughs was thoroughly undermined, the Palace was getting on fast. Vanbrugh assured the Duchess that the whole house would be covered that year and the bridge finished; the chapel should be left alone. He too had his troubles: Banks's men were cutting up the best big Portland blocks for paving when smaller stuff would do. Pebbles to pitch ten thousand yards would be necessary. That winter, his mind full of disquiet, the Duke came down to gaze upon his house. Would it ever be finished? Would he ever live in it? His hold was running out: it was becoming a race between the finishing of the house and the retention of his position at the head of the Allied armies. He was still ordering materials: hundreds of yards of stuff from Dutch looms, velvets, designs for his coat of arms for the hangings. The canopy of state which he had ordered for the peace negotiations was to be made in such a way that it could be used for a bed at Blenheim. Alas, there was no peace.

Next year came the thunder-clap of the change of government, of which there had been premonitory rumblings, disturbing the workmen at Blenheim and causing alarm among the tradesmen of Oxford. The debts on the building were very large and the new Tory government had reason to question the position. By 1710 £134,000 had been spent and the house was still not half completed. The Treasury stopped payments, which were already far in arrears. This was a critical moment for the house and for the Marlboroughs. If they admitted the slightest financial responsibility, they might be charged with the debts and the arrears, and still have to complete the building themselves: that would make a heavy inroad into even their fortune.

There were scenes at Woodstock, since there was no money to pay the men and they were in want. A mob assembled—somebody advanced a few hundreds to pacify them: not the Marlboroughs. This was to be a monument of the nation's gratitude: it looked like turning into a monument of ingratitude, said Van. The government sought to inveigle the Duke into taking steps that would involve him in financial responsibility. Sarah was furious and disposed to intervene. The Duke was wiser: 'it is not our best way to give any orders, but to let the Treasury give what orders they please, either for its going on or standing still'. Sarah sent down an order stopping all the work on the building till the Treasury should direct money for it. The Duke was alarmed: 'it no way becomes you or me to be giving orders for the Queen's money. You know my opinion, that neither you, nor I, nor any of our friends ought to meddle in their accounts, but to let it be taken by the Queen's officers, as they always ought to be. She is the mistress of her own money, and consequently of the time of finishing that house.' As for Vanbrugh, on the Duchess' stopping the work: 'I think she has given orders she'll repent of, but be it as she thinks fit. If she orders the house to be pulled down, I desire you'll comply with her.' Godolphin went down to view the distasteful scene: 'Let them keep their heap of stones!' he said. Tempers were rising all round the tempestuous building.

The Queen did not wish it to go to ruin and let the nation's money be thus wasted. Harley asked how much it would cost to cover it in and protect it from damage until a resolution was taken. Vanbrugh replied £8000. Harley allowed £7000—the implied condition being that Marlborough would not lay down his employments and thus weaken the government's hand in making peace. Luckily the building suffered no injury during the stoppage; and next year a further £20,000 was allowed by the Treasury, with the same implied condition that the Duke would not withdraw from his post. This enabled the work to be pushed forward so far that henceforth, though it was still unfinished when the Marlboroughs went into exile, it might be regarded as safe.

While they were away the building went slowly on, in Vanbrugh's fashion, not Sarah's: that is to say, not finishing the main pile, but on everything else. She was incensed to hear that the new money was to go on the kitchen-court, two grand 'Acroterias' on the bridge and the formal walls that blocked the view from her windows to the east. The interiors of the private apartments were constantly being raised or lowered or altered: they were still not ready for furniture. Vanbrugh continued to live in the manor in great jollity, as he had done for years, and now made himself a closet in the middle, complained Sarah, 'as if he had been to study the planets'. Surely, she was not unreasonable in her view that 'painters, poets and builders have very high flights, but they must be kept down'. From his eyrie Vanbrugh took a hand in local politics in the Whig interest, much to the distaste of Tory Oxford. A letter of his to the mayor of Woodstock was betrayed to Harley, in which he referred to the 'continual plague and bitter persecution' with which the Duke had been most barbarously followed; and for this he lost his job as Commissioner of Works. Sarah made this up to him with £200 a year for his travelling expenses.

On George I's accession the Duke got Vanbrugh one of the first knighthoods of the reign. Marlborough was anxious to know how much fresh money would be necessary to finish the building, over and above the debts which were Crown liabilities; Vanbrugh replied, some £54,000 and, on the understanding that the Duke would meet that himself, the last stage of the works was undertaken. But the legal difficulties that flowed from the ambivalent conditions upon which the house was begun continued to dog all parties: Strong, the contractor, now began proceedings for the large debts owing him, not against the Crown, but against the Duke.

In 1716 the Duke had his first stroke and Sarah took complete charge. Now came the time of reckoning for that rascal, Sir John: she was free to quarrel with him to her heart's content: for years she had been storing up her complaints against him. In accordance with what had become a habit with her—for she was really a writer *manquée*—she drew up a thirty-page narrative of all her grievances. Vanbrugh's defence was that he had never done anything at Blenheim without the Duke's approbation. But the Duke was now in the hands of Sarah; without compunction she pushed Vanbrugh out of Blenheim and took over herself. In later years she said it was a 'terrible undertaking', which she would not have ventured on without encouragement; at the time she did not quail.

She was fighting on two fronts: there were the legal liabilities and complexities, which were almost inextricable; there was the house to be finished, decorated and furnished. She was the less successful in dealing with Sir John. Here she found herself up against a professional writer, who could give as good as he got. He described her narrative as 'so full of far-fetched, laboured accusations, mistaken facts, wrong inferences, groundless jealousies and strained constructions, that I should put a very great affront upon your understanding if I supposed it possible you could mean anything in earnest by them, but to put a stop to my troubling you any more. You have your end, madam, for I will never trouble you more, unless the Duke of Marlborough recovers so far to shelter me from such intolerable treatment.' Her treatment of him was intolerable, for she did not propose to pay him for his work: he had the prospect 'of losing (for I now see little hopes of ever getting it) near £6000 due to me for many years' service, plague and trouble at Blenheim, which that wicked woman of Marlborough is so far from paying me that the Duke, being sued by some of the workmen for work done there, she has tried to turn the debt due to them upon me, for which I think she should be hanged.' To all which the Duchess had the simple reply: he should have finished the house long ago.

Vanbrugh's complaint against her was true. She was not going to accept the liability for Strong's debts: they properly belonged to the Crown. In 1721 Vanbrugh reported joyously: 'my Lady Marlborough has been cast by the workmen—the cause held three days—she's outrageous at it, she accuses the judges, and says I have foresworn myself'. So he had: Vanbrugh had withheld testimony to the Crown's liability for the debts on Blenheim, partly because he did not want to do the Duchess a service, partly because he did not wish to risk his post as Commissioner of Works again. This failure to tell the truth was very shocking to Sarah: 'he has been more wicked to me than all the enemies that ever I had put together (which is saying a great deal)'. The case left her dangerously exposed, for a series of claims and lawsuits might now be expected from workmen whose debts were still unpaid. The Duchess immediately appealed, and also filed a suit 'against everybody that had been concerned in the building'—some four hundred persons from Vanbrugh downwards to workmen whose descendants are still living at Woodstock. It was like one of the Duke's own battlefields, out-size like everything to do with Blenheim.

When the smoke of action cleared away, and the Crown accepted proper liability, the Duchess and Vanbrugh were still found confronting each other. Libels and squibs circulated; she handed round papers against him; he invented lampoons upon her. In the end the Duchess was forced to pay him some £1700 he claimed as owing to him for his expenses; and everybody must be glad, for he had been shabbily treated. 'Being forced into Chancery by that B.B.B.B. Old B. the Duchess of Marlborough and her getting an injunction upon me by her friend the late good Chancellor, who declared I never was employed by the Duke of Marlborough and therefore had no demand upon his estate for my services at Blenheim, since my hands were tied up from trying by law to recover my arrears, I have prevailed with Sir Robert Walpole to help me in a scheme I proposed to him, by which I have got my money in spite of the hussy's teeth, and that out of a sum she expected to receive into her hands towards the discharge of the Blenheim debts, and of which she resolved I should never have a farthing. My carrying this point enrages her much, and the more because it is of considerable weight in my small fortune, which she has heartily endeavoured so to destroy, as to throw me into an English Bastille to finish my days, as I began them in a French one.'

These redoubtable combatants were not ill-matched; perhaps we may adjudge Sir John the victor, since, in addition to getting his money, Blenheim came through, in spite of everything, as he, not Sarah, meant it. The money became an article in her indictment against Walpole, her last long quarrel. It was provoking that, for all her money and her will-power, she could not get her way.

All the same we owe it to Sarah's will, perhaps, that Blenheim was finished and furnished at all. In 1715 she writes to her crony and man of business, Mr. Jennings: 'I am employed every morning at least four hours in cutting out, and ordering furniture for Woodstock. My next bed will be for the room you chose, where I hope to see you often, and dear Mrs. Jennings.' To her Sarah writes, 'I shall want a vast number of feather beds and quilts. I wish you would take this opportunity to know the prices of all such things as will be wanted in that wild unmerciful house. I would have some of the feather beds swansdown, all good and sweet feathers, even for the servants.' Ten years later, 'I shall go for ten days or a fortnight to Blenheim, where I shall almost fill the attic story with friends.'

Sarah exerted herself for the Duke's sake. In these quiet last years of his life, a shadow of his former self, nothing delighted him so much as to ride about the grounds, contemplating what he had called up out of the rough ancient forest of Woodstock: his child, his amusement, the temple of his glory. He loved the theatricals that Sarah—an unexpected rôle for her—arranged for him: acted by Mr. Jennings and the grandchildren, Anne and Di

Spencer and Anne Egerton. There was *Tamburlane* with a prologue written to celebrate the Duke's achievements, a tribute he did not decline. There was Dryden's *All for Love,* with its episcopal prologue, written by Bishop Hoadley, flattering the graces of the Duchess. Not all the speeches passed the test of that prim censor. Her own girlhood passed at the Court of Charles II, she was not going to have her granddaughters corrupted by its most splendid poet. 'The Duchess scratched out some of the most amorous speeches, and there was no embrace allowed, etc. In short, no offence to the company. I suppose we made a very grand appearance; there was profusion of brocade rolls etc., of what was to be the window curtains of Blenheim. Jewels you may believe in plenty; and I think Mark Antony wore the sword that the Emperor gave the Duke of Marlborough. The old Duke was so pleased that we played it three times . . . the third time at the Duke's request.'

After his death Sarah went on with the works. She erected the Victory Column in his memory, the inscription reciting his achievements from the pen of his old disciple and then antagonist, Bolingbroke. 'Times change, and things change, and men change.' To the Triumphal Arch she put up, with its enclosed forecourt—the design by Hawksmoor—the townspeople objected: 'I have had a very ridiculous petition from several of the inhabitants of Woodstock who desire not to have the door made up I ordered; but nobody of that town has merit enough to put me to any inconvenience upon their account, and I desire you to proceed without loss of time and do as you are directed'. Then came the chapel, to which her dear Duke's body was transferred from Westminster Abbey, the magnificent tomb by Rysbrack, 'upon the wall of one side the chapel. The rest of it is finished decently, substantially and very plain. And considering how many figures and whirligigs I have seen architects finish a chapel withal, that are of no manner of use but to laugh at, I must confess I cannot help thinking that what I have designed for this chapel may as reasonably be called finishing of it, as the pews and pulpit.' Lastly, as the years rolled away and old resentments gave way to new, the past appeared to her in a mellower light: she commissioned a fine statue from Rysbrack so that the familiar, once loved, figure should dominate the gallery: 'To the memory of Queen Anne, under whose auspices John, Duke of Marlborough conquered, and to whose munificence he and his posterity with gratitude owe the possession of Blenheim.'

CHAPTER SEVENTEEN

The Three Brothers

THE careers of Marlborough's two brothers in the services—George in the Navy, Charles in the Army—naturally followed their famous brother's star: their fortunes rose and fell with his. But they were very independent personalities, each of them men of ability, decision and weight. They made contributions to the success of Marlborough's war that were important in themselves. That of the Admiral was the more weighty: as the right-hand man of Prince George at the Admiralty from 1702 to 1708—really in the position of a First Sea Lord—it fell to him to press forward Marlborough's policy of sea-power, sometimes against the incomprehension of the seamen, and to carry the main burden of the administration of the Navy. To do this, he made a sacrifice of his career at sea; otherwise, we need not doubt, he would have left as familiar a name as Rooke or Cloudesley Shovell in the annals of the Navy, for he was more able and spirited than the one, and more intelligent than the other. Precisely because of this, he was kept at the Admiralty. His sacrifice gained him no credit: it was used to discredit him by jealous rivals and by enemies of Marlborough. At the head of the Admiralty in his brother's best days, he was an obvious target for detraction, much (and unjustly) maligned.

The Churchills were indeed too successful: flesh and blood could not stand it: pull them down! In the curious way in which fate has dealt with the Churchills, the Admiral has been even more unjustly treated than the Duke: he has come down in history, if at all, with his work totally unappreciated, himself disconsidered and traduced.[1] Again, it is only in our time that justice is being done to this long-dead sailor, the detractions of the envious rectified. He was accused in his own time—and the charge has been regularly repeated since—of making a fortune out of his post. This is untrue. The legitimate perquisites of such a post at that time were large; but the Admiral, unlike his famous brother, was not interested in money. Unmarried, and with no family to support, he left only a

[1] Cf. J. K. Laughton's quite unworthy notice of him in *D.N.B.*, biased, unfair and inaccurate in several respects.

moderate fortune of some £20,000 to his natural son and a nephew between them.

The truth is that the Admiral was not a popular personality; he had no charm: he was a Churchill, not a Villiers. One has only to look at his portrait at Greenwich—enormous, full-bottomed wig, luscious velvet coat with gold facings, hand forcefully upon his baton of command—to see that he was exactly like Sir Winston. There he is, heavy-jowled, double-chinned, forceful, uncompromising; the eyes give one a direct, unsmiling stare: a simple, self-willed personality, all of a piece. His portly figure affords a contrast with John, who was if anything too slim—in both senses of the word. It fell to the Duke to push his brother out of office in the end, because of his forthright, unaccommodating Toryism: a sacrifice to the clamorous, monopolising Whigs.

The Admiral—a strong figure of a man, erect, with the fine hands of his family, a more sensitive nostril than his father—was as unyielding as he. There was this difference: like all those childern born in the ambivalent household at Ashe, he was reserved and taciturn. He presents the teasing paradox of a man of strong personality, who yet has a hard impersonal core. The strong man, who knows his own mind and does not give his inner self away—that is always unpopular.

Both of the brothers left an illegitimate son. We have no letters from either of them. It is a fair inference that the youngest, Charles Churchill, the general, presents also this figure of an impersonal man, with yet a marked personality. For he was a fine fighting soldier, who lived a hard life. He bore a distinguished part at Blenheim, where as General of Foot he was responsible for getting the infantry across the marshes of the Nebel. In the Duke's absences from the Netherlands, he was left in command of the British troops there—with complete confidence. Few letters passed between the brothers: it is extraordinary how impersonal their relations were with each other. All that must have been induced in them by the circumstances of their early life, the shabby insecurities, the galling dependence, the callousness of Courts in which they received their first training.

Neither of these brothers lived to be really old: the Admiral died at fifty-seven, the General at fifty-eight. They wore themselves out in the service of their country; they served it well.

With the Court background of impecunious Sir Winston, all three boys began as pages: John to the Duke of York; George to the

Earl of Sandwich at sea; Charles to the King of Denmark, whence he returned to Whitehall with Prince George. In those days there was no exclusive distinction between land-service and sea-service, especially since the corps of Royal Marines was not established till Marlborough's war. George's first service was at the age of thirteen with Sandwich on his mission to Spain, 1666 to 1668: a start for his subsequent appreciation of the importance of the Mediterranean which marked his administration of the Navy. All three brothers had experience of the Mediterranean when young, and this gave them wider horizons than their more *borné* colleagues.

He first became a Member of Parliament on James's accession; no doubt, as a good Tory, a seat was found for him: St. Albans, which he represented in every Parliament for the rest of his life, until his last (1708), when he was returned for Portsmouth. In 1688 he was in command of the *Newcastle* in the Channel fleet awaiting William that stormy autumn: in November he put in at Plymouth, very leaky, and went over to William with everybody else. He commanded the *Pendennis,* 70 guns, at the engagement at Bantry Bay: the ship was subsequently cast away near the Downs. He was promoted to the *Windsor Castle,* 90 guns, in which he fought at Beachy Head; and in 1692 to a first rate, the *St. Andrew,* 100 guns, in which he served with distinction at La Hogue, 'serving as Lord Torrington's second in the line of battle in the first two actions and as Russell's in the third. Indeed, if not an earnest of further advancement at sea, the post of second to the Commander-in-Chief certainly implied acknowledged merit in the captain who held it.'

It was in the direct line of succession to a chief command: Churchill was clearly an able sea-officer, who inspired people's confidence and so far had had no set-back. It was rumoured that he had been made a flag-officer. Instead of that he was involved in his brother's disgrace by William; when Marlborough was forbidden the Court, George surrendered his commission and for several years was out of active service with him. So he, too, made a big sacrifice. The flag was given instead to Aylmer, Churchill's rival, several places junior to him on the list of captains. Aylmer ended up as a peer; Churchill was never even given a knighthood, for all his privileged position with Prince George. One can hardly say that the rewards of favour for him were excessive; but he was not ambitious in this line, and was content for the family honours to be concentrated on John.

When Marlborough came back to favour, George Churchill was

appointed a commissioner of the Admiralty at a salary of £1000 a year—the same figure as Arabella received for her (past) services. With Anne's succession the sun shone: only a few days after he was given the flag for which he had been made to wait ten years. He was promoted Vice-Admiral of the Red and appointed to Prince George's Council *qua* Lord Admiral, since this performed the functions of the Board of Admiralty. Within a week he had himself made at one bound Admiral of the Blue: that was one for Aylmer, who resigned his commission and sulked in retirement for the next seven years—until Churchill was driven out of office, when Aylmer came back to be Commander-in-Chief for the Whigs.

Like the greatest of naval administrators, Lord Barham, Churchill never went to sea as an Admiral: his was a full-time job of hard work at home—the main burden of the administration fell on him—and coping with the tempers of other Admirals. Much trouble was given by the leading Admiral, Admiral of the Fleet Sir George Rooke. He had been William's choice among sailors, and of course he was a competent seaman. He had, however, no strategic imagination: William had supplied all that. With his remarkable strategic insight William had grasped all that the Mediterranean meant for the struggle with France, for the balance of power, for the support of our allies, for the division of France's energies. Marlborough was the heir of his invention: he grasped all that too, and added, so like him, something else: the possibilities for an attack on France, a lunge at Toulon, an invasion—combined operations with Eugene—from the south-east. Before he died William's mind had been set on Cadiz as the key to the Straits and the best base for Mediterranean communications. Marlborough took over these plans, wove them into his immense and flexible strategic schemes and was bent on carrying them out.

The Admiral of the Fleet was opposed to these plans: his mind was hidebound by the responsibility of getting the fleet safe home again through winter seas. Marlborough's bland reply was that once it had a satisfactory base there it need not come home. George Churchill's chief service was to do all he could to advance his brother's strategic plans at the Admiralty. Rooke's objections were met one by one with tenacity and shrewdness. A large fleet was got to sea in 1702 for an attack on Cadiz—it was like Howard and Essex's expedition of 1596 come again. At Cadiz Rooke did absolutely nothing: a complete fiasco, only partially retrieved by the scuppering of the Plate fleet in Vigo harbour—and this was largely the work of the Admiralty in running it down and making it impossible for it to escape. Rooke got all the credit for this with the mob: he was always popular, because stupid. Churchills not: too intelligent.

In 1704 Marlborough brought forward the grand scheme that showed the full extent of his strategic imagination. At the same time as he was secretly planning his march to the Danube, he was projecting a blow between the wide-extended wings of Louis' southern domain, at the centre—Toulon. It was to be a combined attack, co-operating with the Austrian forces penetrating from Italy. The Toulon expedition failed of its objective because the Austrians were unable to play their part by land. Gibraltar, however, was taken as an afterthought: not much credit in the operation, but henceforth Britain had not only a base but the command of the Straits. The command of the Mediterranean was abandoned to the Allies.

Concentration on the proper strategic objectives of sea-power, however, gave ground for increasing complaints from the merchants that the protection of trade was neglected, convoys inadequate. Further, as Louis gave up the hope of sending fleets to sea, France's maritime effort went into commerce-raiding—as with Hitler in the last war. Seamen like Duguay-Trouin and Forbin made their name and fame by preying on commerce in the Channel. Churchill was the prime force behind the strategic use of sea-power; he was also primarily responsible for the convoy system. Whatever fell victim to French raiders, he was held resonsible for. It was his job to arrange the sailings of the convoys with the different bodies of merchants: Baltic and North Sea, East Indies and West Indies, North America, Guinea Coast, and Levant. He was a hard-pressed, hard-worked man; it does not seem that he was tactful in handling the merchants—a Sir Winston (old style), rather than a Marlborough. Anyway he was a Tory; the big merchants were Whigs.

In 1707 the losses from commerce-raiding at sea reached their height—following a similar pattern in the two wars of our time, the worst fell beyond the half-way line through the war. The legitimate complaints from the merchants grew louder, the cabals of the Whigs sharpened, against the Tory conduct of the Admiralty. Anyone who was responsible for naval affairs in such circumstances was bound to be unpopular: there was a great outcry and Admiral Churchill was there to be shot at. Sarah sent off delighted news of this to the Duke, worried as he was by her quarrel with the Queen and everything else. That sensitive register at once responds: 'I see that I am to be mortified by the prosecution of my brother George. I have deserved better from the Whigs; but since they are grown so indifferent as not to care what mortifications the Court may receive this winter, I shall not expect favour. My greatest concern is for the Queen, and for the Lord Treasurer. England will take care of itself, and not be ruined, because a few men are not pleased. They will see their error when it is too late.'

Marlborough humbled himself to write to one of the leaders of the Whig Junto to spare his brother: Halifax did not deign to reply to the Duke. (They were an arrogant lot, as the Queen thought them.) Events did not come to his rescue: this very year French raiders were at their most effective: 'they had raided three trading fleets, and taken a heavy toll off Brighton, off the coast of Holland, and between Scilly and Ushant, capturing or destroying six battleships of the escorting squadrons'. A Whig peer said in the Lords, 'your disasters at sea have been so many, a man scarce knows where to begin. Your ships have been taken by your enemies, as the Dutch take your herrings, by shoals, upon your own coasts. Nay, your Royal Navy itself has not escaped.'

This was too much for the Admiral. The Duke might humble himself and plead and compromise; not so his brother. The Admiral replied in kind. The Whig war in Spain, which the Tories had never liked, had hit upon disaster with the complete defeat of Galway at Almanza, at the hands of the Admiral's nephew, Berwick. Churchill did not fail to rub this in with caustic comments on the conduct of the operations by the Whig Galway—and with all the more pleasure since his own sympathies were Jacobite, like his father's not his clever brother's. What a liability this was for Marlborough, who was having to rely more and more on the Whigs for the support of the war; and what a handle it gave Sarah in her campaign with the Duke against his brother!

In November 1707 Admiral Churchill laid the Navy Estimate for 1708 before the new Parliament with its Whig majority. He gave them a complete account of the state of the Navy—numbers of ships, complements of men and guns; he added a record of the losses and gains throughout the war, ships captured or destroyed by the enemy, enemy ships destroyed or taken. An Act, of no value in itself, was passed by Parliament for better securing trade by cruisers and convoys. Actually from this deadline the situation began markedly to improve: the destruction of the French fleet in Toulon freed forces from the Mediterranean for the Channel and the North Sea.

The reconstitution of the Admiralty Board to admit Walpole and other Whigs did not please the Admiral, and he made difficulty about taking the new oaths with them, which confirmed people in thinking that he was a Jacobite. There could not be a worse moment for such suspicions at the Admiralty; for at Dunkirk a large expedition was being assembled to land the Pretender in Scotland. The port was blockaded, but gales drove the squadrons away and the fleet slipped out. The young man arrived off Scotland, which did not rise, and he got back again without being captured. This gave the public a great shock—like that when the *Scharnhorst* and the *Gneisenau* escaped up the Channel in spite of the efforts of Navy and R.A.F. The escape was laid at the Admiral's door.

The more hardly he was pressed, the less he gave way: like his father, not his brother. He engaged himself stoutly on the Tory side, taking a hand against the Whigs in the elections and, through his influence with the Prince, shoring up the Queen in her obstinate refusal to admit Whigs into the government. This meant that the Admiral was now pulling clean contrary to the Duke, and had become more than a liability—an encumbrance, virtually an opponent. He told the Prince and the Queen that Walpole had said that the Duke had given away a regiment at Harley's instigation. The report created mischief all round; Walpole was furious and the Duke upset. Then the Admiral went down to Oxford to intrigue in the local politics. Since he continued to enjoy the Prince's complete confidence, his removal became an affair of state. The Whigs, instigated by Sunderland—who took elections very much for his province—were preparing an attack on the Prince and his conduct of the Admiralty, through an attack on Churchill.

Something had to be done to forestall the campaign. Marlborough was appealed to: from the sadness of his tone one sees his kindness towards his brother, his essential gentleness. 'I am sorry that my brother George is gone to Oxford, fearing he may do what I shall not like. I can't hinder being concerned for him, though I find he is not at all sensible for the trouble he is like to have this winter, so that I shall have mortifications upon his account.' He appealed to Godolphin to tell him the truth. Godolphin's reply gives further evidence, if any more were needed, of the delicacy of feeling between these two men in addition to their entire mutual confidence. 'You may do me the right to observe that I never trouble you with stories from hence, being sensible I ought not to make you uneasy, upon whom all our hopes and safeties depend.

But since you required an account of the noise about your brother George and Mr. Walpole, I cannot but think he was very much to blame in that whole affair from the beginning to the end. . . . I must needs add, upon this occasion, that your brother does certainly contribute very much to keep up both in the Prince and in the Queen the natural, but very inconvenient, averseness they have to the Whigs in general . . . and nothing is more certain than that the general dislike of your brother in that station is stronger than ever, and much harder to be supported; but nothing less than your express command should have made me say so much to you upon so disagreeable a subject.'

The Duke turned this over and over in his mind. It was several months before he could bring himself to write his brother a letter of dismissal. 'Finding you still in the Prince's Council, and the Parliament now so near I cannot be so wanting either to you or to myself as not to tell you plainly, with all the kindness of a brother and the sincerity of a friend, that if you do not take an unalterable resolution of laying down that employment before the Parliament sits, you will certainly do the greatest disservice imaginable to the Queen and Prince, the greatest prejudice to me, and bring yourself into such inconveniences as may last as long as you live, and from which it is wholly impossible to protect you.' Marlborough assured him he should enjoy an advantage, 'doubly to what you do now, both in profit and quiet'.

Marlborough thus hoped to spare the Queen the distress of a Parliamentary attack upon her beloved Prince. To avoid it she gave way at the last moment and accepted a Whig administration. What made that all the more bitter was that in the event it did the Prince no good. The actions of both the Queen and Marlborough were rendered superfluous by the Prince's death, upon which the Admiral's appointment lapsed. The Whigs appointed Aylmer as Commander-in-Chief, who did not at all well and was displaced when the Tories came in.

After the Prince's funeral the Admiral retired to his villa at Windsor and the solace of his remarkable aviary. He must have been a rather solitary man. His will reveals that he was on friendly terms with the well-known bookseller and publisher Awnsham Churchill and his nephew William. Awnsham was a kinsman, one of the Churchills of Dorchester and Colliton, who not only prospered in, but made a valuable contribution to, the book-trade in London. It is a fair inference that their best-known publication, *A Collection of Voyages and Travels*—a kind of Hakluyt of Queen

Anne's reign—which began to appear in 1704, owed something to the Churchills' friendship with the Admiral. Having made a fortune in London Awnsham eventually went back to Dorset, where he bought an estate which continued in the family.

The Admiral made Awnsham and William Churchill his executors, leaving each of them £100 to buy mourning, and to the latter 'the picture of the Duke of Buckingham's family', which must have come to him from his mother, 'my diamond ring and my striking gold watch to keep in memory of me'. He was generous to his servants, of whom he had eight or ten: an annuity of £27 to Mary Cook, of £50 to William Murthat, evidently his personal man-servant, a year's wages, money and mourning for the rest. The bulk of his property was to be divided equally between his natural son, George Churchill, who was serving perhaps at sea and was not yet of age, and his nephew, Francis Godfrey, Arabella's son. He was on good terms with Arabella. Only a few months of life in retirement remained to him. On 12 May 1710 he was buried in Westminster Abbey, at the upper end of the middle aisle, on the right hand going into the choir. Twenty years later practically to the day Arabella was buried in the same grave. There they are together.

The memory of this breach at the end must not blind us to the immense service the Admiral gave in the conduct of the war, to the country and to his brother. No such *contretemps* disturbed the relations between the Duke and his youngest brother Charles, with whom he was in constant touch throughout the campaigns of 1702 to 1708. Charles began his military career at the age of eighteen as an ensign in his brother's company of foot in the Duke of York's regiment. In January 1681 he was involved in a duel fought behind Arlington's house as second to a Captain Richardson, who was run through the body: the young bloods had quarrelled over their wine. Next year he was off to Tangier as lieutenant-colonel. We next hear of him serving at Sedgemoor, having brought the siege-train up from Portsmouth. At the Revolution he went over to William at Andover with Prince George and the Duke of Ormonde, and with his senior officer, Brigadier Trelawny.

Thenceforward we follow his regular promotion step by step—a most competent officer—with no set-backs. Since he was abroad fighting at the time, he was not involved in his brother's disgrace. He had fought under him in Ireland, leading the infantry across the tidal estuary at the siege of Cork. He was left as Governor of

Kinsale. At the battle of Landen in 1693 we have seen that he had the good luck to capture his nephew, Berwick; for this William allowed him 20,000 guilders of ransom. Of this £1205 15*s*. 3*d*. in English money he was able to invest £1000 in government loans in the autumn. Three years before he had invested £200, presumably on the winding up of Sir Winston's estate, which it fell to him to do.

With the accession of Anne he, too, shared in the favour, and the solid advantages, that accrued to his family. Promoted Lieutenant-General, he was made Lieutenant of the Tower and Deputy Lieutenant for the Tower Hamlets. We must remind ourselves that this meant work—to which none of the Churchills objected. In the Prince's regiment which he commanded his illegitimate son, another Charles, served under him. For the war Marlborough asked that his brother be made General in command of all the English infantry; he wanted him as his right hand: and his confidence was not misplaced. Charles never at any time failed him: his service was of the highest order. He obeyed his brother's wishes implicitly, carried his instructions into execution, and took his place at the head of the English troops—not of course of the Allies'—as his brother's deputy in his absence. Their collaboration is seen at its best in the Danube campaign.

It is fascinating to read their internal correspondence from the Army, as the well-drilled machine rolled on to its ordained rendezvous. Everything goes to show the high standards of duty, public spirit, care and consideration for the men which we expect from Marlborough and his brother. The result was that when Charles crossed the Danube with twenty battalions of foot, and the Duke passed the rest of his troops across that and the Lech to join up with Eugene before Blenheim, the troops were all in fine fighting trim. That they were so was as much due to Charles's silent hard work as to the Duke's vigilant care over them all.

In the battle of Blenheim he bore a foremost part, getting his infantry safely across the swamp of the Nebel, when Tallard had judged it not possible and regarded its accomplishment with dismay. Later Churchill was responsible, with Orkney and Cutts, for the reduction of the twenty-seven battalions shut up in Blenheim, assaulting the besieged village again and again. After the battle he was given the honour of escorting Tallard and the captured French officers back to England and to their comfortable quarters at Nottingham and Lichfield. Churchill's reward was to be made full General of Foot, which gave him seniority over Slangenberg, the Dutch general who detested Marlborough, had a poor opinion of his generalship and impeded his operations. The year 1705, we recall, was that when the Dutch placed the greatest obstacles in Marlborough's way, the year of the unfought Waterloo.

The General was in command of the British infantry, under the Duke, through all the operations of these years: at the forcing of the Lines of Brabant in 1705; in the splendid achievements of the year of victory, 1706—Ramillies, the crossing of the Dyle, the capture of Brussels (of which he was made Governor), the siege of Dendermonde, which he directed. For his services he was given the governorship of Guernsey, upon which he resigned the Lieutenancy of the Tower. Such a life of strain brought on a stroke, which incapacitated him, in March 1708. Marlborough was just leaving England for the campaign. He put it off until he had seen his brother. It does not seem that his brother was able to play an active part in the war thereafter: their best days together were over. Charles Churchill continued nominally to hold his appointments, and no doubt to draw its emoluments, until the Tories came in: in February 1711 he was replaced by General Erle.

Charles Churchill spent his declining years at Minterne. He was, we have seen, the appointed heir of Sir Winston. In the year of his good fortune, 1702, he married Mary Gould of Dorchester, who was something of an heiress. This enabled him to complete the work Sir Winston had begun and build a substantial, if plain and unassuming, Queen Anne house, which survived until rebuilt at the beginning of this century. There still remain, however, interesting relics of the General at Minterne: a pretty staircase of the period, a fine Thornhill ceiling which he evidently owed to the Duke's patronage of the artist, and which Charles Churchill no doubt commissioned at the time of Thornhill's work at Blenheim. Even more, the tapestries in the house remain as a memento of the association of the two brothers: the tradition is that they were presented by the city of Brussels at the time when Charles was Governor. He probably purchased others for his house, like his brother, the Duke: they are very fine and fresh in colouring, in a beautiful state of preservation. One other relic has a more popular tradition: an elegant French mirror, *verre églomisé*, and a glass-topped table, of which the glass was cracked, it is said, when the General learned that his estate was not freehold but leasehold. There is often something in a tradition and—though the fact was clear all along—it was matter for annoyance, especially if he wished to purchase and was refused.

The General's marriage, it seems, was a happy one, though there were no children of it. On his death in 1714 he left his property to his widow, who left it to her own relations, the Goulds. By Charles Churchill's will there was charged upon his estate an annuity of £50 for Elizabeth Dodd, who was probably the mother of his son. To 'my natural son, Colonel Charles Churchill', he left £2000. This son, a Charles the second, served under his father in the Netherlands—there is a reference in the Duke's despatches to his nephew. He was a soldier of merit and lived a life of much gaiety. He was for a time Governor of Plymouth and finished up as a Lieutenant-General. When Sarah's friend, Arthur Maynwaring, died at Holywell—the Duchess often in tears by the death-bed of that cherished companion—he left his scanty property to the beautiful Miss Oldfield, the actress, by whom he had a son. Miss Oldfield's acting in the part of the virtuous Marcia had contributed greatly to the success of Addison's *Cato*; it was only her inability to hold out any longer that compelled the ending of its run: for the last performances she was said to have a midwife in the wings in case of necessity. After Maynwaring's death she did not remain long unconsoled: Brigadier Churchill came to comfort her. 'He made it his sole busines and delight to place her in the same rank of reputation (to which her own natural deportment greatly contributed) with persons of the best condition.' By him she had a son, the third Charles Churchill. When she died in 1730 she was given a funeral in Westminster Abbey; the General wished to erect a monument to her memory: this the Dean refused. She left her not inconsiderable property to her two sons, making the General, as a tribute of respect, her residuary legatee.

When George I came in, Marlborough did his best to get this gallant soldier placed as Groom of the Bedchamber to the Prince of Wales, but 'could not prevail upon the account of his birth, so that my Lord Marlborough came out and told the Duke of Argyle they must insist no more on't for it would not do'. No wonder George I asked if there was not something wrong with the Archbishop of Canterbury, since he had spent half an hour with him without his asking anything for his relations. Later Churchill seems to have got some such Court appointment: his birth presented no serious impediment to his career.

In 1714 the Hanoverian dynasty began its prosperous career with the most famous soldier in Europe at its right hand. And that, when we think of his career—his long attachment to the Stuarts, his experience with William and again with Anne, the equivocations of fortune—was both an achievement and a happy augury. Perhaps the upshot of it all was less extraordinary than it seems, when we reflect that John Churchill was a very English figure in his ambivalence and reserve, his combination of subtlety and common sense. He was extraordinary only in his ambition and his genius.

Once more his family surrounded the throne. Of his sons-in-law, young Godolphin was cofferer to the royal Household, Bridgwater Lord Chamberlain to the Prince of Wales; the Duke of Montagu was given a regiment, the Duchess made Lady of the Bedchamber to the Princess of Wales, the intelligent redoubtable Caroline. (She had been chosen for wife to the heir by clever old Sophia, the Electress, who had only just failed by a head to inscribe on her tomb 'Queen of Great Britain'.) Sunderland came back to office again. Marlborough's earlier protégés, Walpole and Cadogan came to the head respectively of the Treasury and the active administration (under the Duke) of the Army.

Marlborough was the least vindictive man in the world; but almost by accident, he took an effectual revenge upon Bolingbroke, against whom he had no ill will though plenty of reason for it. Bolingbroke's nerve broke under the strain of the events of 1714. His gamble had failed; the Tory party was broken. He came to Marlborough, of all people, to ask his advice. The Duke advised him to leave the country: his life was in danger. It must have been a source of wry amusement to the Duke when his former disciple, later enemy, acted on it. No one could have foreseen that Bolingbroke would ruin himself in this way. Oxford pursued a more honourable course. He remained in the country and defended himself in the Lords against the attacks upon him for the desertion of the Allies and the Peace. He was the only person against whom Marlborough felt resentment: Harley had prevented him from making the peace in Paris. The Duke pressed his impeachment; but once the excitement of 1714 and 1715 was over moderation asserted itself and Oxford was discharged. Marlborough was much moved, and recorded his protest. It was in regard to this that Dr. Johnson wrote his famous line in 'The Vanity of Human Wishes':

> From Marlborough's eyes the streams of dotage flow.

He was too much exhausted and worn out for serious application to business; though he was consulted over appointments and had his say in decisions. He presided over the arrangements to defeat the Jacobite Rising of 1715, the landing of his old patron's son, the Pretender, in Scotland. In 1716 we find him engaged in an important consultation, along with Stanhope and Townshend, with Bernstorff, the Imperial envoy, from which the Triple Alliance resulted. That spring he had a stroke. At the time of his illness he was taking a hand in a new political combination, which would bring in some of the Tories. It is fascinating to see that at the very last he reverted to what he had been all along: a moderate, a man of the middle, a Trimmer. And who can doubt that this line would have been better for the dynasty and for English politics than the rigorous monopoly of power by the Whigs, the rancorous exclusion of the Tories? For him it was now all too late. Marlborough's first stroke followed close upon the death of his favourite daughter Anne, Lady Sunderland, the only one who could keep the peace with her mother. Shortly after the Duke suffered a lesion of the brain which deprived him of speech and paralysed his limbs; but under the care of Sarah, who was a devoted nurse, and the excellent doctor Garth, a good friend of the family, he made a quick recovery. He was able to go down to Bath for the summer, where he was received by the civic authorities, a long train of nobility and gentry, bell-ringing and multitudes—not very good, one would have thought, for a man recovering from a stroke. On his way back he paid a visit to Blenheim, where he was at length pleased with the progress made: he had entered upon another race, the completion of the house before his death. Sarah described herself as 'working like a pack-horse' in these years to get it finished.

In November 1716 Marlborough had a second and more severe stroke. Again he recovered; but now he was much more frail and, though he retained his faculties as clear as ever, his speech was somewhat affected. In August 1717 Sarah and pleasant Dr. Garth took the Duke to Tunbridge Wells. Here Steele, who had won the hearts of the Marlboroughs by his stout defence of the Duke both in Parliament and the press, when things were at their worst in 1712, visited them and made one of the party. His famous pamphlet, *The Crisis*, had been the only effective counter-blast to Swift, and Steele suffered for it. It was not only this that endeared Steele to the Duke: his gaiety and good humour made him a welcome guest at Blenheim. What the Duke liked best was to be out every day on horseback, or walking round his grounds, especially at Blenheim where Sarah at length got them installed in 1719. A favourite spot was Vanbrugh's bridge, about which there had been so much fuss.

Here the Duke would post himself to survey the operations, no less a field of battle than Blenheim or Ramillies—one sees that lean and graceful shade resting against the parapet, looking up at the Palace of his creation. Here too victory was in sight.

As the Duke's hold on life slackened, Sarah came into her own and took control. She may indeed be said to have taken the field. Within a short time she was on the worst of terms with Sunderland, who had married again—Sarah considered, beneath him and to the prejudice of her daughter's children. By the time he came into power in 1718 there was a complete breach, and she blamed him for the South Sea Bubble, of which she thoroughly disapproved and from which she profited hugely. She was as much of an asset from the business point of view as she was a liability from the political. At the height of the South Sea fever—Sarah said that it was all madness, and it was—she forced the Duke out of the market and added a round £100,000 to their enormous fortune.

Even so it was a high price to pay for the squabbles and quarrels with which she made him uneasy—worst of all, those with her daughters. Henrietta Godolphin and the Duchess of Montagu were too much of their mother's disposition to get on with her: they had all her positiveness without any of her wit and vivacity. She had been unwise and unaffectionate in her treatment of them, and when they grew up they gave as good as they got. Henrietta ignored her mother as much as she could: the heir to the dukedom, she was very lofty—at the same time compromising herself, in her mother's view, by her association with a 'low poet', the dramatist Congreve. (His company was of the most enchanting kind.) Mary Montagu took pleasure in flouting and tormenting Sarah, who allowed herself to be tormented very easily, though she was not unaware of her failing.

She was, I have suggested, a frustrated writer: she would have been far happier if only she could have written—but she had never been educated. She was a naturally clever woman with genuine interests of mind that ran into the sand. This must have been a source of insatisfaction and restlessness, which her practical capacity did not provide for. With pen frequently in hand she confided her troubles to her Green Book. 'After the great illness that the Duke of Marlborough had in 1716, I was determined to bear whatever she [the Duchess of Montagu] would do rather than hinder any of the Duke of Marlborough's children from coming to my house when he was sick. And this was so great an encouragement to all manner of ill behaviour, that what I had hid so long they made public; for they never came to see their father in a morning, but at the hours when company was there, going up towards him without taking any notice of me, as if they had a pleasure in showing everybody that they insulted me.' We need not suppose that Sarah had taken much trouble to keep these family wrangles 'hid': years before Marlborough had warned her against giving the town an opportunity to take part in them.

Marlborough loved taking a hand at cards. In his last year we find his daughter Mary writing him: 'if you could have the least pleasure in the variety of coming here any afternoon, it would be a great one to me, and to anybody, I am sure, that you would let meet you. My Lord Sunderland is a very good whist player, and my sister Godolphin can play and would be pleased with it (I know) in your company.' It was very provoking: not one word of her mother: the party would be more like a cabal of her personal enemies. The Duke replied, gently as always, but with sadness: 'I thank you for your letter, my dear child, but I observe that you take no manner of notice of your mother; and certainly when you consider of that, you can't imagine that any company can be agreeable to me who have not a right behaviour to her. This is doing what is right to yourself as well as to your affectionate father.' Mary Montagu did not give way: she wrote at once justifying herself and charging Sarah with having done 'what no mother did'. Infinitely weary her father went into it, but could not find 'that you had any reason for your complaint, but she had a great deal. Praying God Almighty to turn your heart to what is certainly most just and what has always been my earnest desire.' Later still in a trembling hand he wrote: 'I am not well enough to write so long a letter with my own hand; and I believe I am the worse to see my children live so ill with a mother for whom I must have the greatest tenderness and regard'.

He was at Windsor Lodge in the high summer of 1722 when his last illness fell on him. Sarah recounts this last sad scene. 'The afternoon before her father died, I was mightily surprised and troubled at what I did not expect, that the Duchess of Montagu and my Lady Godolphin were without.... At the time I thought my soul was tearing from my body and that I could not say many things before them, yet I would not refuse them to come in, for fear I should repent of it.... They stayed a great while and, not being able to be out of the room longer from him, I went in though they were there and kneeled down by him. They rose up when I came in and made curtseys, but did not speak to me, and after some time I called for prayers. When they were over, I asked the Duke of

Marlborough if he heard them well, and he answered, "Yes, and he had joined in them".' When it was getting dark the Duke was carried on his couch into his own room and there, at dawn on 16 June, he died.

The Duke's body was embalmed and borne to Marlborough House, where he lay in state. On 9 August a funeral procession of semi-regal magnificence bore him to Westminster Abbey, where he was buried among the kings of England. The Abbey Registers have the entry: '9 August 1722. The most noble Prince John, Duke of Marlborough, Marquis of Blandford, Baron Churchill of Sandridge, Baron of Aymouth in Scotland, Prince of the Roman Empire, Knight of the most noble Order of the Garter.'

Those titles are familiar milestones to us in his full and toilsome life: he had come a long way from Ashe.

Marlborough's will made a great sensation, though there is nothing in it to surprise us. His two chief cares were Blenheim and Sarah. He left Sarah £15,000 a year for life—she was already immensely rich herself—and £10,000 a year for five years for the completion of Blenheim. The estate at St. Albans was at her own disposal; she was to have all the furniture, plate and jewels there, except the gold plate given him by the Elector of Hanover, the Emperor's diamond sword, and the George and collar of the Garter, which were to go as heirlooms with the title. Sarah was to have Blenheim and Marlborough House for life; after, they were to go with the Dukedom. The succession to the remaining estates was provided for along with the title; first Henrietta's children, the Godolphins; after them, if they failed (as they did), Anne's children, the Spencers (who did not). No less than £400,000 was set aside in trust to buy estates to settle on his right heirs, and by an exceptional provision an act was to be obtained from the legislature for settling future purchases on his representative in the title. We see his determination not only to leave his name in history, but to provide for his posterity in supporting it. We need not go into the complexities relating to its contingent provisions, the details of lands and moneys. We know that Arabella was not forgotten—nicely provided for, in fact. He expressed his wish to be buried 'in my chapel in Blenheim house' at Sarah's direction, *i.e.* when completed.

On the news of Marlborough's death Swift, who could not forgive him his fame and power and wealth, distinguished himself with a mean poem, 'A Satirical Elegy on the Death of a late Famous General':

His Grace ! impossible ! what dead !
Of old age too, and in his bed !
And could that Mighty Warrior fall?
And so inglorious, after all ! . . .
Come hither, all ye empty things,
Ye bubbles raised by breath of kings;
Who float upon the tide of state,
Come hither and behold your fate.
Let pride be taught by this rebuke,
How very mean a thing's a Duke;
From all his ill-got honours flung,
Turned to that dirt from whence he sprung.

There could be no better evidence of how contrary Swift's feelings were to those of common humanity.

CHAPTER EIGHTEEN

Sarah in Old Age

SARAH was now free—and rich enough—to indulge her likes and dislikes, her loves and hates, her feuds and quarrels, her prejudices, whims, opinions, propensities for building, politics, cards, decorating her own (and other people's) houses, interfering, moving about the country, giving advice (often sound) where it was not asked, laying down the law to everybody, though most people took no notice. Not that the Duke had ever seriously cramped her style in these ways—as he ought to have done from the beginning. As long as he lived her vagaries were kept within some bounds; his life and care gave polarity to her existence. With him gone her life lost its centricity: she was free to become a rich and glorious eccentric.

Her indefatigable energies of mind and body boiled over: sometimes usefully, as in business affairs, where she continued to pile up money and landed estates; sometimes to no purpose whatever, as almost always in politics—for which she had a hopeless itch, for ever meddling and for ever checkmated and defeated. In personal relations her touch varied: sometimes successful, more often hopeless. There was no middle way with her: she either took to a person, and then was apt to be warm and generous, or she took against them, and then nothing they did was any good.

And yet, intolerable as Sarah was, she was not a bore: she had too much vivacity and wit. Anyway, with pen constantly in hand, tongue never still, crawling upstairs and downstairs on crutches, or having herself carried in a chair between two poles when she grew too gouty to walk, she has left us a portrait of herself more complete than any other woman of the age.

It did not take her long not to be on good terms with the Hanoverian Court and its peculiar denizens.

To begin with all was deceptively well. Her family were provided for, and Sarah had no wish to return to the drudgery of office. In spite of the victory of her side Sarah was politically as restless and factious as ever. She was now at daggers drawn with her son-in-law Sunderland, who was at the head of the government; which did not prevent her from being on equally bad terms with his rivals,

Townshend and Robert Walpole. Secretary Craggs she had quarrelled irretrievably with; Cadogan she had sued in the courts. Here was the whole of her party alienated: what a woman, what a lesson!

When the Duke died Caroline wrote Sarah a kind letter of consolation; but there was no affection. It was perhaps impossible for these two women to get on: each so positive and self-willed, especially since the younger was an educated woman with both intellect and political judgment. One of her first acts on arrival was to buy the complete works of Bacon. The girl who had been brought up by the Electress Sophia and shared the conversation of the philospher Leibniz was more than a match for Sarah. Sarah was jealous—one detects the familiar accent: the reverend Dr. Clarke had once told Sarah that 'her Majesty knew as much as he did, but that was when he hoped to be a bishop'. At Scarborough Sarah saw a woman with an expression of fatuity on her face such that she looked even 'happier than her Majesty the day of her coronation'. She could not bear powdered hair, 'like the Queen's when she came first into England, clotted all over with powder, when I fancy the best thing I had was the colour of my hair'.

This being the situation, it was to be expected that Sarah would take a hand in the scandalous squabbles in the royal family, between Caroline and her miserable first-born, Frederick, Prince of Wales; and that Sarah, actuated as usual by emotion and resentment, should have taken the Prince's side and brought defeat upon herself. He was a cad and a cur—all that his mother said publicly about him. But in order to score off Caroline Sarah was prepared to sacrifice the happiness of her adored, enchanting granddaughter, Di Spencer, and marry her to the creature. The Duchess offered to settle £100,000 on her granddaughter, if the Prince would marry her secretly. What an ambition!—like Bess of Hardwick marrying her daughter into the succession to the throne. It was resentment even more than ambition that inspired the intrigue—what a score that her descendants should occupy the throne of Great Britain! The Prince of Wales was willing. The hated Sir Robert got to hear of it and of course Sarah was checkmated.

In the way stood the bulky, but agile, body of the extremely competent Sir Robert. The provoking man had no sense of the obligations he owed to the Marlborough family. Besides, had she not done him a service by lending his government a large sum of money, for which he had given her very inadequate returns? Even in small matters he was disobliging: he withheld her permit for passing through St. James's Park, going to or from Marlborough house, a liberty which had not been withdrawn by Queen Anne in her worst days. She proceeded to say exactly what she thought of Sir Robert in all companies. As time went on and there seemed no prospect of ever shifting him from power—he had the constant backing of Queen Caroline—Sarah pursued him with rancour, taking a hand in all the cabals against him, joining with her old enemies the Tories (in particular with Bolingbroke) against him, leaving large sums of money in her will to his foremost opponents.

Not all her money could ever shift him. It is amusing to watch how invariably her efforts were frustrated.

Sarah's great defect in politics was the feminine one of looking at matters in excruciatingly personal terms. No one ever impugned her business capacity: in this field her masculine propensities came into play. In the year after the Duke's death, she bought the Winbledon estate of Sir Theodore Jansen, who had been ruined in the South Sea crash. Thereafter hardly a year passed but what she bought an estate or two, until at her death she left some thirty in all.

For all her experience at Blenheim she was building again: in this, too, another Bess of Hardwick. She was clearly bitten with the pleasures of building, or, perhaps more exactly, of furnishing. She was very hard to please. She pulled down the half-finished house she had purchased with the site at Wimbledon, and asked Lord Burlington, whose later buildings she did not approve—in particular the lovely Assembly Rooms at York—to plan another. This too did not please her: not simple enough; so she demolished it and made him try again. This passed muster, and it gave her much pleasure in the 1730's to furnish it and fill it with things.

Now she was buying a marble chimney-piece from Southampton House for her dining-room. It was a fine one, but 'there is a good deal of carving upon it, which is not at all to my taste. . . . I am determined to have no one thing carved in the finishing of my house at Wimbledon, my taste having always been to have things plain and clean from a piece of wainscot to a lady's face.' She had bespoken a set of blue and gold leather hangings, which was as fresh now as when put up, for one of the rooms at Wimbledon. By 1734 all the pictures were finished except those of young Marlborough, her dear Di and her husband the Duke of Bedford. 'When the house is furnished it will be a delightful place to my taste. . . . If I had had only myself and the Duke of Bedford's bricklayers it would have been the finest place in the world. But I have always had the misfortune to suffer very great mischiefs from the assistance of architects. The cutting through the terrace is almost as bad as setting the house in a pit. And the wall of it is so very ill done that I believe it must be pulled down a third time.'

Her favourite house remained Marlborough House; and there within, under the accretions of Victorian and Edwardian royalty, we see—Sarah. The great saloon, going up to the full height of the original two storeys, with its splendid door-cases, is not much changed. During the years of exile Laguerre was at work painting the Battle of Blenheim upon the walls: there is the Duke holding his baton, seated on his white horse, his generals following behind. On the main staircase is the Battle of Ramillies, on the east staircase, Oudenarde or Malplaquet. Sarah was proud of Wren's staircase. The stairs at Bedford House, 'though they were Inigo Jones's doing, certainly are not handsome and looked too much pinched in the middle. . . . It would be much handsomer if it was made with a flight of stairs like those at Marlborough House with large half paces.' There she occupied a red damask bed less than five feet broad: she could not resist advising Di that her small bedrooms should not have big beds in them.

Her letters to Di show how much her mind ran on such things: though no aesthete, she had the instincts (and the competence) of a good housekeeper and we are left in no doubt, here either, of her tastes. She liked the effect of rich red hangings upon white paint, with long pier glasses between windows to enhance it: the architecture plain and unobtrusive in the background. She did not like the proportions disguised or cornices concealed by top-heavy furniture. She hated beds that came up to the ceiling: as Di's bed did not reach the ceiling, 'your upholsterer has gratified this passion and likewise the modern architects by making two things to stand upon the feet of the bed, which I call Gimmey-Gommenys'.

Perhaps we may conclude that her taste was plain and good.

As she grew older she turned more to the pleasures of literature, both of reading and of writing. The appearance of *Gulliver's Travels* gave her extreme pleasure: she was ready to forgive her old enemy for the delight he had given her. Pope and Gay wrote off to Swift: 'the Duchess Dowager of Marlborough is in raptures at it; she says she can dream of nothing else since she read it; she declares that she has now found out that her whole life has been lost in caressing the worst part of mankind, and treating the best as her foes; and that if she knew Gulliver, though he had been the worst enemy she ever had, she should give up her present acquaintance for his friendship'. She was capable of greater magnanimity than ever Swift was: we find her writing in 1736: 'Dean Swift gives the most exact account of kings, ministers, bishops and the courts of justice that is possible to be writ. He has certainly a vast deal of wit; and since he could contribute so much to the pulling down the most honest and best-intentioned ministry that ever I knew, with the help only of Abigail and one or two more, and has certainly stopped the finishing stroke to ruin the Irish in the project of the halfpence, in spite of all the ministry could do, I could not help wishing that we had had his assistance in the Opposition; for I could easily forgive him all the slaps he has given me and the Duke of Marlborough, and have thanked him heartily whenever he would please to do good.' She had never seen Swift in her life, but she was 'prodigiously fond' of *Gulliver* and was re-reading it in 1736.

Spending some part of the summer of 1734 in an empty London, she diverted herself by reading Sir William Temple in Swift's edition of his early patron. She transcribed for Di's benefit what she thought both true and pretty: 'the greatest pleasure of life is love, the greatest treasure contentment, the greatest possession health, the greatest ease is sleep, the greatest medicine is a true friend'. Not all her reading on the subject of friendship was equally inspiring. She was reading, too, a history of the reign of James I. 'There is a great deal so tedious that I pass it over,' she tells Di, 'but his love letters to the Duke of Buckingham are incomparable. . . . I believe it will make you laugh if you read what his Sacred Majesty did and said.' By this time, kings and queens are 'Sacred Majesties' to her, and she writes: 'were I a man, I freely own that I would not adventure anything that I could avoid for any king that I know or that I have heard of. As princes are not the best judges of right and wrong, from the flattery they are used to, not to say worse of them, I think the best thing for them and the whole nation is not to let them have power to hurt themselves or anybody else.' It is a very Whig sentiment.

In the autumn of 1727 Voltaire paid a visit to Blenheim. The Duchess had already written one Vindication of her conduct in relation to Queen Anne, which Walpole had advised her to suppress—no doubt because its tone was too bitter. From time to time she would turn over her papers: 'I am at present altering my account of Queen Anne's character. I have begun to love her again since the present lot have become our governors.' She had the idea of asking the brilliant young Frenchman to put her materials together for her. But the *rusé* Voltaire realised how many enemies it would make for him in England to have a hand in that pie; he already had enough in France: he declined the commission. It was a pity, for thereby we missed what might have been a masterpiece. The Duchess was much vexed: 'I thought the man had sense, but I find him at bottom either a fool or a philosopher'. She had met more than her match in Voltaire: it was he who profited by the encounter. He was writing his *History of Charles XII:* Sarah gave him a vivid account of Marlborough's mission to Charles and his impressions of the warrior-king. Of this he made good use. He seems also to have got an anecdote about Sarah's deliberately upsetting a glass of water over Abigail's court-dress, upon which Scribe based a celebrated play, *Le Verre d'eau.*

Sarah was certainly going to go down in literature. On Bolingbroke's return from exile these two old enemies joined together on the basis of opposition to Sir Robert. The Duchess turned to Marlborough's former disciple who had had such an admiration for him, for an inscription for her Victory Column. Bolingbroke obliged with ringing words: 'The battle was bloody: the event decisive. The woods were pierced: the fortifications trampled down. The enemy fled.' The Duchess was touched to the heart. 'When I first read it, I thought it the finest thing that was possible for any man to write and as often as I have read it I still wet the paper.' She was not without literary feeling: here too her taste was for the plain and unadorned, the simplicity that commands.

In her last years Sarah was much concerned with how posterity would view not so much herself as her actions; she wished to put her case and an official biography of the Duke to be written. It is curious, though perhaps understandable, how much difficulty each of these gave. For years she had been fiddling at her memoirs, and at last she got a reputable man, Nathaniel Hooke—friend of Pope and a good Roman historian—to put them into final shape for her. This must be the circumstance that accounts for the story that the old Duchess, though ill in bed, dictated with perfect clarity for six hours at a stretch. No one who reads the book can mistake that the language is Sarah's own, though Hooke may have toned it down; not even Sarah's resentments, however, were as bitter as they had been. The book, *An Account of the Conduct of the Dowager Duchess of Marlborough, From her first coming to Court to the year* 1710, was published in 1742 and made a sensation.

In the *Gentleman's Magazine* Dr. Johnson wrote a review which is as remarkable for its general reflections on writing history as it is for the exposure of his own prejudices. He goes on to show that he was incapable of doing any sort of justice to William, saying that he was 'arbitrary, insolent, gloomy, rapacious and brutal'—how one detests these facile literary condemnations of people involved in the toils of action—and describes Queen Anne as 'little more than the slave of the Marlborough family', which we know was not the case. However, the great man did allow that from Sarah's book 'the historian may trace the progress of great transactions, and discover the secret causes of important events. And, to mention one use more, the polite writer may learn an unaffected dignity of style and an artful simplicity of narration. The method of confirming her relation by inserting at length the letters that every transaction occasioned has not only set the greatest part of the work above the danger of confutation, but has added to the entertainment of the reader.' This is just.

Sarah's book, like everything about her, at once became a subject of controversy. On the whole she got off lightly: the extraordinary old lady had survived so long that after a lifetime of unpopularity and envy the British public—with its usual mixture of sentimentality and gallantry—had practically taken her to its bosom. Fearlessness—not caring what anybody thought—and eccentricity had their usual reward. At George II's coronation the old Duchess, gouty and weary with standing, had called for a drum in Palace Yard and sat down on it comfortably in all her finery, blazing with jewels, to the enjoyment and cheers of the populace.

The unkindest, and the most effective, criticism came from the American-born writer, James Ralph of Philadelphia—former associate of Benjamin Franklin, now working as an impecunious journalist in London. He devoted a whole book, *The Other Side of the Question,* to traversing Sarah's book point by point. It is rather fun to see the egalitarian American reduced to defending monarchs like William and Mary and Anne against the irreverent remarks of a lady bred up at Court: no idea, evidently, how independent-minded courtiers can be. The Duchess at the height of her troubles had declared with some improbability—like Oliver Cromwell at a similar juncture—that she would emigrate to America. The Continent at that time would hardly have been big enough to hold her. Attacked by this queasy American, Sarah had the fortune to be defended by the generous, full-blooded Fielding: he could appreciate a great woman when he saw one—he 'never contemplated the character of that Glorious Woman but with admiration . Fielding was a gentleman and a chivalrous fellow: he rushed out his *Full Vindication of the Duchess Dowager of Marlborough* before *Joseph Andrews* was clear of the printers. It may be concluded that Sarah had the better in this warfare.

There remains the family: where Sarah's touch was as fallible as in the field of politics. She was on bad terms with her eldest daughter Henrietta, who on her father's death became Duchess of Marlborough in her own right. She had a good deal of her mother's temperament, with the amorous disposition of the Villierses. She was as opinionated and self-willed as Sarah, but more warm-hearted; her combination of haughty grandeur with being no better than she should be was a difficult one to carry off: she managed it with more dignity than most.

She was married at eighteen to Godolphin's only son by Margaret Blagge, aged twenty: intelligent parents, intelligent stock in every direction: nothing could be more appropriate. They soon produced a son, called after the King, William: in the family Willigo. The marriage may be regarded as successful, as marriages go. But the younger Godolphin was as easy-going as his father and as little ambitious. Hervey tells us that he had plenty of natural ability and that he was a man of sense; but his real passion was for horses and he preferred the company of stable-boys. We can hardly blame Henrietta for finding that disappointing and her husband rather tame.

With her spirit and ambition she was more taken with the wits and preferred the company of poets, particularly polite ones who knew how to commend their parts to ladies. When her brother Blandford died, leaving her the heir, the agreeable Mr. Congreve sent her sympathetic verses, 'The Tears of Amaryllis for Amyntas'. Verses were better than horses. The year of Ramillies Congreve strengthened his claim by a Pindaric Ode in honour of the Lord Treasurer; when he and Vanbrugh opened their new playhouse, Henrietta was referred to, as she longed to be, as 'the learn'd Minerva'. It was natural enough: here was ground where her mother could not meet her. Soon Mr. Congreve, who was a delightful companion, was a welcome visitor at Godolphin House, playing at cards and other things. Congreve, Gay, the detested Vanbrugh—this was not a combination that pleased Sarah. She called and found her daughter 'at ombre with Mr. Congreve and a woman that I did not know. I thought he looked out of countenance, but showed more willingness to talk to me than you did; I soon put you at ease by going away.'

We see the kind of woman Henrietta was at this time from her portrait at Lancaster House. In colouring fair like her mother, fine eyes and, like all the women of the family, an elegant figure. There she sits forcefully, in plain scarlet dress with a blue gown draped loosely round her; a gold scarf trailing from her hair, her literary pretensions explicit in the book drooping from her hand. Henrietta's liaison with Congreve was the great affair of her life, recognised by everybody. But it was never recognised by Sarah. It led to vehement reproaches, appeals to the Duke, quarrels, reconciliations, scenes, letters—many of which Sarah afterwards burnt in resentment: the regular gamut of her attempts to destroy the Queen's passion for Abigail, and equally fruitless. Her direct assaults and violent interferences only wedded them closer. And so it was with Henrietta, who owed the happiness of her life to Congreve.

Their visit to Bath proved fruitful: the waters were apt to have 'a wonderful influence on barren ladies, who often prove with child, even in their husbands' absence'. Godolphin, who had not been much in the habit of cohabiting with his wife, wrote complaisantly to his daughter, 'you will, I dare say, my dear child, be glad to hear that your Mama is very well, after having been brought to bed, about two hours ago, of a little girl'. Lady Mary Wortley Montagu —who was jealous over the possession of Congreve—was less kind: 'she is as much embarrassed with the loss of her big belly', she wrote, 'as ever a dairymaid was with the getting one'.

Not long after, Congreve died and was buried in Westminster Abbey. Henrietta did not hesitate to erect a monument to him with an inscription in her own name: 'to whose most valuable memory this monument is set up by Henrietta, Duchess of Marlborough, as a mark how deeply she remembers the happiness and honour she enjoyed in the sincere friendship of so worthy and honest a man, whose virtue, candour and wit gained him the love and esteem of the present age, and whose writings will be the admiration of the future'. Henrietta Churchill was not lacking in the courage of her family. Her mother commented, 'I know not what pleasure she might have had in his company, but I am sure it was no honour'. When it was found that Congreve had left almost all his fortune to the little girl, people felt sure that it was his child.

Henrietta's son, the second Blandford, was the next heir to Marlborough's dukedom. In him the easy-going strain of the Godolphins slackened the fibre still further and, like a lot of rich young men of the eighteenth century, he took to drink early. As a result of Sarah's influence on the Duke in making his will, the young heir had been made independent of his mother, Henrietta; and this made for bad blood between mother and son. Sarah's relations with her grandchildren followed the psychological patterns usual with such types: the boys could do what they liked and get away with it. On a visit to Holland the young heir did the only positive thing he ever managed: he fell in love with a rich burgomaster's daughter and married her before the family could stop him. She had a dowry of £30,000, but that was inconsiderable for the heir to the Marlboroughs.

There was uproar in the family. The Godolphins were alarmed and on the alert. The one person who took it well was Sarah: she proceeded to do her best for the young couple. No doubt she felt responsible for him, and this was a way of getting her own back on Henrietta. Then it was found that the young Dutch lady was 'charming and agreeable; I envy her nothing but her good understanding and her sweet even temper; they stand her I believe in great stead. He is very kind to her in his way and she carries it mighty prettily to him.' Unfortunately the young man was a confirmed drunkard by this time. One day in August 1731 he went to Oxford to attend a meeting of a club, where a drinking bout at Balliol brought on a high fever, of which he died. Sarah was with him at the end: 'I would have given half my estate to have saved him', she said; 'I hope the Devil is picking that man's bones who taught him to drink'.

Among the things this young man had omitted to do was to give his wife a baby. Thus died the hopes of the Godolphins, who would otherwise have succeeded to the dukedom. And so they pass out of our story.

When the Godolphins went out, the Spencers came in.

With Sarah's Either-Or mentality two of her Spencer grandchildren, Diana and Jack, the younger ones, were her favourites; the other two, Anne and Charles, she did not care for. Indeed Anne, Lady Bateman was her aversion: she answered her grandmother back, gave as good as she got, and led the cabals in the family and in society against the notorious old lady. Sarah after some particular provocation blackened her portrait at Blenheim and wrote underneath, 'She is more black within'. The Lady Bateman was as much of a tartar as her grandmother and exerted a great influence over her elder brother Charles, Earl of Sunderland, who now succeeded as third Duke. Sarah was convinced that his sister had arranged his marriage to—of all people—the daughter of one of the twelve peers unforgivably created in 1712. Marlborough's widow could not swallow this. 'I do believe that my Lord Sunderland, who is certainly a very weak man, will always be governed by his sister.' On the other hand Jack Spencer was the apple of her eye. 'I think your brother John has good nature, sense, frankness in his temper (which I love), and in short a great many desirable things in him; but still he wants a great deal to get through this world in the manner that I wish he should do.' He, unlike his brother, had made a marriage of which she could approve.

Diana had been brought up by her grandmother, and had her mother's art of managing the old lady. Sarah loved her passionately and—as her way had always been—jealously: she could not bear to think that any other woman was closer to her. It evidently fell to Diana to do what she could to bring the family together and restore her brother to his grandmother's affections. In this she succeeded. The young Duke paid Sarah a visit which charmed her. Soon, Sarah is 'labouring like a pack-horse every day to save him from the cheats'. Unfortunately Charles was both extravagant and negligent: he simply could not keep up with her energy or answer her multifarious business letters. 'I cannot help saying to you that it is very unpleasant to go through so much drudgery for one that will not trouble himself to write ten lines in answer to things that only concern himself.' The Duke did not displace plain Jack Spencer as his grandmother's favourite, nor—unfortunately for the Churchills—as the chief beneficiary of her will. The joke is that Jack was hardly less extravagant than his brother.

It was their sister Diana, however, who had Sarah's heart. 'Your desiring me to take care of myself for your sake is very kind, and I return it by assuring you that I desire to live only for you.' When the girl married John Russell Sarah gave her a dowry of £30,000 and designed to leave her £100,000. Her husband succeeded his brother as Duke of Bedford. 'This letter is writ by my new secretary, the Duke of Bedford, which you will read with more ease than my ridiculous hand. He has turned Di out of her place of my secretary, which you know is a common thing in this age for ministers to trip up one another's heels. He is the best servant and minister that ever I had, and he is so far from being lazy that he copies out all my papers that I have. He is certainly a perfect miracle of his age. I think Providence designs to make me amends for some of my past sufferings by the goodness and kindness of this young man.'

Sarah took to calling Diana 'Cordelia'. That is the name I intend to call you for the future, which is the name of King Lear's good child, and therefore a proper title for you, who have been always good to me. . . . You are charming in all your thoughts and actions.' The name was ominous of tragedy. Already Di's health was not as Sarah could wish it. She hoped that the girl would go into the air on every fine day: it was impossible it could do any hurt. To aid her take the air Sarah sent her Marlborough's famous tent. 'I wish it may be of any use and please you, but I think the chief value of it is, to think that it was your dear grandfather's tent, when he did such wonderful things to secure the nation from being enslaved by the French king, besides the great provisions he made for his whole family, all which I think should make his memory dear to every one of them.' Sarah did not realise that no further provision would be necessary for her Cordelia: she was dying.

Di's death left the old woman's life empty of love. The soulless round continued—indomitable activity, politics, business, society, people, dragging oneself round to the last. But at heart there was emptiness. 'It is impossible that one of my age and infirmities can live long; and one great happiness there is in death, that one shall never hear any more of anything they do in this world.' Religion, the consolation of them that have not love, meant nothing to her. What her real belief had been is revealed in her saying, 'I have always thought that the greatest happiness of life was to love and value somebody extremely that returned it and to see them often'. She died in her eighty-fifth year at Marlborough House, her favourite residence, on 19 October 1744. She had been born, an age before, only a few days after the happy Restoration of King Charles II.

Her will was as full and crowded as her life had been, and much more generous. It was governed by the decision that since Charles Spencer, the elder brother, had succeeded to the dukedom, the younger should have Althorp and the succession to the Spencer estates. John Spencer, ancestor of the Earls Spencer, became her chief legatee: that is how most of her personal belongings come to be at Althorp. The bulk of her lands and estates went to him and his heirs, on condition that he should not 'accept or take from any King or Queen of these Realms any pension or any office or employment, civil or military'. That must have made the young Duke regret that he had returned to the government fold and accepted office before her death. Marlborough House went to John Spencer for life, afterwards to go with the dukedom. All the furniture that she had bought there was for John; that bought by her husband went to Charles. The furniture at Blenheim went to

Charles, provided he left the goods and furniture of Althorp to John, who was also to have the house in Grosvenor Street. His son and heir was to have £2000 a year on coming of age. A sense of duty to Marlborough's dynastic feelings made her direct £3000 a year for the sons of Blenheim. Their successors had reason to wish that more of her substance had been devoted to the upkeep of that house.

For an exceedingly generous list of legacies to other people followed. Over a score of people were given annuities. Her man of business and trustee, James Stephens, was left £15,000 and £300 a year. (Multiply by ten.) Her companion Grace Midgley, a girl whom she picked up at Woodstock and made her Abigail, got £15,000, £300 a year, a miniature of Marlborough, a locket portrait of him and one of Sarah by Kneller, and the Duke's striking watch. Grace's daughter was left £3000. The Earl of Clancarty, Sarah's neighbour at Marlborough House, £1000 down and £1000 a year. All her gold and silver plate, her seals and trinkets and small pieces of japan were for John Spencer; her best diamonds for his wife. Her diamond solitaire, gold snuff-box with portraits of Marlborough, a string of pearls with other pictures of him were left to his daughter Mary, Duchess of Montagu; to the Duchess of Devonshire 'my box of travelling plate', to the Dowager Countess of Burlington £1000 and her bag of gold medals, to the Duke of Leeds £3000, his niece £1000; to the Duchess of Manchester, a granddaughter, the house in Dover Street. To the Godolphins nothing: they had failed in the race. Her wish was to be buried 'near the body of my dear husband' at Blenheim.

They had been long apart. At length there together they lie.

BOOK II

THE LATE

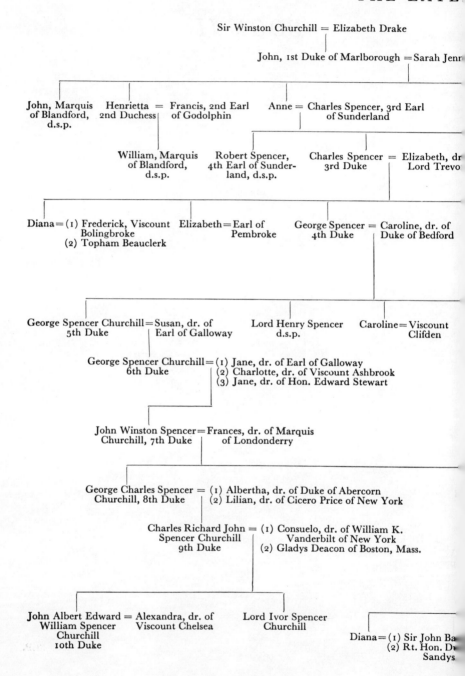

Sir Winston Churchill = Elizabeth Drake

John, 1st Duke of Marlborough = Sarah Jenn

John, Marquis of Blandford, d.s.p.

Henrietta 2nd Duchess = Francis, 2nd Earl of Godolphin

Anne = Charles Spencer, 3rd Earl of Sunderland

William, Marquis of Blandford, d.s.p.

Robert Spencer, 4th Earl of Sunderland, d.s.p.

Charles Spencer 3rd Duke = Elizabeth, dr Lord Trevo

Diana = (1) Frederick, Viscount Bolingbroke (2) Topham Beauclerk

Elizabeth = Earl of Pembroke

George Spencer 4th Duke = Caroline, dr. of Duke of Bedford

George Spencer Churchill 5th Duke = Susan, dr. of Earl of Galloway

Lord Henry Spencer d.s.p.

Caroline = Viscount Clifden

George Spencer Churchill 6th Duke = (1) Jane, dr. of Earl of Galloway (2) Charlotte, dr. of Viscount Ashbrook (3) Jane, dr. of Hon. Edward Stewart

John Winston Spencer Churchill, 7th Duke = Frances, dr. of Marquis of Londonderry

George Charles Spencer Churchill, 8th Duke = (1) Albertha, dr. of Duke of Abercorn (2) Lilian, dr. of Cicero Price of New York

Charles Richard John Spencer Churchill 9th Duke = (1) Consuelo, dr. of William K. Vanderbilt of New York (2) Gladys Deacon of Boston, Mass.

John Albert Edward William Spencer Churchill 10th Duke = Alexandra, dr. of Viscount Chelsea

Lord Ivor Spencer Churchill

Diana = (1) Sir John Ba (2) Rt. Hon. D Sandys

CHURCHILLS

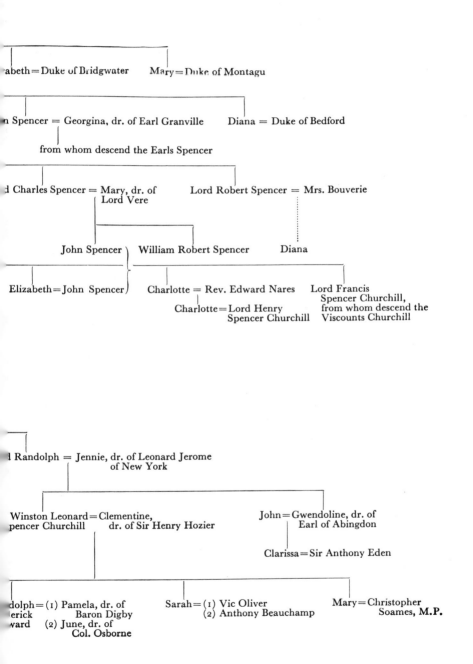

abeth = Duke of Bridgwater

Mary = Duke of Montagu

n Spencer = Georgina, dr. of Earl Granville

from whom descend the Earls Spencer

Diana = Duke of Bedford

d Charles Spencer = Mary, dr. of Lord Vere

Lord Robert Spencer = Mrs. Bouverie

John Spencer

William Robert Spencer

Diana

Elizabeth = John Spencer

Charlotte = Rev. Edward Nares

Charlotte = Lord Henry Spencer Churchill

Lord Francis Spencer Churchill, from whom descend the Viscounts Churchill

d Randolph = Jennie, dr. of Leonard Jerome of New York

Winston Leonard Spencer Churchill = Clementine, dr. of Sir Henry Hozier

John = Gwendoline, dr. of Earl of Abingdon

Clarissa = Sir Anthony Eden

dolph = (1) Pamela, dr. of Baron Digby
erick
ward (2) June, dr. of Col. Osborne

Sarah = (1) Vic Oliver
(2) Anthony Beauchamp

Mary = Christopher Soames, M.P.

CHAPTER ONE

Charles, Third Duke : at Home and Abroad

AGAINST the background of his private life—happy in marriage, unhappy about money in spite of all his grandfather's wealth coming to him—we may turn to Charles the third Duke's, public career.

It was natural that, with his family associations, he should belong at his entry into politics to the heart of the opposition to Walpole at the height of his power. There was Sarah—and for some years Charles may be regarded as her representative in the House of Lords; there was his brother-in-law the Duke of Bedford, with whom he acted in close concert; there was Lord Carteret, John's father-in-law, and Lord Chesterfield, Sarah's favourite, to give the group intellectual leadership. In the Commons there were the Boys, the young Patriots, of whom Lyttelton and Pitt were outstanding, whose popular line was to attack the Hanoverian commitments of George II's government. Lord Hervey tells us that George II had always shown a dislike to Charles while he was Lord Sunderland, on account of his father, George I's minister, who could hardly help being involved in the quarrel between the King and his eldest son. Charles did not take much part in the proceedings of the Lords as Earl of Sunderland; when he did, it was to register an Opposition protest in accordance with Sarah's wishes and the policy of the group.

On succeeding his aunt, Henrietta, as Duke of Marlborough he was introduced, in January 1734, by the Dukes of Bedford and Manchester, with all the paraphernalia proper to such an occasion. In February the Opposition took the opportunity of the dismissal of the Duke of Bolton and Lord Cobham from their commands in the Army, for opposing Walpole's Excise scheme, to bring in a Bill to prevent officers from being deprived of their commissions other than by the Houses of Parliament or court-martial. This was regarded by George II as personally insulting, as it certainly was an infringement of his rights in regard to the Army. The young Duke brought in the Bill, and, though it was negatived, there was a strong muster of Opposition peers to sign the Lords' Protest.

In the 1730's Opposition found a head, though a very unsatisfactory one, in George II's son, Frederick Prince of Wales. There was nothing to be said in his favour—except for his characteristically German love of music—and his mother and father were not given to saying it. The King said of his son, when he left St. James's Palace after the *accouchement* of his wife, that he hoped he would never see the puppy again. The Queen said that her 'dear first-born is the greatest ass, and the greatest liar, and the greatest *canaille*, and the greatest beast in the whole world, and I most heartily wish he was out of it'. There was much to be said for their point of view, but English society was hardly accustomed to these Hanoverian antics in its royal family—such a contrast to the dignity, and fair family relations, of their predecessors.

Political dissension in such a close society did not interfere with the enjoyments of social life—it added a spice to them. That winter party-feeling and court-division extended itself to the realm of music. The Prince of Wales, with Charles's assistance, undertook a campaign against Handel, who was the King's favourite composer. They engaged an Italian company for the Opera in Lincoln's Inn Fields, where they opened their season with an *Ariadne*. Handel replied with a rival *Ariadne* at the Haymarket. The Italians then brought over the most famous of *castrati,* Farinelli, who made a fortune out of his favour in the Courts of Europe. Frederick's passion for music overcame his political feelings and he ultimately made it up with Handel. These pleasurable feuds had their reflection in literature. Towards the end of the winter Fielding put on his tedious play, *The Universal Gallant*, which in opposition to Walpole he dedicated to Marlborough with a resounding platitude: 'Poverty has imposed chains on mankind equal with tyranny; and your Grace has shown as great an eagerness to deliver men from the former as your illustrious grandfather did to rescue them from the latter'. When Fielding published his *Miscellanies* the subscribers were headed by the Prince, followed by Bedford and Marlborough and what reads like a roll-call of the Opposition.

At Frederick's marriage in 1736 Charles, resplendent in white and gold, almost eclipsed his friend the Prince—we may imagine the dazzling scene at St. James's, the flowered silks and damasks, the jewelled headdress of the ladies, a thousand candles reflected in the mirrors, the thronged corridors and galleries. The Duke remained to put the Prince and Princess to bed in the formal

French fashion—the King putting on the Prince's shirt, the Princess undressed by her ladies.

More important for Marlborough was his friendship with Henry Fox, which was a factor in the political grouping of the time and had consequences for the family into the next generation, for the best part of a century. Their friendship was a case of mutual attraction that went back to early days—'my most intimate and dear friend from childhood', Fox wrote of Charles when he died. The Foxes had followed a course somewhat comparable to the Churchills. Starting as a West Country family in Wiltshire, they moved into Dorset; they were Royalists and subsequently Tories, tarnished with Jacobitism. They too were Household officials to the Stuarts, Sir Stephen Fox, like Sir Winston, an officer of the Board of Green Cloth; but as Paymaster he made a large fortune, honestly gotten and unenvied, 'which is next to a miracle', said Evelyn.

When Henry Fox fell in love with the Duke of Richmond's eldest daughter and won her parents' intense disapproval—for he was a younger son and they could not foresee that he would become one of the richest politicians of the time—Marlborough stood by him. Lady Caroline eloped from her parents' house and was married privately in Sir Charles Hanbury-Williams's residence in Privy Gardens; Marlborough as a friend of the Richmond family gave her away. The affair made a sensation and they were much abused for their part in it. Society, as usual in these affairs, took sides—mostly the side of the Richmonds, who were implacable and cut their daughter off, refusing to see her for years. In the end, they had to recognise that the marriage was blissfully happy and their unwanted son-in-law a foremost figure in politics: that mollified them. Whatever we may think of Henry Fox as a politician, in private life he displayed loyalty and charm. On the back of Richardson's portrait of Marlborough at Holland House he inscribed these words: 'Lord Holland loved and still loves his friend Charles Spencer better than any man living'. When Charles died Fox had to seek a change of scene to prevent 'continual thinking' of his dead friend. There must have been something very attractive in Charles to inspire such devotion.

The long ascendancy of Sir Robert Walpole was drawing to a close under increasingly successful challenges to his policy and power. When the colonial war with Spain merged into a general European war and Walpole's policy lay in ruins around him, a concerted attack was made on his prosecution of the war, which he was as ill-fitted to conduct as Neville Chamberlain was that of 1939. In February 1741 addresses to remove Walpole were brought forward with large support in both Houses of Parliament. Thereupon Marlborough came to Walpole's defence against attainder or impeachment with a resolution in the Lords 'that any attempt to inflict any kind of punishment on any person without allowing him an opportunity to make his defence, or without proof of any crime or misdemeanor committed by him, is contrary to natural justice, the fundamental laws of this realm and the ancient established usage of Parliaments; and it is a high infringement on the liberties of the subject.' This was carried by 81 to 54.

But nothing could save Walpole now with the war-fever heightening. In February 1742 he resigned. The Prince of Wales paid a visit in triumph to the King; crowds attended Frederick at Carlton House, where he refused to speak to Marlborough who had defended Walpole to the last. There was talk that he would be rewarded with a command in Flanders; and in fact he did go on active service as brigadier to the Netherlands this year, and to Germany on the Dettingen campaign the year after.

Next year, 1746, brought a shock: the early death of his brother Jack Spencer 'at the age of six or seven and thirty', according to Horace Walpole, 'and in possession of near £30,000 a year, merely because he would not be abridged of those invaluable blessings of an English subject, brandy, small beer and tobacco'. It is more likely to have been from the consumption all these children inherited from their mother. Jack had lived just long enough to get the bulk of Sarah's immense fortune, in addition to the Sunderland estates handed over to him by Charles. Now from the grave Jack administered a worse shock to his brother. 'The great business of the town is Jack Spencer's will, who has left Althorp and the Sunderland estate in reversion to Pitt, after more obligations and more pretended friendship for his brother the Duke than is conceivable. The Duke is in the utmost uneasiness about it, having left the drawing of the writings for the estate to his brother and his grandmother, and without having any idea that himself was cut out of the entail.' To this had their relations come after the years of friction with and around Sarah, the bickerings and the increasing distrust; it is sad to think of, after the closeness and mutual affection of their youth and early manhood.

England's duel with France, which was the dominant theme of foreign affairs for most of the century, reached an inconclusive truce with the Peace of Aix-la-Chapelle in 1748. The rule of the Pelhams, in the years before and after, was described by Horace Walpole as 'a system of lethargic acquiescence in which the spirit of Britain, agitated for so many centuries, seemed willingly to repose'. This was the Augustan age of Georgian England: everywhere country houses were being built or rebuilt in classic beauty, elegance of decoration and proportion, in admirable dignity and repose, or mere decency according to the good standards of the age. They embodied an ideal of civilisation that was at the same time urbane and founded upon sane and healthy country foundations, pursuits, obligations. Never can there have been a better balanced, a more satisfying, way of life. Everywhere the rural landscape was being brought into order and improved; the lines of woodland and plantation, park and wild, that have endured until our own unhappy day were then being laid down. These were the years when the Duke was making his park, with its lakes and plantations, at Langley and rebuilding the house there in the plain symmetry and distinction demanded by the taste of the time.

For the politicians there was the perennial sport of domestic politics, the ins and outs, the ups and downs, the snakes and ladders of office. Dukes—except for the absorbed Duke of Newcastle—sat more loosely to the game, though their stake in the country and their rank demanded some attention. Marlborough belonged to his brother-in-law Bedford's group, whose leading spokesman in the Commons was Henry Fox. Fox, who knew him well, described the Duke of Bedford as 'the most ungovernable governed man in the world'—for he was much under the influence of his second Duchess. Marlborough was equally dilatory and unwilling to support the routine burden of office. Perhaps being a Duke was a full-time job in itself. It was not that he was without ambition, or qualification for office. Even Horace Walpole, in his disparaging way, allowed that he had good judgment. 'The Duke of Marlborough had virtues and sense enough to deserve esteem, but always lost it by forfeiting respect. He was honest and generous; capable of giving the most judicious advice and of following the worst. His profusion was never well directed, and a variety of changes in his political conduct having never been weighed previously or preserved subsequently, joined to the greatest bashfulness and indistinction in his articulation, had confirmed the world in a very mean opinion of his understanding.' We see how right Sarah had been to tell him to speak up, if he wanted to be a British senator—we observe too Charles's natural diffidence that haunted him all his life. Nevertheless, in spite of these disadvantages, pride and his sense of rank kept him to his last as a senator. In 1749 he was appointed Lord Steward of the Household; in spite of diffidence and inarticulateness he spoke in the Lords when necessary.

In 1753 there was a prodigious fuss about suspected Jacobite leanings among the preceptors of Prince George, heir to the throne. Two years before his father had died, regretted by no one: 'he had his father's head and his mother's heart'. The education of the boy who became George III was a matter of state importance. The old King appointed as his governor Lord Waldegrave, who was a personal favourite with him. Waldegrave was a great-grandson of James II by Arabella Churchill. The Hanoverians were as royalist in their prejudices as the exiled Stuarts. The charges against the young Prince's tutors created much excitement. Marlborough was called upon to put the matter in its proper proportions and to report the sentence of the Cabinet Council, which gave no credence to the charges.

Since Sarah's death the Duke had been installed at Blenheim and we find him extending his interests in Oxfordshire. In 1751 Clarendon's descendant, Lord Hyde, was forced to sell beautiful Cornbury, which marches with Blenheim. Marlborough's trustees bought the estate for £61,000, including the Rangership of Wychwood Forest. For the next century and a half this captivating property remained in the possession of the Duke's descendants, for part of the time under the name of Blandford Park. The name did not stick.

In January 1755 the Duke got the high political post of Lord Privy Seal, which gave him an influential voice in affairs and brought him into the forefront of the political manoeuvres on the eve and during the first years of the Seven Years War. It is impossible to describe these in detail—anywhow they are quite well known. The clue to the situation was the weakness of Newcastle's administration in the Commons, where the two leading figures were Fox and Pitt; the problem how to accommodate them, or one or the other of them, without giving him control of the ministry. Marlborough's interest in the matter was very close, through his personal friendship with Fox. We shall see that he acted a part that was sincere in relation to his friend, self-sacrificing in regard to himself, and governed by his sense of duty to the country.

At the end of the year Newcastle was forced to bring in more of the Bedfords. To make this easier Marlborough stepped down from his post as Lord Privy Seal to make way for Bedford's brother-in-law. Instead he accepted the office of Master General of the Ordnance. We may be sure that the change, though a demotion, was congenial to him: no more speechifying in the Lords, but a return to the Army. Moreover, it was an office his grandfather had held.

Hitherto Pitt and Fox had been as friendly as two pre-eminent rivals can be expected to be. One thing that drew them together was that Newcastle wanted neither of these men of superior abilities. But the country was drifting into war and the sense of crisis was sharpening the conflicts of policy and power. There was only one man who could surmount the crisis and carry the country through to victory: William Pitt. All the politicians were united to keep him out. He owed nothing to party and had few friends. Possessed by his own genius, cut off by illness and perhaps schizophrenia from normal commerce with human beings, he soared alone. He had contrived to alienate many people in his twenty years in Parliament. The King detested him for his fulminations against Hanover, his self-consciously and highly dramatised patriotic line, and maintained a rigid veto against admitting him to any office that would bring him into contact with him. In all those years the King had only once spoken to him; at his levees George II was unable to recognise the greatest orator in the kingdom. Perhaps people may be forgiven for not discerning underneath the orator, the 'daring pilot in extremity', the man who would dare all for his country and out of frustration and defeat raise her, in those years from his assumption of supreme power to the outbreak of the American Revolution, to the loftiest height she ever attained.

Horace Walpole points the contrast between these two, Marlborough's friend Fox and no one's 'friend' Pitt—for he did not regard anyone else as his equal. Pitt was by far the greater speaker, Fox the better debater. Not far below the surface in Henry Fox was an inextinguishable jealousy of Pitt: one recognises the familiar smell in his comment, after a superb speech of Pitt's, 'Pitt is a better speaker than I am; but, thank God, I have better judgment.' Some quality in Pitt daunted Fox: as the Prince of Vaudemont had said of John Churchill, there was 'something inexpressible' about him—we remember that Pitt was a kinsman of the Churchills. Next year, when the country was bewildered by a succession of defeats, Pitt told the Duke of Devonshire calmly, 'My lord, I know that I can save my country, and that nobody else can'.

Henry Fox was that rare thing in English politics, a confessed cynic. He knew what people are, and he did not mind. Now at this juncture Newcastle offered him a Secretaryship of State without the management of the Commons: in other words, that he should have the responsibility for the conduct of the war without the power. Marlborough, who did not lack courage, had at first advised his friend not to accept office without power and argued that Newcastle was at his mercy. Now Fox was left dependent on Newcastle, having to defend the government's failures in the Commons, without power. The war meanwhile was going from bad to worse. It had been brought on by Boscawen's attacking a French fleet off Louisbourg, capturing only two ships while all the rest of the ships got safe into harbour: the operation should either have been completed or not attempted at all. General Braddock's army was completely cut up by the French in the Ohio country and himself killed. Then came the surrender of Minorca. The country was both frustrated and furious; it was on this wave of indignation that Pitt was irresistibly borne forward, like his remote kinsman in 1940.

The urgency of the war suspended the scuffling of factions for a time; in the summer of 1756 invasion was expected. The Foot Guards were encamped at Cobham and to raise morale a grand military parade was staged. Horace Walpole tells us that all the world was a-soldiering and that the great drum was to pass by to Cobham. 'The Duke of Marlborough and his grandfather's triumphal car are to close the procession. What would his grandame, if she were alive, say to this pageant? If the war lasts, I think well enough of him to believe he will earn a sprig; but I have no notion of trying on a crown of laurel before I had acquired it. The French are said to be embarked at Dunkirk.' When the emergency passed Marlborough was stationed at Byfleet in command of the artillery.

Pitt was planning an attack on the French coast, to offset the ill posture of affairs in Germany and in the hope of diverting French forces; from this arose the Rochefort expedition. He found the Duke spirited and co-operative. As usual at the beginning of Britain's wars amateurishness and unpreparedness exacted their penalty: the expedition was a complete fiasco. The country did not hold Pitt responsible; he appointed a court of inquiry into the miscarriage, of which Marlborough was the leading member. Everyone appreciated the fairness with which the inquiry was conducted, though not everyone understood the artfulness of the move politically or its intention to stiffen the morale of the army command. Pitt was full of expedients and schemes; he was ready to try anything. A new spirit was at work. What he liked was officers who, instead of making difficulties, found expedients to carry out his plans.

Pit had another command for Marlborough in view, another attack on the French coast—this time St.-Malo, the chief base for enemy privateers at the western end of the Channel. A considerable striking force was got together: a powerful fleet to cover the operations, a lesser force under Commodore Howe including transports for the troops to be landed: combined operations. Marlborough's name recruited a large number of aristocratic volunteers; he took his eldest son, Blandford, with him and the enchanting Di accompanied them to their embarkation at St. Helen's. They set sail on 1 June, but for several days were held up by contrary winds off the French coast and landed their troops only on 5 June in Cancale Bay, several miles from St.-Malo. That spiked the enterprise from effecting a surprise, or else at the first onrush St.-Malo might have been taken, strongly fortified as it was.

From Marlborough's letters to Pitt we may watch the expedition almost day by day: the landing carried out by the troops in excellent order and discipline, the march to St.-Malo through enclosed country with very bad and narrow roads through which it was impossible to get the artillery, finding it impracticable to invest the city with their small forces so that enemy reinforcements and supplies poured in hourly. Marlborough had sent small detachments into St.-Servan under General Waldegrave, while General Boscawen threw up entrenchments to cover their withdrawal—one sees what a close circle conducted affairs in the eighteenth century: here were two family connexions of the Churchills under Marlborough's command. These measures enabled them to hold on long enough to fire the shipping in the harbour and burn the naval stores: practically all the privateers of 30, 20 and 18 guns, were consumed—perhaps a hundred vessels.

Meanwhile the fleet and transports were wind-bound in Cancale Bay and could not get out. The Duke took the opportunity to reconnoitre Granville with Lord George Sackville and the engineers; but they found it too well fortified and guarded by too strong forces to attempt. By 24 June the fleet had got clear of the Bay and was off Hogue. After reconnoitring the Normandy coast, Marlborough and Howe decided on an attack on Cherbourg. All the preparations for a landing on 29 June were made. At the last moment the wind blew so hard as to make it impossible: the transports would have been dashed to pieces. By this time they had only three days' hay left for the horses, the water for the troops was very bad and the men had grown sickly. There was nothing for it but to return to Spithead.

The small results of the expedition may fairly be put down to the stormy weather that summer. Even so it may have had some effect in withholding French reinforcements for Germany—Prince Ferdinand of Brunswick was polite enough to say so. Nor was Pitt discouraged: the effect on him was to make him reverse his veto on sending British troops to Germany. He determined to use the returned expeditionary force, refreshed and recruited in strength, to aid Prince Ferdinand. He at once made Marlborough Commander-in-Chief, with Lord George Sackville as second in command. By the end of July the Duke had already landed at Emden before the first regiments were embarked. He was back once more in the country he had known so well when he was young, in the days of the Dettingen campaign. Now he was Commander-in-Chief.

Campaigning in Germany once more produced the old jealousies between English and Hanoverians that had made such a mark on the Duke's mind fifteen years before. He was incensed at an Hanoverian general being made full General of Foot over his head: this placed the Hanoverian next to Prince Ferdinand in rank and might have the deplorable consequences that ensued in the Dettingen campaign. Charles at once wrote to Pitt demanding a commission as full General dating from the time he was made Master General of the Ordinance—or he would retire from the Army and all employments for ever. Pitt at once got him his commission out of the King: no delay, no obstacles allowed to stand in the way now. And this was reflected in the good relations Marlborough established with Prince Ferdinand on joining up with him at Coesveldt.

A worse enemy than the French was stalking the lines of the British army. The wet summer had brought much sickness in its train; now dysentery spread through the ranks. In October the Duke was struck down. Jacob Bryant, his boys' former tutor whom he had taken with him as secretary, reported the event in his stilted language to Fox: 'after much strength exerted and a train of favourable symptoms that served only to amuse and deceive, the affair came yesterday [20 October] to a crisis and at last fatally determined. Lord Blandford (I cannot yet call him by any other title) is well, but in much trouble. In a few days, I imagine, he will set out for England.' Bryant added that the 'poor Duke's lungs were so gone that had he survived this illness he could not have lived a year'. We see the background, the consumptive inheritance from his mother, against which his life's effort appears all the more gallant. A month before he had sent home a messenger to Elizabeth with a ring of his own, 'rather too large for a lady's hand, yet you must keep it for my sake'. It was the last token she received from him.

CHAPTER TWO

George, Fourth Duke, and Blenheim

WHERE the affections of the third Duke were fixed upon Langley, which was largely his creation, his son's were indubitably upon Blenheim. The pull of the place began to exert itself on the family which had taken so long to become acclimatised to the grandeur of the first Marlborough's conception. Now in the third generation from him Blenheim—disliked and neglected by Sarah, never occupied by Henrietta and only intermittently so by Charles—came into its own, became finally the centre and magnet of the family. And so onwards into the future.

Sir Lewis Namier has a perceptive passage on the importance of the 'place' for the continuity of the family. 'English history, and especially English Parliamentary history, is made by families rather than by individuals. . . . The English political family is a compound of "blood", name and estate, this last being the most important of the three. . . . The name is a weighty symbol, but liable to variations; descent traced in the male line only is like a river without its tributaries. The estate, with all that it implies, is in the long run the most important factor in securing continuity through identification, the "taking up" of the inheritance. The owner of an ancestral estate may have far less of the "blood" than some distant relative bearing a different name . . . still, it is he who in his thoughts and feelings most closely identifies himself, and is identified by others, with his predecessors.'[1]

George, fourth Duke, ruled at Blenheim far longer than any other member of his family—for just on sixty years; it is only natural, therefore, that he should have left an impress on it second only to John Churchill, first Duke, himself. Above all, we owe to the fourth Duke the dominant feature in the setting of the Palace as we see it today: the drowning of the river-valley of the Glyme to make that magnificent half-moon of lake upon which all the western windows look, that so enhances the fairy-tale quality of the scene and brings out the inherent romanticism of so classic a pile.

[1] L. B. Namier, *England in the Age of the American Revolution*, 22.

That wonderful house—a martial palace, a festive castle, conjured up out of the imagination of a dramatist—was almost as little appreciated in the Georgian age as it was in the Victorian. Horace Walpole paid the place another visit just about this time, the high summer of 1760. 'We went to Blenheim and saw all Vanbrugh's quarries, all the Acts of Parliament and gazettes on the Duke in inscriptions, and all the old flock chairs, wainscot tables, and gowns and petticoats of Queen Anne that old Sarah could crown amongst blocks of marble. It looks like the palace of an auctioneer who has been chosen King of Poland and furnished his apartments with obsolete trophies, rubbish that nobody bid for and a dozen pictures that he had stolen from the inventories of different families. The place is as ugly as the house, and the bridge, like the beggars at the old Duchess's gate, begs for a drop of water and is refused.' This last criticism—the absurdity of such a magnificent bridge crossing so insignificant a stream—was just. Everybody recognised that it was unsatisfactory. An attempt had been made to reduce the marshy little Glyme to formal order, to canalise it and fill two ponds with its inadequate waters, one on either side of the immense bridge. It was this that was now to be transformed by a grand stroke of imagination.

The Duke's father had had no money left over from his works at Langley to spend on building at Blenheim, though he had thought of it. From the moment his son settled down to the possession of Blenheim he began to apply himself to embellishing it. He called in Sir William Chambers, the most fashionable architect at the time, with his French tastes and the patronage of George III, to lighten the declamatory effects of Vanbrugh. Chambers designed a superb state-bed—bell-like baldachin and corner-plumes, pink silk and Sarah's lace—and went on to lighter and more elegant cornices to ceilings, chimney-pieces, pier-glasses. Outside he mitigated the severity of the east portal, with its cannon-balls supporting the piers, by laurel-wreaths on the superstructure. For the park he designed a Temple of Diana and a Tuscan gate, at Bladon an exquisite bridge across the Glyme; for the town of Woodstock a town hall of noble proportions, standing between the two streets that lead to park and Palace, a building that gives an air of foreign distinction to the Cotswold architecture of the little market-place.

Then the Duke called in a new man, Capability Brown, the leading exponent of the Back-to-Nature school of landscape-gardening, a conductor of the gathering romantic impulse of the time. Where the classic age had imposed the architectural forms of the house upon its environment, to extend the idea of the house to the garden, the new school sought to bring Nature right up to the doors. And this Brown, during the ten years he was employed at Blenheim from 1764 to 1774, proceeded to do with a vengeance.

It is extrardinary that that sensitive, compromising man, the Duke, should have allowed Brown to bring about such a revolution in his surroundings. But the Duke was a man of taste and fashion, a connoisseur, and he was young: it is doubtful if he would ever have undertaken such vast works later. Brown began by damming the river and creating the expanse of water that laps the Palace on its western side. As the valley filled and the lake came into existence, it gave sense to Vanbrugh's noble bridge at the same time as it reduced its size by drowning the ground-storey. Proportions were improved; a marvellous new scene created: from across the lake the Palace floats on the horizon, its gathered towers and turrets, the whole fantastic roofscape taking the skies.

Now Brown proceeded to bring the park up to the Palace. The bridge leads up to the grand and very formal entrance front—so grand it might almost be Escorial or Vatican. Brown grassed it over. On the south side of the Palace lay the *chef-d'oeuvre* of Henry Wise, gardener to Queen Anne, who had designed and laid out the gardens at Blenheim. This was an immense six-sided citadel of a garden—with Louis XIV's head taken from Tournai looking down on it—built within walls with bastions at each angle, walks and lime-alleys and fountains within; two great parterres running the whole length of the Palace, 'enriched with dwarf evergreens and coloured sands', raised walks from which one could look down the steep slopes to the valley, back to the house, forward to the tower of Bladon church on the axis running through park, garden, house, across the bridge to the Victory Column and beyond to the other horizon. All on a scale no other house in England could rival.

This superb formal garden was swept completely away. We must for ever regret it. Nothing took its place, nothing but grass: grass coming right up to the garden-front, grass extending in every direction, grass to infinity, nothing but grass and an immensity of sky. It, too, is rather magnificent in its way; but it is boring—as boring as a cricket-pitch, which it is, where once the fountains plashed and sun gleamed on evergreens or printed variegated patterns down those vanished alleys. Perhaps Brown thought that the plain expanse of green set off his lake, as it certainly is a foil for it. One has to admit that on balance Blenheim gained greatly by his work: nothing could surpass the setting he gave the house; his natural romanticism curiously complements the rhetoric of Vanbrugh. Everybody feels this—that the strange house has now the providentially right setting.

Nor was this the end of Brown's works. The whole park, except for the north and east avenues and the kitchen garden, was replanted in Brown's famous belt-and-clump style. Beeches surrounded the park and guarded the Grand Bridge; chestnuts, limes and sycamores hung over the water; while in places of honour, for contrast and for their own peculiar grandeur, stood the cedars, in time to grow massive and lofty, spreading plane upon plane of dark foliage for the pale heron to rest on.'[1] In addition Brown wanted to see the park, the Palace itself romanticised. He managed to castellate High Lodge; he made detailed plans for a new granary, battlements and all. Where were the ramparts that should transform the Palace? He made a sketch to illustrate the effect of his plan, 'which would have involved not merely castellating the park walls but treating in like manner the walls of every visible Woodstock building. . . .'

It was time to call a halt. For the years 1764 to 1774 the Duke paid Brown some £16,437 14*s*., and this can have been only a part of the total sums spent on the improvements at Blenheim: money that was well spent: the country has this lasting memorial to show for it.

Whatever his expenses, the Duke continued to collect, for this was a collectors' age: 'an eclectic and acquisitive age', says Namier, 'primarily an age of collectors, with a passion for accumulating no matter what—books, manuscripts, shells, pictures, old coins or the currency of the realm'. It was only in this last class that these later Marlboroughs were remiss. As early as 1762 Walpole, himself a most distinguished specimen of the collectors' class, tells us that the Duke had bought most of the Zanetti collections of gems at Venice. And this was only a beginning. The theme is brought into Reynolds' magnificent portrait of the Duke and his family painted in August 1777. In this canvas, painted in the grand manner with its architectural background, the Duke is holding a large cameo, while the heir is holding one of the crimson cases that held the Marlborough gems. The collector's mania was to run riot with this boy and ruin him.

Ten years later we find the Duke still bidding for gems. He went

[1] David Green, *Blenheim Palace*, 187.

up as far as £120 for a damaged cameo of Augustus, but the Duke of Portland was determined to have it and his resources were now greater. In earlier years Marlborough stinted himself of nothing: we find one goldsmith's account, for a set of two dozen gold knives, forks and spoons engraved with his arms, for altering and adding festoons to a large tureen and gilding two ice pails—£332 5*s.* 7*d.* It was with the fourth Duke as it had been with his father: this state of affairs could not go on. Between 1763 and 1782 the Duke had sunk just £100,000. It was necessary to retrench and, as with his father, we find a paper of suggested economies. As early as 1766 the Duke was writing, 'I don't know what we shall do for money to pay the quarter's bills'. In the next year or two the number of servants was reduced from eighty-eight to some seventy-five. Nothing would do, however, except a major measure; and in 1788 he took the resolution to sell Langley. It must have fetched a very large sum and effected a considerable relief so far as this Duke was concerned. In the latter half of his life he was much less profuse and far more careful; his virtual retirement to Blenheim aided him to live within his income. But by this time his son had come of age and he proved the most extravagant and wasteful of this spendthrift stock.

The Duke and Duchess went about a good deal, every year to Bath, and later on to fashionable Brighthelmstone where they had a house next the Pavilion; in London they lived at Marlborough House. But they moved about alone; they had always been wrapped up in each other since they were first married and they were sufficient to themselves. In time this cut them off from society so much that they became rather eccentric—the Duke notoriously so; but it had its effect on the Duchess too: as sometimes happens with very happy and exclusive marriages, husband and wife echoed each other, grew together.

In their curious withdrawn state from the world the Marlboroughs came to rely increasingly on John Moore's letters —the Duke's former tutor—for what was going on, as well as for counsel as to what they should do. It was the Duchess who kept the contact going; the Duke scarcely put pen to paper. Fortunately Moore was a good letter-writer and his letters to her form a moving picture of their lives and concerns. In 1771 Moore became Dean of Canterbury and it was while he was there that we first hear of trouble with young Blandford, the heir. The boy was delicate and spoiled; it seems that Coxe, his tutor, was not successful in dealing with him. Moore, as usual, was called in to advise. He thought that Coxe had not shown enough firmness in dealing with the boy's fits; while his personal servant had taken advantage to demand new terms for himself. The Dean had no patience with this: if he did it again he should be turned out at an hour's warning. In all this correspondence we find the solid grazier's son trying to steel the Marlboroughs' resolution as they got odder and odder and more incapable of making up their minds.

Meanwhile Moore had been made Bishop of Bangor and in the summer of 1776, while momentous events were taking place on the other side of the Atlantic and Congress was issuing its Declaration of Independence, was peacefully perambulating his diocese. In the summer of 1777, when Howe was occupying Philadelphia and Burgoyne on his way to Saratoga, the bishop was rambling in Anglesey, Sir Joshua painting at Blenheim. 'It will amuse your Graces to have him there and it is a very good season for him to go on with the picture. I have no doubt but he will make a fine picture; but I hope the resemblances will be striking. I would have the countenances I have so long been used to see with pleasure handed down just as they are to posterity.' Thus Sir Joshua accomplished his most sumptuous and famous family portrait. The children, as so often with him, are particularly delightful: there is the smallest girl who was frightened of being painted, caught shrinking back, holding on to her sister's skirts; there is the little girl hiding behind the mask, the young heir looking fragile, the air of weakness already on him. The magnificent Duke displays his handsome calves while the Duchess is the centre of the whole. But the family, which no doubt meant herself, considered she was done least justice. So next year Romney was employed to paint her portrait alone. The Bishop added that 'within this month or two people here have somehow heard of the rebellion in America and begun to talk of it'. Not until the surrender under the chestnut-tree at Saratoga did the country wake up to the seriousness of the situation in America and the task they had been let in for by the mismanagements of the past decade.

Saratoga brought France into the war and later Spain. Britain declared war upon Holland; and the hostile armed neutrality of the Northern Powers was formed against us. Soon Britain was fighting not only her revolted Colonies but half Europe, the more powerful half—fighting alone, without an ally, for her very existence. It was an extraordinary effort that she mounted, but it should never have come to such a pass. Sensible, conservative Coxe wrote from Italy, 'I know nothing in which our blessed Ministry are more blameable than in not having one ally. The moment that a war with America was necessary, they ought to have foreseen that one with France and Spain was unavoidable, and as well they ought to have formed some alliance with Russia, Denmark, Holland.' That alliance had been Chatham's objective in 1766, but it was rejected by Frederick of Prussia. Pitt's genius had elevated Britain to a dangerous ascendancy, for it raised up a world of jealous enemies biding their chance. Everything should have been done to purchase an ally; the combination of a defensive alliance in Europe with concessions to America would have made us safe and kept the Empire intact. This had been Chatham's policy. But he was a dying man, whom illness and the King had kept out in the years that mattered. The politicians gave themselves up to domestic dissensions—and the country, sunk in its eighteenth-century quiet, took no notice of what was piling up on the other side of the Atlantic: it was too far away, another world.

The unrespectable Lord Pembroke had been more sensible. He was now writing, 'Lord Chatham is not only the first Man, but alas the only man who can save this Nation.' And then, 'Lord Chatham came down to the House today . . . a feeble shocking sight, a wreck . . . yet he made a spirited, short speech. A few minutes after he sat down and whilst the Duke of Richmond was speaking he—what they called fainted, fell back and was carried out. . . . I fear the attack was more than fainting.' Within a few weeks the great man—that 'trumpet of sedition' as the King had called him—was dead; George III was against his being given a state funeral. The country's affairs were less safe in the hands of those second-rate men, George III and Lord North, Sandwich and Lord George Germaine, than in those of the dangerous man of genius.

There had been a rumour in 1776 that Marlborough was moving into opposition; it seems that in June he was offered the Lord-Lieutenancy of Ireland and declined it. But by 1778 it was as much as he could do to review the local militia. Moore wrote to congratulate him on summoning up his resolution and to steel him to do it again. 'I have seen with pain how much your Graces have both withdrawn yourselves from the world of late, and I have feared it would grow upon you. . . . Your children are now growing up apace and they *must* mix with the world and how much better under your own eyes?' Moore was right as usual: their withdrawal was a factor in what happened to their eldest son. He held up the example of the Duke's brother, Lord Charles, who 'is so universally beloved in the militia' and whose example contributed 'much to the steadiness of your interest in the county'. Both Lord Charles and Lord Robert had jobs in the Administration, Charles as a member of the Board of Admiralty and Robert as a member of the Board of Trade and Plantations—both of them since the formation of Lord North's government in 1770. Now in 1779 Gibbon was coming to join Lord Robert as a sinecure member, along with the indispensable William Eden, now Moore's brother-in-law. We see what a family-party government was.

In 1779 Spain came into the war, with the object of taking Gibraltar and getting back Minorca and Florida. The first consequence was that a combined Franco-Spanish fleet of sixty ships-of-the-line entered the Channel where at first there was nothing to oppose them. They hovered off Plymouth threatening invasion. Moore's cool head makes an interesting assessment of their chances. He does not think highly of the state of the Spanish ships or of their willingness to fight under a French admiral. The English fleet is better manned and full of ardour—so that the combined fleets are not likely to gain such an ascendancy as to enable enough transports to cross and invade successfully. And so it turned out. Before the combined fleets appeared an immense fleet of merchantmen from the West Indies, one hundred and twenty-five sail, arrived home safe; and immediately after the enemy fleets had left, another equally big convoy came in from the East Indies. The combined fleets got back to Brest, ravaged with sickness, having accomplished nothing. The island-power was called on to make yet greater exertions; she was now fighting not only half the world but, now that conflict raged in India too, over half the world.

The trouble, however, was that the country was not united. United enough against its old enemies and to withstand invasion, it was not united against its own kith and kin across the Atlantic. Some of the best minds in England were with the Americans. From the moment France intervened, Charles Fox's friend, Fitzpatrick, declared, 'all people see the necessity of withdrawing the troops from America'. It is true that neither were the Americans united: in some colonies there was a large number of loyalists or at least neutrally inclined. It was a revolutionary minority that was bent on breaking the connexion. But in England, at the top, there was irresolution. Ten years before, even Henry Fox had at last wished to see Chatham in power, on the ground that he was the only man who did not know what it was to want resolution. Now the country was caught in a war that its minister Lord North had never believed in, driven on by the stubbornness of the King and the country gentlemen.

All these currents and cross-currents came to a head in the next few years of continual crisis until peace was made and Chatham's son came into power to give the country a long period of stable government. We cannot go into these complexities or the issues here: only show how they affected this particular family, the head of which was an intelligent man but afflicted with a paralysis of the will. As the crisis deepened he did not know where to turn—except to Moore for counsel.

Party-spirit had invaded both navy and army. In January 1779 the Admiralty, of which the wicked Lord Sandwich was head, precipitately ordered the court-martial of Admiral Keppel. This was widely unpopular in the country and with the mob—and Keppel was a Whig. On this issue Lord Charles disagreed with the First Lord and determined to resign. Marlborough, sensitive as ever, was now feeling qualms about the Court's proceedings and, fearful for his brother, forbade him to attend Parliament during the trial.

In February 1780 Lord Pembroke resigned his Court appointment and the King dismissed him from the Lord-Lieutenancy of Wiltshire. He instructed Lord North that 'a civil communication should be made to the Duke of Marlborough that regard to him alone made me not remove his brother-in-law; but he having chosen to resign, I could not think it right to leave the Lieutenancy in his hands'. The pull of his family away from the government put the Duke into a great state of mind. At the same time Lord Robert's financial difficulties—the result of his mania for gambling—resulted, like Fox's, in bankruptcy. In regard to both worries the Duke had resort to Moore, who addressed his longest and most interesting letter to the subject.

Moore never allowed himself to think of unpleasant circumstances until the matter was settled. 'I am afraid that emphatical word *Fuss*, which your Grace uses, is not always confined to one side of the fire. Indeed if that word was struck out of the language, or rather the thing itself turned out of the doors at Blenheim, I do think it would be the pleasantest place and the possessors of Blenheim would be the happiest persons in the world. But, alas, there is not resolution enough to resist his intrusions. In some shape or other he conveys himself into the house daily and hourly. If no visitor introduces him before dinner; if Mr. Cole does not convey him into the house in the course of the day, still it is a hundred to one but he comes by the post and, seeing himself made so much of, it is no wonder that he is not in a hurry to quit the house'.

As to the Duke's anxiety about what line he should take towards the government: 'when the judgment of his brothers and sisters is unprejudiced and dispassionate and their arguments are conclusive to his own unbiased judgment, that judgment being formed by the best information he can get, let him come into their sentiments and act accordingly. But I hope he will never give up his own understanding, nor abandon the respectable and manly character he maintains, to mere importunity and teasing. He will hold a very inferior rank in the minds of all men, if he should cease to support government because Lord Robert is the friend of Mr. Charles Fox, or because Lord Pembroke is an enemy of the Administration—or because Lord Charles, with the best of hearts but a ductile mind, is now and then impressed strongly with the sentiments of warm party men with whom he lives in habits of friendship.'

'The Duke of Marlborough is the head of the family by birth and in parts has as good judgment as any of them.' The Bishop sees nothing like perfection in the present Administration, 'but have we another administration to look to of sounder hearts, or sounder heads? I don't see where it is to be found. . . .'

'As to the other points mentioned in your Grace's letter, the necessity of employment, society, etc., I have stunned your ears and rung the changes upon them so often that I have been quite ashamed of myself. . . . The truth is the Duke of Marlborough need never want employment, nor either of your Graces society. But both will be wanted till the Duke resolves not to be afraid of a little employment and both your Graces resolve not to be afraid of society. At present the Duke uses himself to look too much at difficulties in everything that comes in the shape of employment, and I much fear that both your Graces would look upon it as a distress if four or five of the best friends you have in the world should be announced to you unexpectedly any day in the week. While this is the case you will never enjoy society as other people do. The same people are not the same thing to you as to others. They wish to do so, but they can't. They are *gênés,* because they see your Graces so, for there is no distemper more catching.'

There is the whole position set out: the Bishop was a true confessor, and a very rational and sensible one. Here was the upshot of a too happy, too exclusive marriage upon over-refined, over-sensitive temperaments. The position was, in fact, beyond repair.

Lecky says that 'the aspect of affairs at the close of 1780 might indeed well have appalled an English statesman. Perfectly isolated in the world, England was confronted by the united arms of France, Spain, Holland and America; while the Northern league threatened her, if not with another war, at least with the annihilation of her most powerful weapon of offence. At the same time, in Hindostan, Hyder Ali was desolating the Carnatic and menacing Madras; and in Ireland the connexion was strained to its utmost limit and all real power had passed into the hands of a volunteer force which was perfectly independent of the government and firmly resolved to remodel the constitution.'

Strangely enough, in this situation, at war with half the world, the country was not appalled. The tremendous struggle swung to and fro with varying fortunes. Gibraltar, surrounded on all sides and subjected to a terrific bombardment, refused to yield and held out unconquered to the end of the war. With the capture of St. Eustatius Rodney took one hundred and fifty merchantmen of all nations, enormous stores on the island and a Dutch merchant fleet to boot. In America Washington was anything but confident: he knew that it depended entirely on whether France made an effort large enough to turn the scales. At last she made a supreme effort: dispatched a fleet of twenty-five ships of the line under de Grasse, a convoy of between 200 and 300 ships, and 6000 regular soldiers; enough to turn the scales and force Cornwallis to surrender at Yorktown, October 1781.

At the news of Yorktown Lord North, pacing up and down his dining-room, exclaimed, 'Oh God, it is all over!' It was with him, and the Whigs came in—led by Rockingham and Shelburne who had opposed the war all along—to end it, make the peace and introduce the reforms which were to diminish the influence of the King, and the number of placemen, in the Commons. One of the first places to go was that of Lord Charles at the Treasury. Shelburne took his interest under his wing. Rockingham Lord Robert's as a follower of Fox: the ministry was divided between these two sections. Shelburne wrote to Marlborough his regret that it was impossible to save Lord Charles and suggested, rather Jesuitically, to the King that he should express his regret to Lord Rockingham at Lord Charles's being left out of the government and his Majesty's great consideration for the Duke. Shelburne had already sounded the Duke whether he would accept the office of Groom of the Stole: he desired time to consider this.

We see the amount of time and energy expended in this aristocratic age on places and pensions, providing for younger sons, the consideration for great families, keeping them sweet, keeping them together.

Events did not stand still for these manoeuvres and petty disputes. It was conceded that the war was over in America, independence virtually recognised. In the last stages of the war, however, the island-power showed both toughness and resource. Rodney's great victory over a big French fleet at Les Saintes in the West Indies, with the destruction he wrought upon it, and the triumphant resistance to the last combined assault on Gibraltar, enabled peace to be discussed in a better atmosphere. Shelburne favoured the most generous concessions to the Americans—far more so than the French wished. The Peace of 1763 had recognised the country across the Great Lakes and to the Mississippi as forming part of Canada. Now Shelburne with his long-sighted vision of Anglo-American partnership was all in favour of handing over these vast interior territories to the new nation. In the last stages of the peace-preliminaries there came into being an understanding between English and Americans against the French—to the indignation of the latter who had bankrupted themselves in support of the American Revolution and were now on their way to a revolution of their own. Shelburne was bent on an English-speaking future for the North American continent; the new nation came into existence with many immediate difficulties but tremendous ultimate prospects.

In November, with the preliminaries of peace under discussion, Moore wrote to spur the Duke on to do his duty. 'The moment is indeed very critical: too important in my opinion for a man who has such a stature as yours in the country to allow himself to be absent from the great scene of business. I hope therefore your Grace is coming.' Marlborough's name was being once more brought forward for office. Lord Carlisle had resigned as Lord Steward and Shelburne thought of the Duke, but was apprehensive that he might hesitate, 'especially as there is no offering it to him except by letter'. Nothing came of this and, in any case, Shelburne was shortly after turned out of power—not by the King but by the majority of the House of Commons. It is difficult to understand the detestation with which this remarkable man—of political imagination and even vision, a genuine reformer, a man of ideas whose ideas were in line with the future—was regarded by everybody. The fact was that, though a politician, he was not a professional: he was not one of them. Something of a doctrinaire who cared for ideas rather than men, he did not trust people and they did not trust him. A devious and secretive man, they called him 'the Jesuit of Berkeley Square'. The King bitterly resented his resignation: *he* had more nerve and would have faced it out. George III was even more furious at what took his place: the famous, and unprincipled, Coalition of Charles Fox with, of all people, Lord North.

Fox had spent the greater part of the American War—such time as he could spare from the gaming-table—in attacking Lord North and his policies with the utmost moral indignation. Fox, now the leader of Rockingham's Whig Party, was a leading advocate of reform, the violent assailant of the royal power in politics; Lord North, its incarnation during twelve years of rule, representing all that the Foxites meant by corruption. The Coalition effected an astonishing, and rather shocking, transformation of the political scene; Fox himself said with something of his father's cynical candour: 'Nothing but success can justify it'. And it looked certain to succeed, for it had an irresistible majority in the House.

For months George III tried to resist this servitude, tried to find someone who would undertake the government and deliver him from the yoke of Charles Fox. But the King could find no one willing and had to submit. At the end of the year Fox's India Bill gave him his chance. Fox, knowing that he could never win over the King, brought in a Bill which would have the effect of annexing the vast patronage of the reconstructed East India Company to the government and thereby make it independent of royal power, himself the arbiter. This roused the intense hostility of most of the East India interest in the City, increased the distrust of the unscrupulous Coalition in the country and gave the King his opening. Fox's Bill passed the Commons with large majorities, in spite of the antagonism it aroused outside. In the Lords the King let it be known that whoever voted for it he would regard as an enemy; and the measure was defeated. Having ascertained that Pitt was now prepared to form a government, considering in his strangely mature judgment that the moment was at last ripe, the King contemptuously dismissed the ministers, still in possession of their large majority in the Commons.

George III did all he could to strengthen the hands of the young minister fighting against such odds, and there is an interesting exchange of letters at Blenheim that illustrates the efforts he made. The King wrote from Windsor, 29 December 1783: 'I must call on the assistance of every honest man and I trust the Duke of Marlborough will zealously engage his friends to support Government in the present most critical occasion. I know too well the Duchess of Marlborough is ever friendly to me and hope she will also warmly espouse my cause, which is indeed that of the Constitution as fixed at the Revolution and to the support of which my family was invited to mount the throne.' The draft of the Duke's reply from Blenheim the same day confesses that he did not see the East India Bill in a dangerous light: he thought that it was calculated rather to increase than diminish the power of the Crown or he should not have given his proxy in support of it. This was a polite negative to the King's request: the Marlboroughs were with the Fox-North Coalition.

Fox could at first hardly take the young Pitt's government seriously and was convinced that the Coalition must necessarily return in a short time to power. Pitt held on with unshaken tenacity throughout these months. Lecky is right in saying that there is nothing in English parliamentary history more wonderful than the fight he put up. He showed that he possessed all his father's indomitable political courage and much more sense. All the time, like his father, he had his eye on opinion outside the House. The night came when he had worn down the Opposition's immense majority to one, and when he had got the necessary business through the Commons he did not hesitate any longer to seek a Dissolution. Nothing was neglected in the appeal to the country, no chances lost. John Robinson summed up the prospects. The Duke of Marlborough had five seats at his disposal. At Woodstock 'probably the Duke of Marlborough will again return the same members'. He returned one of the two members for the county of Oxford, one for the city and one for Heytesbury. No money would pass in this case. Lord Charles, like the Duke, was something of a waverer: Robinson, writing before the change of government, said that he 'is now *con* as in office, but on a change would be *for*'. But he was wrong in this forecast; nor did the Duke make any move till later. In January 1784 the Duke of Dorset reported: 'the Duke of Newcastle and the Duke of Marlborough are both come over and Robinson says *it will do*'. It did. The Opposition went to the constituencies fore-doomed to ruin and were utterly shattered. A hundred and sixty of their members were driven out of Parliament. The nation had found in Chatham's son a leader, and a long period of stable government ensued under his direction.

In the interval between Shelburne's resignation and the Fox-North Coalition coming in, the King had made Moore Archbishop of Canterbury. With his conscientious desire to get the best man instead of a party-appointee the King had offered it to the two most distinguished prelates in the Church, Bishops Lowth and Hurd, both of whom refused and concurred in recommending Moore as the man. The King communicated his nomination first to Marlborough as a mark of favour. 'The Duke of Marlborough will, I am certain, receive the intelligence of my having just wrote to Lord Sydney that the *congé d'élire* and recommendatory letter to the Chapter of Canterbury in favour of the Bishop of Bangor be prepared. I hope the Duke will acquaint the Bishop that he must kiss hands tomorrow.' With this appointment the former tutor now takes precedence of the Duke. In the next few years Moore's correspondence with the Duchess flags: no doubt he had plenty to do on becoming Archbishop of Canterbury.

Then there was a dreadful rumour that a royal visit to Blenheim was intended: it materialised in the summer of 1786, when the King and Queen paid a visit to Oxford. The Duke was thrown into a state of agitation and had to be led firmly up to the hurdle by Archbishop Moore. Oxford would take a day and 'if proper invitation is given, Blenheim another at least'. Moore urges that 'nobody has so fine a family in so fine a place to show and my lord Duke will be amply paid for all his misgivings on the occasion by the reflection that what is done is right and that the omission would scarcely be doing justice to his family or himself, and certainly condemned by the world, as well as crossing the reasonable expectations of the Royal Family. Long deliberation won't do—your first thoughts will deserve to be followed by immediate act; and I am sure you will all think it right when over.'

Thus firmly propelled, the invitation was given. An attempt had recently been made on the King's life, so that the royal visit to loyal Oxford took place in an atmosphere of emotionalism that was more characteristic of the Regency. The Duke, as High Steward of the university, received the royal family in the Sheldonian—Miss Burney discreetly in attendance, noting it all down. A loyal Address was read, the Princesses wept, there were tears in even Queen Charlotte's eyes, hardly a dry eye in the Sheldonian. There was much kissing the King's hand, old dons who couldn't get up from their knees, others who tried to walk backward and fell down, the mix-up and general confusion one knows so well on these occasions.

Next for Blenheim. The Duchess reports to Moore: 'Considering the shortness of the notice, it all went off very well. They stayed here from eleven till six. We had breakfast for them in the Library and, after they returned from seeing the park, some cold meats and fruit. Lord and Lady Harcourt told us we were to sit as lord and lady of the Bedchamber all the time they stayed here; and poor

Lord Harcourt seemed quite happy to be able to rest himself, the Duke of Marlborough found him sitting down behind every door where he could be concealed from royal eyes. We were just an hour going over the principal floor as they stopped and examined *everything in every room*; and we never sat down during that hour or indeed very little but while we were in the carriages, which fatigued me more than anything else. Lord Harcourt told the Duke of Marlborough that he had been full-dressed in a bag and sword every morning since Saturday; but the Duke of Marlborough could not follow his example in that, as he had no dress-coat or sword in the country. He desires me to tell you that he had no misgivings. All the apprehensions were on my side. Nobody could do the thing better or more thoroughly than he did.'

The King was very much taken with everything and his comment, 'We have nothing equal to this', very gracious. King and Duke shared a keen interest in astronomy, which was becoming an obsession with Marlborough: he was fitting up one of Vanbrugh's towers as an observatory. At the end of August George III wrote, 'the Duke of Marlborough is so skilful and practised an astronomer that I am happy in having got Dr. Herschel to complete the 10 ft. telescope so soon after his return from Germany. I can answer for the excellency of this instrument, having twice compared it with the one in my possession and indeed sent the one that proved the most perfect.' Family man spoke to family man: 'I am certain the Duke, who is a tender father, will share in my joy at my third daughter being totally now without complaint'.

Next year there was talk of another royal visit to Blenheim and the Duke wrote expressing his apprehensions to the Archbishop. The Duchess was unwell. It would be too much. It did not take place.

The children were growing up, on the threshold of their entry into the world; in the background—or rather in the foreground now at Lambeth—there was Moore, willing as ever with counsel and more practical help over this generation as he had been with their parents and all along. He was an elderly man now, but in a position to advance the interests of his old friends' children.

Nothing much could be done with Blandford, though he was not without talent. Indeed a marked vein of talent appeared in both these generations, as it had not done in the previous one, that of Sarah's grandchildren—to her intense annoyance. This young Blandford was at Eton during the years of the American War, 1776 to 1783. When he left the Duke sent him to Paris for three or four months with a tutor, Mr. Hind. 'What a man to send,' wrote Lord Herbert to Coxe, 'a very good scholar, a very good University tutor, but totally ignorant of any modern language except his own mother tongue and as ignorant of the world. What strange people they are!' It did not answer and Moore was called in to advise. He thought they should come home: 'two or three months more abroad can produce no material improvement. They will be thrown away at best. When he comes home your Graces will consider whether he shall go to Oxford or abroad.' The Duke replied with a fine haunch of venison, which came very conveniently for a New Year's dinner at Lambeth. The young man was sent to Christ Church, where no doubt he enjoyed himself.

The hopes of the family rested on the second son, Henry, who was a clever boy of much promise. At Eton he was, with Canning and Hookham Frere, one of the founders of *The Microcosm*, earliest and most famous of school periodicals. At Christ Church he was, again with Canning, and with one of a group of young men of brilliant promise who came under the celebrated Dean Cyril Jackson. To all the family charm—and family reserve and shyness—he added a keen wit and precocious ability. He was marked out for diplomacy, and one cannot but think that it was old Moore who marked him out. For he was brought into the foreign service under the wing of Moore's brother-in-law, the very able administrator William Eden, now Lord Auckland. Eden was an Eton and Christ Church man who had come into Parliament under the patronage of the Duke, who returned him to Parliament as one of his members for Woodstock from 1774 to 1784 and for Heytesbury in the election that confirmed Pitt in his tenure of power. Eden, in conformity with the Marlboroughs, had belonged to the Fox grouping, their sympathies inclining them to the Opposition. Eden went over to Pitt and a good thing he made of it; for Pitt was anxious to recruit young men of ability and used Eden's capacities to the full to negotiate the commercial treaty with France and subsequently in diplomacy. No doubt it was through this connection that Moore made his Eden marriage. We see how these things tie up so nicely for those who are in the swim. Lord Henry was safely launched: he was to go abroad as secretary to Lord Auckland, ambassador to the Netherlands, where the young man, left in charge of the embassy at a critical time, had a resounding success.

Time indeed went slow over those slopes, to Vanbrugh's bridge and up to the Victory Column, over lake and parkland and pasture, in the last decades of those long lives while Mr. Pitt ruled and the country was once more at war, the never-ending struggle with Revolutionary France and Napoleon. Not much changed in that household in the grip of a lethargy so deep it might be inhabited by a Sleeping Prince and Princess under their gathered towers beside the lake. Taxes went up: Mr. Pitt's new taxes upon menservants, on horses and carriages, houses and windows—there were hundreds of windows in Blenheim. Costs went up; servants' liveries, from Scarpelain and McCarty, consumed £166 a year. Marlborough House too was a burden, with the taxes upon it. Before the end it was let to the Princess Charlotte and Prince Leopold—the Duke no longer subscribed his guinea for watering the Mall in summer. On his death Marlborough House would revert to the Crown.

News of the war sometimes penetrated the gathering silence. The Archbishop communicated the news of the victory of the Nile and of its effect on the lower sort. 'They are always captivated with bravery and success', he wrote. Thousands who were disaffected were made friends to government by this victory. 'Last year when Mr. Pitt dined in the City he had to change his carriage for security; this year the horses were taken out and his carriage drawn in triumph by the very mob who would have pulled him to pieces—*varium et mutabile vulgus*.' Such was Georgian England. But when the victor of the Nile himself turned up with Emma and Sir William Hamilton on a July day in 1802, during the peace—as sooner or later everybody did turn up to see Blenheim—it was more than the Duke could do to summon up the spirit to receive him. 'After a lengthy pause, refreshments in the park for Lord Nelson and friends were announced', wrote a Woodstock cleric—to be refused with indignation. The questionable trio were mightily offended, but Lady Hamilton's 'superior mind' rose to the occasion. She said that if Marlborough's services had been rewarded with Blenheim it was because a woman had then reigned and 'women have great souls': if she were queen, Nelson should have had a principality such that Blenheim Park would be only a kitchen garden to it. The hero with the woman's sensibility was mollified and touched to tears.

Old friends were dropping away. In 1805, the year of Trafalgar, died the former tutor and friend of the family, old Moore, Archbishop of Canterbury. Carefully folded away by the Duchess in the archives at Blenheim among the newspaper cuttings recording these faithful lives are others, of which she was evidently not less proud, tributes to her and the Duke's charity and goodness to the poor of Woodstock over many years, the continual happiness he and she reaped from the 'pleasing domestic scene', his 'probity and disinterested justice in public life, benevolence and conjugal affection in domestic retirement'. She herself built the almshouses for poor widows one sees along the road into Woodstock—plain, decent Georgian buildings in honey-coloured Blenheim stone beside the East gate. Then, rendered unhappy by the character, the scrapes, the extravagance of her eldest son, full of foreboding for the future, in 1811 she died.

The Duke retired further than ever into himself, into his passion for astronomy, communing with the stars. There are pages and pages of astronomical calculations, corrected by Dr. Hornsby, Savilian Professor at Oxford, with a paper of the Duke on the Harvest Moon.[1] Nothing disturbed the silence—until one day on the announcement that, clamouring at the gate to get in, was the famous, the aggressive, the intolerable Madame de Staël, the Duke broke out to his astonished attendants with 'Take me away! Oh, take me away!'

It was his last recorded utterance. When he died in 1817 a great change came over Blenheim.

[1] Blenheim MSS., F.I. 44 and 45 contain these. It may be said that the Duke's election as Fellow of the Royal Society in 1786 was rather more appropriate than that of his ancestor Sir Winston Churchill. He presented the university with a large telescope, as well as a number of paintings.

CHAPTER THREE

Whig Frolics

FROM the seventeen-eighties onwards one discerns a new tone, a new spirit abroad in society, and with the coming of age of the Prince of Wales this found its leader at once glamorous and questionable. As Edwardian society took shape long before the end of Victoria's reign, so we see Regency society coming into being, with all its fruity characteristics, and taking possession of the scene years before the Prince became Regent. The keynote of his world was a somewhat promiscuous joyousness; its characteristics a taste running to fantasy, sentiment and sensibility that easily overflowed into insincerity, an attention to fashion and the *chic* that was yet spontaneous and unselfconscious, a lack of self-control, an extravagance that went with chronic indebtedness. In the highest ranks of this society one wasn't quite sure who slept with whom or who was whose child—as Lord Melbourne said, 'Who the devil knows who one's father is, anyway?' (his own father was probably not Lord Melbourne but Lord Egremont); illegitimacy ran riot; a fine old time was had by (almost) all. It was like the Restoration come again; the *beau monde* shaded off into the *demi-monde*.

All this was in marked contrast to the domestic life of the dear King and to no small extent in direct reaction to his dull, economical, restrictive virtues. There was much shaking of heads in the royal circle and among respectable persons like Archbishop Moore and his elderly friends at the capers and the behaviour of the younger generation. But there was nothing they could do about it, except tighten the reins financially and shorten the allowances—and then the young men piled up mountains of indebtedness upon their expectations. Before George III's heir became Regent he had accumulated debts amounting to £630,000—and some £160,000 had once before been met. Before Marlborough's heir succeeded as fifth Duke, his father had tried keeping him short: the young Marquis simply borrowed at outrageous interest on his expectations—and there was no Parliament to meet his indebtedness.

Respectability, and his troubles, had endeared George III to the heart of the English middle class. Nothing about the Prince Regent endeared him to that great organ, for there was nothing about him that was quite respectable: neither his morals nor his politics, his marriage nor his finances, his companionships nor his taste. Perhaps it was his taste that offended most: it was so shockingly regardless of what they chiefly valued, decorum, running as it did to the Oriental fantasy, the minarets, domes and turrets, the lacquer and gilt of the Brighton Pavilion. A Regency poet wrote:

> In Xanadu did Kubla Khan
> A stately pleasure-dome decree;

another Regency artist called into being an evocation of those lines, in bricks and mortar, by the seashore at Brighton. (The irreverent Sydney Smith said it was as if the dome of St. Paul's had gone down by the sea and pupped.)

Within was the exquisite gilt dolphin furniture, all curves and plush and fish-tails; the pretty wallpapers patterned like muslin, festooned and wreathed; the Chinese screens and lanterns, the corridors lighted behind coloured glass; the tented ceilings from which hung astonishing chandeliers, like Oriental fruits dropping succulently above the guests feasting off the gold plate Parliament had ultimately to pay for. At Carlton House was the ebony furniture for which the Regent had a fancy, the magnificent collection of snuff-boxes and *étuis* that now adorns Buckingham Palace. There was his patronage of artists, of the brilliant, too scintillating Lawrence; his purchase of the Dutch pictures that are now a glory of the royal collections; his admiration for Walter Scott and Miss Austen—a set of whose novels appeared chastely among the more exotic ornaments (and personages) in each of his residences.

It was the personality above all, the character, that counted. Along with the feeling, the aesthetic sensibility, there was a levity, an absence of *suite* that gave the tone to so much of his doings and made him a figure of fun. There was the utter disregard of money in reaction from the economy of his father, the lack of any self-control, the romantic fantasy ministered to by such spirits as Sheridan and Lawrence, Nash and Wyatt, that announced a new age. His life was a romantic extravaganza; his personality well summed up by Wellington, 'the most extraordinary compound of talent, wit, buffoonery, obstinacy and good feeling—in short a medley of the most opposite qualities with a great preponderance of good—that I ever saw in my life'. The preponderant good, however, was apt to be nullified in other people's opinions by the fact that the First Gentleman of Europe was also a good deal of a cad. Of course he was a German, and all his characteristics were German: place him beside those subjects who made the glory of his age and rule—Wellington and Nelson, Pitt and Fox, Wordsworth and Scott—and one sees the difference. Like many Germans who are good-looking in youth, he grew gross when old.

However, he had the vitality and the gifts to set the tone to the society of his day and for his extravagance we have at least something to show—the fantasy of the Pavilion at Brighton, the skyline of Windsor with all its gathered towers and battlements, the fragments left of his splendid conception of the West End of London from Carlton Terrace, up the Quadrant through Regent's Street to the grandeur of Regent's Park, however much fractured and fissured by the combined Philistinism and squalor of later times.

Such was the background to our story.

Of Marlborough's brothers and sisters, Diana and Robert were prominent figures in the social life of their time, and they were much the closest together of the family. Diana's contribution was the more valuable and idiosyncratic, for she became an accomplished artist. In her art all the charm that was in this family achieved a most appealing form; while its characteristic notes—gaiety, enjoyment of life, naturalness and fantasy, all in a feminine key—made it a no less authentic expression of the society they created and lived in.

After her deliverance by divorce from what she called Court-slavery, Lady Diana, through her new husband, Topham Beauclerk, became free of the society of the most gifted men of the time—Johnson and Gibbon, Reynolds, Garrick, Horace Walpole, Charles Fox. It was a profitable exchange for the conversation of Queen Charlotte, the life of boredom and thraldom that wore down the sprightly Fanny Burney. Not that Diana had not a good deal to put up with from Topham. As sometimes happens with men of extreme charm, he had a corresponding vein of cruelty in him, and this came to be exacerbated by many illnesses through which Diana dutifully nursed him. Like his great-grandfather, Charles II, he was dissolute. 'The moral, pious Johnson and the gay, dissipated Beauclerk were companions,' said Boswell. 'What a coalition! I shall have my old friend to bail out of the Round House,' said Garrick. Beauclerk was one of those handsome men who do not like washing; when the Beauclerks went to stay at

Blenheim the very correct Duchess complained that 'his habits were beyond what one could have thought possible in anyone but a beggar or a gipsy'.

Topham could plead the excuse of being a bibliophile. He collected an immense library; when he added on a room to his house in Great Russell Street to hold it, Horace Walpole said that it reached half-way to Highgate. There was no doubt about the charm; one sees it in his pleasant threat to the Earl of Charlemont, if he won't come over from Dublin, to bring over all the Club upon him in Ireland: 'Johnson shall spoil your books, Goldsmith pull your flowers and Boswell talk to you'. Neither of the Beauclerks had any idea of money, and Diana was always busy, always in a hurry. From Bath she ends a letter, 'part of this letter was dictated by Mr. Wade; part by my footman; part by my maid; which makes an agreeable mixture of style: I hope you like it'.

Well-off as Topham was—his father had been a shameless *captator*, a legacy-hunter—the day came when he needed money so badly that he mortgaged his library to the Duke for £5000. On his death in 1780 the sale lasted forty-nine days and each day the money was paid over to the Duke: it totalled £5011. Diana was forced to resort to her brother for cash; but in contrast to his earlier open-handedness, she complained that he did not omit to take interest on it and dunned her when she had not five guineas in her purse.

Quit of men at last she was free to deploy her own talents, to develop her remarkable gift as a painter. She had a house at Twickenham, near Horace Walpole, Little Marble Hill—lawns sloping down to the river, garden designed by Pope; and there she proceeded to decorate the rooms in her own delightful festive style. Old Horace grew lyrical about her work, and her. One room was festooned with lilac painted on a pale green background; geranium, ivy, periwinkle in the panels at the base. Horace wrote a poem about it. He describes for us another room painted with honeysuckle wreathed round children—Diana adored children, her art, like her life, came to be designed round them: 'there is a baby Bacchus, so drunk! and so pretty! borne in triumph by Bacchanalian children'.

Nearly all her decorative work has perished with the houses she decorated; but her pastel portraits remain, her water-colours and designs for ceilings, illustrations for books, Wedgwood china plates and jars. For she was a prolific artist, quick at expressing herself with spontaneity and freshness, a natural distinction. From her treatment of landscape, especially her trees, we see that she had studied Gainsborough, and from her children, Romney. She delighted in the rose-pink and pale blues of the Regency. Her work conveys the airy lightness, the sense of fun and mischief of her world; its naturalness and superficiality are disarming, while its very femininity saves it from the sentimentality of a Cipriani, the artificiality of a Loutherbourg. Above all, like the time, it was spontaneous and released; there is an innocence about its pastoral fantasy, the woodland Arcady peopled by cherubs and children, Cupids and Pans making love or quarrelling, with the goat-footed creatures lurking in the background to make mischief. (Perhaps these were creditors, for there was never any money.) It is all a transcript into the world of fantasy of her own gay, chequered, sunny life.

She was an amateur and most of her work was known only to the select circle of her friends—though she was besieged by invitations from people who wanted to see her rooms and decorations: she had to issue tickets. It was known to the public chiefly by the engravings made of her illustrations for Horace Walpole's Gothick tragedy *The Mysterious Mother,* for Dryden's *Fables* and her nephew William Robert Spencer's translation of Bürger's *Leonore.* This young man, son of Lord Charles, had his share of the family talents too: he was well known for his *vers de société* and had the distinction of being favourably reviewed by Byron. Horace Walpole was beside himself with admiration for Lady Diana's drawings—no doubt there was a similar element of fellow-feeling in his enthusiasm. 'Such figures! such dignity! such simplicity! Then there is a cedar hanging over the castle, that is more romantic than when it grew on Lebanon.' We see that her art has its place in the immense romantic transition—flood or cataract or geological fault—that marks off the time from the classic eighteenth century.

She did some portraits of the circle she lived in: an enchanting caricature of Gibbon, laurel-wreath and that face Madame du Deffand thought it a *mauvaise plaisanterie* to lay hand on. Gibbon thought Lady Diana 'handsome and agreeable and ingenious far beyond the ordinary rate'. She painted a portrait of the exquisite—and ruinous—Georgiana, Duchess of Devonshire, goddess of that society, 'all flowing elegance, melting glances and shifting silken colour'; the friend of Fox and addict of the gaming-table, who cost her husband (he lived *à trois* with her and her friend Lady Elizabeth Foster) hundreds of thousands in gambling debts. Like Charles Fox, she had constitutional ill-luck. Marlborough paid for this portrait to be engraved.

Lady Diana's relations with Blenheim grew frostier and frostier as she grew poorer—largely owing to the selfishness and pride of the Duchess, whom Queen Charlotte considered the proudest woman in the kingdom. Diana's real friend within the family was her brother Lord Robert. Her letters ring the changes on the constant theme: lack of money. In 1797, 'we are so poor here. I have not means to pay for a letter even.' In 1799 she cannot pay her taxes, 'all my real friends are so poor I will not mention it to them'. That same year, 'my brother Robert has sold his charming house in town and pictures and all from poverty'—all from gambling, in fact. Next year, though she considered Robert 'the real guardian of all the family . . . we are all in a bad way as to money'. Two years later, 'if I can sell some more old candlesticks (as I did last year) I will go to town for two months, as it is too cold for me here all winter'. Then Robert brings her back two beautiful candlesticks from his visit to Paris with Fox. Next year, 'I am poverty itself, and so is everybody I believe except a few great people, and they keep all snug to themselves'.

In 1806 Lord Robert's luck turned with Pitt's death and Fox and his friends at last coming in, after twenty years in opposition. 'Mr. Pitt being gone, Charles Fox and all my friends are just coming in, I believe. When I say "all my friends", I only mean Charles Fox and my brother Robert, for I know few of the others by sight—but they are reckoned to possess all the abilities of this kingdom.' But Diana's sight was going: no more drawing now: nothing to employ her time except visits to Robert, now installed at Woolbeding with the remains of his possessions around him. There, in that charming, comfortable house, surrounded by affection and pretty objects to remind her of the past, she was always happy.

Her friends were passing away, Charles Fox that same year: she had left him her portrait of his closest friend, Lord Robert; now she must alter her will. To Robert she left a portrait of her son; to Lord Bolingbroke, her marble busts and all her pet greenhouse plants; to her son Lord Robert's miniature. Her daughter Mary was provided for: for years she lived with her aunt, Lady Pembroke, who went peacefully on, in spite of her earlier troubles, to a great old age. One day her aunt 'carried her to Marlborough House on a visit! only think of that!' A long vista of separation within the family unfolds—her gladness is touching: shortly after she was dead.

A closer contact with Blenheim was for some years maintained by the second brother, Lord Charles, from Wheatfield. In the theatricals of the seventeen-eighties he was a frequent performer.

In 1790 a marriage between these two branches of the family should have brought them together: the Duke's daughter Elizabeth married the elder son at Wheatfield. Lady Stafford reports that the 'Duchess of Bedford says that it is the *most charmingest* match that can be, that Mr. Spencer is a good actor, a good musician and a good composer, and that they will be very happy.' Then with feminine malice, 'don't you like the reasons her Grace gives to constitute their happiness?' The marriage seems to have led to a quarrel between Blenheim and Wheatfield, perhaps over settlements. Old Moore had, as usual, to be called in and he wrote to the Duke and Duchess enjoining silence and no talk whatever on the matter in public, especially under the present anger.

At the same time there seems to have been a separation between Lord Charles and his wife, though they kept silent about it. The family *penchant* for silence came in useful, for nobody could extract any information. Not even the Archbishop, who could bring about no reconciliation. Everybody in the Regency world had either wife-trouble or husband-trouble—except the ducal couple at Blenheim, and they paid a price for their mutual contentment. The coldness between Blenheim and Wheatfield continued; when Moore went to stay at the latter in 1796 he could still get no information on the subject.

To personal reasons for the breach we may have to add a political one. Lord Charles represented Oxfordshire in Parliament from the day in 1761 when his brother Robert as a boy deputised for him at the declaration of poll right up to 1790. In that year he had to make way for the feckless youth, his nephew Blandford, and remained out for the Parliament of 1790 to 1796. He cannot have liked this, nor can it have been appreciated by the county, for he was a popular member. In 1796 he was returned once more and Blandford was left out in the cold. Not until 1802 was a seat found for the heir—or more probably bought for him, since it happened to be Tregony.

True to the tradition of his family Lord Charles was a good deal of a Trimmer. In Addington's administration from 1801 to 1804 he was a Postmaster-General, along with Lord Auckland. When Pitt resumed power Lord Auckland was dropped—Pitt had not forgotten Auckland's intervening with the King behind his back against Catholic Emancipation. Lord Charles was continued. On Pitt's death Auckland pressed that Lord Charles might remain Postmaster-General: 'I shall hardly venture to write to Blenheim till I know how the matter rests'. A place was found for him as Master of the Mint, but he held it only till October. After that he went into retirement; a pleasant pension of £1000 a year made him comfortable.

Lord Robert was all his life an undeviating Foxite Whig, a pure party-man, as befitted the boon-companion of Charles Fox. They were at Oxford together. Lord Malmesbury describes the very pleasant life they enjoyed there, the bone-idleness, while waiting to take the chances held open to these fortunate youths in Parliament, the law or the Church. 'Our life was an imitation of High Life in London; luckily drinking was not the fashion, but what we did drink was claret, and we had our regular round of evening parties to the great annoyance of our finances. It has often been a matter of surprise to me how so many of us made our way in the world, and so creditably. Charles Fox, Lord Romney, North, Bishop of Winchester, Lord Robert Spencer, William Eden (now Lord Auckland), were amongst the number'. It is no surprise to us: Foxes, Spencers, Norths—the world was theirs for the taking. Trevelyan describes theirs as 'that most enviable of all the aristocracies of history, the men who look out from the canvasses of Gainsborough and Romney with a divine self-satisfaction, bred of unchallenged possession of all that was really best in a great civilisation. . . . They felt themselves above the censure of any class but their own, and they had not yet been frightened by the French Revolution or reclaimed by the Evangelical Revival'.

The mania of that society was its insatiable passion for gambling. All the literature of the time bore witness to it—and not a few roofless country-houses and ravaged woods. 'The gaming', writes Horace Walpole, 'is worthy the decline of our Empire. The young men lose five, ten, fifteen thousand pounds in an evening.' At the age of sixteen Charles Fox and his brother cost their father £32,000 for three days and nights' play. Some ten years later Fox's debts amounted to £140,000, which his father met with hardly a complaint—such had been the profits of the Paymaster-General's office. They were mad.

If White's were not sufficient to lose a fortune, there was Brooks's across the way; if London flagged, there was Paris. Fox and Lord Robert were in Paris together in 1771. They were often at Madame du Deffand's: those blind eyes saw through the young Fox, 'dur, hardi, l'esprit prompt', she said. As for Robert, he neither spoke nor ate but played tric-trac the whole time with the Marquise de Boufflers, who tried to fleece him. 'Ce petit Milord est bien borné: l'oiseau de proie s'en était emparée et aurait bien voulu le plumer.'

(What had Sarah warned his father years before about these French women cheating silly young Englishmen?)

But Brooks's offered one incomparable opportunities of ruining oneself in the best company, the irresistible company of Charles Fox, and this Lord Robert proceeded to do. Before long he was in financial difficulties and had to resort to his brother to help him. This meant calling in Moore, who drafted the letters that passed, for the Duke could not bear the thought of it. Moore had extracted a promise from Lord Robert that 'certainly went to leaving off play, to living upon his income, to contracting no more debts'. What was the value of a promise from these young addicts?—the Duke 'must consider him as having broken his word'. By 1777 Lord Robert was reduced to selling his estate.

In the early seventeen-eighties the financial affairs of Fox and Lord Robert, always unsteady, reached a crisis along with their politics. They were constantly together: in the notices of the time their names are inseparable: at parties given by the Prince at Carlton House, going down to Norfolk with him, dining at Fox's with General Burgoyne returned from Saratoga. George Selwyn gives us frequent news of the circle, breaking frequently—as their habit was—into French. Early in 1781, their opposition to Lord North and the American War coming to a head, Lord Robert resigned from the Board of Trade and Plantations and went bankrupt.

In May the bailiffs took possession of Fox's effects in St. James's Street: his furniture was thrown out into the street—everybody noticed what a filthy lot of odds and ends it was; for two days the Jews were filling carts with his goods, his clothes and books—presentation copies from Gibbon and so on. While this execution was going on in one part of the street, in another Fox and his friends were holding a faro bank of £3000, by which they soon got near £2000. 'Lord Robert since his bankruptcy and in consideration of his party principles is admitted to some small share.' Is it any wonder that George III objected to these young men having any share, however small, in running the Treasury?

However, the faro bank prospered. In June it made £2300; Hare and Lord Robert had their six guineas an hour, likely to produce more than the pension of a Lord of Trade. 'He has let his own house to Sir George Rodney's son and is now in Foley House: *voici les ouvrages de la fortune.*' By November Selwyn thought that between Foley House and the run of Mr. Bouverie's kitchen, with his credit at Brooks's, his share in the opulent faro bank and flourishing trade, Lord Robert might find a subsistence. He did. On Christmas night one of their friends lost £7000 to the bank, in which Hare and Lord Robert had a twelfth. They proposed that their share should be raised to an eighth. 'The whole manoeuvre, added to their patriotism, their politics etc. are incredible.'

Trevelyan says that 'it is indeed hard to discern any principle, least of all of a Liberal character, in the actions of the Opposition during the years when they were denouncing Pitt's Free Trade and pacific policy towards France and plotting to climb back to power on the shoulders of the Prince Regent'. Lady Holland tells us, years afterwards, that 'the fashion was to be in Opposition; the Prince of Wales belonged to it; all the beauty and wit of London were on that side'. However, common sense and responsible statesmanship were on the other, led by a man who was as much above these aristocratic irresponsibles in integrity and loftiness of purpose as he was far more than a match for them in tactics. It was not they, for all their brilliance and wit, who caught him out; he invariably caught them out. He ruled the country for practically the rest of his life; he gave his life to it.

The long years passed in the twilight of Opposition. These people who considered themselves so much cleverer than ordinary mortals proved again and again how much sillier they were. As France, with the unfolding of the logic of Revolution, became more aggressive and more dangerous to Europe, Fox, who had opposed Pitt's admirable commercial treaty on the ground that France was 'the eternal enemy,' now became the champion of Revolutionary France. When France passed over from the defensive to become a danger with the victory of Valmy in 1792, 'no public event, not excepting Saratoga and Yorktown, ever happened that gave me so much delight', he brayed. Next year, for his services to the country, his party raised another enormous sum to pay off his debts once for all and allow him an annuity to live in comfort for the rest of his life with Mrs. Armisted.

This lady (it does not appear that there ever was a Mr. Armisted), though the daughter of a Methodist shoemaker, spent her early life in frolicsome company. Lord Bolingbroke first raised her from the lower ranks of her profession and introduced her into polite society. She became Lord Derby's mistress, had a turn with the Prince of Wales and finally hooked Charles Fox. In those capacious arms she rested, and in 1795 Fox married her, though they did not declare the marriage till seven years later, when he took her on his celebrated visit to Paris, with Lord Robert, after the

Peace of Amiens, to see the pacific First Consul. The fact was that Mrs. Fox was a good sort, a kind heart, devoted to looking after her famous husband: their marriage was idyllically happy. As Lord Egremont, who knew, truly said: 'Mrs. Fox is a very kind-hearted woman and now very religious. And she seems to have taken the good qualities of our God Almighty without his atrocious ones, by showing mercy unto the third and fourth generation of, not quite, thousands of those who have loved her and kept her commandment.'

Politically a disastrous lot, privately they had a very good time. The grandest houses were open to them (without Mrs. Armisted): Devonshire House and Holland House in London, Woburn and Holkham in the country. And how they enjoyed themselves! Every year they had a large party of friends at one or other of their houses; there they spent the time riding, shooting, walking and talking, reading, playing games or making love. But above all in talking, listening to Charles Fox's talk, for there was no doubt about the fascination or the energy of his mind. One sees it in his letters, where he is capable of breaking off and finishing in Spanish, for he has been reading Cervantes, or in Italian, having just finished Ariosto; passages of Latin or Greek come no less spontaneously to his mind or easily to his pen. No very exact scholar, he was a naturally intellectual man and theirs a cultivated society; while, when Fox was among friends—he was not good-natured with opponents—'a lazy sunshine of good humour shone round them, softening the edge of their sharpest sayings'. His good temper was such that, long after he was dead, his memory was carried on far into the Victorian Age: old gentlemen who had known him could not hear his name without tears bedewing their ancient cheeks. He is still the tutelary deity at Brooks's.

The wry Wraxall tells us, 'no sooner had the shooting season commenced than he constantly repaired to Norfolk. Lord Robert Spencer generally accompanied him; and after visiting various friends they sometimes hired a small house in the town of Thetford, rose at an early hour and passed the whole day with a fowling-piece in their hands, among coveys of partridges and pheasants, for successive weeks during the autumn'. Thus they restored the health they had prejudiced by late nights at Brooks's and in the House of Commons. So they enjoyed London at its most elegant, the English countryside at its loveliest. War might rage on the Continent or in America, but they were safe, behind the wooden walls of the Navy. Their double security gave them ease and naturalness, 'that delightful unassertive confidence', Lord David Cecil tells us, 'possible only to people who have never had cause to doubt their social position'. It was this too that accounts for the paradox that they were the more democratic politically as they were more aristocratic socially: they could afford to be the one because they were the other.

And so it came about that Fox never failed to be elected by the popular electorate of Westminster, the beautiful Duchess canvassing for him assiduously, voluptuously (an Irishman said he could light his pipe at her eyes), the Prince, taking a hand in the election, sporting a fox's brush and escorted by a bevy of prize-fighters. When the famous election of 1796 was over, Fox was drawn in triumph in Lord Robert's carriage from Devonshire House to a popular dinner at the Shakespeare Tavern. The Prince gave a public breakfast in the garden of Carlton House with singing and dancing, while his father drove mutely by in state to open Parliament.

The war went on and on, with its increasing burdens on the country. When a truce was established at Amiens in 1801, the whole of Whig society flocked to Paris to make up to the famous First Consul. Charles Fox took Mrs. Fox abroad with him, recognising her publicly for the purpose; people who did not in the least mind his having a mistress were shocked at his having married her, above all at having been married so long without their knowing. Lord Robert and his friends were there, and both Fox and he had audiences at the Tuileries. Napoleon regretted the necessity for a great military establishment; his inclinations were all for peace and he was 'to the last degree' opposed to war with Britain. When however, he attacked Pitt with the disgraceful lie that he was party to plots for his assassination, Fox came to Pitt's defence, asserting the impossibility of such an idea. Napoleon turned away in silence. He talked to Lord Robert about his admiration for his ancestor Marlborough—which was genuine; a figure of the Duke was being set up on the Tuileries at the time.

They came home persuaded that all the First Consul wanted was peace; nor were they perturbed by his annexation of Piedmont and Elba in the interval, nor by the 'mediatization' (*gleichschaltung* was the word in our time) of Switzerland. Fox was, however, disquieted by Napoleon's unrepublican claim to Sicily for his brother Joseph. When the spectre of Napoleonic aggression all over Europe was at length laid, after years of war, and the man was laid by the heels in St. Helena, Lord Robert sent him the Life of Marlborough they had talked about at the Tuileries in 1802. Lady Holland bustled about among her Whig friends organising sympathy and sending out presents. The cult of the First Consul with these intellectual liberals was almost as silly, though nothing like so disastrous, as the appeasement of Hitler in our time.

In 1803 Creevey supped with Fox and the Whig leaders at Mrs. Bouverie's—she lived in tranquil amity with Lord Robert, Mr. Bouverie raising no objection: he formed the third in a friendly, inseparable family-trio. Creevey was astonished at 'the vigour of body, the energy of mind, the innocent playfulness and happiness of Fox. The contrast between him and his old associates is the most marvellous thing I ever saw—they all having the air of shattered debauchees, of passing gaming, drinking, sleepless nights, whereas the old leader of the gang might really pass for the pattern and the effect of domestic good order.'

Pitt returned to power in 1804, with the renewal of the war, to carry its burden virtually alone; for the King would not have Fox, and the others would not come in without him. Pitt knew that it would cost him his life; after the news of Austerlitz, that look never left his face. Within a few weeks he was dead, those last words—'Europe is not to be saved by any single man'—still ringing in the ears of his countrymen, to inspire a decade of effort to free Europe. He was forty-six, utterly worn out, having been Prime Minister for twenty years. It needed a coalition of All the Talents to take his place, and at last George III had to have Fox to lead it.

Fox at once inherited the difficulties that had overwhelmed Pitt. In one respect, worse; for everybody rushed upon him for office, places, pensions, harmless little jobs for their relations. 'Can I give up Jack Townshend, or Fitzpatrick, or Lord Robert for any of these young Lords? Indeed, indeed, my friends are hard upon me.' Lord Robert became Surveyor-General of Woods and Forests—a small reward for twenty years in Opposition. He and Mrs. Bouverie joined forces to press for promotion in the Church for a son of Bouverie's. A worse disillusionment awaited Fox when he opened peace negotiations and found that Napoleon did not mean business. 'It is . . . the manner in which the French fly from their word that disheartens me. It is not Sicily but the shuffling insincere way in which they act that shows me they are playing a false game.' To make concessions would only be to betray our allies. So Pitt had been right after all; in the last months of Fox's life, too late, he found himself following in Pitt's footsteps. Before the year was out he too was dead; we remember how the news affected Wordsworth when he heard it on a remote road in Cumberland.

Fox's will mentioned by name all those he loved as his oldest companions, all those who, devoted as they had always been, waited anxiously for news as he lay dying. It was Lord Robert who, finding words at last, spoke the truest eulogy of his friend: 'beloved, esteemed, renowned, lamented', he began. With Fox gone the centre went out of their lives; nor was it long before the Talents showed their silliness of judgment once more, lost office almost by inadvertence and went once more into Opposition for which their talents were better fitted. They spent another twenty years in the wilderness, while other, more sensible men got on with the laborious job.

The social life of the Whigs continued, vivacious, convivial, controversial: dinners at Holland House, visits to the Pavilion at Brighton, nights at Brooks's. Coming back from Brighton Creevey would look in at Brooks's to find all the regular gang there—Whitbread, Fitzpatrick, Morpeth, Sefton and Lord Robert. Lord Robert had the appellation of 'Comical' among his friends: there must have been something amusing about him, in expression and turn of speech. During Fox's life Lord Robert had often acted as a channel of political communication between him and his friends. For long after an active political rôle was over, he did not cease to be a sprightly humorous figure in society. In 1828 Creevey had to do the honours to him, and 'really my *tête-â-téte* with old "Comical" was both curious and entertaining. He, aged eighty-one, was just returned from a visit to his sister, Dowager Pembroke, in Richmond Park, aged ninety-four and quite well. In our unreserved moments his criticisms upon men were quite delightful. He considers the wit Sydney Smith as a "boisterous mountebank".'

Lord Robert was a little man; however, he was man enough to give Mrs. Bouverie pleasure. In 1810 her husband died and Lord Robert was free to marry her. Before this rather superfluous event, after so many years, they made an excursion together to stay with Grey, the new leader of the party, at Howick. 'Their marriage (which it is to be presumed will soon take place) is a Comical enough event', considered Lord Dudley. One of Mrs. Bouverie's children, Diana, was thought to be Lord Robert's: 'the tell-tale Bouverie,' wrote Lady Louisa Stuart, 'for there never was such a perfect indisputable Spencer, Lord Robert's walking picture, and the very prettiest creature that ever was seen.' To her he left Woolbeding, with his treasured possessions: so many mementoes of them all, of his sister, Diana Beauclerk, and the friends of Charles

Fox, in that undisturbed temple of Foxite doctrine and Whig society.

When Lord Robert sold his town-house and the greater part of his collection of pictures in 1799 he moved the remainder and his fine library to Woolbeding, the country-house near Midhurst which his gains from the faro bank had enabled him to buy. It was a pretty place, which he proceeded to improve by attentive care and judicious planting. Charles Fox's nephew visited it in 1823 and found it a pleasant contrast to the vast discomfort and untidiness of Petworth: 'small, comfortable and quite luxurious from the perpetual attentions of its owners to the comfort and convenience of their guests and of themselves—the eating and the whole *façon de vivre* exquisite. The fault of the house is the excessive violence of their politics ... to me such party-violence and such bigoted opinions are quite incomprehensible.' A lifetime in opposition is hardly a recipe for political good humour—only the temper of a Charles Fox could support that; Lord Robert died, a very old man, just before his party and his opinions triumphed with the Reform Bill.

A few years before, Mr. Creevey paid Woolbeding a visit and his account corroborates the impression of charm, breeding, taste. 'This place is really exquisite—its history not amiss. This venerable grave old man and offspring of Blenheim purchased it thirty-five years ago with the money he won as keeper of the faro bank at Brooks's, and he has made it what it is by his good taste in planting etc. . . . There is only one fictitious ornament to the place and the "Comical" seems to have shown as much address in converting it to his property as he did in winning the estate. It is a fountain, by far the most perfect in taste, eloquence and in everything else I ever saw. I am always going to it. It came from Cowdray, three miles off, Lord Montagu's. When Cowdray was burned down thirty years ago, this fountain, being in the middle of a court, was greatly defaced and neglected. Lord Montagu was drowned in the Rhine with Burdett's brother at the precise time his house was burnt and so never knew it; and as there was no one else on the spot to look after the ruins, Bob thought it a friendly office to give the fountain a retreat in his grounds. It cost him £100 to remove it and put it up here.'

And there it still is.

CHAPTER FOUR

Regency Generation

LORD ROBERT'S long career spanned the lives of several of the generation younger than his own. Of these two interest us.

Lord Henry, the second son at Blenheim, was the hope of the family. We left him under the kindly wing of Archbishop Moore, on the threshold of his career, going to be presented at Court. In 1790 he was returned for the family seat at Woodstock. Next year he got his first diplomatic post as secretary of legation at The Hague, where Lord Auckland was ambassador. When Lord Auckland came home on leave, full responsibility fell upon a young man totally without experience. However, there was a lull in foreign affairs; Mr. Pitt's government had managed so well that there was not even any concern for what was happening abroad.

During these months the novice acquitted himself with much credit in the slow, intricate negotiations taking place with Holland and Austria in regard to the Austrian Netherlands. The object was to spin these out and maintain the *status quo*. Having achieved this there was not much else to do; 'but you must not flatter yourself that in this eventful age', wrote Lord Auckland, 'you will be long without occasion to exercise both your judgment and your activity'. Curiously enough, this was some time in coming: we had no wish to embroil ourselves in the sequence of events unleased by the French Revolution and were pressing Holland not to take part with Prussia and Austria against Revolutionary France. Already Lord Henry was winning golden opinions; the Foreign Secretary himself, the cool, unexcitable Lord Grenville, wrote: 'it is not possible to have acted with more judgment and good sense than he has done'. The King spoke of him with marked kindness; when the Duke feared that parental partiality led him to think too well of his son, George III assured him it was 'impossible to think better of him than I do'.

After such a promising start, what next for the young man? In the summer of 1792 he was sent *en mission* to Vienna to compliment the Emperor on his accession—a distinction that gave much pleasure to the Marlboroughs and their friends. On his way there he fell in with that lady who became celebrated as Lady Holland: he may be said to have had a narrow escape.

Lady Webster, as she then was, was talented, vivacious, perhaps beautiful, unhappy—and rich. Partly Jamaican and partly American, she had been married at the age of fifteen to a man twenty-three years older, and in her defence it must be said that he was moody, unkind, inclined to be stupid and no company for her. She was not the woman to put up with it. In these years she was journeying about the Continent sometimes with her husband, more often without him. Whatever may be said against the famous Lady Holland—and many people detested her, her minatory manner, her domineering voice, her egotism and caprice—nothing gives a worse impression than what she wrote about herself. At Dresden in July 1792 was a numerous company of English: 'Lord Henry was there on his way to Vienna, whither he was to carry the compliment upon the accession of the Emperor. He was then Secretary at The Hague under Lord Auckland. His abilities were spoken highly of.... His shyness embarrassed him and rendered his manner awkward. He was very witty and possessed a super-abundant stock of irony. In short, he became ardently in love with me, and he was the first man who had ever produced the slightest emotion in my heart.'

In the autumn Lord Henry came home on leave—at the time when revolutionary fervour was reaching a new height with the September massacres in the prisons of Paris and the call for a war of aggression to carry the Revolution across the frontiers. The English upper classes were at last thoroughly alarmed—as well they might be, not only for themselves but for the country. At Blenheim Lord Henry, evidently a Pittite without qualification, was disturbed by reports that Tom Paine's book had been translated into Erse and was in the hands of the common people in the Highlands; the book was being read by all the factory hands in Manchester and had appeared recently in Welsh. In December he made his maiden speech in the House, much to the point, and, since he was able to contradict Fox on a point of fact, it was considered effective. On kissing hands at going abroad again he had a very kind reception from the King, who was 'distressingly gracious' and said he had read all Lord Henry's reports—as no doubt he had, for he was very conscientious.

Lord Henry did not want to go back to the boring Hague, where there was not enough to do; he was ambitious and he wanted an independent post. However, back he had to go. Lord Auckland stayed there until the French advance on Holland was halted and then returned: Lord Henry would have a fine position taking his place there. The young diplomat inquired whether he could have the rank of Envoy and an increase of pay? In July he got his first independent posting, as Minister to Sweden: he was not at all pleased at being sent to a country where there was no business to transact. According to Lady Holland he was out of spirits, complaining of solitude—naturally, away from her. In August, 'Lord Henry talks of coming to meet me; he can be absent from The Hague only by stealth. Wrong as it will be, my inclination would get the better of my reason if I had the measure to decide upon, but as I have *not*, it must take its chance; only I do not think he can arrive before I go. My children are perfectly well.'

The lady returned to England in no very good temper. In her circle she was bored by Gibbon's 'tedious witticisms'; for his part he could not bear her. She went down to Brighthelmstone, where 'the Prince chose to *combl*er me with every attention and civility. . . . I heard from Lord Henry, very miserable at not being able to catch me anywhere on my return, but ordered to repair immediately to Stockholm.' Across northern Europe he made his solitary way, pausing in Copenhagen which charmed him. At home the Dutch Grand Pensionary was in England, but Lord Henry had not given him letters to his family, 'because I did not choose to put it into their power to be rude to him. You will perhaps have an opportunity of explaining to him that we are an odd set of people.' (When an Austrian Archduke visited Blenheim a few years before, he was not asked even to have a glass of wine, nor, though rain kept him in the house some four hours and in the very room where the table was laid, given anything to eat.) Auckland replied that he had apprised the Duke and Duchess of the Grand Pensionary's visit, but 'I apprehend they will not have the courage to molest him'. However, for once they did their duty and received him: could it have been the stirring of some ancestral memory of the first Marlborough's relation to the celebrated Heinsius, or, more likely the desire to advance their brilliant son's career?

He was meanwhile being bored to distraction in Stockholm. Foreign diplomats were hardly received at Court, and etiquette prevented them from being welcomed in the homes of the Swedes. Lord Henry had not met with such a way of life since he left college. Winter was approaching and there were six hours of daylight. It was as if a man had suddenly fallen into a coal-pit. Lord Auckland consoled him with the miseries *he* had endured on his way across the Atlantic in December 1778: every December had been a source of happiness to him ever since. For some time Lord Henry had no news to communicate worth knowing from his Eddystone Lighthouse, then suddenly life was enlivened by all the excitement of a plot: an attempted *coup* by the adherents of the late murdered king, on behalf of a foreign power, a lady at Court, mistess of the exiled leader, love-letters—all the agreeable ingredients of a melodrama.

For some time Lord Henry had been destined for a much more important post—at Berlin where matters were becoming critical: the pro-French party led by Prince Henry was pulling Prussia out of the war. Before leaving Stockholm Lord Henry had an unpleasant surprise. It was usual for monarchs to give miniatures of themselves set in brilliants to departing envoys: the young King Gustav presented Lord Henry with an indecent picture. This must, of course, be regarded in the light of a calculated insult: it was firmly returned to Court and the incident reported in the proper language of diplomatic cant.

Lord Henry was suddenly ordered to hurry to Berlin in the depth of winter. There the peace negotiations were far advanced, and on his arrival he reported that he expected the peace-treaty with the French Convention to be followed by an alliance between the two countries, as against the triple league of Russia, Austria and Britain. 'Under these circumstances', he wrote to the Foreign Secretary, 'I apprehend that the presence of an English minister at this Court would be as little advantageous to the public service as agreeable or creditable to himself and that I may look forward with a great degree of confidence to the leave of absence which I have so long solicited for my private affairs. (What were these affairs?—thoughts of marriage, pursuing his far from reluctant lady?) Lord Grenville replied with a snub, which at the same time reflected the high value he set upon Lord Henry's services: 'it will, I am persuaded, be sufficient for me to mention to you the importance of an English minister of your lordship's rank being resident at Berlin at the present moment in order to induce your lordship to abandon a request which I should not think myself justified in recommending to his Majesty at so critical a period'.

So Lord Henry stayed. The game was by no means lost. Though Prince Henry of Prussia was pro-French, the King was friendly to Britain, and Lord Henry had an influence with him through his mistress who was amicably disposed. Lord Henry's letters continue vigorous and informative; then suddenly, in the heat of July, he was struck down by fever and died.

With this young man there died the hope of the family, not only for this generation but for the next. Everybody was struck by his loss. Mr. Pitt himself wrote the news to the Foreign Secretary; Lord Spencer wrote to inform the Archbishop, who had entertained such hopes; Lord Auckland had to break the news to the Duke. Lord Grenville lamented the loss to the public service on every account, 'having always entertained the highest opinion of his talents, his discretion and his principles'. From abroad even Prince Henry of Prussia, 'whose disposition in general is adverse to English characters, has shown peculiar attentions to our late excellent young friend, whom he constantly mentioned as one of the best young men that he had ever seen from any country'.

It was Lady Holland, as usual, who had the last word. In the summer of Lord Henry's death she hooked Lord Holland. Four years later, down at Saltram, 'I had the misfortune—and a most severe, heartfelt one it was—to lose my faithful companion, my attached Pierrot'. This was the pretty yellow and white Blenheim spaniel one sees in her lap in a portrait of her. 'He died! . . . He was the gift of Lord Henry. He faithfully maintained the love for me his master felt whilst living. Peace to them both!'

Another blow that befell the Marlboroughs in these years was entirely their own fault. Closest to Henry among his sisters was Charlotte, just a year older; and among his Oxford friends was a very good-looking Merton man, son of Judge Nares—fine large nose, blue eyes and a mass of fair wavy hair. The Blenheim theatricals threw these two much together and Nares became an intimate of the house. Years after he wrote, 'those who have been at Blenheim since can have no idea how princely the whole establishment was at that time and yet how little the family mixed with the world at large'. They lived in an enclosed world of their own.

The theatre was fitted up to hold from two to three hundred people, scarlet cloth boxes for the family on either side of the stage. Each performance was given on four successive nights; invitations went out to the neighbourhood, the town of Oxford, the university, the county, friends—each audience ascending in the social scale. On the fourth night of the November performances 1789 the authors of the two plays presented sat in the front row before the stage: Horace Walpole's friend, Field-Marshal Conway, who had written the comedy *False Appearances,* and General Burgoyne, who, more accomplished on the stage than at warfare, was the author of *Maid of the Oaks*. All the younger generation acted; Lord Charles came over from Wheatfield to take a part, and young Mr. Nares from Merton won much applause at his first appearances.

In the years following he appeared frequently at Blenheim and won more than applause: he captured Lady Charlotte's heart. No other more eligible suitors appeared and these girls were allowed little contact with the world. Lady Charlotte was a bridesmaid at the unhappy marriage of the Prince of Wales to the dotty Caroline; but Lady Charlotte was not to leave Blenheim until the Princess had actually landed. (It was proposed that the Duke should carry the sword of state at the wedding: he declined on the ground that he was not strong enough.) Nares was given no reason to suppose that his attentions to Lady Charlotte were unwelcome; they had known each other for seven years and she was over twenty-seven when he asked the Duke for her hand and got a direct refusal. It seems that the Duchess was responsible; Horace Walpole said that her 'wavering weathercockhood always rests at forbidding the banns'.

The couple took matters into their own hands; in April 1797 they went over to Henley and got married. Next day the steward from Blenheim informed Lady Charlotte that the Duke would allow her £400 a year, but they were forbidden the house, and she never saw her home again. Nares got a living in Kent—he had been ordained five years before—to which he took his wife. She bore him a daughter and they were tenderly devoted to each other; but after five years she died, leaving him deeply afflicted.

Lady Diana Beauclerk's kind heart was touched by her niece's fate. 'Poor thing, the story is too horrid to write. Her husband behaved with the utmost affection during her illness (others not so!); there are sad hearts about the world.... Her parents' hard heartedness helped to break her heart, I fear—they really are become callous to all (but themselves), when I say "they" I mean more particularly the female.' And this seems to have been the case, for after the Duchess's death the Duke invited Nares to bring his and Lady Charlotte's daughter to Blenheim. It was in December 1813 that he came back—sixteen years after; the old ones among the servants remembered him with affection and Nares was touched. The old Duke was confined to his bedroom, but Lord Francis showed him up after dinner, and both the Duke and Nares were deeply affected.

Next day he was gratified by the news of Nares's appointment as Regius Professor of Modern History at Oxford, and henceforth relations were renewed. As Professor coming up to deliver his lectures, Nares became intimate with Lord Charles's family, while Lord and Lady Churchill came in to Oxford from Cornbury specially to meet him and his daughter. In May 1814 the Regius Professor was presented to the Regent—he went to the levee from Marlborough House. Later on they stayed with Blandford at Whiteknights. Nares, who never had an ill word for anyone and had borne with the treatment he had been accorded without a murmur, put in a good word for the spendthrift Blandford and pointed to 'the many disadvantages under which he laboured. . . . I shall always consider him an injured man.'

Another close tie re-knitted the family. Lady Charlotte's daughter married Blandford's son, Lord Henry Spencer Churchill—the old name had been resumed. He died young and his widow looked after his mother, now Duchess, to the last; she is remembered in her will. This girl had been handsomely provided for as his grand-daughter by the old Duke: first £6000 in trust and then another £3000. A more touching thought appears in a last codicil: he asked that his daughter's body might be brought back to Blenheim to rest beside him.

The heir to Blenheim, the Marquis of Blandford, first burst upon public attention on account of the celebrated, the fantastic Gunning scandal of 1790-1. Appropriately enough, for he was a fantastic character, though it must be added that in this case he was not to blame. His marriage was naturally the concern of all the designing mothers in town, but no one could have supposed that it would take on all the elements of a Regency novel in real life. Blandford was a figure made after the model of the Regent, both gifted and absurd. Their personalities had several points in common: neither of them was a bad man, in both sentimentality and kindness of heart prevailed; each of them lived in a dream world, each had his 'pleasure-dome' floating flashily and crazily on a foundation of debt. In the case of the Regent Parliament paid up; in Blandford's case not all the remains of the Marlborough fortune were enough to meet his liabilities. The edifice of dream in which he had lived so long at length crashed about him.

In 1781 his mother was laying a scheme to marry him to a great fortune—Sarah Child, who was as beautiful as she was good and, more important, was the only offspring of the immensely rich banker of Osterley Park. The Pembrokes were scheming after her too, but she went to the Earl of Westmorland. Some years later, the young man being still unprovided with a wife, Mrs. Gunning the novelist took a hand—and the novel she proceeded to write with these materials, for she had a daughter to marry, rivalled the Pavilion in proportions, in exotic decoration and labyrinthine detail.

Mrs. Gunning was the sister-in-law of the lovely Gunning sisters, one of whom was twice duked. (This one had first married the Duke of Hamilton surreptitiously with a ring of the bed-curtain, according to Walpole, and secondly the Duke of Argyll.) Mrs. Gunning fancied a duke for her daughter and her choice fell upon the Marlborough heir. The daughter preferred the Argyll heir, but the mother brushed this preference aside. Her husband, the Irish General Gunning, had done not badly at Bunker Hill; he played an humiliating part in the matrimonial drama that ensued, being completely taken in by the tricks of his women-folk and rendered a ridiculous figure.

In August 1790 the news broke upon the town that another Gunning was to become a duchess, and that Miss Gunning was to have the same generous jointure as her future mother-in-law, the Duchess of Marlborough. The match-making old Duchess of Bedford was behind the scheme: 'it took its rise solely in poor old Bedford's dotage, that still harps on conjunctions copulative, but now disavows it, as they say, on a remonstrance from her daughter'. But the rumour grew mysteriously, with a number of letters being bandied about, with affirmations on one side, denials on the other. Then the newspapers came out with a statement of the General's descent from Charlemagne, to prove that his daughter was equal to any such match.

Meanwhile more and more love-letters reached Miss Gunning from the Marquis, until the General considered it his duty to ask him in form what his intentions were with regard to his daughter. The Marquis denied that he had ever entertained any. At that the General confronted him with all the letters. The Marquis immediately owned the few letters disclaiming any inclination for Miss Gunning and disavowed the rest. Her father proceeded to lay the matter before the Marlboroughs, sending his own groom, who returned with a letter saying how delighted they were 'at their son's having made choice of so beautiful and amiable a virgin for his bride . . . and how chagrined they were that, from the lightness and inconstancy of his temper, the proposed alliance was quite at an end'. People hardly knew what to think, for the Marlboroughs were regarded as so odd in their conduct to their children that this might well be true. The General was ready to take proceedings when the groom confessed that he had been bribed by Mrs. Gunning. Revealed as a dupe all along, Gunning turned his wife and daughter out of house; the latter, the fair Gunnilda, was taken in by the Duchess of Bedford, who continued to support her cause.

The saga was by no means at an end. Gunnilda stuck to her story that the Duchess of Marlborough had given her every encouragement; so 'the Signora Madre took a post-chaise-and-four and drove to Blenheim; but not finding the Duke and Duchess there, she inquired where the Marquis was and pursued him to Sir H. Dashwood's: finding him there, she began about her poor daughter; but he interrupted her, said there was an end put to all that, and desired to lead her to her chaise, which he insisted on doing and did'. It was said that Mrs. Gunning tried to get the Marquis into her chaise, but that he would not venture being carried to Gretna Green and married by force. Miss Gunning remained with his Bedford grandmother.

She now confessed to her preference for Lord Lorne, of the two ducal victims, and this brought in the Argylls with affidavits and counter-affidavits as to her, her mother's and the groom's veracity. A new narrative was sent down to Blenheim maintaining Gunnilda's story that she had passed three days with them that summer, when it was in fact but three hours. The Duchess of Bedford interceded on behalf of her darling with the Argylls. The scandal reached enormous proportions with prints beginning to appear: one, 'The New Art of Gunning', depicted 'Miss astride a cannon firing a volley of forged letters at the castle of Blenheim, and old Gertrude, emaciated and withered and very like, lifting up her hoop to shelter injured innocence, as she calls her'. Mrs. Gunning followed with a whole book of 246 pages replying in kind to the aspersions on her with aspersions on everybody else in the farce, with 'endless tiresome encomiums on the virtues of her *glorious darling* and the unspottable innocence of that harmless lambkin'. They then went off to France.

Further pamphlets appeared in the Gunnings' absence and many squibs were passed about, one of them sung to the tune of 'The House that Jack Built': 'this is the note that nobody wrote, this is the groom that carried the note that nobody wrote', etc. etc. It became apparent that most of the Blandford letters had been fabricated by Mrs. Gunning, though when she and her daughter returned from Paris they were still upheld by the Bedford grandmother. The Marquis had had such a narrow escape that he perhaps felt that there was safety only in marriage; so a match was suddenly patched up for him that summer 'with a little more art than was employed by the fair Gunnilda. It is with Lady Susan Stewart, Lord Galloway's daughter, contrived by and at the house of her relation and Lord Blandford's friend, Sir Henry Dashwood; and it is to be so instantly that her Grace, his mother, will scarce have time to forbid the banns.'

His mother resented the marriage, and good old Moore had to patch things up: he wrote that he was glad Lord Blandford had married into a family of rank and good connections. He advised the Duke and Duchess 'as soon as possible to receive both son and daughter and give them every mark of your love and forgiveness'. The truth was that the Marlboroughs were disappointed in their eldest son, and at the back of their disapprobation was his frivolity and thriftlessness. They therefore kept him on a short allowance, one that was insufficient for a person in his position. While the Duke and Duchess resided in state at Marlborough House, he lived in lodgings at Triphook's in St. James's Street. The consequences were what might be expected: Blandford had recourse, in regular Regency fashion, to moneylenders who advanced him large sums at exorbitant rates of interest on his expectations. The very length of his father's life made the situation worse: when Blandford succeeded to the dukedom the whole edifice was undermined.

To music, botany, gardening, the Marquis added another expensive interest—a mistress. Lady Mary Ann Sturt was the wife of a rich Dorset M.P.; her brother, Cropley Ashley, was married to one of Blandford's sisters, so it was all within the family. When Mr. Sturt brought his case before the courts the celebrated Whig advocate Erskine surpassed himself in moral objurgation. This was all by way of asking for large damages.

The connection was not denied and letters were read which revealed the Marquis in a very sentimental light—much in the style of the Prince Regent, as it might be to Mrs. Fitzherbert. Blandford regarded his Mary Ann as his spiritual wife, and wrote after the birth of a child, 'that that Providence which has watched over you in your recent dangers may ever continue to shower down its choicest blessings on the worthiest object of its care is and ever shall be my constant prayer. To one point we must both look—the education of the dear pledge of our eternal love. My wife, my dear wife, the adored mother of my beloved child, my affection to you is ten millions of times stronger than ever. Suffer this innocent babe to cement our union, so that it may know no end. Love the little

Georgiana for the sake of your George, of your Blandford, of your faithful husband.'

The injured husband deposed that the guilty couple dressed very fine; 'Lord Blandford's fingers were loaded with trinkets, while his wife was bedecked with ear-rings, necklaces, lion clasps and handsome gowns the Marquis had given her; he made her presents which would have been more properly bestowed on the Marchioness'. On the discovery of their correspondence the Marquis wrote that he was 'on his way to Switzerland, that he might indulge his melancholy amidst the horrors of the Alps. One consolation he would have in his solitude: he carried along with him a miniature of his Mary Ann, which he had received from her in the days of their love.'

It transpired in the course of the case that the injured husband was not so innocent: he was more or less accessory to the footing upon which the Marquis stood with Mary Ann, while himself 'had been living for several years past in adulterous concubinage with Madame Krumpholtz, who played upon the harp and by whom he had five children'. In place of the £20,000 damages hoped for, the jury awarded him £100.

This extravagance was nothing compared with the money Blandford spent on curious plants and rare books, on music and musicians—he was a fair amateur composer, though we do not know if he composed for Madame Krumpholtz's harp. At Whiteknights near Reading he had a place with a superb garden kept up like a royal residence with more than twenty gardeners. The King of Prussia sent his head gardener there to pick up tips. There was a vineyard producing and a shrubbery of forty acres in which rare American plants only just beginning to be known in England were cultivated. The Marquis thought nothing of paying £500 for a rarity. In the greenhouses aquatic plants from the Ganges were kept afloat in tepid water. Some exotics unique in England he reared with his own hands, for he had exceptional botanical knowledge.

His attitude to books and music was similarly in the family vein of expensive connoisseurship. He collected a fine library at Whiteknights, which contained the fifteenth-century Duke of Bedford's Missal and the Valdarfer Boccaccio, for which he paid £2260. The purchase of this *Decameron*, it seems, was the occasion of the founding of the Roxburghe Club of which he was an original member. When Nares went to stay with him a military band of seventeen musicians played all through dinner. The Marquis himself composed: in 1798 he published a collection of twelve glees, for three and four voices. Like many people of an extravagant turn of mind and no aptitude for business, he longed to manage something—perhaps with a feverish hope of recouping his losses. Wyatt's Pantheon in Oxford Street had twice burned down; Blandford took it over in an unsafe condition to run it as an opera house. The Lord Chamberlain ordered it to be surveyed before reopening to the public; characteristically Wyatt could not be traced. When found he reported that it was unsafe: nothing but a new roof and walls would do. The Lord Chamberlain insisted on the public being warned if the Pantheon opened, and then refused a licence.

The consequences were what one would expect. A solitary note of interest due during eighteen months, June 1808 to January 1810, speaks volumes. There was interest to be paid on his bond for £6000, on a first mortgage for £11,360 12*s.*, on a second for £5472 8*s.* 8*d.*—simply in interest £2488 9*s.* 6*d.* engulfed. There were the accountant's costs for preparing different securities. But this did not discourage his ostentatious extravagances: coachmaker's work for 1808, £482 4*s.*, for 1809, £805 8*s.* He was a great fool, in spite of his varied talents. When Captain Gronow travelled down with him to Whiteknights in his coach, he opened a cupboard, constructed in the side of the roomy vehicle, that contained a capital luncheon with different wines and liqueurs. Another cupboard contained a secretaire with writing materials and a large pocket-book with a wad of fifty Bank of England notes for £1000 each, borrowed the day before from Levy, to whom he had given a post-obit on his father's death for £150,000. Even if we allow for exaggeration, it hardly misrepresents the situation: 'You see, Gronow, how the immense fortune of my family will be frittered away. But I can't help it; I must live. My father inherited £500,000 in ready money and £70,000 a year in land; in all probability when it comes to my turn to live at Blenheim, I shall have nothing left but the £5000 a year on the Post Office.' And that was about what came to pass.

There was nothing that the Duke could do effectively to protect the family from this idiocy. As early as 1793 the Duke was hardly on speaking terms with his son: Lord Henry wrote that his father would not return to Blenheim when Blandford was to be steward of the Oxford races. After Henry's death Lord Francis became the favourite son on whom his parents relied. Blandford was not put up for Parliament again either for the county or for Woodstock. His brother, Lord Francis, represented the county from 1801 up to

1815, when he was made a peer; and he took what should have been his brother's place in the life of the county, commanding the Oxfordshire Cavalry volunteers, then the Oxfordshire Militia, lastly the Yeomanry all through the long war and beyond.

His father rewarded him and marked his disapprobation of his eldest son so far as he could. He was anxious to have Lord Francis made a peer and to have the name and title of Churchill revived in him. To this end he settled the Cornbury estate upon him and the manors and lands purchased from the Earl of Clarendon, away from the Dukedom. In his will he left him for life the beautiful house in Oxford Lord Francis occupied—now the Judge's Lodgings in St. Giles's; all the books, prints and drawings in his dressing-room, together with bronzes and china, to his wife. In 1812 the Duke wrote to the Regent soliciting a barony for his son; the Regent was willing, the Tory Prime Minister Perceval against. However, they got in in 1815, and Lord Francis became Baron Churchill of Wychwood, the first of a cadet line.

Two years later Blandford succeeded as fifth Duke and took back the old surname of Churchill. This may have been partly out of rivalry with his brother, but perhaps even more inspired by these years of victory culminating in Waterloo and the thought of the earlier military glories of John Churchill. On a summer evening in 1817 the new Duke invited over seventy people to dinner to celebrate his accession. The arrangements were in accordance with the elaboration of his taste: the stable people stationed on the steps when the company arrived, lamps round the court, steps and portico lighted at nine, the other servants in the hall to conduct the company through the Bow Window room to the Grand Cabinet. The band played in the hall and then in the dining-room while the guests passed to the saloon later, in the Library while refreshments were served in the colonnade.

The new Duke's fantastic tastes soon displayed themselves in the gardens. He added wings to the Temple of Health to form an aviary for his exotic birds, and soon gardens were forming down the slopes below it: an Arcade Flower Garden, the Botany Bay Garden, the Chinese and Terrace Gardens, the Dahlia and Rose Gardens. Admittance to the Rock Garden was through a revolving mass of rock that gave way to the touch, opening upon a picturesque scene. The Bernini fountain was at last set up; there was also a Druid's Temple, with romantic altar supported on unhewn monoliths overgrown with moss, a Garden of Springs, a Valley of Streams, grottoes, rustic bridges, islands. Within doors, under the

Long Library, the Duke fitted up a room in Waterloo-blue drapery hung from an immense rosette in the ceiling. This room looked out on the Arcade Flower Garden and a new octagon pavilion of coloured woods. Further apartments were formed: an Italian refectory of *verd d'antique* and Sienna marble, a Japanese drawing-room with a fresco of an Indian tiger-hunt.

It is the same spirit of Regency exoticism that was at work in Beckford's mind, at Sezincote and the Brighton Pavilion.

Who knows what the fifth Duke would not have made of Blenheim as his plaything if creditors had not shortly called a halt? The vultures came home to roost—bailiffs in the Palace; the melancholy mournful knell of Debt clanged in his ears for the rest of his life. It was only on succeeding as Duke that he could pay the Rev. Vaughan Thomas for the charges he had incurred for his sons at Eton and the interest that had mounted up since: these included Montem expenses, a portrait of Sarah bought at an auction and a marble chimney-piece for Whiteknights—in all £637 10*s.* 6*d.*, discharged in 1817. His own personal collections there had to go under the hammer; the Boccaccio he had paid £2260 for was sold to his cousin, Earl Spencer, for 875 guineas; the whole library fetched £14,482, far less than he had spent on it.

Before Whiteknights was sold the Duke of Wellington rode over with a large party from Strathfieldsaye to see the gardens. It was January, but 'from the profusion of evergreens the place looked quite like summer and it is impossible to express the beauty of the American plants.... It has been seized by a Sir Charles Cockerell, to whom the Duke owes a large sum of money. It is said that the gardens have cost the Duke £40,000 or £50,000 and that he owes Lee and Kennedy of Hammersmith £10,000 for plants.' Meanwhile, at Blenheim when one of the younger generation of Foxes was asked to dinner, 'I was very much amused with the Duke and surprised at the splendour of the establishment. The party were chiefly (with the exception of some hungry curates) Oxonians. The house ill-lighted and all the servants, I believe, *bailiffs.* I was astonished at the invitation, for I never had seen him in my life. [To be a Fox was no doubt enough.] He is pleasant, but looks like a great West India property overseer.'

When Wellington took Mrs. Arbuthnot to see Blenheim in 1824 she 'could not but regret the difference of times which rendered it impossible for a second Blenheim to be erected to the hero of Waterloo. Such a house could not be erected under millions.... The family of our great General is, however, gone sadly to decay and are but a disgrace to the illustrious name of Churchill, which they have chosen this moment to resume. The present Duke is overloaded with debt, is very little better than a common swindler and lets everything about Blenheim. People may shoot and fish at so much per hour! and it has required all the authority of a Court of Chancery to prevent his cutting down all the trees in the park. He did melt and sell the gold plate given the great Duke by the Elector of Bavaria, substituting ormolu ones to deceive the trustees. His second son took the benefit of the insolvent act lately.' Nor was the elder son, it must be added, in a way to retrieve the position.

At some point there had been an execution in the Palace. The Rev. Vaughan Thomas thought that Marlborough's famous note to Sarah from the battlefield of Blenheim had been abstracted 'by some of the gang of bailiffs let into Blenheim upon Neate's execution—Neate and Bartlett forced open the latticed press which used to be under the Van Dyck picture of Charles I in the drawing room and seized the papers'. As the years went on the Duke was forced to close down more and more on the establishment; for years he was more confined within the walls of Blenheim by debt than even his father had been by eccentricity. Of course he could jog along on the game and venison from the park, beef, poultry and eggs from the estate, fish out of the lake, and he had a good cellar of wine. But he could obtain credit neither in London nor Oxford, nor did he dare to show his face there. His melancholy forecast that he would come to depend on the famous Post Office pension of the first Duke was fulfilled. It was fortunate for the family and the future that the Blenheim estate and the heirlooms were strictly entailed, or they would surely have gone the way of the rest.

In this reduced state the Duke had the honour—and, like his father before him, the anxiety—of a royal visit: in October 1835 Queen Adelaide and her sister descended on him. The Duke in a great state had to ask Lord and Lady Churchill to come over and help him do the honours: it does not appear that his Duchess was living with him. The Churchills arrived in time, shortly before the Duke of Wellington. Lord Churchill's band was stationed in the Grand Court, at the centre gate of which the royal party entered, which had a good effect. The Duke handed out the Queen and Lord Churchill her sister. After seeing over the Palace there was a handsome luncheon, and an address from the borough of Woodstock. 'Everything went off *surprisingly* well', reported Lady Churchill to the absent Duchess.

The heir, known as Lord Sunderland while his father was still

Marquis of Blandford, was not the man to retrieve the situation. His schoolfellow at Eton, Lord Monson, described him as 'one of the handsomest lads I ever saw'; but at that ancient house of learning he signalised himself, so far as is known, only as the ringleader in the riots against the ferocious Keate, the headmaster. Dr. Keate, however, bore no malice, nor did the boys. When all the English flocked to Paris after Waterloo they were astonished to see the Doctor eating an ice at Torloni's on the Boulevard like any other human being. His pupils—many of whom had suffered as much from him as Dr. Busby's—determined to give him a dinner at Beauvillier's, the best dining place in Paris. There were Sunderland and his friend Lord James Stuart; the dinner was an immense success, the Doctor ate as he had never eaten before and paid his addresses in large bumpers to every description of wine. *Floreat Etona!*

In those blissful Waterloo years the young Duke of Devonshire was being hunted down by scheming mothers for their daughters, with all the vulgarity, according to Gronow, of the British matron in full cry after a duke. Lady Conyngham, the Regent's Egeria, was after him for her daughter, Lady Elizabeth. (The Duke of Devonshire remained obstinately, inexplicably, the Bachelor Duke.) Lord Sunderland, more susceptible, fell desperately in love with Lady Elizabeth and proposed to her. Her mother refused him, hoping against hope that the besieged Duke would yield.

Whether off the rebound or no Lord Sunderland—who, everybody agreed, was a fine young man—engaged immediately in an adventure for which he more than merited Dr. Keate's cane. At twenty-three he wanted a girl and he found one aged between sixteen and seventeen, the daughter of parents in a respectable position. Whether there was collusion between the mother and the Marquis or no, the way to the girl's charms was a marriage ceremony. The young lord had a brother who was a clergyman, he said, and would perform it. The ceremony took place privately in the mother's presence and in her room—she must have known that it was not legal, though she may not have known that the 'clergyman'-brother was actually an army officer. The ceremony was entered up in the Prayer Book and the young woman received a 'settlement' of £400 a year. On that she went to live with the Marquis—his father had just become Duke—as his wife in private.

When he went down to Scotland for the grouse-shooting next summer he travelled in his own carriage with his valet, 'Mrs. Lawson' went by the Edinburgh mail with her child and one servant. It was this that got him into trouble subsequently; for twenty years later a horrid paper, the *Satirist*, claimed that 'his was a Scots marriage by recognition and admission' and invalidated his subsequent marriage to his Galloway cousin. This was a matter of the first importance to his son, heir to Blenheim in turn, and a case was brought before the courts to settle the issue. There had been no legal marriage with the girl, of course, and subsequently she herself married. The Marquis's mother, the Duchess, paid her her £400 a year for a number of years, in return for which she gave up many of his letters signing himself as her husband. Like father, like son: both lived in a world of Regency extravaganza and fantasy.

Blandford added political divergence to other disagreements with his father. The family representatives in both Houses had been so silent for so long that it is curious to find this member of it speaking frequently and fully during a very short period, the sessions of 1829 and 1830, before silence descends again. What makes it all the odder is that he gives the impression of an accomplished speaker, rather stylish, with quotations from Bacon and Locke, Chatham and Burke. One would say that he was on the way to becoming a figure in politics, except that his position was such an eccentric one; and then something cut it short. Altogether it makes an odd episode.

The differences between Lord Blandford and his father were reflected in the representation of Woodstock, the family borough. In 1830 Blandford was returned with his brother, Lord Charles Spencer Churchill, for the two seats. In 1831 Blandford was left out and Viscount Stormont took his place: no doubt the Duke disapproved of his extreme Reform views. The Reform Bill reduced Woodstock to one seat, and in 1833 Blandford had it. In 1835 he made way again for Lord Charles. In the election on Queen Victoria's accession in 1837 Lord Charles was defeated at his own gates by an Oxfordshire gentleman, Henry Peyton. The majority was only ten; Lord Charles petitioned against Peyton's return on the ground of bribery and corruption. Lord Charles did not enter into recognisances in respect of the petition—he was probably unable to—and so it was discharged. However, Peyton had the goodness, or was prevailed on, to withdraw, and in May 1838 there was a by-election in which Blandford fought his brother, Lord John. Now Lord John petitioned the House that his brother's election had been procured by bribery, undue influence, the admission of persons not qualified to vote. The House rejected this plea, declared Blandford's election valid and pronounced the disqualification of three Woodstock voters.

When Blandford succeeded as Duke in 1840 Frederick Thesiger got the seat. On Thesiger's appointment as Solicitor-General in 1844 he resigned for re-election; but the new Lord Blandford took his seat and when he resigned it after a year, it was to Viscount Loftus who made way for a younger son of Blenheim, Lord Alfred Spencer Churchill. This Blandford's resignation was due to a disagreement with *his* father in turn—over Free Trade. The father on becoming Duke became noticeably more conservative than he had been; and, in spite of his earlier Reform ideas, had never approved of Free Trade. It is refreshing to see the differences that could take place in regard to policy within the bosom of a privileged landed aristocracy—even if we observe that the views of the holder of the title and estate conformed more closely to what he considered his economic interest than those of the heir: politics were not simply a question of class-interest. This Blandford sat henceforth for Woodstock until his succession as Duke in 1857, when his brother, Lord Alfred, followed him.

The spendthrift, spend-all fifth Duke, the Regency buck who had undermined the family's finances, died in 1840. He left a curious brief will, leaving 'all and singular my goods, chattels and effects unto Matilda Glover now living in my family at Blenheim. And I do hereby nominate, constitute and appoint the said Matilda Glover to be the sole executrix of this my will.' The will was made in 1838; it was attested as valid in 1841 and proved by Matilda Glover. Who was Matilda Glover? I do not know.

The Duchess died next year, leaving a large number of small legacies—but nothing to Matilda Glover. It does not seem that the Duchess had been living at Blenheim, but occupying a grace-and-favour lodging at Hampton Court. She had a little money to leave, a little furniture and a number of family miniatures by Craig copied from Cosway. Nothing attests the decline of the family fortunes more than this pathetic bequest. On the Duke's death the *Annual Register* recorded that the collections he had made were dispersed in his lifetime, and 'during the latter years of his life he lived in utter retirement at one corner of his magnificent palace: a melancholy instance of the results of extravagance'.

Of the rule of the sixth Duke at Blenheim there is nothing to say, for he left instructions at his death for all his personal papers to be destroyed—the fragmentary evidences of the life of the man who had been the handsomest boy at Eton. He made three marriages: the first to his cousin of the Galloway family—his mother's family.

She had been born at Blenheim in 1798, and died there in 1844. He next married a daughter of Lord Ashbrook, who died in 1850. For his third wife he went back to his mother's family and married a Galloway cousin; but, strangely enough, in his will he says nothing about her and leaves her nothing. She lived up to the threshold of our day, dying in 1897, one of the five Duchesses of Marlborough above ground at one and the same time.

The various vicissitudes, financial, matrimonial, personal, of these two dukes did not prevent the university of Oxford from honouring their great neighbours. The fifth Duke had received the degree of D.C.L. as long ago as 1792; the sixth after his accession at the Encaenia of 1841. He was also Lord-Lieutenant of the county from 1842 till his death; not all the mighty shades of Blenheim could prevail on the Crown to make his bankrupt father its representative.

It is only from the will of the sixth Duke that we glean some pathetic particulars about him. He was dying in 1857, not old, only sixty-three, leaving a family of young children to provide for, about whom he was anxious. For the past seven or eight years he was an invalid, confined to a wheeled chair. He had been a sportsman, keen on shooting, fishing, yachting. He left his chronometer, ship-watch, sextant and telescope to his son, Lord Alfred; all his sea-telescopes, some Vulliamy clocks and a painting by Condy of the *Wyvern* yacht to Lord Alan; his guns, fishing-rods and tackle to be divided between them. His daughter, Lady Clementina, was to have, when twenty-one, the diamonds her mother had converted after her marriage into 'a splendid tiara'; a guardian was appointed for her, while his eldest son and heir was to be sole guardian of young Lord Almeric during his minority, with the express wish that he should go to Eton and then to Oxford. So we deduce that there was entire confidence between the sixth Duke and his eminently respectable, public-spirited successor.

The will is of immense length and complexity, for there were various trusts to provide for these younger children; the entailed estates to go to Blandford, with the addition of most of the household goods, furniture, garden tools and wines in the Blenheim cellars. A more touching reference is provided by the Duke's solicitude for his housekeeper, Sarah Licence: she had £50 down, £3 a week for life, the Duke's little brass bedstead, his black marble clock and rosewood writing-table, 'also the large arm-chair with high wheels in which I have daily sat for the last five years'. This was in 1854. Later that year, solicitous for her, he purchased a house for her to dwell in for life. His funeral expenses were not to exceed £100—a far cry from the magnificence of the funeral of John Churchill, first Duke.

CHAPTER FIVE

The Complete Victorian

WITH John Winston, seventh Duke, respectability set in with its usual severity. No more Whig frolics, no more Regency extravaganzas. From his early youth this Blandford, unlike his predecessors of that name, was sober-sided and serious-minded, devout and chaste, devoted to the interests of the Church, for most of his life his horizon bounded by ecclesiastical legislation. A one-track mind, he was yet a man of ability, pertinacious and industrious in the cause he served; needless to say, he was a Tory of a narrow dispensation. The astonishing house of Marlborough holds yet another surprise for us: for the first (and last) time it produces a complete, full-blown, Victorian prig.

It is a sobering thought that this was the grandfather of our Sir Winston, and it is difficult to account for him: John Winston was decidedly a sport in the line. But there is this historical interest in such an apparition: it shows how the family reflects the varying temper of the society—a continuing theme of this book.

Is he to be accounted for by his education, as the original Sir Winston was? We saw that the first Winston remained always what St. John's College at Oxford made him—High Church but obstinately Protestant, a royalist and divine-right-of-kings-man, a loather of Puritans and Republicans. His descendant, John Winston, may have similarly been affected by his Oxford college; for, contrary to family tradition, he did not go to Christ Church—which was apt to be broad-minded in all senses of the word—but to Oriel, the seminary of the Tractarian movement, and at its critical apogee in the midst of the *Tracts for the Times*. He matriculated from Oriel in the Michaelmas term of 1840 and remained there under the tuition of a devout clergyman who died young. John Winston seems always to have been affected by the Tractarian influence, though later something confirmed his Protestantism to the point of being anti-Roman, as so many Victorians were. This circumstance may equally have been his marriage to a strong-minded Ulster-woman, the influence of his cousin, Lord Shaftesbury, or the reaction against the creation of a Roman hierarchy in

England.

There was no challenge to virtue in dining at Blenheim with this Duke—nothing but confirmation of one's prejudices. Mrs. Jeune, the wife of an Oxford don on his way to becoming a Victorian bishop, dined there on a cold night in November 1858: 'furs and hot-water bottles kept us warm and prevented any evil results'. There were Lord and Lady Shaftesbury, the Dean and Mrs. Liddell from Christ Church. Conversation was not very lively: 'the Duchess sat evidently racking her brains for some subject for conversation, but was unsuccessful in finding any sufficiently interesting to excite more than a sentence or two from either of her two supporters. She seems a kind-hearted motherly sort of person—neither clever nor at all handsome. The Duke also is a "plain" man in all its meanings, but it is in itself an immense merit to be a religious Duke of Marlborough, and this his Grace has.'

John Winston became well known, some years before he succeeded as seventh Duke, for his prolonged campaigns for Church reform. When he died, having widened his experience and interests as Lord President of the Council and as Lord-Lieutenant of Ireland, *The Times* said of him, 'perhaps his name will be held longest in remembrance as the author of the Act which he helped to pass as Lord Blandford and which bears that name, for the purpose of strengthening the Established Church in our large towns by the subdivision of extensive parishes and the erection of smaller vicarages or incumbencies'. It is unlikely that anyone remembers the Act of that name now, but to get it passed involved Blandford in a strenuous one-man campaign over some years.

In 1851 Blandford raised the question of Church Extension, 'an object which ought to be upon the hearts of all good men . . . but the interest which is shown in ecclesiastical affairs is not great'. He proceeded to devote his energies entirely to them, becoming a kind of Lord Hugh Cecil of his time. He embarked on a campaign for the subdivision of parishes, for founding new parishes in over-burdened industrial districts with no clergy or church provision; he demanded an inquiry into the surplus revenues of the bishops and of the deans and chapters, which might be devoted to this purpose. He proposed an Address to the Queen 'to lay the wants of the people at the feet of Her who in this country is the fountain of worldly honour, ecclesiastical as well as civil'. The Radical member Hume was able to get some of his own back by drawing public attention to a document on the revenues of the bishops 'so tardily furnished by themselves'. From this it appeared that the Archbishop of Canterbury had averaged over the past seven years £22,907 a year, the Bishop of Durham £26,786, the Bishop of London £16,513, the Archbishop of York and the Bishop of Winchester over £12,000 each. In all, a sum of £192,024 a year went on twenty-six bishops. It is the world of Trollope, of Barchester and scuffling for preferments, of Mrs. Proudies and underpaid starveling curates.

This state of affairs forced Blandford, with his passionate concern for the welfare of the Church, to become a reformer in his way. He urged that the management of Church lands should be placed in the hands of laymen: was it fitting that persons of spiritual character should spend so much of their time managing property? He wanted a central body to take over the estates of the Church. The member for the university of Oxford—a largely clerical constituency—thought this would be fatal to the Church's interests. The proposal was lost in the Lords, where the bishops sat in strength. But Blandford persevered: years of parliamentary time and acres of Hansard went on this campaign for sensible reforms.

In 1854 Blandford brought forward his Bill again. The Crimean war had now begun. He thought that 'if it was desired to obtain the Divine blessing for the country—its prosperity at home and its immunity and protection from invasion from without—no surer method could be adopted . . . than by that House having due regard to the spiritual interests of the people'. Some people thought that in the midst of a war other things were more important than Lord Blandford's Episcopal and Capitular Estates Bill. Not so John Winston: with characteristic obstinacy he brought it forward again—this was peculiarly the time to bring down the favour of God on the people of this country. He ferreted out a few more damaging facts; he found that the Dean and Chapter of Canterbury, out of a revenue of £25,000 a year, devoted £71 to augment their poor vicarages and £1306 for schools and charitable purposes. Durham Cathedral Chapter, with an income of £60,000 a year, provided £4000 for these purposes; Westminster, with £30,000 a year, ear-marked £474 for their vicars and £426 for charities. Truly these deans and canons were at ease in Zion: the earth was theirs and the fulness thereof. They were not letting go so easily. Blandford was once more checkmated by the Church he wished so ardently to serve.

In the summer of 1856 Blandford at length got his Bill for the subdivision of parishes through—the reward of long pertinacity. But it was only one part of his programme: he was unable to get his clutches into the fat surpluses of bishops, deans and canons. He had been radical enough to propose putting these prelates and clerical persons on fixed incomes. No such luck: these birds eluded him. Meanwhile he went after such of the bishops as were too debilitated to perform their functions. He raised the question of suffragans. He had great respect for prelates, but it was necessary to bring forward the matter 'in consequence of infirmities over which those reverend personages had no control'. In consequence of their state of health 'several of the prelates of the Church were unhappily disabled from attending their dioceses'. Wiser now, Blandford proposed no disturbing measure, merely asked that the Act of Henry VIII (!) for Suffragans might be put into force.

This frightened a brace of moribund bishops into retirement. Whereupon an impolite Liberal M.P. pointed out that the Bishops of London and Durham over a period of twenty years had together absorbed a matter of £973,000. The good old days were beginning to be over when these Victorian reformers got to work. Blandford was one of them. He himself had pointed out that over the past thirty years £191,000 had been paid to the Dean and Chapter of Durham alone, simply for fines on the renewals of leases: no portion of this had been funded for the benefit of the Church, it just went into the pockets of the Dean and canons. 'When we remember that this is the return from one proprietary only, we shall be able to form some estimate of what enormous sums are being annually lost to the Church.' In March 1857 Blandford introduced an Ecclesiastical Corporations Bill into the Commons. It was withdrawn, and shortly he left the Commons for the Lords. However, there is no doubt that in the end his campaign bore fruit: in strengthening and recasting the Ecclesiastical Commission, and so on. In our time his proposals have come about: the properties of the Church are administered by the Commissioners; bishops, deans and canons live on fixed stipends. Mrs. Proudie's day (financially speaking) is over.

In spite of his religious preoccupations the seventh Duke led a more effective social life, much more in the public eye, than any of his three predecessors. In 1843 he had married a daughter of the Marquis of Londonderry, 'a woman of remarkable character and capacity, judicious and tactful', as the *Complete Peerage* tells us. She was a figure in her own right, warm-hearted and forceful, ambitious for her brilliant younger son, Lord Randolph. Together the Duke and Duchess proceeded to revivify the life of Blenheim, melancholy and moribund for so long; and there they gave entertainments such as the Palace had never seen. The new Duke succeeded to the Lord-Lieutenancy of Oxfordshire and certainly did his duty by the county, city and university.

Mrs. Jeune describes for us a ball given for the Prince of Wales when staying at Blenheim in 1859. It was November and cold again; but 'it looked *very* grand, well lighted and with a dozen footmen in the showy Marlborough livery drawn up at the entrance —when the servant conducting us, being evidently on the watch, turned and announced "the Prince is coming". H.R.H. was coming from his rooms with his suite and in his gracious pleasing manner advanced at once to us to shake hands, and then we followed him into the Grand Cabinet where a large party was already assembled.' There, too, were the inevitable Liddells from Christ Church, along with the Austrian Ambassador and Ambassadress, Macclesfields, Portarlingtons, Vanes and who not in the county of Oxford.

Dinner was in the Grand Saloon, brilliantly lit by candles and gas below, dark suggestive shadows in the high vault above. Little Mrs. Jeune was dazzled by the display of jewels around the table, the Ambassadress's shoulder-knots of rubies and diamonds, the Duchess's necklace, Lady Macclesfield's tiara. At ten the evening company began to arrive and they all proceeded to the ballroom. There was dancing in two of the Tapestry rooms too, and all would have been perfect 'if the Duchess had requested those who knew more of her company than she knew herself to make more introductions; but she has not very agreeable manners herself and is very deaf, which gives her an appearance of awkwardness unfortunate in her position'. However, his Royal Highness enjoyed himself thoroughly with the ladies, dancing 'every dance of every kind and was still dancing the Cotillion when we left a little before four o'clock'.

The Prince was there again for an even grander party another year. He had come to shoot with three or four friends, including Colonel Keppel. After the shoot there was a banquet *à la russe* in the Grand Saloon, with a vast bill of French fare. There was an evening party for three hundred; 'the display of diamonds and jewellery was dazzling in the extreme'. All the apartments along the whole south front of the Palace were illuminated and thrown open to the autumn night and the gaze of hundreds of spectators gathered on the site of Henry Wise's vanished parterres. The first and second state drawing-rooms had been furnished anew for the occasion, the Prince's apartments fitted up in enamelled white and gold furniture. Altogether, the newspaper concluded, it was the most brilliant spectacle in the county for a century.

The Bishop of Oxford, in the intervals of trying to squash Bishop Colenso and make T. H. Huxley look ridiculous, found time to stay at Blenheim. In November 1865, for example, there was a large party for Blandford's coming of age, with the Duc d'Aumale, Lord Hardwicke, etc. etc. 'The Duke is doing it very handsomely and I want to back him up in everything. He is quite a capital fellow really.' Two years later the Bishop was invited to meet Disraeli. 'Nothing can be kinder than the Duke and Duchess have been. I enjoyed meeting Disraeli. He is a marvellous man. Not a bit of a Briton, but all over an Eastern Jew; but very interesting to talk to. He *always* speaks as if he did believe in the Church.' Dizzy always knew which side his bread was buttered: was he not the Conservative leader, and had he not described the Church of England as the Conservative party at prayer?

However, the grandest society would not be what it is without its mortifications to complain about and cause the blood to flow. At the wedding of the Prince of Wales to Princess Alexandra in St. George's chapel at Windsor in 1863, space was so limited that though Mr. and Mrs. Disraeli were bidden as the Queen's guests, the Marlboroughs were not. 'There is no language which can describe the rage, envy and indignation of the great world. The Duchess of Marlborough went into hysterics of mortification at the sight of my wife, who was on terms of considerable intimacy with her, and said it was really shameful after the reception which the Duke had given the Prince of Wales at Blenheim.'

By now Dizzy had 'climbed to the top of the greasy pole'— a remark that earnest Victorians could hardly approve. (Can one imagine Mr. Gladstone making it?) Marlborough was a friend of Dizzy's and was first given office as Lord Steward of the Household —a post the fourth Duke had held—in 1866. Next year there was a reconstruction of the cabinet upon the resignation of Cranborne (later Lord Salisbury) in disgust at Disraeli's democratic Reform Bill. Disraeli replaced him by no less than three dukes, of whom Marlborough became Lord President of the Council. It was an arrangement that provoked many a smile: so characteristic of Dizzy—an artful combination of reactionary dukes with democratic measures. The author of *Coningsby* and *Sybil* was writing a novel in real life.

Disraeli, however, was not without effect in influencing the minds of his dukes: he reported with some complacency to the

Queen Marlborough's speech in favour of his Reform Bill. The Duke 'spoke with much ability on the point and adjured his colleagues to take the step of necessary boldness'. In a few years Marlborough had come a long way from divine-right-of-kings nonsense. But at the end of the year he was alarmed by Fenian news from New York: a couple of small vessels had left harbour carrying armed Fenians who planned to murder the Queen. The Queen for her part was not alarmed, merely irritated, and refused to leave Osborne. 'It is most unpleasant to feel one's liberty now so much interfered with, and every step and turn having to be calculated.' The dreary Irish question was beginning to raise its head in its usual murderous form.

In this last year of Derby's administration, with the Prime Minister away at Knowsley nursing his gout, Disraeli willingly shouldered the burden of government. In January Disraeli reports, 'the Duke of Marlborough has been with me all this afternoon and has unfolded the project of the Council Office. I think it excellent: large, I would almost say complete, and yet moderate and prudent. But it is a scheme which would require frequent cabinets and minute discussion.' As Lord President the Duke had to concern himself specially with education, since there was no Minister of Education and the question of introducing a national system was coming to the fore. Marlborough took up the matter with his usual energy and keenness. Disraeli reported to the Queen that the Duke wished 'the Lord President to be the ex-officio Education Minister on a great scale, which is not an arrangement which would be popular in the House of Commons, as it would seem to close the House of Commons to the Minister for Education'.

Within the month, February 1868, Disraeli became Prime Minister; he wanted Marlborough to lead the House of Lords. After the Lord Chancellor, 'I think the Duke of Marlborough the most competent man in our ranks to address a senate. He has culture, intellectual grasp and moral energy—great qualities, though in him they may have been developed, perhaps, in too contracted a sphere.' Naturally Dizzy preferred a duke, and the Duchess's mother, Lady Londonderry, was one of his most intimate friends. But Marlborough told the Prime Minister that Lord Malmesbury, who had filled the place in Lord Derby's frequent absences, had the prior claim and he insisted on standing down.

In April Gladstone carried a resolution against the government in favour of disestablishing the Irish Church, and Disraeli decided on a dissolution of Parliament, hoping for gratitude from the electors he had enfranchised on so generous a scale. Marlborough disagreed with the policy: he preferred a simple resignation, leaving the onus upon Mr. Gladstone to form a government. The Duke was ready to resign from the cabinet, but Malmesbury dissuaded him. He remained to introduce the Education Bill upon which he had been at work. 'It had the great merit of recognising the importance and dignity of education by constituting a comprehensive education department under a Cabinet Minister, a reform which Disraeli had advocated in 1855 but which Parliament did not accept till 1899.... It was a measure, in Disraeli's word, "preliminary, but of magnitude"; but there was no time to consider it, and the whole question was left over to the next Parliament.'

On appealing to the country Disraeli's new electorate expressed their gratitude by throwing out his government and returning his opponents with a triumphant majority. Disraeli and Marlborough alike spent the next six years of Mr. Gladstone's government in opposition.

The Duke's short experience as Lord President had expanded his mind and enlarged his interests considerably. Forster's Elementary Education Bill of 1870 he welcomed and, surprisingly, accepted its conscience clause which embodied a compromise between the Church and the Nonconformists on religious teaching: roughly, the Bible but no Church Catechism. The Duke was indeed becoming more broad-minded; it was not to be expected, however, but that he should urge extending the voluntary schools instead of pressing on the building of national schools, and argue for more religious instruction. In 1872 we find him speaking on a variety of subjects—the peculiar question of the Marriages of Friends or, in case anyone misunderstands, of Quakers; on Church Seats, the Resignations of Deans and Canons, and the more appealing topic of the Brigade of Guards.

On the return of the Conservatives to power in 1874 Disraeli was faced with the familiar difficulty of finding a suitable Lord-Lieutenant for Ireland. This exalted position under the Crown, viceregal in state and consequence, was a place of great responsibility where a career might be marred—though it might not be made, for the position was now without power. On the other hand, it cost a fortune to maintain its pomp and circumstance: regular Courts at Dublin Castle, balls and official receptions, at Viceregal Lodge in Phoenix Park week-end parties, the unceasing hospitality of Irish life expected and given; a glittering staff, a retinue of servants, postilions and outriders; races and hunting, feasts and charities. It may be seen that the number of political persons from whom to draw upon to support all this was comparatively few and select. Disraeli turned first to Marlborough and proposed his name to the Queen, who minuted 20 February 1874: 'I saw Mr. Disraeli at quarter to three today. He proposed the Duke of Marlborough for the post of Lord Lieutenant and thought the Duchess and her daughters would do well there. I approved this.' But the Duke of Marlborough was no longer a rich man and there were troubles enough at Blenheim to detain him. For the time he had to refuse.

When we scrutinise this apogee of the Victorian age we are struck by the fantastic wealth of a number of the peers at the head of English society. The Earl of Derby had a revenue of over £150,000 a year from Lancashire alone; the Duke of Northumberland had over £160,000 within his county: both these magnates had estates elsewhere too. From Dumfries, Lanark, Roxburgh and Edinburgh the Duke of Buccleuch drew some £160,000 a year. The Duke of Bedford enjoyed an income of £120,000 from his agricultural estates, while his London properties yielded at least as much again. So too with the Duke of Westminster. While the Duke of Norfolk's revenues from Yorkshire were some £231,000 a year—though this was gross and would far exceed the net income; Sussex yielded him nearly £30,000 a year to jog along on.

In comparison with these magnates the Marlboroughs were no longer wealthy. Their Oxfordshire estates brought in £35,541 a year, Buckinghamshire £5135—a total of not much above £40,000 a year, and with the immense expense of a Palace to keep up. They had reason to regret the fourth Duke's alienation of Cornbury to a younger son—an estate of 5000 acres worth another £6000 a year. There the cadet branch of the Churchills, with a separate peerage, was in possession. The family had still more reason to regret the fabulous extravagance of Charles, third Duke, the £100,000 sunk on the gardens at Blenheim by the fourth Duke, the incalculabe and ruinous waste, ending in virtual bankruptcy, of the fifth Duke. Even the seventh Duke had himself not been niggardly in his expenditure. And not a single one of the whole lot of them had as much as married an heiress.

The result was that circumstances at Blenheim in relation to the demands upon it were decidedly pinched—and this at a time when the agricultural depression of the mid-1870's was bringing ruin to many landowners. In addition there was the family now grown up to provide for—six daughters as well as two extravagant sons, both addicted to society with all its expensive allurements. Blandford was a sad disappointment to the Duke, for all Soapy Sam's moral support; no one now had any expectations of him, though he was not without odd talents—like his great-grandfather, the botanising Blandford of Whiteknights: a return to the Regency. Lord Randolph, early addicted to politics and the hope of the family, in 1874 married Jennie Jerome, daughter of the celebrated Leonard Jerome of New York, who, having made two fortunes on the Stock Market and lost them, now had not much to bestow. Nor had the Duke.

What was he to do? Where was he to turn for money?

It is ironical that where the Regency rips and rakes, the Georgian extravagants, had left the treasures and heirlooms of Blenheim fairly intact, the virtuous Victorian should have begun its systematic spoliation. But then, dead keen as he was on religion and the Church, there is no evidence that he had any taste. Lady Randolph observed on coming into this Victorian family, surrounded by magnificent pictures, Rubenses and Van Dycks, that none of its members ever looked at them. The Duke may have been proud of the splendid Sunderland Library that occupied the Long Gallery, for in 1872 he got the Rev. H. O. Coxe to catalogue it and had the result printed in fine big quarto; but it was he who nine years later sold it.

There naturally had been sales of surplus stuff from Blenheim at intervals before—usually upon the demise of a duke and the beginning of a new régime. On the death of the fifth Duke there was a four-day sale at Oxford of surplus books, mostly light literature but some earlier editions, a collection of prints and drawings, another of musical instruments. One sees the interests of this curious man in the botanical prints, American Ornithology, Cruikshank engravings; the quantities of music, including his own compositions, *Arie composte dal Marchese di Blandford,* in two volumes. In London Thorpe sold a quantity of rarer books he had himself collected, including an early Dekker item and the Roxburghe Club volumes he had initiated. In 1853 more music and engravings were sold, with several parcels of English and French literature, and a few miscellaneous items which had belonged to the great Duke, including—of all things—his badge of the Garter in onyx. (Was this perhaps the one that came into the possession of the Wellington family, and that one sees now at Apsley House?)

In 1856 a still larger collection of the fifth Duke's music and musical instruments was sold: pianofortes, harps, violins, cellos; plate, bijouterie, clocks, china, Sèvres and Wedgwood. There was a small library, then the Duke's own glees, Moore's Irish melodies, Czerny, Haydn and Beethoven, Crotch, Green and Purcell, Croft and Handel, with full scores of Mozart and Donizetti: a complete Georgian and Regency collection. In 1870 a selection of duplicate and surplus books was sold. In 1875, hard put to it, the Duke decided on the sale of one the greatest treasures of Blenheim, the famous Marlborough Gems.

As we have seen, the formation of this collection was the real life-work of the connoisseur fourth Duke: it was on this that he spent his time, his money, his passion. To collect it, to get rare gems—antique, Renaissance or modern—into his possession he had been in correspondence with agents all over Europe. In this channel and in the collection of pictures we see something of the acquisitiveness of his great-grandfather, John Churchill, reappear. It was over his gems that he pored hour after hour with Jacob Bryant, getting their scholarly descriptions right for the superb volumes he had printed, in Latin and French, with the Bartolozzi engravings, to present to the crowned heads of Europe. There they were, these exquisite works of art, 739 in all in their red morocco cases: about a half of them he had collected himself; the remainder contained such collections as the Earl of Arundel's cabinet, the second Earl of Bessborough's, the Earl of Chesterfield's. Some of the gems were signed by famous gem-cutters, like the celebrated example of the dog-star Sirius, a ring-set gem cut into a splendid garnet. Of the Pallas with helmet, breast-plate and Medusa's head *The Times* said, 'nothing can be more singularly fascinating than this gem into which one looks as into deep water, to discover a beautiful vision of the stern goddess'. And of the collection as a whole, 'most of the finest cameos and intaglios are cut in Oriental stones of rare quality such as are scarcely ever met with in modern commerce'. There were chalcedony and onyx, sardonyx and sard, amethyst, garnet, sapphire and agate, occasionally lapis lazuli.

The sale at the end of June at Christie, Manson and Woods created much excitement, all the leading amateurs and experts from Britain and the Continent being present. A reserve price of £35,000 was put on the gems. After a brief pause, Mr. Agnew bade 35,000 guineas—to the loudest applause ever heard in the saleroom. The collection, it was understood, passed *en bloc* to a Mr. Bromilow; what happened to him or it subsequently I do not know. On the whole the Duke must be held to have been lucky to realise such a price with so little trouble. Only Blenheim was the poorer.

Upon the family, Blandford's vagaries brought increasing trouble. He had alienated the Prince of Wales by his affair with Lady Aylesford, and Lord Randolph, taking his brother's side with an effective aggression that was characteristic of him, wrecked his friendship with the Prince for several years to come. Lord Randolph found himself, newly married, ostracised by the society of which he and his wife were already scintillating ornaments. It was a bitter experience. Clever old Disraeli, now Lord Beaconsfield, took his opportunity to renew the offer to the Duke to go to Ireland as Viceroy, adding the argument that if he took Lord Randolph over with him resentment in London would blow over the sooner in his absence. The Duke reluctantly consented, Sir Winston tells us: 'Blenheim was handed over to housekeepers and agents and its household was bodily transported to the Viceregal Lodge'. The Duke had hoped that Lord Randolph might go over as his official secretary; not at all: he had to pay for him out of his own pocket.

From a photograph published at this time by the London Stereoscopic Company, we derive a convincing likeness of the Duke on the eve of his Viceroyalty. It is a very Churchillian face, square and set; there is the pugnacious lower lip thrust out, the short snub nose with long upper lip, and the extraordinary expression of those strange eyes, full of latent vigour. The countenance has a dogged, muffled expression—the melancholy of the virtuous Victorian, chaste and stern, somewhat remote and very aristocratic. Such was the man who disembarked from the *Connaught* at Kingstown on 12 December 1876, to preside over the last years of comparative quiet before the Irish question was given a new and bitter twist by the personality of Parnell, and the rising storm over Home Rule divided and bedevilled British politics for half a century. It was bitterly cold and the people on the landing pier waited with exemplary patience. The Viceroy was accompanied by Lord Randolph and was received by the Household and the viceregal staff. There was a special train and a state entry into Dublin; in the procession that followed was Lady Randolph with her child, the two-year-old Winston.

In spite of the assassination of Lord Leitrim in Donegal, Marlborough's first year was fairly quiet. Over in England, in July 1877 he was able to give a good report in the Lords of the diminishing number of outrages: in 1870 there had been 4321; in 1872, 3238; in 1874, 2096: now in 1876, 2048. Agrarian crimes had gone down from 767 in 1870 to 212 in 1876. Occasionally, when over in England, we find him taking the opportunity to speak on Irish matters—railways, inland navigation, piers and harbours. But 1878 was excessively rainy; the potato crop failed and there was a fuel shortage. Ireland's agrarian economy existed on a shoe-string and no one could do much about that. The Duchess came to the fore with a vigorous campaign for a Relief Fund; she got a warm response from the English press and a lot of money was subscribed—though never enough. Not to be outdone, the Catholic Lord Mayor of Dublin initiated a rival fund. The Dublin Municipal Council passed a resolution in favour of public works: no response from Disraeli's government. (Disraeli was preoccupied with the Russo-Turkish war and the Congress of Berlin.) Parnell, an Irish Protestant landowner himself, took the opportunity to launch an Anti-Rent agitation and to press for a more aggressive Home Rule policy. Hitherto the Irish members in the House of Commons had followed the gentlemanly lead of Isaac Butt—with whom Lord and Lady Randolph were on friendly terms. Parnell's slogans—'No rent to the landlords, the land of Ireland restored to the people of Ireland'—were effective in capturing the leadership of the Home Rule movement from Butt.

Lord Randolph threw himself with his usual gusto into Irish life, which had, as always, a hospitable warmth and charm to make up for its political disagreeableness. He and Lady Randolph lived in the Little Lodge, a short distance from the Viceregal Lodge in Phoenix Park, and here they too kept open house, entertaining company far too Nationalist for the Tory grandees that surrounded the Viceroy. Soon Randolph knew everybody and had travelled all over the country. He hunted every winter with the Meath and Kildare hounds; he fished the lakes and streams, or sailed in Dublin Bay; he went after snipe in Donegal or Connemara. 'But wherever he went, and for whatever purpose, he interested himself in the people and studied the questions of the country.' It was not long before Lord Randolph was speaking about Irish affairs in a tone not agreeable to Tory ears. At Woodstock in 1877 he proclaimed, 'I have no hesitation in saying that it is inattention to Irish legislation that has produced obstruction. There are great and crying Irish questions which the government have not attended to, do not seem to be inclined to attend to and perhaps do not intend to attend to . . . and so long as these matters are neglected, so long will the government have to deal with obstruction from Ireland.' It may be noted here that Lord Randolph's subsequent obstructive tactics against Mr. Gladstone's government owed something to Parnell's example.

This outburst created trouble for his father, the Viceroy, who had to answer the remonstrances of the Chief Secretary. 'The only excuse I can find for Randolph is that he must either be mad or have been singularly affected with local champagne or claret. I can only say that the sentiments he has indulged in are purely his own; and, more than this, I was as much amazed as you in reading them, and had no conception that he entertained such opinions.' The Duke had to point out that Randolph's position was quite unofficial and that it was unwarrantable to represent Randolph's views as his father's. But Lord Randolph, as usual, was unrepentant. In 1878 he pushed forward a motion in the House of Commons for a Select Committee to inquire into the condition of the (Protestant) endowed schools of Ireland to report on how far they were promoting intermediate education there without distinction of class or religion. This pleased the Irish Nationalists as much as it disgusted the Irish Tories. In the course of the work of the commission appointed, he 'travelled all over Ireland—north, west and south—collecting information and examining schools'. In fact it may be said that Ireland provided Lord Randolph's real political apprenticeship.

Lady Randolph enjoyed her time in Ireland no less. The Marlboroughs took various houses in different parts of the country so that they saw a great deal of it. 'At Knockdrin Castle in Westmeath, where we stayed for a few months, we enjoyed the hunting, for the foxes were as wild as the people were untamed. . . . One winter my father-in-law had Lord Sligo's place at Westport, County Mayo, where the snipe-shooting afforded excellent sport. They went to Galway and Connemara, and often stayed at Muckross Abbey on the Lake of Killarney, from which they visited Kenmare, one of the showplaces of Ireland then.' Altogether they hunted with almost every pack of hounds in the country: what better way of seeing it?

Lady Randolph herself did not go unobserved. Lord D'Abernon, a notable amateur of women's beauty, describes her as she was in those years. 'I have the clearest recollection of seeing her for the first time. It was at the Viceregal Lodge at Dublin. The Viceroy was on a dais at the farther end of the room surrounded by a brilliant staff, but eyes were not turned on him or his consort, but on a dark lithe figure, standing somewhat apart and appearing to be of another texture to those around her, radiant, translucent, intense. A diamond star in her hair, her favourite ornament—its lustre dimmed by the flashing glory of her eyes. . . . With all these attributes of brilliancy, such kindliness and high spirits that she was universally popular. . . . Her courage not less great than that of her husband—fit mother for descendants of the great Duke.'

The youthful eyes of one of these descendants were beginning to take in the scene. By one of those pleasant proprieties of history the first memories of our Sir Winston go back to the town where the first Sir Winston ploughed away at the land-settlement of Ireland in the draughty King's Courts of Restoration Dublin. (That land-settlement was now in the throes of dissolution, about to be undone.) 'I can recall scenes and events in Ireland quite well, and sometimes dimly, even people. . . . I remember my grandfather, the Viceroy, unveiling the Lord Gough statue in 1878. A great black crowd, scarlet soldiers on horseback, strings pulling away a brown shiny sheet, the old Duke, the formidable grandpapa, talking loudly to the crowd. I recall even a phrase he used: "and with a withering volley he shattered the enemy's line". I quite understood that he was speaking about war and fighting, and that a "volley" meant what the black-coated soldiers (Riflemen) used to do with loud bangs so often in the Phoenix Park where I was taken for my morning walks. This, I think, is my first coherent memory.'[1]

There were other memories. There was the long dark procession of men whom his nurse took to be Fenians approaching and the house amid the shrubberies where the Under-Secretary lived, Mr. Burke, who gave the boy a drum. It was at the Little Lodge that he was first 'menaced with Education. The approach of a sinister figure described as "the Governess" was announced.' When 'the fateful hour struck and the Governess was due to arrive, I did what so many oppressed peoples have done in similar circumstances: I took to the woods'. The 'woods' were the shrubberies amid which the Chief Secretary, Lord Frederick Cavendish, and Mr. Burke were murdered two or three years later.

For the political situation deteriorated rapidly in the last months of Marlborough's Viceroyalty. In October 1879 the National Land League was formed; seven of its first chosen officers were either Fenians or ex-Fenians. The government, alarmed by further murderous attacks on landlords and their agents, suddenly arrested four of the agitators, including the popular Michael Davitt. After some days, realising that no jury would convict them, the government released them—and was ridiculed by both sides all over the country. There is never any satisfactory dealing with such situations: they are intractable.

[1] Winston S. Churchill, *My Early Life,* 15.

Nothing remedied the distress owing to the persistent bad harvests in Ireland since 1878, and the relief measures introduced by the government on Marlborough's advice were as persistently obstructed by the Parnellites in Parliament. At length Beaconsfield, deciding on an appeal to the country, sought to make Ireland the issue. In a historic letter to the Duke he stated that 'a danger, in its ultimate results scarcely less disastrous than pestilence and famine, and which now engages your Excellency's anxious attention, distracts that country. A portion of its population is attempting to sever the constitutional tie which unites it to Great Britain in that bond which has favoured the power and prosperity of both.' This uncompromising statement united both sections of the Home Rule movement, moderates and Parnellites, against the government and helped to give Mr. Gladstone a sweeping majority.

Before the Viceroy laid down his charge the Duchess was able to report to the public on the work accomplished by her Relief Fund. Her grandson sums up: 'she was a woman of exceptional capacity, energy and decision, and she laboured earnestly and ceaselessly to collect and administer a great fund'. Its purposes were to supply food, fuel and clothing, especially for the aged and weak; to give grants to schools for free meals for children; to provide seed potatoes for tilling. In spite of the rival fund set going by the Lord Mayor of Dublin, the Duchess ultimately raised £135,000; of which £80,000 went in relief through local committees, £37,000 on seed, £10,000 on clothing. The working expenses were under £1700, for all the viceregal family were brought into the work. The Duchess was proud of the work she had accomplished, and treasured the personal letter she received from the Queen in recognition of it. Just before her death she gave the letter to her grandson for the archives at Blenheim, with the touching words, 'I may seem a useless old woman now, but this letter will show you I was once of some importance and did good in my day'. In that are expressed two sides of the Victorian spirit.

The Duke came back from his ungrateful charge to find everything at Blenheim wanting attention. His grandson tells us that the 'estates had suffered from the absence of their owner and those dependent upon them felt acutely the diversion to Ireland and Irish purposes of that personal sympathy and care' which was customarily devoted to the neighbourhood of Blenheim. The life there that Lady Randolph observed with a fresh eye—the family took it all for granted—was resumed. But Randolph had a deep ancestral pride in the place: it was a pity that he was not the heir—except that if he had been a duke the career of his famous son would, nowadays, have been impossible. As the young married couple had been drawn by the loyal inhabitants of Woodstock through Sarah's archway and the scene suddenly, as he had planned, opened out before them, Randolph said to his American bride, 'This is the finest view in England'.

She found the life conducted by the elderly Duke and Duchess of an old-fashioned formality. 'At luncheon rows of *entrée* dishes adorned the table, joints beneath massive silver covers being placed before the Duke and Duchess, who each carved for the whole company, and as this included governesses, tutors and children it was no sinecure.' Sir Winston recalled that after the meal it was the regular thing for the Duchess to fill small panniers with the food that remained over for the children to distribute among the sick and poor of Woodstock and Bladon following the list she gave them. He had the impression that there was nothing to waste or indeed much to spare at that time.

Under the rule of the Duchess when the family were alone the big household went like clockwork: part of the morning devoted to the newspapers, for the conversation at dinner was invariably political; in the afternoon drives to visit neighbours or in the grounds; dinner a rather solemn full-dress affair, and afterwards all would repair to the Van Dyck room. However sleepy, 'no one dared suggest bed until the sacred hour of eleven had struck. Then we would all troop out into a small ante-room and, lighting our candles, each in turn would kiss the Duke and Duchess and depart to our own rooms. . . . The Duke was extremely kind and had the most courteous and *grand seigneur* appearance and manner. His wife was a very remarkable and intelligent woman with a warm heart, particularly for members of her family, which made up for any overmasterfulness of which she might have been accused. She ruled Blenheim and nearly all those in it with a firm hand. At the rustle of her silk dress the household trembled.'

Blenheim still possessed most of its treasures. There had been a serious loss when, in February 1861, part of the north-east quadrangle was burnt out and the Titian gallery with all its pictures destroyed. When the intelligence spread to Oxford that the Palace was in flames, 'with equal rapidity several fire-engines and thousands of persons on horseback and on foot were on the way to the spot'. This fine room had contained the series of nine large paintings, attributed to Titian, on gilt leather and given to the great

Duke by Victor Amadeus II of Savoy. It also contained a Rubens 'Rape of Proserpine' and a number of family portraits. What a treasure-house Blenheim must have been! Lady Randolph writes, 'when I first went there the far-famed Sunderland Library was still in existence. The beautiful old leather bindings decorated as nothing else can the immense long gallery with its white carved bookcases and vaulted ceiling. Cabinets of Limoges enamels gave the old-world look and Renaissance colouring to the Duchess's sitting-room. There, too, were the Marlborough Gems, besides rooms full of priceless Oriental, Sèvres and Saxe china. And what of the four hundred and fifty pictures all recklessly sold regardless of the remonstrances and prayers of the family and without a thought of future generations! Little did Lord Cairns think when he made his Act affecting the sale of heirlooms that it could be stretched to such a point.'

The Lord Chancellor was a colleague and the Duke was enabled to put through the Blenheim Settled Estates Act in 1880, by which the argument that the Sunderland Library was deteriorating 'through age and other circumstances' was allowed to over-rule the entail. The Duke felt forced to sell the Library, but he cannot have realised what a flood-gate he was opening for his miscreant of an heir to take advantage of. *The Times* urged that this famous Library should be bought for the nation and suggested a figure of £40,000. But those were the days of *laisser-faire* and privileged Philistinism in the highest quarters—the Prince of Wales could have bought it with a fraction of what he spent on his vulgar social life, or the Queen easily from what she saved for her family.

The Duke needed to sell, and this splendid collection of books, monument to the scholarly tastes of the third Earl of Sunderland, passed under the hammer. It contained a fine body of early editions of the classics, a large section of Bibles and Testaments in various languages from early presses; more congenial, there was a large collection of Renaissance authors, including a Valdarfer Boccaccio; a greater number of early books printed on vellum than any private library in Europe possessed, large collections of English county histories, medieval chronicles and of Americana. There was an extraordinarily full section of English pamphlets and tracts ranging from Elizabeth I to Anne, a large number of books on canon and civil law and a unique collection of French controversial tracts of the sixteenth and seventeenth centuries. The Library was sold in two portions, each taking ten days in December 1881 and July 1882. It realised altogether £56,581 6*s*.

This sum, by the Act, had to go back into the family estate, but the Duke was allowed £2000 to convert the Library into a picture gallery. The splendid early Georgian woodwork of the bookcases was torn out to instal inferior family portraits ransacked out of obscure corridors. Shortly before he died the Duke sent from Blenheim to the saleroom the very fine collection of over eighty Limoges enamels, mostly of the Renaissance. The sale drew a large attendance of amateurs and dealers, but the prices did not reach the figures of the recent Hamilton Palace sale. Several of the items did not come up to their reserve, and Marie-Antoinette's table of Sèvres with painted panels and ormolu was withdrawn. A sum of merely £8226 was netted: one can imagine the prices these things would fetch today.

The combination of Victorian piety and politics was not propitious to the arts.

With his Irish experience fresh in mind, the Duke's interventions in the Lords were, in these last years, wholly devoted to that topic. Indeed it dominated British politics throughout Gladstone's second administration and beyond. The Irish Land League, Parnell's obstruction in Parliament, his agitation outside, in Ireland and America, the increasing demand for Home Rule, the deterioration of law and order in Ireland reinforcing the Tory determination against it, the mounting bitterness of the conflict—the dreary question was entering a new and more sinister phase. Marlborough's withdrawal coincided with the effective spread of the weapon of 'boycotting' and the miraculous appearance of the Virgin Mary at Knock, to which thousands of pilgrims arrived from all over the country, though it did not prevent the murders from continuing. In 1880 Lord Mountnorris was murdered, and a deputation of more than a hundred landowners and agents laid their position before the new Liberal Viceroy, with their recommendations of means for restoring law and order.

Mr. Gladstone's government was anxious to meet the Irish case and began by suspending coercion. Marlborough expressed the doubt whether they were warranted in so doing, with the situation becoming not less but more threatening. Inevitably there was a further increase in crimes and outrages. The Duke, who knew, pointed to the activities of the secret societies as 'the kernel of the whole state of things'. He had had to witness a record of outrages—murders for which not a tittle of evidence was found, destruction of property without any information coming to light, the collision of arms-carrying processions; it was not possible to control such a situation if the government removed the mild measures of repression that were necessary in the interests of public order. And so indeed the government found—much against Mr. Gladstone's liberty-loving convictions. As J. L. Hammond points out, Ireland's best friends were increasingly alienated by Irish lawlessness.

It was against this background that Gladstone introduced his Bill for Irish land reform. In August 1881 the Duke made an effective speech against the measure. He said that it was the result of the agitation of the Land League, and there he was right: the British government was conceding to violence and crime what it had not granted to justice and reason. The result was soon to see: 'the number of agrarian outrages, instead of declining, had risen by 60 per cent, while the number of homicides and cases of firing at the person had trebled'. The Liberal Viceroy and his Chief Secretary resigned, and their places were taken by Gladstone's friend (and Marlborough's remote cousin) Earl Spencer, with Lord Frederick Cavendish as his Chief Secretary. After the pageantry of the state-entry, Lord Frederick and Mr. Burke, the permanent Under-Secretary, were surprised within sight and hearing of the Viceregal Lodge by the emissaries of a Dublin murder-club, who hacked them to death with long surgical knives. Even the iron Parnell was appalled. The Duke paid his tribute in the Lords to Mr. Burke, acknowledging that it was he who had foreseen the famine and scarcity of the winter of 1879-80 and that it was due to him that steps were taken which were 'the means of preventing a vast amount of want and distress in that country.'

The Duke's last appearance in the Lords, in June 1883, was to make a long speech on a more congenial subject, the Marriage with a Deceased Wife's Sister Bill. One would have thought that the long record of his heir's misconduct, which was now public property through a divorce case before the courts, might have made the old Duke take this subject less seriously. Not so: he ended, as he began, with the defence of the Church. It is somewhat difficult, after the experiences of our age, to feel with their full intensity the force of the sacred objections to marriage with a deceased wife's sister.

The Duke did not rest his case upon an Old Testament prohibition, for there was none; but with Christianity 'a higher law and a higher morality had been introduced'. A Liberal Earl had said that the universal opinion in America was in favour of these marriages.

The Duke read a letter from a clergyman in Ohio to the effect that repugnance to them was growing. Moreover, a resolution against the marriage of relations was about to be presented to the General Convention of the Episcopal Church in America. 'A large portion of the American people looked with great interest to the vote their lordships might give on that occasion.' (Was this likely? The Victorian Duke never at any time betrayed, among his immense possessions, a sense of humour.) This was the Duke's last battle on behalf of the Church. He had not been able to accomplish much, to arrest the movement of the time; but he managed to hold up a small fraction of the tide at this point. The vote on the Bill in the Lords was a near thing: 140 voted for it, including, very sensibly and understandably, the Prince of Wales; 145 voted against, including 18 bishops, and with the Duke as Teller.

The result was that this matter remained over to waste more parliamentary time and people's tempers in the next generation. And appropriately enough the subject was made the special concern of that confirmed bachelor, Lord Hugh Cecil, the Duke's successor as the self-dedicated defender of the Church. The Duke's grandson tells us that he had scarcely got into Parliament when Lord Hugh 'drew me into his vehement resistance to the Bill for allowing a man to marry his deceased wife's sister. I was myself at first sight inclined to think this might be a very excusable and often reasonable arrangement. . . . But when I pointed out these considerations to Lord Hugh Cecil, he was scandalised at my ignorance of Ecclesiastical Law.' Lord Hugh bore him down with a complexity of arguments 'enforced with splendid eloquence and flame of faith which induced me to assist Lord Hugh in the prolonged and successful obstruction of the Deceased Wife's Sister Bill of 1901 in the Grand Committee'. After weeks of obstruction—during which Lord Hugh *loitered in the lobby!* and the venerable Hicks-Beach 'literally crawled inch by inch across the matting which led to the portals where the votes were counted'—the Bill was killed: an enjoyable time had been had by all, except the Deceased Wives' Sisters.

Years after, Sir Winston admits that 'in the growing tolerance of the age I was ultimately induced to acquiesce in the legalising of a man's marriage with his deceased wife's sister'. It is obvious that he can no longer remember what it was that he found so compelling in Lord Hugh's arguments against this sensible measure. Perhaps it was the sheer joy of obstruction.

A few days after his last speech in the Lords the Duke died, of a sudden heart-attack on 5 July 1883. His body was taken to Blenheim where he lay in state; some three thousand people passed before the coffin, a genuine tribute to a man worthy of respect. There was fine weather for the funeral—the mayor and corporation of Woodstock in their robes, tenantry lining the steps, a gathering of his political colleagues, Blandford and Lord Randolph present. The coffin was lowered into the vault at the foot of Rysbrack's monument to the great Duke, while they all sang 'I heard the voice of Jesus say'. There was a *contretemps* over the solitary cross of white lilies, roses and maidenhair said to have been placed there for the Marchioness of Blandford, now definitely parted from her erring husband; two days later this was contradicted—it had been placed there, of course, at the express wish of the widowed Duchess. Lord Randolph incontinently left Blenheim for the Continent.

There is little to reveal this reserved, discreet, dutiful man in his will. The long and wordy document is chiefly content to recite and confirm previous settlements: little that is personal in it. His Duchess was provided for by the terms of her marriage settlement; but the Duke left her £2000 for her immediate use and convenience, all the contents of his town-house in Berkeley Square, from Blenheim what furniture she should select, with all the jewellery and trinkets she wore, 'except the three large diamonds set now in her necklace and which have been substituted for diamonds formerly set in the sword of John Duke of Marlborough and subjected to the trusts and provisions affecting the said sword as an heirloom'. (This was the famous sword that Sarah had refused to make over to her grandson Charles, on the ground that he would pawn the diamonds.) Several clauses are concerned with the settlements he had made on his daughters at the time of their marriages, Lady Wimborne, Lady Rosamond Fellowes, Lady Fanny Marjoribanks, the Duchess of Roxburghe—each of whom had received £8666 13*s.* 4*d.*; and there were two unmarried daughters. His aim seems to be to raise their portions to £10,000 apiece. The residue of his personal stocks and shares were to form a trust, with the income for his widow for her life, afterwards to go to Lord Randolph.

Nothing in his life contradicts, everything corroborates, the verdict on him of the *Dictionary of National Biography*: 'a sensible, honourable and industrious public man'.

CHAPTER SIX

Edwardian Reaction

LONG before Queen Victoria died Edwardian society proclaimed itself and took possession of the scene. It was with her reign as it had been with her grandfather's—with George III and the Regent—the withdrawal of the monarch from general society left the heir to the throne to take the lead and set the pace. And in both cases a very fast pace was set—a marked reaction from the sedateness and sobriety of the parents. In both cases it was very understandable. Queen Victoria's exaggerated grief for the Prince Consort, the cult she vowed to his memory and morosely inflicted on her family and entourage, with the impression she gave of resentment against Providence for taking him from her—one sees it in the expression of her face, the turned-down corners of the mouth—all testified to the emotional extremism of her pure German blood. Nothing could be more un-English. Though the heir to the throne again spoke English with a German accent he was at least gay, did enjoy life, was a sport—though perhaps not always a sportsman—and was in full touch with the commoner currents of the nation's life.

The Prince of Wales was a kind of Prinny come again, with all his social gifts, his immense gusto and conviviality; wherever he went a troupe of companions surrounded him, of both sexes: he was never alone and never in the same place for long. If he had not the Regent's artistic flair, his fantasy or his taste, he was even more an amateur of the beauty of women. Apart from that he had as good as no taste at all. With him dress and the punctilios of social behaviour took the place that high politics, and the affairs of her family, took in his mother's mind. He could not bear women, for whom he had such a nose, to be ill-dressed. To the remarkable Lady Salisbury, who had a mind above such things, he one day said reprovingly: 'Lady Salisbury, I think I have seen that dress before'. 'Yes, and you'll see it again', replied that lady, undaunted.

By the 1870's society had found its acknowledged leader: people looked to Marlborough House and Sandringham, where the Prince and Princess of Wales ruled and entertained continually, as in the earlier years of the century they had looked to Carlton House and the Pavilion at Brighton. Marlborough House had undergone some interesting changes since the Marlboroughs' lease had come to an end: first came Princess Charlotte and her husband, Prince Leopold, then William IV's widow, Queen Adelaide. Latterly it had been a National School of Design: the pictures were removed to the National Gallery, the drawing classes to South Kensington and the house a good deal altered to make room for Albert Edward and Alexandra. A large state dining-room was added for their entertainments, three of Sarah's original small rooms on the ground floor were thrown into one long Red Drawing-Room; a third storey was added to spoil the proportions, the windows given plate-glass to impair the look of the house. Yet not even these characteristic Edwardian improvements—they might have been worse—succeeded in destroying the distinction of the house Wren, and Sarah, conceived.

The Marlborough House set led the younger generation and was in every way more liberal-minded, more Continental in its outlook, its manners and modes, than the stuffy closed atmosphere of the Court, ruled by the standards of the Queen and her ladies, intensely conservative, dedicated to duty without pleasure, the monotony of endless work and routine—Windsor, Balmoral, Osborne, with rare appearances in London. Marlborough House was essentially cosmopolitan, its *habitués* as much at home at Auteuil, Longchamps, Chantilly as at Newmarket, Ascot, Goodwood; the Prince and Princess of Wales were accustomed to spend several months of the year abroad, their regular routine including Biarritz, Homburg, Marienbad, with frequent appearances in Paris or at Monte Carlo. (When the great Lord Salisbury made one appearance there he was, to the delight of his family, rejected from the Casino on the ground that he was unsuitably dressed.) To the familiar figures of the Austrian and Portuguese ministers, Count Mensdorff and the Marquis de Soveral, Marlborough House added a distinctive American element: there were Minnie Stevens of New York, later Lady Paget, Mrs. Cavendish Bentinck, and Consuelo, Duchess of Manchester. Upon these followed Jennie Jerome, who married Lord Randolph Churchill, and later Consuelo Vanderbilt, who became Duchess of Marlborough.

The America of those days must have been essentially a man's world: the movement of menfolk was westward to its wide-open spaces and wider opportunities, while it was the women who came east, crossing the Atlantic to lay London and Paris at their feet.

They were not without the prizes of conquest: Lady Randolph Churchill herself noted that nowhere in the world had women so much influence in politics as they had in London.

And what a time they all had! These were the last days of a privileged society to whom all the earth was open: from Vladivostok or Kyoto all the way across the Old World and the New to Wyoming, where there were buffalo still to be shot. The massacre of big game all over the world at the hands of these gentlemen—tiger-hunts in India, lions, rhinoceros, elephants in Africa—makes characteristic (and sickening) reading. 'He was a magnificent specimen, 9 feet 7 inches in length, and a splendid skin, which will, I think, look very well in Grosvenor Square', writes Lord Randolph home to his wife. 'Tigers in the Zoo give one very little idea of what the wild animal is like.' Or it is, 'yesterday we hunted one leopard, which ultimately escaped after being much fired at and, I think, grievously wounded. I shot a very nice swamp deer, and Thomas a nilghai or blue bull. We also shot pea-fowl, bustards and partridges, and every variety of bird. We have fifteen elephants, and these creatures are an unfailing source of interest and amusement.'

At home it was much the same sort of thing: massed battues of birds over thickly-preserved coverts in East Anglia or Yorkshire; or the expensive routine of deer-stalking in Scotland. Every county had its hunts, though hunting was at its most opulent in the Midlands, especially Leicestershire. There was the still more extravagant interest in horse-racing. All these avocations went with constant entertaining, large country-house parties, complete with baccarat, bridge or billiards, with the singers, variety artists, orchestras of the day to help to entertain them. At the top it was a European society with its Courts all the way from St. Petersburg to Seville, in which its glittering denizens were—if not equally, at any rate everywhere—at home.

What added a peculiarity to the English version and gave it its flavour was that here there was a national sport, in which the privileged and the unprivileged were equally judges of form: politics. Nothing could exceed the passionate interest taken in politics in that age, whether by society in the narrow and exclusive sense or by society at large—when the appearance of a national figure like Mr. Gladstone or Lord Randolph Churchill could hold up the traffic and suspend the life of a large city for hours. Lord Randolph's son, who was born in that age, tells us how things were: 'I was a child of the Victorian era, when the structure of our country seemed firmly set, when its position in trade and on the seas was unrivalled, and when the realisation of the greatness of our Empire and of our duty to preserve it was ever growing stronger. In those days the dominant forces in Great Britain were very sure of themselves and of their doctrines. They were sure they were supreme at sea and consequently safe at home. They rested therefore sedately under the conviction of power and security.'[1]

Such was the high Victorian position. We may not be wrong in diagnosing an increase of tempo, a certain loosening of morale, a feverishness and a brittleness, that differentiated the Edwardian tone from the high Victorian. Some of its glitter we may impute to the phosphorescence of decay.

The two sons of the seventh Duke were yet another George, Marquis of Blandford, and Lord Randolph—a new name to appear in the family: whence it came I do not know. Throughout their short, and rather hectic, lives they remained firmly attached to each other—except for one brief interval, when they had a serious quarrel, and not without good reason. The elder was born 13 May 1844, the younger 13 February 1849. Both were sent to Eton, though with such a gap in age between them they did not overlap.

Young Randolph's home-letters from Eton remind one of his ancestor's, the fourth Duke, when a boy: there are the similar concerns of their small world, the family's doings, the dogs and ponies, sport, the birds, the successes of the Heythrop hounds, occasionally some political event that impinges, an election at Woodstock or a visit from Mr. Disraeli. Subsequent letters show the terms of mutual concern and confidence upon which the Duke was with his gifted son. Randolph: 'I cannot tell you how delighted I was when you wrote and told me that you had accepted the office of Lord President of the Council. I think it is just the office that you would like best.' One notices the characteristic 'I think'. Pride in his younger son did not induce the Duke to spare him censure for some equally characteristic act of rebelliousness: 'to tell you the truth, I fear that you yourself are very impatient and resentful of any control; and while you stand upon some fancied right or injury, you fail to perceive what is your *duty*, and allow both your language and manner a most improper scope'. That scored a bull's eye: it remained true of Randolph all his life, his greatest failing. As his mother who adored him wrote, with touch-

[1] Winston S. Churchill, *My Early Life* (*A Roving Commission*), 9-10.

ing humility, 'Alas! had I been a clever woman, I must have had more ability to curb and control his impulses, and I should have taught him patience and moderation. Yet at times he had extraordinary good judgment, and it was only on rare occasions that he took the bit between his teeth, and then there was no stopping him.' It must be said that there was a Churchillian vein of unamenability in him, that all his life he was incorrigible.

After Eton he went up to Oxford, at the same time as the schoolfriend who became Lord Rosebery. There their friendship was confirmed for life: after the Conservative leader's early death the Liberal Prime Minister wrote the most perceptive and the most generous account of his personality. In yet another generation the house of Blenheim refrained from sending its son to Christ Church: Lord Randolph went to Merton, where he came under the encouraging tutorship of the politic Creighton. Here he narrowly missed a First in the Schools—no mean achievement for a young aristocrat who was giving the greater part of his energies to the Blenheim Harriers he had started and whose affairs he was conducting most methodically.

Meanwhile, his brother was serving as an officer in the Blues, enjoying all the delights of life proper to a young man of his station. After a considerable experience of these he fell in love with a beautiful daughter of the Duke of Abercorn: Lady Albertha Hamilton was as good as she was beautiful, as pious as she was innocent, and really rather stupid. He was neither pious, nor innocent, nor stupid. In fact he seems to have been a clever man whose cleverness ran all to seed; a hedonist whose pursuit of pleasure (in the form of women) brought him no satisfaction; a very *désabusé* man of whom no one approved, a man to whom life gave a decided chip on the shoulder. Everyone keeps quiet about him, he was so very much disapproved of in his day: his elusive, unhappy, buried personality intrigues one the more. There was some inner source of restlessness incapable of satisfaction in him, as there was in his brother. There was an element of reaction against the religiosity of their parents—though both sons, natural rebels as they were, deeply respected their father, while Randolph adored, and was spoiled by, his mother. Perhaps it was too high breeding: too many marriages within an exclusive aristocratic circle, and what was wanted was a good middle-class marriage like that which revivified the stock with the Cecils—or an American marriage bringing in a renewal of spirits, confidence in life, boundless zest and unfaltering courage. That was on the way for one of the brothers—with what incalculable results!

The Marquis of Blandford married his ducal bride in Westminster Abbey, 8 November 1869, and was at once bored with his treasure. Her chief accomplishment seems to have been practical jokes. At a Blenheim dinner-party she once placed small bits of soap indistinguishably among pieces of cheese. A rich guest, too polite to spit this out, was rendered extremely sick and—'Fancy, he never forgave me'. Her husband would open a door, to receive the contents of an ink-pot on his head. When he took up chemistry, in which he became passionately interested—like the fourth Duke in gems and astronomy, the fifth in botany and music—Albertha mixed up his chemical experiments for him. As if these were not sufficient grounds for divorce, he added others, more savoury, on his part.

A few years later Lord Randolph found for himself a most unexpected bride. In the high summer of 1873, now aged twenty-four, he was at Cowes when a ball was given in honour of the Czarevich and the Czarevna who had arrived in the *Ariadne*. Here he met Miss Jennie Jerome, whose mother had taken a cottage there for the summer. Next night he went to dinner with them. The third evening he went for a walk with Miss Jerome, proposed to her and was accepted.

This sudden train of events was not easy to explain to Blenheim. To the Duke he wrote, 'I must not any longer keep you in ignorance of a very important step I have taken—one which will undoubtedly influence very strongly all my future life. . . . I know, of course, that you will be very much surprised and find it difficult to understand how an attachment so strong could have arisen in so short a space of time; and really I feel it quite impossible for me to give any explanation of it that could appear reasonable to anyone practical and dispassionate.'[1] In short, this was, what one often hears about but seldom meets, a romantic instance of love-at-first-sight. And her family? 'Mr. Jerome is a gentleman who is obliged to live in New York to look after his business. I do not know what it is.'

This could hardly be expected to be thought good enough by the Duke, who wrote back, 'it is not likely that at present you can look at anything except from your own point of view; but persons from the outside cannot but be struck with the unwisdom of your proceedings, and the uncontrolled state of your feelings, which completely paralyses your judgment'. Blandford was now able to support this view with a set of witty, but presumably unprintable,

1 Winston S. Churchill, *Lord Randolph Churchill,* I. 41-43.

verses on what happens to those who marry in haste.

Who was Jennie Jerome anyway?

She was the daughter of one of the finest men, certainly one of the sunniest and most golden natures, to arise out of the hurly-burly of New York in the middle of the nineteenth century. Leonard Jerome, born at Syracuse in New York State, was descended from an old Huguenot family of La Rochelle who had left for America as early as the time when the Tories were coming back into power under Queen Anne and Marlborough was on his way out. As a boy Leonard Jerome had moved westward to Palmyra, whence he went to Princeton quite poor, though this did not prevent him from enjoying himself, as he did everywhere all through life with a zest that people, but especially women, found irresistible. Tall, good-looking, abounding in vitality, he married dark Clara Hall, who was one-quarter Iroquois from those woods. So that her eldest grandson, Sir Winston, in the middle of some war-time dispute with the Americans, was able to claim in his own right, 'Tell them I was there before they were!' This, in addition, to an unbroken male descent five generations back on his mother's side to a lieutenant in Washington's army.

Leonard Jerome brought his bride to New York in 1850, where he proceeded to make (and lose) his first fortune, make a second and bigger one on Wall Street, and fall for the singing of Jenny Lind—hence his second daughter's name. Appointed consul at Trieste for a time, he gave himself up to the delights of sailing in the Adriatic as he had done to making money and music, making up to women. Mrs. Jerome lost her heart to Europe, and when she paid a visit to Paris later—the adorable, gimcrack Paris of the Second Empire, of Eugénie and Princesse Mathilde, of Morny and Offenbach and Meyerbeer, of the brilliant blue uniforms of the Imperial Guard, parties at Compiègne and the new boulevards of the Baron Haussmann—'I have found the Court I want', she said.

Back at home it was the New York of *The House of Mirth*. In partnership with Commodore Vanderbilt—Consuelo's grandfather—Leonard Jerome could only prosper, but he knew how to spend his money more agreeably. It is said that some $10 millions ran through his fingers; it is certain that he gave a quarter of a million dollars to the sufferers from the New York riots of 1863. He owned one-quarter of the *New York Times* at one time, and on the conclusion of the war he backed the Southern Relief Fund: 'we must ease the bitterness', he declared. No more generous spirit ever existed, and no more joyous. He built himself a house on Madison Square with a private theatre and a stables at the back. From the one he brought forth the singers he launched upon their careers—Minnie Hauk, America's first prima donna, and Fanny Ronalds, her second; from the other he produced the horses with which he created and refined flat-track racing in America and became, with August Belmont, a Father of the American Turf.

He was the first in the States to drive four-in-hand. One sees him driving up the more spacious, rattling Fifth Avenue of those days, soon reaching country where now Central Park begins—'gay and laughing ladies in gorgeous costumes filled the carriage. Lackeys, carefully gotten up, occupied the coupé behind; Jerome sat on the box and handled the reins. With a huge bouquet of flowers attached to his button-hole, with white gloves, cracking his whip, and with the shouts of the party, the four horses would rush up Fifth Avenue, on toward the Park, while the populace said, one to the other "That is Jerome".'[1] They were on the way to the race-track he had created: Jerome Park. Not content with triumphs on land, he backed the *Henrietta* on the first ocean sailing race, sailed the Atlantic in her through the storms of mid-winter, narrowly missed being presented to Queen Victoria on landing at the Isle of Wight—and won $100,000 on the result.

Everyone had to admit that Jerome made his money honestly: 'that damn fellow has cashed in on honesty'. But in the years after the Civil War his luck turned: he suffered enormous losses on Pacific Mail, and in a default on Indiana bonds; he was involved in a friend's failure with Georgia stock. With the remains of his fortunes he was engaged in giving the best he could to wife and daughters now set up in Paris in the last days of the Empire.

His daughter has written well on what life was like in those years. 'The last flicker of the candle, the last flame of the dying fire, is ever the brightest; and so it was with Paris in 1869. Never had the Empire seemed more assured, the Court more brilliant, the fêtes more gorgeous. The Bois de Boulogne and the Champs-Elysées, where we were living at that time, were crowded with splendid equipages. I remember often seeing the Empress Eugénie, then the handsomest woman in Europe, driving in her daumont, the green and gold liveries of the postilions and outriders making a brave show.'[2] But it was not a question of observing this pageantry, these cavalcades, from the outside: *la belle Américaine* and her

[1] Anita Leslie, *The Fabulous Leonard Jerome*, 85.

[2] *Reminiscences of Lady Randolph Churchill*, 4-5.

daughters were invited not only to the formal receptions at the Tuileries, but to the Empress's favoured *petits Lundis*, the Emperor's hunting parties at Compiègne.

It was after one of the *petits Lundis* that a sinister note was sounded by a German diplomat. Count Hatzfeldt remarked, 'I never saw their Majesties in better spirits than they were last night, and God knows where they will be next year at this time'.[1] He knew. In the interval Bismarck had his war; the Second Empire crashed in ruins and that is how Mrs. Jerome and her daughters came to be spending the summer at Cowes. She had meant to marry her daughters to French noblemen. Fate (in the shape of Bismarck) ordained otherwise: all three of them married Englishmen, so that all Leonard Jerome's grandchildren—himself the most American of men—grew up English.

Mr. Jerome, who was as proud as any duke, was displeased by the Duke's attitude; he considered his daughter good enough for any duke's son—as indeed she was. And yet the Duke's attitude was not at all unreasonable: how could he be sure, especially with Blandford's experience before his eyes, that Randolph's three-day infatuation would last, was a strong enough foundation for marriage? He knew, none better, his son's impulsiveness, his wilfulness and impatience. He did not reject Lord Randolph's request; he imposed a year's delay: 'if this time next year you come and tell me that you are both of the same mind we will receive Miss Jerome as a daughter and, I need not say, in the affection you could desire for your wife'.[2]

The fact was that the Duke was expecting an election this year and was determined that nothing should stand in the way of his brilliant son being returned for Woodstock. 'It is for this that they have kept me idle ever since I left Oxford, waiting for a dissolution', he wrote to Jennie. 'I have two courses open to me: either to refuse to stand altogether unless they consent to my being married immediately afterwards; or else—and this is still more Machiavellian and deep—to stand, but at the last moment to threaten to withdraw and leave the Radical to walk over. All tricks are fair in love and war.' One recognises the authentic Churchillian note.

The election came early in 1874 and Lord Randolph—perhaps his situation aroused sympathy—got a record majority. He reported to Jennie: 'the poll was not declared till eleven, and the hours of suspense were most trying; but when it was known, there

[1] *Ibid.* 7.

[2] Winston S. Churchill, *Lord Randolph Churchill,* I. 49-7.

was such a burst of cheers that must have made the old Dukes in the vault jump. . . . There is nothing more to be done except to pay the bill, and that I have left to my father.'[1]

After this there was no more resistance on either side. The Duke capitulated; Mr. Jerome capitulated, and added £6000 a year to the young couple—never enough as it was, at the pace they went and the rate they spent. What was more, Mr. Jerome became the staunchest believer in Lord Randolph in all his ups and downs: he recognised a man after his own heart, a man ready to take his life in his hands, a gambler and a sport; though he complained that none of his grandchildren was American, Randolph's son, named Leonard after him, was always his favourite grandchild. And indeed the boy turned greatly after him.

The impatient young couple were married in Paris in April; we have noted their welcome to 'the leafy glories of Blenheim in the spring'. At the end of November Lady Randolph, prancing about with too much vivacity for her condition and out in the park that very day with the guns—the child no doubt eager to arrive on the public scene and start his career without further delay—had to be hustled back into the house and there, in a drab downstairs room, gave birth. This room had been the original chaplain's, Dean Jones—the gluttonous-looking old cleric one sees painted by Laguerre in the saloon—who was said to haunt it still. Such was the force of the new arrival, or the influence of the event, that it exorcised that baleful presence; at any rate he has not been seen there since. The boy was given the names of his two grandfathers: Winston Leonard Spencer Churchill.

With this agreeable event out of the way Lady Randolph was able to throw herself and her younger sister, Clara, into the delights of London society, and a dazzling season they had of it in 1875. For Jennie there was entertaining the Prime Minister, fascinating old Mr. Disraeli, to dinner at their little house or being taken by Lord Rosebery to the opening of Parliament. The purely social side of life is depicted in Clara's artless letters to Mrs. Jerome; and from them we see that there was a certain *froideur* between the elderly Marlboroughs, of Queen Victoria's generation and outlook, and the Randolph Churchills who were at once taken up by the Prince of Wales's fast set—Jennie was made much of by them—and made free of Marlborough House.

At the end of the season the Prince proposed himself for an Indian tour—tiger-hunting included. The Queen took alarm at the

[1] *Ibid.* I. 55.

proposal: there was her jealousy of her position as Queen, there was her specifically Hanoverian jealousy of the heir who was to succeed her. (At this time she could not look at him without shuddering, she said, and communicated with him through her Cabinet ministers.) The proposed tour raised the critical question of expense. It would not do to do it on a fairly simple scale, as the Prince had done on his tour of the Colonies. His friends advocated that everything should be done on an Imperial scale, with ample provision for the exchange of presents demanded by Oriental courtesy—and no doubt for other little things too.

Disraeli proposed a vote of £60,000 for the Prince's personal expenses in addition to the costs of the journey. His friends thought that inadequate: they saw themselves accompanying him at official expense. So did the Queen. They got up a letter to *The Times*, which Disraeli describes as 'written by Randolph Churchill, under the dictation of Blandford and Bartle Frere. Under their inspiration he had prepared a Marlborough House manifesto, and utterly broke down, destroying a rising reputation. The letter is a mass of absurdities. It assumes the P. is to make presents to the 95 reigning Princes. If he visited them all, his tour wd. be six years, not six months. He will visit only about five.'

Next came the question of who was to accompany him. The Queen wanted him suitably encased in an entourage of serious-minded personages. The Prince, in his determination not to be bored, insisted on half a dozen of his Marlborough House cronies—Lord Charles Beresford, Lord Carrington, the Duke of Sutherland, above all the Earl of Aylesford, a champion pig-sticker and polo-player, otherwise 'Sporting Joe'. Thereby came the fall. For Lord Aylesford had an attractive Welsh wife, to whom the Prince had been paying marked attention and even writing letters. It would not do to leave Sporting Joe out of the party; the malicious said that the Prince was afraid to leave him behind.

As it happened, the Indian tour in the cold weather of 1875-6 was an immense success, as the Prince had felt it would be: he took care to make it so. But Lord Aylesford had to return in the middle of it; for his frail lady had another admirer: Lord Blandford. He took the opportunity of Sporting Joe's absence to move his horses down to an inn not far from the Aylesfords' house for a good winter's hunting. Someone took the trouble to write Joe a letter to come home. Surprisingly enough he did.

The result was that he threatened to take proceedings that would incriminate Blandford, and the Prince backed his cause warmly. It was here that Lord Randolph came to his brother's rescue most effectively, but rashly, without counting the consequences, and in the event unwisely. Who was the Prince to intervene against his brother? He declared that if proceedings were taken he would publish the letters the Prince had written the lady. We can only infer that the lady had placed them at his disposal and that this was her way of defending her lover. In fact, there was a regular—or, rather, irregular—affair between them; for in the spring of 1876 Blandford refused to give up the lady: he preferred to part with his wife.

For the Prince this was a terrible rebuff from a future subject, still more from a young man he had made his friend: deeply as he disapproved of Blandford's conduct, he had been made to withdraw by a threat. Lord Randolph's best friend could not approve of his action, so we must conclude that the Prince was more in the right: he was standing, if not for the proprieties, at any rate for the rules of the game. But for Lord Randolph this had been a fatal step socially. The Prince let it be known that he would not set foot in any house that received him, and this meant complete social ostracism. It was a bitter experience for a young couple, just as they were launched upon a brilliant course. One sees traces of the bitterness in Lady Randolph's sunny-natured *Reminiscences*. All the fashionable world held aloof from them, no longer invited anywhere: 'most people in the course of a lifetime get to know the real value of the Mammon of Unrighteousness, but few learn their lesson so early. We both profited by it. Personally I would never give up anything by which I really set store for the sake of its unsatisfactory approbation.' But Lord Randolph was a young politician dependent on the world to make his way in it. There is no doubt that the iron entered into his soul; from this time a more corrosive strain appears in his wit. All this had put him wrong with society, and in the singular way in which these mixtures work out in human motivation—a dash of iron, a drop of poison—this experience gave an edge to his ambition, which had so far not declared itself, not even been aroused: it awoke in him a determination to make himself felt, and as he was impelled to declare war on humbug this took an increasingly restless, uncompromising and even Radical form.

For the moment, to make themselves scarce and obtain some distraction, the Churchills went off on what was Randolph's first visit to America. They visited Niagara in a heat-wave and took refuge at Newport, Rhode Island, which they found altogether more urban than Cowes. Thence they went to the Philadelphia Exhibition, which they were shown round by Jennie's uncle and much enjoyed. When they got back to London they found that the Duke had accepted the Irish Viceroyalty, largely in their interest; and Ireland, with few visits to London, was their refuge for the next four years.

This however, was no solution for Blandford. In 1877 Lord Aylesford and his wife were separated. Next year Lady Blandford, unable to obtain a regular income from her husband—we have seen that money was tight—got a deed of separation executed securing a maintenance. However, Lady Blandford refrained from insisting on her rights; she—as they used to say—'forgave him' on condition he 'sinned no more'. In July 1878 they began to try living together again until they found in April 1882 that they could stand it no longer.

It must have been during this period that Lady Blandford thought up the best (or worst) of her practical jokes. One morning at breakfast the Marquis, on lifting the cover concealing his bacon and egg, was greeted by a small pink baby doll. Lady Blandford can hardly have known that in November 1881 Lady Aylesford gave birth to a son at 8 Avenue Friedland in Paris, whose reputed father was the Marquis. But breakfast is no time for practical jokes. The Marquis departed: this time for good. In February 1883, on his wife's complaint of desertion, she was granted a divorce. It is evident that nothing could have made those two compatible.

These things must have grieved the last years of the pious old Duke, even if they did not cause him to question the gravity of marriage with a Deceased Wife's Sister. When he died in July 1883 both brothers received a shock: he had been for so long the dominating figure in their landscape. Especially for Randolph, who was deeply moved, gave himself up for hours, to reading over his father's letters and went down to Blenheim to remember the past. 'It is very melancholy here—sad recollections at every moment. Nothing can be nicer than Blandford to everyone.' At this moment of grief the brothers were drawn close together. The new Duke joined Randolph in Switzerland in August and they came home together. While abroad Lord Randolph had been infuriated by the opposition to his brother's election to the Carlton Club. 'And now how can anyone occupy a more unpleasant position than Blandford does? He has publicly changed his politics, to please me more than for any other reason, and owing to H. Chaplin's action his overtures to the Conservatives are spurned. . . .' From which we can only infer that Blandford had enjoyed a spell of Liberalism: on acquaintance he becomes more and more like his ancestors, the fifth and sixth Dukes.

However, the new master of Blenheim had better fish to fry. He persuaded Lord Randolph to start up the Blenheim harriers again, and many a good day's hunting they had that autumn and winter. Together they pressed forward the Duke's scheme of bringing the railway from Oxford to Woodstock: which resulted in that delightful meandering single-track line across the meadows, with the little railway station, closed in our time. The eighth Duke was a modern-minded man, and this we see with a vengeance in his next venture.

It was, ironically, the virtuous seventh Duke who set his son the worst of all possible examples in the dispersal of the Blenheim treasures. He had only to follow in his father's footsteps. His father had been driven by necessity, but there is no reason to suppose that he would ever have contemplated what his son proposed and proceeded to carry out—a clean sweep of all the Blenheim pictures, not to mention a trifle like the china and porcelain, which in itself took a three-day sale to disperse. The eighth Duke was no fool, and for some time he had been watching the trends of sale prices, the immense figures given for favourite old masters. Perhaps he was influenced by the fabulous sums realised by the Hamilton Palace sales—some £400,000 in 1882—the result of the doings of another miscreant duke. When the family realised what he proposed to do a stiff struggle was engaged, Lord Randolph taking the lead. The brothers had stood together in their fortunes hitherto; now there was a violent quarrel, an open breach, and no wonder.

For a couple of years before the great sales took place in 1886 it had been known that the new Duke intended to disperse the whole of the famous Blenheim collection. *The Times* said that this news had engaged the attention of the art world for the past two years. Under the Chancery order obtained by the Duke's father, twenty-five of the finest pictures had been offered to the National Gallery for £400,000. This was a steep price, and the nation acquired only the Ansidei Madonna for £70,000 and the equestrian portrait of Charles I for £17,500. The best prices had been obtained for sales by private contract; auction prices were generally below their standard.

As *hors-d'oeuvre* before the feast the Teniers Gallery—120 small copies by Teniers of great masters, which had hung round the billiard room at Blenheim—were exhibited for months at Davis's in the hope of selling them *en bloc*. They were of varying merit and interest and ultimately were sold one by one, mostly to Agnew's, at small prices. The total brought £2031. The first main portion, sold by Christie, Manson and Woods, 24 July 1886, contained all the Rubenses, some eighteen in all, a number of Van Dycks, a couple of Rembrandts, a Breughel, a fine Jordaens' 'Deposition', several Snyders, Teniers, Wouvermans, Cuyps. *The Times* reported that, in a period of depression such as the present, prices had not reached the levels of the Hamilton Palace sales—whence the Berlin Gallery got so many of its pictures; nor were the European galleries represented as they had been then. Some of the finest pictures had not reached the figures offered for them previously. All the same the total for the first day was considered handsome—£34,834 11*s*. Several of the best pictures had been sold privately for no very high sums compared with auction-room prices. Most of the canvases were purchased by private collectors, notably Lord Ardilaun, who bought several of the Rubenses. Sir John Millais bought the beautiful Van Dyck of 'Time Clipping the Wings of Cupid' for £241 10*s*. Among the art-dealers Agnew and Colnaghi led, Agnew bidding the highest, for the Rubens 'Venus and Adonis'—7200 guineas—to enthusiastic applause. Subsequently it was learned that this picture and the splendid Rubens 'Anne of Austria' had been bought in. The prices fetched by the Rubenses were considered very disappointing.

The second portion consisted mainly of historical portraits. There were eight Van Dycks of Charles I's Court, a fine Mytens of Buckingham all in white, a Reynolds of a Marquis of Tavistock, a Gainsborough of the fourth Duke of Bedford, Gheerardts's portrait of the wicked Countess of Essex. In addition, Watteaus, Lancrets, Claudes, a Pater, a Poussin, a Stubbs and a group of Reynolds studies. No doubt this last group was collected by the connoisseur fourth Duke, as well as the Gainsborough portrait of his father-in-law. The last was bought for the National Portrait Gallery; the National Gallery of Ireland got a bargain in a fine William Dobson family group for £22. The two Lancrets sold for £27 and £11 respectively; two Watteaus for £35 and £11. The Mytens made more than expected; the Van Dycks and the portraits of the seventeenth-century school much more. Colnaghi bought the wicked Countess of Essex (I have come across her somewhere in America).

The third portion consisted mainly of Italian seventeenth- and eighteenth-century pictures: Carraccis, Marattas, four by Luca

Giordano, six Ricci landscapes, Panninis, Carlo Dolcis, along with a Borgognone, Bassano, Tempesta; two Titians and a Veronese 'Europa'. As one would expect of the nineteenth century, these Italian baroque and mannerist pieces fetched very low prices: they were disconsidered then. But now! . . . Altogether they raised only £11,411 11*s*. 6*d*. There was one exception, Carlo Dolci's 'Madonna delle Stelle', which the late Duke had often been pressed to sell: Lord Dudley had offered 20,000 guineas for it. In those times of depression Agnew gave 6600 guineas: top price, to much applause. In those August days were sold large collections of china and porcelain belonging to Blenheim. One of these, consisting of Chinese, Japanese and Chelsea porcelain, had not been formed by any Marlborough but had been 'presented to Blenheim by a Mr. Spalding on certain conditions as an appendant to Blenheim'. From 1813 onwards it had been exhibited in a special building near the Home Lodge: full of rare and old pieces, Mr. Spalding's ranked among the finest collections. It was bought by dealers, Duveen's name appearing for the first time, for £2326 8*s*. A second portion of the china, mainly English—Bow, Bristol, Derby, Wedgwood, Worcester—fetched £3646 12*s*. A third day devoted to old Chinese and Japanese porcelair brought the total for china up to £7313.

From *The Times* we gather that Sebastiano del Piombo's famous 'La Fornarina' had been sold to the Berlin Gallery for about 10,000 guineas; Rubens's 'The Graces' to Baron Rothschild for 25,000 guineas, his two magnificent portraits of himself and his wife to Baron Alphonse Rothschild for 55,000 guineas, the 'Andromeda' and 'Lot and his Daughters' to a Paris dealer for some 15,000 to 20,000 guineas each. The Van Dyck, 'Mrs. Morton and Mrs. Killigrew', had been sold for a large sum just before the sale. So far the total sales had achieved some £350,000. *The Times* concluded with a justified rebuke: 'considering that the original cost of these treasures was something utterly insignificant compared with their present value, we cannot wonder that owners who are not enthusiastic lovers of art prefer to realise upon them as a luxury that can be dispensed with when the time comes'. The sale catalogue contained no less than 227 pictures: 'we must conclude that the Duke determined to have a great clearance sale', clearing out numbers of queer things that fetched next to nothing, along with the Rubenses and Van Dycks for which Blenheim was famous.

Most of these treasures, many of which had hung on the walls there since John and Sarah's day, left the country. It would be an interesting task, though it is no part of my purpose, to trace where these pictures went and where they have come to rest now. Already on his visits around Europe Lord Randolph, who cared for these things, had the mortification of recognising former belongings of Blenheim: at St. Petersburg in 1881 an Italian cabinet his father had sold; at Berlin in 1888, 'the picture gallery in which I observed three Blenheim pictures—the Fornarina by Raphael (now called a Sebastian del Piombo), the Andromeda of Rubens and the great Bacchanalian picture by Rubens. . . .' As the result of these triumphant operations, over a period roughly equal to the campaigns of the great Duke, Blenheim now lay despoiled. The eighth Duke, who cared for none of these things, now had plenty of money to spend on what he did care for: science and agriculture. Most of the money went on equipping the farms, putting up farm buildings and, for himself—where the Titian gallery had been in old days—hot-houses.

There was still something wanting to his life—someone suggested to him that he might find it in America—a wife, with money. Here golden-hearted Mr. Jerome came in handy: he had always been on good terms with this erring young Duke, who for his part was an admirer of the older man. In New York there was a very rich and good-natured widow, Mrs. Hammersley, who was known for her habit of festooning the whole room at the back of her box at the theatre with orchids. But she objected to her name Lilian because it rhymed with million, and insisted on her friends calling her Lily—with who knows what thoughts of rivalry with the lovely 'Jersey Lily'? The New Jersey Lily was not beautiful, but unlike Mrs. Langtry, she had been left very far from poor.[1]

Marlborough—he continued to be referred to as Blandford still in the family circle—went over in 1888 to have a look for himself. Leonard Jerome reports for us with his usual good humour. 'The Duke has gone off this morning with Lawrence [*i.e.* Jerome's brother] and a party to the Adirondacks trout-fishing, to be gone a week. I rather think he will marry the Hammersley. Don't you fear any responsibility on my part. Mrs. H. is quite capable of deciding for herself. Besides I have never laid eyes on the lady but once. At the same time I hope the marriage will come off as there is no doubts she has lots of tin.[2] Before the month was out Jerome

[1] She was the daughter of Cicero Price, Commodore of the U.S. Navy. Her wealth had come to her from her husband.

[2] Anita Leslie, *op. cit.* 280-2.

reports, 'Well, Blandford is married! I went with him to the Mayor's office in the City Hall at one o'clock today and witnessed the ceremony. The bride was looking very well and all passed off quietly. I took charge of his cable to the Duchess [*i.e.* his mother], also sent one of my own to Jennie. I dine with them at Delmonico's this evening: a dinner given by Mr. and Mrs. Clews to the Duke and his bride. I shall go down to the *Aurania* in the morning to see them off. They had great difficulty in arranging the religious marriage. The clergy refused, he being a divorced man. However they found a parson of the Methodist persuasion who consented to perform the service. An hour ago it was all done.'

With his new bride to help, the Duke felt that some reparation was due to Blenheim. Central heating and electricity were installed. The Long Gallery, robbed of its book-cases, had a Grand Willis organ installed in the bay Sarah had dedicated to Rysbrack's Queen Anne. There after dinner music was made. Leonard Jerome's old flame, Fanny Ronalds, came to sing—what but 'The Lost Chord'? Plunket Greene sang 'O Star of Eve'. We are in the flood-tide of Edwardian sentimentality.

Yet nothing assuaged this sad, strange man's ache at heart. All who knew the Duke testified to his talents, alas unfulfilled. Lady Randolph's brother-in-law was an admirer: 'I have known one or two quite first-class minds whose achievements have been nil. Take George, eighth Duke of Marlborough, an almost incomparable mind; indeed in receptivity, range and versatility, hardly to be matched.' This may be an exaggeration; but there is Lord Ribblesdale—'a youth of great promise marred by fate, shining in many branches of human endeavour, clever, capable of great industry, and within measurable distance of reaching conspicuous success in science, mathematics and mechanics'. Something had gone wrong with him; sex was clearly a nuisance to him, but perhaps that was a symptom of some deeper unrest: he seems all his life, as to some extent his brother was, reacting against the too formidable, too righteous Victorian parents, wedded to standards impossible to achieve and perhaps not desirable to accept.

When Consuelo Vanderbilt came to Blenheim as Duchess she found the mantelpieces in the bedrooms inscribed with expressions of the dead Duke's rancour against life, which had somehow cheated him. 'One woke up in bed to find staring at one in large black letters, "Dust. Ashes. Nothing"; in another room, "They say. What say they? Let them say."—Which I gathered he lived up to', is her unsympathetic comment; for in these phrases one looks into the emptiness, the desolation, of a soul. He cannot have found happiness with Lily—or perhaps with anyone; but he at least had confidence in her. Suddenly one day in November 1892 he died of heart-failure: he was only forty-eight. It was a severe shock to Lord Randolph, already nearing his bourne, though five years younger: some nervous overstrain, some over-strung sensitivity, made life hard to bear for these two brothers.

His will—more personal than any of the Marlborough wills—gives us some insight into the heart of this unknown, disapproved man. He made his wife Lily his executrix and left to her absolutely all the residue of his real and personal estate which he could dispose of. He also at the last had another friend: 'I bequeath to Lady Colin Campbell as a proof of my friendship and esteem the sum of twenty thousand pounds absolutely'. Of his live or dead farming stock he left it to his son and heir to select £5000 worth. The rest of his will recognised his obligations to Blenheim: a trust-fund of £5000 to be invested and accumulate a sum at the end of twenty-one years to be applied to renovate the roof and outside of the Palace; generous bequests to his servants—£100 to each of them who had been in his service five years, £50 more if they had been ten years. He noted his wife's intention to devote £3000 to the repair of Bladon church. Then comes the most interesting clause, in which the dead man speaks his life-long maladjustment from the grave: 'I dislike particularly the exclusiveness of family pride and I wish not to be buried in the family vault in Blenheim Chapel, but in any suitable place that may be convenient in which others of my own generation and surroundings are equally able with myself to find a resting place together'.

All this must have been not without its effect on the mind of the young man who, barely twenty-one, now succeeded to the heritage of Blenheim and all its responsibilities. He had been born in November 1871 at Simla, where his father had left Lady Blandford to the kind offices of the Viceroy and Vicereine and gone off to enjoy the hospitality, the scenery, the pleasures of Kashmir. On her recovery she had to make her way home with the child and an ayah; but the boy was given a traditional grand christening at the Chapel Royal, St. James's. For his school Lord Blandford broke with tradition by sending him to Winchester: no member of the family had had contact with that monastic seminary since the early Churchills leased Minterne from it. From there Sunderland, as he was known—hence the familiar name of 'Sunny' by which he was called all his life—was sent to Trinity College, Cambridge:

another breach with tradition, for the Churchills had gone to Oxford all along. The boy thought himself bullied by his father; he is much more likely to have been neglected.

And yet, how like his family this boy was! Intelligent, moody, pernickety rather than difficult—like his father; with something of his father's unrest of spirit; fastidious and fussy—for at bottom he was an aesthete, with a cult of perfection, whether in riding or architecture, buildings, landscape, dress or women. In him the taste, the connoisseurship of his Spencer ancestors burned bright and clear: it was the inspiration of his blood that drove him to sacrifice everything, his own personal happiness first, for the rehabilitation of Blenheim. It was the real passion of his life: in that he found such happiness as life held for him. It was incomplete.

This being so, and such the set of his mind and temperament, it was necessary to look for a wife, a great fortune.

On the other side of the Atlantic a very determined pair of eyes were on the look-out for him: those of Mrs. William K. Vanderbilt, daughter-in-law of the old Commodore who had left his immense fortune equally between his two elder sons. Like Mrs. Jerome's, Mrs. Vanderbilt's ambitions were purely social, in her case concentrated on an only daughter, with a ferocious intensity—according to the daughter: Consuelo, named after her godmother who had become Duchess of Manchester. Mrs. Vanderbilt had made up her mind early to marry her daughter, who was both lovely and well-educated, either to the Duke of Marlborough's heir or the Marquis of Lansdowne's. Marlborough's heir was now the Duke and willing to sacrifice himself for the sake of Blenheim—in itself a sufficient indication of a remarkable nature in so young a man.

In the summer of her eighteenth birthday Consuelo was brought over for a brief visit to Blenheim. The boy was inhabiting the vast Palace practically alone. His unmarried sisters sometimes came to stay; his mother, Lady Blandford, was seldom asked. (It should be explained that though her husband had become Duke before their decree was made absolute, she preferred to remain Lady Blandford; while Lilian, otherwise Lily, though married to Lord William Beresford, retained her more honorific title as Lily, Duchess of Marlborough. No wonder foreigners find the vagaries of English aristocratic nomenclature incomprehensible.) Consuelo immediately liked Marlborough's sister, Lady Lilian—who had no such objection to the name as Lily Duchess, nor the reason. There were two or three young men to join the party; but Consuelo felt that they were lost in so vast a house.

Next day, Sunday, the young Duke showed her his estate. 'We also drove to outlying villages, where old women and children curtsied and men touched their caps as we passed. The country round Blenheim is rural, with ploughed fields and stone fences. The villages are built of grey stone and the lovely old churches delighted me. Each cottage had its small garden gay with flowers. I realised that I had come to an old world with ancient traditions and that the villagers were still proud of their Duke and of their allegiance to his family.'[1] The country round about, the villages, the churches, the cottage gardens have not much changed: all that is wanting is the spirit of the thing, irretrievably broken in the revolution of our time.

When Consuelo returned to Marble House, Newport,where even the gates were lined with sheet-iron, she found herself under the strict surveillance of her formidable mama, until Marlborough arrived on what he declared would be his one and only visit to America, to propose to her. 'It was in the comparative quiet of an evening at home that Marlborough proposed to me in the Gothic Room, whose atmosphere was so propitious to sacrifice.'[2] Perhaps it is ungallant to reflect that the sacrifice was not all on one side. Marlborough was giving up the woman he loved for the sake of his house, his family—for Blenheim; in the way that royal personages are supposed to do, though not all are equal to the sacrifice.

The marriage was fixed for 5 November, when the Duke remembered that this was Guy Fawkes day and had it changed to 6 November. 'I could not understand why Guy Fawkes's attempt to blow up Parliament almost three centuries before should affect the date of our marriage, but this was only the first of a series of, to me, archaic prejudices inspired by a point of view opposed to my own.' That comic difference was a symptomatic pointer to what lay ahead: there was bound to be trouble between those two. There was too the significant difference between English and American in Marlborough's rooted objection to being married on Guy Fawkes day—impossible to explain: the one looking to the past, the other attitude a virgin soil. One can only say that the former is a richer soil, as indeed, for all Consuelo's beauty, spirit, warmth of heart, his was a subtler nature.

It does not appear from her reminiscences that, though a more generous and candid spirit, she wholly appreciated that. Each of

[1] Consuelo Vanderbilt Balsan, *The Glitter and the Gold,* 35.

[2] Consuelo Vanderbilt Balsan, *op. cit.* 40.

them a remarkable person in his (and her) own right, they were temperamentally opposed and incompatible. Yet the marriage had its compensations. The girl of eighteen was born to be a duchess, and move an elegant and incomparable leader in an international society in its last days. England took her to its heart: 'I would stand all day in the street to see Consuelo Marlborough get into her carriage', said Barrie. As Duchess of Marlborough she was taken into the innermost of that society, given all it had to offer, sharing its experiences, a shining figure in its ritual and its *décor*. As she witnessed the coronation of Edward VII—after a lifetime as Prince of Wales becoming King at last—her husband bearing the crown, she 'realised that she was more British than she knew.' There was all the magnificence of her visits to the Coronation Durbar in India, to the Imperial Court at St. Petersburg, before it vanished under the waters. There was—what she may have appreciated more, where she certainly did good work and was much loved—the devotion of those villagers and cottagers round Blenheim.

Marlborough gave her all this, and more: he gave her a Palace for a home, and children whom she adored. What, perhaps, in the end gives her the last word in the argument that has now entered into history: he could not give her love.

After a prolonged honeymoon tour of the Continent Consuelo arrived at Blenheim to acclimatise herself to the stratified and congealed intricacies of English life, the arrogance of an aristocratic society. At Blenheim there was some distaste between the Churchills and the Hamiltons—Lady Blandford's clan. Consuelo thought her 'a typical *grande dame* of the late Victorian era—Disraeli had made her the heroine of one of his novels'. In fact she is the Lady Corisande of his *roman à clef, Lothair*. The clever Churchills thought Albertha a fool, and at Consuelo's presentation at Court she showed herself to be one. With Consuelo's beauty and extreme elegance it was not but to be expected that she would add lustre to the age-long ritual, the dazzling scene. Lady Blandford assured her, 'I must tell you that no one would take you for an American'. Really!—But this was but one instance of what Americans had to put up with from these aristocrats: the intolerable patronage and bad manners betraying a real *impolitesse du coeur*.

From all sides of the family it was impressed on the new arrival that she was, above all, the 'link in the chain': that her most important duty was to produce the next heir. This formed the riveting subject of her first interview with the formidable Dowager

Duchess. She hoped to see Blenheim restored to its former glories and the prestige of the family upheld—this by way of prelude; for, after an embarrassing inspection of Consuelo's figure and extending an ear-trumpet, she came to the point. 'Your first duty is to have a child and it must be a son, because it would be intolerable to have that little upstart Winston become Duke. Are you in the family way?'[1] The old Duchess had never seen eye to eye with Lady Randolph: each of them too dominating and each of them a rival for the possession of Randolph, who escaped them both. It would have astonished that very certain old lady to learn that the 'little upstart Winston' would become one of the glories of Blenheim, in whom the family name would be carried round the world.

In time Consuelo did her duty and produced the heir, very suitably at Spencer House, the town-house of the Althorp branch. There followed the regular Chapel Royal christening, with the Prince of Wales as godfather: the child named John after the great Duke, William after his Vanderbilt grandfather, Albert Edward after the Prince.

Marlborough had now the wherewithal to embark upon his life's work of restoring the glories of Blenheim, in his grand-mother's words: in other words, of rehabilitating it from the indignity to which it had been brought by her husband and her son, pious duke and impious alike. Naturally he began with the interior; we will begin with the exterior where his best efforts were made, his grandest effects achieved.

As the result of Capability Brown's work the Palace had lost its formal setting; it now rose up improbably from a sea of grass, shaggy and overgrown on every side. By a characteristic inspiration Marlborough brought in a French architect and landscape-designer, Duchêne, who understood in his bones the essence of classic form, what the architecture of Vanbrugh intended and clamorously demanded. In 1900 they set to work on the grand northern entrance court which Brown had grassed over. It was a straightforward task for they had early prints to go on, showing how it had been: the *pavé*, the strips of coloured sand, the finished stone paving all round the edge at the foot of the walls, the terrace with steps approaching the house. The restoration of this Great Court of three acres was a triumph; if, with its square tubs of orange-trees formally placed, it has a French flavouring it is all the better for that: the Palace makes its salute to Versailles, as it should.

[1] Ibid, *op. cit.* 57.

The east side of the Palace presented a quite different problem. This was the side upon which the private apartments gave, Sarah's bow-window in the centre, from which she looked out without favour upon boundary walls. These had been swept away, the beds overgrown, all sense of form lost. The solution adopted by the Duke was ideally right: in this case a sunken garden from which Vanbrugh's east front rises up with heightened proportions and into which the windows looked with all the more effect of colour and shape. A mermaid-fountain with a lily-pool to plash in, symmetrical flower-beds with elaborate patterns in box and figured box-edging. Again the idiom is slightly French; but then the inspiration of Vanbrugh's house is not so much English as Continental.

The greatest problem of all was that of the western slopes from the Palace into the lake. The Duke was not able to approach this until the 1920's, after the first German war—with diminished resources, but with far greater experience of what was necessary. There was nothing to go upon, for Vanbrugh had been dismissed by Sarah before he had got round to the treatment of this western prospect, which he had recognised as far the finest from the house and planned an orangery to overlook.

The Duke conceived a series of water-terraces from the house all the way down to the lake, marrying the two by the imaginative use of water. 'The problem for M. Duchéne is to make a liaison between the façade of Vanbrugh and the water-line of the Lake made by Brown. To reconcile these conflicting ideas is difficult. The difficulty is not diminished when you remember that the façade of the house is limited and the line of the Lake is limitless. As an example, if you turn your back to the Lake and look at the façade, your parterre, basin etc. is in scale to the façade, but if you look at the same parterre from the rotunda to the Lake it is out of scale with the panorama.'[1] M. Duchêne's plan aroused the Duke's enthusiasm: 'it is certainly a stroke of genius on your part bringing the water-line up to the first terrace. I certainly should not have thought of this idea myself and I doubt any English architect would have.' Alas, the plan in full was found to be impracticable: 'I find in looking at old documents that the bed of the river runs at the water's edge. The depth is considerable and I fear the earth would slide into the middle of the Lake.'

He had to be content with two great terraces covering most of the slope to the lake and to the design of these he gave the utmost attention and thought. For hours he would stand there considering

[1] q. D. Green, *Blenheim Palace,* 205-6.

every detail, every alternative—rather like the first Marlborough standing on the bridge watching the house being built. At last he had found a use for the Bernini fountain: a second obelisk was executed to give symmetrical *points d'appui* on the terrace. 'I want you to work more in the spirit of Bernini than of Mansard or Le Nôtre. The value of the obelisks is this, that they give an architectural transition between a lateral line of stone and the perpendicular effect of the trees. Pray therefore do not despise them. I think we can get a magnificent effect. Something like the Trevi fountain or the Fontana Hispana in Rome.'

When all was done—the Duke was afraid he might not live to see it finished—he was at last content. 'Pray tell M. Duchêne that the ensemble of the Terraces is magnificent and in my judgment far superior to the work done by Le Nôtre at Versailles. The proportion of the house, the Terrace and the Lake is perfect.'[1] M. Duchêne was anxious that there should be movement in the water. 'I shall not contradict you. Bear in mind however that the situation is grandiose. Limpidity of water is pleasing and possesses a romance. You have got this effect in the basins and in the large area of water contained by the Lake. Be careful not to destroy this major emotion which Nature has granted to you for the sake of what may possibly be a vulgar display of waterworks which can be seen at any exhibition or public park. Turn all these matters over in your mind when you are at rest in the evening, for it is only by thought, constant thought, and mature reflection that artists have left their great works for the enjoyment of posterity.'

We see from his letters what a remarkable man in his own right the ninth Duke was: the true successor of the art-patron of George III's reign. His work on the lake-front was the one major addition to the beauty of Blenheim since the lake itself. Would he have gone on to restore Henry Wise's Grand Parterre on the south front? There can be no doubt that he would have liked to. But he was now a sick man, too weary and discouraged by the way things had gone in his time, by the frustrations of his personal life. His cousin and friend—one notes points of similarity in style, 'Pray' this or 'Pray' that—pays well-deserved tribute to this gifted man, unhappy in his life: 'always there weighed upon him the size and cost of the great house which was the monument of his ancestor's victories. This he conceived to be almost his first duty in life to preserve and embellish. . . . As the successive crashes of taxation descended upon the Old World it was only by ceaseless care and management, and

[1] q. *Ibid.* 217-18.

also frugality, that he was able to discharge his task. He sacrificed much to this—too much; but he succeeded; and at his death Blenheim passed from his care in a finer state than ever.'[1]

Let us turn to the interior, where he was less successful. His own sternest critic, where aesthetic matters were concerned, he wrote: 'when I was young and uninformed I put French decoration into the three State rooms here. The rooms have English proportions . . . and the result is that the French decoration is quite out of scale and leaves a very unpleasant impression on those who possess trained eyes.'[2] It may be added that few possess such eyes; it was the very desire for perfection that made life so difficult for him.

However, within the house he pulled things together, after the disastrous Victorian interlude. The Long Gallery returned to being a library, book-cases re-installed, books collected once more, beautiful books bought: now one would not think that books had ever been missing from there. He employed a trained historical scholar to put his archives in order—and a good job was made of it, as I can testify. He salvaged the remains of the collection of china that had once bulged in the house, disposed the pieces to the best advantage. Tapestries were puchased, the pictures again added to—though nothing could bring back the wonderful Rubenses and Van Dycks. Not even his scientifically minded father had had the face to sell the bulk of the family portraits. The superb Reynolds canvas of his predecessor, the fourth Duke with his family, remained.

In 1905 Marlborough decided to give this a companion-piece with a portrait of his own family; nor did he make a mistake in calling in Sargent, in whom the Edwardians saw their age, their society, mirrored. This celebrated large canvas has the brilliance, the *panache,* demanded by its subject; it is not unworthy of the Reynolds. Once more the family is dominated by the Duchess, in this case markedly so with the Velasquez inflection of her beauty accentuated, her dominating height, the stylishness of the figure. She possesses the two children, the younger one of a Lawrence prettiness that betokened the distinguished connoisseur he, too, was to grow up to be. There are all the accessories: the two Blenheim spaniels, the bust of the great Duke looking down on them, the Blenheim standard with its fleurs-de-lys above. And then to one side, a little aloof from it all as if displaying it, is the Duke himself, the expression of a refined melancholy, disillusionment in the eyes.

[1] *The Times,* 2 July 1934.

[2] q. D. Green, *op. cit.* 204.

The *train-de-vie* was what such a house, such a master dictated, with its boredom for the beautiful girl growing up with a personality, a will of her own. There was the elaborate stratification of the household, sanctioned, like the ritual, by centuries: the Duke would not be the one to question it; for him it was the necessary order of life. There was still a groom of the chambers, as there had been in the eighteenth century; the butler could not put a match to the fire, even if asked: a footman must be rung for to do that. As for their life when the doors were shut and they were alone together—'how I learned to dread and hate those dinners, how ominous and wearisome they loomed at the end of a long day. They were served with all accustomed ceremony, but once a course had been passed the servants retired to the hall; the door was closed and only a ring of the bell placed before Marlborough summoned them. He had a way of piling food on his plate; the next move was to push the plate away, together with knives, forks, spoons and glasses—all this in considered gestures which took a long time; then he backed his chair away from the table, crossed one leg over the other and endlessly twirled the ring on his little finger. While accomplishing these gestures he was absorbed in thought and quite oblivious of any reactions I might have. After a quarter of an hour he would suddenly return to earth, or perhaps I should say to food, and begin to eat very slowly, usually complaining that the food was cold! As a rule neither of us spoke a word. I took to knitting in desperation and the butler read detective stories in the hall.'[1]

But the immense house woke up at the week-ends when there were parties. Then the Long Gallery came to life with music, for the Duke had an organist: C. W. Perkins. (In an obscure corner behind the organ are these tell-tale words: 'C. W. Perkins how often · has thy genius · beguiled · my sad heart'. Whose were they? Marlborough's father's or his own?) Sometimes there were concerts given, like those in aid of the restoration of Woodstock church in October 1896, when Lady Randolph was among the eminent artists and would play a piano solo, C. W. Perkins give a recital and George Grossmith a humorous sketch; or in December 1897 when the Duke and Duchess, Lady Randolph, Ladies Lilian and Norah and Lord Churchill from Cornbury took part in a new musical burlesque.[2] From the musty bills, with their old-fashioned provincial lettering, arises the aroma of those Edwardian days—as the announcement of a lecture in Woodstock Town Hall one day in

1 Consuelo Vanderbilt Balsan, *op. cit.* 60.

2 Bodleian, G. A. Oxon, C. 317 (19).

1892 by G. Bernard Shaw on 'The Progress of Social Democracy' foretells the sentence passed upon their order.

For some time the going was good, the years golden, the pace of life gentle and slow. On hot summer days the Indian tent would be set up under the cedars on the lawn. 'Sometimes we played tennis or rowed on the lake, and in the afternoon the household played cricket on the lawn. The tea-table was set under the trees. It was a lovely sight, with masses of luscious apricots and peaches to adorn it. There were also pyramids of strawberries and raspberries; bowls brimful of Devonshire cream; pitchers of iced coffee; scones to be eaten with various jams, and cakes with sugared icing. No one dieted in those days and the still-room maid, who was responsible for the teas, was a popular person in the household.

'Winston was then the life and soul of the young and brilliant circle that gathered round him at Blenheim. . . . Whether it was his American blood or his boyish enthusiasm and spontaneity, qualities sadly lacking in my husband, I delighted in his companionship.'[1] So also did the husband, it is agreeable to note: their affection and respect were mutual. It is a tribute to both that these cousins, so different in temperament, should have been drawn to each other. Political divergence, when Winston joined the Liberal Party and was vilified by the Conservatives, made not the slightest difference: it provided only the more fodder for friendly argument. In these very years Winston was writing his first big book, the biography of his father: when finished he dedicated it to his cousin 'in all faithful friendship'. It is clear, too, how much Sir Winston owed to the inspiration and encouragement of the Duke over his historical masterpiece, the vindication of their ancestor. That was a subject that must have been often discussed between them.

Sometimes there would be a more august visitor and a grander party: the Prince of Wales or the German Emperor, on one occasion the two together with the jealous problems of placing and seating that such a visitation provoked. The Kaiser lectured them all on the great Duke's battles: the Duchess was 'amused by his evident desire to shine, but William II seemed to me no more than the typical Prussian Officer with the added arrogance and conceit his royal birth inspired. Indeed I was surprised at his undistinguished appearance, which was perhaps due to the fact that he was not in uniform, without which Germans usually appear at a disadvantage. He seemed to have inherited no English characteristics [which is not surprising considering that he had no English

[1] Consuelo Vanderbilt Balsan, 103-4.

blood] and had neither the charm nor the wisdom of his uncle, the Prince of Wales. During the South African War, soon after this visit, his jealousy and hatred of England became evident.'[1]

The South African War may be taken to announce the end of their care-free world—if ever any world can be said to be care-free. The Duke, who had political ideas and ambitions, had been made a Privy Councillor in 1894 and was Paymaster-General in Lord Salisbury's last government, from 1899 to 1902. In 1900 he went out to South Africa and was on Lord Roberts' Staff. On his return he was made a Knight of the Garter, as four of his predecessors had been; in Mr. Balfour's administration he was Under-Secretary for the Colonies, 1903-5. But the long rule of the Liberals, which raised his cousin to power, kept him out. He made only a brief return to government in 1917 as Parliamentary Secretary to the Board of Agriculture.

Already his private griefs were thickening on him. We need not go into these: the story has been told by Consuelo Duchess—though we may remember that, since he is dead, we have not heard his side of the case. In the end, we may reflect—considering how incompatible their temperaments were—how much they together accomplished, and would certainly not have done without each other. No doubt it involved a sacrifice of personal happiness on both sides; but achievement always demands sacrifice. What remains now is the achievement; remarkable as it was, we have reason to be grateful for it. Consuelo Duchess did after all do her duty as a 'link in the chain': she continued the family. She was a shining figure in the society she adorned with her gifts; warm-hearted and democratic in her feelings, she was loved in the neighbourhood of Woodstock, the heart of England. Then, too, there was Blenheim, saved, revivified, restored: as a work of art in its present state a national possession we owe in good part to them.

[1] *Ibid,* 101-2.

CHAPTER SEVEN

The Rise and Fall of Lord Randolph

SUCH is the background against which we have to see the most tragic career in British politics of the nineteenth century:[1] that of Lord Randolph Churchill. What struck contemporaries so forcibly was the suddenness of his rise, to such a commanding height of leadership so young, the completeness of his fall. Politics is never without an element of the dramatic; but a couple of years, 1884 to 1886—as disturbed and as decisive in their outcome as those we have observed in 1782 to 1784—saw Lord Randolph's drama played out: ascent, apogee and fall.

The historian of the period tells us, 'aged only thirty-seven he was the youngest Chancellor of the Exchequer and leader of the House after Pitt. From the age of thirty-one his rise had been meteoric. On public platforms his party had no equal to him; in the election fight against Home Rule he had been its mainstay throughout the constituencies. He seemed predestined to be Prime Minister at no distant date; and might but for the events of the previous year [1885] have stepped into Disraeli's place already. Yet ere 1886 ended, from his sudden eminence he fell sheer.'[2]

To suppose that Lord Randolph might have succeeded Disraeli immediately is, in my opinion, rather to exaggerate his power—as Lord Randolph did himself: chief reason for his fall. But it is clear that we must not underestimate him, when Lord Rosebery regarded him as 'incomparably the most formidable Tory in the House of Commons and probably in the country', and as 'one of the most remarkable men, with perhaps the most remarkable career, of my time'—strong tributes coming from that quarter.[3] He goes on to add that in all the century Lord Randolph's career was only less dramatic than that of Disraeli.

[1] With the single exception of Parnell's.

[2] R. C. K. Ensor, *England, 1870-1914* (*Oxford History of England*), 173.

[3] Lord Rosebery, *Lord Randolph Churchill*, I. 14.

This gives us a clue to the inwardness of that brilliant, hectic, short life: Lord Randolph saw himself as Disraeli's successor in rejuvenating the Tory party, in renewing its contacts with the people, giving it a popular appeal, a programme with which to outbid and beat the Liberals. And not unreasonably. After Disraeli died there was no one among the Tories to take his place in the eye of the people. Lord Salisbury had no demagogic arts; in the House of Commons there was only blameless old Sir Stafford Northcote to lead the Tory remnant, and he was almost as much under the spell of the Grand Old Man, the incomparable Parliamentarian, as the Liberals themselves. 'In 1880 we were all thrown out of office by Mr. Gladstone', writes Sir Winston—himself then aged six.[1] Mr. Gladstone had returned from supposed retirement to active politics, and come back to power not only with an immense majority but with the conviction that the Almighty had put him there. It was this personal ascendancy of the grandest figure in the politics of the time that Lord Randolph went straight for—a young man who had hitherto not taken much of a part. In the next year or two, almost within a matter of months, the certainty and cohesion of the large Liberal majority were undermined, the moral authority of the government dissipated, the ascendancy of Mr. Gladstone questioned and shaken in the House, if not yet in the country. All this was largely the work of Lord Randolph Churchill—an extraordinary achievement in one so young. He showed that in Parliament he was a match for the greatest of Parliamentarians; he went on to prove that in the country he could equal Mr. Gladstone as a draw, as a compelling power with the mob—and even, at his best, draw larger crowds. Then, in a handful of years, all was over.

What kind of man was it, the strangeness of whose career made such an impression on his time?—certainly the complexity of his personality made him very little understood.

He was a little man, full of vibrant nervous energy, with large moustaches that endeared him to contemporary caricaturists, beneath which one glimpses the Churchill under-lip. Then there were the familiar prominent eyes—'My, what poppy eyes those Churchills have!' said a tourist going the round at Blenheim. In short he was a good deal of a Churchill in appearance; Queen Victoria thought that he had a look of his grandfather; if so, he was like him in more ways than one. Lord Rosebery, his friend from Eton days, tells us: 'he was a born party leader, reminding one of Bolingbroke in the dashing days of Harry St. John. He was

[1] Winston S. Churchill, *My Early Life*, 21.

brilliant, courageous, resourceful, and unembarrassed by scruple; he had fascination, audacity, tact; great and solid ability welded with the priceless gift of concentration; marvellous readiness in debate, and an almost unrivalled skill and attraction on the platform; for he united in an eminent degree the Parliamentary and the popular gifts.'

What then was lacking to rob these brilliant gifts of their full fruition?

It cannot be said that Lord Randolph was as wise as he was shrewd; that he was as good a strategist as he was a tactician; as dependable a colleague as he was an opponent. Though a very quick and piercing judge of a situation, his judgment was not really reliable. He was self-willed and impulsive, above all impatient. If he had only had patience all the rest would have come into line. But he had the defect of the artistic temperament, what we in our day of psychological jargon diagnose as the manic-depressive alternation—tremendous high spirits and racing energy on the upward bound, depression and discouragement on the down. This rhythm is present in a more or less marked degree with all persons of creative capacity, particularly in the arts. And clearly this strongly artistic strain we have observed in the stock came out in him, as it has done again in his son. But where in Sir Winston it has been accorded the foundation of rude health, a rock-like character, Lord Randolph was betrayed by ill-health: nervous instability and over-excitement wore away a fragile, sensitive system, so that the tensions of politics were often accompanied, or relieved, by bouts of illness. We have to see Lord Randolph's political activities in that context; for some years before his death he was a failing man. He was dead at forty-six.

The large Liberal majority of 1880 might well have daunted the Conservatives, depressed as they were by Disraeli's retirement to the Lords; but almost immediately an issue was found that wrought the maximum confusion in the government ranks—the squalid affair of Bradlaugh, the militant rationalist Member who wished to make an affirmation instead of the usual oath on the Bible. That this affair should have reached the proportions it did, consumed parliamentary time and obstructed government business, was due to the ineptitude of Speaker Brand and the advantage taken of it by Lord Randolph. It seems to have been in badgering the government over this that the ginger-group of youngish men led by him came together on the Opposition benches. They were never more than four; but they made as much noise as forty and took up as much time as a hundred and forty.

They were always on their legs speaking, or protesting, or asking questions, or moving motions or amendments. There was Lord Randolph, pertinacious and marvellously quick to seize an advantage; there were Sir Henry Drummond Wolff and John Gorst with his invaluable legal equipment and longer experience. They were usually joined by young Arthur Balfour, who concealed beneath his lackadaisical manner a will of steel, a subtle intellect and a very cool detached judgment—for he was by blood a Cecil, a nephew of Lord Salisbury. They were for ever asking for explanations, for more information. Mr. Gladstone, now seventy-one, could not resist that. Was there not a good deal of the Scotch pedagogue in him, the misplaced don? Was he not the Headmaster in the House? Night after night he would reply with unfailing courtesy, and at unfailing length, to these young men; until one night his lieutenant, Sir William Harcourt, dared to protest to the G.O.M., 'if you speak again we shall be here till morning'.

Lord Randolph had got his measure. Though we need not suppose that religion meant much to him, he made the fullest use of it to embarrass Mr. Gladstone over Bradlaugh. It was he again who insisted on their little group being accorded the name and consideration of a Fourth Party.

Lord Beaconsfield observed these beginnings with a certain amused sympathy. He could never forget that he had been young himself and not altogether respectable. Years ago Disraeli had reported to Queen Victoria of Lord Randolph's maiden speech, 'Lord Randolph said many imprudent things, which is not very important in the maiden speech of a young member and a young man; but the House was surprised and then captivated, by his energy and natural flow and his impressive manner. With self-control and study he might mount. It was a speech of great promise.' Then came those bitter years when Lord Randolph was mostly out of the country.

Now in 1880 the old tired statesman wrote to encourage the young man, coupling with it a warning. 'I fully appreciate your feelings and those of your friends, but you must stick to Northcote. He represents the respectability of the party. I wholly sympathise with you all, because I never was respectable myself. . . . Don't on any account break with Northcote; but defer to him as often as you can.' If Beaconsfield had lived he would have exercised a sympathetic restraining influence on Lord Randolph, who for his part never had any intention of deferring to a Stafford Northcote. The situation was intensely irritating to an impatient young man, for here was his own leader, the leader of the Opposition, deferring to Mr. Gladstone, visibly unable to emancipate himself from the spell of those eagle eyes of his former chief at the Treasury. Sir Stafford was an amiable West Country gentleman; Lord Randolph was not altogether a gentleman, but he was a man of genius. It was maddening to sit under the authority of such nerveless leadership. Restive, audacious, self-willed, Lord Randolph soon began to show symptoms of gerontophobia: the old men were in the way. His campaign against the government became in large part a campaign against the leadership of his own party too: against the Old Gang in general, and the Goat (Northcote) in particular. These were Lord Randolph's own elegant terms, expressive of his feelings. Meanwhile he set the pace.

Beaconsfield's visible exhaustion and withdrawal, followed shortly by his death, left the question of the leadership of the Conservative party open. It was by no means settled, and we must not ante-date the long ascendancy that Lord Salisbury ultimately won. For the present there was a dual leadership—Lord Salisbury in the Lords, Northcote in the Commons; and very unsatisfactory it was to impatient spirits like Lord Randolph. He exerted himself to have Lord Salisbury declared leader—with the irony usual in such things, for in the end it was Salisbury who destroyed him. But before the end of the year (1880) he had got him to come down to Blenheim and appear on the platform with him in his constituency at Woodstock. The aged eyes of Lord Beaconsfield, that perceived everything, had seen how things were. His last judgment of Lord Randolph, delivered not long before he died to a Liberal who was expressing admiration of the young man's parliamentary instinct and his gifts, was prophetic as ever: 'Ah, yes, you are quite right: when they come in they will have to give him anything he chooses to ask for and in a very short time they will have to take anything he chooses to give them'.[1]

In those days before universal suffrage the attention of the nation was focused on the parliamentary arena with an intensity that today would be devoted to a football stadium or the pools, and it was not long before the nation noticed the form of the new performer. An aristocratic demagogue, a lord who was a good deal of a *gamin*, he touched people's imagination; he appealed especially to youth. Here was a new note: wit, cheek, imagination, insolence—he was great fun to listen to; there could not be a

[1] Winston S. Churchill, *Lord Randolph Churchill,* I. 155.

greater contrast with that other great master of the demagogic art, the G.O.M. Only Lord Randolph dared to say what was what about him—or at any rate half what was what. ' "Vanity of vanities," says the Preacher, "all is vanity." "Humbug of humbugs," says the Radical, "all is humbug." Gentlemen, we live in an age of advertisement, the age of Holloway's pills, of Colman's mustard, and of Horniman's pure tea. The Prime Minister is the greatest living master of the art of personal advertisement. Holloway, Colman and Horniman are nothing compared with him. Every act of his, whether it be for the purposes of health, or of recreation, or of religious devotion, is spread before the eyes of every man, woman and child in the United Kingdom on large and glaring placards. . . . For the purposes of recreation he has selected the felling of trees; and we may usefully remark that his amusements, like his politics, are essentially destructive. Every afternoon the whole world is invited to assist at the crashing fall of some beech or elm or oak. The forest laments, in order that Mr. Gladstone may perspire.'[1]

It was immensely enjoyable; but underneath was a deadly ability, as we can see from the style of the invective. Mr. Gladstone, for his part, was a gladiator worthy of him; he rode these waves undaunted, quite unquelled. One night, meeting Lady Randolph at dinner after one of Randolph's most effective performances against him, the old man inquired kindly, without irony, 'I hope Lord Randolph is not *too* tired after his magnificent effort'. If there was one thing that was irresistible about Gladstone it was his unfailing courtesy. Lady Randolph adored sitting by him at dinner. In fact the two people she most liked having beside her at dinner were Mr. Gladstone, her husband's chief target, and Lord Salisbury, who ruined him. When Randolph was in India he wrote home to her, 'any Hindu who dies at Benares, and whose ashes are thrown into the Ganges, goes right bang up to Heaven without stopping, no matter how great a rascal he may have been. I think the G.O.M. ought to come here; it is his best chance.'

The running against the government in these years, both in Parliament and in the country, was made by Lord Randolph. The serious side of what he had to say was this. ' "Trust the people"—I have long tried to make that my motto; but I know, and will not conceal, that there are still a few in our party who have that lesson yet to learn and who have yet to understand that the Tory party of today is no longer identified with that small and narrow class which

[1]q. *Ibid.* 282-3.

is connected with the ownership of land; but that its great strength can be found, and must be developed, in our large towns as well as in our country districts. . . . Trust the people, and they will trust you—and they will follow you and join you in the defence of that Constitution against any and every foe. I have no fear of democracy.' These were rather questionable sentiments coming from a Tory at that time. Lord Salisbury had no intention of putting his trust in the people or in anything human. He was a philosophic sceptic, taken in by nothing in human affairs—and for the rest a profoundly religious man. He had always distrusted and feared democracy—had resigned office rather than approve Disraeli's Reform Bill enfranchising the urban working men. It was Lord Salisbury who reaped the benefit of Lord Randolph's trust in the people, who was the residuary legatee of the younger man's efforts.

Nevertheless, though Lord Salisbury was philosophically right, Lord Randolph was not wrong either. It was indispensable if the Tory party was to survive in the new circumstances, with a newly enfranchised electorate of several millions, with working men exercising the vote in the towns and soon to achieve it in the country, that the party should make both effective contact with, and appeal to, the mass of the people. It is perhaps Lord Randolph's chief claim to a place in history that he grasped this, alone among the Tory leaders, and also saw how it was to be done. The foundation upon which the constitution rested had completely changed: 'your new foundation is a great seething and swaying mass of some five million electors, who have it in their power by the mere heave of the shoulders, if they only act with moderate unanimity, to sweep away entirely the three ancient institutions and put anything they like in their place. . . .'

This was what the Tory Democracy that Lord Randolph preached came to in essence—we need neither give it a greater importance as doctrine than it had, nor must we underrate it: the acceptance, generously and without reluctance, of the cardinal new fact of democracy in politics; the putting forward of a proper programme to appeal to it, a policy that took account of its interests. The seriousness of Lord Randolph's campaign and his platform has been often questioned—partly because he was a man dangerously devoid of humbug and of a cynical turn of wit. I do not think we need question his fundamental seriousness at all. He was the kind of person who—beneath the extravagant rhetoric, beneath the high spirits, the invective and the fun—meant what he said.

There was enough bitterness in his experience of high life to make him mean it too, to give a cutting edge to his advocacy; and that won for him dangerous enemies on his own side. He was to drink of the cup of bitterness a great deal more deeply yet before he had finished.

So far as the new electorates were concerned things worked out with an unexpected twist. This came into evidence with the elections after Gladstone's Reform Bill of 1884. The working-class vote in the big towns came to provide a solid foundation for twenty years of Tory rule. To that extent Lord Randolph had been right and was a prime agent in making it so. The enfranchisement of rural labourers brought an accession of strength to the Liberals who now dominated the county constituencies. The unity of the landed interest in a Tory sense was broken. So much for the feudal view of the countryside entertained by the landowning class: a very direct disclaimer on the part of their dependants!

All over the country Lord Randolph was the star-turn of his party as a speaker. A follower of his wrote, 'the work of inspiring a beaten party with hope and courage was substantially left to one man'. Meeting the people face to face was very far from Lord Salisbury's ideal of pleasure: 'this duty of making speeches', he wrote to Queen Victoria, 'is an aggravation of the labours of your Majesty's servants which we owe entirely to Mr. Gladstone'. Now the womenfolk were able to lend a hand and Lord Randolph was quick to perceive the use that might be made of the idea of the Primrose League, founded to keep Dizzy's memory green. Official orthodox Conservatives regarded this venture with distaste; most of their papers treated it with scorn and ridicule. It was only gradually that it took hold and conquered upper-class aversion. Wasn't it all very vulgar, a Conservative woman once asked Lady Salisbury. 'Of course, it's vulgar,' replied that common-sense lady, 'that's why we are so successful.'

Lord Randolph recruited his mother to become President, his wife as a member of the Ladies' Grand Council. Here was a platform on which the old Duchess and her daughter-in-law, who did not always see eye to eye, could unite. Together they battled and worked and canvassed for Randolph. He was so busy in Parliament and so much in request to speak in the big cities that sometimes the ladies had to carry the burden of the election for him in his own constituency at Woodstock. Driving about the leafy lanes of that delectable countryside, summer at its height, in their smart turn-out, the horses decorated with Randolph's racing colours, pink and brown, in at the gateways into the fields where the men were working, climbing the hayricks after shy or dumb voters—what a time they had! The rustic voters often did not know whether they were Conservative or Liberal, but only for which colours they voted, red or blue. Those were the days of old-fashioned gallantries, of election songs—

> Bless my soul! that Yankee lady,
> Whether day was bright or shady,
> Dashed about the district like an oriflamme of war . . .

When Lady Randolph went to Birmingham to canvass for Mr. Burdett-Coutts, she found that urban voters were apt to know a thing or two more. A waverer with whom Lady Randolph was pleading said that if he could get the same price as the beautiful Duchess of Devonshire had once given for a vote she could have his. Not a bit abashed the Yankee lady returned, 'Thank you very much: I'll let the Baroness Burdett-Coutts know at once'.

A much tougher struggle ensued within the Conservative party for the control of the party-machine. Its affairs and finances were governed by a Central Committee, virtually self-appointed, responsible to no one, utterly out of touch with the rank and file in the constituencies. Lord Randolph was very unpopular with the panjandrums of the party, entrenched in the central offices, at the Carlton Club as on the Opposition Front Bench. Several of them had taken a toss at his hands. The inseparable Sir Stafford Northcote and Sir Richard Cross had been guyed as 'Marshall and Snelgrove'—very insulting in those days when 'trade' was hardly respectable. Rich Mr. W. H. Smith, of the bookshops, very much a *parvenu,* had expressed the thought that the inhabitants of Irish mud-cabins hardly qualified for a vote. He was treated to the following from Lord Randolph. 'I have heard a great deal of the mud-cabin argument. I suppose that in the minds of the lords of suburban villas, of the owners of vineries and pineries, the mud-cabin represents the climax of physical and social degradation. But . . . the difference between the cabin of the Irish peasant and the cottage of the English agricultural labourer is not so great as that which exists between the abode of the right honourable member for Westminister [*i.e.* rich Mr. W. H. Smith] and the humble roof which shelters from the storm the individual who now has the honour to address the Committee.'[1] He proceeded to add insult to

[1] Churchill, *op. cit.* I. 345.

injury by quoting Latin—it was not known whether Mr. Smith knew Latin:

> Non ebur, neque aureum
> Mea renidet in domo lacunar;
> Non trabes Hymettiae
> Premunt columnas ultima recisas
> Africa.

Here was a by no means gentle art of making enemies. 'Vineries and pineries' stuck. But it was Mr. Smith who had the last word.

Nevertheless, it was essential that the party-machine should be reconstructed effectively on a broad popular basis. Joseph Chamberlain was at this time showing how it could be done: his Radical caucus at Birmingham was the foundation of his growing appeal as a national figure. Something similar in their position and temperaments drew these two, Chamberlain and Churchill, together. When Lord Randolph invited Radical Joe to dinner, the old Duke was scandalised. Was he not a republican? Had he not refrained from drinking the Queen's health at a public function in Birmingham, had doubts about driving in the same carriage as Mayor with the Prince of Wales? What company Randolph kept!

It is curious to think back over the lapse of time at the mutual attraction and exclusion of Joe Chamberlain and Lord Randolph, still more at the dichotomy exhibited in the careers of their sons. A good deal of recent English history has passed between the ranks of those two families.

But this anticipates; it is sufficient to observe that the victory of Lord Randolph within the party-machine would necessarily bring him a large accession of power.

Where the Central Committee possessed all the power and the cash, the National Union of Conservative Associations represented the constituency parties, the active workers. It was to this national body that Lord Randolph appealed, and at the Birmingham Conference in 1883 he won their backing. His argument was a powerful one. 'The Conservative party will never exercise power until it has gained the confidence of the working classes.' From that he made the transition to the point that 'the great bulk of the Tory party throughout the country is composed of artisans and labouring classes. . . . No party management can be effective and healthy unless the great labouring classes are directly represented on the Executive of the party.' From this he drove home the conclusion that he wished to see 'the control and guidance of the organisation of the Tory party transferred from a self-elected body to an annually elected body. I wish to see the management of the financial resources of our party transferred from an irresponsible body to a responsible body.'

Upon this the Conference passed a resolution directing a new Council to take steps to secure for the National Union its proper influence in the party organisation. Impossible to recount here the complicated (and boring) party manoeuvres that ensued. Lord Randolph's supporters obtained a slight majority on the new Council, with himself as chairman. Lord Percy had been chairman of the Organisation Committee, and Lord Salisbury continued to make his communications to him—and gave offence to the majority. On realising this Lord Salisbury made a tactical retreat and wrote to Lord Randolph, 'I hope, however, that there is no chance of the paths of the Central Committee and the National Union crossing: for there is plenty of good work for both to do'. One recognises familiar language from that agile tactician: that was not the point.

It is clear that Lord Salisbury was not giving way. After some months of intrigue and counter-intrigue it transpired that all business relating to elections and candidates was to remain in the hands of the Central Committee—in other words, the Old Gang. At that Lord Randolph resigned his chairmanship and let it be known that he would withdraw from politics. Consternation in the Tory ranks; he was re-elected chairman unanimously. At the Sheffield Conference next year, in time for the general election, Lord Randolph won a complete victory. He was at the head of the poll; the Old Gang made every effort to maintain control, but in vain. The Central Committee was dissolved, the organisation of the National Union on a democratic, representative basis was confirmed. Lord Salisbury and Lord Randolph were reconciled and met to form an alliance and plan strategy. But they met as two comparable powers—and observe that Lord Randolph had attained his object by a timely resignation.

In Parliament he continued to drive his furious pace. But there was calculation in his aggression: he considered it indispensable to attack, to destroy the personal ascendancy of Mr. Gladstone if the Tory party were ever to regain the initiative. The Liberal plan for further extension of the franchise, with yet another Reform Bill, looked like putting the Tories in a permanent minority. An unfriendly critic on the Tory side bore reluctant witness to Lord Randolph's effectiveness. Whenever the Bradlaugh case came up, as it did again and again in this unhappy Parliament, he used it to distract the government and disrupt its majority. He showed himself no less contemptuous of his own Front Bench. It was not only Sir Stafford's deference to Gladstone that infuriated him, but his total lack of punch, the very conventionality of his character. This encouraged Lord Randolph to take a line of his own, and impose it: he did not care whether it was the party-line, approved by his accredited leaders, or no. In his inner mind they were not his leaders; his relations with Sir Stafford were purely formal and barely civil; he had undoubtedly passed sentence of exclusion upon him when his day came. The impression on his fellows may be gathered: 'on one side he was a genius, on the other a spoilt and naughty child; but in either capacity he always trampled on the weak and irresolute . . . as he rose in popularity so he became more dictatorial and unreasonable. . . . Provided he could embarrass the government, the after-effect of his action was of little concern to him. . . . Still, it must be admitted that Churchill's actions and speeches, impolitic and risky as they often were, did much to rehabilitate the Tory party as a fighting organisation and a living force.'[1]

In foreign affairs he was a Little Englander. He was opposed to intervention in the Sudan, calling it a 'bondholders' war': a very advanced line for the time and one not calculated to please the bondholders. The view of Dilke, with whom Lord Randolph had broken, was that his fierce attacks on the Khedive of Egypt were 'without one atom of truth in them', and he regarded it as a curious example of his flightiness that when he went to Egypt a few years later, he was struck with wonder at the Khedive's refusal to receive him. Even as a very young member Lord Randolph had been opposed to his party's pro-Turk policy. He was himself pro-Russian and pro-French—an alignment very much in advance of his time, though it may be said that his party ultimately came round to it with the Anglo-French entente of Lord Lansdowne and its sequel. This meant that he did not share his party's fears of a Russian advance on the North-West Frontier of India. Altogether Lord Randolph's temperamental leanings and prejudices were those of a Radical, except for the dominant question of the day: only Home Rule kept him a Tory.

The Irish question was coming more and more to dominate internal politics and with Mr. Gladstone's conversion to Home

[1] Lord George Hamilton, *Parliamentary Reminiscences and Reflections,* 1868-85, I. 200.

Rule to divide and wreck the Liberal party. On this subject Lord Randolph had a special equipment and point of view of his own. Unlike most Tories he had a genuine sympathy with, and understanding of, the Irish character. He was in favour of concession, except for the ultimate one of Home Rule. He was liberal about extending the franchise and argued for the application of the Reform Bill of 1884 to Ireland. He put forward good cynical reasons for this course—after all, he knew Ireland. He argued that the Fenian proclivities of the towns would be more than counterbalanced by the increased power given to the peasantry. The incidents of agricultural life, he observed, are unfavourable to revolutionary movements, and the peasant is even more under the proper and legitimate influence of the Roman Catholic priesthood than the lower classes of the towns.

In the end it was not so much the Irish Catholic bishops as the odious English Nonconformist conscience that ruined Parnell—with infinitely tragic consequences: the demand for Home Rule was stifled for two or three decades, to emerge in the murderous form of Sinn Fein with all the consequences of murder campaigns, arson and destruction, Black and Tans, civil war and ultimate separation of Ireland from the Commonwealth.

With slow rumination that powerful organ, Mr. Gladstone's mind, was moving, righteously and rightly, to the acceptance of Home Rule. It may have been this that made him ready to accept a minor reverse on an item of the Budget as defeat for the government, Lord Randolph, who had planned it, jumping on his seat below the gangway and leading the cheers of the whole Conservative party. The immense Liberal majority had been at length breached. The Queen, with her usual common sense, expressed surprise that Mr. Gladstone should regard a minor matter as a vital question. But he was determined to go—until an appeal to the country should decide who had its confidence. Meanwhile no one had any doubt whose victory it was.

The political situation was extraordinarily confused, partly because Parnell, alienated by the Liberals' application of coercion, was offering the votes of the Irish Nationalists to the Conservatives in return for—what? No one knew for what. Lord Randolph was playing Parnell for all he was worth. Until the political situation cleared one way or another, Lord Salisbury was called upon by the Queen to form a Caretakers' Government. He proposed to make Sir Stafford Northcote Chancellor of the Exchequer and Leader of the House of Commons. He offered Lord Randolph, who had never held office before, the India Office, then important among the Secretaryships of State. He then found that Lord Randolph would not accept so long as Northcote was to be Leader of the House. The wise old Duchess pleaded with her son: 'I have been thinking very quietly and calmly over your position, and I think you might go to see Lord Salisbury to show him your friendly feeling while you maintain your own position. . . . He told you to consider his offer; so that, it seems to me, you are almost in duty bound to go to see him. There is no doubt that he is in a very difficult position, and may say you require *not* any policy or special measure, but simply that he should *kill* an old friend whom *all* respect.'

But that was precisely what Lord Randolph did require of Lord Salisbury. For himself, he said, 'I am very near the end of my tether. In the last five years I have lived twenty. I have fought Society. I have fought Mr. Gladstone at the head of a great majority. I have fought the Front Opposition Bench. Now I am fighting Lord Salisbury. I have said I will not join the Government unless Northcote leaves the House of Commons. Lord Salisbury will never give way.' As a matter of fact, when he learned that if Lord Randolph would not join the government neither would Hicks-Beach, Lord Salisbury had to give way. Not in the least anxious to form a government—a massive patience which he had developed by sheer force of character and intellect became a great asset to him—Lord Salisbury solved the dilemma by giving the Foreign Secretaryship, to which he himself had every claim, to Northcote and promoting him to the Lords.

While the matter hung in the balance Lord Salisbury informed the Queen of his troubles with Lord Randolph and asked 'if I had any insuperable objection to him, which I said I had not'. The proposal that he should go to the India Office 'rather startled me, but the India Council would be a check on him'. On learning that he would not take office unless Sir Stafford were deposed from Leader—'with due consideration to Lord Randolph Churchill', she did not think 'he should be allowed entirely his own terms, especially as he has never held office before'. When at length all was arranged and Lord Randolph was sworn in as Secretary of State for India, in the Green Drawing-Room at Windsor on a dreadfully hot June day, the Queen was interested to observe that Lord Randolph was 'rather like his sisters, a little like his grandfather'. She had never seen this startling young politician before, now aged thirty-six, who was the talk of her kingdom. Now he was to preside over the government of her Indian Empire. It gave her to think; it gave her a headache later. Only a couple of years before the Queen had taken the initiative in ending the rift between the rising politician and the royal family. The Prince of Wales made it up with Lord Randolph; Lady Randolph attended a Drawing-Room at the Queen's express wish. In July they were bidden to dine at Windsor. 'He is very quiet and has an extraordinary likeness to darling Leopold, which quite startled me . . . Lord Randolph talked sensibly.' She was evidently on hot bricks about him. Did she expect him to bite?

If so, he very shortly did. Lord Randolph had declared himself all along opposed to coercion in Ireland: it was this that had gained the Tories the support of the Nationalists, and he had been the chief procurer of it. Parnell demanded, as part of his price, an inquiry into the trials for murder that had taken place under the Coercion Viceroy, Lord Spencer. The Cabinet resolved against this as setting a very dangerous precedent. Lord Randolph dissented. Whatever his motive, whether out of just indignation or to please the Nationalists, he delivered a violent attack on Lord Spencer and his administration. The Queen was incensed at his language; she expressed her doubts about the policy of trying to govern Ireland without additional powers: it looked like trying to cajole the Nationalists, 'who she feels sure *everyone but* Lord Randolph in the Cabinet *must know* are totally *unreliable*.' She hoped that Lord Salisbury would restrain Lord Randolph as much as he could. Poor Lord Salisbury was called on to explain. One sees the Queen as the most exalted, though not the most formidable, member of the Old Gang.

The result of this affair was unfortunate. Lord Spencer was deeply wounded by the attack; the breach between these two leading members of the Spencer clan was never repaired. On Lord Spencer it had a somewhat paradoxical impact: he concluded that since it was not possible to govern Ireland without coercion, the only alternative was full Home Rule. When the split in the Liberal party came and the Liberal Unionists hived off, he was the only one of the great Whig magnates to remain with Mr. Gladstone on his forlorn journey towards the setting sun and self-government in Ireland.

The Queen was now to experience in her own person, and her own sphere, something of what Lord Randolph could do. Since dear Lord Beaconsfield had made her Empress of India she took a personal interest in its affairs. Might there not be an opening there for her dear Arthur (the Duke of Connaught), who was so keen on his military career? She proposed him for the vacant Bombay command, which carried with it the Commandership-in-Chief and a seat on the Governor's Council. Lord Randolph thought not, on the ground that the post involved political functions, which it would be unsuitable for a member of the royal family to take part in.

At this the Queen consulted the Viceroy for his opinion and rather compromised Lord Salisbury by asking him to forward her telegram. He was in a fix; he could hardly have refused. Lord Randolph: 'I have for some time felt that the India Office, while I was there, had little influence with respect to other matters of great importance. But from what has passed between yourself and the Viceroy about the Duke of Connaught, it must be obvious to the Viceroy that I no longer possess the confidence of the Sovereign or of yourself.' Lord Salisbury: 'I regret very much that you should think I have not shown you confidence. I have done my best to give effect to your wishes as far as I possibly could.' The boring explanations usual in such cases followed and the tangle was straightened out. But Lord Randolph got his way: the Duke of Connaught did not get the Bombay command while he was Secretary of State for India. It was left to Lord Salisbury to mollify the Queen, who could not see how she had offended 'because I had asked privately of Lord Dufferin, through Lord Salisbury, as to Arthur's fitness for Bombay'. However, Lord Randolph 'has since returned to reason, "having taken calomel", as Lord Salisbury amusingly words it, and is not going to resign'.

A few days later Salisbury reported to the Queen the Cabinet decision to hold on to the Zulficar Pass in the delimitation of frontiers with Afghanistan. Lord Randolph had wished to settle without standing out for it; Salisbury and the majority of the Cabinet would not hear of it. 'He spoke of Lord Randolph, in general, as being a great difficulty, but that his state of health had much to do with it.' This jar between them could not but bring home to the Prime Minister the success of his junior partner's technique of resignation or threatened resignation.

For the rest Lord Randolph made an unexpectedly good departmental chief. In spite of his own feeling in presiding over the venerable Council of India 'like an Eton boy presiding at a meeting of the Masters', his officials paid tribute to his instinctive ability for the work. He was quick to seize the essential points, clear-minded and hard-working. What surprised people was that such a man could be conciliatory, sensitive and tactful. Officials found him skilful at devolving subordinate business and remarkably persuasive when he wanted anything. When all was over between them Lord Salisbury singled out as Randolph's greatest gift that of attaching to himself the unlimited devotion of his subordinates. Like Chatham he does not seem to have had the art of working with equals.

Nor would it have been like him if his career at the India Office had not ended with a paradox. The Little Englander annexed Burma outright. Burmese government was in a frightful state of disintegration and decay: murders, massacres, outrages multipled upon its own subjects; upon the foreign trading community vexations, insults, threats. The miserable ruler, King Theebaw, tried to play off the French against the British; this, at the threshold of India, was too much. He was presented with the demand to admit a British mission; Lord Randolph telegraphed that 'its dispatch should be concurrent with movement of troops and ships to Rangoon. If ultimatum is rejected, the advance on Mandalay ought to be immediate. On the other hand, armed demonstration might bring Burmese to their senses.' It did. Neither Lord Salisbury nor the Government of India wished for annexation. But Lord Randolph's will prevailed: for the next half century the Burmese people experienced an intermission from murder, outrage and massacre as methods of government.

Lord Salisbury's conduct of his administration, firm and sagacious over foreign affairs, did much to recover the country's prestige abroad where Mr. Gladstone had lost so much ground. No one was more appreciative of this than the Queen. But the internal difficulties of governing in a minority were insuperable, and Ireland exerted a distracting influence. Lord Randolph despaired of the parliamentary difficulties they met with and was anxious to be quit of the whole business. The Queen was tougher: 'the youngest member of the Cabinet must *not* be allowed to dictate to the others. It will *not* do, and Lord Salisbury must really put his foot down.' It did not do: when Lord Salisbury found in turn that it was not possible to govern Ireland without coercion, Lord Randolph and his friend Hicks-Beach threatened resignation rather than accept it. They were wrong: in a few weeks it had to be resorted to. Lord Salisbury wrote Randolph a very wise, forbearing letter on the duty of the government not being afraid to govern; he had gone all lengths to sacrifice his own opinion for the sake of unity in the Cabinet. 'Internally as well as externally our position as a government is intolerable.... I am feverishly anxious to be out,' and very shortly, in January 1886, he was.

Mr. Gladstone was feverishly anxious to be in and the Liberals anticipated the result of the election with some confidence. They were wrong, and it was precisely the areas where Lord Randolph's appeal was strongest, the big cities, that put them wrong. The election was enlivened by a celebrated trope from him, comparing the Whig leader Lord Hartington to a boa-constrictor having to swallow the various morsels of the Radical programme that Mr. Chamberlain handed out: 'the only difference between the boa-constrictor and the Marquis of Hartington is this—that the boa-constrictor enjoys his food [rabbits out of a hat] and thrives on it and Lord Hartington loathes his food and it makes him sick'. The result of this was to make another enemy, and a very powerful one: leader of the Liberal Unionists to be. The result of the election—the newly enfranchised rural voters coming to Mr. Gladstone's rescue—was a Liberal majority of 86, within which was a dissident wing of almost as many anti-Home Rulers; while Parnell's following of 86 held the balance in British politics. Mr. Gladstone would, even apart from his inclinations, be forced to come out in favour of Home Rule.

What will happen now? a friend asked Lord Randolph. 'I shall lead the Opposition for five years,' he replied. 'Then I shall be Prime Minister for five years. Then I shall die.' This turned out exactly right as to the term of life that remained to him: he must have had some inner knowledge that it would not be long. But the incalculable element in politics utterly falsified his other expectations.

The year 1886 was one of continuous political crisis. Mr. Gladstone introduced his Home Rule Bill and in the struggle over it Lord Randolph took the lead on his side, urgent, aggressive, hectic. We find him in constant touch with Lord Salisbury by letter, and their correspondence affords a fascinating contrast. Where Randolph is urgent, Lord Salisbury is patient and wise; where the junior partner is all for aggression, his leader is much more *rusé*, waiting for the inherent difficulties of his opponents to overwhelm them; where Randolph wants action, Lord Salisbury is content to put the onus on others, to hold himself in reserve until he alone is the master of the situation. It is a masterly object-lesson; it was lost on Lord Randolph.

Over Home Rule Mr. Gladstone divided his party for good. A large section of Liberal Unionists left the ranks. These consisted of two wings: there were the aristocratic Whigs led by Lord Hartington, whose views were naturally conservative and who were happier in association with Conservatives. The other wing, paradoxically, were those Radicals who followed Joseph Chamberlain, the catalytic effect of whose personality was to draw them out of their natural orbit, bring them too into association with the Tories, frustrate the natural development of a strong Radical Liberalism and distract the course of British politics for the next twenty years.

Lord Randolph expressed himself as ready to retire to make way for the Liberal Unionists: 'you will never get Whig support as long as I am in the government, and Whig support you must have. Very indifferent health makes me look forward irresistibly to idleness regained.' Lord Salisbury: 'if retirements are required for the sake of repose and Whig combinations I shall claim to retire with you in both respects'. Politicians are apt to talk like that; but in the event one of them was indispensable, the other found to be expendable. At the height of the contest Lord Randolph went across to Ulster—which Mr. Gladstone had not excepted from his Irish Bill and had put under the rule of a Dublin Parliament—and made a flaming speech. He coined the slogan 'Ulster will fight, and Ulster will be right', which was to be revived with shattering effect in future years and with unexpected impact on his son.

In Parliament an intervention of Lord Randolph's had a decisive consequence. In the excitement of debate he managed to make Mr. Gladstone commit himself to refusing to consider any substantial changes in the Bill as it was. That settled its fate. The Liberal dissidents voted against it; the government was defeated by 343 votes to 313.

The election that followed was an exceptionally critical one; both in the issue—for on it depended the political unity of the British Isles—and in its consequences for the future of parties. Few people at the time could have guessed that it would inaugurate a twenty-year long Tory ascendancy, when the natural thing, with the full extension of the franchise to the working-class, would have been to expect a dominant Liberalism with a Radical impulse. More than any other person, Joe Chamberlain was responsible for the distortions that followed—Tory Imperialism, a brash jingoism, the South African War, the poisoning of relations with Ireland. No wonder he was the most hated man in English politics.

The keynote of the election was set by Lord Randolph, and it was an intensely personal one, vulgar and very effective. Mr. Gladstone was 'the Old Man in a hurry'. This phrase fastened on him and became historic, in the way that only a phrase that speaks a historic truth does. Though one can have no doubt, after all that has happened since, that Gladstone was profoundly right in his intuition that self-government was the only answer to the Irish question, it is probably true that he was over-hasty and premature. If those decades had been given to the Liberals it might have been dealt with gradually, the obstacle of the House of Lords and all. Joe Chamberlain the Radical ruined that hope.

In the strategy of the election Lord Randolph again held a key-place. He more than anyone saw to it that the Liberal Unionists were not opposed by Tories, that the split did the maximum damage to the Liberals. The results were decisive. Lord Salisbury's majority was a composite one, but with the Liberal Unionists it was 118; it gave him a foundation upon which to govern for the next six years, no one could have foretold how securely—and perhaps only Lord Salisbury could have held them together.

Lord Randolph now got his reward. He was at the zenith of his popularity and power—of his powers, too, we may add. The *Yorkshire Post* said that he had 'touched the popular imagination as the eloquence of few men has ever done'; other Tory papers followed suit; even *The Times* became more sympathetic with success. At Bradford an address was presented him by some two hundred and forty Conservative delegates. The Tory leaders were very ready to accept the facts of the situation. Lord Salisbury offered him the Treasury with the Leadership of the House of Commons: at thirty-six he was the youngest since Pitt. John Tenniel in a famous *Punch* cartoon depicted him at the dispatch-box in the Leader's place, with the shade of Dizzy behind saying:

> You stand—at your age—where I stood after years
> Of waiting on Fortune and working on fools.

Dizzy's prophecy of some years before as to the future of Lord Randolph had now come true. A Liberal friend asked him, 'How long will your leadership last?' 'Six months,' he replied. 'And after that?' 'Westminster Abbey.' It lasted less than six months; there was no Westminster Abbey.

From the first the sage Lord Salisbury regarded it as an experiment, and Lord Randolph seems to have recognised that quite well. The Queen confided to her Journal, 'Lord Randolph, whom I felt to be a great experiment, Lord Salisbury said was very nervous, which was perhaps a good thing'. Others too were doubtful. A friend wrote to young Curzon, who started his career as an enthusiastic follower of Lord Randolph and became his assistant private secretary. 'I must confess to being a wee bit anxious as to how he will lead. A leader requires angelic temper: this, I fear, Lord Randolph has not.' A powerful enemy within the party, one of those who had to be removed from his propinquity to the Lords, wrote, 'I should be sorry to think that our future depended upon Randolph Churchill'. He would need to be very circumspect.

And in the first brief September session he was. Even the Cecils had to admit that he surprised 'even his admirers by the dignity and unprovocative skill of his leadership'. It was part of his duty to write nightly reports of the proceedings in the House to the Queen. Nothing could have been more dignified and proper—except that she was amused to find an offending morsel of tobacco in the official red box. From Balmoral she wrote him—writing-paper deep-edged in black, though it was more than twenty years since the Prince Consort died: 'Now that the Session is just over, the Queen wishes to write and thank Lord Randolph Churchill for his regular and full and interesting reports of the debates in the House of Commons, which must have been most trying. Lord Randolph has shown much skill and judgment in his leadership during this exceptional session of Parliament.'

In addition to the Leadership there was the Treasury. That province had been for so long dominated by Mr. Gladstone, where his financial orthodoxy was the prevailing religion, that Lord Randolph's arrival created consternation. 'I forget. Was I a bi-metallist when I was at the India Office?', he inquired gaily. It was like doubting the religion of the Gold Standard in the days of Montagu Norman. When it came to budgetary figures, 'I never could make out what those damned dots meant,' he said. Serious-minded officials, earnest Gladstonians, were shocked at such levity. But, indeed, Lord Randolph would have done better to act on the advice of an Irish friend and leave the Treasury to Goschen; not that he was incapable of running it, but that the double burden for one of his uncertain health and nervous excitement was too much.

His pre-eminence in the Commons and in the country made his position indisputable; and when he made his famous Dartford speech in October, outlining a whole programme of reform, he spoke, as Chamberlain noted, in the tone of a co-Premier. That, however, was not Lord Salisbury's idea, nor was the programme of reform, in which he had no belief. And, in fact, in the ironical way in which things work out in politics, with Lord Randolph's arrival at leadership, the political situation underneath had changed against him. With the secession of the Liberal Unionists he, who had hitherto been indispensable, could now be dispensed with—if it came to the point. Lord Randolph had been most active in paving the way for co-operation with the Liberal Unionists; but when it came about, it immensely strengthened Lord Salisbury's position as the pivot of power between the Tories and them. Some sense of this must have exasperated Lord Randolph—to arrive at the top and find that power was elsewhere; for exasperation was the keynote of his conduct in the following months. When to that was added the complete frustration of his ideas (he could not bear not to get his way), he was driven to despair, to make a desperate challenge.

The cool eye of the Cecils took in the situation. 'In dealing with Lord Randolph', Arthur Balfour's sister wrote, 'Lord Salisbury and his nephew were in the habit of taking long views.' 'The line I took with Randolph Churchill', said his friend, young Balfour, who succeeded to his place, 'was based on the supposition that it was better to have him with us than against us.' The innermost thoughts of Lord Salisbury are revealed in his correspondence with his nephew—blood, however rarefied, is thicker than water—as they waited to catch Lord Randolph out. 'I am inclined to think that we should avoid, as far as possible, all "rows" until Randolph puts himself entirely and flagrantly in the wrong by some act of party disloyalty which everybody can understand and nobody can deny. By this course we may avoid a battle altogether, but if a battle is forced upon us, we shall be forced to win it.'

Relations with Lord Salisbury were now of crucial importance—as his daughter recognises from his point of view: 'that chief, meditating upon its [the government's] prospects, was in fact more occupied with a problem of personality than with one of political programmes'. Lord Randolph did not hesitate to intervene in Lord Salisbury's sphere of foreign affairs, where the chief's judgment would be almost bound to be right. In the previous year Salisbury had engaged in a single-handed struggle to protect the union of Southern with Northern Bulgaria—against Russia and all the Continental powers. And against the wishes of the mercurial Randolph constantly protesting against our exasperating Russia, which had reversed her aggressive line since her war in Turkey, etc. Wise old monolith, how right Lord Salisbury was, and how much he deserved to be leader, when it came to the fundamental interests of the country! He stuck to his point and won against all Europe:

Bulgaria achieved a certain measure of independence with unity.

Now in September 1886 there was another threat of a forward Russian move, and Lord Randolph was not in favour of resisting Russia's advance in the Balkans. Salisbury thought that if Russia attacked Constantinople, we should act in the Dardanelles. Lord Randolph did not mind about Constantinople. Lord Salisbury: 'You are naturally sarcastic about my Dardanelles, and I hope the matter will not come up in our time. But the possession by Russia of Constantinople will be an awkward piece of news for the Minister who receives it.' Not content with opposing the Prime Minister on a matter where he knew far better, Lord Randolph discussed matters with both the Russian and German ambassadors—quite beyond his sphere. Upon this the chief came down firmly and unmistakably. 'I am afraid you are prepared to give up Constantinople: and foreign Powers will be quick enough to find that divergence out.... I consider the loss of Constantinople would be the ruin of our party and a heavy blow to the country: and therefore I am anxious to delay by all means Russia's advance to that goal.'

Who can doubt that the older and wiser man was right? Two world-wars have passed over us, and far too heavy a Russian domination has been imposed upon Eastern Europe. If Constantinople, gateway to the Mediterranean, had been given away then, it would have made an impossible situation.

Lord Randolph's ideas of internal policy were consistent with this little Englandism, and they were Radical ones. At Dartford in October he stood on the pinnacle of his popularity—many thousands of Conservatives to greet him, a hundred addresses from all over the country, celebrations in the town all day, fireworks at night. There were no fireworks in the speech, but he promised a Bill to enable agricultural labourers to acquire freehold plots and allotments—with grateful acknowledgments to Mr. Chamberlain. A Land Bill to make the transfer of land simple and cheap; a gradual transfer of the unpopular burden of tithe to the shoulders of the landlord. A reorganisation of local government with changes in the incidence of local taxation; reform and simplification of House of Commons procedure. Lastly he proclaimed his intention of reducing public expenditure and taxation.

The most deadly opponent of Mr. Gladstone was at work on a Gladstonian Budget. He was in fact bolder and more radical in his proposals than Mr. Gladstone would have been. We need not go in detail into the damned dots, but indicate simply the principles of the thing. His aim was to lighten the burden on the lower middle classes, to transfer it from necessaries to luxuries. He was budgeting for a large surplus to distribute in lower taxes on tea and tobacco, and to provide funds for an important new system of local government grants: he really meant his promises of reform. To get his surplus he aimed at an increase in death-duties and house-duties—hardly palatable to Conservatives or to be expected from a Conservative administration. Income-tax, in accordance with correct Gladstonian principles, he proposed to lower—*O fortunatos nimium*—from 8*d*. to 5*d*. in the pound.

Such was his power that the Cabinet, strange to say, accepted his Budget in principle; but there was bound to be a struggle with the spending departments over the particular economies to be enforced, and his colleagues were nearing the end of their patience. Lord Randolph was in complete disagreement with his colleagues over Local Government reform: he wanted the Radical programme of the abolition of the Poor Law and Boards of Guardians, and placing relief of the poor under the County Councils and District Councils. All this was looking decades ahead. He thought that the Liberal Unionists would support him; but the Whig majority among them was more conservative than the Conservatives. Only the Radical wing under Chamberlain was in sympathy, and Lord Randolph should have concerted his moves with them. He and Chamberlain were taken with the idea of some central combination in politics between them, as his son played with the idea of a National party later on in our time. Sir Winston refers wishfully to 'that solid basis of agreement upon middle courses, which is shared by many sensible people and was in those days abhorrent to party machines. Need one add that the party machines always prove the stronger?'[1]

Lord Salisbury was full of forebodings: he thought that the Cabinet would break up. On his side Lord Randolph was despairing. 'Alas! I see the Dartford programme crumbling into pieces every day. The Land Bill is rotten. I am afraid it is an idle schoolboy's dream to suppose that Tories can legislate—as I did, stupidly. They can govern and make war and increase taxation and expenditure *à merveille*, but legislation is not their province in a democratic constitution. I certainly have not the courage and energy to go on struggling against cliques, as poor Dizzy did all his life.' What he would have liked would be to bring Lord Salisbury—for whom he had a curiously filial feeling, affection and respect mingled with exasperation—over to his side; failing that, to force

1 Winston S. Churchill, *Great Contemporaries*, 15.

him. But Lord Salisbury was not the man to be forced.

The struggle with the tremendous *vis inertiae* of Conservatism at this time was wearing down Lord Randolph. The Queen noticed it when he came to dine at Windsor. 'We remained talking in the corridor till half past ten. Lady Randolph (an American) is very handsome and very dark. He said some strange things to me, which I will refer to later.' She gave Lord Salisbury a full account of their conversation, saying that she thought Lord Randolph looked very ill and winding up shrewdly, 'it looked as if he was likely to be disagreeable and wanted the Queen to agree with him'. Lord Randolph had, according to Salisbury, thrown a fly at the Queen—ought not the Conservatives to agree with the Liberal Unionists as far as possible? She thought it a mistake for Conservatives to alter their principles. Lord Salisbury knew that Randolph was mistaken in thinking the Liberal Unionists were with him.

Salisbury warned Lord Randolph what would happen in a most interesting letter politically. 'The classes and the dependants of class are the strongest ingredients in our composition, but we have so to conduct our legislation that we shall give some satisfaction to both classes and masses. This is specially difficult with the classes—because all legislation is rather unwelcome to them, as tending to disturb a state of things with which they are satisfied.' He thought the policy of hitting the 'classes' hard and trusting the democracy to see one through would fail. 'I do not mean that the "classes" will join issue with you on one of the measures which hits them hard, and beat you on that. That is not the way they fight. They will select some other matter on which they can appeal to prejudice, and on which they think the masses will be indifferent; and on this they will upset you.'

The breach came over the Services. Lord Randolph was determined on economies on both Army and Navy. He managed to get Lord George Hamilton at the Admiralty to cut down his estimates by £700,000—a very large sum then. Mr. W. H. Smith at the War Office was made of sterner stuff. He would not give way, and if he were made to, he would go. With the crude finality of a *nouveau riche* in these aristocratic discussions, he put the issue: 'it comes to this—is he to be *the* Government? If you are willing that he should be, I shall be delighted, but I could not go on on such conditions.'

When it came to the point Lord Salisbury was with the Services, as Lord Randolph expected. The outlook on the Continent was black, there was a distinct possibility of war: it was no time to be disarming. Lord Randolph was on his way to Windsor, when he told Lord George Hamilton quite casually that he meant to resign. But he said no word of it to the Queen, with whom he had a long and friendly conversation. On her writing-paper he wrote his resignation to Lord Salisbury— without a word of consultation with his friends, with Hicks-Beach who had made way for him and would certainly have dissuaded him; without consulting his wise old mother, or even his wife; without concerting any measures with sympathisers like Chamberlain. Lord Salisbury replied in a letter which, we now know, was not intended as an acceptance of resignation, but placed the onus squarely on Lord Randolph—acceptance of his, the Prime Minister's, decision. Lord Randolph was not the one to submit: he felt too much committed. He sent word of his resignation to the newspapers.

When the final word reached Hatfield a ball was in progress; Lord Randolph's mother and sister were members of the house-party. Next morning Lord and Lady Salisbury were to be up early to see them off. The sagacious Prime Minister, knowing what to expect in *The Times* that morning—as skilful a tactician in small matters as in great—decided that they should oversleep. The guests departed without any awkward farewells.

The resignation was for the moment a tremendous blow to the government—the suddenness of it, the unexpectedness by the public, in whose eyes Lord Randolph stood forth as the popular champion. Moreover, was he replaceable? On the Conservative side there was no one to replace him. For a few days the government rocked, and people expected it to fall. But it was precisely in adverse circumstances that Salisbury's strongest qualities came to the fore. He made the masterly move of once more offering to make way for Hartington; of course, the Liberal Unionists could not form a government. But out of the manoeuvre he recruited their ablest financial brain, Goschen—superior in this sphere to anyone else in the House—as Chancellor of the Exchequer. At the Treasury, then, Lord Randolph was most successfully replaced—and this is the significance of his best known, but perhaps apocryphal, remark that he 'forgot Goschen'. For Leader of the House the Prime Minister turned to Mr. W. H. Smith. It was Mr. Smith of the vineries and pineries who had brought brilliant Lord Randolph down. He made a most successful Leader of the House. He received his reward: the family of Smith was ennobled, recruited to the peerage and, a more select accolade, intermarried with the Cecils. Had not the great Lord Burghley said, centuries before, 'What is gentility but ancient riches'?

For Lord Randolph the resignation was mortal; and a moment afterwards, in a flash of self-knowledge, he recognised that it was so. 'In inflicting on the Old Gang this final fatal blow, I have mortally wounded myself.' He had indeed; there was to be no forgiveness, no remission for him. So far as the Tory party was concerned he had committed the irreparable offence: he had imperilled the unity of the party, and even its existence, for the sake of playing his own hand. Now that he was down all the antipathies he had provoked could come into the open; now that he had lost power it was safe for anybody to attack him. There was no protection, no quarter given; for his was the unpardonable offence. For the rest of his life Lord Randolph was a marked man; there was never any return. Lucifer had fallen from among the stars.

Salisbury's daughter has an admirable phrase to describe, fairly neutrally, the 'strongest force at work' against him: 'the instinctive British recalcitrance to an exaggerated personal claim'. It is true that there is something un-English about the personality of Lord Randolph: he is much more like Celts we have known. Perhaps that is why he had an instinctive sympathy with the Irish and got on so well with them. And it may be by the same token that he was so exasperated, as Celts are apt to be, by the imperturbable impersonality of the English, a certain immobility that looks like sheer insensitiveness. Is it possible that the three generations of Stewarts from whom he was descended—mother, grandmother, great-grandmother—brought some such influence into his blood? For all his characteristics are so very much those of the Celt: the surface gaiety and effervescence, the melancholy and depression underneath; the mixture of extreme charm with aggression, of sensitiveness and tact with a biting tongue and willingness to wound; the very personal colouring of his judgment and of his reactions, the emotionalism; the quickness of perception, the lack of staying power; the quivering self-esteem, the streak of genius and ultimate defencelessness.

He was up against a very powerful English type in Lord Salisbury, with the legions behind him. The Prime Minister made an interesting comment on the political reasons for his fall: he ascribed it to 'his resolution to make the interests of his Budget overrule the wishes and necessities of all the other Departments and, secondly, his friendship for Chamberlain which made him insist that we should accept that statesman as our guide in internal politics'. Of the Prime Minister Lord Randolph never said anything harsher than 'What a fool Lord S. was to let me go so easily!'

But Lord Salisbury was never at any time a fool about anything: it is fairly safe to say that the younger man never penetrated the reserves of wisdom, the recesses of subtlety, of the older man's mind. Yet he had a vast respect for it. Lord Salisbury had, he said, 'a mighty intellect'; to argue with him was like 'arguing with a rock'; and then, with a curiously feminine movement of mind, 'he might have made what he pleased of me'. That would have been a whole-time job, and Lord Salisbury had the country to govern, his party to manage.

Their last exchange was a very moving one. Old Sir Stafford Northcote, now Lord Iddesleigh, was dropped from the Foreign Office on the reconstruction of the government. By some misunderstanding he learned of his demotion before Lord Salisbury could see him and explain to him what he had in mind. When he came to see the Prime Minister at 10 Downing Street, the old man was suddenly struck down and died in his presence. Lord Randolph at once wrote a letter which Salisbury's daughter describes as exemplifying 'the qualities which, in spite of all defects, made him so singularly attractive a character to his fellows'. Lord Salisbury responded even more remarkably. 'I had never happened to see anyone die before—and therefore, even apart from the circumstances, the suddenness of this unexpected death would have been shocking. But here was, in addition, the thought of our thirty years' companionship in political life, and the reflection that now, just before this sudden parting, by some strange misunderstanding, which it is hopeless to explain, I had, I believe, for the first time in my life, seriously wounded his feelings. As I looked upon the dead body stretched before me, I felt that politics was a cursed profession.'

In that, for once, the reserve is pierced and one looks into the heart of a man who knew all about the underlying tragic element in life.

The remaining years of Lord Randolph offered a sad anticlimax to such a career. Mr. Gladstone, with his immense experience of politics, judged that he was one of the rare cases of those who had committed political suicide. He noted in his Journal that the method of the resignation was an 'outrage' as against the Queen and also against the Prime Minister: 'this, of course, they will work against him'. They did.

For the next three years, nevertheless, he remained a leading figure in politics, though an isolated one. He continued to speak at the top of his form. One of his speeches has a masterly passage about Podsnap and Podsnappery in politics—and that was one of his troubles: he was too candid: he had no humbug. Lourdes, for example, he thought, 'a monument to *la bêtise humaine*'. His speeches continued to be reported in full, as only those of the Prime Minister and Mr. Gladstone were. He remained always 'news'. And not only in this country: when he journeyed on the Continent, visiting Berlin and St. Petersburg, people wondered what he was up to now. But politics is about power: he was a political leader without power. He was left to eat his heart.

One observes his increasing realisation of this in the accents of his letters. In 1887: 'when the Old Gang with their ideas are quite played out and proved to be utter failures, then, perhaps, people will turn to the young lot. Till this time comes, and I do not think it is far off, I must wait patiently.' A little later: 'I own W. H. Smith has done better than I expected, for I expected a complete breakdown'. Mr. Gladstone judged Lord Randolph's Budget speech of that year 'excellent'; but it was no consolation to the latter that the government was now adhering to his ideas on economy with regard to the Services. That, too, often happens.

In this year he and Chamberlain were attempting to co-operate. It ended in bitter disappointment for Lord Randolph. In Birmingham he had a large working-class following, and his supporters wished him to stand for a seat there. Then he found that his friend Chamberlain not merely had no intention of sharing any power with him in his own preserve, but was not even willing to permit Lord Randolph's candidature for one of the seats. This ended those prospects of co-operation.

Over Ireland he came into open conflict with his party. So long as Parnell remained all-powerful there could be no peace in Ireland without Home Rule. The Tories were determined to snatch at any and every chance to ruin him; and by this time understandably sickened by the methods of Irish resistance—the maiming of cattle, arson and wanton damage—they wanted Ireland governed with a firm hand anyway. They now got it from of all people, Randolph's junior associate in the Fourth Party, Arthur Balfour: the Prime Minister's nephew displayed unexpected courage and resource in the Irish Chief Secretaryship, while his debating ability in the House indicated that soon Lord Randolph would have an equal. The latter retained his sympathies with the Irish people and resented the strong hand—the imprisonment of Irish M.P.s, coercion—the Tories had always wanted. When the party snatched at the forged Pigott letters to discredit the Irish leader, and on the discovery of the forgery found themselves faced with the prospect of a Liberal and Nationalist victory, Lord Randolph, genuinely ashamed and shocked, assailed the Tory party in the most furious of his invectives. When he paused, exhausted—for he was already ill—no one in the ranks around him would so much as fetch him a glass of water.

His breach with his own party seemed complete: he should really have gone over to the Liberals. But he did not agree with them over Home Rule. This left him isolated and utterly impotent.

When he travelled abroad the Old Gang had their eye on him. In the winter of 1887-8 when he went to Russia and to Germany, and had conversations with the Czar and with Bismarck, the Queen wrote to Lord Salisbury to see to it that foreign governments and the country knew that Lord Randolph was going simply on a private journey in no way charged with any message or mission from government, nor was likely to return to it. Lord Salisbury did not need telling: he assured her that the information had been relayed to St. Petersburg, Berlin and Vienna. *The Times* had been plainly instructed. The visit had been encouraged by the Prince of Wales, whose friendship now proved constant and strong. He had highly approved of Randolph's appointment as Leader and Chancellor, and after his fall proved a good friend to him in adversity. They were constantly together at race-meetings, and of this the Queen disapproved, warning the Prince that intimacy with one 'so changeable and indiscreet' was compromising. On his return from Russia Lord Randolph reported at length on his conversations to the Prince. That would give no pleasure to Queen Victoria, who continued to withhold official papers from him on the ground that he was not sufficiently responsible. She was merely jealous, in the Hanoverian manner.

In his long conversation with the Czar Lord Randolph observed perfect propriety and loyalty to Lord Salisbury, whom the Czar regarded as an enemy to Russia. On his return he duly reported his impressions to the Prime Minister, who forwarded an account to the Queen. But, he added, Lord Randolph did not mention some things which 'we know he said to Herbert Bismarck.' His policy is for us to line up with France and Russia: France will give way to us in Egypt, Russia will not molest us in India. 'It is odd that so clever a man should attach the slightest value to such a promise on the part of Russia.' He had told his friends that the post of all others he would like is Viceroy of India. 'Of course it is impossible; his reputation for rashness is too pronounced. But it is odd that he should desire it. It is said that his pecuniary position is very bad.' One observes the accents of dislike: Lord Salisbury and Lord Randolph who should have been complementary were now antithetical.

In these circumstances of complete frustration he ceased to speak in the House and went more and more abroad. In 1891 he accepted an invitation from Cecil Rhodes to go to South Africa and travel up-country to Mashonaland, and he went in search of health and peace of mind. At once his journey was 'news', and the *Daily Graphic* offered him a large sum of money for a series of letters describing it. These were published next year as a book, *Men, Mines and Animals in South Africa.* Received in an unfriendly critical spirit, it is a characteristic production and makes interesting reading: vividly and well-written, though its manner is off-hand and disillusioned. The fact was his heart was in politics at home; as happens to politicians he could not do without the drug.

He left Dartmouth in the *Grantully Castle,* in which Mr. Gladstone had performed his much-advertised 'periplus' round Britain, of which Randolph had made such fun in happier years. Arrived in South Africa he made amends by praising the magnanimity of Gladstone's peace giving up the Transvaal ten years before: it had won the confidence of the Cape Dutch, which Cecil Rhodes was now enjoying. Without it there would have been no confidence—though he had no illusions about the up-country Boers. 'The Dutch settlers in Cape Colony are as worthy of praise as their relatives, the Transvaal Boers, are of blame. The former loyal, thrifty, industrious, hospitable, liberal, are and will, I trust, ever remain the backbone of our great colony at the Cape of Good Hope.' He wished they might transmit some of their good qualities to 'their backward brethren in the Transvaal'. The Transvaal betrayed their bad and lazy farming, the thousands of acres carrying only a few hundred head of cattle; roads in a frightful state, even the main highway from Johannesburg to Pretoria, a mere thirty-five miles, in a shocking condition. There was the insolent denial by the Boers of all political or even municipal rights to persons other than of Dutch birth, in addition to their 'vicious and cruel sentiments to the native races'. These names, Pretoria, Potchefstroom, Mafeking, were soon to re-echo round the world.

At Mafeking he heard news that brought back all the old bitterness and at the same time made him long to be home. 'So

Arthur Balfour is really Leader—and Tory Democracy, the genuine article, at an end! Well, I have had quite enough of it all. I have waited with great patience for the tide to turn, but it has not turned, and will not now turn in time. . . . More than two-thirds, in all probability, of my life is over, and I will not spend the remainder of my years in beating my head against a stone wall. I expect I have made great mistakes; but there has been no consideration, no indulgence, no memory or gratitude—nothing but spite, malice and abuse. . . . All confirms me in my decision to have done with politics and try to make a little money for the boys and for ourselves.'

However, when the election came and the Liberals took office once more, though in a minority, he could not resist the drug: his party had need of him in Opposition and everybody thought that opposition would recover his powers. His disease was gaining upon him, and his articulation was not what it had been. It was noticed that Mr. Gladstone, now over eighty—with his customary courtesy, his manners so much better than those of the aristocrats—was always in his place to hear what Lord Randolph had to say. He reported to the Queen on the Home Rule debate that his 'renewed participation in a great discussion, after two years of absence or silence, excited interest in the House and was greeted with warm cheering by his own party'. Mr. Gladstone added that his criticisms were less incisive than Balfour's, 'perhaps owing to the fact that he did not for the moment seem to be at the highest level of his physical energies'. Harcourt thought that the speech regained some of his old influence with his party; but the truth was that he was going down-hill physically.

In these last years his views took an even more Radical turn. He had always had a peculiar, possibly a premature, sensitiveness about the way things were to go in society, perhaps with too little regard for the way they were at the moment. Now he sensed the emergence of the working-class as the foremost thing in the politics of the future. His views took on a collectivist tinge. He was anxious for the House of Commons to examine the demand for an eight-hour day; without further ado he expressed himself in favour of an eight-hour day for the miners—on this he was more radical than Mr. Gladstone, who always remained an addict to Manchester doctrines. Lord Randolph wrote, with perceptive foresight: 'the Labour interest is now seeking to do itself what the landed interest and the manufacturing capitalist interest did for themselves when each in turn commanded the disposition of State policy. Our land laws were framed by the landed interest for the advantage of the landed interest, and foreign policy was directed by that interest to the same end. Political power passed very considerably from the landed interest to the manufacturing capitalist, and our whole fiscal system was shaped by this latter power to its own advantage, foreign policy being also made to coincide. We are now come, or are coming fast, to a time when Labour laws will be made by the Labour interest for the advantage of Labour.'

We see that, on the essential point, neither Lord Salisbury nor Lord Randolph had much to learn from Karl Marx.

The Cecils, as we know from Lady Gwendolen's cool appraisal, never took Tory Democracy seriously. From this point of view, now that it is all long over—though it made an immense perturbation in their day—we can see that his split with Lord Salisbury had a certain historical rightness. They did not mean the same thing. Lord Randolph both meant his Radicalism and thought it was the way to revivify the Tory party. The Tory party did not and therefore found him intolerable. As it happened, the orthodox Tories were right in the short run: the split in the Liberal party made it unnecessary to resort to Lord Randolph's ideas, while he himself could be dispensed with. Lord Salisbury's nephew, Balfour, took his place. Lord Randolph may be said to have had his delayed revenge with his sons's going over to the Liberals in time for the great landslide of 1906 in their favour.

It is possible that had he lived he would have moved over to the Liberal party—such is the conclusion that suggests itself from his son's biography—and that would have been a development consistent with his ideas. By the time of their victory he was long dead. After a last world-tour in 1894, in vain search of health, he came back to die in his mother's house, 24 January 1895. His friend Lord Rosebery, who knew him best, pays him the best tribute. 'He had a faithful and warm heart; from childhood he had been the best of sons; and the whole soul of his mother was with him to the end. Nothing could exceed the pathos of her devotion to him in political adversity, or to his memory when he had passed away. . . . I see, as all the public saw, many faults; but I remember what the public could not know, the generous, lovable nature of the man. I cannot forget the pathos of the story; I mourn as all must mourn that he had not time to retrieve himself, not time to display his highest nature; I grieve, as all must grieve, that that daring and gifted spirit, should have been extinguished at an age when its work should only have just begun.'

Lord Salisbury lies on his tomb in Westminster Abbey, majestic and serene. Lord Randolph lies in the country churchyard at Bladon, among the grey slabs on the sunny south side of the church—Jennie beside him—just across from the park and the great house that gave him birth.

CHAPTER EIGHT

The Young Winston

IT would have been a great surprise to Lord Randolph to learn that his son would qualify for the Westminster Abbey burial he himself missed. Lord Randolph had been the kind of bright boy not unusual at school; his elder son was backward in an unusual way, not through lack of intelligence, but through sheer self-will and because his interest was not intelligently engaged or aroused. Where it was, he did well enough and even won a prize or two; but the ordinary classical grind of Victorian times both at his private and his public school—dominantly concerned with Latin and Greek, excruciatingly linguistic and grammatical—put him off. Even at this early age he was not going to have it, and he did badly. It is obvious that Lord Randolph was disappointed in his offspring.

We may surmise that he was always rather a handful. Lady Randolph reports to her mother when he was five that he was a good boy and getting on with his lessons, 'but he is a most difficult child to manage'. After what we know of his father, and of his American grandfather, we need not wonder. The one person who could manage him, and that by unstinted love, was his nurse Mrs. Everest—suitably named, we may suppose, for her task. His mother 'shone for me like the Evening Star. I loved her dearly—but at a distance. My nurse was my confidante. Mrs. Everest it was who looked after me and tended all my wants. It was to her I poured out my many troubles, both now and in my schooldays.'[1] Not even she could always command obedience; once when he could not get his own way he threatened, as the wickedest thing he could think of—for Mrs. Everest enjoyed a very Low Church form of piety—that he would go and 'worship idols'.

The usual feminine jealousies intervened to complicate matters. His grandmother, the old Duchess, wanted him at Blenheim: 'I must say I am very much disappointed at Winston's not being

[1] Churchill, *My Early Life,* 19.

allowed to come here for a few days. I had made every arrangement to take great care of him knowing he is susceptible to colds, and I do not think there could have been as much danger as there is in going to Pantomimes in London. Besides I feel it's all an excuse of that horrid old Everest to prevent my having him and his being happy with his cousins without her. . . . I hardly ever see him, and must say I am very much vexed. He is not fit to go to Harrow if he is not fit for a visit here. The house is quite warm.' Blenheim Palace in December, before the days of central heating!—it is evident that her ideas of warmth were of a Spartan Victorianism. It is also evident that Everest had defeated the Duchess—and perhaps this was one reason for her not liking the boy who remained right up to twenty-three, curious to think, heir presumptive to the dukedom and to Blenheim.

Affection for his nurse survived the adolescent cynicism of the atmosphere of a public school, or rather the young Winston was impervious to it. His cousin relates as a marked example of moral courage that when his old nurse came down to see him at Harrow in her poke-bonnet, he walked her all round the school and in public kissed her goodbye. He was a subaltern at Aldershot when she fell dangerously ill; he at once rushed up to London to be with her at the last: 'she had been my dearest and most intimate friend during the whole of the twenty years I had lived'. He cites her life as having given him an impulse towards building the fabric of social insurance, sickness and old age pensions he took part in under the Liberal government of 1906. On a more personal note we see early displayed the loyalty of his nature, the fidelity and good heartedness so strong in his make-up: I think we may say, for a politician, so exceptionally strong.

School tore him away from Mrs. Everest, and he did not like it. At home there had been the mechanical toys of the nursery, a magic lantern, a real steam-engine, and almost a thousand lead soldiers. (One sees those that are left still at Chartwell.) His cousin, Clare Sheridan—Clara Jerome's daughter—was much impressed. 'He filled me with awe. His playroom contained from one end to the other a plank table on trestles, upon which were thousands [*sic*] of lead soldiers arranged for battle. He organised wars. The lead battalions were manoeuvred into action, peas and pebbles committed great casualties, forts were stormed, cavalry charged, bridges were destroyed—real water tanks engulfed the advancing foe.' With all young animals the play-instinct foreshadows the future.

At his first private school he made the acquaintance of Latin, and a very funny account of the experience he gives. Declining *mensa* was not recommended in any way to his reason, so he declined to regard the subject with any respect and was frequently flogged. He makes a useful pedagogical comment: 'perhaps if I had been introduced to the ancients through their history and customs, instead of through their grammar and syntax, I might have had a better record'. Taken away from this horrid school, which he hated and where he was made ill, he was sent to a less pretentious place where he was happy and learned things that interested him: history and poetry and French, above all, riding and swimming. And there were some delightful volumes of cartoons from *Punch*, which early aroused an interest in politics and recent history—even if their suggestions as to remoter history were apt to lead one a little astray. Mr. Gladstone, for example, often appeared looking like Julius Caesar; it was long before the young Winston learned that Julius Caesar was not at all what a virtuous Victorian like Mr. Gladstone should be. From *Punch* too he gained his first interest in the American Civil War—not at all a bad source. Then there were the cartoons of his famous father, depicted always as a very little man though he was really of 'quite a passable stature'.

From here he went on to Harrow where he met the classics in even more august array. His first term was marked by a collision with a sixth-former, a short, squat boy whom he took to be a junior and, coming up behind him, pushed into the swimming-pool. The boy turned out to be immensely strong and swift, head of his house, champion at gym and what not. An explanation with apology was necessitated: 'I mistook you for a Fourth Form boy. You are so small.' A sense of the inadequacy of this made him recover himself with, 'My father, who is a great man, is also small'. This was better received and formed the foundation of a life-long friendship with Leo Amery, colleagues as war-correspondents, in the House of Commons and in various Cabinets. It is nice to have all been at the same school together.

Latin, however, remained a stumbling-block: either he could not, or more probably would not, learn it. So he learned English instead from an admirable master who taught it properly—as it was not taught in the public schools—to whom he confesses his indebtedness as a writer subsequently. Who can doubt that this was a better idea? 'When in after years my school-fellows who had won prizes and distinction for writing such beautiful Latin poetry and pithy Greek epigrams had to come down again to common English, to earn their living or make their way, I did not feel myself at any disadvantage. Naturally I am biassed in favour of boys learning English. I would make them all learn English: and then I would let the clever ones learn Latin as an honour, and Greek as a treat.'

However, this kept him in the lower school; he never got into the upper: he stagnated in the bottom form until he went with the other dunces into the Army class. He was an odd case, for at the same time he won a prize for reciting twelve hundred lines of Macaulay's *Lays* without a mistake, could quote whole scenes from Shakespeare and had no hesitation in correcting the masters if they misquoted. He was building up a prodigious memory, subconsciously strengthening his tough mental aptitudes by feeding on what he liked and refusing what he did not like. He was evidently a fair terror. Mr. Amery remembered him as a rather inky small boy, grubby and obstinate. Another contemporary tells us that 'he consistently broke almost every rule made by masters or boys, was quite incorrigible, and had an unlimited vocabulary of "back-chat", which he produced with dauntless courage on every occasion of remonstrance'. Not interested in football or cricket either, and making no pretence of it, he was pretty clearly not a popular figure.

'I was on the whole considerably discouraged by my school days,' he concludes, 'I am all for the Public Schools but I do not want to go there again.' He adds a comment not without malice, and another not without pathos. 'Most of the boys were very happy, and many found in its class-rooms and upon playing fields the greatest distinction they have ever known in life. . . . I would far rather have been apprenticed as a bricklayer's mate, or run errands as a messenger boy, or helped my father to dress the front windows of a grocer's shop. It would have been real; it would have been natural; it would have taught me more; and I should have done it much better. Also I should have got to know my father, which would have been a joy to me.'

In later years he has made it up with Harrow. In the autumn of 1940, after all the strain and glory of the events of that year, after the Battle of Britain had saved the country, he went back there as Prime Minister. Perhaps he felt some need for renewed contact with his youth, some unconscious sense of putting it right with his remote past: there could not have been a better moment for rehabilitation. Once more he sat there in the Speech Room with the other boys, singing the famous Harrow songs, tears in his eyes.

Called on to speak—after half a century—he said, 'I like the song "Boy", although when I was at the school I did not advance to that position of authority which entitles one to make that call'. He had only been a fag to other boys—perhaps a useful apprenticeship for doing the nation's chores. Reconciliation effected, he took pleasure and found solace in going back every year to his old school amid all the strain and anxieties of the war and post-war years. On one visit, in November 1942, just after the landings in North Africa, he paid tribute to what the Harrow songs had meant for him: 'You have the songs of Bowen and Howson (whom I remember well as housemasters here) with the music of John Farmer and Eaton Fanning. They are wonderful; marvellous; more than could be put into brick and mortar, or treasured in any trophies of silver or gold. They grow with the years. I treasure them and sing them with joy.'

It is clear that he was a disappointment to his father, who decided that, since he was not clever enough to go to the Bar, the Army had better be his lot. But this also involved examinations: it took him three tries, and a special crammer's, to get him into Sandhurst. The monster in the path here was not Latin but mathematics—another, and more sympathetic, allergy. After his second attempt, when on holiday, he had a dreadful accident which might well have ended any further attempts at anything. He was playing a game with his cousins in a chine at Bournemouth when, to avoid capture, he jumped off a bridge hoping to catch the branches of a fir-tree and fell thirty feet to hard ground. He was very badly injured, with a ruptured kidney among other things, was for days unconscious and in bed for more than three months. 'It is to the surgeon's art and to my own pronounced will-to-live that the reader is indebted for this story [*My Early Life*]. But for a year I looked at life round a corner.' I have heard it said, and it is probable enough, that it was this long illness that matured and ripened his faculties, gave him time to ponder, something to think about.

When he recovered he passed into Sandhurst, qualifying for a cavalry cadetship, which was easier than an infantry one, since life in the cavalry was so much more expensive. Lord Randolph, who was now heavily in debt, did not hold with this: 'he thought it very discreditable that I had not qualified for the infantry'. A certain embarrassment appears in the attitude of Lord Randolph towards his son. A quick and well-trained mind like his must have been baffled coming up against such an odd case: one sympathises with his vexation at finding, after all the money spent on his boy's education, that he did not know what the Grand Remonstrance was. The boy, on the other hand, was genuinely puzzled why his father thought it so important. The time was coming when he would want to know all about it himself, and then he would appreciate its importance. What is so striking is the sudden, and belated, awakening.

This did not take place, alas, till the father was dead. On the son's side there had always been devotion and a partisan pride. He was aware of the tragedy of his father's life and of the bitterness and resentment that were gnawing at him. 'Although in the past little had been said in my hearing, one could not grow up in my father's house, and still less among his mother and sisters, without understanding that there had been a great political disaster.' He longed to take up the cudgels on his behalf, most of all that his father would admit him to his confidence. 'But if ever I began to show the slightest idea of comradeship, he was immediately offended; and when once I suggested that I might help his private secretary to write some of his letters, he froze me into stone. . . . Had he lived another four or five years, he could not have done without me. But there were no four or five years!'

He had just passed out of Sandhurst and was in his twenty-first year when his father died. 'All my dreams of comradeship with him, of entering Parliament at his side, and in his support, were ended. There remained for me only to pursue his aims and vindicate his memory.'

They were all living under the old Duchess's roof in Grosvenor Square at the time to save expense. On his South African tour Lord Randolph had made a very fortunate investment in the Rand. If he had lived he would have been a rich man from it; now, when sold, it was just enough to pay his debts—some £70,000. Jennie was provided for by her marriage settlement; but as for the young cavalry officer, 'I was now in the main the master of my fortunes'; in other words, he had his way to make for himself—as much as any working-class or middle-class lad moving out into the world, except that he had the advantage of all those connexions, family and political, with Blenheim always in the background. Then, too, there was his mother—worth a whole Army corps in herself: 'she soon became an ardent ally, furthering my plans and guarding my interests with all her influence and boundless energy. She was still at forty young, beautiful and fascinating. We worked together on even terms, more like brother and sister than mother and son. At least so it seemed to me. And so it continued to the end.'

In those days, the summer training season over, all good cavalry officers settled down to five months' hunting in the autumn and winter. This young subaltern could not afford that—besides, he had spent all his money on polo ponies. So he decided to go off and attend a war in progress. 'Rarity in a desirable commodity is usually the cause of enhanced value; and there has never been a time when war service was held in so much esteem by the military authorities or more ardently sought by officers of every rank.' Spain was having trouble in Cuba, last of her American possessions. It was a guerrilla war on a considerable scale, with Spain having to keep a quarter of a million men at the end of the long Atlantic line; a war on the pattern that soon became familiar in South Africa, Malaya, Indo-China, Cyprus. And it ended in the intervention of the United States upon her first grand incursion into benevolent imperialism. Theodore Roosevelt, Colonel of the Rough Riders—perhaps the closest in temperament to Churchill of all modern figures—was in at the end; Lieutenant Churchill, his junior by sixteen years, was in at the beginning.

It was his father's old partner in the Fourth Party, Sir Henry Wolff, ambassador at Madrid, who got all the necessary passes and documents from the Spanish authorities. Arrived in Cuba young Churchill joined a mobile column under General Valdez at Sancti Spiritus, a place very unhealthy with yellow fever and smallpox. Here he got the experience he had travelled thousands of miles for, on money he could ill afford, of being under fire. The fire does not seem to have been much, but fire it was on several occasions as the column wound its way along like a snake in the humid jungle. Once he received some shelter from the neighbouring hammock where hung a Spanish officer of substantial physique, 'indeed one might almost have called him fat. I have never been prejudiced against fat men.' The Lieutenant slept all the sounder. But he might easily have perished of yellow fever, or enteric, or smallpox, or typhoid. Instead, when the column got back to the coast Lieutenant Churchill, perfectly sound and better informed, sailed for home: his well-spent leave was up.

When he first left school for Sandhurst he had been kept for several months in the Awkward Squad, containing those who needed bringing up to scratch. When he passed out, it was with honours, and he was eighth in a batch of a hundred and fifty: his interest had been engaged and from this moment one sees him making firm strides. There was plenty of leeway to make up, and there were still apt to be the *contretemps* that are such a worry when one is young. Invited down to Deepdene by Lilian Duchess to meet the Prince of Wales, the subaltern was late; he had hoped to slip in unnoticed, but without him the party was thirteen. Edward couldn't bear unpunctuality; on the other hand, he wouldn't dream of sitting down thirteen at table; 'Don't they teach you to be punctual in your regiment, Winston?' he said severely. But it was here that he met Sir Bindon Blood, a foremost Indian Frontier commander, to whom he owed his next experience of action.

His regiment, the 4th Hussars, was posted to Bangalore in Southern India: excellent climate, 3000 feet up, a bungalow wreathed in roses and purple bougainvillea to share with one's friends, a butler, a boy to attend to one's wants, a syce to the ponies'—what more delightful for young men who were polo-addicts, for whom polo was the serious business of life? But there was one of them who found the long afternoon hours invaluable and it was then that he took his education in hand. He got his mother to send him packages of books. Someone had told him that his father admired Gibbon, had known whole pages by heart; so—'all through the long glistening middle hours of the Indian day, from when we quitted stables till the evening shadows proclaimed the hour of Polo, I devoured Gibbon. I rode triumphantly through it from end to end and enjoyed it all.' Next followed Macaulay, with whom he was more closely engaged in later years—and emerged victor from the struggle. He had long loved the *Lays*, but had never read a page of the *History*. Now he galloped through Macaulay, *Essays* and all. It is not surprising that, when he came to write, the joint influences are Gibbon and Macaulay—though at the same time, from the very first, a personal voice is heard, idiosyncratic, already recognisable.

Four or five hours a day he read: Plato and Aristotle, Malthus and Darwin, Lecky and Winwood Reade. It was very remarkable: this was his university, out there in a cavalry regiment in a British cantonment, in the intervals of polo. And he began for the first time to envy the young men who had had no difficulties with Latin and who were at the university where there were scholars to tell them what to read and what was what about it. There was the problem of Ethics, for instance: what did it mean? No one to tell him on the parade-ground at Bangalore. He began to read books that challenged the religious views received—or customs observed—at Harrow. He came to a dominantly secular view. 'I adopted a system of believing whatever I wanted to believe, while at the same time leaving reason to pursue whatever paths she was capable of treading.'

What one learns for oneself in this rough, tough fashion one is liable to hold on to more tenaciously. Another autodidact, picking up ideas for himself in the slums of Vienna not long after, became possessed of some very tenacious ideas. But the trouble with Hitler's demonic genius was that his *Weltanschauung* was at bottom uncritical: parts of it were utterly crazy, in the German manner, and he did not know whether it made sense intellectually or no. There is everything to be said for a strong tradition of tested common sense in a society and its schooling; and Churchill, though he was unaware of it at the time, imbibed that unconsciously at Harrow. Many years later when he went back, in the throes of the mortal struggle with Hitler, December 1940, he said—'Hitler, in one of his recent discourses, declared that the fight is between those who have been through the Adolf Hitler schools and those who have been at Eton. Hitler has forgotten Harrow.'

While he was at home on leave in the hot weather of 1897 a chance of action suddenly appeared on his horizon.The Pathans of the North-West Frontier broke out in revolt against the retention of an outpost at Chitral in their country and the construction of the military road leading to it: like the Britons in Roman Britain they knew too well what it meant: *Pax Britannica.* Lieutenant Churchill was at Goodwood, but he at once telegraphed Sir Bindon Blood, who had been placed in command of the Field Force to suppress the irruption, reminding him of his promise. Duchess Lilian's husband, of the powerful Beresford clan, was also brought into play. At Bombay Sir Bindon left a message that, since he had no vacancies, Churchill might come up as a war-correspondent. While he was getting leave of absence from his regiment, to report the war for the *Pioneer* newspaper, his mother arranged for these letters to be published in England by the *Daily Telegraph* at £5 a column, paying all his own expenses. ('I have improved upon this figure in later life.')

Hence a thrilling experience, of which he made the most, and his first book: '*The Story of the Malakand Field Force, An Episode of Frontier War.* By Winston L. Spencer Churchill, Lieutenant, the 4th Queen's Own Hussars.' The title-page has a motto drawn from Lord Salisbury: 'They (Frontier Wars) are but the surf that marks the edge and the advance of the wave of civilisation'. The book is dedicated to Sir Bindon Blood, to whom the author was indebted 'for the most valuable, and fascinating, experience of his life'—

with charming ingenuousness, for the author was only twenty-three and would have some more valuable experiences before he had finished. (A certain ingenuousness has always been a part of that personality made in a simple mould, direct and sincere.)

A lot of men could have played their parts in such an expedition, gone through the dangers and had the adventures he had—thousands did on the North-West Frontier; but only a very promising one could have written this book at twenty-three. He sees the Imperial theme—the influence of Gibbon is there: 'looking at the road running broad and white across the valley; at the soldiers moving along it; at the political officers extending their influence in all directions; at the bridge and fort of Chakdara; and at the growing cantonment on the Malakand Pass, it needs no education to appreciate its significance. Nor can any sophistry obscure it.'[1] But to this he adds a romantic feeling, to which he can already give unforced expression. At Mardan, the entrance to the pass up which the Force went to action, 'the passer-by should pause to see the guides' cemetery, perhaps the only regimental cemetery in the world. To this last resting-place under the palm-trees, close to the fields where they have played and the barracks in which they lived, have been borne the bodies of successive generations of these wardens of the marches, killed in action across the frontier line. It is a green and pleasant spot. Nor is there any place in the world where a soldier might lie in braver company.'[2]

The scene is very well set and the descriptive passages throughout are vivid and well written: one sees the places. Even more striking is the way in which, with a shock of recognition, one meets the sage of half a century later—such is the force of personality, the continuity of style. Of a Hindu saint by the banks of the Indus: 'the longer his riparian reflections were continued, the greater his sanctity became'. 'The religion of blood and war is face to face with that of peace. Luckily the religion of peace is usually better armed.' And naturally the personal accent, with such an individual, is stamped on every page: it could not be otherwise. Here he sees himself at both ends of the news: 'how different are the scenes. The club on an autumn evening—its members grouped anxiously around, discussing, wondering, asserting; the noise of the traffic outside; the cigarette smoke and electric lights within. And, only an hour away along the wire, the field, with the bright sunlight shining

[1] Churchill, *The Story of the Malakand Field Force* (ed. 1898), 34-5.

[2] *Ibid*, 16, 22, 41, 141.

on the swirling muddy waters; the black forbidding rocks; the white tents of the brigade a mile up the valley; the long streak of vivid green rice crop by the river; and in the foreground the brown-clad armed men. I can never doubt which is the right end to be at. It is better to be making the news than taking it; to be an actor rather than a critic.'

The letters to the *Daily Telegraph* had been well received in England, and now the book was an immediate success. The Prince of Wales, continuing his interest in Randolph's progeny, wrote him a letter of warm congratulation, adding 'you have plenty of time before you, and should certainly stick to the Army before adding M.P. to your name'. More important, he was summoned for an interview with Lord Salisbury, who had read his book with much interest. There was 'the Great Man, Master of the British world, the unchallenged leader of the Conservative Party, a third time Prime Minister and Foreign Secretary at the height of his long career' in that spacious room in the Foreign Office 'in which I was afterwards for many years from time to time to see much grave business done in Peace and War'.

The young officer appreciated the tremendous air about the old statesman and the grave courtesy with which he met him, conducted him to a small sofa in the vast room and said that the book had enabled him to form a truer picture of the fighting in the Frontier valleys than from any of the documents which he had had to read. In dismissing Randolph's son he said,'I hope you will allow me to say how much you remind me of your father, with whom such important days of my political life were lived. If there is anything at any time that I can do which would be of assistance to you, pray do not fail to let me know.' There very shortly was to come such an opportunity.

On his return to Bangalore he entertained himself in the long hot afternoons writing a Ruritanian romance, *Savrola*, which appeared in *Macmillan's Magazine* in 1897. In spite of his consistently urging his friends to abstain from reading it, it is well worth reading: not so much for the story, though that holds the attention, as for the light it throws upon the author and forward upon coming events. In the way Nature has of imitating Art, with the climax of bombardment of an insurgent capital by the Fleet, it might be about happenings in Buenos Aires. The novel has a love-interest: the revolutionary leader Savrola is in love with the wife of the President who is defeated. But who but Churchill would describe the situation with the words—'he was a young man, and Jupiter was not the only planet he admired'? His fellow-officers, to whom the book was dedicated, 'made various suggestions for stimulating the love interest which I was not able to accept'.

We recognise the hero sixty years back: 'his highly wrought temperament exaggerated every mood and passion; he always lived in the superlative. . . . Under any circumstances, in any situation, he knew himself a factor to be reckoned with.' The dreams of the youth reveal the man: here are the principles governing his life announced early. 'Would you rise in the world? You must work while others amuse themselves. Are you desirous of a reputation for courage? You must risk your life. Would you be strong morally or physically? You must resist temptations.' The naïveté, the egoism are patent and harmless; the fighting value of the convictions has received triumphant justification.

In 1898 Kitchener, the British Sirdar in command of the Egyptian army, judged that the moment was ripe for the re-conquest of the Sudan from the tyranny of the Dervish Empire. This was necessitated by the position of indirect rule, and certainly responsibility, Britain had taken on in Egypt as the result of Mr. Gladstone's bombardment of Alexandria. Since that detonating event the squalid and corrupt rule of the Khedives in Egypt had gradually given way to the fostering care of Lord Cromer, with the usual results. A hitherto bankrupt state now had surpluses to spend on internal improvements; the delights of party faction-fights had to give way to irrigation, agriculture, growing cotton. This, of course, was Imperialism; but ordinary folk prospered better under it, as even Wilfrid Scawen Blunt, the romantic anti-Imperialist and friend of the Egyptian Nationalists, had to admit. With the revival of the country and the progress it was making, there was the obligation to recover the Egyptian position in the Sudan. Egyptian rule there had been rapacious and incompetent; but the Dervish Empire was worse, a fanatic military barbarism extending its sway dangerously. There were the French to forestall, and Gordon to avenge. (It was Lord Randolph who had first raised the question of General Gordon's safety in those months in 1885 when Gladstone would take no action.)

After the tragedy and humiliation of Khartoum 'the British people averted their eyes in shame and vexation from the valley of the Nile'. Now the position was to be rectified. Kitchener had already got as far as the confluence of the Nile and the Atbara, where his mixed army of British and Egyptians had destroyed the Khalifa's lieutenant in a fierce battle. There remained the difficult advance up the Nile—cataracts, rapids, desert, disease—to Omdurman and the final reckoning with the whole strength of the Dervish Empire. Lieutenant Churchill was 'deeply anxious to share in this'.

He found himself up against unexpected resistance. Hitherto in the Army he had had pretty much his own way. Now he met a prevalent attitude that what he needed was a long period of discipline and routine; harsh words like 'self-advertiser' began to be used about him—from which he was hardly ever to be free till late in life. Other junior officers of his rank were accepted, while he was refused. When his own time came he never rejected such requests for service: after all, 'they are only asking to stop a bullet'. Kitchener himself regarded the young applicant with disapproval and vetoed his appointment when recommended by the War Office. The fact was that he had been heard of; it was still more objectionable that he was successful, perhaps worst of all, that he made no attempt to conceal his desire to shine. Other human beings find this outrageous; it is usually found more tolerable to camouflage conspicuous talents; less confident persons adopt various methods of concealment. Henceforth he would always find, right up to 1940, this difficulty in his way in his relations with other people: too straight, too ingenuous, and taking no trouble to disguise his self-confidence or anything else. It is like the jealousy his ancestor John Churchill had to contend with all his life; though a subtler man, artful and 'brimful of policy', the one thing he did not trouble to disguise was the superiority of his talents.

Lieutenant Churchill came home from India to argue his case. He brought Lord Salisbury's promise into play: not even the Prime Minister could prevail upon Kitchener. Only by chance did the subaltern learn that the Adjutant-General at home much resented Kitchener's interference with the posting of officers, and a direct appeal to him resulted in Churchill's being seconded to the 21st Lancers. A little late, he was nevertheless in time for the final phase of the campaign, in time for Omdurman. He was to go at his own expense, and if he got himself killed or wounded he was to be no charge to the British Army. Such terms justified his doubling the rôle of cavalry officer and war-correspondent again: this time he was to write a series of letters, at an improved fee, for the *Morning Post* and to this circumstance we owe his second war-book, *The River War*.

It is an altogether more mature and substantial book than the first, as the Sudan Campaign was an altogether more important affair than what was, after all, only 'an episode of Frontier War'. In fact it is a fine book, giving one a full account of the Mahdi's movement, of the Dervish Empire and its victories, its final struggle with the Anglo-Egyptian army, its collapse, the Fashoda incident and the pacification of the Sudan. Its evocation of the scene is masterly, the extraordinary country all sand and rock and scrub for hundreds of miles, only alive along the confines of the majestic river upon which all depends. There are many excellent descriptions, moments to remember, as when the sun goes down in the desert and 'the smell of grass was noticed by the alert senses of many, and will for ever refresh in their minds the strong impression of the night. The breeze which had sprung up at sundown gradually freshened and raised clouds of fine sand, which deepened the darkness with a whiter mist.'[1]

The personal element that gives the book character, colour and warmth is firmer, though not less in evidence than before. Good nature and magnanimity shine forth in the sympathetic account he gives of the Mahdi: his sympathies are wholly with him and his followers against the miserable Egyptians, whose only aim had been to exploit the Sudanese. As for the expeditions they sent to recover their stranglehold: 'they came, they saw, they ran away'. It is with no reluctance that he relates that, when at Omdurman the 7th Egyptians began to waver and tried to bolt, they were turned round to face the right way by two companies of British behind them with fixed bayonets. Of many observations by this young man several remind us of the wisdom of the older. 'Few facts are so encouraging to the student of human development as the desire, which most men and all communities manifest at all times, to associate with their actions at least the appearance of moral right.' 'All politics are a series of compromises and bargains, and while the historian may easily mark what would have been the best possible moment for any great undertaking, a good moment must content the administrator.' 'The human element—in defiance of experience and probability—may produce a wholly irrational result, and a starving, outmanoeuvred army win food, safety and honour by their bravery.' There is a reflection that points straight to far graver events in 1940, an early indication of the spirit, not without an element of calculation, that endured through such experiences as Dunkirk. Nor is the end of the story without a moral: 'it is pleasing to remember that a great crisis found England united. The determination of the Government was approved by the loyalty of the

[1] Churchill, *The River War* (ed. 1951), 232.

Opposition, supported by the calm resolve of the people.'

In action Lieutenant Churchill had two strokes of luck. On the day before Omdurman he was sent to report to Kitchener the advance of the Dervish army, which was expected to attack then and there. It was a dramatic confrontation, Kitchener riding alone in front of his staff, his two standard-bearers immediately behind him, and the irrepressible subaltern who was there contrary to his wishes. Nothing was said outside the matter in hand—but what an introduction for these two who were to be brought together, and clash, again in the first German war! Next day took place the battle he would not have missed for anything. 'Nothing like the battle of Omdurman will ever be seen again. It was the last link in the long chain of those spectacular conflicts whose vivid and majestic splendour has done so much to invest war with glamour. Everything was visible to the naked eye':[1] the Nile with its flotilla of gunboats (Lieutenant Churchill made the acquaintance of Lieutenant Beatty serving in one, a bottle of champagne thrown down to the thirsty shore); the *zeriba* behind which the small Anglo-Egyptian army was drawn up, back to the river; between them and the Mahdi's sacred city, the brown dome of his tomb rising above it, the hordes of the faithful, over fifty thousand of them in their battle-formations. In the battle he had the luck to be in the celebrated charge of the 21st Lancers: he was luckier still to get out of it alive, for there were two or three thousand Dervishes in the water-course the squadrons had to cross, and they had heavy casualties.

Lieutenant Churchill lived to tell the tale to much effect: letters, articles, books, appearances on lecture-platforms all in good time. On the proceeds he was determined to leave the Army, live inexpensively with his mother at home and earn a better living with his pen than her Majesty could afford him. (From that day onward he earned his own living by pen and tongue; though as a reward for virtue there descended upon him after the War of 1914-18 an ancient but considerable legacy under the will of his great-grandmother, the Duchess's mother.) First, however, he had to return to Bangalore to wind up his affairs and play in the team that won the Polo Tournament that year. On his way back to England he was able to submit the early chapters of *The River War*, with their account of Egyptian and Sudanese affairs, to the censure of Lord Cromer. He took the task seriously: 'one of the very few things which still interest me in life is to see young men get on'.

[1] Churchill, *My Early Life*, 186.

Churchill had been shocked by what he considered the brutal desecration of the Mahdi's tomb, knocking the knob off with a howitzer, and still more by Kitchener's carrying the prophet's head off as a trophy in a kerosene can. No respecter of person himself, he seems always—with no exaggerated rationalism of outlook—to have had a respect for their superstitions, their beliefs. This generosity of outlook much commended itself to Liberals as a weapon with which to beat Kitchener for winning Omdurman. *The River War* when it came out was then another score against this young man in the eyes of Kitchener—and a recommendation of him to the Liberals.

On his return to England he would have liked to go up to Oxford to go on with the formal education he had come, belatedly, to appreciate. That for a young man of his years and experience, with the books he had written, was something quite exceptional in those days, and there was no way to fit him in. He went so far as to make inquiries about how to get there: 'I was, I expect, at this time capable of deriving both profit and enjoyment from Oxford life and thought'. Alas, the twin spectres of Latin and Greek guarded the gate and he could not bear the idea of going back to Greek irregular verbs after having commanded British regular troops. He could not see why he could not have gone and paid his fees (well earned by himself), listen to the lectures, argue with the professors and read the books. He might well have been disappointed, but he would certainly have enjoyed himself.

Nothing would have prevented him from enjoying himself: such zest, healthy and inexhaustible, is more like that of Leonard Jerome than it is of Lord Randolph, in whom there was a too highly-strung strain. His son enjoyed everything: soldiering, horses, polo, campaigning, good food and wine, writing. What fun it was writing a book! One lived with it; it went everywhere along with one. It was like building a house or planning a battle or painting a picture—all of which would come in time. As for the years, 'from the beginning of 1895 down to the present time of writing I have never had time to turn round. I could count almost on my fingers the days when I have had nothing to do. An endless moving picture in which one was an actor.' The most exciting experience of all, to date, was just ahead of him.

Before *The River War* could well get going the Boer War had got going instead: 'we all had other things to think about'.

The events of the 1960's have thrown an illuminating searchlight into the genesis of the war in South Africa. We no longer have to accept the comfortable Liberal illusions as to British responsibility for it. It is true that Cecil Rhodes was disastrously impatient and that Dr. Jameson made a shocking mistake, but what made the war certain was something more profound: the determination of the extreme Dutch Nationalists to impose their nationalism on South Africa.[1] As to that we are better informed today. Bringing it to a point was the readiness of the aged, but very agile, President Kruger of the Transvaal for a war of independence to achieve a United States of South Africa. Louis Botha, best and wisest of the Dutch, was opposed to the war; but mistakes on the British side—in particular, the understandable impatience of Milner, confronted with a monumental intransigence—played into the hands of the Transvaal extremists.

When the war broke out, the wonder is that the Boers did not win it at the first rush, for they had all the advantages. Even with the first British reinforcements, the Boers were two to one in the field; their armies of mobile marksmen—and they were superb horsemen—were ideal for the veldt, their own terrain of which they took fullest advantage. Within their hill and mountain frontiers the Boer republics had the advantage of interior communications, of intelligence service, the sympathies of the countryside and hence facilities for surprise. Their Krupps guns, with Germans as usual to lend a hand, were superior to the types of British artillery then in use. Why, then, did the Boers not win? Because of a strategic misconception of the war at the beginning. The British were unprepared, fighting at the end of several thousand miles of supply line (as in the 1770's) and made every conceivable mistake of generalship in the field. But their fundamental stategy was sound and, in the end, superior resources were bound to tell.

There was not much appreciation of all this at the outset of the war; mistakes were made, and there was much mutual ignorance, on both sides. Though Lord Salisbury's strong Cabinet had every desire to avoid war, there was an unpleasant atmosphere of swagger and bellicosity among the mob at the end of the 1890's. Though this is not to depreciate him, for he was a man of many-

[1] Cf. the following from an Orange Free Stater: 'the only thing we are afraid of now is that Chamberlain, with his admitted fitfulness of temper, will cheat us out of the war and consequently the opportunity of annexing the Cape Colony and Natal and forming the Republican United States of South Africa.'—q. L. S. Amery, *My Political Life,* I. 105.

sided genius, it was the age of Kipling, the apogee of his fame; on one side he was the laureate of these impulses, his spirit spoke to theirs, expressed the spirit of the time—very rarely indeed, and hardly ever with a poet, has there been a writer more immediately in touch with the moods of a people, who so made himself their voice.

> Truly ye come of The Blood; slower to bless than to ban,
> Little used to lie down at the bidding of any man.

Not for nothing did he come from Nonconformist stock:

> Fair is our lot—O goodly is our heritage!
> (Humble ye, my people, and be fearful in your mirth!)
> For the Lord our God Most High
> He hath made the deep as dry,
> He hath smote for us a pathway to the ends of all the Earth!

The war meant a grand opportunity for the most promising of British war-correspondents, and the *Morning Post* came forward with a higher offer than had yet been made in British journalism: £250 a month, plus all expenses, complete freedom of movement and expression.[1] What larks, indeed! Churchill travelled out in the same ship as the Commander-in-Chief, Sir Redvers Buller, of

[1] His vivid letters are reprinted in two volumes, *London to Ladysmith via Pretoria* and *Ian Hamilton's March,* 1900. These give one a more immediate sense of the war than any other books I know, along with some illuminating shafts as to its origins. In the course of one of many discussions a Boer said to him, 'Is it right that a dirty Kaffir should walk on the pavement—without a pass too? That's what they do in your British Colonies. Brother! Equal! Ugh! Free! Not a bit. We know how to treat Kaffirs.' We see that theirs was the uncompromising, unyielding mentality of the Southern States in the American Civil War. Churchill comments, 'probing at random I had touched a very sensitive nerve. We had got down from underneath the political and reached the social. What is the true and original root of Dutch aversion to British rule? . . . It is the abiding fear and hatred of the movement that seeks to place the native on a level with the white man. British government is associated in the Boer farmer's mind with violent social revolution. Black is to be proclaimed the same as white. The servant is to be raised against the master; the Kaffir is to be declared the brother of the European, to be constituted his legal equal, to be armed with political rights. The dominant race is to be deprived of their superiority; nor is a tigress robbed of her cubs more furious than is the Boer at this prospect.'—*London to Ladysmith,* 133-4.

whom the war-correspondent was to form an unfavourable opinion. For indeed Sir Redvers Buller was of a slow, monumental stupidity. Because he was a Liberal, because he was a West Countryman, and perhaps because he was so stupid and people could understand him, there was still a Buller cult in the West Country in my childhood: people thought that he was unfairly treated. It would have saved the lives of thousands and shortened the war if he had been thrown out earlier. Kipling spoke for the ordinary soldier when he wrote:

> The General 'ad 'produced a great effect',
> The General 'ad the country cleared—almost;
> The General 'ad 'no reason to expect',
> And the Boers 'ad us bloomin' well on toast!
> For we might 'ave crossed the drift before the twilight,
> Instead o' sittin' down an' takin' root;
> But we was not allowed, so the Boojers scooped the crowd,
> To the last survivin' bandolier an' boot.

Arrived at the frontier outpost of Estcourt in Natal, Churchill was able to set up his tent with Leo Amery, who had turned up as war-correspondent of *The Times*. At once there followed the adventure of the armoured train. A general had the idea of sending this helpless monster, with several hundred troops, into enemy country to reconnoitre—helpless, for remove a few feet of railway line and it would be stranded, like a whale on the coast of Patagonia. Something of this sort happened: two or three trucks left the line, the train came to a standstill while they were all under Boer fire. Churchill, ever to the fore, got out to investigate, formed a plan to clear the line, made his way up to the engine; there he left his pistol behind him. On his way back, scrambling along the cutting he found himself being headed off by a couple of Boer marksmen. He made a dash for cover, but in no time found himself covered by a Boer rifle. There was nothing for it but surrender: thus early in the war he was a prisoner. It did not mitigate matters at the time that his captor was Louis Botha: this was their first introduction. Some years later, when Botha was attending a banquet for Dominion Prime Ministers in Westminster Hall and his former prisoner was now Colonial Under-Secretary, the Boer leader paused to say to Lady Randolph, 'He and I have been out in all weathers'. In the years before 1914 whenever Botha came to London he always sought Churchill out, faithfully warned him what to expect of the Germans, enjoined on him to be prepared.

When the war came his services to this country and the Commonwealth were immeasurable.

Nothing of all this could be glimpsed in that railway-cutting or in the prison-camp at Pretoria to which Churchill was removed. Naturally he made all the fuss possible: he was a Press correspondent, who had been taken unarmed.[1] (It seems merely a chance if he were without his pistol, and he was a very combative, if not combatant, correspondent.) But his importance, and his name, were appreciated by the Boers, who decided to retain him. Upon hearing this, Churchill decided that they should not. He was not, so far as he could help it, going to miss the entire war. He planned to escape, and he did.

> When by the labour of my 'ands
>   I've 'elped to pack a transport tight
> With prisoners for foreign lands,
>   I ain't transported with delight.
>
> I know it's only just an' right,
>   But yet it somehow sickens me,
> For I 'ave learned at Waterval
>   The meanin' of captivity.

Familiar as we have become with the escape-stories of the last war, Churchill's story of his escape never ceases to be thrilling—as exciting as *Kidnapped*, which he read with all the more interest while he lay concealed by the friendly mine-captain at Witbank. It should be read in his own words: how he boarded the coal-train moving east at night from Pretoria, got off it, wandered in the veldt, had fantastic luck in falling in with the one English household in the vicinity and a brave man who planned his escape in a hide-out among the bales of wool on a goods-train bound for Delagoa Bay. For years he could recite the names of the stations,

[1] There is some conflict of evidence here. Field-Marshal Smuts's son says that the 'defiant young man' was brought before his father 'dishevelled and most indignant and claiming immunity as a non-combatant. It was pointed out, however, that he was carrying a pistol when captured and so he was sent on detention to Pretoria. . . . It appears that my father had developed quite a liking for the high-spirited young man he had interrogated and so, some days afterwards, he persuaded General Joubert that there was not much point in detaining him. . . . His release was therefore authorised, but before it could be put into effect he had escaped.'—J. C. Smuts, *Jan Christian Smuts*, 50-1.

that journey into freedom made such an impression: Witbank, Middelburg, Bergendal, Belfast, Dalmanutha, Machadodorp, Waterval Boven, Waterval Onder, Elands, Nooitgedacht and so on to Komati Poort. He turned up at Durban to find himself a popular hero. Today one of the most treasured possessions at Chartwell is the Pretoria poster offering a reward of £25 sterling

> 'to anyone who brings the escaped prisioner [*sic*] of war
>
> CHURCHILL
>
> dead or alive to this office'

The story of his escape made him famous, thus young, all over the English-speaking world. It was a piece of individual pluck and audacity against the background of Black Week contemporaneously, the dreadful week in which three incompetent generals all suffered staggering defeats at Stormberg, Magersfontein and Colenso, which opened people's eyes to the seriousness of the situation and the magnitude of the effort required to retrieve it. Churchill's single-handed victory at once produced an equal current of reaction, of jealous disparagement. No doubt the self-advertiser had contrived it; it was held against him that he had escaped at all—who was he to escape? He had broken his parole; he had escaped alone, without bringing the others with him, etc. This surf of criticism was advanced against him for years—by the envious, by the third-rate, always those people with pretensions of their own who never achieve anything themselves. One knows the type well. Churchill had them at his heels all his life long, right up to 1940, when the nation in danger had need of such a man.

The situation was not improved by the tone he held towards the third-rate. In his dispatches home he told the truth. 'It is foolish not to recognise that we are fighting a formidable adversary. The high qualities of the burghers increase their efficiency. The individual Boer, mounted in suitable country, is worth from three to five regular soldiers.' That gave much offence, in clubs, dug-outs and such places: the brash young whipper-snapper was being disloyal now to the Army. Kipling, with the similar intuition of genius, knew better:

> Ah, there, Piet!—'is trousies to 'is knees,
> 'Is coat-tails lyin' level in the bullet-sprinkled breeze;
> 'E does not lose 'is rifle an' 'e does not lose 'is seat.
> I've known a lot o' people ride a dam' sight worse than Piet.

The war-correspondent did not hesitate to suggest a war-policy.

'We should collect overwhelming masses of troops. It would be much cheaper in the end to send more than necessary. There is plenty of work here for a quarter of a million men. More irregular corps are wanted. Are the gentlemen of England all fox-hunting? Why not an English Light Horse?' In the end a quarter of a million soldiers had to be sent, the larger disparity he had mentioned—five British regulars to one Boer. To be thus corroborated does not make one more popular. It is probable that, great as was the *réclame* he collected, by the end of the war he had collected as much unpopularity in influential quarters, in the Army, among politicians, his equals and competitors. Simpler people are, of course, above such mean resentments.

Buller rewarded the young man's enterprise by giving him his wish—a commission in the newly recruited South African Light Horse. So there he was once more in the rôle that made people so envious, doubling the soldier with the correspondent. The rule against this had been specially made because of him; he was made the first exception. The General squared his conscience: 'you will have to do as much as you can for both jobs. But you will get no pay for ours'. Thus he returned to the Army under Colonel Byng (later Lord Byng of Vimy), who let him roam where he liked when they were not engaged in fighting and he 'lived from day to day in perfect happiness'.

The war proceeded on its slow course. Churchill was present at the fearful mess Buller made at Spion Kop, whence he announced that he had 'effected his retreat'—in the phrase Kipling took up. However, the new Lieutenant of the S.A.L.H. vastly enjoyed the two months' fighting for the relief of Ladysmith, in the course of which he came across his brother John. At home Lady Randolph had exerted herself to recruit benevolent American support to provide and equip a hospital-ship, the *Maine*, on which she served as a nurse. The first casualty she received was her younger son; the elder shortly joined them for a few good days together. Back at the front in Natal, Buller made his fourth attempt to relieve Ladysmith—this time in the right direction—and thus 'we all rode together into the long beleaguered, almost starved-out Ladysmith. It was a thrilling moment.'

With Buller's supersession as Commander-in-Chief by Lord Roberts, Kitchener as his Chief-of-Staff, a transformation came over the war: henceforward it was fought on intelligent, and intelligible, lines. With his much larger forces concentrated, Roberts was moving forward from Cape Colony upon the Orange

Free State, outflanking the Boer invasion of Natal. The Lieutenant of Light Horse at once transferred himself on to his other foot as war-correspondent and got leave of absence to take part in what was going forward on the now more active front. Lord Roberts had been a friend of Lord Randolph, who had appointed him Commander-in-Chief in India over the head of Lord Wolseley. But neither Roberts nor Kitchener would recognise the existence of the too active, or too expressive, war-correspondent who broke all the rules—or rather, had a genius for getting his own way without actually breaking the rules. Nor would General French, to whose cavalry division the correspondent attached himself: there was a line-up of the generals against so irregular a case of a regular soldier who yet was irrepressible, could not be got at by discipline and reported home exactly what he thought about generals as well as everybody else.

This did not prevent him from enjoying himself as he marched north with Roberts' army: 'a jolly march, occupying with halts about six weeks and covering in that period between four and five hundred miles. The wonderful air and climate of South Africa, the magnificent scale of its landscape, the life of unceasing movement and of continuous incident' made a lasting impression, folded away in that astonishing treasure-house of memories. Some of the incidents were somewhat equivocally amusing, asking for trouble, as before. Arrived at the outskirts of Johannesburg he could not wait to enter, though it had not yet been evacuated by the Boers. He bicycled straight down the main road into the city. It gave him a distinct sensation of adventure: 'according to all the laws of war my situation, if arrested, would have been disagreeable. I was an officer holding a commission in the South African Light Horse, disguised in plain clothes and secretly within the enemy's lines. No court-martial that ever sat in Europe would have had much difficulty in disposing of such a case. On all these matters I was quite well informed.' However, the risk was taken: ambivalence has its rewards, it seems.

On his staff Lord Roberts had no less than three dukes—to the scandal of the Radical press—Norfolk, Westminster and Marlborough. It was decided to retrench Marlborough, who was despairing at the thought of being left behind in the advance. The effective war-correspondent managed to get his friend Ian Hamilton to take the Duke on to his staff. Thus it was that the two cousins rode together at the head of an infantry column into Pretoria. These two made at once for the prisoner-of-war camp. 'We were only two, and before us stood the armed Boer guard with their rifles at the"ready". Marlborough, resplendent in the red tabs of the staff, called on the Commandant to surrender forthwith, adding by a happy thought that he would give a receipt for the rifles.' Thus happily in appropriate family company, he returned to the starting-point of so many excitements and adventures.

Mr. Churchill came back from South Africa to find himself, thus young, famous. Already the music-halls had caught up with him:

> You've heard of Winston Churchill;
> This is all I need to say—
> He's the latest and the greatest
> Correspondent of the day.

Across the Atlantic another Winston Churchill—who presumably, with that Christian name, was an offshoot of the old stock, for there were Churchills in Virginia quite early—was at the same time winning fame with his admirable novels. Our Winston at first liked to think that some of the literary tributes he received were due to a belated recognition of the merits of *Savrola*. Inevitably there was some confusion between these two literary aspirants and a pleasant correspondence followed in which the Transatlantic Churchill considered signing himself 'The American', while the English—or, shall we say, the Anglo-American—Churchill solved the problem by affirming the Spencer along with the Churchill.

He returned in time for Chamberlain's Khaki Election of 1900, which gave the Unionists a thumping majority and the control of power for the next five years. He was asked to stand again for Oldham, which had rejected him on his first try before going out to South Africa. In that by-election Mr. Balfour's Clerical Tithes Bill hung about his neck like a Deceased Wife's Sister, until the candidate threw the liability overboard—and found, to his surprise, that 'it is not the slighest use defending governments or parties unless you defend the very worst thing about which they are attacked'. Mr. Balfour said, 'I thought he was a young man of promise, but it appears he is a young man of promises.' Having lost that election, he found that 'everyone threw the blame on me. I have noticed that they nearly always do. I suppose it is because they think I shall be able to bear it best.'

Now he was received at Oldham like a conquering hero and when he told his audience the story of the Oldham man who had helped to conceal him in the Witbank Colliery, Lancashire shouted back, 'His wa-af's in the gallery.' Sensation. There was no resisting that. On winning the seat he was in request to lend a hand all over the country—in those leisurely days 'before the liquefaction of the British political system had set in', when a general election was spread over several weeks—and he appeared on both Chamberlain and Balfour's platforms and 'never addressed any but the greatest meetings'.

After this there was the more remunerative experience of a lecture-tour—hardly ever less than £100 a night, with Lord Wolseley to take the chair in London, Lord Rosebery at Edinburgh, the Duke of Marlborough at Oxford. In America he had a more varied reception, depending on the place, for there was a good deal of pro-Boer feeling. When at Chicago the audience found that he had as much admiration and sympathy for the Boers as they had, their good nature prevailed and hostility turned to friendliness. At Boston a strong pro-British demonstration was staged; but the height for him was reached in New York, where he was thrilled to have for his chairman Mark Twain, beloved companion of his youth and of as many boys on this side of the Atlantic as on the other.

As the result of all his efforts, articles, books, lectures, he had £10,000 to invest and live on for the next few years, since in those days Members of Parliament were unpaid. That sum made the difference of ten years between his and his friend Amery's entry into Parliament. 'If I had not been caught, I could not have escaped, and my imprisonment and escape provided me with materials for lectures and a book which brought me in enough money to get into Parliament in 1900—ten years before you!' He has always held strong views about the importance of chance in human affairs.

With all this behind him, though the youngest member of the House, with the expectations aroused from Lord Randolph's son, his maiden speech was awaited with attention, by himself with intense nervousness. For the truth is that he was not a good natural speaker. Not for him the deplorable fluency of so many people who have nothing to say. He had a great deal to say—there were inexhaustible resources pent up within him—but he had great difficulty in saying it. There was, as Amery notes, not only the lisp, but a tendency to stutter when excited and a voice that was harsh and unpleasing. How different the voice of the speaker before him in the debate, that of the Radical Lloyd George, already ten years a Member—that voice we still remember, the natural music of its cadences, the purity of the Welsh vowel-sounds, the soft caressing quality of it with its extraordinary range and variety of expression, the command in the voice of anger and scorn, humour and mischief, pathos and every kind of sympathy. In later years Churchill said of Lloyd George that 'at his best he could charm a bird off a tree'.

To Churchill speaking did not come naturally: he had to learn it like Demosthenes. (Somebody said that on the way back from South Africa on board ship he would practise his harangues, like Demosthenes, to the waves.) His speeches were carefully prepared, learnt by heart beforehand; that gave him a certain immobility in debate, for they could not be changed when the arguments he had to answer were different. The airy but agile Balfour, who prepared nothing, one day scored against him over this. Here, too, we notice a contrast with his father, who was a natural orator, fluent and precocious. On the night, however, everyone was kind; no one interrupted to put off the neophyte who, breathless and dripping with nervousness, stuck to it to the end, when 'the usual restoratives were applied and I sat in a comfortable coma till I was strong enough to go home'. In fact the content of the speech was excellent, for it had been well got up; he had a line of his own: a very individual voice was heard and that was remarked on. The Speaker, for example, thought that Churchill spoke 'most effectively and marked himself out at once as a young man of great ability who would have to be reckoned with in the future'.

Lloyd George's pro-Boer speech had been very scathing against the government; though Churchill spoke from the opposite side he insisted that 'no national emergency short of the actual invasion of this country itself ought in any way to restrict or prevent the entire freedom of Parliamentary discussion'. It is interesting that this theme appeared thus early: he affirmed it again and again during the years 1940-5. A commonplace in itself, it was shrewd to assert it, for, though no doubt sincerely held, it was also flattering to the self-esteem of Parliament. He went on to speak of the war: 'from what I saw of the war—and I sometimes saw something of it—I believe that, as compared with other wars, especially those in which a civil population took part, this war in South Africa has been on the whole carried on with unusual humanity and generosity'. This was before the terrible experience of the concentration camps which were so ravaged by disease—the result of sheer military incompetence rather than any inhumanity.

A friendly feeling towards the Boers was evident in the phrase, 'if I were a Boer fighting in the field—and if I were a Boer I hope I should be fighting in the field' . . . Mr. Chamberlain made an impatient movement on the Front Bench: 'that's the way to throw away seats', he muttered. The new member went further: 'I have often myself been much ashamed to see respectable old Boer farmers—the Boer is a curious combination of the squire and the peasant, and under the rough coat of the farmer there are very often to be found the instincts of the squire I have been ashamed to see such men ordered about peremptorily by young subaltern officers, as if they were private soldiers'.

His plea was that the government's policy should be 'to make it easy and honourable for the Boers to surrender'. Nothing should be left undone 'to bring home to those brave and unhappy men who are fighting in the field that whenever they are prepared to recognise that their small independence must be merged in the larger liberties of the British Empire, there will be a full guarantee for the security of their property and religion, an assurance of equal rights, a promise of representative institutions and, last of all, but not least of all, what the British Army would most readily accord to a brave and enduring foe—all the honours of war'.

Here was a new note, which was recognised by the Liberal speaker following him: 'the tone was different from what we sometimes hear with reference to this deplorable conflict'. We recognise it, the note of a chivalrous magnanimity continuous throughout his career. Before sitting down the new member had thanked the House for its kindness: 'it has been extended to me, I well know, not on my own account, but because of a splendid memory which many honourable members still preserve'. Chamberlain, who was the dominating figure in the House, paid his tribute to 'a speech which I am sure that those who were friends and intimates of his father will have welcomed with the utmost satisfaction in the hope that we may see the father repeated in the son'.

His father's image was constantly before his mind in this arena where he had been such a dazzling figure. The son took up his father's cause of retrenchment in a long speech a few months later. He proceeded to cite Lord Randolph's views at length and his struggle with the Secretary of State for War: 'in the end the government triumphed and the Chancellor of the Exchequer went down for ever and with him, as it now seems, there fell also the cause of retrenchment and economy. I suppose that was a lesson which Chancellors of the Exchequer were not likely to forget in a hurry. . . . I am very glad that the House has allowed me, after an interval of fifteen years, to lift again the tattered flag I found lying on a stricken field. . . . If such a one is to stand forward in such a cause, no one has a better right than I have, for this is a cause I have inherited, and a cause for which the late Lord Randolph Churchill made the greatest sacrifice of any minister of modern times.'

This speech marked the beginning of an effective campaign against the scheme for reorganising the Army propounded by Brodrick, Secretary of State for War. The War Office wished Britain to become a military nation with a considerable expansion of the regular Army; the plan was inspired on German lines—six Army Corps, three for home defence, three to form an expeditionary force, if necessary, to Europe. The young speaker had an unanswerable objection to this: 'one is quite enough to fight savages, and three are not enough even to begin to fight Europeans'. The speech now took a remarkable turn: he had been in the House a very short time, but he was 'astonished to hear with what composure and how glibly Members, and even Ministers, talk of a European war'. They evidently had no idea of the great change that had overcome war and society. 'Democracy is more vindictive than Cabinets. The war of peoples will be more terrible than those of kings.' He enforced the point that the British Empire could never depend on the Army: 'the Admiralty is the only office strong enough to insure the British Empire . . . the only weapon with which we can expect to cope with great nations is the Navy'. He ended by adducing the moral force which had been so strongly with us and had been a factor in our security in the past century, which it would be a fatal mistake to sacrifice for the aggressive gestures implied by 'the costly, trumpery, dangerous military playthings on which the Secretary of State for War has set his heart'.

The House was much impressed by this remarkable speech—which it had taken him six weeks to prepare and which he had learnt thoroughly by heart that he might not be thrown out of his stride; the Conservatives were startled, the Liberals wholly with him. It marked the beginning of his divergence from his party. Mr. Brodrick replied with some acerbity: he expected that Parliament 'which was not afraid to part company with a brilliant statesman in 1886 will not sleep the less soundly because of the financial heroics' of the son. He hoped that the son's 'judgment would grow up to his ability, when the hereditary qualities he possesses of eloquence and courage may be tempered also by discarding the hereditary desire to run Imperialism on the cheap'. At Cambridge he replied to

Brodrick: 'We are all Imperialists nowadays. It is not only a political faith, but the prevailing fashion. I am an Imperialist, too—though I do not like the name—and perhaps I shall remain one when it is less fashionable, and from an electioneering point of view less profitable than at present.'

This was the beginning of a duel with Brodrick that went on for the next couple of years. It seems that Brodrick had unwittingly had some part in Lord Randolph's fall; at any rate, consciously or unconsciously, the son was avenging him upon the War Office. In addition to this he was, on the whole, right. The cavalry officer was not blinkered by the regular soldier's point of view; his speeches were full of military images, but the speaker was not a militarist. Indeed, he was in the true tradition of British defence-policy, and as the campaign proceeded he did not fear to proclaim constructively what that should be. In the first place, reliance on the Navy. At some point, Brodrick was so unwise as to defend his scheme by the 'possibility of our, at any time, losing the command of the sea'. If that went, no amount of army reorganisation could save us: that showed a fundamental failure to grasp our necessary strategy. The conception of the Army proper to our needs was that of a smaller, picked force distributed at strategic points within the Empire: while home-defence should make full use of volunteer forces.

At the outset Churchill was entirely alone in his campaign against the proposed Army reorganisation, the only Conservative member who voted against it. As he went on, people began to see that his criticisms were justified; but 'political prophets are always unpopular, especially when they happen to be right'. Nevertheless, his constituency supported him and he gradually gathered a band of young Conservatives who went into the lobby with him against Brodrick. It became clear that Brodrick's scheme was both financially burdensome and on unsound lines. His opponent was able to claim, 'now after two years I have no hesitation in saying that Mr. Brodrick's scheme of 1901 is a total, costly, ghastly failure'. He did not spare Brodrick from ridicule, or his addiction to German models, methods, uniforms. He did not spare the generals—we have seen that he was not popular with them in South Africa; he thought that not the least remarkable feature of the British Army was the number of its generals. He considered that there was a serious military prejudice against the Volunteers.

None of this endeared him in orthodox quarters either in the Army or the Conservative party. Brodrick's scheme was breaking down under the weight of criticism in the House and from its own impracticability. It was left to the Liberals when they came in, and to Haldane, to produce a better. As a move in his campaign Churchill published his speeches in a little book, *Mr. Brodrick's Army*. He did not mince his language: he described the scheme as 'The Great English Fraud', and in his Preface he arrayed himself once more under his father's standard.

The summer of 1901 saw Unionism at the meridian of its political power and Blenheim chosen for its demonstration. There Chamberlain and Balfour appeared together on a hot August day on a platform beneath the Corinthian portico, supported by a score of lesser dignitaries and a hundred M.P.s. Thousands of people were gathered on Capability Brown's vast lawn to hear Chamberlain triumphing over the divided Liberals, taunting them in his characteristic way. But events were gradually bringing that party together again and providing matter for dissension within the Unionist majority. For one thing the war had by no means ended with the capture of Pretoria; it entered a new and more difficult phase of dispersed guerrilla warfare. The Boers were still holding out for nothing short of independence.

In regard to the conduct of the war Churchill expressed his dissatisfaction in a strong private letter to Chamberlain. 'There is no plan worth speaking of in the operations except hammer, hammer, at random. The troops, which are numerous everywhere, are overwhelming nowhere. The thousands of superior men are intermingled with and consequently reduced to the level of the inferior soldiers. The mobility of the Army is that of the slowest mounted man.... What I want is that the Government should localise, delimit and assign the functions of the C.-in-C. in Africa. Should reorganise the Remount and Intelligence Depts. Should lay the army by for a short period of rest and refreshment. Should organise a picked force. Should make some sort of peace: and make sure that we end the matter with the next bitter weather, whatever happens.'

Throughout 1902 we find Churchill concerning himself with every aspect of military questions; at one moment proposing to use 30,000 Indian troops to bring the war to a speedier end; congratulating poor Mr. Brodrick on abandoning 'the fatal and foolish theory of conscription'; dissociating himself from 'pious tributes to Ministerial infallibility'. Now he is horrified to find that the Military Intelligence Department had only sixteen or twenty officers, where the German had two hundred. He made various suggestions for small economies, though he opposed that of bringing in business experts. Next he brings forward a motion for a Select Committee on the reduction of national expenditure. Mr. Balfour, now Prime Minister, found this a bore and tried to forget it. He was not allowed to.

It was an arduous, industrious apprenticeship, for in spite of speaking frequently, 'in those days, and indeed for many years, I was unable to say anything (except a sentence in rejoinder) that I had not written out and committed to memory beforehand'. Once now and again he makes the point, rather pathetically, that not having been to a university he had not had the experience of those young men in debating and discussion, in impromptu speaking of all kinds. He noticed this all the more because he was one of a group of younger members led by Lord Hugh Cecil—the Hughligans—whose mind was of a very academic dialectical turn, while the Hatfield of that generation and the next was a debating society in itself.

The year 1903 marked the beginning of the breach within the ranks of the Tories, the recovery of the Liberals, with Chamberlain's departure from Free Trade, coming out in favour of Imperial Preference. Churchill had several times tried to draw him on the subject in the House: it was acutely embarrassing to the government, which was deeply divided on the issue. Now Churchill came forward with an uncompromising Free Trade declaration—Oldham was Free Trade, his father had been, he was himself. 'This move means a change, not only in historic English parties, but in the conditions of our public life. The old Conservative Party, with its religious convictions and constitutional principles, will disappear and a new party arise like perhaps the Republican party of America—rich, materialist and secular—whose opinions will turn on tariffs, and who will cause the lobbies to be crowded with the touts of protected industries.' He wrote to the Duke of Devonshire, leader of the Liberal Unionists, protesting against Chamberlain's Protectionist propaganda circulating through all the channels of the Conservative party. 'We are on the eve of a gigantic political landslide. I don't think Balfour and those about him realise at all how far the degeneration of the forces of Unionism has proceeded, and how tremendous the counter-current is going to be.' This turned out a true prophecy.

In these years he was writing his biography of his father, devoting himself to it with his intense power of concentration and his artistic conscientiousness, collecting his letters—he already had his speeches by heart—seeing and consulting everybody who had known him well. The moral of his father's career cannot but have become increasingly clear to him: not to follow one's convictions into the party that agrees with them and will give effect to them is to condemn one's self to complete frustration. We have seen that intellectually Lord Randolph was genuinely Radical; he chose to remain inside the Conservative party, which had no further use for him and wasted his life: there was the real political suicide. In the couse of writing his biography his son consulted Rosebery, who, to begin with, did not much approve of Winston—like a good many people, until they got to know him. The relationship between these two became rather touching: the young man avid to hear everything he could learn about the famous father who had held himself so aloof from him, whom he had never got to know. One observes in his attitude to Rosebery something of a filial feeling, looking to him in place of the father he had lost. In these circumstances Rosebery became his mentor and that could not but have pulled him towards the Liberal party.

Others too had their influence. 'I found that Asquith and Grey and, above all, John Morley seemed to understand my point of view far better than my own chiefs. I was fascinated by the intellectual stature of these men and their broad and inspiring outlook upon public affairs, untrammelled as it was by the practical burden of events.' A hardly less remarkable associate of his father met him at this moment for the first time: this was Wilfrid Scawen Blunt, poet, diplomat, Sussex squire, anti-Imperialist, breeder of fine Arab horses, opponent of the Egyptian occupation, of Sudan ventures—and that had brought him into contact with Lord Randolph, also a Little Englander. Randolph's son interested Blunt intensely and he gives us the best impressions of him in these years, for they became fast friends. (Blunt, with the optimism of his kind, for long hoped to turn him into an anti-Imperialist too.) 'He is a little, square-headed fellow of no very striking appearance', wrote the tall and very striking poet, 'but of wit, intelligence and originality. In mind and manner he is a strange replica of his father, with all his father's suddenness and assurance, and I should say more than his father's ability. There is just the same *gaminerie* and contempt of the conventional and the same engaging plain-spokenness and readiness to understand. As I listened to him recounting conversations he had had with Chamberlain I seemed once more to be listening to Randolph on the subject of Northcote and Salisbury. About Chamberlain he was especially amusing, his attitude being one of mingled contempt and admiration, contempt for the man and admiration for his astuteness and audacity. In Opposition Winston I expect to see playing precisely his father's game, and I should not be surprised if he had his father's success. He has a power of writing Randolph never had. . . . He interested me immensely.' Here is a remarkably perceptive view so early: the poet's personal intuition was much better than his generalised judgment when it came to political affairs.

By 1904 Mr. Balfour's Cabinet was breaking up and Churchill visibly preparing to move over to the Liberals. Balfour made no effort to retain him; years after Chamberlain said that he was 'the cleverest of all the young man, and the mistake Arthur made was letting him go'. But no doubt it would have been impossible to stop him and, like Disraeli, he 'had his way to make'. Like the major figures in English politics, as opposed to the lesser ones, he was not a good party man: he transcended those narrow limitations. He wrote to a Liberal candidate at a by-election wishing him success in the common Free Trade cause. In the Budget Debate he supported an Opposition amendment, with a good deal of banter against his friend Austen Chamberlain, now Chancellor of the Exchequer. But he was not going to quote figures: 'it was quite enough to say that the government of the country cost half as much again as it did when the Unionist government in 1895 came into power. Was it governed half as well again?' This was a mere debating point, in fact his quarrel with the government was now irreparable, and it had been essentially on the question of finance all along.

From this time he had to meet constant barracking from his own side. Several times the Conservatives tried to howl him down. Once when he rose to speak, as he now did very frequently, the Prime Minister left the Front Bench and all the Conservatives walked out of the House by a spontaneous demonstration, stopping at the door to jeer while Churchill stood waiting. It needed courage to persevere in these circumstances; what is more remarkable is that he retained his customary good-humour and courtesy.

Such a situation could not long endure. He accepted an invitation to stand at the approaching election as a Free Trade candidate for North-West Manchester, and crossed the floor of the House to sit beside Lloyd George. It was not long before he was moving an Opposition amendment about the tax on tea: he would have preferred to raise money by placing *2d.* or *3d.* on income-tax. In July he was joining with Lloyd George to attack the Prime Minister for not listening to representations from the mining industry against the coal-tax. Several times Balfour left the House when he rose to speak, and he was constantly faced with Conservative interruptions. Amery tells us that the Conservatives hated him, as the Liberals did Chamberlain for leaving them. Chamberlain himself warned him from bitter experience, 'you must expect to have the same sort of abuse flung at you as I have endured. But if a man is sure of himself, it only sharpens him and makes him more effective.' All the same, even after his return to the fold twenty years later, there always remained an irreducible element of antagonism to Churchill in the Conservative party, particularly in the party organisation, where hidebound orthodoxy was at its most congealed. On the other hand, it is pleasant to think that in a few years it was precisely these contestants, Balfour and Churchill, Austen Chamberlain and Lloyd George, who became fast friends and held together in Coalition days. Churchill, bursting all the bonds, may be said to have had Coalitionism in his blood.

By this time he had lost his early diffidence, had himself become a marked figure in the House, was speaking—always with preparation—on every conceivable subject, frequently told by the Chair to keep to the matter in hand. These subjects ranged from Customs in the Isle of Man, Shop Hours, Reform of the Militia, Savings Banks, Sugar Duties, Chinese Labour in the Transvaal, all Army and most Budget questions, to the Tibet expedition. Clearly such energy, such industry, was crying out for office: a large machine would be required for such a dynamo.

Balfour had missed the opportunity to harness him to his government; now it was too late: the Cabinet itself was disintegrating under the contrary pressures of Chamberlain and the Conservative Free Traders. Chamberlain described Balfour's attempts to evade declaring himself, by frequently walking out of the House, as 'humiliating'. Churchill was more trenchant. 'The government are now doing penance for the disingenuousness of years. All their shams, all the shuffles, all their manoeuvrings, all their scurrying from the House of Commons, all their ingenious devices of the gag and the guillotine are of no avail.' Balfour had inherited the greatest governing instrument possible from Lord Salisbury, which he had now wrecked in a couple of years, 'simply by weak and vacillating action, by not having the courage to state his opinions boldly on great controversies, he had wrecked his party, lost his friends and broken up his government'. This was followed by a series of personal attacks on the Prime Minister for 'the gross, unpardonable ignorance' he exhibited on public business, for his 'slip-shod, slap-dash, haphazard manner of doing business'. The

Prime Minister was often away from the House; Mr. Churchill supposed, on one occasion, to write his philosophical Address to the British Association—and that may well have been so. The failing administration received a characteristic parting shot: 'the dignity of a Prime Minister, like a lady's virtue, was not susceptible of partial diminution'.

All this, of course, was unfair: the small change of party controversy—and Churchill was now wholly with the other side. In truth, Balfour was never wanting in courage, personal or political; under the lady-like appearance there was the quality of steel. Moreover, his government had a fruitful legislative record: its Education Act (1902) was one of the grand constructive measures of a century: our educational system today is built on it. It simply was that after twenty years of Tory rule the country was looking to a new deal, the social reform that would have come twenty years earlier if Chamberlain had not apostatised from the Liberals.

During these years Churchill was labouring at his biography of his father—it would no doubt have surprised Lord Randolph to know who the author would be and what a satisfying job he would make of it. The book was a fine piece of work, firmly constructed, full in its documentation, just in its presentation of the subject and his companion figures, living and warm in its sympathies. And this from a man of thirty who had been so backward in his beginnings. The book had the reception it deserved: it delighted the great world that read it and for whom it was written; at the same time they were again rather surprised that the author had it in him to produce such a work.

The last stages in its composition were marked by a slight *contretemps* with Lord Rosebery, who intended to contribute his character-sketch to it. This contained the Etonian expression 'scug' to characterise Lord Randolph; and though Rosebery explained that the expression was harmless—it means a boy who does not play games, and is to that extent derogatory—Winston was not going to have it in his book. The mutual affection between him and his father's friend survived the strain. The book was written over some three years in the House, 'in spite of some political distractions', and in his bachelor rooms in Mount Street. There he worked away surrounded by his few treasured possessions: the entrance-hall hung with cartoons of his father, himself seated in the carved oak chair presented by the city of Manchester to Lord Randolph, dipping his pen into the immense inkstand that had been his father's. There were photographs of Lady Randolph, a portrait of the old Duchess and an engraving of the Duke playing chess—no doubt less objectionable than playing cards. Looking down on the work going forward was a print of the great Duke, whose biography also he would one day write. On the cabinet between the windows, in the most honoured place, stood a photograph of his old nurse.

Here Scawen Blunt came one day to visit him. 'He is astonishingly like his father in manners and ways, and the whole attitude of his mind. He has just come in from playing polo, a short, sturdy little man with a twinkle in his eye, reminding me especially of the Randolph of twenty years ago. He took out his father's letters, which I had left with him six weeks ago, from a tin box and read them to me aloud while I explained the allusions in them and gave him a short account of the political adventures of the early eighties in which Randolph and I had been connected. There is something touching about the fidelity with which he continues to espouse his father's cause and his father's quarrels. He has been working double shifts this session in Parliament, and looks, I fancy, to a leadership of the Liberal Party and an opportunity of full vengeance on those who caused his father's death.'

The Liberal landslide of 1906 certainly saw full retribution upon the Tories; his life of his father did him full justice at last and put the record right. With his call to office under the Liberals and the appearance of his first masterpiece—the Preface dated from Blenheim—we may regard the long and arduous, but immensely varied and enriching, apprenticeship as over.

CHAPTER NINE

Liberal Minister

FROM 1906 onwards the most fabulous, outsize career in our modern history begins to flow in full spate. We can no more describe it in detail, its ups and downs, its checks and chances, with the ever-mounting creative contribution to legislation, political action and the life of the nation, than we could the military campaigns of his ancestor. As with the great figure among the early Churchills, so with his descendant, the emphasis must be on the person and the personal, events forming the patterns in the tapestry.

We observe a certain parallel in the significant rhythms of their careers. Just as John Churchill made his strenuous ascent from difficult, though not unpropitious, beginnings to be thrown back for a decade out of favour and out of office under William III, so the later Churchill's career has had its set-backs and remarkable recoveries. From 1906 to 1915 Winston Churchill's course was one of steady ascent and increasing importance as a minister and a national figure until, as First Lord of the Admiralty in 1914, he held one of the three or four key-positions in the conduct of the war. From that he fell almost sheer, and went off to fight as a soldier in France, until he was rescued by Lloyd George and brought back to be Minister of Munitions. The end of the Coalition in 1922 left him stranded once more and, for once, ill. ('In a twinkling of an eye I found myself without an office, without a seat, without a party, and without an appendix.') Saved from this dismal condition by Mr. Baldwin, he was offered the Chancellorship—'of the Duchy?' 'No—of the Exchequer.' As such he was a ruling figure until he separated from Mr. Baldwin, opposed the Conservative party leadership and was out of office and of any power throughout the contemptible decade that led to war in 1939. His being out of office and the neglect of his counsels—indeed the opposite line was taken by the second-rate men who took his place—was a considerable factor in bringing the war upon us in the most unfavourable conditions. From 1940 to 1945 he was the chief instrument of resistance and victory, as Marlborough had been from 1702 to

1711—to be thrown out of office, as Marlborough was, before victory was quite complete and his own conditions for peace properly secured. Marlborough came back in his sixties when the Tories were ousted in 1714; Winston Churchill came back in his seventies when Labour lost power in 1951. Their lives are not dissimilar in their rhythms, the ebbs and flows of power, the recessions and strokes of fortune, in their military inspiration and strategic concern for their country. Both of them were men of the sensible centre, one of them a Trimmer by nature, the other with Coalitionism in his blood; neither of them what is called 'a good party man'. Each of them might claim, though with a rather different emphasis, 'some men change their party for the sake of their principles; others change their principles for the sake of their party'.

The Liberal Prime Minister, Campbell-Bannerman, took the opportunity that Balfour had missed to make Churchill Under-Secretary of State for the Colonies. (Actually he was succeeding his cousin the Duke in the post, so Blenheim still had a voice, and a more powerful one, in the management of the Empire.) On this news the Prince of Wales wrote home to King Edward that Lord Elgin, the new Secretary of State, 'will have to look after him!' But we do not hear of Lord Elgin again. Since he was skied in the Lords, the voice we hear is that of the Under-Secretary in the Commons; and since in these years the settlement of South Africa after the war was the foremost question in politics, Churchill came immediately to the fore with it.

On the personal side we see him henceforth from the interesting angle of his private secretary, Edward Marsh, whom he appointed somewhat irregularly and who accompanied him faithfully from office to office until they arrived together at the august, but somewhat uncongenial, portals of the Treasury. This partnership was in itself irregular: tribute to the dog-like, or perhaps more truly cat-like, devotion Winston aroused in this rather feminine type—in himself a remarkable man, who became a public-spirited patron and encourager of artists and writers. This faithful partnership took its rise from a party at which Marsh was put across Winston by a forceful aunt. The moral Marsh drew was never to miss parties. Actually he had already met Churchill and found him overbearing; but Lady Lytton assured him that 'the first time you meet Winston you see all his faults, and the rest of your life you spend in discovering his virtues'. And so it proved.

Together they sallied off to Manchester to fight the election, where they explored the slums, Winston fascinated and horrified. He had never seen such places before: 'Fancy living in one of these streets—never seeing anything beautiful—never eating anything savoury—*never saying anything clever*!' Marsh was entranced to find that Winston had never so much as heard of a lodging-house. He fell completely for his new master and tells us that it was the officials who saw most of him who liked him best: they soon saw that there was no ill-will in his asperities or his impatience, no malice and hardly any guile—rare for a politician. And yet his manner of speaking in these early years was apt to arouse intense hostility. Marsh says that it was partly due to the difficulty he had in articulation, the harshness of utterance which could be very effective when aggression was called for, but which sounded aggressive when it was not intended.

A speech about Lord Milner in retirement, who had become a hero to the displaced Tories, gave much offence, particularly a phrase about 'this disconsolate pro-consul'. King Edward at Biarritz was alerted; when the Prime Minister attributed the party-rancour that had arisen to Milner's own intemperateness, 'I cannot consider Lord Milner's speech in the House of Lords was intemperate. If it was, what were Mr. W. S. Churchill's speeches in the House of Commons?' We observe King Edward's almost paternal interest in his old friend's son, commenting like a headmaster on his form, pleased when he improves; performing his duty as a monarch in toning down asperities, helping to keep things together. Another phrase of Churchill's that became notorious and was frequently flung back at him was when he described some unwelcome statement as a 'terminological inexactitude'. The born writer's fondness for words and phrases became sometimes a liability to the politician.

More serious matters were to the fore and it fell to Churchill to put them to the King. There was the question of the new Transvaal Constitution: were the Boers to be granted complete self-government so soon after the war they had made? The Liberal government was in favour of taking the risk. The King put his finger on the crux of the matter in his letter to Churchill. Would this increase or diminish the chance of an English majority? Would it encourage immigration from England or choke it off? 'The King can well understand that the onus of all these discussions in Parliament was thrown upon your shoulders, and no doubt severe criticisms were made from both extremes, but his Majesty is glad to see that you are becoming a *reliable* minister and above all a serious politician'—here Edward VII took up the pen himself to add, '*which can only be attained by putting country before party*'. The junior minister replied with an immense letter of thirteen pages: too much for the King; he did not reply.

In July, however, Churchill concluded his speech recommending the Transvaal Constitution to Parliament with a magnificent appeal to the Tories, showing how much above mere party-spirit he was and foreshadowing the things to come. 'I will ask them whether they cannot join with us to invest the grant of a free constitution to the Transvaal with something of a national sanction. With all our majority we can only make it the gift of a party; they can make it the gift of England.' They did not respond: to the party-Tory he was for long anathema. Later, he gave expression to his vision of the future of small nationalities—a subject on which Stalin, himself a sprig of one of them, was to specialise, with how different results!—'If the near future should unfold to our eyes a tranquil, prosperous, consolidated Afrikander nation under the protecting aegis of the British Crown, then, I say, the good as well as the evil will not be confined to South Africa . . . everywhere small peoples will have more room to breathe, and everywhere great empires will be encouraged by our example to step forward—it only needs a step—into the sunshine of a more gentle and more generous age.'

Then came the offer of the Cullinan diamond—the largest ever to come to light—to the British Crown by the Transvaal government as a peace-offering, a token of its loyalty within the Commonwealth. Small-minded people at both ends were opposed to this generous act, but the Under-Secretary through his friendship with his former captor, Botha, now Prime Minister of the Transvaal, was able to advance it. He had his way, and in recognition of his part in it he was presented with a replica of the diamond. When the object was taken round his luncheon-table on a silver salver for the guests to see, his aunt Lady Lilian, after one look at what she took to be a not very well-strained white jelly, replied, 'No, thank you.'

In the winter of 1907-8 Churchill and Eddie Marsh went off for a tour of the East African territories in their charge. In those spacious days the tour gave them four months off and commissions for the Under-Secretary to write a series of articles for the *Strand Magazine,* his private secretary for the *Manchester Guardian.* When Marsh applied to the Treasury for some item of equipment on the ground that Winston was taking one, Lord Chalmers replied, 'I dare say he is, but *you're* not a Blenheim spaniel'. Before leaving, Churchill finished an article for the *Daily News* with the question, 'Where is the statesman to be found who is adequate to the times?' and told Charles Masterman that if he were eaten by some horrible tsetse fly in East Africa this was his last message to the nation. The statesman who was the answer was shortly to be found in East Africa, but he was taking no chances with the tsetse fly: Eddie Marsh observed him in the heat muffled up like Father Christmas. They had had a leisurely journey out through the Mediterranean and Red Sea; the officers on board the *Venus,* who began with a strong prejudice against the Minister, ended up at his feet.

When the articles came out as a book, *My African Journey*, they contained some Radical sentiments. 'I have always experienced a feeling of devout thankfulness never to have possessed a square yard of that perverse commodity called "land".' Something must have converted him by the time he set eyes on Chartwell and gradually acquired that delightful Kentish valley with its sidelong prospect away to the South Downs. 'I am clearly of opinion that no man has a right to be idle, whoever he be or wherever he lives.' This, which had a Radical ring in 1908, has quite a different application today.

The theme of the book is that of the immense possibilities of development, which thrilled Churchill's imagination. He spent hours at Ripon Falls watching the waters and revolving plans to harness them: 'so much power running to waste, such a coign of vantage unoccupied, such a lever to control the natural forces of Africa ungripped, cannot but vex and stimulate imagination.... And what fun to make the immemorial Nile begin its journey by diving through a turbine.' His mind leaped forward at the prospect of controlling the system of Central African waters, the levels and flows, improving and co-ordinating the channels; he imagined the railway routes connecting up with steamers across the Great Lakes to form an uninterrupted chain of communication from Mombasa to Khartoum and thence to Cairo.

When he got to Khartoum he could see what British enterprise had accomplished in only the ten years since the Dervish empire had been shattered at Omdurman: Khartoum rebuilt in some splendour, quays giving upon the river, a fleet of steamers going up and down, a railway running more than a thousand miles to Cairo; in the immaterial realm, slavery abolished, the population restored and their education begun. In East Africa his hopes were upon Uganda as a most fertile and promising country, and he rejoiced that physical conditions were such as 'to prevent the growth in the heart of happy Uganda of a petty white community with the harsh and selfish ideas which mark the jealous contact of races and the selfish exploitation of the weaker'. Such was the message not only of English enterprise but of English humanity.

Much of what he foresaw has come to pass in the half-century since he bicycled considerable stretches along the native tracks between the Great Lakes. Whole areas at that date had been depopulated by the ravages of sleeping sickness: not even he could foresee the work of recovery wrought by the achievements of twentieth-century medicine.

Along with this there went the inexhaustible capacity of his temperament for sheer enjoyment, and the book is full of vivid descriptions bringing the exotic scenery to the eye: the wonderfully coloured butterflies feeding upon the filth, the orchids, the flowers, the tangle of vegetation, the sunlight upon falls, the wild life, a whole river-bank that slid into the water at a shot—crocodiles packed together like sardines. There were the delights of shooting rhinoceros and pig-sticking: one wild pig with Winston's spear in him took refuge in a deep hole 'from which no inducements or insults could draw him'. He had the pleasure of meeting (and shooting) one of the rare Burchell's White Rhinoceros: Eddie, who was caught at the encounter with only an umbrella, which he hoped to open with a bang, thought it looked rather a subfusc rhinoceros. However, the vegetation alone was such as to astonish; 'as for our English garden products, brought in contact with the surface of Uganda they simply gave one wild bound of efflorescence or fruition and break their hearts for joy'.

The fact was that they saw the world at its best—before 1914.

On Campbell-Bannerman's death Asquith formed his very able administration, on the personnel of which British politics subsisted almost up to the Second World War. Not afraid of superior talents, Asquith drew round him a government that included Lloyd George, Sir Edward Grey, Haldane and Lord Morley; and to these he proceeded to promote Churchill at thirty-three. There were people who were opposed to his inclusion in the Cabinet: such readiness to serve, such obvious ambition to work hard and make his contribution, called for obstruction. There was a question whether he should go to the Local Government Board; but that had not the recommendation of a seat in the Cabinet. Churchill preferred the Board of Trade; he declined, he said, to be 'shut up in a soup-kitchen with Mrs. Sidney Webb'. But he did not thus escape the Webbs; he walked straight into their parlour, where were spun so many plans for remaking English society on the Fabian model.

The grand opportunity for social legislation and reform which had been lost when Chamberlain dropped the Radical leadership over Home Rule now fell to this Liberal government and was grasped effectively and energetically by Lloyd George and Churchill. It was to this campaign for social services—labour exchanges, unemployment and sickness insurance benefits, old age pensions with the concomitant campaign for economy on Army and Navy—that the fruitful partnership between these two dated.

The formidable Beatrice Webb had her eye on them for her own (entirely public-spirited) purpose. She had already met Churchill; her first impression can hardly be described as favourable: 'restless—almost intolerably so, without capacity for sustained and unexciting labour—egotistical, bumptious, shallow-minded and reactionary, but with a certain personal magnetism, great pluck and some originality—not of intellect but of character. More of the American speculator than the English aristocrat. . . . Bound to be unpopular—too unpleasant a flavour with his restless, self-regarding personality, and lack of moral or intellectual refinement. . . . No notion of scientific research, philosophy, literature or art: still less of religion. But his pluck, courage, resourcefulness and great tradition may carry him far unless he knocks himself to pieces like his father.' I leave this as a monument to the superciliousness of the intellectual, the readiness to condemn on a very superficial acquaintance and little knowledge. Beatrice Webb was nothing if not cocksure—a quality that led the Webbs ultimately to their stupefying credulity about 'Soviet Communism', which completely took them in. John Burns, the old Labour leader who formed a (rather stupid) member of the government, had a better opinion of its youngest member: he thought Winston cleverer than his father and possessing a sounder political instinct.

Further acquaintance modified Mrs. Webb's harsh judgment of Churchill; indeed for some time he became her white-headed boy, upon whom her chief hopes were placed. (I fear that with the Webbs, who judged by types rather than individuals, by the general rather than the concrete, their opinions of people went up and down according to whether they served their public purposes or not.) On Churchill's appointment to the Board of Trade they had him to dinner along with Masterman and Beveridge, the inventor of the scheme of Labour Exchanges. Churchill had agreeably 'swallowed whole Sidney's scheme for boy labour and unemployment. . . . He is most anxious to be friendly and we were quite willing to be so. . . . Winston has a hard temperament, with the American's capacity for the quick appreciation and rapid execution of new ideas, whilst hardly comprehending the philosophy beneath them. But I rather liked the man. He is under no delusions about himself.' This from the woman who had rejected Chamberlain, though rather in love with him, on the ground that he had delusions about *him*self, was no small compliment.

Before succumbing completely to Beatrice's charms, Labour Exchanges, organisation of labour and all, Winston took an important step towards fortifying himself: he decided to marry. We hear the news first from Wilfrid Blunt. 'Blanche Hozier writes from Blenheim that her daughter Clementine is to marry Winston Churchill. She says of him, "yesterday he came to London to ask my consent, and we all three came on here. Winston and I spoke of you and of your great friendship with his father. He is so like Lord Randolph, he has some of his faults, and all his qualities. He is gentle and tender, and affectionate to those he loves, much hated by those who have not come under his personal charm." It is a good marriage for both of them, for Clementine is pretty, clever and altogether charming, while Winston is what the world knows him, and a good fellow to boot.'

The poet made one of his rare visits to London to attend the wedding at St. Margaret's, Westminster, on 12 September. 'It was quite a popular demonstration. Lord Hugh Cecil Winston's best man, and the great crowd of relations, not only the church full, but all Victoria Street, though that may have partly been for the Eucharistic Congress. . . . At St. Margaret's I arrived late when all the seats were taken, but Blanche Hozier found me one in the family pew. . . . The bride was pale, as was the bridegroom. He had gained in appearance since I saw him last, and has a powerful if ugly face. Winston's responses were clearly made in a pleasant voice, Clementine's inaudible.' He tells us, in the concluding sentence of *My Early Life,* that he lived happily ever afterwards. (That autumn, too, saw another Churchill marriage: of Winston's brother, John, to Lady Gwendeline Bertie, who became mother of Clarissa, later wife of Sir Anthony Eden.)

The marriage was approved of by Mrs. Webb for her own high reasons. In October 'we lunched with Winston Churchill and his bride—a charming lady, well bred and pretty, and earnest withal—but not rich, by no means a good match, which is to Winston's credit. Winston had made a really eloquent speech on the unemployed the night before and he has mastered the Webb scheme, though not going the whole length of compulsory labour exchanges. He is brilliantly able—more than a phrase-monger I think—and he is definitely casting in his lot with the constructive state action.' Now her mandibles close upon Lloyd George: 'a clever fellow, but has less intellect than Winston, and not such an attractive personality—more of the preacher, less of the statesman'. I think we may conclude that Lloyd George was less susceptible to the influence.

In fact Churchill showed himself much more audacious and energetic than the Webbs or even Beveridge hoped. At the dinner-party at which the Minister first met Beveridge, that superior young man from Balliol was not 'as much impressed by his cleverness as I expected to be, he was or appeared to be rather tired and inconsecutive'. He noticed, however, Churchill's horror of being called a Liberal. Stimulated by the Webbs and Beveridge, Churchill took Eddie Marsh off with him to Germany to study its system of Labour Exchanges on the spot. The Germans were astonished at the easy terms upon which the private secretary was with his official superior, never once clicking heels to attention. In the intervals of doing their home-work they toured the battlefields of the Franco-Prussian war in Alsace, Winston giving far more lucid explanations of the battles than he could yet give of the principles of Labour Exchanges.

He got it all mastered in time; the scheme was immense in its scope: there was the necessity for him to convert the Prime Minister and the Cabinet first. Having done that he obtained their assent to implement the Reports of the Royal Commission on the Poor Law and Unemployment six months before their publication—to young Beveridge's surprise. In November he gave a large breakfast at the Board of Trade to all the Labour M.P.s, at which he used the Webbs to explain the theory of the proposed Exchanges. Their purpose was to help the community and industry by organising the supply of labour. This might have been done on a purely local basis, experimentally and sporadically, offering to supplement existing facilities with government assistance where desired. Instead of this he opted for a full-blown national system of Labour Exchanges, taking over the existing facilities and weaving them into the scheme. He had his eye on something further: their use for the purpose of a national system of unemployment insurance, if and when called into operation. As usual, he was before hand: he asked Beveridge and Llewelyn Smith to try their hands at preparing a practical scheme of unemployment insurance. The scheme they drafted was that put into effect in 1911.

This was after Churchill had moved on to other spheres of activity. But what energy he generated: the Trade Boards Act, the Labour Exchanges Act, both in 1909. He made Beveridge Director of Labour Exchanges and these began to be set up from 1910 onwards. Beveridge cites Churchill's Presidency of the Board of Trade as a striking illustration 'of how much the personality of the Minister in a few critical months may change the course of social legislation'. And what fun he was to work for! These Oxford men found that 'the President has a mind about everything—and it's a mind one must attend to'. This rather surprised them, for to them he was still uneducated. One day at a dinner-party he picked up a book: 'Matthew Arnold's poems—who's Matthew Arnold?—do you know anything about Matthew Arnold?' They had no difficulty in telling him all about Matthew Arnold. 'Oh,' said Winston, 'this public school education!' Then, shaking his fist, 'If ever I get my chance at it!' He had not forgiven Harrow; if Arnold had been an Harrovian he might perhaps have heard of him.

Anyhow, it was more important to have a genius for action. Beveridge pays tribute to it. In the midst of the first election campaign of 1910, when he was in demand as a speaker all over the country—and was notoriously generous in going to the help of his friends—Beveridge went to him one morning in bed, after an all-night journey, with a list of the first women divisional officers for the Labour Exchanges. 'Let there be women', he said and signed without further ado. Even Lord Esher, the King's confidant, who had started with a prejudiced view, was now ready to admit that Winston had 'very nearly, if not quite, a first-rate intellect'. It is extraordinary the amount of prejudice he created and had to batter down in consequence. A homely dinner-party in Eccleston Square seems to have completed Lord Esher's conquest. 'He has a charming double room on the first floor, all books. A splendid library. It was a birthday dinner. Only six people. But he had a birthday cake with 35 candles. And *crackers*. He sat all the evening with a paper cap, from a cracker, on his head. A queer sight, if all the thousands who go to his meetings could have seen him. He and she sit on the same sofa, and he holds her hand. I never saw two people more in love. If he goes out of office, he has not a penny. He would have to earn his living, but he says it is well worth it if you live with someone you love. He would *loathe* it, but he is ready to live in a *lodging*—just two rooms—with her and the baby! They have a cook now, two maids and a man. *She* ran down to the kitchen before dinner to see that it was all right. And an excellent dinner it was!'

Their first baby to arrive, in the midst of all this activity in social legislation, was a girl—another Diana, a return to the eighteenth century for a name. Lloyd George was able to offer his congratulations as they sat on the Treasury Bench together. 'Is she a pretty child?' said the Chancellor of the Exchequer. 'The prettiest child ever seen,' said the President of the Board of Trade. 'Like her mother, I suppose?' said L. G. 'Not at all,' said Winston gravely, 'she's the very image of me.'

A sterner critic than Lord Esher loomed up in Mrs. Webb. One day she and Winston met on the Embankment—chaste assignation. 'Well, how do you think we are doing, Mrs. Webb?' '*You* are doing very well, Mr. Churchill, but I have my doubts about your Cabinet: I don't believe they mean to do anything with the Poor Law.' This was because the government was not for accepting the Webbs' scheme of breaking up the Poor Law and bringing it to an end. 'Oh, yes, they do,' replied Churchill, 'we are going in for a *classified* Poor Law.' This was not good enough for Mrs. Webb; she recognised, however, that Lloyd George and Churchill were favourable to its supersession but were pledged to the introduction of their insurance schemes first. She gave them credit for this: 'The big thing that has happened in the last two years is that Lloyd George and Winston Churchill have practically taken the *limelight*, not merely from their own colleagues, but from the Labour Party. They stand out as the most advanced politicians.' She envisaged their young Fabian followers, 'fully equipped for the fray—better than the Labour men—enrolling themselves behind these two Radical leaders'.

That was hardly likely, even if these early blissful beginnings of the Welfare State—to which these two men made such contributions—had not been shadowed by the sinister developments abroad, the threat constituted by twentieth-century Germany.

The curious thing is that Churchill, though he had the privilege of a personal invitation to the German Army manoeuvres in 1906 and again in 1909, was slow to perceive it. He was always a man of intense power of concentration; when engaged on a job, nothing else existed for him: in that sense, though a man of many ideas, a man of one idea at a time. And this provides the clue to the constantly recurring mistrust we find expressed as to his judgment. For such was his energy of mind and the battering force of his personality that he was apt to weigh down the weightier considerations on the other side.

Sir Edward Grey and the Foreign Office knew well how grave these were. They had had long experience of Germany's ill-will and continual attempts to exert pressure and force demands upon us. There had been ebullitions of it all through the Boer War, which went far beyond mere unfriendliness. They were expressions of characteristic German *Schadenfreude* and of a deep-seated jealousy of Britain, a determination to displace her, if possible. Childishly envious and on edge with inferiority complex as the Kaiser was—in this, that fatuous and somewhat winged peacock was a fair expression of his people—even he could assert that he was more friendly disposed than most Germans. Their ambassadors here, both Metternich and Lichnowsky, were convinced that British opinion was more friendly to Germany and her claims than ever German opinion was to Britain. To the Germans—apart from socialists and such people—to the dominant forces in the nation Britain was the enemy *par excellence*, for Britain stood in the way: a war with Britain was 'in the logic of history'.

And this was the real purpose of the powerful navy they were determined to build.[1] By no stretch of imagination could it be described as merely defensive. As Grey pointed out, without any fleet at all Germany would still be the most powerful nation on the Continent. Metternich himself admitted that the Germans could not expect to possess both the strongest army and the strongest navy in the world. Again and again he warned his government faithfully that fear would not compel Britain to accept terms: he was untimately sacrificed for telling the Germans what they did not wish to hear. For, as Grey said, with the candour and sincerity of his nature, a margin of naval superiority was a matter of life and death for Britain; for Germany it was not. Britain must maintain it at all costs, while willing to accept the fact of Germany's military pre-eminence.

The more one studies the history of those years the more it is brought home to one that nothing would deflect the German leadership from their naval challenge to Britain, and there is

[1] Bebel said that they wanted it for use in an offensive war against England. E. L. Woodward, *Great Britain and the German Navy*, 29.

evidence that they could hardly desist from it in face of public opinion in Germany. Reasonable accommodation would have been regarded as capitulation. How familiar the attitude and mentality are from the 1930's; continuous from the 1900's! Every time the Liberal government proposed a friendly slackening, it was taken for weakness; any offer for mutual reduction or slowing up of construction was regarded as an interference with Germany's sovereignty and her internal affairs. If Britain slackened her building, Germany took advantage of that fact to increase hers, hoping to overtake her. In the end Britain had to make it clear beyond all doubt that she could never afford to risk her very existence by allowing Germany to outbuild her. Even so, when 1914 came—and even with the aid of France and Italy—her margin of naval security was only just sufficient.

At the turn of the century Germany had rejected Chamberlain's overtures for an alliance. Bülow was convinced that time was on Germany's side, that Britain would have to accept her terms, that she had no alternative. When an alternative was found in the Entente with France, an attempt was made to break it by a threat of force. The Tangier incident—when the Kaiser was sent off, against his better judgment, to Tangier to assert the German interest in Morocco against France and Britain—only had the effect of strengthening the Entente. The Emperor, who considered that British statesmen sometimes had 'lucid intervals', was sometimes permitted moments of perception himself; but he would never, or never dared to, give way on German naval ambitions. An American observer of the European scene, Ambassador Page, saw clearly what was the root of the trouble and where it was leading. When war came in 1914, he wrote: 'no power on earth could have prevented it. The German militarism, which is *the* crime of the last fifty years, has been working for this for twenty five years. It is the logical result of their spirit and enterprise and doctrine. It *had* to come.'

But in these years, when the threat was developing that was to overshadow our lives, Churchill was immersed in social legislation. There was a spirit of friendly rivalry between Lloyd George and him. 'Sometimes when I see Winston making these speeches I get a flash of jealousy', said Lloyd George, 'and I have to say to myself, "Don't be a fool. What's the use of getting jealous of Winston?" ' In fact there was no doubt which was leader: in addition to his eleven years' seniority, his longer experience of Parliament, his greater flexibility and adaptability, his appeal to the masses with his brand of oratory, Lloyd George had the immense advantage of his standing within the Liberal party. He was the leader of the Radical wing, the second man in the party; Churchill was a recruit from Conservatism: he would have to work his passage.

Together, as advanced social reformers, they took the lead of the campaign for economy on arms, whether for the Army or Navy. In this Churchill was being faithful to his father's old line and consistent with his own; but it would soon cease to make sense. Meanwhile it gave much trouble to both Haldane at the War Office and McKenna at the Admiralty, and it vexed King Edward. At Swansea in August 1908 Churchill assured the miners that there was no German menace, that there was nothing to fight about except tropical plantations and coaling stations, and that even if Britain were defeated the status of the Colonies and India would remain unchanged. How unwise this was the experience of the first half of this century has taught us. He was young then, and he did not know. It is no part of a historian's purpose to show that his subject was always right, but rather how a great man learns from mistakes and matures with experience. And what this makes clear is that Churchill had no anti-German prejudice: the facts themselves instructed him.

In 1905 the Admiralty was convinced that the Germans were accelerating their programme and that security at sea could only be maintained by building six new dreadnoughts. This programme was strenuously resisted in the Cabinet by Lloyd George and Churchill, supported by Morley and young Harcourt. King Edward was annoyed at their intrusion into foreign affairs, which he considered the domain of the Prime Minister and the Foreign Secretary. We have a view of what the King's intimate adviser, Lord Esher, thought in his Diary: 'Winston works tremendously hard, but gets involved in subtleties. Ll. George realises that in 1912 we shall be in danger of having hardly a *one* power naval standard. Winston cannot see it. I pointed out to them that the great majority of the country is against them. To resign upon the point would ruin them.' Eventually they accepted the inescapable facts of the situation; by 19 March 1909 Asquith was able to assure Grey that 'the course of things this week has been a complete débâcle for them and their ideas, and the two cannot help reflecting how they would have looked at this moment if they had resigned, with (as Winston predicted) 90 per cent of the Liberal party behind them'.

The truth is that he was never an expert party-politician in the narrow sense and his judgment of party-reactions and manoeuvres was often at fault and rather naïf. The Admiralty got its dreadnoughts and the country was, for the time, safe—until the German Navy Law of 1912 announced an immense increase: which it fell to Churchill as First Lord of the Admiralty—poacher turned gamekeeper—to meet. We need not blame him overmuch: at the Board of Trade and at the Home Office it was not his business to build battleships. When he went to the Admiralty his point of view changed: no one could have done better. Meanwhile, having brought him into line in time for the election campaign, the Prime Minister gave him a headmasterly certificate of conduct to the King, drawing his attention to 'the moderation of tone, and the absence of personalities and bad taste—as well as the conspicuous ability—which have characterised Winston Churchill's campaign in Lancashire'.

So too Lord Crewe and Grey thought, and agreed that Churchill 'has shown marked improvement during the elections of 1910, in grasp and tone'. At this time they thought 'the other one' (Lloyd George) incorrigible. The fact was that, under the rhetoric necessary to keep his end up with the masses and in the party-hierarchy, Churchill was a moderate. Masterman found him ready to praise 'government by aristocracy and revealing the aboriginal and unchangeable Tory in him. . . . Winston, of course, is not a democrat, or at least, he is a Tory democrat.' Lloyd George said, apropos of his Radical Budget of 1909 which provoked the Lords to reject it and so brought on the prolonged constitutional crisis and the two elections of 1910, 'if we put a special clause in the Budget exempting Sunny [Marlborough] from taxation, Winston would let us do what we liked'.

However, for the two electoral handicaps of 1910, he put forth a popular volume of selections from his speeches on the leading issues—the House of Lords, the Land, the Budget and Free Trade: *The People's Rights*. The House of Lords being the main issue, the statesman's thoughts are summed up under such headings as:

> 'Has the House of Lords ever done right in any of the great controversies of the last 100 years?'

It did not appear that they had.

> 'The power of the Peers in Finance is only a power to wreck.'
> 'The House of Lords is Representative of Nobody.'

It was thought that the effect of his strictures upon the Lords in general, and upon dukes in particular, was somewhat diminished by this descendant of so many dukes, with a duke for his cousin, going to stay with him at Blenheim that Christmas.

Nevertheless he scrambled through the two elections of 1910 successfully, with no pretence of enjoying those orgies indispensable to democratic life. Having fought more parliamentary elections than any other member of the House of Commons—'each taking at least three weeks, with a week beforehand when you are sickening for it, and at least a week afterwards when you are convalescing and paying the bills'—he reckoned that considerably more than a year of his life had been spent under these trying conditions. There were the old jokes to endure trotted out for the thirty-third time, and 'nothing is so ludicrous as a large number of good people in a frantic state, so long as you are sure they are not going to hurt you'. Worst of all, there is the grief of one's supporters when defeated: 'men and women who have given weeks of devoted and utterly disinterested labour, with tears streaming down their cheeks and looking as if the world had come to an end!'

The resistance of the Lords to Lloyd George's Budget probably cost the Tories a hundred seats at the election of January 1910. Thus the Liberals were returned again, though dependent on Irish votes for a majority—which made the question of Home Rule once more a foremost issue in politics. At once Churchill won his well-earned promotion to a Secretaryship of State: he went to the Home Office. Here it fell to him to report the proceedings in the Commons to the King, who much enjoyed his Disraelian accounts of them—it would be nice to have them to read—though he had not much relished Churchill's allusions to the Crown in regard to the creation of peers in the course of the election. This is the last we hear of the kindly, almost avuncular, relations that subsisted between King Edward and his old friend's son, for in May the King died.

Whatever Churchill now said, nothing could mitigate the animosity of the Conservatives towards him or the rancour with which they pursued him. They hated him much worse than they hated Lloyd George, a more dangerous opponent, for he was a genuine Radical who had no use for the class-system: Churchill was a renegade from his class. One duke announced—rather comically, the image was so appropriate to the public's idea of a duke—that he would like to put them both in the middle of twenty couple of his hounds. Conservative leaders in the Commons said that his conversion to Radicalism coincided with his personal interests; a Cecil said that he was entirely without principle and 'ready to follow any short cut to the Prime Ministership'. (And, indeed, why should he not? Was that not what they were all out for? It was merely that he was obvious and direct, where they were oblique and devious.) A Lyttelton said, with some mixture of metaphor: 'He trims his sails to every passing air. One might as well try to rebuke a brass band.' There was brass, as there should be, in the Churchillian orchestra.

What is interesting is to observe that underneath this chorus of abuse, Churchill sat—like his ancestor the great Duke, and true to the tradition of his family—somewhat loosely to party. It was to this year 1910 that his first suggestions of a national coalition dated, a junction of parties to settle the Irish and constitutional issues that were becoming so embittered as to poison political life, and to prepare against the German menace now clearly visible to anybody of intelligence. In this endeavour he found a kindred spirit in F. E. Smith, later Lord Birkenhead. This brilliant lawyer had this quality, among others, in common with Churchill, that within the partisan claptrap there was a sound core of patriotic spirit. F. E. Smith's father had been a humble follower of Lord Randolph in the country; the son was at first unwilling to meet Churchill, who had left his father's party. But once they did meet they found each other: 'from that hour our friendship was perfect. It was one of my most precious possessions. It was never disturbed by the fiercest party fighting. It was never marred by the slightest personal difference or misunderstanding.' Thus Churchill on that famous friendship. There was much else they shared too, the amenities, the pleasures, the excitements of life; those gay festive Christmases at Blenheim.

Now these younger men made their first attempt to bring their elders together. It is significant that Lloyd George and Balfour were willing. It was the second-rate who were not, in particular that very uninspiring man, Bonar Law, shortly to be leader of the Conservative party. A man of no imagination, he always had a rooted objection to Churchill. It would have saved a great deal of bitterness, avoided many hazards, if only the parties could have come together to face them. Again and again in the mounting tension over Ireland—Home Rule, Ulster, Curragh and the whole dangerous course—Churchill made attempts across the party-barriers to achieve a settlement by coalition and agreement. They were always rejected until, during the war, the Conservatives made their own terms, the first of which was that Churchill should be kept out. He was their prime victim.

Meanwhile, at the Home Office 1910-11, he threw himself into his new job with characteristic zest. Wilfrid Blunt paid him tribute in an unexpected quarter. The old socialist leader Hyndman brought Blunt the information from Bebel and the socialist leaders in Germany that the dominant forces there meant aggression, and that war could not be prevented since German democracy was really powerless. This had no effect on Blunt in his comfortable Sussex squire's ivory-tower. Hyndman, who was in favour of compulsory military training in England, went on to ask about Churchill, of whom he had heard nothing good. Blunt told him that 'there were three things of value in him, great ability, honesty in politics, and a good heart'.

Warmth of heart was evident in the enthusiasm with which he embarked at once on prison reform, calling for the programme Blunt had put forward, usefully for once, and himself making a tour of the prisons. He was moved by the number of boys in prison, with nothing of the criminal type about them and incarcerated for nothing much. It was scandalous that so many of them should be there, often for merely sleeping out: a way to create criminals. Where previous Home Secretaries had been content to administer the system as it was, Churchill, with his instinct for action, got powers to reform it. Blunt was pleased with him: 'he is quite thorough about the reforms and said he would have liked to adopt the whole of my programme only public opinion was not yet ready for it'. One reason why he wanted a coalition to deal with the House of Lords issue and end the interminable chaffer about it was to get on with the practical job of alleviating misery. 'If we could only get it shunted,' he would say to Masterman, 'think of all we could do: boy prisoners, truck, feeble-minded.' Eddie Marsh tells us that Churchill went to see Galsworthy's play *Justice* and was moved by it. Lady Randolph gave a dinner to bring them together. All not without its effect: Churchill got his powers enacted to initiate the modern era of prison reform. The pity is that no successor of similar courage and calibre appeared in that office to carry the campaign to its proper conclusion and remove the most notorious derogation from justice in Britain, bringing it into accord with civilised standards in other countries.

When Churchill went down to stay with Blunt that autumn, 'he was dressed in a little close-fitting fur-collared jacket, tight leggings and gaiters, and a little round hat, which, with his half-mischievous face, made him look the exact figure of Puck'. But he 'is going on energetically about prison reform, and will push it much beyond what he has already announced publicly. He means to arrange matters so that next year there will be 50,000 fewer people sent to prison than this year.' Someone else in conversation with him discovered the anguish the consideration of death-sentences—the most distasteful part of the Home Secretary's duties—cost him.

Other duties there were in plenty. Two celebrated affairs, Tonypandy and the Battle of Sidney Street, cost him much unpopularity and some obloquy. As the result of a strike in South Wales one district became greatly disturbed and there were riots. He might have moved in troops, as the Conservative party demanded; he contented himself with moving in a large number of Metropolitan police, keeping the troops in reserve. Order was preserved, and the general in charge attributed it entirely to these dispositions, which were Churchill's own idea. But this added unpopularity with Labour people, especially among the miners, to that which he already enjoyed with the Conservatives.

Nor was his own idea, of taking part in the Battle of Sidney Street, altogether a happy one. The trouble was that he could not keep away from trouble. Some suspicious Eastern European characters, who were armed, had barricaded themselves in a house in the East End and killed several of the police trying to round them up. It was thought that they were Anarchists; it is certain that they were burglars. At any rate the Home Secretary, in fur-lined coat and top hat, went down to the East End to have a look and could not resist conducting siege-operations. Unfortunately he was photographed in various attitudes and even appeared on cinema-reels. This was more than the conventional and respectable could stand in those days. The new king, George V, took exactly the same line as his father or grandmother would have done: what was a Cabinet minister doing down there in such a position, peeping round corners among the bullets? Mr. Balfour asked a sarcastic question in the Commons. 'We are concerned to observe photographs in the illustrated newspapers of the Home Secretary in the danger-zone. I understand what the photographer was doing, but why the Home Secretary?' When he got back from the scene of action there was an irate civil servant to chide him for his misdemeanour. 'What the hell have you been doing now, Winston?' said Masterman, bursting into the Minister's room. '*Now* Charlie,' said the Minister with his imitable lisp. 'Don't be croth. It was such fun.'

It must have been irresistible to serve such a Minister, who had the heart of a boy.

In the summer of 1911 Germany precipitated a dangerous crisis upon Europe, with the Agadir incident, which clearly foreshadowed the outbreak of war three years later. It seems clear that the Germans did not intend the war at that moment: their preparations were not yet complete, the widening of the Kiel Canal, to enable them to pass their fleet to and from the North Sea and the Baltic, would not be finished until August 1914. Their action in dispatching a cruiser to Agadir to assert their (largely non-existent) interests in Morocco was really to test the ground. Since their last similar action in 1906 they had forced a stinging defeat upon Russia, by supporting Austria's annexation of Slav Bosnia-Herzegovina. The result of that was that no Russian government could accept a further defeat at the hands of the Germans, and the Russians came to an understanding with Britain, compromising their differences. Now, since the Germans understood nothing in diplomacy save blackmail and bullying, this was to be put to the test of force.

The reaction surprised them. The Anglo-Russian Entente survived the shock and was strengthened by it, as the Anglo-French Entente had been in 1906. Holstein, the *éminence grise* of the Wilhelmstrasse—a more psychotic type than Bülow—believed that Britain would break any agreement she had entered into rather than be entangled in a Continental war. Those Radical and Pacifist elements in Britain did a grave disservice to peace, therefore, who gave him ground for thinking so. The unmistakable German threat shocked the more sensible among these elements into sense for the moment. Above all their leader, Lloyd George, whose underlying patriotism was stronger than the illusions he entertained. His Mansion House speech was a direct warning to the Germans that Britain would not purchase peace from them at any price and would defend her vital interests.

Churchill tells us that this came 'as a thunder-clap to the German government. All their information had led them to believe that Mr. Lloyd George would head the peace-party and that British action would be neutralised. Jumping from one extreme to another, they now assumed that the British Cabinet was absolutely united, and that the Chancellor of the Exchequer of all others had been deliberately selected as the most Radical Minister by the British government to make this pronouncement.' So like their clumsy stupidity, we may add, for the predominant sentiment of this Liberal government was pacific until it was overwhelmed by events in 1914.

Winston Churchill was among those who received a salutary shock and, being a sensible man, the impression remained. He was no longer to be found among those hampering the efforts of Grey at the Foreign Office, Haldane at the War Office, McKenna at the Admiralty, who were working to defend their country against a growing danger. He had hitherto been Lloyd George's closest associate in social reform and economy on the services; he had not been concerned with foreign affairs or defence. Henceforth he saw how the facts lay: the aggressive threat to Europe and to Britain constituted by Germany, the overriding necessity to prepare ourselves. This did not mean that he passed over to the aggressive. As to this we have the best testimony, that of Grey. Churchill 'followed the anxieties of the Foreign Office with intense interest.... He followed all the diplomacy closely, but never either in Council or in conversation with me did he urge an aggressive line. It was only that his high-mettled spirit was exhilarated by the air of crisis and high events. His companionship was a great refreshment.' The days had passed when Grey could regret chaffingly that the young Winston 'would soon be incapable of any post in the Cabinet but that of Prime Minister from sheer excess of mental energy'. The weary Foreign Secretary, longing for the country delights, the coolness of Fallodon in that hot summer in London, was grateful for the support of his younger colleague with all his superabundant energy. In the afternoons, after the anxieties of the day, they would go down to the Automobile Club together, where 'he would cool his ardour and I revive my spirits in the swimming-bath'.

That autumn—the immediate crisis over, the ultimate collision ever more certain—the Prime Minister saw fit to harness that dynamo of energy to the Admiralty. Asquith asked Churchill if he would like to become First Lord—actually a lower grade in the ministerial hierarchy. He answered, 'Indeed, I would'. It was a momentous task that he undertook, and at such an hour. For the whole security of Great Britain and the Empire, the existence of her people, then depended entirely on the Navy; and there is no doubt that the Navy needed to be revivified, brought up to date, magnetised, given new ideas. No one need doubt the courage or the patriotism of the senior fighting service from top to bottom of its ranks, but its very ascendancy for over a century had encrusted it with tradition, clogged it with conservatism, getting in the way of new methods necessary in an increasingly technical age.

Sir John Fisher, who was First Sea Lord 1907-10, had already tackled the task and brought about tremendous changes. An extraordinary man of near-genius, who apprehended all the demands of a machine-age and envisaged revolutionary solutions to new problems—the essential factor of speed, gunnery of a quite different order of magnitude, the development of submarines and naval aircraft—he had been responsible for the introduction of the modern battleship, which had jeopardised the margin of superiority and given the Germans a more equal chance. Fisher's work had demanded a superhuman effort and had been done at great cost: it divided the Navy from top to bottom; it created feuds and maddened Fisher. Moreover, when he retired on reaching seventy in 1910, it was not yet half done: the reconstitution of the Navy was but in its beginnings. Churchill writes, with magnanimity considering what ultimately happened between them in the fires of war: 'there is no doubt whatever that Fisher was right in nine-tenths of what he fought for. His great reforms sustained the power of the Royal Navy at the most critical period of its history. He gave the Navy the kind of shock which the British Army received at the time of the South African war. . . . But the Navy was not a pleasant place while this was going on. . . . Fisher was maddened by the difficulties and obstructions which he encountered, and became violent in the process of fighting so hard at every step.'

Churchill wished to bring back Fisher to carry forward the policy he had initiated; but though this proved impossible till the war came, he kept constant contact with the old sea-officer, whom he found 'a veritable volcano of knowledge and of inspiration; and as soon as he learnt what my main purpose was, he passed into a state of vehement eruption'. Thus began the famous unofficial partnership which ended so miserably under the stress of war. Years before they had taken to each other: when on a Mediterranean cruise in 1907 King Edward had found them 'most amusing together. I call them the "chatterers".' The old Sea-Lord had found the young Minister keen to fight his battles for him: 'it was rather sweet: he said his penchant for me was that I painted with a big brush!' Now it was from the astonishing old Admiral who had found in the civilian head of the Admiralty a favourite son: 'Yours to a cinder', 'Yours till Hell freezes', etc. The day came between them when it did freeze.

Churchill's main purpose, and what he was sent to the Admiralty to accomplish, was to bring the Navy up to war-standard and the highest fighting efficiency in time of peace, when more than half the government and its supporters would hardly recognise the necessity or the reality of the danger. (Left Liberals always preferred to accept the information coming from German sources to their own government's.) Churchill was therefore fighting on two fronts; on the naval front to bring it up to fighting form, on the political to get supplies to carry out his task. He was the man to do it, and no doubt that was why Asquith had replaced McKenna by him. There was a certain irony in that Churchill had opposed McKenna's programme of dreadnoughts a few years before: McKenna had no love for Churchill after that; for his part Churchill never bore him any ill will. Asquith evidently appreciated that the Navy needed his dynamism.

The first necessity was the creation of a navy war staff—something parallel to the organisation that Haldane was engaged in working out for the Army. Along with this went the necessity for co-ordinating plans for sending the British Expeditionary Force to France on the outbreak of war. Admiral Wilson, who had succeeded Fisher as First Sea-Lord, did not see the need for either of these, and shortly he went. For his Naval Secretary Churchill took—contrary to advice—Beatty, the youngest flag-officer, whom he had met years before at Omdurman. There was general agreement about promoting Jellicoe, the cleverest of the Admirals, over the heads of several of those senior to him, to take supreme command.

Thus equipped and supported, Churchill gave himself up to the crucial task in preparing England's defences for war. Always placable himself, he insisted on the absolute cessation of the vendetta Fisher had started. His policy was in the main Fisher's policy without his methods. But there was not time enough to carry through the titanic task to anything like the degree demanded by the technique of modern war: hence 'many untoward events' later. 'At least fifteen years of consistent policy were required to give the Royal Navy that widely extended outlook upon war-problems and of war-situations without which seamanship, gunnery, instrumentalisms of every kind, devotion of the highest order, could not achieve their due reward. Fifteen years! And we were only to have thirty months!'

Thus began a new life of intense, and as usual single-minded, concentration upon a fresh subject. We may easily suppose that, new as he was to naval matters, they appealed more deeply to his nature than social reform. The main axis of his life's interest, whether as subaltern, Minister in his prime or Prime Minister, called back to office or in retirement, as historian or statesman, in action or in the bulk of his writing, was the subject of war—a unique qualification among democratic politicians.

Eight months of every year were now spent afloat, inspecting naval bases, dockyards, ships, establishments, in the Admiralty yacht *Enchantress.* This was really a miniature liner of 4000 tons with a Board Room, a good cellar and plenty of accommodation for guests, naval, political or simply social. Admiral Beatty could not bear these trips: he preferred to be either at sea with the Fleet, or else in the hunting-field. Or perhaps he found it hard—like Brooke later—to support the unceasing battery of what Baldwin called 'Winston's 100 horse-power mind'; for he now talked nothing but the Sea and the Navy, forcing Beatty to think out every aspect of a naval war with Germany and perpetually discussing its problems. Elderly Asquith, who sometimes came on these excursions and whose mind was more cultivated than war-like, was to be found peaceably reading Baedeker with comments to an appreciative circle. So too Eddie, who says in his engaging way that in 1911 'we moved to the Admiralty', which he found the most agreeable of all their offices together; he records with enthusiasm those Whitsun cruises to inspect Gibraltar, Malta and anything else worth inspecting—Paestum, Spalato, Ragusa, Corfu.

In 1912 they were brought smartly to attention by the new German Navy Law, providing for 'an extraordinary increase in the striking force of ships of all classes immediately available'. Even the socialists in the Reichstag did not dare to oppose. Commenting on this challenging measure Churchill said, 'the purposes of British naval power are essentially defensive. . . . The British Navy is to us a necessity and, from some points of view, the German Navy is to them more in the nature of a luxury.' This reflection provoked a storm of abuse in Germany—all the usual symptoms of their psychotic state. Haldane had been sent on a mission to Berlin to see if some agreement could not be reached on reduction of naval armaments. In the course of the discussion the Kaiser handed him the new naval programme. The unspeakable Tirpitz commented on his departure, 'after Haldane's visit, when our extravagant desire for an understanding led the English to believe for a time that they could treat us like Portugal, the government in London refused an agreement on neutrality'.

In all the negotiations and discussions raised by the Liberal government to stop the race in naval armaments, the German demand was always the same: that England should remain neutral in a Continental war. In other words, that Germany should have a free hand in Europe to crush France and deal with Russia—leaving us to confront a German-controlled Europe. How could they suppose that we should be such fools? (Under the able conduct of our affairs before 1914 there was no likelihood of that; under the confused conduct of our affairs in the 1930's we very nearly arrived at just that—only succeeded in extricating ourselves by the war of 1939, which the whole course of our action, or rather inaction, had brought upon us.)

The Liberal government's reply to the failure to get agreement was immediate and right: a speeding up and an increase of building, 'a maintenance of naval superiority known to be a matter of life and death to an island power, dependent upon imported foodstuffs'.[1] A further measure of immense importance which was decided on Churchill's Mediterranean cruise this year was an agreement with the French by which they concentrated their Navy in the Mediterranean, while Britain concentrated hers in the North Sea. That this was the consequence of his policy seems to have been lost on the ineffable Tirpitz, who wrote, even after the war should have opened his eyes: 'in order to estimate the strength of the trump-card which our fleet put in the hands of an energetic diplomacy at this time, one must remember that in consequence of the concentration of the English forces which we had caused in the North Sea, the English control of the Mediterranean and Far Eastern waters had practically ceased'. Churchill expresses himself astonished at such incomprehension. Later, Tirpitz considers that 'seventeen years of fleet-building had, it is true, improved the prospects of an acceptable peace with England'. Churchill describes him as 'a sincere, wrong-headed, purblind old Prussian': one might equally well describe him as a crazy lunatic, if he had not been characteristic of the ruling forces in Germany.

The truth is obvious: nothing would stop them. The occult forces that ruled in Germany, the General Staff, Army and Navy—to whom the Kaiser was but a vain posturing mascot, with his fatuous letters to the Czar addressed from 'the Admiral of the Atlantic to the Admiral of the Pacific'—were determined on their all-out throw for *Weltmacht*. To think that a great nation's affairs should have been governed by such people!—many millions of good fellows perished because of it in the twentieth century and all our lives been darkened. Whole libraries of books have been and continue to be written on the origins of the war of 1914-18 or that of 1939-45. We really do not need to waste much time on them: the origins are perfectly clear, the determination of Ger-

[1] E. L. Woodward, *Great Britain and the German Navy*, 11.

many's ruling forces, backed by most of the nation, to ride roughshod over everybody else and achieve world power at whatever cost. Churchill sums up the situation completely though briefly: 'to create the unfavourable conditions for herself in which Germany afterwards brought about the war, many acts of supreme unwisdom on the part of her rulers were necessary. France must be kept in a state of continued apprehension. The Russian nation must be stung by some violent affront inflicted in their hour of weakness. The slow, deep, restrained antagonism of the British Empire must be roused by the continuous and repeated challenge to the sea-power by which it lived. Then and then only could those conditions be created under which Germany by an act of aggression would bring into being against her a combination strong enough to resist and ultimately to overcome her might.'

The German outbreaks against the peace of the world were continuous, two waves of the same movement. This passage relating to the war of 1914 may stand also for that of 1939—except that the ineptitude of Baldwin and Chamberlain converted the unfavourable conditions for Germany in 1914 to favourable conditions in 1939; and where the methods of the Kaiser's Germany were those of bullying and blackmail, those of Hitler's Germany were of a bestiality hardly imaginable—which yet must not be forgotten.

Churchill stuck to his job with all the energy of which he was capable: we may say that upon him and his work in these years rested the safety of the nation. 'The stakes were very high. If our naval defence were maintained we were safe and sure beyond the lot of any other European nation; if it failed, our doom was certain and final.' From 1912 was carried through the conversion of the fleet from coal-burning to oil-burning, greatly increasing speed and mobility. In 1913 he twice made proposals for a 'naval holiday' to Germany. No response, save the ingenious offer from Tirpitz of a ratio of construction which would have the effect of lowering 'the British security'. The alternative was the three programmes of 1912, 1913 and 1914, 'which comprised the greatest additions in power and cost ever made to the Royal Navy.... All through 1912 and 1913 our efforts were unceasing.' By 1914 even Tirpitz was ready to acknowledge that Germany could not out-build Britain; he went so far as to urge that any further increase in the German Navy would be 'a great political blunder'. The acknowledgment made nonsense of all his work, the whole course which he pressed on since 1900.

Impossible here even to sum up in detail the work Churchill

accomplished in those few years at the Admiralty—and unnecessary since he has described it himself: we may more usefully cite the impression it made upon a privileged observer, the King's confidant. Lord Esher began by expressing doubts as to his appointment as First Lord. He thought that he would have only one eye on the Navy, 'the other on the Radical tail'. He very soon revised his opinion when he saw that Churchill meant business about the formation of a Naval Staff: 'the most pregnant reform which has been carried out at the Admiralty since the days of Lord St. Vincent.... It is bound to have far-reaching results not only as regards the Navy but as regards our whole national and Imperial methods of preparing for war.' Lord Esher, who was himself a member of the Committee of Imperial Defence, expressed himself pleased with the details of Churchill's scheme. Later he wrote to Fisher, 'you must have been mightily pleased with Winston. He has done splendidly. It was a hard job for him too. What a tragedy it would be if this government were to be displaced by Bonar Law & Co.'

As to that we need not be in much doubt.

Churchill's intense preoccupation with the Navy did not mean that other things stood still. Within the country, too, events were moving to a grave crisis. Not for many years had there been such bitterness of party-spirit—the Churchills found themselves proscribed from many houses where they had formerly been welcome; once, after an attack on her friend Mrs. Asquith, Mrs. Churchill packed her bags and left Blenheim. Fortunately there was always the variegated and eccentric hospitality of Wilfrid Blunt's Sussex home. In October 1912 Churchill was there with George Wyndham and began a political argument that went on from tea-time all through dinner till midnight. 'It was a fine night, and we dined in the bungalow, dressed in gorgeous Oriental garments, Clementine in a suit of embroidered silk, purchased last year in Smyrna, Winston in one of my Baghdad robes, George in a blue dressing gown, and I in my Bedouin robes.... Winston was very brilliant, and though he kept on at the madeira he also kept his head, and played with George's wild rushes like a skilled fencer with a greatly superior fence. He is certainly an astonishing young man, and has gained immensely within the last two years in character and intellectual grip.' This was a tribute coming from such a source, for Blunt was a pro-German along with his other eccentricities; it was even more evidence of his tolerance that Winston could put up with him.

The Home Rule Bill brought party-dissension to a feverish pitch. Actually within the Cabinet Lloyd George and Churchill urged some measure of exclusion for Protestant Ulster. At Blenheim that summer of 1912 there was a big Unionist demonstration, attended by Bonar Law, F. E. Smith and Carson, with a hundred and twenty M.P.s and forty peers. The unionist leader had the ill-judgment to appeal to force: 'in our opposition we shall not be guided by the considerations or bound by the restraints which would influence us in an ordinary constitutional struggle. . . . I can imagine no length of resistance to which Ulster can go in which I should not be prepared to support them.' No wonder such a constitutionalist as Asquith had such a contempt for Bonar Law: this came very near to inciting the country to civil war. There were disorderly scenes in the Commons, such as have never been seen since; in one of them an Ulster M.P. hurled a book with accuracy and force at Churchill's head.

Yet Churchill remained a moderate. He maintained his friendship with F. E. Smith, in spite of the latter's extreme pro-Ulster stand. When Asquith wished to approach the Tories to see if some agreement were not possible, he used Churchill. It was only when Carson rejected Asquith's conciliatory offers that Churchill sent the 3rd Battle Squadron of the Fleet to Lamlash: a warning to Belfast. The unity of the United Kingdom was in danger of dissolution when the war broke out. Churchill had addressed a direct appeal to Carson: 'foreign countries never really understand us in these islands. They do not know what we know, that at a touch of external difficulties or menace all these fierce internal controversies would disappear for the time being, and we should be brought into line and into tune.'

Germans could hardly be expected to understand that, and perhaps it would not have mattered if they had. For their intention was already certain. The historian of these years tells us, 'it is clear that in January 1913 a decision was there [at Berlin] taken, that war between the Triple and Dual Alliances had become inevitable, and that Germany's business was to prepare for it instantly and bring it about when she was ready—in her time, not her enemies'. . . . Who made the decision at Berlin? The General Staff. There are reasons for thinking that from the inception the date worked towards was the beginning of August 1914.'[1] Herr Ballin, the distinguished head of the Hamburg-Amerika line, who knew opinion in England and America well, has left on record his conviction that 'even a

[1] R. C. K. Ensor, *England, 1870-1914*, 469-70.

moderately skilled German diplomatist could easily have come to an understanding with England and France, which could have made peace certain'. When the full fatality of his people's atavistic impulses came home to him, the great shipping magnate sought a way out in suicide: an eloquent comment on the whole course upon which they were bent.

In England the situation was very different. Though the Conservatives were staunch—as they were not on the renewal of the menace in the thirties—they did not reciprocate Churchill's wish for a coalition to conduct the war. The Liberal Cabinet was overwhelmingly pacific: it looked at one time as if the majority would resign rather than do their duty and resist Germany. 'Nothing less than the deeds of Germany', says Churchill, 'would have converted the British nation to war.' The delay meanwhile was agonising to those who knew all that depended on it: above all to Grey, who knew the extent of our moral obligation to France, who fully realised what our own fate would be if we did not resist, and yet the hope of whose life, the maintenance of European peace, lay now in ruins.

The invasion of Belgium, the evident determination to smash France, resolved all doubts. The greatest of all Grey's services to his country was, ironically for such a man of peace, to have brought the nation united into the war. He could at last speak all his mind to the Commons: 'when he came to deal with the Belgian question, it became apparent for the first time that almost the whole House approved. The news that "they have cheered him" was carried to the Foreign Office, causing inexpressible relief to those who knew better than the public that if we stood arguing together on the verge of war the Germans would be in Paris in a few weeks and England left shamed, friendless and foredoomed.'[1] In reading of those days, it makes one weep—to think of all that was involved in it, the nation's existence, itself unaware, the struggle Grey had had, all he had gone through. That night, as the lamps were being lit in the Park, Grey stood at the window of his room and said to a friend, 'the lamps are going out all over Europe; we shall not see them lit again in our life-time'. Nor, in a sense, have they ever been.

By good fortune, in those last days of July the fleet was mobilised on a war footing at the conclusion of its summer manoeuvres. With anyone else than Churchill at the Admiralty it might have been dispersed in accordance with routine. In that last week on his own

[1] G. M. Trevelyan, *Grey of Fallodon,* 265-6.

responsibility he kept it together. The outbreak of war found the strategic concentration of the Fleet in the North Sea accomplished, no longer open to the hazards of such a move. Grey himself, in quiet reflective fashion, recognises the immense service that this was: 'it was an accident that the end of the naval manoeuvres coincided with the diplomatic stage of a foreign crisis; the fact that full advantage was taken of this good fortune was due to the vigour and alertness of Churchill. . . . Undoubtedly the country owes much also to Churchill for the great advantage that war found us with a strong Fleet in an exceptionally good state of preparation.'[1]

When, in the course of the disappointments and frustrations of the war, the Tories got their revenge upon Churchill for the years between, his old opponent Kitchener paid him the most moving of compliments, that which went most to his heart: 'there is one thing at any rate they cannot take from you: the Fleet was ready'.

[1] Grey, *Twenty-Five Years,* II. 64.

CHAPTER TEN

The First World War

THERE is a revealing phrase that appears first in a letter Churchill wrote to Grey in the distress of the Dardanelles operations, and that would recur again and again at critical junctures in the second German war—adjuring him not to 'fall below the level of events'. (The letter was not sent, for Grey never did.) The phrase is a clue to the man: it springs out of a rare imaginative perception of the historical quality of events as they are proceeding; further, it implies a duty not to be unworthy of them, to play one's part to the full. There goes along with this a willing acceptance of responsibility, unhampered by any unworthy preoccupation with the consequences to oneself. Churchill tells us that he interpreted his duty as the head of the Admiralty before and in the first war thus: 'I accepted full responsibility for bringing about successful results, and in that spirit I exercised an unlimited power of suggestion and initiative over the whole field, subject only to the approval and agreement of the First Sea Lord on all operative orders'.

What a contrast to the spirit of the men who were all-powerful in the thirties, whose main preoccupation, so far from being not to fall below the level of events, was to see that they did not fall out of office themselves. It is odd, considering the intellectual inferiority of their conduct of our affairs, that *they* should have thought themselves so indispensable. On the other hand, they could have observed the consequences to Churchill in his own career of his simple, rash and honest acceptance of responsibility. These men were cleverer where their own interests were concerned; for we shall see that when things went wrong Churchill, with his *naïveté* of spirit and the unpopularity that genius often arouses, was made to bear the brunt of it, readily, enjoyably, vindictively.

The war began with the Germans, according to plan, overrunning Belgium, threatening to overwhelm France and making for the Channel ports to cut communications with Britain. The British Expeditionary Force—a solid, compact, efficient little army of six divisions, which had been built up by the able work of Haldane at the War Office—was in France, transported by the Navy without a single loss. As the Belgian forts fell with astonishing rapidity and the Channel ports were uncovered, Sir John French sent a despairing message to fortify Havre. Kitchener himself brought it over to Churchill at the Admiralty: 'I forget much of what passed between us. But the apparition of Kitchener *Agonistes* in my doorway will dwell with me as long as I live. It was like seeing old John Bull on the rack!'[1]

Churchill considered himself 'sufficiently instructed to derive an immense refreshment of judgment from personal investigation'; in other words, he could not keep away from the scene of action, and the First Lord of the Admiralty crossed over to make a tour of the front that appeared to be crumbling. Driven round by the Duke of Westminster, he witnessed the scenes 'that were afterwards to become commonplace: but their first aspect was thrilling'. As the German lunge threatened to envelop Antwerp he saw the strategic necessity to intervene and arrest it, if at all possible. For Antwerp was not only all that was left for a nucleus of Belgian national resistance, it was the true linch-pin of the Allied front. If a line from Antwerp to Lille could only have been held, it might have shortened the war by many months and many thousands of lives.

In this fearful emergency any action that offered a chance of staving off the disaster was worth trying—and Churchill was not thinking of reputation at such a moment. 'There is always a strong case for doing nothing, especially for doing nothing yourself.' He was ready to go over at a few hours' notice, with what could be got together of a naval division and a few naval guns, to throw himself into Antwerp in the path of the oncoming Germans. But it was no Omdurman over again: these were a different sort of barbarian hordes, highly trained and technical, with vastly superior equipment, masters of the art of modern war, inspired by the belief that the proper end of society is to make war. 'I now found myself suddenly, unexpectedly and deeply involved in a tremendous and hideously critical local situation which might well continue for some time. I had also assumed a very direct responsibility for exposing the city to bombardment and for bringing into it the inexperienced, partially equipped and partially trained battalions of the Royal Naval Division. I felt it my duty to see the matter through.'[1] The matter did not continue more than five days: there was no resisting the overwhelming forces the Germans brought to

[1] Churchill, *The World Crises,* I. 221, 235, 306.
[1] *Ibid.* 316, 322.

bear and which it was not realised they would have at their disposal. Meanwhile, the First Lord of the Admiralty was away from his post. It was not wise: 'no doubt had I been ten years older, I should have hesitated long before accepting so unpromising a task'. People said it was like the battle of Sidney Street over again. When Antwerp fell it was remembered against him; he would be made to smart for his gallant attempt to save it. Meanwhile, we may record at this moment of dejection his own golden rule in warfare: never to acquiesce in the will of the enemy, but to seek always to impose your will on him.

Other events came, through no fault of his own, to impair his authority. There was the torpedoing of the three old cruisers, *Aboukir, Cressy* and *Hogue* while on patrol. It was true that they should not have been on patrol, but it was not Churchill's business to interfere with the routine operations of ships. Actually orders had been issued to withdraw them; before these were received the disaster had occurred. People then said that the First Lord had overridden the advice of the Admirals and sent the squadron to its fate. Next came the torpedoing of the *Audacious.* The British public has always been more sensitive to losses of ships than to any other losses in war. The indignation with which these sinkings were regarded partly reflects the over-confidence engendered by a century's complete security at sea: the public somehow expected the Navy to conduct war without breaking any of its ships. Losses had not yet come to be seen as in the nature of war: the public mind was still that of peacetime—and this was a factor in frustrating what should have been the grandest and most original contribution towards winning the war: the Dardanelles campaign. No credit accrued for successful actions, like that of the Heligoland Bight, or for the fundamental operation of bringing the Fleet up to its highest strength and efficiency: that was taken for granted, simply expected.

These untoward events coincided with a shocking press-campaign against Prince Louis of Battenberg, the admirable sailor who was First Sea Lord, on account of his German origin.[1] Prince Louis resigned and Churchill decided to do what he had wanted to do four years before and bring back Fisher, now aged seventy-four. King George V regarded this appointment with the utmost misgivings and appealed to Asquith to prevent it. The King knew from experience the politics of the Navy and the distrust aroused by the

[1] Father of Admiral Earl Mountbatten and great-uncle of Prince Philip.

personality of Fisher, who had risen from small beginnings and antagonised many people of social position and influence. Churchill overrode these objections: he held Fisher to be the greatest naval officer since Nelson; the Admiralty needed strengthening, and so did his own position. The old man came back, as full of energy, ideas and resource as ever. The unofficial liaison was regularised, so to speak. Since Fisher worked best in the early hours of the morning and Churchill worked far into the night, they made 'very nearly a perpetual clock', in Fisher's words. He also said, referring to Churchill's minutes in red ink and his own in green, that they were 'the port and starboard lights'. Churchill comments, 'we had established a combination which, while it remained unbroken, could not have been overthrown by intrigue at home or the foe on the sea'. Alas, the day came when the combination ended in a fierce explosion, as was Fisher's way: it ended his career and brought Churchill's star plunging downwards into the night of exclusion from conduct of the war and even from office, relegating him to fighting in France, at his own desire, one of the hundreds of thousands of British soldiers engulfed there.

It was all over the Dardanelles campaign, for the failure of which, since he was its initiator and whole inspiration, he was made the victim.

This abortive campaign, indeed the very conception of it, was for long the subject of acute controversy and a considerable literature has grown up about it. For long it was regarded as a reckless gamble and Churchill, by implication, as the gambler. Then, when out of office after the war, he wrote *The World Crisis*, a large part of which was occupied by the issue. A conception, a project, a campaign that has the united judgment behind it of both Churchill and Attlee, who fought in it as a young officer, can hardly be dismissed out of hand. If it had succeeded, the war might well have been shortened by a year or two. And success at that point would have saved Russia from defeat and perhaps from so extremist a Revolution with its malign consequences for millions of human beings. Moorehead writes: 'It was the greatest amphibious operation which mankind had known up till then, and it took place in circumstances in which nearly everything was experimental: in the use of submarines and aircraft, in the trial of modern naval guns against artillery on the shore, in the manoeuvre of landing armies in small boats on a hostile coast, in the use of radio, of the aerial bomb, the land mine, and many other novel devices. These things led on through Dunkirk and the Mediterranean landings to the invasion of Normandy in the second world war. . . . Gallipoli was a mine of information about the complexities of the modern war of manoeuvre, of the combined operation by land and sea and sky; and the correction of the errors made then was the basis of the victory of 1945. The next time, as Kitchener had once hoped, "they got it right".'[1]

When Turkey came into the war, the plan at first was to rush the Dardanelles by a naval attack while they were weakly defended. Old battleships, which were anyway due to be scrapped in a few months, could be profitably expended in bombarding the forts. The Greeks were anxious to co-operate by taking the Gallipoli peninsula in flank. Admiral Carden on the spot was optimistic and put up a plan of operations that was decidedly promising. Churchill took it up and made it his own: here was the one chance of turning Germany's European flank, of making the war mobile instead of settling down to the static holocaust of the Western Front. Churchill got Fisher to agree to the plan, and then persuaded Kitchener on the basis of its being a purely naval operation. He turned his batteries on Cabinet and War Council; Lloyd George witnesses that when Churchill 'has a scheme agitating his powerful mind, as everyone who is acquainted with his method knows quite well, he is indefatigable in pressing it upon the acceptance of everyone who matters in the decision'. The War Council he carried 'with all the inexorable force and pertinacity, together with the mastery of detail he always commands when he is really interested in a subject'.

From the first everything began to go wrong to a degree hardly exampled in the history of war. Even when we remember that all was experimental, ill thought out and ill prepared, in a field of combined operations—sea, land, air, submarine, mines—of which there was as yet no experience to hand and the techniques of which would not be worked out until the second German war. Even so, beyond the normal hazards of war, beyond all the mistakes that were made, the needless confusion created, everything seemed loaded against the operation, down to personal accidents. There is no doubt now that it could have succeeded, *might* have succeeded at a dozen turning-points, if chance had not been always against. This is what makes Gallipoli such sickening, such tragic reading—the heroism and sacrifice of individual men's lives, the confusion, the abdication of leadership at the head, and then every chance turning malign. The brilliant prospects offered by a Greek landing

[1] Alan Moorehead, *Gallipoli,* 364.

on the Gallipoli flank were vetoed by Russia—the power that stood to gain most from the opening of the Dardanelles, 'failing, reeling backward under the German hammer, with her munitions running short, cut off from her allies'.[1]

Then Admiral Carden, whose plan of a naval attack had been adopted, fell ill. He was succeeded by a commander, de Roebeck, who never believed in the operations, and after an initial check made scarcely any effort to go on—though the Turks were short of munitions and there were few forces in the peninsula. At home Fisher had never favoured the project: he had a wild scheme of his own for an impossible landing in the Baltic. It became clear that troops would be necessary; Kitchener had got the decision to send them reversed, the transports were countermanded. When at length the need was recognised there ensued weeks of delay, while the Turks, stiffened by Germans, fortified the peninsula under Liman von Sanders.

On the spot de Roebeck abdicated action and put the onus on the Army; the newest and most powerful battleship, *Queen Elizabeth*, which had been added to the armada, never fired a gun. Too late Kitchener undertook to storm the peninsula with the Army—on the assumption that the Navy would exert continuous pressure in support. But the Army was left to flounder and bog down in the sands of Gallipoli, now strongly held and fortified, where so many bleached bones lie. At home 'never again could I marshal the Admiralty War Group and the War Council in favour of resolute action. Never again could I move the First Sea Lord. "No" had settled down for ever on our councils, crushing with its deadening weight what I shall ever believe was the hope of the world. Vain was it for Admiral de Roebeck a month later, inspired by the ardent Keyes, to offer to renew the naval attack. His hour had passed. I could never lift the "No" that had descended, and soon I was myself to succumb.' The fighting in the peninsula settled down to as grim a contest of attrition as the Western Front; all hope of mobility, of seizing the initiative had passed. Even so the battles of July and August narrowly missed victory; just when the Turkish defenders had been worn down and at last were prepared to admit defeat the order for evacuation was sent out. But Churchill had now ceased to have any active part in the decisions.

We cannot here go into the operations, the hopes and despair of those agonising months: we are concerned with their effect on the personal fortunes of Churchill. He was borne down with them. All

[1] Churchill, I. 620.

the evidence shows, and it is completely in keeping with his character, that his mind was so set upon winning the war that he was hardly aware of the political repercussions going on around him, the undermining of his position. He knew that he was the target of a good many people's hatred. One day before the war he had opened his heart to his old friend Blunt on the subject: he bore no one any malice, yet he was the best-hated man in the country, the most mistrusted and traduced. Whatever the reasons for it, and they are complex—some inherent, some fortuitous—he could never command the popularity that came so easily, so unfairly to some men. Not until the country was in mortal danger in 1940, and he in his seventh decade, was this reversed. It is a very strange historical case: the more one thinks of it the stranger it becomes.

Lord Beaverbrook, who was in a position to know, says of this crisis in his fortunes: 'his attitude from August 1914 onwards was a noble one, too noble to be wise. He cared for the success of the British arms, especially in so far as they could be achieved by the Admiralty, and for nothing else. His passion for this aim was pure, self-devoted, and all-devouring. He thought of himself not as holding a certain position in relation to Liberal colleagues and a Tory Opposition, but as a National Minister secure of support from all men of good will.'[1] In short, the war was to him the only issue; he was above party-spirit, he ceased to be a party-man. It was honest, sincere, innocent of him. For he was confronted by people who had no good will for him, especially among the Tories who had never forgiven him for his defection. Now was their opportunity, their chance to get back at him was coming. Beaverbrook says that 'belief in the naval and military experts and intense opposition to Churchill were dominant articles in their creed. Churchill did not understand all this, largely because he shut himself up in the Admiralty and hardly ever went to the House of Commons except as a form.... His ambition was in essence disinterested. I do not say that he was always wise—but his patriotism burnt with a pure flame throughout. Hard fighter as he is in debate, he is a man devoid almost of rancour. A defeat does not sour him, even though it depresses him, nor does it turn him into a hater of the successful half of political mankind. And he possesses another virtue—exceptionally rare in politics—or, for that matter, almost anywhere. He is strictly honest and truthful to other people, down to the smallest details of his life.'

He was now to find that these virtues are at times disadvantages.

[1] Lord Beaverbrook, *Politicians and the War, 1914-1916,* I. 131-2.

His old mentor and comrade, Fisher, turned traitor to him; he not only went over into fierce opposition to the Dardanelles campaign while it was still at its most critical, he got in touch with the Tory Opposition, particularly Bonar Law, its most dangerous opponent and Churchill's personal enemy. Fisher now declared that he could no longer continue as Churchill's colleague and, without himself resigning, pulled down his blinds at the Admiralty and refused to serve at his post. Churchill addressed him a *cri de coeur*: 'in order to bring you back to the Admiralty I took my political life in my hands—as you know well. You then promised to stand by me and see me through. If you go now at this bad moment and thereby let loose upon me the spite and malice of those who are your enemies even more than they are mine, it will be a melancholy ending. . . .'

But the old Admiral insisted. He replied: 'YOU ARE BENT ON FORCING THE DARDANELLES AND NOTHING WILL TURN YOU FROM IT—NOTHING'. This explosion precipitated a Cabinet crisis. Mr. Asquith's weakened government was forced to look to the Tories to strengthen itself by a coalition. Absorbed in his own problems, Churchill 'still had no knowledge whatever of the violent political convulsions which were proceeding around me and beneath me'. In the formation of the Coalition in May 1915 the Tories at last got their revenge: they insisted as an absolute condition on Churchill's exclusion from the Admiralty. All his experience there, all the work he had put in at that proud, cherished post were to go by the board. At that moment the news came to him that the German Fleet was coming out: 'the political crisis and my own fate in it passed almost completely out of my mind'.

The moment passed. He was to be excluded. Fisher presented an ultimatum to the government, revealing a state of advanced megalomania, demanding that he should have complete charge of the war at sea, together with the sole disposition of the Fleet and the appointment of all officers of all ranks whatsoever. His resignation was at once accepted. Admiral Wilson, the man whom Churchill had displaced on coming to the Admiralty, was to succeed Fisher as First Sea Lord. Then a strange thing happened. Wilson, whom Churchill had disregarded, had been so much impressed by his work and devotion that he refused to be First Sea Lord under anybody else. Churchill was touched to tears by this testimony at such a point in his fortunes—and from such a quarter.

Lloyd George, who was a prime mover in the formation of the

Coalition, hoped to see Churchill placed at the Colonial Office, 'where his energies would have been helpfully employed in organising our resources in the Empire beyond the seas; and I cannot to this hour explain the change of plans which suddenly occurred'. It seems to have been due not only to Bonar Law's sentence of exclusion but also to a loss of confidence in him on Asquith's part. He was made to take all the blame for the miscarriage of the Dardanelles, which Lloyd George considered as 'due not so much to Mr. Churchill's precipitancy as to Lord Kitchener's and Mr. Asquith's procrastination'. Churchill was now relegated to the Duchy of Lancaster, 'a post generally reserved either for beginners in the Cabinet or for distinguished politicians who had reached the first stages of unmistakable decrepitude. It was a cruel and unjust degradation.... The brutality of the fall stunned Mr. Churchill, and for a year or two of the War his fine brain was of no avail in helping in its prosecution.'

What the country lost by this we can infer from his adaptability of mind in regard to the techniques of war, when the mentality of the War Office was ossified by stupidity and tradition. Take the case of tanks—a cardinal invention in modern warfare. The War Office never saw the point and simply refused to carry on the experiments that led to their production. While at the Admiralty Churchill took the matter under his wing, though it was no business of his. (If people never ventured beyond their 'own business' the war would have been lost.) He took 'personal responsibility for the expenditure of the public money involved, about £70,000. I did not invite the Board of Admiralty to share this responsibility with me. I did not inform the War Office, for I knew they would raise objections to my interference in this sphere.... Neither did I inform the Treasury.' The experiments he had initiated and encouraged went slowly forward, hampered by every obstacle and discouragement in his absence. It took the High Command two years before they first brought a few tanks into action on the Somme. 'This priceless conception, containing if used in its integrity and on a sufficient scale, the certainty of a great and brilliant victory, was revealed to the Germans for the mere petty purpose of taking a few ruined villages.'

Perhaps we may reflect back here to the similar discouragements Marlborough experienced in the conduct of William III's war, the wooden unimaginativeness, the sticking to convention, the static slaughter—and the change that came about with the second war, the mobility, the far better generalship, the mastery. We observe a like contrast between the two wars of our time. And with this goes a further reflection. Churchill's instinct for war has often been suspect, by a confusion of thought, as if there were something inhumane about it. The exact converse is true. A war of manoeuvre and surprise would have been vastly less costly in lives. 'All such ideas had received their quietus. Good, plain, straightforward frontal attacks by valiant flesh and blood against wire and machine-guns, "killing Germans" while Germans killed Allies twice as often, calling out the men of forty, of fifty, and even of fifty-five, and the youths of eighteen, sending the wounded soldiers back three or four times over into the shambles—such were the sole manifestations now reserved for the military art.' These thoughts run like a recurring knell through Churchill's book, *The World Crisis*. There can be no doubt at all that he was right, nor that his conception of the war was the more humane.

Perhaps the conclusion one must draw from the Dardanelles campaign is that he could not hope to impose his conception without supreme power. His remaining in the government at all in such an humiliating position, after such a stunning fall, was only due to a sense of duty to the men still engaged in Gallipoli, to a desire to help forward in any way he could the operations in their last phase. He remained a member of the War Committee of the Cabinet and was at first treated with consideration; after all, he had more experience and knowledge of war than any other civilian minister. He continued to press for reinforcements for the peninsula; his desire to go there himself was vetoed. Someone back from Gallipolli who saw him at this time thought he looked years older and very much depressed; at dinner he was dejected and silent, until he burst forth into a long harangue on the subject that obsessed him—into the sympathetic ears of his mother. At the very moment when at last the fleet at the Dardanelles had got a competent commander, Admiral Wemyss, the decision was taken to evacuate. This was under the insistent pressure of Bonar Law, now in a position of decisive power in the government—though no one need suppose that that decent, melancholy, monochrome man had any instinct for war.

With the end of the Dardanelles and the reconstruction of the War Committee to include Bonar Law, Churchill was excluded. There was no place for him in the conduct of the war. He drew his own conclusions, decided 'to relinquish a well-paid sinecure office which I could not bear longer to hold at this sad juncture in our affairs', and go and fight in France.

It was in these tormented months that this extraordinary man became a painter—without ever having taken any interest in pictures before. But he felt the need for a distraction, an outlet. The sudden change from the intense executive activities of the Admiralty to the sinecure duties of a Chancellor of the Duchy of Lancaster left him gasping. 'Like a sea-beast fished up from the depths, or a diver too suddenly hoisted, my veins threatened to burst from the fall in pressure. I had great anxiety and no means of relieving it; I had vehement convictions and small power to give effect to them. I had to watch the unhappy casting-away of great opportunities, and the feeble execution of plans which I had launched and in which I heartily believed.' Here was painting, an unknown territory in which to advance; after all, it was not unlike a campaign. Eddie Marsh tells us that he swooped upon a shop, and bought up practically the whole stock of easels, canvases, brushes, palettes, tubes. He soon discovered that 'painting a picture is like fighting a battle; and trying to paint a picture is, I suppose, like trying to fight a battle'.

For the first time in his life he seems to have been afflicted with diffidence: there was the canvas extended dauntingly before him, like the empty paper before the incipient writer awaiting the words. He hesitated. He had never had any lessons. Lady Lavery bore down upon him, took the brush from his arrested hand. 'Splash into the turpentine, wallop into the blue and white, frantic flourish on the palette—clean no longer—and then several large, fierce strokes and slashes of blue on the absolutely cowering canvas. Anyone could see that it could not hit back. No evil fate avenged the jaunty violence. The canvas grinned in helplessness before me. The spell was broken. The sickly inhibitions rolled away. I seized the largest brush and fell upon my victim with Berserk fury. I have never felt any awe of a canvas since.'

It was indeed an achievement to make himself, from such beginnings and at the improbable age of forty, into a recognised painter. He seems to have received some tips and wrinkles from Lavery, Orpen and Sickert; but for the most part he went his own wilful way, a boy at school again—the inspired autodidact. It was not until he happened to be painting one day on the Côte d'Azur that he fell in with one or two painters who revealed to him the methods of French Impressionism. Thus he found himself as an artist: that is the kind of painter he became. It is astonishing, everything else considered, that he should arrive at exhibiting in the Academy—the Honorary Academician Extraordinary—and having his pictures collected by the galleries. When one observes his work in bulk, as one does at Chartwell, where staircase, corridors, passages are lined by his paintings, one sees something more significant—that his painting represents another, much less realised side to his nature, the gentler and more sensitive; it represents the feminine side in the complex that makes for genius.

At that time, Lord Beaverbrook tells us, Churchill was 'a character depressed beyond the limits of description. When the government was deprived of his guidance, he could see no hope anywhere.' He turned with relief to the idea of a command in the field, ready to take his chance with the rest. The night before his departure Beaverbrook went to see him. 'The whole household was upside down while the soldier-statesman was buckling on his sword.' Downstairs, Eddie was in tears; upstairs, Lady Randolph 'in despair at the idea of her brilliant son being relegated to the trenches'. Mrs. Churchill seemed to be the only person who remained calm and collected: she must have become used to such scenes.

In France Churchill's old enemy of Boer War days, Sir John French, offered him the command of a brigade, which his experience as a Regular well warranted. Churchill 'did not feel incapable of discharging the duties in question', but considered that he must first learn for himself the special conditions of trench warfare. So he was posted off for instruction, as a Major, to a battalion of the Grenadier Guards—Marlborough's own regiment—in the line. There he received the somewhat frosty reception that might have been expected, not so much as a failed politician whose dizzy descent from the stars looked like a parallel to his father, Lord Randolph's, but as a new boy at school once more. He was firmly put in his place; the colonel had not been consulted in the matter of his coming to his battalion, etc. Before ten days were out his irresistible *bonhomie* prevailed, and 'I might as well have been an absolutely blameless Regular officer who had never strayed from the strict professional path. . . . It will always be a source of pride to me that I succeeded in making myself perfectly at home with these men and formed friendships which I enjoy today.'

One or two episodes in especial, while serving in the trenches, corroborated a conviction that had long held force in his mind—that the element of chance, luck, destiny, providence exerts a dominant and formative power upon a man's life. One day he was summoned out of the trenches for a rendezvous several miles behind the line with a general, whom he missed after all. It seemed so purposeless, until he got back, wet through in the rain, to find that he had missed another rendezvous: a shell-burst on the shelter had blown off the other occupant's head. It is such coincidences and escapes that build up in the fabric of human egoism the concept of destiny. Nevertheless, we have reason to be grateful for the hand that had been 'stretched out to move me in the nick of time from a fatal spot. But whether it was General ——'s hand or not, I cannot tell.'

He gives us the story of another such episode, when he had moved on to the command of the 6th Royal Scots Fusiliers in Flanders. He was then working upon a memorandum for the High Command on the secret projects in which he was so much interested, in particular the use of tanks for the offensive. Nor was this the only new development in warfare upon which his mind was working. He was using his interstices of leisure while at the Front to think out the methods of amphibious warfare that would come to dominate the second war. As he has told me himself, while Lloyd George was working his way back for him with the Tories, he was preparing a scheme for the capture of the Frisian island of Borkum. The essence of the plan was to use tanks to run ashore from specially-constructed landing-craft on the beaches. How all this looked forward to the beaches of North Africa and Italy, Okinawa and the Pacific islands, and at length Normandy! There were the essential ideas—the bullet-proof lighters, the tanks in large numbers, the flat-bottomed barges or caissons of concrete out of which came the mulberry harbours of 1944. Here is the sphere in which he regards himself as having made an original contribution to the art of warfare; it was 'by the mercy of providence', that he had not published this paper in *The World Crisis*, where it would certainly have been noticed and taken up by the Germans in their second war.

Lloyd George was so much impressed by this paper that he had it printed and circulated to the Admiralty and the War Cabinet. For by the end of 1916 he had arrived, not a day too soon, at the supreme direction of the war. The simple truth behind all the dissatisfactions and the political manoeuvres of that year was that Asquith was totally lacking in dynamism; the war, the country needed dynamic leadership and only Lloyd George could provide it. The war was proceeding in the most unsatisfactory fashion, and there was a growing danger of a peace by negotiation—which would in effect mean a German victory or a second bid when it suited them. In the field in France Churchill was as effectively frustrated as he had been at home. He should have been put on the staff at High Command, where his fertility in ideas, his invention and resource might have transformed the war. Suppose if tanks had been employed on the scale he conceived—it could have broken the stalemate on the Western Front. But Bonar Law would not hear of his having anything to do with the conduct of the war in France; he was not even allowed the command of a brigade he had been promised.

With the mounting dissatisfaction at home, champing for action, he allowed himself to be impelled back to Parliament by Carson and Beaverbrook to play his part among the ginger-groups calling for a new direction. But when Asquith fell, Lloyd George, who was anxious to harness Churchill's energies to his government, was not allowed to recruit him. He found himself confronted by Bonar Law's unshakable veto. When Lloyd George put the case for including Churchill even negatively—would he rather have Churchill against him?—the Tory leader replied, 'I would rather have him against us every time'. Why were the Tories so bitter and implacable against him, when they were ready to accept Lloyd George? It was simple revenge for his desertion: 'had he remained a faithful son in the political household in which he was born and brought up, his share in the Dardanelles fiasco would have been passed over'. Then, too, 'it was interesting to observe in a concentrated form every phase of the distrust and trepidation with which mediocrity views genius at close quarters'. It was not for some six months, July 1917, that Lloyd George felt himself sufficiently strong to invite Churchill into his administration. And then it rocked the government, placed it in jeopardy according to Lloyd George; the Tory leaders were furious.

Since the war had become one of attrition a key-position was the Ministry of Munitions, which Lloyd George himself had created. Supplies were now all in all; other opportunities having been lost, we could only win by making full use of superior resources. This vast new war-time department had grown out of all proportion, proliferating sub-departments in all directions. Only an outsize Minister could grapple with it. Lloyd George was determined on Churchill. In consequence, 'at the Ministry of Munitions I worked with incomparably the largest and most powerful staff in my experience'. But 'all the main and numberless minor decisions still centred upon the Minister himself. I found a staff of 12,000 officials organised in no less than fifty principal departments each claiming direct access to the Chief, and requiring a swift flow of decisions upon most intricate and interrelated problems.'

He set to work to change all this, and group the fifty departments into ten large units, each in charge of a head directly responsible to the Minister. These ten heads then formed a council like a Cabinet. 'The relief was instantaneous. I was no longer oppressed by heaps of bulky files. Every one of my ten councillors was able to give important and final decisions in his own sphere. . . . Once the whole organisation was in motion it never required change.' As to the results Lloyd George is the best witness: 'owing to the energy which Mr. Winston Churchill threw into the production of munitions, between March 1st and August 1st the strength of the Tank Corps increased by 27 per cent, and that of the Machine Gun Corps by 41 per cent, while the number of aeroplanes in France rose by 40 per cent.' He was at last making an effective contribution once more to winning the war.

With this vast machine running efficiently behind him he was able to tour the Front again with Eddie, whom we last saw crying at the foot of the stairs. Eddie had been so worked up over Jackie Fisher's falseness to Winston that he had torn up his signed photograph, 'Yours till Hell freezes', and now regretted it since the 'ever-placable' Winston had made it up with Fisher. Here, Beaverbrook noticed, was one of the sources of Churchill's charm: 'it lies so largely in his unexpectedness and in his belief that everybody takes everything as charmingly as he does'. Beaverbrook was quite unable to fathom the mystery how Churchill could command such depths of devotion in Eddie. At the Front Eddie was rather surprised at not feeling the least frightened at being under fire—Burchell's White Rhinoceros had been much worse. Together they visited Jack Churchill, now a Camp Commandant, of whom Winston observed, 'Jack is an extraordinary fellow—quite unborable'. There was a pleasant encounter when the American Winston Churchill came to drink coffee with the English one; another, crossed with more reflections, when they met Mr. Asquith visiting his son at the Front. The Minister who provided the munitions was as pleased as Punch at the men recognising and cheering him. Action had quite recovered his spirits. He specially went up to Arras to visit his old regiment, the Royal Scots Fusiliers, in the line. The spectacle of a daylight raid was found irresistible, though it put the time-table two hours out. 'Winston's disregard of time, when there's anything he wants to do, is sublime—he firmly believes that it waits for him.' Perhaps in a way he was right.

The war was moving to its conclusion, though it could yield no satisfaction to contemplate. The generals' whole conception of waging it, unimaginative and stupid, through the head-on offensives of 1915, 1916, 1917, with their fearful losses, never ceased to revolt him. When victory came, it came as a relief from exhaustion. 'I was conscious of reaction rather than elation.' The last words of his Memoirs of that war are, 'Surely, Germans, for history it is enough!'

Yet, twenty-five years later, they attempted it all over again.

John Morley's prophecy that 'if there is a war Churchill will beat L. G. hollow' had been singularly falsified. The successful conclusion of the war raised Lloyd George to the heights of world fame; at Paris he figured as a world-statesman, along with President Wilson, and for the next three years he dominated British politics. The best Churchill could do for himself was to shelter under David's mantle. His first impulse after the prolonged conflict, which had been largely won by the blockade, was to rush a dozen food-ships to Hamburg, and this he urged upon Lloyd George. But the idea was too uncongenial to the public after what they had suffered at the hands of the Germans.

Upon the reconstruction of the Coalition government after the election Churchill might have gone back to the Admiralty—just where he was years before. But grave difficulties blew up in regard to demobilisation and Lloyd George sent him to the War Office, the post of danger. This was to be combined with the Air Ministry. 'Whew!' wrote Sir Henry Wilson, Chief of the Imperial General Staff, in his diary, and inquired acidly on meeting his new chief why the Admiralty had not been thrown in as well. Why not, indeed?—it would have constituted the joint Ministry of Defence which he shortly came to think the answer to the problem, which he advocated all through the thirties and to some extent constituted in himself in the forties, and which in the fifties at last came into existence, headed by his son-in-law.

The difficulties of demobilisation were acute and dangerous. There were close on four million men under arms, clamouring to be released all at once. This could obviously not be done: the labour market was crowded with the intake from the munitions factories and there might easily be an uncontrolled mass of unemployment. A rational scheme had been drawn up to release the key-men wanted in industry first; but these were the very men who had been called up to the forces last. There were demonstrations in Glasgow and Belfast, and several hundred men marched to Horse Guards

Parade to vent their grievances. With the background of the Russian Revolution—and the initial hope offered to the working classes of the world by it—there was much underlying fear of social unrest in those years. (It accounts in part for Churchill's obsession about Bolshevism.) Now he acted with speed: he scrapped the War Office plan, drew up another based on length of service and war-wounds and put it across the men with complete success. Always at his best in dealing with soldierly matters, he soon got the rate of demobilisation flowing at 50,000 a day and the unrest subsided.

There remained the other side of the task, reconstituting quite a large Army for the various commitments with which the country was saddled: the occupation of Germany, Ireland and the Middle East. Churchill produced a plan and was soon able to report that volunteers were coming in at the rate of a thousand a day. Next year he brought forward the government's scheme for reoganising the Territorial Force. It was like being Mr. Brodrick, after the cataclysm.

What was new was the Air. 'Except for the year 1916, I was continually in control of one or the other branch of the Air Service during the first eleven years of its existence.' We know that at the Admiralty he had been responsible for the creation of the Royal Naval Air Service; both he and Fisher had been very much alive to the possibilities of the new arm, so that the Navy started the war ahead of everyone in this field. At the Ministry of Munitions he was in charge of the design, manufacture and supply of all kinds of aircraft. Now, from 1919 to 1921, he was Air Minister as well as Secretary of State for War.

As such he had plenty of adventures; a long series of fatal accidents which he narrowly missed corroborated his conviction that Chance is not mere chance, but a kind of external power reaching out a hand to safeguard its favourites. It would certainly seem so. 'The young Pilot Instructor who gave me my first lesson at Eastchurch was killed the day after we had been flying together.' A few weeks later he made a long and completely satisfactory flight in a new experimental sea-plane and sailed off happily to Sheerness in the *Enchantress*. No sooner had he arrived than he learned that the plane had nose-dived into the sea, killing all her officers.

As Minister of Munitions he had frequently to be on the other side of the Channel and he usually travelled by air. Thus he had a number of forced landings, and missed engagements. When Air Minister he flew more frequently than ever before, usually in a dual-control machine, 'and I had become capable, with supervision, of flying under ordinary conditions and performing the usual vertical turns'. Once the plane caught fire: the pilot made an erratic fall of a thousand feet, surprising Churchill who did not know what was happening, and, by leaving the machine to take care of itself, had managed to stop the flames with a fire-extinguisher before they reached the petrol-tanks. 'I was extremely glad to find myself once more on *terra firma*.' On another occasion, when their plane crashed, the pilot and he looked so ridiculous hanging upside-down from the fuselage that, bruised and cut, they scrambled out laughing.

In these immediate post-war years his mind was obsessed by the dangers of Bolshevism, the threat that the Russian Revolution and the spread of international Communism constituted to the civilised world. For, remember, ideas were much more apt to go to his head than with any average politician. With his usual disregard of consequences, he made himself the leading spokesman against Communist Russia and thus came to be regarded as the fugleman of Reaction. Lloyd George disagreed with him and wanted to come to terms with the Russians: 'his ducal blood', he said of Churchill, 'revolted against the wholesale elimination of Grand Dukes in Russia'. There was much more to it than that. Churchill always had a real detestation of tyranny, of dictatorship of any kind; his historical sixth sense enabled him to see that, once the safeguards of freedom have been removed, *anything* may be perpetrated; he sensed, with the sense of history that so distinguished him among statesmen, the appeal the evil thing would have, the overtowering menace upon all our lives it would grow into, if left to itself to foster and spread.

His championship of this view, the ardour with which he pressed it, led to a grave misrepresentation of his positive action, which had ill consequences for himself. In fact he had no responsibility for the origins of our military intervention in Russia—and yet once more he had to take the blame for it in the public mind. When Lenin took Russia out of the war, Britain was still fighting the Germans; it was only natural that she should seek to stiffen what resistance she could to them inside Russia, safeguard the munitions and supplies she had sent to Archangel, prevent the oil-wells of Baku from falling into German hands. Hence the British forces at Archangel and in the Caucasus. It fell to Churchill to extricate these forces from these entanglements and bring them home. What he wanted to see was the anti-Bolshevik forces among the Russians prevail against the Communists.

Supplying the Russian counter-revolutionaries was a waste of breath and good supplies—like the Americans supplying the Chinese Nationalists. It all went down the drain. In the kingdom of the blind the one-eyed were kings and the Communists emerged from the scramble on top. Churchill expressed his conviction that the great powers 'would learn to regret the fact that they had not been able to take a more decided and more united action to crush the Bolshevist peril at its heart and centre before it had grown too strong'. It may not have been practical politics, but are many practical politicians capable of taking such long-term views? Looking at the history of the world since, at the sufferings men have been made to endure by the Russian Revolution, can we say that he was wrong? Nevertheless, he disclaimed the sending of British troops to Russia; short of that he had 'done everything in his power to help the loyal anti-Bolshevist forces'.

For that he would have to pay with the prolonged distrust and hostility of all the forces of Labour, political and industrial, over the next two decades: he became the enemy *par excellence*. Not until the disastrous consequences of Tory appeasement of Hitler came home to us, and his own constant good record stood out clear in contrast, was he allowed to have worked his passage. Then—such are the ironies of politics—it was the Labour Movement that made Churchill Prime Minister in 1940; while it was his good record as an anti-Bolshevik that enabled him to put the alliance with Russia across the Tories in 1941.

However, there were consolations at the War Office (and Air Ministry). Eddie had made friends with Ivor Novello, already famous as the composer of *Keep the Home Fires Burning;* and Lady Randolph arranged a lunch for the Minister to meet the young man, 'very spruce and taking in his smart new Air-Force uniform'.[1] At once there was brisk talk of old music-hall songs, of which Winston had a large repertory from Sandhurst days and where Ivor was a specialist, not caught out until the Minister said suddenly, 'Do you know, *you* ought to be in a home?' Everybody was taken aback, until the statesman scored with *You Ought to be in a Home* from old days. While at the War Office Churchill continued to play polo, but to preserve the serious character of the

[1] Lady Randolph, vivacious and active to the last, died 29 June 1921, aged 67. Asquith paid tribute to her as 'an amazing reservoir of vitality and gay and unflinching courage', 'a woman who had lived every inch of her life up to the edge,' and to Winston as 'best and most devoted of sons.'

Minister's engagements-book it went under the French title of 'Collective Equitation'.

Shortly, in Eddie's phrase, 'our next move was in 1921 back to our primeval Colonial Office, where Winston was to cope with the complicated problems of the Middle East'. As to this Churchill confessed at his first interview with his expert adviser that he had a virgin mind; to which that official replied, 'I'm here to ravish it'. The fact was that the war, the break-up of the Turkish Empire, and British interests in that immense area made a most complex tangle. There had just been suppressed a dangerous rebellion in Iraq, but 40,000 troops at a cost of £30 million a year were necessary to maintain order. This could not be borne; here was the danger-point and Churchill was moved to it.

He at once formed a Middle East Department at the Colonial Office to grapple with these problems, and, greatly to everybody's surprise, succeeded in recruiting Lawrence of Arabia to it. For Lawrence had been bitterly disappointed, at the Paris Peace Conference, at the failure to recognise the help received from the Emir Feisal and his brothers in defeating the Turks and clearing them out of Arabia, Syria and Palestine. Now was his chance, in concert with Churchill, to rectify all this; it was in working together on this basis and to make a settlement of the Middle East that there came together these two men of genius, and their lasting friendship was founded. (We find Lawrence saying of Churchill in the doldrums of 1929, 'I want him to be Prime Minister somehow'.) Now Churchill called a conference at Cairo and the tangle was sorted out.

If it was Lawrence's ideas that mainly prevailed, it was nevertheless a brilliant settlement for which Churchill was responsible. Against all the probabilities—and the Middle East was in an alarming state, out of which it was unlikely any settled order could be wrested—Churchill made a peace-settlement that endured up to the Second World War and beyond. It was a prime service to Britain; but because the country was then less conscious of Middle Eastern affairs—they were regarded as the specialist's field—and because he shortly after lost office, perhaps even because the settlement was so signally successful, the country lost sight of it.

Even the self-tortured Lawrence declared himself contented, and was free to immure himself in the Army once more—his form of seclusion from the world. 'Churchill', he wrote, 'in a few weeks made straight all the tangle, finding solutions fulfilling (I think) our promises in letter and spirit (where humanly possible) without sacrificing any interest of our Empire or any interest of the peoples concerned'. And then he vanished, 'a small cloud of dust on the horizon'. Some years later he inscribed a copy of *The Seven Pillars of Wisdom*, to 'Winston Churchill who made a happy ending to this show. And eleven years after we set our hands to making an honest settlement, all our work still stands: the countries having gone forward, our interests having been saved, and nobody killed, either on our side or the other. To have planned for eleven years is statesmanship.'

Churchill's services were, however, not rewarded. When Bonar Law withdrew from Lloyd George's government in 1921, thereby gravely weakening it and preparing the way for a pure Tory administration, Churchill did not succeed to the Chancellorship of the Exchequer, though he was now the second man in the government and evidently expected it. A business man, whom everyone has now forgotten, Sir Robert Horne, was appointed. Beaverbrook reported to Bonar Law abroad: 'Winston is very—very—very—very angry'.

Nevertheless, he took his full share in the negotiations for an Irish settlement, long overdue. It was time the Coalition attempted a settlement, for only a coalition could carry it through, as Lloyd George and Churchill had long seen; the withdrawal of Bonar Law made a settlement more possible, on the other hand the Coalition was being undermined. It was a race for time. He had some compunction about negotiating with Michael Collins, or 'shaking hands with murder', as it was called. And Collins proved difficult to deal with, moody and defiant: 'you hunted me day and night. You put a price on my head.' 'Wait a minute,' said Churchill, 'you are not the only one.' He fetched down the Boer poster offering a reward for his capture. 'At any rate it was a good price—£5,000. Look at me—£25 dead or alive. How would you like that?' After that Collins conceived a real liking for Churchill. He went back to face death at the hands of his own countrymen, sending a farewell message, 'Tell Winston we could never have done anything without him'.

Subsequently it fell to him as chairman of the Cabinet Committee on Irish affairs to operate the Treaty, to help the Irish government establish itself and perform its functions in spite of the murder-campaign with which it was dogged. At one point he had to issue a warning that, if it continued, the British government would have to regard the Treaty as violated and resume liberty of action. On the other hand, he had to protect the integrity of

Northern Ireland which insisted on remaining part of the United Kingdom. All this needed tactful yet firm handling, and people were surprised to find beneath the orator always at concert-pitch, who could be trusted to raise the temperature of an issue and make it too interesting, a patient, tireless, sagacious conciliator. Could it be that within one breast there were two men?

Both facets of this complex personality appear in the last months of the Coalition. There was the convinced Coalitionist—the man who for eleven years past, long before the war, had advocated a coming together of the men of good will to settle the outstanding issues of Ireland and the Constitution, and defend the country in danger. It may be opined that he was never altogether happy as a Liberal, any more than he was to be altogether happy as a Conservative returned to the fold. Such men as Churchill and Marlborough are not made to be defined or circumscribed by party-ties. After the cataclysm of the war, with the rise of the Labour Movement and socialism becoming the dominant issue in internal politics, he could not see that there was any real division of principle between Liberals and Conservatives. Why could they not unite to combat socialism, which was as harmful to Liberalism as it was pernicious to the interests of the Empire? However, differences which are invisible or insignificant to really big men are all in all to small ones. Perhaps, without them, there would be the less reason for their existence. The Liberals, long an absurd anachronism in the circumstances of British political life, continue in holes and corners to encumber the scene.

Near the Dardanelles there blew up a crisis that brought down Lloyd George's government. Lloyd George was passionately pro-Greek and had sanctioned a Greek expansion in Asia Minor which brought about a war in which the Greeks were now being driven into the sea. Churchill had not shared these illusions, nor was he anti-Turk in this matter. Nevertheless, he was not prepared to see the victorious Turks under Kemal back in force in Europe. When they drew near to Chanak it happened to fall to him to draw up the ultimatum warning them off. He did so in no uncertain Churchillian terms: if they made any infraction of the neutral zone of the Dardanelles or crossed the European shores they would find themselves faced by the forces of the British Empire.

The interesting thing is that this strong language had its effect upon the Turks at once: they withdrew from Chanak and shortly signed an armistice. It was the British public that was alarmed: above all, no more war.

The back-bench Tories, long straining to free themselves, decided that this was the moment to get rid of Lloyd George—he had served his purpose and won the war—and get back to normal, peacetime, party government. In the disturbed circumstances of international affairs, since nothing had settled down in Europe, the best brains in British politics were in favour of continuing a national administration, retaining the world-wide prestige (and the genius) of Lloyd George. On Lloyd George's side was Churchill, among the Conservatives Balfour, Austen Chamberlain and Birkenhead: the best heads and hearts. On the other side were Bonar Law and Baldwin (the 'cabin-boy') and all the Cecils. A vote at the Carlton Club withdrew the Tory party from support; Lloyd George at once fell—and for ever. Bonar Law formed his administration and appealed to the country in the name of 'Tranquillity'—as if there could be any tranquillity in twentieth-century affairs! To lead people to suppose so was to mislead them. However, a Tory government 'of the second eleven', as Churchill called it, was installed. He himself, out on a limb, lost his seat. 'The avenging march of the mediocrities' had begun.

CHAPTER ELEVEN

Between the Wars

THE next decade hardly saw Churchill at his best. Nor the country either: the war had been too great a strain for Britain, and now she found herself wanting the ability and talent of the best of a generation massacred. To the historian the contrast between the grasp and distinction of the Liberal government before the war and the mediocrity of Conservative government after it is both pointed and poignant. Yet Churchill made an active and busy, a leading, figure in both. It must be that the times were unpropitious for him, in spite of the attainment (after some scuffling) of high office; that the environment was somehow uncongenial, in so many ways discouraging, as it was certainly confused in purpose and without leadership.

Something of what Churchill felt about it he expressed at the end of that decade in his Romanes Lecture of 1930. 'These eventful years through which we are passing are not less serious for us than the years of the Great War. The grand and victorious summits which the British Empire won in that war are being lost, have indeed largely been lost in the years which followed the peace. We see our race doubtful of its mission and no longer confident about its principles, infirm of purpose, drifting to and fro with the tides and currents of a deeply-disturbed ocean. The compass has been damaged. The charts are out of date. The crew have to take it in turns to be Captain; and every captain before every movement of the helm has to take a ballot not only of the crew but of an ever-increasing number of passengers.'

Even so, it was not inevitable, it was not absolutely essential, that the confused twenties should have been succeeded by the disgrace and humilation of the thirties. Perhaps now we can see it in historical perspective for what it was: a stage in the decline of the nation.

The war, the Coalition that had been necessary to see it through, and perhaps the profounder shifts underneath of a society in transformation, produced a period of political instability and confusion. Even when that was resolved with a steady Conservative majority in 1924, there was still uncertainty, hesitation and no real leadership. When leadership, of a kind, came with Neville Chamberlain it was in a fatally wrong direction: appeasement of Hitler. What a background these decades make for a Churchill! What a galling experience it must have been in the first decade to have to play second fiddle to a second-rate man, and how bitter in the next decade to have no place at all, to have less and less influence, while all the mistakes possible of omission and commission were made, Hitler handed his triumphs on a platter and the war rendered inevitable!

We can observe the effect upon Churchill in his restiveness, the implicit duel with Baldwin coming now into the open, the challenge to his leadership, Churchill's defeat and turning to expedients each more hopeless than the last to get rid of the incubus; in the end being reduced almost to despair. That he did not altogether despair was one of his prime services to the country: a lesser man might well have done so.

A series of unexpected accidents brought Mr. Baldwin to the leadership of the Conservative party and made him the most powerful politician in the country for the best part of these two decades. In itself this was a surprising eventuality—a Worcestershire industrialist of a sound classical education (though also at Harrow) now turned country gentleman, a man who had never had to fight for anything, either for a living, or a seat in Parliament or office, and had made half a dozen speeches in the House in the years before the war, when Churchill was already a European figure making history. Those men of superior abilities, Asquith and Lloyd George, Birkenhead and Churchill, could never quite believe it and never acclimatised themselves to Baldwin's ascendancy, the cabin-boy made captain. It cannot have made it any the more tolerable to reflect, as Amery does, that if Churchill had remained with the Conservative party he would almost certainly have become its leader and Prime Minister in 1922.

All the same these superior men were astray in their estimate of Baldwin, for all was not so simple as meets the eye. This so very typical Englishman, whose political fortune rested on typifying the English so nicely, was not an Englishman but a Celt. He had at heart that romantic dream of England which those who are not English are apt to entertain and find profitable. Not for nothing was he a Macdonald on his mother's side—this affinity was to have important political consequences in 1931. 'Understand Baldwin?' said Lloyd George; 'of course you can't; he is one of us. He is a

Celt.' Of his own mental processes Baldwin said, 'there is a cloud round my mind, it takes shape, and then I know what to say'. The emphasis was all on intuition, perception, sympathy. For this strange man—he was very far from being the ordinary man he made himself out to be—was a good deal of a poet, like his Macdonald cousin, Kipling. He was man of an exquisite tact and good feeling, infallible in personal matters; a shrewd committee-man and party-manager—Churchill said with some exaggeration, 'the greatest party-manager the Conservatives had ever had'—a master of the art of persuasion. In the end, a nice man, moral and religious, respectable and kind.

Great countries require more than that its leaders should exemplify the domestic virtues. For, like Louis XV, who also had never had to fight for anything in his life, Mr. Baldwin had the incurable vice of indolence; he had the inertia that went with a kind of fatalism, a scepticism that did not believe in *doing* anything. Thereby he nearly ruined his country. The most powerful politician in England, he took no single action to avert the war. When foreign affairs came up in Cabinet, 'wake me up when you are finished with that', he would say.[1] His biographer observes that between him and Churchill there was a hopeless divergence of temper. 'Then comes Winston with his hundred-horse-power mind and what can I do?' Baldwin complained. 'I wish I had more energy; then I might have done something, and I have done nothing. But one must not expect to see results. I am always telling Winston that.' The English people felt when war came—as to which he had never even alerted them—that they had been taken in, betrayed by the man to whom they had given all their confidence, a trust such as few have been given in politics.

'War is fatal to Liberalism', Churchill had declared many years earlier. This was perhaps only a rhetorical declaration, but it proved true. More important than the personal feud between the Asquith and Lloyd George wings into which the party had split, its social and class-foundations had given way, so that it lost its *raison d'être* beyond any hope of revival. It became more evident with every year that passed that it was a waste of time, of good men, and a disservice to the country, to go on with it. What was Churchill, now nearing fifty, to do in those circumstances?

In the election of 1922 he lost his seat at Dundee. When the inexperienced Baldwin precipitated an election in 1923 over Pro-

[1] G. M. Young, *Stanley Baldwin*, 63, 77, 106.

tection, which he believed in—he never made that kind of mistake again—Churchill as a Free Trader came out as a follower of Asquith, titular leader of the apparently reunited Liberals. Once more Churchill was rejected, this time by the electorate of West Leicester, in his search round the country for somewhere to represent. The result was that he was out of Parliament during the first Labour government.

He had made himself anathema to the working-class with his campaign against Bolshevism in Russia and socialism at home: it was fairly certain that henceforth no industrial seat would return him. This was the consequence of his attempts to make anti-socialism the basis of a centre-party at this time—his way out of the prevailing confusion among parties.

A year out of Parliament enabled him to bring out the first two volumes, of four, of his War Memoirs, *The World Crisis*. It looked as if there was no future for him in politics; even his admirers Lloyd George and Birkenhead thought at this time that he would be remembered merely as a writer rather than a statesman. His book provoked even more furious controversy than his speeches or his actions: he raised the temperature of everything he touched. Balfour reported agreeably that he was reading Winston's autobiography disguised as a history of the universe. The fact was that Churchill was bent on substantiating his case, particularly in regard to the Dardanelles. This let loose a flood of controversy. Everywhere at elections he was pestered by fatuous hecklers, 'What about the Dardanelles?' His reply, 'the Dardanelles might have saved millions of lives', naturally made no impression.

Meanwhile it was encouraging to be writing away at half a crown a word: some consolation for being out of things. On the proceeds he bought Chartwell, destined to make an historic acquisition for the nation. Asquith had Churchill next to him at Princess Mary's wedding, and was amused to hear his plans for building and developing the little estate. A good deal of bricklaying there was done by Churchill himself, who learnt the art and joined the appropriate trade union. It did not reconcile trade unionists to him; bricklayers were not much interested in competitive records in bricklaying.

How to get back into politics?

In March 1924 there was a by-election in the Abbey division of Westminster, perhaps the most famous, certainly the most publicised, of constituencies. Though official candidates for all three parties were adopted, Churchill determined to break in and stand as an independent appealing to all who were anti-socialist to join together. The implication was—under his leadership. The response made this by-election a memorable one, which might have had decisive results. For, as usual, the impact of his personality had electric consequences. The Conservative Association was torn in two between the official candidate and him; so was the party leadership. Balfour came out in his favour; Baldwin against him. Thirty Conservative M.P.s appeared on his platform, 'Dukes, jockeys, prize-fighters, courtiers, actors and business men, all developed a keen partisanship. The chorus girls of Daly's Theatre sat up all night addressing the envelopes and dispatching the election address. It was most cheering and refreshing to see so many young and beautiful women of every rank in life ardently working in a purely disinterested cause not unconnected with myself. . . . Incomparably the most exciting, stirring, sensational election I have ever fought. I must confess I thoroughly enjoyed the fight from start to finish.'

He was only just not elected, by forty votes out of forty thousand. But the defeat was decisive; if he had been elected he might have challenged the leadership of the anti-socialist forces. That now fell unquestionably to Baldwin, as everything did, without effort. In May Churchill addressed a large Conservative meeting at Liverpool, accepting the claim of the Conservative party as the bulwark against socialism and offering a small Liberal wing to co-operate with it. Baldwin was happy to accept the recruit, or rather the returned prodigal: it was a surrender to his terms. In September Churchill was adopted as candidate for the safe Conservative seat of Epping. A few days later he was welcomed back by a large meeting of Scottish Conservatives at Edinburgh, presided over by Balfour. It is pleasant to observe the constant good relations later prevailing between him and the leader he had flouted as a very young neophyte. More than a year before, Churchill told Sir Robert Horne, the Conservative industrialist whom Lloyd George had appointed Chancellor of the Exchequer, 'I am what I have always been—a Tory Democrat. Force of circumstances has compelled me to serve with another party, but my views have never changed, and I should be glad to give effect to them by rejoining the Conservatives.'

This he accomplished in time for the election of 1924, which settled the post-war instability of parties with a large Conservative majority. When he took office under Mr. Baldwin as Chancellor of the Exchequer, a good many Conservatives took offence. It was in fact a shrewd move on Baldwin's part, whose prime purpose in politics was to keep Lloyd George out and to that end to re-absorb his chief supporters, Churchill, Austen Chamberlain, Birkenhead, individually. As for Churchill, he was at last, at ten years older, in his father's place; Lady Randolph had faithfully preserved his father's robes as Chancellor for him to wear.

Did he make a good Chancellor of the Exchequer?

Views differ about that; opinion has not yet settled down into a definite form, and his work at that time has become overlaid in the public mind by the achievements of later years. It is noticeable that in the volume devoted to every aspect of his multifarious activity there is not a single chapter devoted to this.[1] And yet he was in charge of the Treasury for five crowded years, 1924 to 1929, and brought in no less than five Budgets. He has been condemned by Keynes and others for his return to the Gold Standard at the pre-war dollar-parity, and he has not said much in his own defence. It is probable that, like his father, he did not take to 'those damned dots' and that this department of state was less congenial to him that any of the numerous others he occupied. There is something endearing about a head of that grim department who could say after dinner one evening, when it was over, 'everybody said that I was the worst Chancellor of the Exchequer that ever was. And now I'm inclined to agree with them. So now the world's unanimous.'

The truth is far different. The economic historian of the period calls him dramatic, resourceful, ingenious.[2] If the return to the Gold Standard at such a high parity was a mistake fraught with ill consequences, he was much less responsible in the matter than the financial experts of the Treasury, above all the Governor of the Bank of England, Montagu Norman. The curious thing is that Churchill's instinct was rather against the measure, and in any other realm where he had confidence in his own judgment, he would have insisted on having his way—to the country's advantage. In the dim mysterious world of high finance—and it is extraordinary what a *mystique* it had in those days—he was not sure of himself. That was where he erred, oddly for him. Himself, he had no particular reverence for gold. 'Are we to be at the mercy of a lot of negro women scrabbling with their toes in the mud of the Zambesi?' he inquired of his experts after a good dinner. He would have done better to follow this up by telling the experts to go to the

1 *Churchill, By his Contemporaries, ed.* Charles Eade.

2 Cf. U. K. Hicks, *The Finance of British Government, 1920-1936.*

devil. As it was, he followed them, and was able to quote Keynes in his defence: 'if we are to return to gold, and in the face of general opinion that is inevitable, the Chancellor, the Treasury and the Bank have contrived to do so along the most prudent and far-sighted lines which were open to them'.

To those forbidding portals the faithful Eddie accompanied him, to be relieved by the beauty of the room they occupied and to be the recipient of such confidences as—'earned increments are sweet, but those unearned are sweeter'. This was the last of their many offices together: Eddie remained with him till their final parting in 1929. Winston, with 'a natural desire to have everything handsome about him', wanted to make Eddie a K.C.M.G., which they interpreted to mean, for such was Eddie's function, Kindly Correct My Grammar. It was in this capacity that Eddie brought down an infuriated mob of grammarians upon Winston's head by passing the word 'choate' which the latter deemed to exist: 'inchoate' existed, what more natural than to suppose therefore that there must be a word 'choate'? Winston did not know (Harrow again!); Eddie, who did know, thought it a useful addition to the language. He did not get his K.C.M.G.; he got a K.C.V.O. instead.

In tearing good spirits, with his usual energy and optimism, Churchill confronted the complicated problems, the arduous labour, of the new department he had desiderated three years before. In the international field there was the inextricable tangle of German Reparations and Inter-Allied War Debts. There was the question of the Gold Standard and dollar-parity. At home there were the depressed industries, especially coal, to dog the government and plague the country; and by consequence, strikes, unemployment, the demand for protection. All this in addition to, and with their repercussions upon, more strictly Budgetary problems. Nothing daunted, Churchill walloped into all these, lashing out about him, more or less at once. Asquith reported to him at this moment: 'he is a Chimborazo or Everest among the sand-hills of the Baldwin Cabinet'.

To fight the war and resist German aggression Britain had had to sell out a thousand million pounds worth of investments built up in America by the enterprise and hard work of preceding generations, and to contract a debt of a similar magnitude. At the same time her allies had incurred a comparable debt to Britain. As Chancellor Churchill insisted on linking these two together: 'I thought that if Great Britain were thus made not only the debtor, but the debt-collector of the United States, the unwisdom of the debt-collection would become apparent at Washington'. It did not become so to the lapidary Coolidge: 'they hired the money, didn't they?' was the extent of his contribution to the problem. 'This laconic statement was true,' comments Churchill, 'but not exhaustive.'

In January 1925 he had to plunge immediately into one of the Reparations Conferences that frequently punctuated those years. At Paris he showed himself sympathetic to the French point of view and consented to France accounting Germany with the cost of the Ruhr occupation—since the Germans were defaulting on Reparations. On the question of Inter-Allied debts he proposed that French payments to Britain should be independent of any sums received from Germany. The French shelved this unwelcome idea by a Cabinet crisis. In August there were further negotiations about the French debt with the pro-German Caillaux—who had narrowly escaped being shot as a traitor during the war. Caillaux's secretary 'leaked' to the press proposals which were far from being up to those Caillaux agreed with Churchill. When the French Cabinet accepted these 'France thereupon fell into the throes of a financial and political crisis which lasted till the end of the year, and, in spite of the agreement, Britain's prospects of receiving any payment from France on account of war-debt remained as uncertain as ever'. The Germans solved their difficulties by importing as much American capital as ever they paid in Reparations; while in the 1930's they spent far more than both on re-armament. So much for Keynes's argument that they were unable to make reparation for the damage they had done—with which he did so much to undermine the moral authority of the Peace.

Lord Esher opined on Churchill's appointment, Gunpowder day 1924, 'I think Winston will be very economical and formidable at the Exchequer'. At once he found himself, like his father, up against the service departments, in this case the Admiralty, which wanted a large cruiser-replacement programme. Early in January Beatty reports, 'yesterday I was vigorously engaged with Winston, and I think on the whole got the better of him. I must say, although I had to say some pretty strong things, he never bears any malice and was good-humoured throughout the engagement.' On Churchill's return from Paris, Beatty had another wrangle of four hours with him and his Treasury myrmidons. After yet another: 'that extraordinary fellow Winston has gone mad. Economically mad, and no sacrifice is too great to achieve what in his shortsightedness is the panacea for all evils—to take 1*s*. off the Income Tax. Nobody outside a lunatic asylum expects a shilling off the Income Tax this Budget. But he has made up his mind that it is the only thing he can do to justify his appointment as Chancellor of the Exchequer.'

The tussle went on day after day, with Beatty expecting a split in the Cabinet and the Conservative party. Occasionally the man of war had 'a rest from Winston for two days. . . . It takes a good deal out of me when dealing with a man of his calibre with a very quick brain. A false step, remark or even gesture is immediately fastened upon, so I have to keep my wits about me.' This is precisely what the soldier Brooke found in the Second World War and his Diary bears frequent witness to: we shall have to bear it in mind in considering the capital question of Churchill's judgment. Here it is enough to record the technique: bringing all the batteries to bear upon an opposing position by way of testing it and then giving way if necessary either to superior arguments or force of circumstances.

In this instance Baldwin came down against Churchill, if 'came down' is the word for a feather-bed. But feather-beds are useful for smothering purposes. Beatty got his way and the cruiser-programme went through. Churchill bore no ill-will, and had reason to be grateful when the Germans renewed the war, as Foch was sure they would. (Of Versailles he had said, 'this is not peace: this is an armistice for twenty years'.)

Churchill was evidently anxious to strike the imagination with something dramatic in his first Budget and this he achieved with the announcement of the return to the Gold Standard. He raised death-duties on all estates save the very largest, while reducing super-tax and income-tax on the lower ranges. The intention seems clear: to encourage productive enterprise. He reimposed the McKenna protective duties, chiefly on imported motor-cars; and in fact each year saw import duties grow up piece-meal at the hands of this Free-Trader. Industrial interests regarded a protective tariff as the only hope of reducing direct taxes, while he needed the money to finance the ambitious scheme of Contributory Pensions, including widows' pensions, which he was introducing: a further step in social welfare, which was continuous with his record in the matter from Liberal days.

The Budget created less sensation than expected. Snowden attacked it as 'the worst rich man's Budget of recent times', which it obviously was not, and taxed Churchill with having changed his mind on the shibboleth of Free Trade. 'There is nothing wrong with change, if it is in the right direction,' said Churchill. 'You are an authority on that,' retorted Snowden. 'To improve is to change; to be perfect is to change often,' concluded Churchill. This was the first of many slanging matches with Snowden, which became a feature of Budget debates year by year, a great attraction to average M.P.s and a bore to sensible men. There was no ill-will between the two duellists: Snowden once ended a rude exchange by abruptly telling Churchill he was really fond of him and wishing him a Merry Christmas, while Churchill assured Snowden in the midst of his attacks, 'the harder my opponent hits me the better I like him'. Churchill's summing-up of his opponent's career is a warm-hearted tribute to someone with whom he genuinely disagreed, even if he has to say, reasonably enough, 'Gladstonian Radicals are a very arrogant brood. To begin with they are quite sure they know all about everything.... The Treasury mind and the Snowden mind embraced each other with the fervour of two long-separate kindred lizards.' The interesting thing is that Churchill excludes himself from this sacred enclosure: he had not 'the Treasury mind'.

The contrast between the two men is brought out in a remark by Snowden on his return to the Treasury in 1929, 'I found that Churchill had altered the position of all the furniture in the room. I at once had it replaced.' And perhaps equally by a remark of Churchill's who gaily assured Snowden on the same occasion that he had left him 'nothing in the till'. Looking over Churchill's tenure of the Treasury and his Budgets as a whole, one sees that he erred on the side of optimism. Britain had indeed made a remarkable come-back after the war, but its international position in trade and finance was in some important respects impaired. He was able to claim that the return to gold made a great saving upon purchases from the United States and on the payment of our war debt. But it had not brought about the restoration of international trade that had been hoped for; the basic industries remained depressed and in especial it dealt a heavy blow to the export of coal. (It is curious to reflect that there was then a redundancy of men in the mines.) In 1927 Churchill introduced a large measure of derating for industry and agriculture, partly consequent upon Neville Chamberlain's reforms in local government and partly designed to help productive industry. Both this and the new Pensions scheme proved more costly than was estimated, and Churchill was reduced to a variety of expedients to raise the money.

Twice he raided the Road Fund's substantial surpluses to stop up deficits. Another year he anticipated the collection of revenue. In 1926 he constructed a Betting Tax, which turned out a complete failure owing to 'the volatile and elusive nature of the betting population'. The fall in liquor consumption and revenue enabled him to contrast 'the results of regulated freedom corrected by high taxation with those which have flowed elsewhere from Prohibition tempered by bootlegging'. Even so his optimism might have been justified if it had not been for the disastrous events of 1926, the General Strike and the Coal Strike that lasted seven months and cost the country some £800 millions. As Churchill's Financial Secretary, Robert Boothby, points out, such a sum 'could have settled it, at any time, on fair terms. It left a legacy of bitterness which continues to this day.' The miners have not ceased getting their own back or holding the community up to ransom.

Churchill bore some responsibility for the handicap the return to gold imposed on what was then an export industry; but it was an indirect one. The direct responsibility must be laid at the door of the government and its leader who failed to lead. A temporary subsidy was being paid to the miners because, in Baldwin's candid words, 'we were not ready'. When they were, the government forced a showdown. This precipitated the General Strike—an extraordinary nine days' wonder which ended in an humiliating fiasco for the Trades Union Congress that had never intended it. As Ernest Bevin emerged the one strong figure on the Labour side, so Churchill came out as the chief voice on the other. With his Bolshevist obsession he charged the T.U.C. with attempting to set up a Soviet. Nothing was further from their muddled thoughts. Mr. Baldwin was more shrewd: he contented himself with out-manoeuvring Labour at every point, while taking care to speak so softly as always to be regarded as a friend.

Churchill's passion for action led him to take over the *Morning Post* plant, recruit a corps of volunteer type-setters and run a government *British Gazette* during this blessed intermission from newspapers. By the end of a week the *Gazette* had a circulation of over two millions. A run of the newspapers is now of some value. Its editor did not know what Baldwin considered the 'cleverest thing' he ever did: 'I put Winston in a corner and told him to edit the *British Gazette*'.

The General Strike defeated, the Coal Strike went on all through the summer. The Prime Minister did nothing more, but went abroad as usual to Aix for August, leaving an intractable situation to Churchill. In his absence Churchill turned round in favour of conciliation and tried to bring the coal-owners to a national conference. They were obdurate and he could not carry the Cabinet with him to force them. This was the kind of impasse that only Lloyd George could surmount: one sees what the country lost by the Tories' exclusion of him. It is evident that Churchill hoped to settle the strike over Baldwin's head, but there was no stealing a march on that bird. When he returned in the autumn—the miners still out—he addressed the Conservative Conference with much complacency, according to the *Annual Register,* and 'treated the coal-stoppage with a philosophical detachment'. Some weeks later the Prime Minister 'adopted a more detached attitude than ever'. The miners were now drifting back to work; after seven months of misery and hunger they accepted surrender terms in November. We pay for that today.

In Parliament Churchill took far more trouble to present the government's case than the Prime Minister, who sat back and received the unearned increment for 'sympathy', though he had not raised a finger. Churchill answered MacDonald with truth that the government had not the powers to coerce the coal-owners to an agreement—an intellectually reputable answer, in contrast to the intellectual disreputability of Baldwin on such a crucial issue, lazy and disingenuous, yet always plausible. It is possible that left to himself Churchill would have enforced a solution; it is probable that Lloyd George would have contrived one. The shrewd party-manager of the Conservatives knew his party better than even to try.

All this darkened the economic outlook of the country and put out Churchill's plans for the future, already of too optimistic a cast—Baldwin did not share his optimism. In these circumstances Churchill's Budget speech of 1927 made up by its brilliance and audacity for the gloom of the deficit: a jeremiad had been expected, but people forgot the artist in him always liable to surprise. He took pride in how little the strength and resources of the nation had been affected by 'the shocking breakdown in our island's civilisation': the country had continued to augment its capital, was still the chief creditor nation and financial centre of the world. (Alas! one reflects forty years on.) However, there was no hope of a reduction of income-tax now and he had to face a Tory revolt against the Budget's attempt to prevent tax-evasion by private companies. He promised to administer the measure leniently, but all to no effect: the revolt went on and he had to introduce amendments later to pacify the rich. The selfishness of the moneyed classes in their heyday has been well answered, and to some extent explains, that of the working-class in theirs.

Next year Churchill gave further offence to a section of the Conservatives by discountenancing their agitation for the protection of iron and steel. Nor, as the election of 1929 drew near, would he make an electioneering contribution by taking 6d. off the income-tax. He had more principle than many who make such a song about it, and the Budget gave no help to winning the election. An ominous fact was the growth of unemployment. Churchill laid the blame on the disturbances of 1926; it was still more the first symptoms of the economic blizzard that swept over the world, destroying so many landmarks of the old order and levelling foundations for a cruel and dreary new one.

It seems that when Churchill left the Treasury in 1929 he was contemplating further measures of expansion, and that, we now know, would have been right—instead of the restrictive deflationary measures the National Government took to deal with the crisis in 1931-2, which were directly contrary to sense. Here, too, Churchill's instinct would have been sounder. We may sum up his Chancellorship fairly with the economic historian: the country would probably have done better with the careful financial orthodoxy of Snowden in the earlier years, and have profited by the unorthodox, expansionist bent of Churchill in the depression.[1] Such is the perversity of things that we enjoyed the exact opposite. As it was, the expenditures that produced the financial crisis of 1931 originated in the expansionist legislation of those earlier optimistic years—pensions and de-rating. In lightening the burdens on small incomes 'Churchill's zeal was almost a match for Snowden's'. Not much credit is due for that: we always knew he had a good heart and anybody can ladle out the taxpayer's money.

The election of 1929 put the Conservatives in a minority, and Churchill left office not to resume it again for the decade that ensued. Baldwin was hurt by the verdict of the electorate: he felt, as politicians are apt to do, their ingratitude for all he had done. But he was soon back again, in altered circumstances. The second Labour government, dependent on the divided Liberals for a majority, lasted no more than a couple of years. With complete helplessness it watched the unemployment figures mount up and up. There were only two things it could do: go off the Gold Standard and devalue the pound, or introduce a general protective tariff. It did neither, and was swept away by the financial panic of

[1] Cf. U. K. Hicks, 15, 236.

1931: really the victim of the world-crisis that threw out the Republican party in American and, more malign, destroyed the Weimar Republic in Germany, preparing the way for Hitler.

The year 1931 was a turning-point for the world, certainly for Britain: our modern period begins here. It does not cease to be any the less heart-breaking looking at the 1930's in perspective, for it was to that time that we must date the responsibility for the relegation of Britain, so long foremost, to a second-rate position in the world. It makes one sick to write about it. Fortunately Sir Winston Churchill has both surveyed it himself, in a spirit that cannot be bettered, and has documented it fully as the events happened and the years rolled on. There is the admirable section, 'From War to War, 1919-1939', all the more forceful for its brevity, that is the prelude to his many-volumed Memoirs of the Second World War; and there is the magnificent array of his speeches covering the thirties in the volume, *Arms and the Covenant.*

The real *raison d'être* of the so-called National Government of 1931 was to keep Labour out—and this they achieved with complete success. So complete a success had very ill consequences for the proper functioning of democratic government: the Labour party was in a hopelessly weak position in Parliament throughout, some of its ablest members were never in the House; its irresponsibility and unrealism were increased, the Movement was riddled with distrust and suspicion, very understandably, at the fraudulent appeals put across the electorate in 1931 and 1935, as in 1924 before. On the personal side the National Government was a coming together of MacDonald and Baldwin, two tired and disillusioned men, to keep out those dangerous activist brains of the first rank, Lloyd George and Churchill. In this they were lucky, for Lloyd George was ill at the time of the government's formation and Churchill already on bad terms with Baldwin. Though Lloyd George had better ideas than anyone for dealing with unemployment, that dynamic energy, unharnessed to office or responsibility, ran into the sand. In these circumstances the only intellectually formidable opposition to the government came from one man. It was a very remarkable performance—not the least so of all his performances, all the more strange when one looks back over it: a one-man Opposition.

During the Labour government he had parted company with Baldwin, and left the Conservative shadow-Cabinet, over India.

This made it impossible for him to co-operate with the Left, for his appeal on India was to the extreme Right, the Tory Diehards, apart from whom he was now left isolated. There is no doubt that he was sincere in his Indian views, his detestation of a policy that could only terminate in the end of British rule and handing over to the Indians. Such a course was contrary to his deepest instincts and his earliest experience, as well as to his strategic sense. His antagonism was no less a challenge to Baldwin's leadership, an attempt to divide the party against him, to rally the old and true Tories to his side. And here he miscalculated: in the realm of party-manoeuvre he was no match for Baldwin, who was a past-master at it, and besides held all the trumps.

Something of his surprise and disappointment may be glimpsed from his speech to the Indian Empire Society he inspired, at a meeting at the Albert Hall, 18 March 1931, presided over by the Duke of Marlborough. 'One would have thought that if there was one cause in the world which the Conservative party would have hastened to defend, it would be the cause of the British Empire in India'. Strangely enough they preferred to follow Baldwin in giving it away—it is always easier to give away—than to follow Churchill in defending it. He appealed to their sense of history, their pride in the past. 'The rescue of India from ages of barbarism, tyranny and intestine war, and its slow but ceaseless forward march to civilisation constitute upon the whole the finest achievement of our history. This work has been done in four or five generations by the willing sacrifices of the best of our race. War has been banished from India; her frontiers have been defended against invasion from the north; famine has been gripped and controlled. . . . Justice has been given—equal between race and race, impartial between man and man. And by the new streams of health and life and tranquillity which it has been our mission to bring to India, the number of its people has grown even in our own lifetime by scores of millions.'

The appeal was in vain. Britain was suffering from what he diagnosed himself as a disease of the will-power, a failure of confidence in itself. He related it specifically to the development of a democracy based on universal suffrage, and indeed it is clear that a democracy does not make a ruling power. He was convinced that the loss of India would mark the downfall of the British Empire and that we should be reduced to the scale of a minor power, like Holland in the eighteenth century.

Nothing that he could say, no efforts that he made, were of any avail. The Conservative party conference of 1933 supported Baldwin against him by a majority of two to one; at that of 1934 the majority was nearly three to one. In the House of Commons he had only the Diehards with him; the bulk of the party were with the Labour and Liberal parties in supporting Hoare's Bill according India responsible government at the centre, a long step towards eventual self-government and independence. Once the Bill was passed Churchill announced with his usual good spirit that he intended 'to bury the hatchet . . . in face of the tasks and dangers that lay before the country'. These had now become flagrantly obvious; but his declaration was not met in a similar spirit. His Indian campaign completed his alienation from the Conservative party and the determination of the men of the thirties to keep him out at all costs. 'He had gone about threatening to smash the Tory party on India,' said Baldwin, 'and I did not mean to be smashed.'

In 1932, in New York, Churchill had a dangerous accident which very nearly brought to an end that inestimable life. He got out of his car on the wrong side, a thing that might happen to any visiting Englishman, proceeded to walk across Fifth Avenue and was mown down by one of those happily-driven, jovial taxis—only it was a Winston Churchill that was beneath it. From this collision he emerged a very bad wreck; it took him two months to recover enough strength to go forward with the full lecture-tour of forty lectures all over the States that had been arranged for him. Even so he accomplished it, 'living all day on my back in a railway compartment, and addressing in the evening large audiences. On the whole I consider this was the hardest time I have had in my life.'

However, those months of returning strength were of importance in enabling him to get to know his mother's country, which in so crowded a life he had so far not had much time to become acquainted with. We have a sketch of him from his American private secretary at this time, very convincing with all his foibles and old-fashioned prejudices. For one thing he thought that women occupied too much of the American scene: American men 'just can't live without women all round them'. (Very unlike the life at Chartwell, we may add, which had something of a collegiate atmosphere, a hive of masculine activity, mitigated by intervals of family life). Perhaps this reflected something of the smart he felt at being routed by Consuelo's mother, that formidable tartar, who for her part used to refer to him as 'that dreadful man'. However, people saw that 'there's a lot of the Yankee in Winston. He knows how to hustle and how to make others hustle too': he was always on the look-out for new and more effective ways of getting things done. This quality was soon to have supreme consequences for his country's survival. We can all recognise the authentic note in the observation on him in America: 'Mr. Churchill's tastes are very simple. He is easily pleased with the best of everything.'

At home, apart from his growing anxiety over the way public affairs were going, especially after Hitler's advent to power, he had the enjoyable time of someone every moment of whose life is crowded with work and agreeable activity. At Chartwell he was building—cottages, terraces, policies, partly by his own hand—and making a garden. He was dictating articles which brought in plenty of money—more than office would have done. He was gathering his friends about him, technical advisers like Professor Lindemann on science, Ralph Wigram the most promising brain in the Foreign Office, soldiers and airmen, for the stormy times that he saw were bound to close in on us now.

At the same time, with the help of expert advice—for it was always characteristic of him to make the best use of experts on their subjects—he was writing an historical masterpiece. It was only one more achievement in this titan's life to have written one of the grand historical works of the time, a book to place beside Trevelyan's *England in the Reign of Queen Anne.* We have seen what an immense injustice Macaulay did to Marlborough's memory and how the power of his pen riveted this travesty of the man upon generations of readers—and also how paradoxical it was that the greatest of English soldiers should have come down to us so traduced and vilified. Churchill set himself to rectify this. He must have often discussed it with his cousin the ninth Duke, who kept the archives at Blenheim closed for his benefit. But it is possible that he might not have tackled it if it had not been that 'two of the most gifted men I have known urged me to it strongly'. It is pleasant to note who these were. The first was Lord Rosebery, whose expert knowledge introduced him to Paget's exposure of Macaulay; the second was Balfour again, always encouraging to his former rebel. No effort was spared to make this work definitive: the archives in Paris, Vienna and London were searched for him, no less than the family records at Blenheim and Althorp. He himself in 1932 followed in Marlborough's tracks along the famous march from the Rhine to the Danube—in the course of which he narrowly escaped a meeting with Hitler.

The first volume came out next year, the year Hitler came to power. This was the really critical volume of the series, for it dealt with the first half of Marlborough's life where Churchill had 'to plough through years of struggle and to meet a whole host of sneers, calumnies and grave accusations'. It became at once fairly evident that the amateur historian had reversed the great professional's judgment, and for good. It seems that to begin with two, or at most three, volumes were intended. In the end there were four, spread across the thirties in which there was so much else to claim attention: a splendid tapestry depicting the age as well as the man, comparable to the series Marlborough had had woven to depict the scenes of his life and hang at Blenheim.

One further reflection, which I owe to an earlier colleague of his: the contemplation of the problems involved in fighting the war of a Grand Alliance against an aggressor, as he saw them through Marlborough's eyes over these years, afforded a providential training for the comparable destiny awaiting Marlborough's descendant. The experience may be taken to have matured him as a statesman.

Perhaps this is the place to confront squarely, as the historian must, the question of Churchill's judgment. For it is a question. It comes up too often and in too many relations—Asquith and Lloyd George, Bonar Law and Baldwin, not to mention Brooke and others who came up against him in the second war—to be ignored. It is not enough to say that the lesser men were all wrong. What was at the bottom of their mistrust?

Lloyd George, Birkenhead and Beaverbrook, all friends who knew him best, have each made revealing contributions to the problem of this outsize personality and its effect upon others. Lloyd George wondered why it was that he was so unpopular with people. 'They admitted he was a man of dazzling talents, that he possessed a forceful and a fascinating personality. They recognised his courage and that he was an indefatigable worker. But they asked why, in spite of that, although he had more admirers, he had fewer followers than any prominent public man in Britain? Churchill had never attracted, he had certainly never retained, the affection of any section, province or town.... What then was the reason? Here was their explanation. His mind was a powerful machine, but there lay hidden in its material or its make-up some obscure defect which prevented it from always running true. They could not tell what it was. When the mechanism went wrong, its very power made the action disastrous, not only to himself but to the causes in which he was engaged and the men with whom he was co-operating. That was why the latter were so nervous in his partnership.'

It was this that Baldwin meant when he said, 'he is often right, but when he is wrong—my God!' And yet the problem is more subtle than this; for, after all, they were as often wrong as he was, and far more disastrously: Lloyd George about Hitler, and Baldwin as to what was necessary for the country's safety over the whole run of these years. The difference here must be that they at least gave the impression of being tellable, of being open to representations, where Churchill gave the *impression*—for it was not wholly true—of being untellable, intransigent, obstinately sticking to his own point of view. We have seen that there was this obstinacy in his character all the way along from childhood. And when right, it was a wholly good thing: it meant an unbreakable courage, resolution in adverse circumstances. It means what the brilliant and sensitive Wigram said in his last message, himself shattered by the lunacy of appeasing Hitler and only too clear-eyed as to where it would all end: 'Winston has always, always understood, and he is strong and will go on to the end'.

What was lacking was some intuitive tactile sense to tell him what others were thinking and (especially) feeling—the quality in which those feline Celtic natures, Lloyd George and Baldwin, were so gifted. Churchill was interested, in a very masculine way, only in the issue in itself, the merits of the case, not at all in its ambience. Baldwin was hardly at all interested in the issue itself, only in the personal ambience: he pondered the imponderables. Perhaps the defect in Churchill came from the very strength of the two natures mixed in him: the self-willed English aristocrat and the equally self-willed forceful American, each with a hundred horse-power capacity for getting his or her own way. Or it came from the excessive force of the mixture: he lacked some ordinariness which ordinary people ordinarily have.

Beaverbrook saw very clearly the two natures: the winning seductive charm, the child-like spontaneity and naturalness—and the change to an intolerable peremptoriness, a ruthlessness called forth by opposition. Birkenhead remarked on the contrast: 'to those who know him well it is very remarkable how complete is the public misconception of the man. He is looked upon as reserved, insolent and even bullying. For these illusions his own demeanour is (unintentionally) much to blame. He has no small talk, and says everything which comes into his mind. Sometimes caustic and disagreeable things come into it though in private life this never happens. . . . He has indeed, in the intimacy of personal friendship, a quality which is almost feminine in its caressing charm. And he has never in all his life failed a friend.' What a tribute! —his loyalty was indeed a shining characteristic, absolute in itself, so much greater than with those who stress personal relations more.

The question of his judgment is bound up with this. The very excess of his mental energy produced a certain obsessive quality: a man of one idea at a time, he was always apt to be possessed by it to the exclusion of other considerations, particularly personal. It is a characteristic of genius to see things with such intensity that other things cease to exist; and those who worked with him say that the concentration on the job in hand was such that nothing else existed at the time. (In this very unlike the supple Marlborough.) Perhaps this gives us some clue to why he was not good as a party-politician, especially at personal manoeuvres, and reached full stature with great issues, great arguments and events. Nor must we fail to note another singularity: that he should have gone on developing all his life so as to overcome these disabilities quite late, and reached maturity as a statesman, having begun so very young, only in his seventies.

Meanwhile, with Hitler's advent to power and Germany setting out on the path to her second attempt, events were catching up on Britain with a vengeance.

First, the question of air-parity, which Churchill made his primary campaign. Its importance was this: only in the air could Germany hope to attain a rapid equality with, and then a predominance over, Britain and France; so everything depended on what we did about that. Churchill points out that 'if Great Britain and France had each maintained quantitative parity with Germany they would together have been doubly as strong, and Hitler's career of violence might have been nipped in the bud without the loss of a single life'. He therefore obtained a solemn pledge from Baldwin that the National Government would 'see to it that in air strength and air power this country shall no longer be in a position inferior to any country within striking distance of its shores'. Mr. Baldwin contributed a memorable phrase, which gave the impression that he meant business, that the frontiers of England were no longer the cliffs of Dover but on the Rhine.

Churchill pointed out at the time that Baldwin 'because of the mass of the people throughout the country who trusted his sober judgment and because he was head of the Conservative party, with large majorities in both Houses, had only to make up his mind what was to be done in the matter, and Parliament would take all the steps that were necessary within forty-eight hours'. But he never did make up his mind on this vital matter. At the end of 1934 Churchill learned from his own sources of information that Germany was already approaching equality in the air, and raised the matter once more in Parliament. Baldwin gave him a categorical denial that this was so or that it was likely to be so; he reassured the country—he was a past-master at reassurance—that in Europe alone we had a margin of 50 per cent. Next year he had to admit that he had been completely wrong and—not that he had misled the country but that—'we were completely misled . . . it is the responsibility of the government as a whole, and we are all responsible, and we are all to blame'. Churchill expected that this shocking admission exposing the country's danger would have immediate consequences—think what would have happened before 1914! Here he was wrong. The very frankness of Baldwin's confession doubled his popularity with a complacent House: one would have thought he had won a famous victory. Churchill 'felt a sensation of despair. To be so entirely convinced and vindicated in a matter of life and death to one's country, and not to be able to make Parliament and the nation heed the warning, or bow to the proof by taking action, was an experience most painful.'

Not content with this from government and Air Ministry, the Admiralty now added its own folly: an Anglo-German Naval Agreement which was not worth the paper it was written on. From the moment Hitler came in the Germans began constructing their battle-cruisers, *Scharnhorst* and *Gneisenau,* 'in brazen and fraudulent violation of the Peace Treaty'; now, in direct contravention of the Agreement, they began laying down the *Bismarck,* which they made the most powerful battleship in the world. But the Agreement was worth a great deal to Hitler: it condoned their breach of the Peace Treaty, it drove a wedge between the British and the French, it was a blow to the League and it encouraged Mussolini to go forward against Abyssinia. Churchill sums up: 'what had in fact been done was to authorise Germany to build to her utmost capacity for five or six years to come'. What a contrast in the conduct of our affairs under the Liberal Government before 1914 and under the Conservative ascendancy that led to 1939!

There followed Mussolini's aggression against Abyssinia, his open defiance of the League and essentially of Britain. The Labour party, under the strong leadership of Ernest Bevin, threw over its pacifism, to implement the League with force if necessary and bring Mussolini to heel. Baldwin took the opportunity to catch the Labour party off-balance and force an election, on the pledge that he would resist aggression and uphold the League without any large increase in armaments. He won a thumping majority from a bemused country. 'Thus an administration more disastrous than any in our history', Churchill sums up, 'saw all its errors and shortcomings acclaimed by the nation. There was, however, a bill to be paid, and it took the new House of Commons nearly ten years to pay it.' On the personal side, 'this remarkable Party Manager, having won the election on world leadership against aggression, was profoundly convinced that we must keep peace at any price'. There had been some expectation before the election that Churchill would be recalled to the Admiralty, where he was certainly needed. Having won it Baldwin lost no time in accouncing that there was no intention to include him in the government. And having defeated the Labour party as the spokesman of collective security against aggression, he revealed his true mind, with cynical alacrity, in permitting Hoare to do his deal with Laval.

At the revelation of this even Baldwin lost caste and the government rocked: instead of resigning himself he threw over Hoare, the Foreign Secretary, and brought in Eden who was a convinced supporter of collective security, in other words a Grand Alliance, to contain and restrain the aggressors. That was, in fact, the only hope of keeping the peace; even so, it needed enforcement and rearming. The Labour party had the sense to see the first, but had not the sense to see the necessity of the second. Churchill saw that the temper of the Labour party was changing, and that 'here was the chance of a true National Government'. He happened to be abroad at the time and he thought later that he ought to have returned: 'I might have brought an element of decision and combination to the anti-Government gatherings which would have ended the Baldwin régime'. This is too sanguine: nothing was more pervasive, more cohesive—or in the long run more disastrous to their world, their country and their social order—than the sense of self-preservation among the Conservatives behind the men of the thirties. They marched together, the lot of them, on their melancholy, deliberate way to Munich and the war of 1939. I hope the survivors of them, when they look round, enjoy the world, the country, the social order they brought about for themselves.

Hitler drew his conclusions from the disgraceful spectacle and shortly after, in March 1936, re-militarised the Rhineland. If this were accepted it meant that there was no further chance of controlling him: he would be free to complete his preparations and strike where and when he chose: only war would stop him. The country was now alarmed; but 'there was an immense measure of agreement open, and had His Majesty's government risen to the occasion they could have led a united people forward into the whole business of preparation in an emergency spirit.... It was astonishing to me that they did not seek to utilise all the growing harmonies that now existed in the nation.' So far from that they altered nothing; thinking themselves indispensable, all their energy went into clinging on to power and keeping everybody else out; they kept the nation divided. Worst of all, they fatally accepted Hitler's move into the Rhineland. They even argued for it: 'wasn't it his own backyard?' was the cliché they used. I had it from Geoffrey Dawson, editor of *The Times* and immensely powerful in pushing in this fatally wrong direction. His friend, Lord Halifax, used it again later: 'to go to war with Germany for walking into their own backyard, which was how the British people saw it'.[1] He was mistaken: it was not the British people who saw it like that; the phrase came from his own circle, from Lothian and Geoffrey Dawson who put it across them. Lothian's friend, Lionel Curtis, assured me that 'Philip Lothian died in the knowledge that he had been wrong'. So were they all, painstakingly, obstinately, determinedly wrong to the last.

But fancy anyone being wrong about Hitler even from the first!

There was nothing now but to prepare for Hitler's war, see that it was met in the best possible circumstances, build up our alliances, strengthen our friends. Within the Foreign Office in December of that year, Churchill's friend, Wigram, died: his 'profound comprehension' of all that it meant and his inability to get the government to understand, let alone take the right action, was too much for him.

As a private citizen Churchill worked manfully to make up for the backwardness of the government in rearming, making the fullest use of his friendship with Professor Lindemann to keep abreast with the developments of science, especially in the air. At the same time as Churchill was attacking the government with severity over all other parts of the field, he was a member of the secret committee working hard to catch up in air-defence. They were only just in time. 'What would have surprised them [the

[1] The Earl of Halifax, *Fulness of Days,* 197.

Germans] was the extent to which we had turned our discoveries to practical effect, and woven all into our general air-defence system. In this we led the world, and it was operational efficiency rather than novelty of equipment that was the British achievement.' It was this that just tipped the scale against superior numbers in the Battle of Britain.

He should, of course, have been made Minister of Defence. But that would not have pleased Hitler—and Hitler's likes and dislikes were a matter of careful concern to this government. Everyone expected that Churchill would be called in. Nothing reveals more the inertness of Baldwin's judgment in regard to the safety of the nation than his appointment of a mediocre Evangelical lawyer, Sir Thomas Inskip, whose real passion was the Prayer Book, as Minister of Defence. His Ministry of Defence consisted of himself, his private secretary, a typist and a charwoman. It was a characteristic piece of wool-pulling over the eyes of the public on the past-master's part thus to answer the anxious demand for a Ministry of Defence. Churchill pressed for a Ministry of Supply; he was answered that that was precisely what Sir Thomas Inskip was supplying.

However, at the end of that year, Baldwin surpassed himself over the sorry business of King Edward VIII, and Churchill's fortunes were reduced to their lowest. People's qualities and their defects are intimately connected, and Baldwin, who could not be got to think out issues of policy on which the country's survival depended, was at his most skilful in the personal business of getting rid of an unsuitable king. Not a step did he put wrong; he thought out every move, took subtle advantage of every mistake made on the other side, committed not a fault of tact and, it must be admitted, served his country well in the hypnotising solo-dance he performed. He was enabled to retire in a cloud of equivocal glory—until profounder responsibilities on more important matters began to rain home.

Churchill's tactile sense, on the other hand, proved to be completely at fault. Never was the contrast between the two men more strikingly revealed. Churchill's intense loyalty of nature, the romantic appeal to his gallantry made by the plight of an unfortunate prince, were bound to put him on the side of the King. And not the less so because of the attitude of Mr. Baldwin. If there was some idea of seizing on the issue to get rid of Baldwin, can we blame him? We have seen him turning now this way, now that in the vain hope of getting rid of the incubus. Would it not have been infinitely better, might it not have spared the nation the war, if he had only succeeded in ridding us of Baldwin, over India, or over the Hoare-Laval pact, over Air-Parity and Defence? The issue of the King—if that was how in part he saw it—was a last hope. It turned out a very nearly fatal miscalculation. He was the only political leader who had the courage to raise his voice on the King's behalf, but when he raised it 'it was on more than one occasion almost physically impossible to make myself heard. All the forces I had gathered together on "Arms and the Covenant", of which I conceived myself to be the mainspring, were estranged or dissolved, and I was myself so smitten in public opinion that it was the almost universal view that my political life was at last ended.'

Neville Chamberlain was able to succeed to his inheritance with no breath of a challenge. Where Baldwin's sins had largely been those of omission, Chamberlain's were those of deliberate commission. For he really believed it was possible to do a deal with Hitler: that was the whole end of his policy and he meant to attain it. On his return from Munich he said that he had 'got the impression that here was a man who could be relied upon when he had given his word'. Anyone who thought that was a fool indeed. But Neville Chamberlain, who was a good Minister of Health and an orderly-minded head of a department, was a blinkered, opinionated, obstinate man with no knowledge whatever of Europe. Those men, his immeasurable superiors, Lloyd George and Churchill, described him accurately enough: the one, 'a good Lord Mayor of Birmingham in a lean year'; the other, 'he viewed world affairs through the wrong end of the municipal drain-pipe'.

It is sometimes thought that the best case made for the men of Munich is that given by Hoare in his Memoirs. If that is so there is no case at all. For what it comes to is that Chamberlain envisaged taking up each point at issue with Hitler and Mussolini *one by one* as a step to a general settlement. Exactly: at the end we should find ourselves with the whole balance of Europe turned against us and facing a Europe arrayed against us. This was the nightmare that had troubled Grey and that he so successfully countered. As the result of the able conduct of our affairs before 1914 we went into the war with the whole balance of Europe with us against Germany; after two decades of dominantly Conservative rule we faced Nazi Germany alone and unprepared with a devitalised and defeatist France.

Why did they not see it? What is so difficult to understand is the ignorance of these men as to the life-interests of their country, the fundamental patterns of the Grand Alliance against any over-mighty aggressor that had been the sheet-anchor of our security throughout the ages—against Philip II, against Louis XIV and Napoleon, against the Germany of the Kaiser. It was all thrown away as against Hitler and Nazi Germany. Why? It is a searching question and one that goes to the heart of the decline of our country, and in our society. In part it was due to the decadence of the governing classes, a failure of confidence and nerve; in part to a muddlement of mind as between their class-interests and the interests of their country: they really thought that Hitler was their ally against Communism—no conception that a defeat by Nazi Germany, with the technical efficiency of its bestial barbarism, would be the end for Britain anyway.

There went along with this a curious mentality on the part of the men of Munich, an interesting psychological phenomenon if it were not so distasteful: a complacent smugness about their course, a fatuous self-satisfaction, an astonishing conceit considering how wrong they were; they behaved extremely badly to those who opposed their fatal course—Churchill, Eden, Cranborne, Duff Cooper and others all had experience of this at their hands. When Eden revealed his disquiet at the course being taken—for the Foreign Office was never wrong in these matters, it was simply thrown over by an opinionated old man with no knowledge of foreign affairs—Chamberlain told him 'to go home and take an aspirin'. Actually he had an understanding with Mussolini's ambassador against his own Foreign Secretary. Duff Cooper tells us that Chamberlain was playing a part: 'while allowing his colleagues to suppose that he was as anxious as any of them to dissuade the Foreign Secretary from resigning, he had in reality determined to get rid of him, and had secretly informed the Italian ambassador that he hoped to succeed in doing so. Had I known this at the time, not only would I have resigned with Eden, but I should have found it difficult to sit in Cabinet with Neville Chamberlain again.'[1]

Eden's resignation reduced Churchill to despair. 'I must confess that my heart sank, and for a while the dark waters of despair overwhelmed me. In a long life I have had many ups and downs. During all the war soon to come and in its darkest times I never had any trouble in sleeping. . . . But now on this night of February

[1] Duff Cooper, *Old Men Forget,* 215. Cf. Churchill's reaction to all this, 'it makes one flush to read in Ciano's diary the comments which were made behind the Italian scene about our country and its representatives', *op. cit.* I. 266-7.

20, 1938, and on this occasion only, sleep deserted me. From midnight till dawn I lay in my bed consumed by emotions of sorrow and fear.' Lord Halifax came to Chamberlain's rescue and the way to Munich was all clear.

Churchill's views on this disgraceful surrender are well known. At the time, with true strategic sense, they all focussed upon the necessity. 'We must get Russia in'. So far from trying to, 'no invitation was extended to Russia. Nor were the Czechs themselves allowed to be present at the meetings' at which their country was maimed for Hitler's benefit and handed over to his mercy. Chamberlain made no attempt to bring over the balance of powers to our side, but simply relied on his own ability to 'do business' with Hitler face to face. It is fairly clear that he had no idea what he was up against and that when he emerged from having made a complete surrender he really believed, what he told the crowd in Downing Street, that it was 'peace for our time'. When Churchill told the House of Commons 'we have sustained a total and unmitigated defeat', he was almost shouted down. Only some thirty to forty Conservatives were prepared to stand with him at this juncture, and they were made the target of attack by the Conservative machine—such was the Munich mentality. 'Each of us was attacked in his constituency by the Conservative party machine, and many there were, who a year later were our ardent supporters, who agitated against us.'

We are near the explanation of the psychological phenomenon of the Munich mentality: the men who were so wrong betrayed by their behaviour an uncomfortable consciousness at the back of their minds that they *were* wrong. That was why they were so determined to make everybody assent to what was crazy—to associate everyone with their guilt.

All they could do now was to go on downhill. In the privacy of his own circle Chamberlain would admit 'all depends on whether we can trust Hitler'. The impossibility of any such trust should have been evident all along—if our political leaders had been sufficiently educated to read *Mein Kampf* they would have known it all beforehand—but it took Hitler's breach of his word to *him*, Neville Chamberlain, the march on Prague and the swallowing up of Czecho-Slovakia to open his eyes. As Lord Halifax sagely observes, 'after March and the final rape of Prague, it was no longer possible to hope that Hitler's purposes and ambitions were limited by any boundaries of race, and the lust of continental or world mastery seemed to stand out in stark relief'. 'It was no longer possible to hope'!—it never had been possible to hope: to suppose that it was—there was the lunacy. After that there followed Chamberlain's scuttle to offer alliances and guarantees to anybody and everybody who would accept them—when it was too late and regardless of whether we could now render them an effective help. Lord Halifax observes, 'if the event showed that Hitler was not to be restrained, it was better that the nations under threat should stand and fight together than they should await German attack one by one'. Of course; but it would have been mere sense to have adopted that line all along, and it might not have been necessary to fight. Stand firm and the break would have come inside Germany—that was the policy of the Grand Alliance or collective security, under whichever name.

Churchill was convinced that at this last moment war might have been averted. I am not so sure. Certainly the key to it was Russia. 'There can be no doubt', he says, 'that Britain and France should have accepted the Russian offer. . . . If, for instance, Mr. Chamberlain on receipt of the Russian offer had replied, "Yes. Let us three band together and break Hitler's neck," or words to that effect, Parliament would have approved, Stalin would have understood, and history might have taken a different course. At least it could not have taken a worse.' In place of that, Chamberlain's 'reception of it was certainly cool, and indeed disdainful'. The Russians drew their own conclusions, reversed their policy and made their pact with Hitler. The war was upon us.

At this point Churchill has a magnanimous sentence upon his fellow-countrymen who had for so long disregarded his warnings: 'it is a curious fact about the British Islanders that as danger comes nearer and grows, they become progressively less nervous; when it is imminent, they are fierce; when it is mortal, they are fearless. These habits have led them into some very narrow escapes.' What followed was a very narrow escape indeed—the narrowest since 1688, when Marlborough was at hand, or perhaps since 1588. As for their leaders throughout all this period Churchill regards them as 'blameworthy before history'. 'That we should all have come to this pass makes those responsible, however honourable their motives, blameworthy before history.'

On 3 September 1939 Neville Chamberlain broadcast to the nation that we were at war with Germany once more. Many of us remember that lugubrious, uninspiring discourse, all about himself: 'everything that I have worked for, everything that I have hoped for, everything that I have believed in during my public life has crashed into ruins'.—As if that were the most regrettable aspect of the matter! No historic conception of the day it was to arouse and steel the nation's resolve: the day of Dunbar and Worcester, of Oliver's 'crowning mercy', the day when that mighty spirit went out in a thunderstorm.

Chamberlain had to take Churchill into his government. He came back to the Admiralty he had quitted a quarter of a century before: the Board had the imagination to send out the signal to the Fleet, 'Winston is back'. There were the familiar things about him once more, his old chair, the maps and charts, the map-case he had himself fixed in 1911, in the room he had last quitted when Fisher broke with him and all the hopes placed upon the Dardanelles foundered. From across the Atlantic there came a no less significant signal. President Roosevelt wrote, 'it is because you and I occupied similar positions in the World War that I want you to know how glad I am that you are back again in the Admiralty. . . . I am glad you did the Marlborough volumes before this thing started—and I much enjoyed reading them.'

Between Chamberlain and Churchill there could be no sympathy, and though Churchill had answered his call and come to the rescue of his government he complained that the Prime Minister did not take him into his confidence. Chamberlain was indeed at sea, had no grasp of the situation. In April 1940 he told his Conservative followers, 'after seven months of war I feel ten times as confident of victory as I did at the beginning. . . . I feel that during the seven months our relative position towards the enemy has become a great deal stronger than it was.' This was just before the avalanche fell upon us: Norway and Denmark overwhelmed, then Holland and Belgium, to be followed by France.

These events broke Neville Chamberlain's government at last. Even the Conservative party was beginning to turn, though in the final vote he still had a majority of eighty-one and could appeal to 'his friends' there—as if that were the question that counted at such a time. Roger Keyes came down to the House in full uniform as Admiral of the Fleet to record his vote against the men of Munich. Amery directed to them the words with which Cromwell had dismissed the Rump: 'you have sat here too long for any good you have been doing. Depart, I say, and let us have done with you! In the name of God, Go!' Lloyd George had his moment of revenge after nearly twenty years—Neville Chamberlain's prime motive in coming into politics had been to keep him out. The man who led the country to victory in 1918 now said that nothing could contribute more to victory in this war than that Chamberlain should go.

He still lingered, held on, hoping against hope, offering office to Amery, to the dissidents. At this moment when the avalanche descended—which everything had been done to bring down on us—nothing but a real National government would do instead of the humbugging simulacrum of the name which had bemused the country for now nine years. It is pleasant to record that it was the Labour party that at last gave Neville Chamberlain his quittance: they would serve under Churchill but not under him. It is even pleasanter to think that Churchill owed his elevation to his old enemies the Labour people. His government, the Churchill-Labour government that fought the war and saved the country, was formed on an equal basis: a coming together of all the men of sense on both sides who had been kept out during that shameful decade. Even so, when Churchill led in his new government he got a very cool reception—it was Neville Chamberlain who got the cheers—from that unspeakable assembly; it is said that Churchill commented, 'any more of that and we'll have an election and wipe them out'. All the world knows what we owed to him in the years to come, the forties; but it is questionable whether we did not owe him as much, all things considered, in those agonising years of the thirties. Looking back over them in perspective one shudders to think where the nation would have been without him.

For himself, 'I was conscious of a profound sense of relief. At last I had the authority to give directions over the whole scene. I felt as if I were walking with destiny, and that all my past life had been but a preparation for this hour and for this trial.'

The nation had found its true leader in time of danger, and that leader had at last found himself.

CHAPTER TWELVE

The Heroic Years

CHURCHILL'S life was virtually synonymous with the history of the country during the heroic years 1940 to 1945. To a degree hardly paralleled in recent centuries—certainly to a greater extent even than with Lloyd George in the first war. Perhaps we should have to go back for a parallel to Pitt's leadership and inspiration in the Seven Years War; or, in more recent times, we may think of Lincoln's heroic Presidency, without whom the Civil War might never have been won. These years were the apogee of our country's history, when its purpose reached the fullest and ripest development. In its resistance to Nazi Germany—for what seemed at the time of going through it an age, alone—it rendered a grander service to Europe than even in its resistance to the Spain of Philip II, the France of Louis XIV and Napoleon, the Germany of Bismarck and William II; for though Britain's existence was at stake, more was involved for others—the survival of European civilisation.

Happy then is the man whose name is indelibly associated with the time he has himself described as 'their finest hour'.

That in itself carries with it an impossibility for the recorder of the family: it is out of the question to describe his life in detail in those years, give it its proper emphasis and proportion. He has himself told his story of the Second World War in six full volumes; and there are almost as many of his speeches, his words at the time. No English statesman has been so documented by himself—it stands in some contrast with the reserved Marlborough. Only Britain produced a leader capable equally of writing the history and of acting it. And there is something significant in that, for politics and literature are the two chief expressions of the English in the arts of life. In combining and expressing them Churchill may therefore be regarded as the most representative of Englishmen, as Luther is of the Germans in his combination of music and unreason.

Here, then, we must concentrate on Churchill's personal contribution in those years to winning the war, attempt to *préciser* what that was—in itself a formidable enough task.

We may say at the outset that for Britain in 1940 Churchill's contribution made the difference between defeat and resistance, or at any rate effective resistance. The slightest hesitation, the least faltering or any sign that we were prepared to consider terms—and we should have been done for. For, except for the Channel, Britain was defeated and Western Europe lay unexpectedly at Hitler's feet. At the moment Churchill was called to power, 10 May 1940, Holland and Belgium were being submerged and France, undermined and eaten out from within, was ready to crumble. All Englishmen who were alive at the time remember Churchill's words at that moment, the very tones of his voice, sombre and harsh, angry and defiant, thrilling with resolve to fight on or go down fighting. Indeed the whole story might be told in his words, to the best advantage, for never have words exerted a grander compulsion, a nobler impulse to such effect upon his hearers—or perhaps not since the words of Elizabeth and Drake in the summer of 1588, historic memories that came often to mind to sustain him.

On becoming, at last, their leader when all was crashing around them he told government, Parliament and people, 'I have nothing to offer but blood, toil, tears and sweat. We have before us an ordeal of the most grievous kind. We have before us many, many long months of struggle and of suffering. You ask, What is our policy? I will say: It is to wage war, by sea, land and air, with all our might and with all the strength that God can give us: to wage war against a monstrous tyranny, never surpassed in the dark, lamentable catalogue of human crime. You ask, What is our aim? I can answer in one word: Victory—victory at all costs, victory in spite of all terror, victory however long and hard the road may be; for without victory, there is no survival. Let that be realised: no survival for the British Empire; no survival for all that the British Empire has stood for, no survival for the urge and impulse of the ages, that mankind will move forward towards its goal. But I take up my task with buoyancy and hope. I feel sure that our cause will not be suffered to fail among men. At this time I feel entitled to claim the aid of all, and I say, "Come, then, let us go forward together with our united strength".'

Even now, nearly three decades after, with the dust lying upon so much ardour along the dreary way, one can hardly see for tears in transcribing those words that bring back that glorious, unforgettable summer, the long hot days full of catastrophe and suspense, the country's sudden and complete uncovering, the mortal danger we stood in. Consider the situation he had to confront: the French army crumbling at the moment he was engaged in forming his government, himself flying to and from Paris attempting in vain to stiffen resistance while recruiting his ministry at home. It was not contemplated that France would collapse: it is fairly clear that he envisaged the second German war in terms of the first, the large French army, in which he placed his trust, holding the Germans until British man-power and resources were fully mobilised and engaged. When the Germans began their break-through, Churchill asked the French High Command, as a soldier naturally would, where were their reserves, the mass of manoeuvre to deploy in this situation? He was told there were none. It was one of the worst surprises he had ever had in his life. And there was the British Army—small, it is true, but all we had with its equipment—increasingly exposed to being cut off on the northern flank, under a French command that believed all was irremediably lost. But 'where were we British anyway, having regard to our tiny contribution—ten divisions after eight months of war, and not even one modern tank division in action?'

However, to the British people on the eve of the decision in France: 'Today is Trinity Sunday. Centuries ago words were written to be a call and a spur to the faithful servants of Truth and Justice: "Arm yourselves, and be ye men of valour, and be in readiness for the conflict; for it is better for us to perish in battle than to look upon the outrage of our nation and our altar. As the Will of God is in Heaven, even so let it be." '

At this moment, the hand of the great President in Washington, who understood all that was at stake, was stretched out to sustain him; and to him he could confide his innermost thoughts. 'I do not need to tell you about the gravity of what has happened. We are determined to persevere to the very end, whatever the result of the great battle raging in France may be. We must expect in any case to be attacked here on the Dutch model before very long, and we hope to give a good account of ourselves. But if American assistance is to play any part it must be available soon.' And again, 'our intention is, whatever happens, to fight on to the end in this Island, and, provided we can get the help for which we ask, we hope to run them very close in the air battles in view of individual superiority'. Here a factor of extreme importance, an element indispensable to winning the war and Churchill's own vital contribution, is already adumbrated: the effect of his courage and confidence upon Roosevelt, persuading him that we were not a lost cause—against all the evidence—but worth supporting. A German victory would leave America unprepared and exposed to a hostile Europe on the Atlantic front, when she already had a hostile Japan facing her across the Pacific. We were a risk doubly worth taking; but Churchill's relations with the President, his own American blood enabling him to feel along with the Americans, clinched it as a Chamberlain could never have done.

On the eve of the battle of Dunkirk, on which the fate of the Army depended, for it was there surrounded on every side but the sea, there was a service of Intercession and Prayer in Westminster Abbey. 'The English are loth to expose their feelings, but in my stall in the Choir I could feel the pent-up, passionate emotion, and also the fear of the congregation, not of death or wounds or material loss, but of defeat and the final ruin of Britain.' In fact, we all remember that these were glorious moments in which to be alive; Churchill not only voiced them but embodied the hour. When he let drop almost casually in Cabinet—many of whom had supported Baldwin and Chamberlain all the way along—the words, 'of course, whatever happens at Dunkirk, we shall fight on', there occurred an extraordinary demonstration of emotion unexampled in the long history of British Cabinets. One resolve united government and people, was incarnate in one man, for so long unheard, disconsidered, disregarded.

All the same, by the light of cool reason it is difficult to see how, if the Army had been destroyed at Dunkirk, we could have fought on. But now Europe witnessed one of those miraculous transformations—perhaps the last and finest in our history—which sea-power can accomplish. Overhead the R.A.F. contested the air with the Luftwaffe above the entrenched army within its contracting perimeter. The very night after the service in Westminster Abbey, 'a great tide of small vessels began to flow towards the sea, first to our Channel ports, and thence to the beaches of Dunkirk and the beloved Army'. That is the only time in our history that I can remember the Army being described as 'beloved'; yet strangely enough that was discovered to be what was at the bottom of all our hearts. Only Churchill could have said it.

And now the advantage of being a seafaring people came to the rescue—the crest of a wave going back a long way beyond 1588. The brunt of the Dunkirk evacuation was borne by the Navy, especially by the destroyers and minesweepers; but everybody else who had a boat joined in, fishing trawlers and drifters, tugs and motor-boats, yachts and pleasure-boats, old Thames steamers and river-craft of every kind. The great majority of the ships in that Armada in reverse, that plunged into the inferno of those waters, were little boats. One-third of them all were lost; but the bulk of the Army was saved. We remember them as they came back from the Channel and passed through the ports and railway-stations, where civilians brought them food and cigarettes—blackened, dirty, disarmed, but not at all dismayed by their ordeal: in fact, in high spirits, their general reaction, 'Give us the arms and we'll give Jerry some of his own back'.[1] Notice that their attitude towards the odious people who had let loose this inferno a second time upon Europe was not even unfriendly. But note Churchill on leaving to meet the President on 4 August 1941: 'it is twenty-seven years ago today that the Huns began their last war. We must make a good job of it this time. Twice ought to be enough.' *They knew.*

When it was known that the bulk of the Army was saved an immense feeling of an almighty deliverance spread through the nation. Anyone would have thought that it had been a great victory, instead of a very narrow escape; but the English apparently take more pleasure in narrow escapes. Churchill noticed that 'the sense of fear seemed entirely lacking in the people', and that was true. Simple folk at the time were relieved after the fall of France—they felt that now they could go forward and fight the war better by themselves. That, of course, was pure ignorance; the intelligent realised that we were in mortal peril. The importance of Dunkirk was that now the bulk of the trained men were safe we could build a bigger Army anew upon their cadres. But the whole of their equipment had been lost, all the *matériel,* artillery, machine-guns, automobiles, rifles that had at least been brought together in the improvident years. It would take years to train and equip an Army capable of re-entering Europe. Meanwhile, the country was stripped bare militarily: there was the Navy and the R.A.F., for the rest, very few guns, hardly even rifles and only one armoured regiment in the country. Could we hold on? Could we hold out? Could we resist invasion?

Here again Churchill's resolve, his very character, was of inestimable value: everybody knew he would not give in. In reporting the issue of Dunkirk to the House he made his famous declaration, which owed something to his memory of Clemenceau's words in 1918:[2] 'we shall go on to the end, we shall fight in France, we shall

[1] These were the very words I heard from a group of them passing through a southern railway-station.

[2] 'I will fight before Paris, I will fight in Paris, I will fight behind Paris.' Cf. Romier, *History of France,* trans. Rowse, 452.

fight on the seas and oceans, we shall fight with confidence and growing strength in the air, we shall defend our island, whatever the cost may be, we shall fight on the beaches, we shall fight on the landing grounds, we shall fight in the fields and in the streets, we shall fight in the hills; we shall never surrender, and even if, which I do not for a moment believe, this island or a large part of it were subjugated and starving, then our Empire beyond the seas, armed and guarded by the British Fleet, would carry on the struggle, until, in God's good time, the New World, with all its power and might, steps forth to the rescue and the liberation of the Old.'

It was this spirit that turned the scale with the President and his Secretary of State, and impelled them to their resolution of turning over the mass of arms that could be spared from the minimum requirements of the American Army: half a million rifles from 1918, cartridges, machine-guns, field-guns. Cordell Hull says quite simply, 'the President and I believed Mr. Churchill meant what he said. Had we had any doubt of Britain's determination to keep on fighting, we would not have taken the steps we did to get material aid to her.' Without that we should not have been able to resist in case of invasion.

For Churchill especially the fall of France was a harrowing experience: he had always been the most French in sympathy of British political figures, had maintained his confidence in the French Army, alongside of whom he had fought on the Western Front in 1916. Now that Pétain had surrendered to Hitler, Churchill had to take an agonising decision: to eliminate what remained expendable of the French Navy at Oran. With Britain's back to the wall, with the Italian Fleet now in the war against her in the Mediterranean, she simply could not take the risk of the French Fleet there being added to her enemies. They were given the choice of coming over or being put out of action. It was a terrible decision to take. There is no doubt that it was Churchill's and, though Vichy was able to exploit anti-English feeling by it, he felt sure that the French people would understand the hard measures that were necessary for our common salvation. Moreover, the action at Oran brought home to all the world that the British government would stop at nothing to make sure the command of the sea and continue the war. After the Battle of Britain and our own agony that autumn, Churchill was able to address the French people with a personal appeal, assuring them that all would come right in the end, and this, in spite of everything, went home to their hearts. 'Goodnight then: sleep to gather strength for the morning.

For the morning will come. Brightly will it shine on the brave and true, kindly upon all who suffer for the cause, glorious upon the tombs of heroes. Thus will shine the dawn. *Vive la France!* Long live also the forward march of the common people in all the lands towards their just and true inheritance, and towards the broader and fuller age.'[1]

The country was now expecting invasion. Hitler was expecting our surrender; but, as the Duke of Windsor said, he 'did not know Winston'. He had previously met a number of feebler specimens among our politicians, and a lunatic fringe of pacifists, appeasers, defeatists, do-gooders, whose total efforts had done much to bring the war down on us. At the surrender of France the Führer of the German people danced his extraordinary jig of joy, but this was somewhat premature after all: he danced his last jig in the macabre environment of the underground Bunker in Berlin. Dizzy with success, the Führer waited a little, even made a peace-offer of which no notice was taken, and then, somewhat at a loss and rather belatedly, gave the orders for the assault on Britain to be set in motion.

All that fine summer while we were waiting, the lorries crashed down to the coast night and day; gun-emplacements, hide-outs, machine-gun posts, trenches, tank-traps, barriers were feverishly constructed—one comes across them in quiet English countryside still—the American rifles and ammunition handed sparely out. By the end of the summer those of us living on the exposed coast, looking across to France, felt not quite so naked. From the centre an utterly new spirit went forth vibrating through the country. Week by week the Prime Minister assembled his full Cabinet, as a member of it has told me, to inject his resolution into them, tell them what he expected and what he demanded of them. A message from him went through the country's governing machine: 'the Prime Minister expects all his Majesty's servants in high places to set an example of steadiness and resolution. They should check and rebuke the expression of loose and ill-digested opinions in their circles, or by their subordinates. They should not hesitate to report, or if necessary remove, any persons, officers, or officials, who are found to be consciously exercising a disturbing or depressing influence, and whose talk is calculated to spread alarm and despondency. Thus alone will they be worthy of the fighting men who, in

[1] Churchill, *Into Battle,* 297. I should add his immense service to France in getting de Gaulle away in 1940, in supporting him and forwarding his cause throughout the war.

the air, on the sea, and on land, have already met the enemy without any sense of being outmatched in martial qualities.'

How different a spirit from that of the thirties! An admirable historian friend of mine brought home to me the change of spirit within the governing machine, where he served, with Churchill's advent to power. Before, he said, one could not see that the war could be won; after a short time, though one still could not see, one began to feel that it might be. It was like Pitt in 1758. He did not know how it was done. It is not difficult to understand, if one allows oneself to.

Actually, though the danger was acute, the outlook grim and no one could tell what the upshot would be, Churchill's confidence was a reasoned one: it was not mere bravado. He reckoned that in our own skies, over the island and its waters, the R.A.F. could beat the larger German Air Force; and upon that condition the Navy could hold the seas around us and destroy the enemy setting their course for us. He himself told me he was sure they could not land. But if they had landed every inch would be contested. No surrendering London as Paris had been surrendered: 'you may rest assured that we should fight every street of London and its suburbs. It would *devour* an invading army, assuming one ever got so far, We hope however to drown the bulk of them in the salt sea.' If they got so far as to land he intended to use the grim, inspiriting slogan, *You can always take one with you*. In these 'white-hot weeks' he had two brave spirits very close to him, Ernest Bevin and Beaverbrook; if the government had had to disperse over the country, he told me, he had an idea of a triumvirate with them. The government would never leave the island. Of those summer weeks, while German planes sneaked across the coasts, spying out the land, probing our defences, and the country steadied itself for the trial, he writes, 'this was a time when it was equally good to live or die'.

Meanwhile, the withdrawal of the French Navy left us perilously strained at sea, especially in destroyers, what with the losses at Dunkirk, and from U-boats, aircraft and mines. Laid up in American harbours were fifty old destroyers from the first war, now unused. All that summer Churchill exerted his powers of persuasion with the President to sell, give or hand them over. 'Mr. President, with great respect I must tell you that in the long history of the world this is a thing to do *now*.' The President was nothing loth: his difficulties were political and they seemed insuperable. After all, he was supposed to be neutral; we recall the crazy neutrality-legislation that hampered the cause that was in essence as much America's as Britain's. But the President was not a superlative politician for nothing—immensely Churchill's superior in these arts: after the Battle of Britain was fought and won Roosevelt thought up a way of releasing the destroyers, in return for the lease of bases on British territory around American shores. It may well be considered that the United States had the better of this bargain; but the aid those destroyers gave was something in 1940, while resources were so strained and before new building came in. It was one of the factors that enabled us to hold out, and Churchill's gratitude to the President for his confidence in him was profound. But already he was looking further than the personal factor: 'this process means that these two great organisations of the English-speaking democracies, the British Empire and the United States, will have to be somewhat mixed up together in some of their affairs for mutual and general advantage. For my own part, looking out upon the future, I do not view the process with any misgivings. I could not stop it if I wished; no one can stop it. Like the Mississippi, it just keeps rolling along. Let it roll on—full flood, inexorable, irresistible, benignant, to broader lands and better days.'

In August and September the Battle of Britain was fought out in the skies, the country saved in the lives of our fighter-pilots. If an invasion was to be attempted it was indispensable for the Luftwaffe to establish an ascendancy over the R.A.F., and this by a narrow margin it failed to do.[1] With his irresistible desire to be on the spot, Churchill was at the headquarters of Fighter Command at Uxbridge on the culminating day of the battle, 15 September—like Waterloo, he recalled, fought on a Sunday. In his Memoirs he describes this critical air-battle, which proved the turning-point; after that the Luftwaffe gave up the attempt and turned to bombing: the invasion was off. With his mind always sustained, as well as enriched, from the wells of history, Churchill thought of Drake and his little ships in 1588 while action raged in the skies. Even more striking was his appreciation of the complicated technical matters involved. And then we are reminded of his experience earlier at the Air Ministry, his constant interest in developments in the air, his learning to pilot an aircraft, his part in Britain's air rearmament, unbeknown to the Germans, just in time for the war.

[1] For an interesting account of the German bafflement at the result see the American observer, William L. Shirer, *Berlin Diary* (New York, 1941), 553-7.

His work with Lindemann had a share in achieving that operational efficiency by which the R.A.F. survived and triumphed, 'the like of which existed nowhere in the world' at that time. When the issue was decided he was able to sum it up in an unforgotten phrase in the Commons: 'never in the field of human conflict was so much owed by so many to so few'.

Defeated in battle, the Germans turned to the methods of indiscriminate *Blitzkrieg* which had won such results in Poland and Norway, upon friendly Rotterdam. That autumn they made London their target. It was difficult to miss, and Londoners were treated to the fascinating, dangerous, unbelievable spectacle of their city going up in flames. The King and Queen had a narrow escape from a salvo of bombs which fell on Buckingham Palace, giving them the exhilaration of feeling that they were sharing the dangers equally with their subjects. It was difficult to restrain the Prime Minister from going up on the roofs at night to have a look. As the blitz grew heavier he went to visit the worst-damaged quarters: he seemed to be everywhere, the familiar bulky figure clambering over the smoking ruins, cheering the bombed-out with his sympathy, his jokes, his spirit.

Early on one day in Peckham, where there had been a large amount of damage in a very poor district from a land-mine, a crowd surrounded his car when he was recognized, 'cheering and manifesting every sign of lively affection, wanting to touch and stroke my clothes. One would have thought I had brought them some fine substantial benefit which would improve their lot in life. I was completely undermined, and wept. Ismay, who was with me, records that he heard an old woman say: "You see, he really cares. He's crying."' It was that that put him into the people's hearts: none of the middle-class fear of emotion, their inhibition in expressing it: the old aristocrat was much nearer the people in spirit. And in his reactions, too, direct and natural, uncomplex and understandable. When the Peckham crowd had shown him round the crater and the devastation, 'Give it 'em back', they cried, and 'Let *them* have it too.' 'I undertook forthwith to see that their wishes were carried out; and this promise was certainly kept.' It was a regular feature of those days and of the winter of bombing that followed to see groups of the bombed and houseless telling him 'Stick it, Winnie'—as if he needed the adjuration. The spirit in Britain was certainly very different from what the malign *Schadenfreude* of Hitler and Goebbels fancied, the characteristic German mixture of envy and spite.

At the end of that wonderful year an unexpectedly complete victory came to cheer the company of the faithful. At the moment of the fall of France, Mussolini, fearful he would be too late to join in the spoils, entered the war, begging Hitler that Italian aircraft might share in the attack on Britain. Churchill, who had never had any animus against Mussolini—in that mistaken, in my view—sent him a personal message, half-appeal, half-warning. But Mussolini was convinced that Britain was finished. At the height of her preparation against invasion Churchill took the daring resolution to counter the Italian attack on Egypt and Suez by sending half the tanks she had left, two armoured regiments, to reinforce the garrison there. Thus stiffened, Wavell's small army inflicted an overwhelming defeat upon the Italian Army, several times its size, that was invading Egypt. At Sidi Barrani five Italian divisions were destroyed; 38,000 prisoners were taken for the loss of 133 British killed. By mid-December Egypt was completely cleared of the enemy. It must be said that the Italians showed up very badly—which only proves how easily they could have been dealt with in 1935 and the disastrous run of events thereafter stopped.

By the end of the year 1940 a remarkable transformation had come over the outlook. The Battle of Britain had defeated all serious threat of invasion; Suez was firmly held and one of the Axis partners had been started on the road to defeat, humiliatingly and without reversal. If only France had continued the fight from North Africa the duration of the war would have been halved.

For us the year 1940 must ever rank with that other *annus mirabilis* 1588. Transcendent as were the services yet to come from Churchill, 1940 must rank as his finest hour, along with the nation's, for in that year his contribution made the difference between defeat and survival.

At the same time, though we had survived, one could not see how it would all end, how we were to win, alone against a German-controlled Europe. My own view at the time, the argument I steadily put forward to depressed friends, was that Britain's fundamental interest against German domination was one with Russia and the United States: the moment that latent common interest became realised in action we were safe, though the fighting still remained to be done. This conception of our common interests—it was what was implied by 'collective security' and should have dominated our policy in the ignorant thirties—was clear enough in the Foreign Office[1] and must have been present to Churchill's mind. He put it rather differently, on one occasion saying that the mistakes of our enemies would come to our aid; they would certainly be taken full advantage of.

There is a revealing conversation that he had had in 1937 with Ribbentrop, the egregious creature whom Hitler sent to London as ambassador. Ribbentrop made Churchill the suggestion that bemused so many Chamberlainites: a German guarantee of the British Empire in the outside world in return for a free hand for Germany in Europe. Churchill said Britain would never disinterest herself in the Continent to the extent of accepting a German domination of Central and Eastern Europe. Ribbentrop replied, 'in that case war is inevitable. The Führer is resolved. Nothing will stop him and nothing will stop us.' (That short interchange should have been enough to enlighten Chamberlain's government as to Germany's real intentions—as if, even so, it should have been necessary!) Though a mere private Member of Parliament whom not more than twenty Tories would follow then, Churchill gave Ribbentrop a solemn warning, which Germans would have done well to take heed of—it was really the same warning their ambassadors had given them before 1914, which they would not listen to. 'When you talk of war, which no doubt would be general war, you must not underrate England.... Do not judge by the attitude of the present Administration. Once a great cause is presented to the people, all kinds of unexpected actions might be taken by this very government and by the British nation.' He repeated, 'do not underrate England. She is very clever. If you plunge us all into another Great War, she will bring the whole world against you like last time.' But Ribbentrop, so like a German, wouldn't take telling: he rose in heat and said, 'Ah, England may be very clever, but this time she will not bring the world against Germany'.

But this was just what was now about to happen.

In the spring of 1941 we find Churchill very early alerted about Hitler's troop-movements against Russia, correctly assessing his intentions, ready to pounce and take the utmost advantage of this transformation of the war. As early as 3 April he transmitted a warning personally to Stalin through our ambassador, Sir Stafford Cripps. He got no reply. The extraordinary thing was that, though the Soviet leaders were well aware of the conflict between German

1 Once and again in those years a word of encouragement reached me from the Foreign Office in my own small campaign on these lines, cf. my *End of an Epoch*.

and Russian interests, and between Nazism and Communism, they preferred to 'trust' Hitler rather than the Western democracies. Like calls to like, gangster to gangster, thug to thug. Both were tyrannies, both were barbarous and cruel—even if one were ultimately rational, the other ultimately insane; both had their hands imbrued in men's blood; neither of them had any belief in truth, or honesty, or common decency. And so Stalin preferred Hitler's assurances to Churchill's warning—with the result that, when the German assault came, a considerable part of the Soviet Air Force was destroyed on the ground and the Russians were caught at a great disadvantage. Molotov's wonderful reaction to the German ambassador was—'your aircraft have just bombarded some ten open villages. *Do you think that we deserved that?*'[1]

With the German attack on Russia, Britain no longer stood alone: she had an ally in fact, if unwilling and surly. Actions speak louder than words; facts are stronger than tempers. It was Churchill's immense service to clinch the alliance at once, without hesitation or leaving a moment for mistrust cr doubt to fester. No one was in so strong a position to reconcile doubters to our new ally. This was the beginning of our deliverance and there must be no faltering about it. There were plenty of doubters where Russia was concerned—understandably enough. The year before, when Russia was engaged in her war against Finland, there had been people so lunatic as to urge our helping the Finns and taking on Russia in addition to Germany. And indeed, at bottom, it was anti-Communism that had split the mind of the governing class in Britain and ruined all hope of a coherent policy before the war—made them give the game away to Hitler as to Mussolini and Franco.

There was no confusion of mind, no hesitation with Churchill; in the struggle with Nazy Germany the existence of the nation was at stake: if one is in mortal combat with a tiger, and a crocodile or great bear comes to one's aid, is it sense to reject it? The very day of the German attack on Russia, 21 June, Churchill broadcast to the nation making clear all the implications of the new state of affairs—more, grappling them to its use. Anyone else might have

[1] It is not absolutely certain that Molotov had no sense of humour, or if so, here is his one recorded joke. On his visit to Ribbentrop in Berlin, November, 1940, a British air-raid was laid on for their benefit. They had to finish their conversation in an air-raid shelter. 'England,' said Ribbentrop, 'is finished. She is no more use as a power.' 'If that is so,' said Molotov, 'why are we in this shelter, and whose are these bombs which fall?'

hesitated; it was over this that Chamberlain's government had hesitated and brought on the Soviet-German Pact and the war. It is to be noticed that much of the argument of the broadcast was addressed to the doubters; but no one could address them so compelling an argument as he with his long record of anti-Bolshevism. 'No one has been a more consistent opponent of Communism than I have for the last twenty-five years. I will unsay no word that I have spoken about it. But all this fades away before the spectacle which is now unfolding. . . . I have to declare the decision of His Majesty's government—and I feel sure it is a decision in which the great Dominions will in due course concur—for we must speak out now at once, without a day's delay. I have to make the declaration, but can you doubt what our policy will be? We have but one aim and one single, irrevocable purpose. We are resolved to destroy Hitler and every vestige of the Nazi régime. . . . Any man or state who fights on against Nazidom will have our aid. . . . It follows therefore that we shall give whatever help we can to Russia and the Russian people. . . . The Russian danger is therefore our danger and the danger of the United States, just as the cause of any Russian fighting for his hearth and home is the cause of free men and free peoples in every quarter of the globe.'

There is the argument in as many sentences: it could not be better put, considering all the susceptibilities, the awkwardnesses, his own past record of intervention in Russia, the so recent indifference of our new-found ally to our survival. The broadcast gave also something of the pattern the future would take. One great wing of the Grand Alliance was taking shape; it could hardly be doubted now that the other would form in due course. Of all Churchill's services in following up his promise of aid to Russia, putting up with Stalin's surly responses and insults, himself, though the older man, journeying to Moscow to get relations on to a better footing, at length establishing a not ungenial if uneasy camaraderie for the purpose of the war, nothing exceeds his firm initial grappling of Russia to our side and the unequivocal ending of our isolation.

All through 1941 President Roosevelt was gradually bringing the United States towards a full and open share in the Grand Alliance. In the New Year he sent his most intimate confidant to Churchill with the message: 'the President is determined that we shall win the war together. Make no mistake about it. He has sent me here to tell you that at all costs and by all means he will carry you through, no matter what happens to him—there is nothing that he will not do so far as he has human power.' Churchill and his government were deeply grateful for all the support, moral and material, that they received from the President and his country in this time of tribulation. The remarkable correspondence between their two leaders continued with ever-growing intimacy—there had been absolute and entire confidence from the first, such as was perhaps only possible between two leaders of English-speaking peoples—with favourite quotations from the Bible and exchanges of verse. The President wrote out and sent over Longfellow's verse—

> Sail on, O ship of State!
> Sail on, O Union, strong and great!
> Humanity with all its fears,
> With all the hopes of future years,
> Is hanging breathless on thy fate.'

With the transformation of the war by the entry of Russia, and with the growth of the aid to her without which she would not have been able to withstand Germany's onslaught—as in 1917—Roosevelt and Churchill both felt the need of a meeting, to know each other's full minds and plan their future course of action. A rendezvous was arranged for August in Placentia Bay, Newfoundland, the President arriving in the *Augusta*, the Prime Minister in the *Prince of Wales*. Churchill has a poignant description of the scene that summer morning in the quiet sunlit bay, when the President came aboard the *Prince of Wales* with all his staff and several hundred representatives of all ranks for Sunday service, 'the close-packed ranks of British and American sailors, completely intermingled, sharing the same books and joining fervently together in the prayers and hymns familiar to both. I chose the hymns myself—'For Those in Peril on the Sea' and 'Onward, Christian Soldiers'. We ended with 'O God, our Help in Ages Past', which, Macaulay reminds us, the Ironsides had chanted as they bore John Hampden's body to the grave. Every word seemed to stir the heart. It was a great hour to live. Nearly half those who sang were soon to die.'

Churchill brought with him the original draft of the Atlantic Charter—his own composition, he records with glee as a riposte to the tales of his reactionary, Old World, imperialist outlook. As the upshot of their talks the President and he issued a full declaration of war-aims and sent a joint message to Stalin. The Americans made an important further move towards entering the war by taking over the America-Iceland stretch of the Atlantic, a considerable help when the Battle of the Atlantic was at its height, losses from U-boats were enormous and the Navy still under continuous strain. There was nothing more Hitler could do about it.

But at Pearl Harbour on 7 December the Japanese took a hand. As Churchill says, madness carries with it the advantage of surprise—as we had found with Hitler. As the Germans in 1940 had gained by it the (temporary) domination of Europe, so now Japan by a sudden treacherous stroke had gained the (temporary) command of the Pacific. It is difficult for a sceptical historian to appreciate why people will attempt these things in history: they so rarely last. The immediate disaster was grievous, though it might have been even worse: the aircraft-carriers were away on other duties, and it was by them ultimately that the Japanese Navy was defeated. Meanwhile the American Pacific Coast was exposed: Churchill's reaction was at once to think of sending the *Prince of Wales* and the *Repulse* from Singapore across the Pacific to reinforce what was left of the American Fleet. The next thing he heard was that they were at the bottom of the sea. When he heard the news, 'I was thankful to be alone. In all the war I never received a more direct shock.' Years afterwards, he expressed to me the horror of that moment, and indeed we all of us felt its heart-sick anguish.

Churchill's instinct, as always, was for action and he decided that he must go to Washington at once to establish complete understanding for the conduct of the joint war. For the Americans were now in it up to the neck: Hitler had characteristically given orders to sink all American shipping wherever found, three days before declaring war upon the United States, and there followed innumerable sinkings off the Atlantic coast. But the fact that America was now fighting beside us gave us the certain assurance of victory, whatever further disasters and trials we should have to endure together. And at this grim moment Churchill had a message for the American people based on our own long endurance: it was the message he had given us on Trinity Sunday, 1940: 'Arm yourselves, and be ye men of valour, and be in readiness for the conflict'. Not that the Americans needed any steeling of their resolve: the mood was one of cold anger at these dastardly blows and no one need doubt their fighting toughness—the Germans were so stupid to ignore and belittle that as they did, unteachably, in the second war as in the first.

However, Churchill himself was a visible embodiment of

courage and resistance when the world was falling around one; he felt one with the Americans, they too were his own people. As he put the point in that wonderful speech to Congress we all remember listening to, for it was relayed to us across the Atlantic: 'I cannot help reflecting that if my father had been an American and my mother British, instead of the other way round, I might have got here on my own'. And then, chuckling, 'in that case I should not have needed any invitation, but if I had, it is hardly likely it would have been unanimous'. The revealing moment came with the question—the accent stern, angry, defiant: 'what sort of people do they think we are?' and the roar of response that came from the representatives of the whole American nation assembled there. For, a foreigner and yet one of their own, he had touched the dominant chord in the assembly, he had voiced the will-power of the nation. After that, he was never a foreigner in the United States again; the American people took him to their hearts, for good, as the British had done in the stress of 1940.

For himself that Christmas in the White House was crammed with work, both future planning and current business, speeches to prepare for the Canadian Parliament as well as for Congress. From it there issued the Anglo-American accords: directives for the joint war, the offensives planned, operations decided. There were consolations—not only warmth and kindness on every hand, but the ever-present sense of history, of making history in the present continuous with the living past. When he wheeled the President in his chair in the drawing-room of the White House inhabited by memories of John Adams and Andrew Jackson, Lincoln and Woodrow Wilson—he thought of himself as Sir Walter Ralegh spreading his cloak before Queen Elizabeth. On Christmas Day the President and he went to church together, and found peace in the simple service and well-known hymns. 'Certainly there was much to fortify the faith of all who believe in the moral governance of the universe.'

Though the ultimate configuration was now secure, the disasters and set-backs of the winter of 1941-2 reacted upon Churchill's position. We were all suffering from the sickness of hope deferred. In North Africa the entry of Rommel's Afrika Corps reversed Wavell's brilliant victories against the Italians: it was sickening to see the loss of Libya and Cyrenaica after they had been so largely won. In the Far East the loss of Malaya and the fall of Singapore were even more shattering: Australia was now exposed—and reproachful, though there was nothing more we could have done. In these circumstances the campaign in Britain, voiced by Aneurin Bevan and the Left, for opening up a Second Front in Europe for the relief of Russia was nothing short of suicidal: it could not be mounted without at least a year's preparation in landing-craft, tanks, *matériel*, training; to try it prematurely was the one way to lose the war, and to fail, as it would have done, would mean hundreds of thousands of casualties for nothing. It is difficult to have any patience with politicians who would throw away men's lives. Nor did Churchill need any pushing on the subject of a Second Front: all along he had been only too anxious to open one up, he was often tempted by the thought of a return to Norway, at this time his mind was set on 1943 as the target for the Second Front. If there was any ground for criticism it was that he was too impatient, too anxious for immediate results, always in favour of the offensive. The campaign for a Second Front simply had the effect of weakening him in his dealings with Stalin, exposed him to further recriminations when he was doing all he could for Russia, sending vast stores of equipment we badly needed ourselves through the Arctic convoys with their frightful losses.

A sense of dissatisfaction with the conduct of the war was spreading and the Press was full of suggestions that, though he should remain Prime Minister, he should cease to be Minister of Defence and leave the direction of the war to others. It was ominously like 1916 again. At this moment Sir Stafford Cripps chose to return from his embassy in Moscow, bearing himself, as Churchill says, 'as if he had a message to deliver'. (The phrase persuades one that the joke, 'there, but for the grace of God, goes God'—one of many that circulated throughout the dark days of the war to rejoice us—must be authentic.) The Prime Minister invited him to join the government as Minister of Supply; but this was not good enough: he held himself in majestic reserve. Churchill called for a vote of confidence, and won it, with unexpected completeness, by 464 to 1—the one, plus his two tellers, being members of the idiot I.L.P. The President cabled his congratulations: 'it is fun to be in the same decade with you'.

Upon this Churchill gained the adhesion of Sir Stafford Cripps by inviting him to become Leader of the House of Commons, where he was not very successful. This involved a reconstruction of the government, though the Prime Minister's personal position was no longer involved. He did not suffer from any desire to be relieved of his responsibilities: 'all I wanted was compliance with my wishes after reasonable discussion'. In the Far East the Japanese progress continued: Burma was invaded, India now threatened. In June, Churchill was in Washington for his second visit, when the President handed him a telegram with the news of the fall of Tobruk with 25,000 prisoners: 'I was the most miserable Englishman in America since Burgoyne'. The root of the trouble was the failure in tanks. The Americans were better than their word: they put three hundred Sherman tanks at once at his disposal, and these played their part in Rommel's defeat in the end. He came home to face a vote of censure—which was lost from the start by its seconder, Admiral Sir Roger Keyes, insisting that it would be a disaster if the Prime Minister had to go: he only wanted him to sack his Chiefs of Staff. The vote was supported by a mere twenty-five—exactly the same number as had voted against the younger Pitt's conduct of the war in 1799. This was very consoling to the historically-minded Prime Minister; the vote gave equal pleasure to the President. Harry Hopkins cabled, 'your strength, tenacity, and everlasting courage will see Britain through, and the President, you know, does not quit'.[1]

Such was the sum of our internal political difficulties in the Second World War, in striking contrast with the first. There was no further question about Churchill's position. On Chamberlain's resignation, to die, in 1940 Churchill had at last become Leader of the Conservative party, and this gave him an inexpugnable position, for the Conservatives retained the immense majority over all parties they had won by Baldwin's fraud in 1935. There was some question whether the truly national leader Churchill had become ought to be a party-leader at all; but after the experience of the first war there could be no doubt for him. Supported by loyal colleagues

[1] Churchill, *The Second World War,* IV. 366. The Nazis had regarded these difficulties with great hope and put their money on Cripps. Cf. Goebbels, 11 February 1942: 'the Führer agrees that Cripps is a real treasure for us, to be guarded carefully. His latest effusions have created such a sensation in neutral countries that we may in future expect all sorts of good things from this white-headed boy.' 13 February 1942: 'Cripps continues to carry on agitation on behalf of the Bolsheviks. For us he is a propagandist whom we simply could not pay with money. . . . It is claimed that Hore-Belisha and Cripps intend to found a new anti-Churchill party. It would be best, of course, if Churchill were defeated and Hore-Belisha took his place. Today we would most heartily welcome a Jew as Prime Minister.'—*The Goebbels Diaries,* trans. Louis P. Lochner, 42, 44. One sees what a fantasy-world these maniacs inhabited.

from all parties—the Chamberlainites now at a discount, one of them relegated to Madrid, another to Washington, a third to the Woolsack, others demoted or dropped—he was left free from the daily routine of internal administration to devote his energies wholly to the war.

So far we have been considering mainly Churchill's contribution in the realm of politics and morale—one might almost say, the spirit. We must now confront the much-debated question of his specifically military contribution.

Here the essential thing, we observe, is that his instinct was all for action; he was always on the aggressive. In the darkest days of defeat he was thinking of the come-back, ways and means of bringing the war home to the enemy, no mere resistance but a resumption of the offensive as early as possible. He was impulsive, impatient, self-willed, as he always had been; but if he had not been like that we should not have held out and might never have won through. That quality, though morally of the utmost value, led to some mistakes, though these are not to be compared with the positive achievement.

He was always urging his generals on to action. His mood was very much like Chatham's, who chose Wolfe because, where other officers made difficulties, he found expedients. That was what Churchill liked; he hated obstruction, difficulties being created: he suspected inertia. At the beginning of his close and long co-operation with Brooke as Chief of the Imperial General Staff—to whom we owe our most intimate portrait of him in directing the war—there was a midnight scene when the Chief of Air Staff objected to Churchill promising to send Russia ten squadrons from North Africa at the end of the Libyan offensive. This course was both too risky and too magnanimous. There was an outburst: 'we were told we did nothing but obstruct his intentions, we had no ideas of our own and, whenever he produced ideas, we produced nothing but objections, etc. etc. . . . God knows where we should be without him, but God knows where we shall go with him!'[1] But, note: next day he came round to their view: he did not overrule them. He hated negativeness, troops standing by idle, unemployed. 'Those damned planners of yours', he one day said to Brooke, 'plan nothing but difficulties.' And again a year later when Montgomery's offensive against Rommel was delayed: 'he started all his worst arguments about generals only thinking about themselves and

[1]q. from Brooke's Diary, Sir Arthur Bryant, *The Turn of the Tide*, 298-9, 505.

their reputations and never attacking until matters were a certainty; of never being prepared to take any risks, etc. . . . At the root of it all lay his everlasting desire to speed up the date of all attacks irrespective of the effect such measures might have on the preparations.' Again, note: when Brooke told him so, he accepted the rebuke and adjusted his orders to the Chief of Staff's view.

Here is a marked contrast with Hitler and one that underlines the superiority of democratic methods. Hitler too was a man of intense fertility in ideas—we must not deny that evil genius this justice. But no one dared contradict the Führer; his ideas did not have to go through the sieve of equal discussion; he frequently overruled his professional advisers and contributed largely by his mistakes to Germany's defeat. Churchill never overruled his Chiefs of Staff when they were united in their judgment. But he submitted them to the gruelling test of all-in argument day and night. Tough men of action quailed before the ordeal, as Beatty had done. The large-hearted and very able C.I.G.S., Dill, preferred the gentler clime of Washington, where the President did not interfere with professional military matters. Churchill, as an old professional, interfered with everything. Brooke complained that hardly six hours went by but he was called up by the Prime Minister; he could not bear the night sessions Churchill liked, the interminable discussions wore him down.

However, the end of it all was this, in C. M. Woodhouse's just summing-up: 'what he did, and had every right to do, was to test the firmness of their judgment to the uttermost limits of endurance, so that no conceivable possibility became recognised as an impossibility until it had been through the fire over and over again. That is not ignorance of strategy; it is leadership, and a peculiarly British kind of leadership—the kind that beat Hitler.' Over any specific issue, 'it would not be so certain that that policy was correct if Sir Winston had not insisted, with all his superlative and appalling powers of advocacy, on the examination of half a dozen other policies as well. . . . The last word rests with Sir Winston: "in war you do not have to be nice—you have only to be right".'

Then, too, he had so much of his own to contribute, not only ideas and expedients, but his share in specialised techniques. We have seen the pride he took in the suggestions he made during the first war for landings on Borkum, landing-craft for tanks, cement-caissons out of which developed the mulberry harbour, the technique of amphibious warfare. There is his striking readiness to listen to the promptings of science in every field; he owed a great deal to his close friendship with Professor Lindemann, nevertheless such flexibility of mind is all the more remarkable in so inflexible a man.

There remains the final question of grand strategy about which there has been so much controversy. It is clear that Brooke did not think highly of Churchill as a strategist: 'Winston never had the slightest doubt that he had inherited all the military genius of his great ancestor, Marlborough. His military plans and ideas varied from the most brilliant conceptions at the one end to the wildest and most dangerous ideas at the other. To wean him away from these wilder plans required superhuman efforts and was never entirely successful in so far as he tended to return to these again and again.' The root of the difference was that between the intuitive mind of the artist, and the logical methods, carefully calculating and working out pros and cons, of the military scientist. General Marshall in Washington had the same professional distrust of the brilliant amateur and an even greater fear of what he considered Churchill's diversionary predilections. The two professionals, however, were at logger-heads with each other. Brooke stood for the concentric strategy of making the best use of sea-power to close in on Germany from the perimeter, beginning with the Mediterranean. Churchill was at one with him on that; however much he tested and tried Brooke at home, when it came to the Combined Chiefs of Staff in Washington we find Churchill standing firmly with Brooke, as we see from Hopkins' *White House Papers*. On the other hand, Churchill sympathised with the American desire for the invasion of Europe as early as 1943: it turned out to be impossible for simple reasons of logistics. It is difficult to see that he was wrong on either of these prime issues—though he may have been wrong about Norway, Greece and Singapore.

The main charge made against Churchill all his life, as we have seen, was on the ground of his judgment. People feared the peremptoriness in him, the strongheadedness, the impetuousness like that which had taken him over the bridge as a boy at Bournemouth. He did not take us over the bridge, after all, in the second war: he controlled his impulsiveness to a remarkable degree, put up with a long catalogue of defeats and disappointments in an exemplary manner, and fought the war with the least expenditure of lives—only a quarter of those lost in the holocaust of the first. Most important—and a discriminating test of judgment—he chose the right men. He chose Brooke and Montgomery and Alexander, Mountbatten and Slim. No one has made that point, yet it is the final test of the statesman, without which everything else goes wrong. Like Chatham, like Elizabeth I, he chose right.

The co-operation of Churchill and Brooke, the man of intuitive genius and the brilliant strategical brain, was the right one: they were complementary to each other and produced historic results. Brooke wrote, 'he is quite the most difficult man to work with that I have ever struck, but I would not have missed the chance of working with him for anything on earth'. There were certainly compensations: there was a great deal of fun and it was a source of never-ending interest watching and studying him. At Chequers, March 1941: 'P.M. suffering from bronchitis, came down to dinner in his "siren-suit", a one-piece garment like a child's romper-suit of light blue. He was in great form and after dinner sent for his rifle to give me a demonstration of the "long port" which he wanted to substitute for the "slope". He followed this up with some bayonet exercise!' In June 1942 they were flying to America, 'at a time when the Atlantic had not been so very frequently flown, we were both somewhat doubtful why we were going, whether we should get there, what we should achieve while we were there, and whether we should ever get back'. This did not depress the Prime Minister, who arrived 'dressed in his zip-suit and zip-shoes, with a black Homburg hat on the side of his head and his small gold-tipped malacca cane in his hand. Suddenly, almost like Pooh-Bear, he started humming, "We are here because we're here—We're here because we're here".' The only person who could call him to order was his butler-valet, Sawyers. For Washington Winston had changed into a Panama hat turned up all round: the Prime Minister looked like a small boy going down to the beach to dig in the sand. Sawyers refused to let him get off the plane: 'the brim of your hat is turned up, does not look well, turn it down!' The Prime Minister, rather red in the face, turned it down. Sawyers, standing aside to let him pass: 'that's much, much better!'

In August 1942 they were in Cairo, where the Australians were delighted to see him. They would have been still more so if they could have seen him in some of his off-moments—after a long day motoring in clouds of sand, addressing the troops, talking with officers, taking a second bathe in the sea (contrary to doctor's orders) and being rolled over by the waves, coming in upside-down doing the V-sign with his legs. Or resting in an improbable bed in Cairo, in a Moorish alcove with a religious light shining on either side, the bed with light-blue silk covering six inches deep in lace; 'and there in the bed was Winston in his green, red and gold dragon dressing-gown, his hair, or what there is of it, standing on end, the religious lights shining on his cheeks, and a large cigar in his face!' Or there was the march-past of the famous 51st (Highland) Division, the wild music of the pipes bringing a lump into Brooke's throat while the tears streamed down Winston's face. Or Winston in bed with pneumonia, looking very ill but protesting at the reduced number of papers reaching him, when his temperature was only 100° and he was quite ready to joke. No wonder Brooke thought him the most wonderful man he had ever met and doubted if any historian of the future would ever be able to paint him in his true colours.

These journeys told on Churchill more than he knew. After the strain of the Casablanca Conference and his tour of North Africa, the Eighth Army, Cyprus and Cairo by air and home again to an English February, he had a bad bout of pneumonia. I well remember the country's anxiety at the news. The doctor described the disease as 'the old man's friend'. Winston asked innocently, 'Why?' 'Because it takes them off so quietly.' He noticed with some disapproval the marked diminution in the number of official papers that reached him; however, he consoled himself with *Moll Flanders*. (Defoe has long been an admiration of his and provided something of a model for his Memoirs.) An unknown gentleman kindly presented him with a lion, with good wishes for his recovery. 'I do not want the lion at the moment either at Downing Street or at Chequers, owing to the Ministerial calm which prevails there. But the Zoo is not far away, and situations may arise in which I shall have great need of it.' President Roosevelt sent him, with orders to obey the doctor, a photograph of an American Civil War General Churchill, a direct descendant of the Dorset Churchills, with a marked resemblance to Winston.

In spite of his being senior to both Roosevelt and Stalin, it fell to him to make the journeyings between both Washington and Moscow. And this in spite of Roosevelt's conviction that he could 'personally handle Stalin better than either your Foreign Office or my State Department. Stalin hates the guts of all your top people. He thinks he likes me better, and I hope he will continue to do so.' In August 1942 Churchill paid his first visit to Moscow, flying via Cairo and Teheran, to establish a personal relationship with Stalin, who was so inaccessible, and see if they could not achieve some harmony, a measure of trust for the common purpose of defeating Hitler. Stalin's reponses so far had been curt and ungracious: no recognition of the drain upon Britain of the Arctic convoys. Nothing but the Second Front would do.

Churchill had the unpleasant task of informing him that there could be no Second Front in 1942—or at any rate, no invasion of Europe. The atmosphere of this first meeting was very glum. Then Churchill imparted to him the joint Anglo-American plans for the landings in North Africa, the assault upon 'the soft under-belly' of the Axis powers, himself drawing the picture of a crocodile and unfolding the maps. Stalin's interest was very much excited and in the shortest space grasped all the strategic implications. Churchill was much impressed. 'It showed the Russian Dictator's swift and complete mastery of a problem hitherto novel to him. Very few people alive could have comprehended in so few minutes the reasons which we had all so long been wrestling with for months. He saw it all in a flash.' At the end of Churchill's exposition Stalin, quite moved, said, 'May God prosper this undertaking'. The atmosphere improved; the relationship—one of comradeship in the struggle against Hitler, mutual wariness about what would happen thereafter—was established. There is no disingenuousness in Churchill; 'I was very active in the intervention,' he said to Stalin, 'and I do not wish you to think otherwise. Have you forgiven me?' Stalin replied, 'all that is in the past, and the past belongs to God'. With Stalin, who had had the advantage of a seminary education, the word 'God' was frequent upon the lips.

Anglo-American co-operation was a very different matter. When Eisenhower and Mark Clark came to London 'we talked all our affairs over, back and forth, as if we were all of one country'. When Churchill was on his third visit to Washington in May 1943 and one day passed through the town of Frederick with the Roosevelts, he inquired about Barbara Frietchie and her house. Harry Hopkins came out with the lines everybody knows,

> 'Shoot, if you must, this old grey head,
> But spare your country's flag', she said,

No one else could say any more of Whittier's poem, so Churchill started,

> Up from the meadows rich with corn,
> Clear in the cool September morn,
> The clustered spires of Frederick stand
> Green-walled by the hills of Maryland . . .

and went on to the end, while they all joined in the chorus—*She said*. He took a schoolboy pleasure in this demonstration, for which he received full marks from the President of the United States; but then we remember his schoolboy accomplishment of reciting hundreds of verses at pleasure. Gettysburg he had already seen and knew the story of the Civil War, its battles and its heroes, in detail such as perhaps few Americans do. That story was familiar to Englishmen of his generation, but with Churchill, after all, it was part of the family tradition.

In August he was back on the American continent for the first Quebec conference planning the invasion of Normandy. After the hard work was over, 'I remained for a few days in the Citadel, pacing the ramparts for an hour each afternoon, and brooding over the glorious panorama of the St. Lawrence and all the tales of Wolfe and Quebec'. With the fall of Mussolini the Axis was beginning to break, but there remained the Germans to be got out of Italy—a far tougher proposition. The new situation brought with it further problems and he went down to Washington to discuss them. When the President left for his home at Hyde Park, he put the White House at Churchill's disposal with a characteristic generosity. Thus the Prime Minister was enabled to preside over the Combined Chiefs of Staff—the most remarkable instrument of Anglo-American co-operation to emerge from the war—in the Council Room of the White House. What could be more appealing to the historic sense, or more striking evidence of entire mutual confidence?

The last phase of the war was, perhaps, bound to bring out divergences between the Allies, both with regard to the operations and the shape of things after the war. But it is always sad to watch the dissolution of an historic comradeship. Earlier, in 1942, over India—a question which Roosevelt envisaged in terms of the American War of Independence—Churchill wrote, 'anything like a serious difference between you and me would break my heart'. Differences were now widening between them, though there seems to have been no derogation from their mutual respect or even—on Churchill's side—of affection. The President was at heart a lonelier man, less accessible and more inscrutable, more of a politician and a too sanguine nature; moreover, he had carried an inhuman burden, in circumstances of intense physical strain, for years: he was nearing his end.

The root of the strategic difference between Churchill and the Americans was the old distrust of his 'diversions' from the main ground of attack. They had the rules of classic strategy on their side; they had also a factor not fully known to either of us: the Germans were working at their V-bombs and rockets, which next year would put London and the southern counties once more under a strain like that they had endured in 1940-1. The Americans turned out to be right in wanting to hurry up the direct assault upon Hitler's Europe planned for Normandy. They wanted to put everything into that and nothing to be deflected from it. But the British had a fine army fighting the Germans in Italy: if it could be sufficiently reinforced it would fight its way through to Vienna, whence the Western powers would be able to influence events in Central Europe and the Balkans. Churchill had his eye on the balance of forces there at the end of the war, and wanted the West to end it in no unfavourable position. 'I was very anxious to forestall the Russians in certain areas of Central Europe. The Hungarians, for instance, had expressed their intention of resisting the Soviet advance, but would surrender to a British force if it could arrive in time.' Would it not have been better for us all, Hungarians included, if he could have had his way?

Stalin favoured the American plan of an advance up the Rhône valley to aid the assault on Normandy—naturally: anything to keep us out of the Balkans. The Americans were rather slow to appreciate the point of this: they were much more conscious of British 'imperialism' than of Russian. Roosevelt felt that he was committed to this project and did not wish to prejudice his good relations, or what he considered his influence, with Stalin. To be just, he may not have been wholly mistaken—if he could have remained alive to exert the influence. This became a prime issue at the Teheran conference in November, at which Roosevelt and Stalin met for the first time. The Russians arranged for the President to share their compound. Churchill, who was unwell with a return of his pneumonic symptoms, felt left out. Perhaps the President thought it more important to establish relations with Stalin on a friendly footing for post-war purposes. When Churchill took up these arguments somewhat warmly with Stalin, to his surprise he found the President arbitrating between them rather than supporting him. The shadow of Poland was coming to loom between them. It had an even greater significance.

As D-Day approached and all the preparations along the Channel came to a head for the liberation of Europe, the return to France from which we had been driven in 1940, the end of the long nightmare, the Prime Minister could not contain his anxiety, or conceal his intention, to be there on the day for which he had laboured with all his might so long. The King, who as a young man had been present at the battle of Jutland, wished to be there too. The Prime Minister did not favour this risk. The King thought that if it was not right for him to go, neither was it for Churchill. The Prime Minister had a reply to that: he considered that in his capacity as Minister of Defence it was his duty to go. The King's secretary came to his master's rescue: he thought that 'his Majesty's anxieties would be increased if he heard his Prime Minister was at the bottom of the English Channel'. Still Churchill did not give up: it took a letter from the King, just as he was setting out, to stop him. He must have been sad.

Those days before and after D-Day in the summer of 1944 were indeed unforgettable to all of us who lived through them. It was like the summer of 1940 again, but this time with the burning hope that all would be put right at last. The mood of the whole country was a mood of prayer: everyone understood what was at stake: everyone had somebody involved in it, in danger. No one knew what the casualties would be—the word went round fifty-fifty. By now people were steeled to bad news, the V-bombs were falling on London; this was the last hope, this the moment for which all had waited and many had died. People that day stood in the streets waiting every hour for news, strangers speaking familiarly to each other. Every morning at dawn people in the south of England awoke to hear the planes go over to aid the landings. Not to be there was like not being there on St. Crispin's day.

'How I wish you were here', wrote Churchill to the President. As soon as Montgomery launched his offensive Churchill went over to see for himself how things were going and encourage the men. He visited every sector within our restricted foothold and ended up with the field hospital where casualties were coming in. One poor fellow was on the operating table, and Churchill was about to slip away when the soldier said he wanted him. The Prime Minister came to his side; the wounded man smiled wanly and kissed his hand.

At Yalta death's hand was already upon the President. Himself unwell, Churchill went by plane to meet him in Valletta harbour. 'As the American cruiser steamed slowly past us towards her berth alongside the quay wall I could see the figure of the President seated on the bridge, and we waved to each other. With the escort of Spitfires overhead, the salutes, and the bands of the ships' companies in the harbour playing "The Star-spangled Banner" it was a splendid scene.' The President was looking frail and ill. A young British sailor who saw him disembarking told me how harrowing it was to see the effort it cost him to move, the sweat pouring down his face: he was going, careless of the personal cost, to his death. However, he took full part in the sessions of the conference, seven out of eight of which were devoted to Poland. At the end a joint declaration was issued: 'we re-affirm our common desire to see established a strong, free, independent, and democratic Poland'. We know how that promise was kept.

Churchill did not see the President again. When he said goodbye to him he felt that his contact with life was already slender, his mind remote. The Prime Minister returned to the rejoicings over the crossing of the Rhine and victory in sight. But 'Britain, though still very powerful, could not act decisively alone. I could at this stage only warn and plead. Thus this climax of apparently measureless success was to me a most unhappy time. I moved among cheering crowds, or sat at a table adorned with congratulations and blessings from every part of the Grand Alliance, with an aching heart and a mind oppressed with forebodings.' In April came the news of the President's death. It struck him as a physical blow. And so it did the people of Britain. No leading figure outside this island has ever meant so much to ordinary simple folk within it: he was a figure beside everyone's hearth. They all felt, not obscurely, that he had come to their rescue. That day an intense sense of the presence stilled, the image of the friend gone from the world, was with us all: every English house was a house of mourning.

The days of the government that had saved Britain from being so nearly lost were numbered. It is fairly clear that its best members did not wish it to break up, neither Churchill nor Bevin, Eden nor Attlee. Victory against Hitler was won. On Victory day one saw Churchill at the head of the House of Commons lead them proudly in procession, head high, across Parliament Square to give thanksgiving in St. Margaret's, their parish church. Those leaders knew how much remained to do, the problems left by the defeat of Hitler, a Europe in dissolution, ready for the strongest and most unscrupulous to take advantage of, the Russian advance into the centre of the Continent. It would have been better for Britain and the world if the government could have kept together a little longer, utilising its experience and authority. But the forces of party and the pressure of lesser men had their way.

Stalin never had any doubt that the Conservatives would win. At Yalta he had asked politely who could be a better leader than he who had won the victory. Churchill explained that we had two parties in England and that he belonged to only one of them. 'One party is much better,' said Stalin with conviction. Later, at Potsdam, with the certainty that attaches to Russian orthodoxy, Stalin was able to assure Churchill that he would have a majority of about eighty. After all he had considerable experience of foretelling the results of elections in Russia. Churchill himself was not unconfident—he even hoped to reconstitute the coalition with which he had saved England, to save Europe if possible—until the night before the results were declared. He awoke with an intuitive certainty, that was almost a stab of physical pain, that he was beaten. 'The power to shape the future would be denied me. The knowledge and experience I had gathered, the authority and goodwill I had gained in so many countries, would vanish.'

The day confirmed this foreboding. There was an immense majority for the Labour party—or rather, against the twenty-year rule of the Conservatives that had brought Britain to such a pass. It was in keeping with the fatuity of human affairs that the man who had delivered us should have to pay the penalty for them. He did not wait to meet Parliament; at the end of the day he handed in his resignation to the King. 'The verdict of the electors had been so overwhelmingly expressed that I did not wish to remain even for an hour responsible for their affairs.'

Epilogue

THUS passed the most famous five years in all our history.

It is impossible to describe the events of the years that followed: we lack the documents, the precise annotated information; we do not know the inner facts. Anyway, we need not envy the chronicler of a squalid age.

The initial relapse to party-politics threw Churchill off his balance; in the changed circumstances, the war-time comradeship over, we do not find him at his best. On the withdrawal of the Labour people from the coalition he formed a 'care-taker government' to carry on over the election and until the results were known. But his appeal to the country struck an unfortunate note, and one that was unworthy of him. Instead of keeping people's minds firmly to the tasks ahead of them, the dangers that would follow, none knew better, from the advance of Soviet Russia in Europe, the increasing rift between East and West, the still overriding need for unity in the nation, he tried to alert the electors to the internal Bolshevik danger coming from the Labour party.

This was very unconvincing, and indeed unfair of him: his friends and opponents, Attlee and Bevin—did they look like Bolsheviks? Attlee considered that this line was due to Lord Beaverbrook's influence and, himself yielding to no one in his admiration for Churchill, points out how necessary it is that the latter should have people about him strong enough to counter an impulsive wrong idea. With characteristic under-statement Attlee says, 'I feel that the line I took was more in accord with the mood of the electors'.[1] Churchill persisted and tried to take advantage of an intervention by Laski, the asinine Chairman of the Labour Party,[2] to place Attlee in a bad tactical position. 'I was generally thought', says Attlee, with meek effectiveness, 'to have had the better of the exchanges.' The truth is that Churchill was not a match for Attlee as a party-tactician. When the large Labour majority over the Conservatives became clear—some 393 members to a Conservative minority of 213, smaller than at any time since 1906—it is said that

[1] C. R. Attlee, *As It Happened,* 140, 144-5.

[2] 'Whose political judgment was not very good', says Attlee. This, too, is an under-statement.

Churchill muttered, 'they should have had Baldwin to lead them, and they wouldn't have lost the election'. This may not be apocryphal: it has the right ring, comic, magnanimous, rueful. (And we may add—maybe, but *he* would have lost the country.) It is really rather irresistible in so great a man to be so bad at the mere party-game that occupies so much of the minds of lesser men. And even here, strange to say, he improved his form, reached maturity—in his late seventies!

Actually these manoeuvres may have contributed little enough to the result of the election of 1945 anyway. The vast majority of the service-men voted Labour. One of the new Labour Ministers. Ellen Wilkinson, told me that, on her tour of the Occupied Zone in Germany, when she asked a young soldier exactly why he had voted Labour, he replied blissfully, 'Well, you know, miss—anything for a change!' And that was about it. In my own old constituency the working people assured me that they had voted Labour, but were very sorry that Mr. Churchill had been defeated. This not only goes to show the good-heartedness rather than the logical sense of the British elector, but that there may be more sense in him than logic. What the country needed at this juncture was the continuance of the Churchill government, with a larger Labour wing.

At such a rebuff anyone else might have given up; there was the long unhappy twilight of Lloyd George's career as a warning; plenty for him to write about, plenty to paint. Not so Churchill. He was Leader of the Opposition, a new job for him, in diminished circumstances, in a House full of new faces that knew not David. People wondered how he would do, how he would accommodate himself to this raw, untutored assembly. They were rather restive at first and, not knowing the great days, inclined to be disrespectful. But the comrades of 1940, who knew who had saved the country, were not wanting in respect, neither Attlee nor Bevin, Morrison nor Dalton; and soon the new House listened with attention to what the 'Old Man' had to say. Though he was not constant in attendance upon the routine business of the House—he had better things to do with his time—he yet spoke on many occasions and on all the leading issues, giving full measure of his experience, warning, advice.

The dominant issues left by the war, as we know too well, were those of an Atomic world, the illimitable prospects of destruction opening up from nuclear fission, the world-advance of Communism, the conflict between East and West, the throttling of liberties over all of Eastern, and much of Central Europe. Here he was much better apprised than most people what to expect. He knew Stalin's record of duplicity and cruelty in the treatment of Poland, the determination to throttle any Polish independence or freedom. It was the more agonising that we could do nothing about it, since we owed Poland a debt of honour. Churchill's only consolation was the thought that 'this is not the end of the story'. Nor is it, indeed; it never is: then why do people go on trying these things in history? It was followed by the extinction of any independence in Roumania, Bulgaria, Hungary; Yugoslavia at that time was an obedient satellite; half Austria and all Eastern Germany were in the Russian grip; notice was served on the West with the Communist *coup* in Czecho-Slovakia, the stifling of her independence, the brutal dragooning of Beneŝ, the murder of Jan Masaryk. It had been a profound mistake at the end of the war to allow the Russians so far forward into the heart of Europe; if only Berlin had been the frontier between East and West, Europe would have been able to breathe more freely.

Churchill himself says that the Americans were slow to grasp what it all meant, and for the first six months Bevin was left to stand in the breach alone. He knew the Communists—had had them to deal with all his life; he was at one on the subject with Churchill. At Churchill's last meeting with his Conservative Cabinet he had spoken sombrely of the country's outlook with a large socialist majority; but he concluded with one consoling thought—Bevin was to be Foreign Secretary, an Englishman and a patriot firm as a rock, in whose hands the country's interests were safe. And so it proved.

One thing we can affirm of these next years: no statesman out of office, except possibly Gladstone, has exerted such an influence by his words alone. And now Churchill's words excited as much attention, if not more, in America. In March 1946 he made there his Fulton speech, which had a wider reverberation round the world than any of his speeches. It was not altogether welcome: he used President Truman's encouragement to give 'true and faithful counsel' to direct the attention of the world to the full implications of Stalin's course of action while it was still in its early stages. 'I shall certainly avail myself of this freedom, and feel the more right to do because any private ambitions I may have cherished in my younger days have been satisfied beyond my wildest dreams.'

His dominant theme was that the American monopoly of the atomic bomb for a year or two gave the Western world only 'a breathing space to set our house in order'. From Stettin to Trieste an Iron Curtain had been drawn across the Continent, all communications of the spirit broken off. At the end of the fighting the American and British armies had withdrawn westwards along a front of four hundred miles, in some places to a depth of 150 miles—territory which the Western democracies had conquered, but handed over to the Russians to occupy. In most countries, except those of the Commonwealth and the United States, 'the Communist parties or fifth columns constitute a growing challenge and peril to Christian civilisation'. He did not believe that a new war was inevitable or that Soviet Russia desired war. 'What they desire is the fruits of war and the indefinite expansion of their power and doctrines.' From what he had seen of the Russians, he was convinced that what counted with them was strength; they despised weakness, especially military weakness. The Western democracies needed then to stand together, organise their forces and parley from a position of strength. To this end he advocated the continuance of the war-time facilities between America and the Commonwealth for the mutual use of naval and air bases all over the world. This would double the mobility of American forces and greatly expand the strength of the British. 'Eventually there may come—I feel eventually there will come—the principle of common citizenship, but that we may be content to leave to destiny, whose outstretched arm many of us can already clearly see.'

Not content with announcing imperative measures of common defence he described—as so rarely—the ends for which these exist, what we mean by the cause of democracy, why it is worth defending and what it has to offer to the world. 'All this means that the people of any country have the right, and should have the power, by constitutional action, by free unfettered elections with secret ballot, to choose or change the character or form of government under which they dwell; that freedom of speech and thought should reign; that courts of justice, independent of the executive, unbiased by any party, should administer laws which have received the broad assent of large majorities or are consecrated by time and custom. Here are the title-deeds of freedom which should lie in every cottage home. Here is the message of the British and American peoples to mankind.'

This speech had a bad reception in Britain, and a worse one in America: people do not like to be told home-truths. This did not discourage him: he had been through that before. 'Last time I saw it all coming and cried aloud to my own fellow-countrymen and to the world, but no one paid any attention. Up till the year 1933 or even 1935, Germany might have been saved from the awful fate which has overtaken her and we might all have been spared the miseries Hitler let loose upon mankind. There never was a war in all history easier to prevent by timely action than the one which has just desolated such great areas of the globe. It could have been prevented in my belief without the firing of a single shot, and Germany might be powerful, prosperous and honoured today; but no one would listen and one by one we were all sucked into the awful whirlpool.'

It is probable that no speech by a politician out of office and power has exerted such an influence on events. For it is to this that we must date the alerting of the democracies to their danger and their mental preparedness to take steps in their own defence. America and Britain, with their essentially civilian outlook, had been far too anxious to return to a peace-time basis and had gone too far, too soon, in unscrambling and dispersing their war-time forces. As Stalin's intentions were progressively revealed, all this was ended. The democracies began to equip themselves once more for their defence; America set up her advanced air-bases in the island, once more the pivot of their joint security. All this went back to the Fulton speech: it cannot be said that it was premature or, alas, unnecessary.

In this, as with regard to world affairs generally, Bevin and Churchill were in much agreement. And it must be said that the Labour government did far better in resisting Stalin than the pre-war Conservatives had done in resisting Hitler. Where Churchill disagreed with them, as he always had done, was over socialist economics. The war left Britain economically exhausted: capital investments abroad eaten up; immense material damage within the country, large cities ruined, areas laid waste; industry run down, railways worn out, nothing replaced or kept up for years, except war-industries; the people suffering from under-nourishment, listless and weary. And that continued to be so for years after the war.

In these circumstances it would be a mistake to expect too much from them. The transition to a Welfare State was inevitable. Churchill had no quarrel with that; indeed, we have seen that he had a large and generous hand in its early beginnings years before. What he did not believe in was the end and aim of socialist doctrine: a planned and regulated society controlled by the state; the economic life of the country held in the strait-jacket of a bureaucracy; a level of taxation penalising enterprise, the operation of incentive throughout society undermined and rendered null. In short, he feared that a socialist society would not be a free society; intellectually he remained, what he had always been, a liberal.

The burden the country was bearing was due to the war: it owed this to the Germans. And without American aid on an immense scale, and of an unprecedented generosity, we could not have carried on or begun to revive. It was natural enough, after such long endurance, that the people should take, with or without leave, a five-day week—though the industrious Germans, to whom these miseries were due, were working all hours to restore their shattered country. But on top of these burdens, at a time when there was so much destruction to replace, and when the prime necessity was therefore work, enterprise, incentive, the socialist government saw fit to burden the economy with larger instalments of the Welfare State than the country could possibly afford, social services, a vast transformation and expansion in education, expensive health services, pensions, socialised medicine, what not. It was too much, all at once and at such a time. Its cost was crippling, at the expense of savings, of proper capital-investment, of capital-formation, of the future. For a socialist society, *unless forced*, consumes the seed-corn.

This is the theme of speech after speech of Churchill's, as crisis upon crisis over foreign exchange succeeded each other throughout the Labour government, gold and dollar reserves were lost, the value of the pound undermined, down to a third what it had been before the war, and the long fever of inflation gained head, from which Britain can hardly recover. I do not see how Churchill's arguments can be gainsaid. On the financial crisis of September 1949: 'in these last four lavish years the socialist government have exacted upwards of £16 thousand millions and spent them—over four times as much every year as was the cost of running the country in our richer days before the war. They have used up every national asset or reserve upon which they could lay their hands; they have taken 40 per cent of the national income for the purposes of governmental administration. Our taxation has been the highest in the world. Large incomes are virtually confiscated. The exertions and rewards of the most active class of wage-earners and craftsmen have been burdened in times of peace by the harsh direct taxation which in war, when we are fighting for life, may be a matter of pride to bear, but which in victory is at least a disappointment, and I believe has been a definite deterrent to production.... As has been well said, we ate the Argentine railways—£110 millions—last year as a mere side-dish.... We have been given or loaned—and have spent—above £1750 thousand millions by the United States. We have been helped to the extent of over £300 millions by Canada, Australia and New Zealand.... In all history no community has ever been helped and kept by gratuitous overseas aid, that is to say, by the labour of other hard-working peoples, to anything approaching the degree which we have been under the present socialist government. And where are we at the end of it all?' The answer was—in a crisis which necessitated an emergency session of Parliament to sanction fixing the pound, as against its pre-war rate of $4·86, at $2.70.

As the election drew near Churchill stated the choice before the nation: 'between two ways of life; between individual liberty and state domination; between concentration of ownership in the hands of the state and the extension of a property-owning democracy; between a policy of increasing restraint and a policy of liberating energy and ingenuity; between a policy of levelling down and a policy of finding opportunity for all to rise upwards from a basic standard'.

These may be political clichés; the realities in Britain were sufficiently dreary and disheartening: a kindly and slack society without sense of quality or enterprise, without colour or discrimination, subtlety or spirit, neither desiring nor valuing achievement, without pride of ancestry, and all too much hope of posterity.

Let us turn, for a moment, from the distasteful subject.

Churchill, with his old-fashioned energy, his prodigious Victorian vitality, had better things to do. Now in his seventies, he was writing his Memoirs of the Second World War. The first volume was ready a couple of years after the fall of his government, in spite of distractions as Leader of the Opposition; it was published in 1948. He modestly refused to describe it as history, in the austere sense of the word, 'for that belongs to another generation. But I claim with confidence that it is a contribution to history which will be of service to the future.' Once more, as with his Memoirs of the First World War, there would be controversy, 'but it would be wrong not to lay the lessons of the past before the future.... One day President Roosevelt told me that he was asking publicly for suggestions about what the war should be called. I said at once "The Unnecessary War". There never was a war more easy to stop than that which has just wrecked what was left of the world from the previous struggle.' He follows this up with the theme of this volume occupying a page to itself, 'How the English-speaking Peoples through their Unwisdom, Carelessness and Good Nature

Allowed the Wicked to Re-Arm'.

We see that he believed in the practical value of the study of history, in drawing its morals and learning its lessons. All the sages of the past have thought that, from Erasmus and Francis Bacon downwards; the lesser academics of today know better. But what is the point of history if we do not learn from it, relate it to life? It is no abstract, pure geometry. Thereafter followed a volume each year until the last, a sixth, which appeared in 1954 when he was Prime Minister again. The theme of that is 'How the Great Democracies Triumphed, and so Were Able to Resume the Follies which Had so nearly Cost Them their Life.'

In his seventy-seventh year, in November 1951, Churchill became Prime Minister and Minister of Defence once more. There had been nothing to equal this since Gladstone.

Labour's ascendancy had been undermined by the constant weakening of the economic position and a consequent failure of confidence, by the death of their real leader Bevin and by the squabbles and divisions endemic in the party, but which he and Attlee had managed to hold in check. In return for Churchill's warnings as to the danger from Soviet imperialism and the necessity to rearm, he was under constant attack from the more irresponsible Labour people at this time as a 'warmonger'. It was exactly what had been said about him by Chamberlainite Conservatives in the 1930's, and it was the exact reverse of the truth. 'One can break one's heart only once', he had said at the time of Munich; but there is every evidence that he was deeply wounded at the renewal of this cruel charge. 'I do not hold that we should rearm in order to fight,' he had to explain; 'I hold that we should rearm in order to parley.' If we had remained disarmed and weak there was nothing to stop Stalin occupying all Europe. He was already trying it out in the Far East, when the Americans had withdrawn from Korea: the real reason for the Korean War: the objective was Japan. If President Truman had not had the courage to resist then and there, the world-balance against Communism would have been lost. Churchill, naturally, saw the whole thing; the lunatic fringe, naturally, not.

However, it was generally thought that this charge made the difference of twenty seats to the Conservatives: they were returned to power with a small majority of only twenty-five—difficult to work on. Churchill's Cabinet leaned definitely to the liberal Conservative side: the Churchillians, not the Chamberlainites—this still remained the primary division in the party—were in the ascendant. On the last day of the year the Prime Minister departed in a gale for America, determined to achieve solvency, warning his countrymen that 'Britons should not expect the Americans to solve their domestic problems', and carrying with him the decision to repay in full the first instalments of the American loan.

All through the first year of his second government the financial situation remained one of feverish debility and intermittent crisis. Immense losses of gold and dollar reserves continued: the truth was that the war and the Welfare State together had seriously impaired the country's economic viability. In 1952 the government was at its lowest strength: if there had been an election Labour would certainly have been returned to power. A member of Churchill's Cabinet has told me that only the old man's will-power kept them together and saw them through: a new-comer himself and a heroic fighting man in the war, he was deeply impressed by the spectacle and the experience. Walter Lippman paid tribute from the other side: he was 'after all the old champion, their champion and our champion. What he has to give, which is his genius and the steadfastness of his people is, on any decent reckoning, the equal of anything he can get in return.' Lippman hoped that 'the alliance would not degenerate into an American empire, surrounded only by satellites and dependencies'.

At the end of this year Churchill went off again for talks with Truman and the incoming President Eisenhower, and for a December holiday in the West Indies. He clearly liked going; but though the use of American bases in Britain was continued, he could not persuade the Americans to contribute a token force in the Suez Canal zone. Not till a year later was the real reason for the visit disclosed: the hydrogen bomb was now well on the way, and he was much concerned at Britain's lack of information. The advance of nuclear fission, the increasing possibilities of destruction for the human race, the urgent necessity for an understanding with Russia, some assured basis for peace—these were the thoughts that obsessed his mind in these last years of office. He longed to bring about a meeting of the three leaders at the summit, as in the days of the war, when pulling together for a common end had been possible in spite of divergences. Now, more than ever, it was a dire necessity. He longed to end his career, not as a 'war-monger' but as a harbinger of peace to the nations. Again and again he suggested a meeting with the Russian leaders. Time pressed—certainly for him. He strained every nerve to bring it about, but American opinion was now, in a changed atmosphere, consistently unfavourable; nor were the Russians willing.

King George VI had died in 1952, still a comparatively young man, but worn out by work, the strain of the war-years, of service to the country. It was thought that the Prime Minister's tribute not even he had surpassed. In May 1953 came the coronation of Queen Elizabeth II, and that moment coincided with a recovery of the country's spirits. Not until then did the mood of weariness and war-exhaustion lift from the people; everybody noticed a new buoyancy, the old gaiety and cheerfulness return to the English after too long an endurance. Not even the Russian menace, and their comparative proximity to it, repressed them. The Coronation junketings helped. One saw him at that marvellous spectacle in the Abbey, leading the procession of the Commonwealth Prime Ministers, pausing to say a word to Lady Churchill in the pew in front before taking his place in his stall in the choir, a billowing figure in the plumes and robes of a Knight of the Garter—a Low cartoon of himself. For over-night he had accepted the Garter he had refused in 1945. He had forfeited the majestic simplicity of Mr. Churchill—it took one a long time to become acclimatised to 'Sir Winston', for all its pleasant long-retarded chime with his ancestor, the Cavalier Colonel. On his way out from the astonishing hieratic scene we had witnessed—its poignancy multiplied a hundred-fold for those in whose minds re-echoed the memories in that place of Victoria, of the young George III and his friend the fourth Duke, of Anne and Sarah and Marlborough, of Elizabeth I and the medieval kings going right back to the Conqueror—one saw him hang back surveying the scene on which the improbable sacrament, the enacted dream of the ages had taken place, looking at it for the last time, then moving on in the procession past the spot where Arabella and her brother are buried, on and out.

The strain of that year was too much for him; in July he had a severe stroke, paralysing all one side of his body, arm and leg. The secret was very well kept, for at the moment his designated successor Eden was desperately ill, undergoing one of those liver-duct operations of which the Americans have perfected the technique, without which he could not have lived. People only knew that the Prime Minister was suffering from strain and was resting down at Chartwell. Hardly anyone was admitted to see him; he was out of action for four months—until people wondered whether he would come back. Not the least of his marvels was his recovery, at such an age, from so severe a thrombosis and coming back to carry on as Prime Minister. In October he returned to public life, to speak to the Conservative Conference. Then it was, 'would the Old Man prove to be his old self again?' His speech provided a triumphant and a moving affirmative: 'if I stay for the time being, bearing the burden at my age, it is not because of love for power or office. I have had an ample share of both. If I stay it is because I have the feeling that I may, through things that have happened, have an influence on what I care about above all else—the building of a sure and lasting peace.'

On his return to the House the better side, the latent good nature, of British politics was made evident. The Opposition declared that it had been 'a duller place in his absence'. After Stalin's death in March Churchill suggested a private conference of the Western allies as a preliminary to conferring with the Russians. The Opposition contrasted the humanity of his approach to the petti-fogging difficulties made by his colleagues while he was away. We may say from this time the Opposition took him to their hearts as in the great years, 1940 to 1945—only with a few leading Chamber-lainites did the rancour remain. Labour had forgiven him every-thing; they nothing. But he was a figure now above the storm, above party.

In June he spent a week-end at Washington with President Eisenhower. 'I come from my fatherland to my mother's land.' He praised the amenities of a Federal system: England 'was once a Heptarchy and it might be a good thing if it were to become a heptarchy again'. There was evidently no response for a meeting with the Russians in that quarter. In July he made a private proposal for an exploratory meeting to Molotov: he got an answer to something different. He was holding on, hoping against hope that something might be possible, some assurance of peace to humanity on which he might go out as a peace-maker.

In November he paid his annual visit to Harrow, where a verse was added to the School song in his honour:

Sixty years on—though in time growing older,
Younger in heart you return to the Hill.

In retrospect perhaps Harrow had not been so bad after all: Time, so long a time, had put it right. At the end of the month his eightieth birthday was celebrated in unparalleled manner by Parliament—members of all parties joining in—and the nation. Addresses, honours, presents showered. The House of Lords had a happy thought: two silver jugs that had belonged to General Charles

Churchill, the great Duke's brother, engraved with his crest and coat of arms and that of his wife, Mary Gould. There was a unique ceremony in Westminster Hall, where both Houses of Parliament assembled to do him honour. His portrait was presented to him, with a felicitous speech by his friend and opponent Attlee, who, as an old soldier in the Dardanelles campaign, did not hesitate to praise it as 'the only imaginative strategic concept of the war'. In Churchill's reply the whole country heard the familiar voice for the last time, on a grand occasion: 'there has never been anything like it in British history and, indeed I doubt, whether any of the modern democracries abroad have shown such a degree of kindness and generosity to a party politician who has not yet retired and may at any time be involved in controversy'. Going back to 1940—all people's minds and emotions were there again—'I have never accepted what many people have kindly said, namely, that I inspired the nation. Their will was resolute and remorseless, and, as it proved, unconquerable. It fell to me to express it, and if I found the right words, you must remember that I have always earned my living by my pen and by my tongue. It was the nation and the race dwelling all round the globe that had the lion's heart. I had the luck to be called on to give'—and here we heard, for the last time, the old harsh defiant note—'the roar'.

It was all in inverted commas now, mellowed and mute. All the same it was impossible to listen without emotion to the V-sign given out upon the drums, Elgar's march accompanying him as he walked down the full length of Westminster Hall out at the great west door to the crowd awaiting him in Parliament Square.

The nation had subscribed its present: a very large sum which the Prime Minister proposed to turn into a trust for the endowment of Chartwell—his creation as it stands, with all its treasures—'as a museum containing relics and mementoes of my long life'. So the nation will have something far more personal and idiosyncratic, if on a much smaller scale, befitting a more egalitarian society, than the magnificent impersonality, at once so eloquent and so reserved, that commemorates John Churchill in Blenheim.

Still he did not resign. He evidently enjoyed the comedy of keeping people guessing; his colleagues might be on tenterhooks, but the Opposition relished the situation—they had become fond of their old enemy and were loth to let him go. In January and February 1955 he presided, for the last time, over the Conference of Commonwealth Prime Ministers. At last he had given up hope of bringing about the meeting he so much desired. His last message on the subject upon which humanity's future rests was that for the next three or four years superiority in hydrogen bombs should give us a breathing-space; that deterence might well prove the road to disarmament; it might be that 'safety would be the sturdy child of terror and survival the twin-brother of annihilation. . . . Meanwhile, never flinch, never weary, never despair'. In that lies all our attenuated hope.

On 4 April he entertained the Queen to dinner at 10 Downing Street, where once more he assembled his war-time colleagues of both parties. In proposing the Queen's health he was able to say that he had enjoyed drinking that toast as a cavalry subaltern 'in the reign of your Majesty's great-great-grandmother'. What a world away that was, the world of Queen Victoria and Mr. Gladstone, Lord Salisbury and Lord Randolph, the hot afternoons at Bangalore in which he had read Gibbon and Macaulay, the first experience of war on the North-West Frontier and of writing it up in *The Story of the Malakand Field Force,* the Empire and the Raj apparently secure as ever. It was an immense span of experience for one life to hold. Queen Victoria's great-great-grandfather was George II, and his was James I: we are back in the age of the first Elizabeth, from which it all sprang.

After his resignation as Prime Minister on 5 April 1955 there still remained to him an unexpected span of life, almost a decade. Like everything about him, this also was unprecedented among English, or even English-speaking, political leaders. For a parallel one has to go back to the eighteenth century, and to France, where Cardinal Fleury was still active at ninety. Declining a peerage that would have taken him out of the life of his beloved House of Commons, he remained a familiar, a parental figure there, though he took no further part in its debates.

Though he was increasingly incapacitated by age, occasional illness and physical mishaps in these years, he took a lively interest in what was going on around him and honours continued to pour in on him from all over the world. In the summer of 1959 the Royal Academy held a representative exhibition of his paintings, and—though these were under-estimated in some critical quarters simply because they were his—they drew a record attendance from the public. Even more made their pilgrimage when the exhibition went on view in the United States. In April 1963 came the greatest honour in his life, when he was declared an honorary citizen of the United States by proclamation at a ceremony in the White

House—again something unprecedented, for this has been conferred upon no one else in the history of the Union.

Early on Sunday, 24 January 1965, he died at his home in London. He was given the funeral of a hero in St. Paul's Cathedral, on Sunday, 31 January, attended by many heads of states, leaders of European peoples and representatives from all over the world. He had always wished to be buried beside his father and mother in the little country church at Bladon, outside the park of Blenheim, to which the story all goes back as a stream to its source. As the funeral train passed through Oxford that afternoon, the flags flying at half-mast all down the High, a pale wintry sunset lighting the west, it bespoke sunset upon the Empire he had loved so ardently and served supremely well.

His life was fortunate beyond belief in coinciding with the finest hour in his country's long history—its apogee, and the moment when its separate history is merging, in the fearful danger of the time we live in, in that of the English stocks across the world. Here, too, his was a chosen life, prophetic of the future; for he drew strength equally from the two main branches of those stocks on either side of the Atlantic and in himself drew them together.

We have observed again and again in the story of this family how singularly it reflects the history of the country. Apart from outriders on the flanks, those party-men on the Right and on the Left, the Cavalier Colonel and Lord Robert, the tradition of the family has been essentially centripetal. Undoctrinaire and undogmatic, however strong their personalities, they have been Trimmers in the true sense of the word—in the sense in which so many of the most intelligent men in politics have been: standing somewhat loosely to party, they have been to be found usually where the interest of the country was to be found.

Though the two peaks with which the family has culminated in its two grand periods, the great Duke and the war-time Prime Minister, stand in some contrast of character, Sir Winston Churchill summed up in his life many of the themes of the family exposed in this book. There is the overriding interest in politics and military affairs of the Churchills; the artistic inheritance of the Spencers coming out in him not only as a writer but also in painting. He was not only a politician but also an artist, even in that trade, both Spencer and Churchill; while the American element in his astonishing personality was as obvious as it was strong, the boyishness, the zest for life, the generosity and magnanimity, the radiance that came through his mother from gallant Leonard Jerome of New York. All these rich elements were brought together, as if prophetically in his name: Winston Leonard Spencer Churchill.

We see in him how the conscious ideal of a family tradition can have a decisive effect in moulding a life—the desire to complete and compensate for his father's broken career, the aristocrat who was a tribune of the people; the return to his mother's soil for renewal and sustenance, to a remoter past with the determination to be the Marlborough in the Grand Alliance of his time.

The miracle was to have achieved it all.

Index